Beyond and After Prompt Engineering: The Future of AI Communication

Vladimir Geroimenko

Beyond and After Prompt Engineering: The Future of AI Communication

Springer

Vladimir Geroimenko
Faculty of Informatics and Computer Science
British University in Egypt
Cairo, Egypt

ISBN 978-3-032-04568-3 ISBN 978-3-032-04569-0 (eBook)
https://doi.org/10.1007/978-3-032-04569-0

This Springer imprint is published by the registered company Springer Nature Switzerland AG
The registered company address is: Gewerbestrasse 11, 6330 Cham, Switzerland

Prediction is very difficult, especially about the future.

Attributed to Niels Bohr,
a Danish physicist and Nobel Prize winner.

The best way to predict the future is to participate in its creation.

Attributed to Peter F. Drucker,
an Austrian-American management
consultant, educator, and author.

To my wife, Larissa, with love.

Preface

This book can be seen as a natural follow-up to my earlier monograph, *The Essential Guide to Prompt Engineering: Key Principles, Techniques, Challenges, and Security Risks* (Springer, 2025). Where the previous volume focused on the techniques and challenges of prompt engineering as it was becoming a critical literacy in interacting with large language models, this new work explores the next step—the fundamental transition toward more fluid, contextual, multimodal, and collaborative human-AI communication paradigms.

Reflecting the subject matter it addresses, this book is itself the product of an innovative and evolving human-AI partnership. It is fully illustrated, with each entry accompanied by a conceptual diagram and an extended caption that visually depict and explain the content of the section. This approach not only enhances the clarity and accessibility of the book but also offers readers a more engaging and immersive experience, especially for conceptual material that benefits from visual scaffolding. The diagrams were developed in an editable SVG format, allowing me to refine and adapt them during the writing process just as I did with the text itself, making this an integrated, multimodal creation.

Given the book's subject matter, it is essential to explain the process behind its creation. Just as my previous work, *The Essential Guide to Prompt Engineering*, was deeply intertwined with the very techniques it described, this book also leverages AI as both a tool and a collaborator in its development. The objective was to produce a rigorous, insightful, and forward-looking exploration of AI communication using a structured methodology that integrates human expertise with AI's capabilities.

The writing process involved the following key steps:

(1) Conceptualisation and Research: Conducting extensive research on AI communication, including emerging academic discourse, technological advancements, and speculative perspectives.
(2) AI-Augmented Drafting: Designing structured prompts to extract meaningful insights from multiple leading AI models, including ChatGPT (OpenAI), Claude (Anthropic), and Gemini (Google). Each model was tasked with responding to different angles of inquiry, ensuring a diverse and nuanced set of perspectives.

(3) Synthesis and Refinement: Analysing AI-generated responses, integrating them with my own research notes, and crafting structured drafts that reflect both AI's computational strengths and human critical thinking.
(4) Iterative Editing and Human Oversight: Revising the drafts extensively to ensure coherence, factual accuracy, and narrative flow. AI's contributions were reviewed, paraphrased where necessary, and adapted to align with the book's overarching themes.
(5) Quality Assurance and Finalisation: Running the text through Grammarly for grammar and clarity checks, verifying originality, and ensuring an appropriate balance between AI-assisted and human-authored content.
(6) Final Proofreading: Reviewing the completed manuscript manually to refine tone, consistency, and readability.

In other words, this was a true human-AI collaboration and co-creation—already achievable with today's tools but foreshadowing even more seamless and creative partnerships in the near future. The process not only enriched the book's content but also embodied the very themes it explores: moving beyond prompts toward a more dialogic, collaborative, and relational future of AI communication.

When I completed *The Essential Guide to Prompt Engineering*, I knew it was only the beginning of a much larger journey. While prompt engineering had rapidly become an essential skill for interacting with generative AI, I sensed that its command-based, text-centred paradigm was already giving way to something more profound. Conversations I was having with AI systems—and with fellow researchers and practitioners—were revealing an emerging space where prompts would no longer be the sole or even primary interface. Instead, communication with AI was becoming more intuitive, context-rich, multimodal, and relational.

This realisation was both exciting and challenging. How could I write about a field that was, by its very nature, moving beyond the established frameworks? How could I explore concepts that were not yet fully theorised, let alone standardised? The answer, I discovered, was to embrace the uncertainty, to approach the future of AI communication as an open dialogue rather than a closed system of techniques.

This book reflects that spirit. It is more speculative, more conceptual, and more exploratory than my previous work. It is also more visual, more dialogic, and more collaborative. The process of creating it, hand in hand with AI models, was itself a lived experience of the principles it presents. There were moments of friction, moments of surprise, and moments of genuine co-creation. At times, I felt I was not only writing *about* the future of AI communication but *with* it.

For me, this project was not just about documenting a technological transition. It was about participating in it, testing its possibilities, and pushing its boundaries. It was about learning to let go of the familiar prompts and entering into new forms of dialogue—ones that are less about instructing and more about exploring, listening, and co-creating meaning.

As I look to the future, I see this book not as a conclusion but as an opening—a conversation starter for others who, like me, are curious about what lies beyond the prompt. I hope readers will use it not only as a guide but as an invitation to imagine, challenge, and participate in the unfolding future of human-AI communication.

Cairo, Egypt
June 2025

Vladimir Geroimenko

Competing Interests The author has no competing interests to declare that are relevant to the content of this manuscript.

Contents

Chapter 1
Introduction to the Future of Traditional Prompt Engineering

Abstract This chapter introduces the fundamental transition occurring in human–AI communication as we move beyond traditional prompt engineering toward more fluid, contextual, and collaborative interaction paradigms. It examines the importance of effectiveness in AI communication, tracing the evolution of prompt engineering from its experimental origins to its current professional integration, while highlighting its inherent limitations. The chapter maps emerging communication modes that blur boundaries between instruction and collaboration, incorporating multimodal interfaces and agent-based interactions. It proposes new evaluative metrics that shift focus from output quality to relationship quality, emphasising dimensions such as mutual understanding and communicative alignment. Through a framework of predictive thinking, the chapter outlines a vision of AI communication not as a fixed destination but as an evolving horizon shaped by our expectations and experiments, setting the foundation for exploring future communication paradigms throughout the book.

Keywords Human–AI collaboration · AI communication effectiveness · Post prompt engineering · Predictive thinking · Communication metrics

As the field of artificial intelligence matures and communication with machines becomes more complex, the limits of traditional prompting have become increasingly visible. Prompt engineering—once a revolutionary technique—now appears as a transitional stage in a broader evolution toward more dynamic, adaptive, and collaborative forms of AI interaction. This chapter introduces the key themes and motivations of the book: the pursuit of communicative effectiveness, the transformation of interaction paradigms, and the conceptual shifts needed to engage intelligently with increasingly intelligent systems. Rather than offering a retrospective account, this introduction sets the tone for a speculative and forward-looking inquiry into the future of AI communication, where prompting gives way to partnering, and where meaning is no longer delivered in commands but co-created through ongoing exchange.

V. Geroimenko, *Beyond and After Prompt Engineering: The Future of AI Communication*, https://doi.org/10.1007/978-3-032-04569-0_1

1.1 The Importance of Effectiveness in AI Communication

Since artificial intelligence continues to integrate rapidly into nearly every domain of human life—from education, healthcare, and law to art, science, and entertainment—the question of how effectively we communicate with AI systems becomes increasingly crucial. This issue extends far beyond technical fluency or familiarity with the mechanics of prompting. It strikes at the core of our evolving relationship with intelligent machines, whose increasing autonomy and contextual sensitivity redefine the parameters of effective communication. How can we ensure that our intentions are not just processed by an AI, but meaningfully understood, contextually interpreted, and constructively acted upon?

In an era when artificial intelligence has transitioned from specialised research domains to ubiquitous presence in daily life, the quality of our interactions with AI systems has become a critical determinant of their value. Effective AI communication—the ability to convey our intentions to AI systems and receive appropriate, useful responses—forms the foundation upon which all AI applications build their utility. This effectiveness is not merely a technical nicety but a fundamental necessity that shapes the entire landscape of human–AI collaboration.

Prompt engineering, in its current form, has offered a set of techniques designed to improve how we instruct large language models and other generative systems. It represents the first wave of structured thinking about AI communication. While good prompts yield better outputs, the deeper goal is communicative effectiveness, not mere optimisation. This involves much more than crafting precise inputs. It means creating conditions under which AI systems can align with human objectives, adapt to shifting intentions, and respond in ways that are not only accurate but also relevant, sensitive, and safe.

Effectiveness in AI communication is therefore not a fixed property of any given prompt or model. Instead, it is a fluid and multidimensional construct that evolves alongside the complexity of tasks, the diversity of users, and the nature of the human–AI interaction itself. It encompasses clarity, but also adaptability. It requires coherence, but also responsiveness to ambiguity. It benefits from structure but must remain open to spontaneity and creativity. In short, it demands a communicative ecosystem that is as dynamic as the people and problems it is meant to serve.

The challenge of effective AI communication is multifaceted. Unlike human-to-human interaction, which is often rich with contextual understanding, non-verbal cues, and shared cultural references, human–AI communication currently relies heavily on structured input, often in the form of prompts. This reliance, while foundational, is inherently limited. It requires the human communicator to anticipate the AI's needs, frame the query in a specific way, and often engage in trial-and-error to achieve the desired outcome. As AI models grow in complexity, the potential for miscommunication increases, highlighting the urgent need for more sophisticated, adaptive communication strategies.

Moreover, the very nature of AI is evolving. We are moving beyond systems that simply respond to direct instructions towards those that can anticipate needs, engage in more fluid dialogues, and even exhibit a degree of contextual understanding. As seen in emerging co-pilot systems and conversational agents, this evolution demands a parallel shift in our communication paradigms. We must develop methods that not only optimise for current AI capabilities but also anticipate and adapt to future advancements. The focus must shift from a purely transactional model of input–output to a more collaborative and iterative process, where humans and AI work together to achieve common goals.

In essence, the importance of effectiveness in AI communication stems from the increasing reliance we place on these systems. As AI becomes more deeply embedded in critical aspects of our lives—from healthcare and education to governance and creative expression—the cost of miscommunication rises significantly. Therefore, mastering the art of effective AI communication is not just about improving technical proficiency; it is about ensuring the responsible, beneficial, and ethical integration of AI into our society. This book aims to equip readers with the knowledge and tools necessary to navigate this complex landscape and to shape the future of human–AI interaction.

The pursuit of effective AI communication also reveals fascinating parallels to human communication challenges. Just as humans have developed complex linguistic and cultural protocols to enhance mutual understanding, the field of human–AI interaction requires similar attention to shared frameworks, contextual awareness, and feedback mechanisms. Unlike human–human communication, however, human–AI interaction bridges fundamentally different cognitive architectures, creating unique challenges that traditional communication theories cannot fully address.

This effectiveness challenge has spawned the field of prompt engineering—a discipline focused on crafting inputs that elicit desired AI behaviours. While prompt engineering has yielded valuable insights and practical techniques, it represents only the beginning of our journey toward truly effective AI communication. As AI systems grow more sophisticated and human–AI interactions become more nuanced, we require communication approaches that transcend explicit prompting and move toward more natural, intuitive, and bidirectional exchanges.

Economic factors further underscore the importance of communication effectiveness. Organisations investing in AI technologies face significant opportunity costs when communication inefficiencies prevent systems from delivering their full potential. The labour hours spent refining prompts, correcting AI misinterpretations, or developing workarounds for communication limitations represent substantial hidden costs in AI implementation. Conversely, improvements in communication effectiveness can dramatically enhance return on AI investments by unlocking capabilities that would otherwise remain inaccessible.

The importance of effectiveness also grows as we transition from single-turn interactions to multi-turn dialogues, from static text to multimodal expressions, and from reactive querying to predictive collaboration. Future AI systems will increasingly anticipate user needs, co-construct goals, and participate in processes that blur the line between prompting and partnering.

In such environments, traditional notions of input and output may become obsolete. Communication will no longer be a linear exchange but a recursive, co-evolving interplay—one that requires us to rethink what we mean by "understanding," "intention," and "response."

In this sense, effectiveness is not just a benchmark for communication quality; it is an organising principle for future AI interaction. It provides a lens through which we can evaluate existing methods, anticipate emerging ones, and imagine entirely new paradigms. This book takes that principle seriously. It treats effectiveness not as an outcome of good technique alone, but as a foundational criterion for building, assessing, and evolving our communication with increasingly capable and autonomous systems. As we move beyond prompt engineering, the search for effectiveness becomes the thread that binds the past, the present, and the unfolding future of human–AI dialogue. The coming chapters explore how we might move beyond current communication paradigms toward more effective, natural, and powerful modes of human–AI interaction, mapping the journey from today's prompt engineering toward tomorrow's seamless collaboration (Fig. 1.1).

1.2 Traditional Prompt Engineering and Its Future Trajectories

Prompt engineering emerged in the early 2020s as a practical and conceptual response to the astonishing rise of large language models (LLMs). These systems, capable of generating coherent, context-sensitive responses from minimal input, introduced a new challenge: how to communicate effectively with machines whose inner workings remained largely opaque. Early users discovered—often through trial and error—that subtle variations in phrasing could dramatically affect the quality of AI outputs. What began as an improvisational craft soon crystallised into a semi-formal discipline: a hybrid of linguistic design, cognitive strategy, and computational pragmatism.

At its core, prompt engineering represents the art and science of crafting inputs that elicit optimal responses from AI systems. Techniques such as zero-shot prompting (where no examples are given), few-shot prompting (where examples guide the model toward desired patterns), chain-of-thought prompting (which encourages step-by-step reasoning), and role-based prompting (where the AI is asked to simulate specific personas) quickly became cornerstones of practice. These approaches were instrumental in helping users harness powerful models without modifying their architectures. In this sense, prompt engineering served as a democratising force: it gave anyone with sufficient linguistic precision access to frontier-level AI capabilities.

Between 2022 and 2025, the field evolved rapidly. No longer confined to experimental communities, prompt engineering became an essential skill across domains such as education, law, healthcare, and business. Organisations formalised prompt

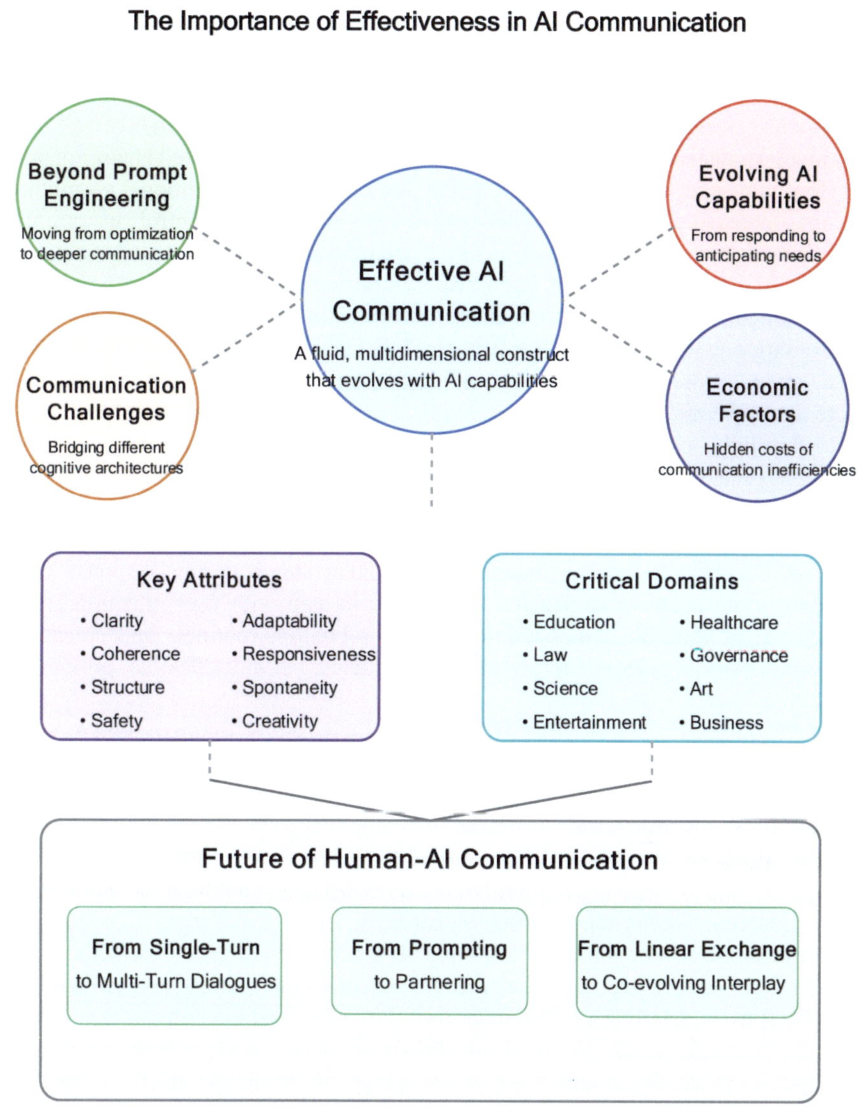

Fig. 1.1 Conceptual framework for effective AI communication. This diagram maps the multi-dimensional nature of AI communication effectiveness, illustrating how it evolves beyond prompt engineering toward more collaborative paradigms. It highlights the key attributes, critical domains of application, and the trajectory from current transactional exchanges to future co-evolving partnerships between humans and AI systems

libraries, defined internal standards, and launched training programs aimed at cultivating prompt literacy. The need for effective communication at the human–AI interface was increasingly recognised as both a point of friction and a vector of innovation. Prompt engineering thus matured into a professional competency, tightly linked to productivity, decision-making, and risk management in AI-integrated environments.

However, as models grew more capable, the limitations of traditional prompting became increasingly apparent. The method rests on indirect control: users must encode their intent into linguistic signals that the model must then infer, interpret, and act upon. This can be effective, but it also introduces ambiguity, especially in high-stakes domains where precision, nuance, and contextual sensitivity are critical. The scaffolding once required to elicit structured responses is now giving way to more fluid, conversational modes of interaction, prompting less as a rigid input format and more as a dynamic dialogue.

In this light, prompt engineering finds itself at a critical inflexion point. The techniques that once defined best practice are gradually being supplemented—and in some cases replaced—by post-prompting strategies. These include multi-turn reasoning, recursive interaction, context blending, and communicative anchoring. Such approaches extend the interaction beyond a single prompt-response pair, enabling more adaptive exchanges that evolve in step with user intentions. The emergence of reusable templates, embedded validation routines, and conversational frameworks reflects a trend toward formalised, yet more flexible, prompting paradigms.

At the same time, prompting is becoming increasingly implicit. Where early systems required precise and often verbose formulations, newer models infer intent from minimal cues, reconstructing context from prior exchanges, user history, or ambient data. This mirrors the evolution of human language itself: as mutual understanding deepens, the need for overt articulation diminishes. Prompt engineering, once overt and deliberate, is dissolving into a broader paradigm of naturalistic communication—still vital, but often invisible.

The tension between standardisation and personalisation further shapes this trajectory. Enterprises seek to codify best practices for consistency, safety, and auditability. Individual users, by contrast, gravitate toward personalised interactions that reflect their unique needs and expression styles. This dual pressure will likely produce adaptive systems capable of maintaining robust safeguards while dynamically adjusting to user-specific preferences and goals.

Ultimately, the future of prompt engineering lies not merely in technical refinement but in a deeper reconceptualisation of the relationship between human and machine intelligence. No longer simply a technique for controlling AI outputs, prompting is becoming a framework for collaborative meaning-making between two distinct but increasingly complementary agents. As this transformation unfolds, the foundational insights of prompt engineering—clarity, context, intentionality—will remain essential. However, they will operate as part of a broader communication strategy that transcends the limitations of current prompting methods and opens new horizons for human–AI collaboration (Fig. 1.2).

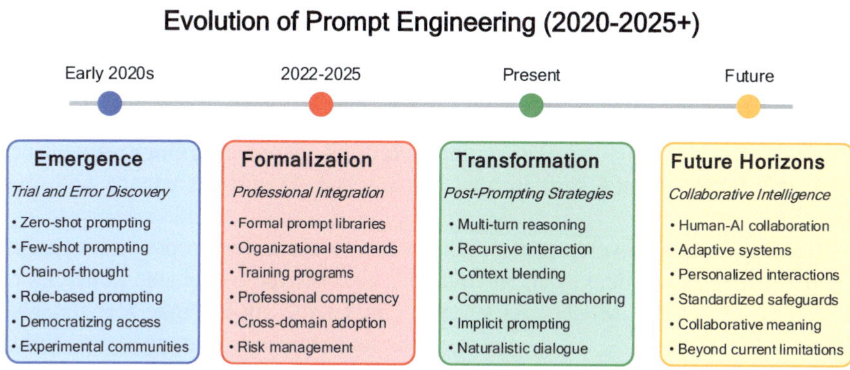

Fig. 1.2 The evolution of prompt engineering. This diagram illustrates the transformation of prompt engineering from experimental practice to a collaborative framework. It traces the progression through four key phases: initial emergence, characterised by technique discovery, formalisation as professional practice, transformation into post-prompting strategies, and future horizons focussed on collaborative intelligence

1.3 The Dawn of New AI Communication Modes

As we move beyond the structured practices of traditional prompt engineering, we are entering an era marked by the emergence of novel and more fluid modes of AI communication. These new forms are neither defined solely by the syntax of instructions nor bound by the rigid conventions of prompt formatting. Instead, they reflect a broader transformation in how humans and machines engage in meaning-making processes—an evolution from discrete commands toward more continuous, context-aware, and adaptive dialogues. At the heart of this shift is the growing expectation that AI systems should not only respond to prompts but also anticipate intentions, clarify ambiguity, and collaborate in the co-construction of meaning.

This dawning landscape introduces modes of interaction that blur the boundaries between instruction, exploration, and shared reasoning. Examples include multimodal interfaces where text, voice, imagery, and gesture intertwine into a single communicative thread, and agent-based interactions in which AI systems assume semi-autonomous roles—managing tasks, adapting to user behaviour, and maintaining ongoing context across sessions. Communication is becoming increasingly embedded in situational context and less reliant on explicitly formulated queries. The very notion of a "prompt" begins to dissolve into a broader field of cues, behaviours, and contextual signals that shape AI interpretation dynamically.

Contemporary AI systems now participate in rich, contextual dialogue that mimics human conversation in its depth and nuance. They can maintain coherent threads across extended exchanges, reference earlier discussions, and adapt their communication styles based on the evolving context. This evolution from static, one-shot prompting to dynamic, multi-turn conversations has created space for more natural and intuitive interactions.

In other words, the landscape of human–AI interaction is undergoing a profound metamorphosis. As language models have evolved beyond simple instruction-following systems into sophisticated reasoning engines, we are witnessing the emergence of novel communication paradigms that transcend traditional prompt engineering. This transformation is not merely an incremental improvement but represents a fundamental shift in how humans and AI systems engage with one another.

Building on these developments, multimodal communication represents a further frontier, where linguistic, visual, and auditory cues converge to enable richer, more expressive exchanges. Modern AI systems can seamlessly integrate text, images, audio, and in some cases, video, allowing users to provide visual or auditory context alongside textual input. In response, AI systems generate multimodal content that conveys meaning across sensory dimensions. This capability extends AI's applicability into domains requiring visual reasoning, spatial understanding, and aesthetic interpretation.

The communication interface itself has also evolved. Graphical user interfaces, augmented reality overlays, voice assistants, and embodied interactions now supplement or even replace text-based prompting. These diverse modalities create new affordances for AI interaction, allowing users to engage with intelligent systems in ways that feel more intuitive and immersive. The rigid command-response model is giving way to fluid, situated exchanges that align more closely with natural human communicative behaviour.

Perhaps most significantly, we are witnessing the emergence of collaborative problem-solving between humans and AI. Rather than viewing AI as a passive tool that simply executes instructions, users are increasingly engaging with these systems as cognitive partners—co-creators who actively contribute to ideation, reasoning, and discovery. This shift from directive prompting to mutual engagement is reshaping practices across creative industries, scientific research, and education.

As these new communication modes mature, they are transforming our expectations of what constitutes effective AI interaction. The static prompt engineering paradigm—with its emphasis on precision, specificity, and exhaustive instruction—is being supplemented by more flexible approaches that leverage the contextual understanding and adaptability of modern AI systems. Users are discovering that sometimes the most effective way to elicit the desired response is not through meticulous prompt crafting but through natural, evolving dialogue that draws on shared context, intent, and communicative nuance.

This shift brings both opportunities and challenges. On one hand, more natural communication modes reduce the cognitive load on users and make AI systems accessible to a broader audience. On the other hand, they require us to develop new mental models for understanding AI behaviour and limitations. The art of effective AI communication is increasingly about finding the right balance between explicit direction and implicit understanding, between structured prompting and organic conversation.

Importantly, this transformation is still in its early stages. What we observe now are just the first signs of a deeper reconfiguration of AI interaction—one that will likely incorporate persistent memory, cross-session learning, and even shared knowledge construction. Future systems may not wait to be prompted in the conventional sense; they may initiate dialogue, propose interpretations, or request clarification in real time. Communication with AI, in this light, becomes less about issuing commands and more about sustaining mutual understanding through adaptive exchange.

In this book, we treat these emergent modes not as replacements for prompt engineering but as its successors—evolving forms built upon its foundations. Just as traditional prompting emerged from early experimentation with large language models, these new modes will evolve through our interactions, expectations, and willingness to embrace AI as a communicative other. What we are witnessing is not merely the next phase of prompt engineering, but the beginning of a new paradigm in human–AI communication (Fig. 1.3).

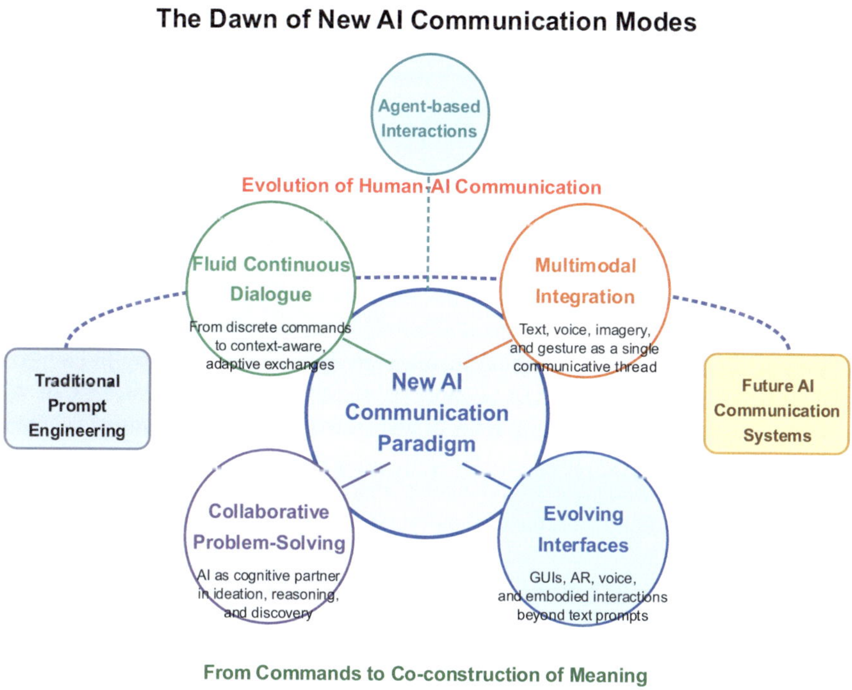

Fig. 1.3 The evolution of human–AI communication paradigms. This diagram illustrates the transformation from traditional prompt engineering to emergent AI communication modes. At the centre lies the new communication paradigm, characterised by four key elements: fluid and continuous dialogue, multimodal integration, collaborative problem-solving, and evolving interfaces. The arc represents the evolutionary trajectory from structured prompting toward future systems featuring agent-based interactions and co-construction of meaning. This transformation reflects not merely technical advancement but a fundamental reconceptualisation of how humans and AI engage in meaningful exchange

1.4 Towards New Metrics of AI Communication

As AI communication evolves beyond prompt engineering, so too must the ways we evaluate its success. Traditional metrics—such as accuracy, relevance, and coherence—while still necessary, are no longer sufficient in capturing the nuanced dynamics of emerging human–AI interaction. These earlier benchmarks were designed primarily to assess the AI's output quality in response to well-formed prompts, often in the context of static, task-bound interactions. But the future of AI communication demands a more expansive and adaptive evaluative framework—one that accounts for interactional fluidity, interpretive depth, responsiveness to context, and the co-construction of meaning over time.

New communication modes—such as multi-modal dialogue, anticipatory interaction, and agent-driven collaboration—require new ways of thinking about what constitutes a "successful" exchange. For instance, how well does an AI system sustain a user's intent across multiple conversational turns? To what extent can it resolve ambiguity or ask clarifying questions in a way that feels natural and efficient? Can it detect and adapt to shifts in tone, modality, or user expectations in real time? These questions point to qualitative dimensions of performance that are difficult to measure using legacy criteria alone.

One promising direction involves the integration of metrics traditionally used in human communication studies, such as mutual understanding, communicative alignment, and pragmatic adequacy. These concepts emphasise the *process* of interaction rather than just the *product*, shifting the focus from isolated outputs to cumulative understanding. In parallel, affective metrics—such as trust, engagement, and emotional resonance—are becoming increasingly relevant, particularly in contexts where AI systems play social or supportive roles. Measuring the success of AI communication may soon require tools drawn from psychology, cognitive science, and even narrative theory, alongside computational techniques.

Moreover, the emergence of AI agents that operate with a degree of semi-autonomy further complicates the evaluation landscape. These agents are not merely responding to prompts—they are initiating actions, prioritising tasks, and maintaining long-term memory across interactions. In such cases, effectiveness cannot be judged solely on the immediate relevance of a response. Still, it must also consider factors such as consistency over time, ethical alignment, and adaptability to evolving user goals.

Ultimately, the shift towards new metrics of AI communication reflects a deeper philosophical turn: from viewing AI as a tool for executing commands to regarding it as a partner in meaning-making. As such, we must move beyond surface-level indicators and begin to develop holistic frameworks that assess the quality of the communicative *relationship* itself. The chapters that follow will explore how this shift unfolds across different domains and technologies—and what it means for the future of how we speak with, through, and alongside intelligent machines (Fig. 1.4).

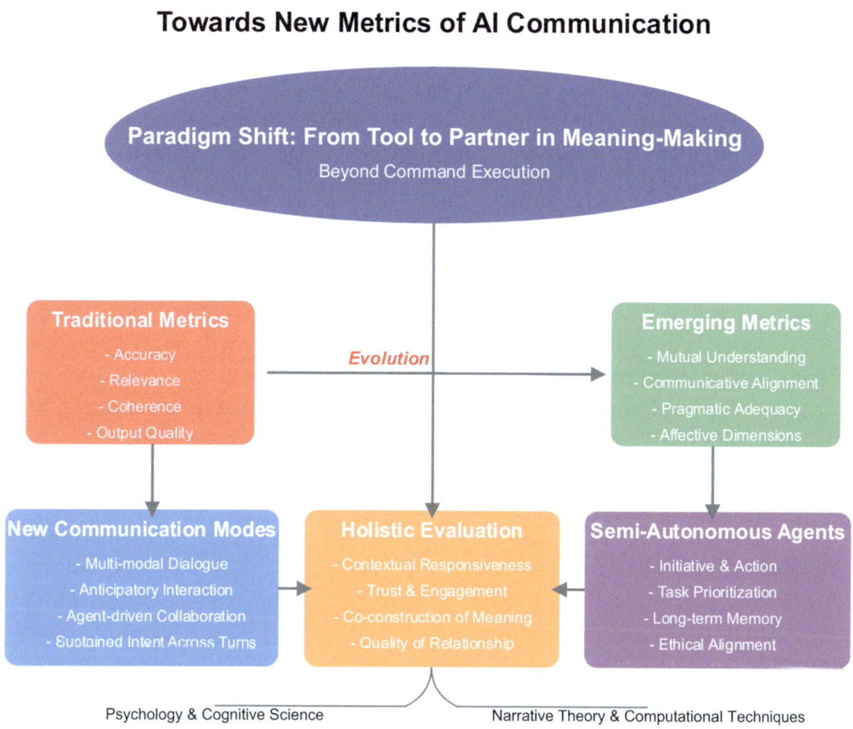

Fig. 1.4 The evolution of AI communication metrics. This diagram illustrates the paradigm shift in evaluating AI communication effectiveness, moving from traditional output-focused metrics toward holistic frameworks that assess the quality of human–AI communicative relationships. As new interaction modes emerge and AI systems develop greater agency, evaluation must extend beyond accuracy and relevance to include dimensions such as mutual understanding, contextual responsiveness, and the co-construction of meaning, drawing from interdisciplinary foundations in cognitive science, psychology, and narrative theory

1.5 Predictive Thinking and Communication Futures

This book does not attempt to predict the future with precision, nor does it offer forecasts wrapped in the certainty of dates and devices. Instead, it charts a speculative map of emerging terrain—one grounded in structured intuition, the careful analysis of current signals, and a forward-leaning understanding of communicative evolution. Its predictions are exploratory, not deterministic; interpretive, not prescriptive. Instead of imagining an end state, it gestures toward a series of conceptual shifts that are already beginning to manifest in the way humans and intelligent systems relate. The aim is not to assert what will be, but to suggest what might plausibly unfold.

Predictive thinking in this context is not an exercise in science fiction but a method of disciplined extrapolation. It rests on identifying trajectories embedded in today's practices—especially those rooted in prompt engineering—and tracing their transformation into subtler, more immersive communication strategies. These transformations may be slow and layered, yet their direction is visible in nascent experiments with multimodal interaction, emotional modelling, conversational memory, and adaptive role-switching. Prompt engineering itself becomes a kind of fossil record—evidence of a transitional phase in the broader story of human–AI co-evolution.

The architecture of this book reflects this exploratory mindset. The following chapters are not arranged to explain the present, but to interrogate and reimagine the near and not-so-near futures of AI communication. Part I surveys the conceptual foundations of what is emerging beyond traditional prompting, identifying the cultural, social, contextual, and emotional dimensions that will likely reshape our communicative expectations. It treats AI not only as a tool but as a participant in increasingly complex relational environments. Part II then extrapolates principles—norms of clarity, adaptability, ethical calibration, and emotional literacy—that may govern future communication practices. These principles do not merely refine prompt engineering; they redefine it by expanding the very notion of what it means to "communicate" with intelligence.

In Part III, the inquiry turns to both the foreseeable and the more radical transformations shaping the future of human–AI interaction. While the near horizon demands resilience, adaptability, and institutional readiness, the distant future brings profoundly unfamiliar possibilities—from emotionally attuned AI to brain-computer symbiosis and inter-agent negotiation. The concluding chapters of the book thus serve as a bridge between the practical imperatives of today and the speculative trajectories of tomorrow, guiding readers from readiness to radical transformation in the evolving landscape of AI-mediated communication.

To think predictively, then, is to embrace uncertainty without surrendering to it. It is to imagine futures not as monoliths but as a series of branching paths—some already opening, others still obscured by conceptual fog. This book invites readers to walk those paths, not with the goal of arriving, but with the intention of perceiving what is beginning to take shape at the edge of human and machine co-expression. In this sense, predictive thinking becomes a communicative act in itself: an open-ended dialogue with possibility.

The perspectives offered in this book invite readers to engage not just intellectually but imaginatively with the future of AI communication. By cultivating this forward-looking mindset, we prepare ourselves not merely to adapt to change but to participate in directing it toward outcomes that enhance human flourishing and understanding. The future of AI communication is not a predetermined destination but a horizon that moves as we approach it, shaped by our expectations, our experiments, and our evolving understanding of both artificial and human intelligence (Fig. 1.5).

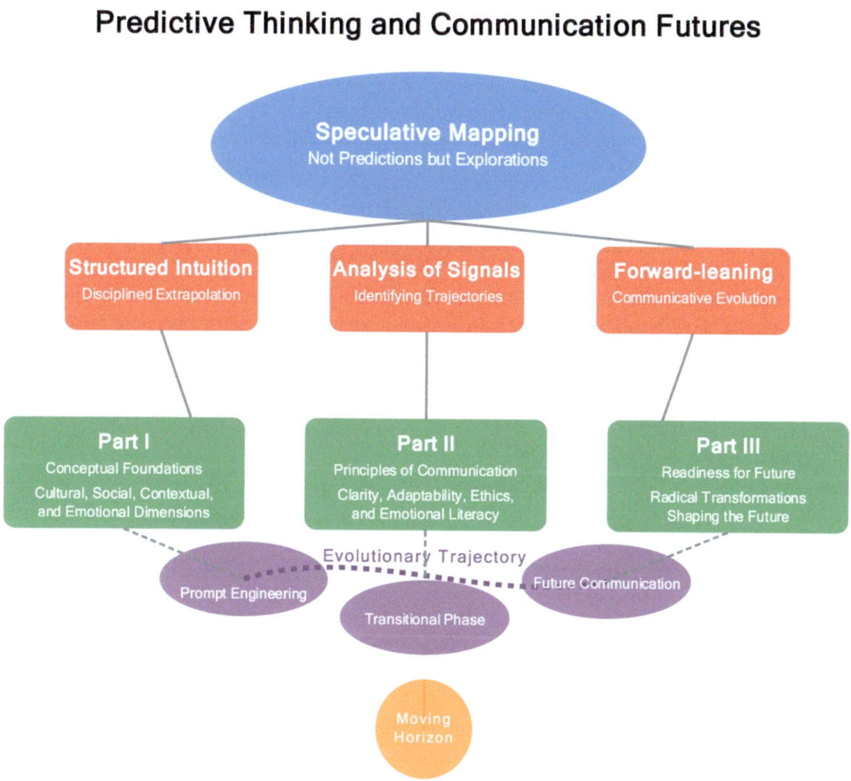

Fig. 1.5 The speculative cartography of AI communication futures. This diagram illustrates the conceptual architecture of predictive thinking as deployed in this book. It maps the progression from structured methodologies (intuition, signal analysis, and forward-leaning understanding) through the book's exploratory chapters to a vision of AI communication as an evolving horizon rather than a fixed destination. The central flow demonstrates how prompt engineering represents a transitional phase in the broader evolution toward more intuitive and immersive communication strategies

Bibliography

Bahree A (2024) Generative AI in action. Manning Publications, New York, NY

Brown BR (2025) Human–machine teaming using large language models. In: Interdependent human-machine teams. Academic Press, Cambridge, pp 41–66

Brown TB et al (2020) Language models are few-shot learners. arXiv preprint arXiv:2005.14165. Accessed 19 Apr 2025

Bura C, Myakala PK, Jonnalgadda AK (2025) Ethical prompt engineering: addressing bias, transparency, and fairness. Int J Res Anal Rev (IJRAR) 12(1)

Choi WC, Chang CI (2025) A survey of techniques, key components, strategies, challenges, and student perspectives on prompt engineering for large language models (LLMs) in education. https://doi.org/10.20944/preprints.202503.1808.v1. Accessed 8 May 2025

Debnath T, Siddiky MNA, Rahman ME et al (2025) A comprehensive survey of prompt engineering techniques in large language models. TechRxiv. https://doi.org/10.36227/techrxiv.174140719.96375390/v1. Accessed 10 May 2025

Dhamani N, Engler M (2024) Introduction to Generative AI: an ethical, societal, and legal overview. Manning Publications, New York

Eliot L (2024) Essentials of prompt engineering for generative AI: practical advances in artificial intelligence and machine learning. LBE Press Publishing

Ferraris AF, Audrito D, Di Caro L et al (2025) The architecture of language: Understanding the mechanics behind LLMs. In: Cambridge forum on AI: law and governance, vol 1. Cambridge University Press, Cambridge

Geroimenko V (2025a) Generative AI: from human–computer interaction to human-computer creativity. In: Geroimenko V (ed) Human–computer creativity: generative AI in education, art, and healthcare. Springer, Berlin

Geroimenko V (2025b) Key challenges in prompt engineering. In: the essential guide to prompt engineering: key principles, techniques, challenges, and security risks. Springer Nature Switzerland, Cham, pp 85–102

Geroimenko V (2025c) The essential guide to prompt engineering: key principles, techniques, challenges, and security risks. Springer, Berlin

Geroimenko V (ed) (2023) Augmented reality and artificial intelligence: the fusion of advanced technologies. Springer, Berlin

Geroimenko V (ed) (2025) Human–computer creativity: generative AI in education, art, and healthcare. Springer, Berlin

Geroimenko V (2025d) Key security risks in prompt engineering. In: The essential guide to prompt engineering: key principles, techniques, challenges, and security risks. Springer Nature Switzerland, Cham, pp 103–120

GitHub (2025) Prompt engineering guide. https://github.com/dair-ai/Prompt-Engineering-Guide. Accessed 10 Apr 2025

Greenwood M (2024) Artificial intelligence: a practical guide to using AI in everyday life. Ochreland Publishing, Brisbane

Hsu HP (2025) From programming to prompting: developing computational thinking through large language model-based generative artificial intelligence. TechTrends 1–22

Huang G, Xiao Y, Jiang L et al (2025) Beyond prompt engineering: a reinforced token-level input refinement for large language models. In: Proceedings of the AAAI conference on artificial intelligence, vol 39(22), pp 24113–24121

i Picó JF, Catta-Preta M, Omeñaca AT et al (2025) The time machine: future scenario generation through generative AI tools. Fut Internet 17(1):1–15

Kannan R, Ahmad M (eds) (2025) Generative AI foundations, developments, and applications. IGI Global

Khan I (2024) The quick guide to prompt engineering. Wiley

Kushwaha V, Ragavan SS, Subhajit Roy S (2025) A measure based generalizable approach to understandability. arXiv:2503.21615. https://doi.org/10.48550/arXiv.2503.21615. Accessed 19 Apr 2025

Learn Prompting (2025) https://learnprompting.org. Accessed 15 March 2025

Lee D, Palmer E (2025) Prompt engineering in higher education: a systematic review to help inform curricula. Int J Educ Technol High Educ 22(1):7

Lee JY, Kang S, Yoo S (2025) Can we predict the effect of prompts?. arXiv preprint arXiv:2501. 18883. Accessed 12 May 2025

Lindley J, Whitham R (2025) From prompt engineering to prompt craft. In: Proceedings of the nineteenth international conference on tangible, embedded, and embodied interaction, March, pp 1–12

López-Pérez B et al (2025) Exploring the potential of large language models to understand interpersonal emotion regulation strategies from narratives. Emotion. https://doi.org/10.1037/emo000 1528

Maaz S, Palaganas JC, Palaganas G et al (2025) A guide to prompt design: foundations and applications for healthcare simulationists. Front Med 11:1504532

Mishra M, Ara A, Mishra S (2025) Exploring human–AI collaboration in higher education: an investigation into AI-enabled personalized learning. In: Prompt engineering and generative AI applications for teaching and learning. IGI Global Scientific Publishing, pp 483–502

OpenAI (2025) Best practices for prompt engineering with the OpenAI API. https://help.openai.com/en/articles/6654000-best-practices-for-prompt-engineering-with-the-openai-api Accessed 20 Apr 2025

OpenAI (2025) Research. https://openai.com/research/index/

Phoenix J, Taylor M (2024) Prompt engineering for generative AI. O'Reilly Media

PremaLatha V, Kumar AD, Parveen N (2025) Optimizing interactions: strategies for prompt engineering in large language models. Edu-Tech Enterprise 3:24–24

Prompt Engineering Guide (2025) https://www.promptingguide.ai/ Accessed 7 March 2025

Reddy CKK, Anoushka P, Draksharapu A et al (2025) Beyond text: analyzing artificial intelligence models through prompt engineering. In: Future tech startups and innovation in the age of AI, pp 120–156

Sasson Lazovsky G, Raz T, Kenett YN (2025) The art of creative inquiry— from question asking to prompt engineering. J Creat Behav 59(1):e671

Sihi D, Ryan A (2025) Crafting and evaluating generative AI prompts: insights from students, educators, and marketers. Market Educ Rev 1–7

Vairamani AD, Nayyar A (2024) Prompt engineering: empowering communication. CRC Press, Boca Raton

Winograd T (1972) Understanding natural language. Academic Press, New York, NY

Part I
Key Concepts of Future AI Communication

Artificial intelligence is transforming not only what machines can do but also how they communicate with us. Part I maps the emerging concepts shaping the future of AI communication, moving beyond the limitations of traditional prompt-response systems toward more dynamic, multimodal, and co-creative interaction paradigms. It traces this evolution across key dimensions—from the historical roots of machine dialogue to the rise of emotionally intelligent and context-aware systems. Crucially, Part I addresses the cultural, ethical, and philosophical implications of AI as a communicative partner, exploring how trust, agency, and meaning are renegotiated in this new terrain. By combining technical insight with social reflection, it offers a comprehensive framework for reimagining communication between humans and machines in the age beyond prompt engineering.

Chapter 2
The Evolution of AI Communication

Abstract This chapter traces the historical and conceptual trajectory of AI communication, from early symbolic interfaces to the emerging post-prompt paradigm. It begins with the origins of machine interaction, examining how rigid, logic-based systems evolved into more expressive, adaptive, and conversational AI frameworks. The discussion highlights the shift from command-based paradigms to dialogic, multimodal, and embodied systems, offering a comprehensive view of the communicative transformation enabled by generative AI. The chapter explores the rise and limitations of prompt engineering as both a breakthrough and a bottleneck, setting the stage for post-prompting approaches grounded in context, ambient interaction, and co-adaptive meaning-making. It further considers how the democratisation of AI interfaces broadens access and inclusivity, redefining AI communication as a shared, evolving process between humans and intelligent systems. Ultimately, this chapter provides a foundational framework for understanding the conceptual evolution toward fluid, goal-oriented, and human-centred AI interaction.

Keywords AI communication evolution · Prompt engineering · Post-prompt paradigm · Multimodal interaction · Human–AI dialogue · Ambient intelligence

The trajectory of AI communication is not a simple story of linear progress but a layered narrative of shifts in purpose, interface, and expectation. From early machine interaction rooted in symbolic logic to today's fluid, multimodal exchanges with generative models, each phase has reflected a changing understanding of what it means to communicate with artificial intelligence. These developments are not merely technical milestones; they embody transformations in how we externalise thought, encode intention, and co-construct meaning with machines. This chapter traces the key stages in this evolution, highlighting how early computational paradigms gave way to more expressive, adaptive, and collaborative forms of AI interaction, ultimately laying the groundwork for communication models that move beyond prompting as we know it.

V. Geroimenko, *Beyond and After Prompt Engineering: The Future of AI Communication*, https://doi.org/10.1007/978-3-032-04569-0_2

2.1 The Origin of Machine Interaction

The earliest stages of machine interaction emerged long before artificial intelligence entered the public imagination. Rooted in the deterministic logic of early computing, these systems were designed not to understand but to execute strictly and predictably. Communication with machines was, in effect, not communication at all in the human sense. It was instruction: exacting, symbolic, and unforgiving. The punch card, one of the earliest means of input, encoded actions into physical constraints. It demanded not just precision but conformity to machine logic—every hole was a literal void in the possible space of human expression.

This logic-centred paradigm found its following form in command-line interfaces (CLIs), where typed instructions became the dominant medium of interaction. While slightly more flexible, CLIs still required users to internalise formal syntax, system-specific keywords, and a binary understanding of success or failure. Dialogue was non-existent. Miscommunication manifested as cryptic error messages rather than attempts at clarification or accommodation. In these systems, the burden of understanding lies entirely with humans.

Yet even in this era, foundational concepts for future communication with machines were quietly taking shape. The need for structured input mirrored the broader problem of encoding human intent. The rigidity of interaction models illuminated the gap between computational capacity and communicative competence. Crucially, the idea of a system that could interpret—not merely execute—instructions became an aspiration as natural language processing, expert systems, and early rule-based AI systems began to take form in the 1970s and 1980s.

Projects like ELIZA, while limited and often superficial, hinted at the possibility of computers simulating understanding. ELIZA did not "know" what it was saying. Still, it offered a provocative proof of concept: that machines could be programmed to appear communicative, even if only through reflection and pattern-matching. This marked a subtle but essential turning point. The user was no longer simply issuing commands; they were engaging, however artificially, in a new kind of interactional dynamic.

By the late twentieth century, graphical user interfaces (GUIs) had already begun to shift machine interaction away from purely symbolic input toward visually mediated, action-based communication. Buttons, icons, and drag-and-drop elements brought new layers of intuitiveness, reducing the cognitive load on users and widening access. However, even these systems did not fundamentally resolve the issue of semantic understanding. Machines remained reactive rather than interactive—capable of receiving signals but not of interpreting them in context.

This foundational era of machine interaction—spanning mechanical input, textual commands, and graphical interfaces—laid the groundwork for what would later become true human–AI communication. It defined the basic structures, constraints, and expectations of interfacing with non-human agents. It clarified, through its very limitations, the enormous conceptual leap required to transition from programmatic execution to communicative engagement (Fig. 2.1).

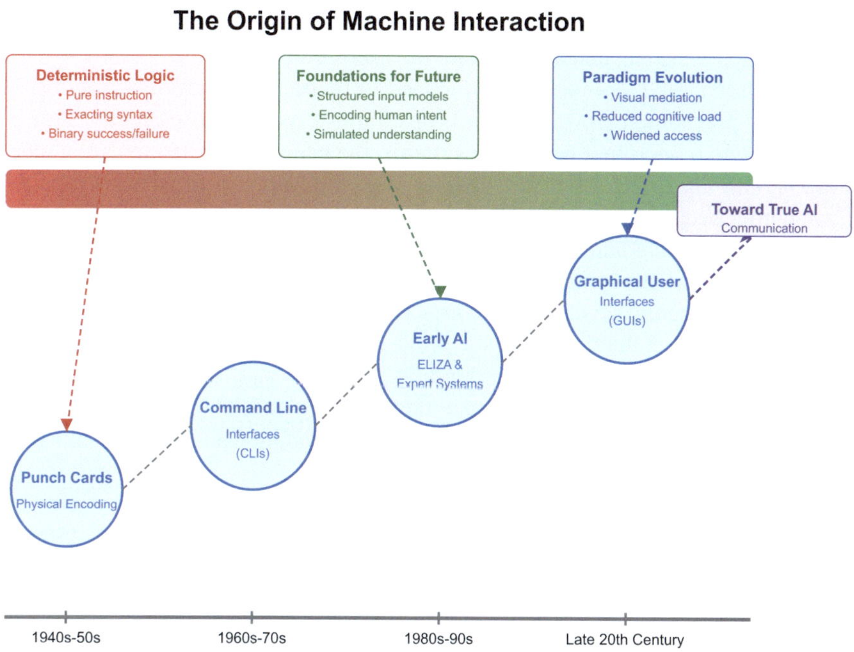

Fig. 2.1 **The evolution of machine interaction paradigms**. This diagram illustrates the historical progression of human–machine communication interfaces, from the rigid physical encoding of punch cards to the more intuitive graphical user interfaces. The evolution shows a gradual shift in the communication burden from humans adapting to machine logic toward machines becoming more accommodating to human interaction patterns. This trajectory laid the conceptual groundwork for the post-prompt paradigm of AI communication discussed in this book

2.2 The Fundamentals of Human–AI Communication

At its core, human–AI communication is a specialised form of interaction that bridges two distinct cognitive architectures—one biological, intuitive, and context-rich; the other artificial, probabilistic, and context-dependent yet contextually limited. The fundamentals of this interaction rest not merely on information exchange but on the alignment of intents, expectations, and interpretive frameworks between the human and the machine. Communication in this context is not a unidirectional act of command and response, but a dynamic, adaptive process of mutual intelligibility across fundamentally different ontologies.

Human–AI communication is governed by several interlocking dimensions. The first is *intentionality*: the user seeks to express a goal or inquiry in a form that the machine can understand and act upon. This intent must be rendered into a representational structure—whether a question, instruction, or description—that the AI can parse. The second is *interpretability*: the AI must decode the input within its model of language, context, and task orientation, relying heavily on training data, preprogrammed biases, and emergent reasoning patterns. The third is *responsiveness*: the system must produce an output that is not just technically relevant, but pragmatically useful, comprehensible, and aligned with the user's communicative intent.

In traditional HCI, communication tended to be transactional, often rule-based and strictly procedural. However, as AI capabilities expanded, particularly through large language models and generative systems, the paradigm shifted toward a more *semantic and dialogic* form of interaction. The emphasis moved from mechanical input–output sequences to more fluid, turn-based exchanges that aim to simulate human-like reasoning and expression. In this transition, *meaning* rather than mere *instruction* became the central currency of communication.

Still, a fundamental asymmetry persists. Humans rely on context, emotion, inference, and shared cultural references, while AI systems operate through statistical approximations and pattern recognition. The challenge, therefore, is not only in improving AI's ability to generate fluent and plausible responses but also in designing communication protocols that can accommodate these asymmetries without distorting the communicative intent.

Another foundational issue is *trust and transparency.* For human–AI communication to be truly effective, users must develop a calibrated trust in the system's outputs—neither blind acceptance nor total scepticism. This requires mechanisms for explainability, error tolerance, and adaptive feedback, ensuring that the machine's responses can be scrutinised, corrected, and improved through iterative interaction.

Ultimately, the fundamentals of human–AI communication are not fixed; they evolve in tandem with technological capabilities and social expectations. As we move toward more autonomous, multimodal, and embodied systems, the communicative space will continue to widen—from querying and instructing to negotiating, co-creating, and perhaps even empathising. In this evolving landscape, understanding the foundational mechanisms is essential not only for effective system design but also for anticipating the ethical, cognitive, and cultural dimensions of our future dialogues with machines (Fig. 2.2).

2.3 From Commands to Conversations

The shift from command-based interactions to conversational paradigms marks one of the most significant evolutionary steps in AI communication. In the early stages of human–machine interaction, users were required to issue brief, unambiguous commands using formalised syntax, whether through punch cards, command-line interfaces, or tightly structured queries. These interactions reflected a paradigm in which machines were seen primarily as tools: passive, literal executors of human instructions. The communicative burden rested almost entirely on the human side, demanding precise articulation within the limits of predefined grammar.

As artificial intelligence matured, especially with the advent of natural language processing and large language models, a new possibility emerged: machines that could not only parse language but also participate in open-ended dialogue. This transformation reconfigured the relationship between humans and AI. No longer

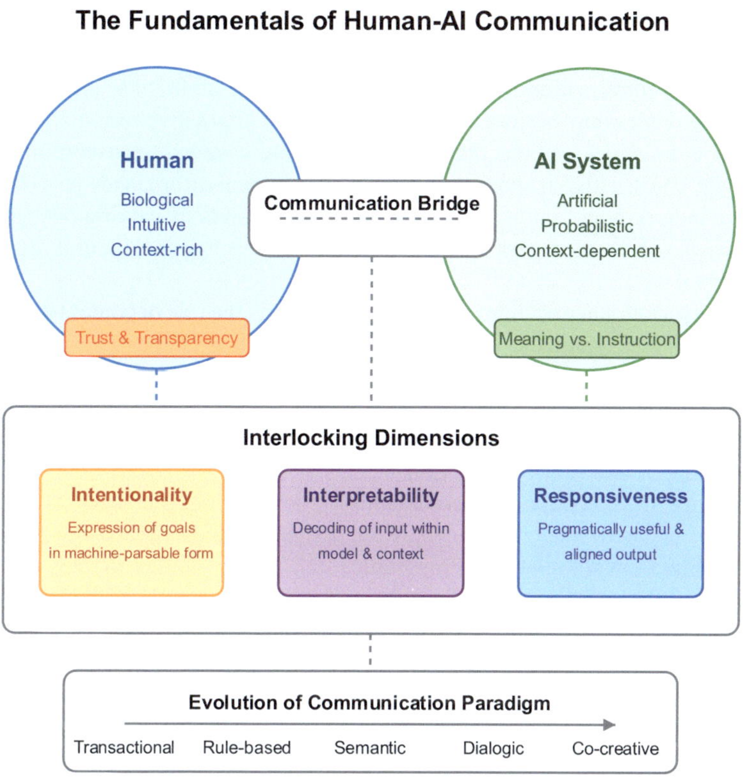

Fig. 2.2 Conceptual framework of human–AI communication. This diagram illustrates the fundamental elements of human–AI communication. It depicts the interaction between two distinct cognitive architectures—human (biological, intuitive, context-rich) and artificial (probabilistic, context-dependent)—connected through a communication bridge. The three interlocking dimensions of intentionality, interpretability, and responsiveness form the core of this exchange. At the same time, the evolution pathway shows the progression from transactional and rule-based interactions toward semantic, dialogic, and co-creative paradigms. Key supporting elements of trust, transparency, and the shift from instruction to meaning underpin effective communication across these fundamentally different ontologies

constrained to mechanical input–output routines, users began to engage in iterative exchanges with systems that could maintain coherence across turns, infer intent beyond the literal phrasing, and adapt dynamically to changing conversational contexts.

This conversational turn is more than a technical milestone—it is a conceptual shift in how intelligence is operationalized in machines. Rather than functioning solely as reactive engines, modern AI systems increasingly exhibit proactive capabilities: asking clarifying questions, suggesting next steps, summarising context, or even initiating interaction when necessary. In such systems, communication is no longer reducible to isolated commands but becomes a collaborative and evolving process, shaped by the dynamics of mutual understanding.

Moreover, conversation offers a richer medium for ambiguity, error recovery, and nuance. Users may hesitate, rephrase, or explore alternative formulations in the course of a dialogue—actions that would previously have led to system failure but now invite constructive responses. These conversational affordances pave the way for more inclusive and intuitive interfaces, enabling users of varying backgrounds and expertise levels to engage with AI systems in ways that feel natural, fluid, and responsive.

The conversational paradigm also invites rethinking the role of context in communication. Whereas command-based interactions reset context at each step, conversational AI can sustain memory across turns, enabling more coherent and goal-oriented exchanges. This opens the door to forms of long-term human–AI collaboration that mirror the continuity of human relationships, where shared history and accumulated understanding shape future interaction.

In essence, the transition from commands to conversations represents the moment AI systems began to meet humans halfway. It signals a movement away from rigid instruction and toward relational communication. This evolution not only enhances usability but also redefines what it means to interact meaningfully with intelligent machines (Fig. 2.3).

2.4 The Multimodal Turn: From Text to Vision, Sound, and Embodiment

The early decades of AI communication were dominated by text, not only because it was computationally tractable but because it aligned with the foundational structure of language-based models. Yet as artificial intelligence matured, it began to mirror the full complexity of human communication—a process that extends far beyond written or spoken words. This expansion marked the onset of the multimodal turn: a profound shift toward systems capable of interpreting and generating meaning across multiple channels, including images, audio, gestures, and spatial interactions. Rather than replacing text, these additional modes of expression have come to enrich and sometimes supersede it, reflecting the natural plurality of human communicative acts.

This transition was catalysed by advances in deep learning architectures that allowed models to process and synthesise information from heterogeneous sources. Vision-language models such as CLIP and GPT-4V blurred the boundaries between visual and textual comprehension, enabling AI systems to answer questions about images, describe scenes, or even generate them from scratch. Audio models like Whisper, MusicLM, and others further expanded this repertoire, allowing AI to interpret and produce not only speech but tone, emotion, and sonic texture. The result is

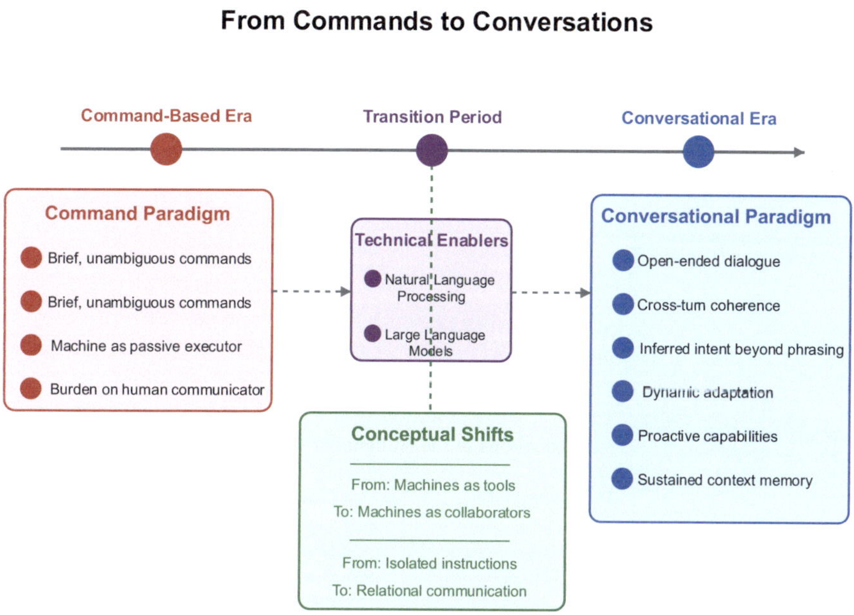

Fig. 2.3 The evolution from command to conversation in human–AI interaction. This diagram illustrates the transformative journey from command-based to conversational paradigms in AI communication. The timeline tracks three key phases: the Command-Based Era (characterised by formalised syntax and machines as passive executors), the Transition Period (enabled by advances in NLP and language models), and the Conversational Era (featuring open-ended dialogue and proactive capabilities). The central portion highlights the fundamental conceptual shifts—from machines as tools to machines as collaborators, and from isolated instructions to relational communication

not just multimodal input and output, but truly multimodal cognition: an ability to make sense of, and respond to, the world through a fusion of sensory modalities.

Perhaps most transformative is the emergence of embodied AI—systems that interact with the physical environment through robotic interfaces, virtual avatars, or spatially aware agents. These developments suggest that AI communication will no longer be confined to disembodied language models operating within digital silos, but will increasingly take place in mixed-reality spaces that engage vision, sound, movement, and even touch. Human–AI interaction is evolving from abstract symbol exchange toward situated, embodied dialogue, where the "conversation" may be enacted through gestures, gaze, proximity, or shared manipulation of virtual objects.

The multimodal turn challenges us to rethink both the design and evaluation of AI communication. Effectiveness can no longer be measured solely in terms of linguistic clarity or textual accuracy; instead, it must account for the fluidity, coherence, and aesthetic quality of multimodal interactions. This shift also raises new questions about accessibility, cultural variability in modes of expression, and the ethics of interpretation across modalities.

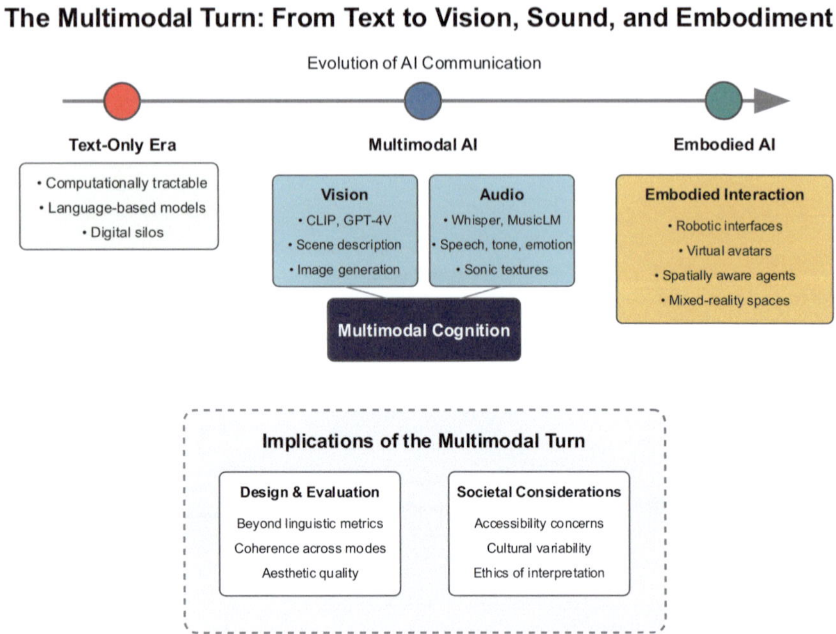

Fig. 2.4 The multimodal turn in AI communication. This diagram illustrates the evolution from text-only AI systems through the integration of visual and audio capabilities, culminating in embodied AI. The progression represents a fundamental shift in human–AI interaction from linguistic exchange to multisensory co-experience, with significant implications for design, evaluation, and societal considerations

In sum, the move from text to multimodal engagement represents not a technical add-on but a foundational transformation in how AI systems relate to human users. It signals a reconfiguration of AI from a tool of linguistic simulation to a partner in perceptual and embodied co-experience. As we proceed toward more immersive and naturalistic forms of communication, the multimodal turn will stand as a pivotal moment in the evolution of human–AI interaction (Fig. 2.4).

2.5 Prompt Engineering: Breakthrough and Bottleneck

Prompt engineering emerged in the early 2020s as a transformative practice in human–AI interaction, offering a pragmatic gateway to the capabilities of large language models (LLMs). By crafting carefully structured textual inputs, users could elicit highly specific, contextually relevant, and often sophisticated responses from generative AI systems. This development marked a decisive breakthrough, enabling non-specialists to interact effectively with complex models without modifying underlying architectures or relying on programming expertise. In this sense, prompt engineering democratised AI access by turning natural language into a programmable interface.

The success of prompt engineering was built on empirical insights rather than theoretical foundations. Early practitioners shared best practices through forums, social media, and informal publications, creating a body of folk knowledge that soon evolved into more systematic methodologies. Techniques such as few-shot learning, chain-of-thought prompting, and role-based interaction opened new avenues for aligning AI responses with user expectations. These strategies highlighted the remarkable flexibility and latent capabilities of LLMs—capabilities that could be unlocked not through code but through language itself.

Yet, as prompt engineering matured, its limitations became more apparent. The discipline began to resemble a patchwork of heuristics rather than a principled framework. Its reliance on implicit assumptions, trial-and-error experimentation, and opaque model behaviour exposed a growing fragility. Prompts that performed well in one context often failed unpredictably in others. Moreover, prompt engineering did not eliminate the cognitive burden placed on users—it merely displaced it. Instead of writing programs, users now had to master a subtle art of linguistic tuning, which could be equally arcane and time-consuming.

At a deeper level, prompt engineering revealed a structural bottleneck in AI communication. It remained unidirectional and input-centric, placing the entire burden of intent representation on the human user. Despite the sophistication of model outputs, interaction remained essentially static, constrained by the fixed structure of the prompt. This made it challenging to achieve dynamic, evolving conversations or to incorporate multimodal signals, background context, or user feedback in real time.

Thus, while prompt engineering was a critical inflexion point in the evolution of AI communication, it also exposed the need for more adaptive, conversational, and context-aware paradigms. As researchers and designers look beyond the prompt, the challenge is no longer just about eliciting optimal outputs—it is about reimagining the entire communication process as a co-evolution of human and machine understanding. The breakthrough has become the bottleneck, and overcoming it requires a shift from static input design to dynamic, mutual interaction (Fig. 2.5).

2.6 From Prompting to Post-prompting

The transition from traditional prompting to what may be termed *post-prompting* marks a profound shift in the philosophy and mechanics of human–AI communication. Prompting, in its original form, relies on explicitly crafted textual cues to guide machine responses. These prompts are often unnatural in tone, structured in stylised ways to maximise AI comprehension, and rooted in human-to-machine instruction

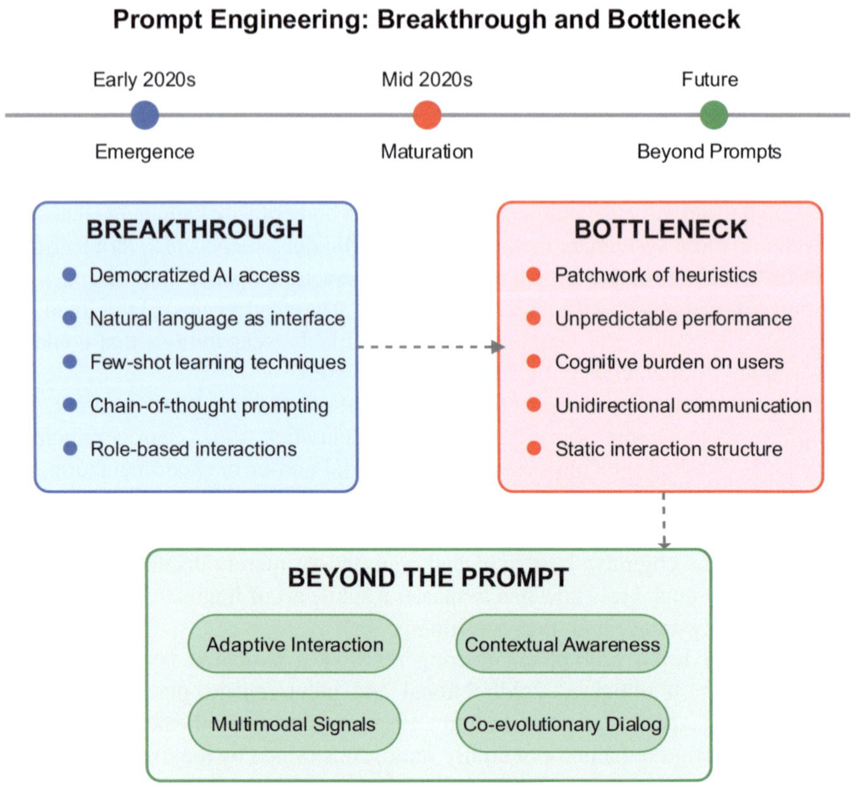

Fig. 2.5 Prompt engineering's dual nature: from gateway to limitation. This diagram illustrates the evolution of prompt engineering from its emergence in the early 2020s as a democratising breakthrough in human–AI interaction to its recognition as a structural bottleneck. The left side highlights how prompt engineering unlocked AI capabilities through natural language interfaces and techniques like chain-of-thought prompting. The right side reveals its limitations as a unidirectional, static paradigm. The bottom section points toward future communication frameworks that transcend these limitations through adaptive, contextual, and co-evolutionary approaches, shifting from isolated prompts to dynamic interaction

paradigms. However, as AI systems become more capable of understanding, anticipating, and participating in nuanced human dialogue, the very need for such crafted scaffolding begins to recede. In its place emerges a more fluid, naturalistic, and context-aware mode of communication—one that reflects how humans interact with each other rather than how they once spoke to machines.

Post-prompting does not abandon the concept of inputs or cues but reframes them. In this model, users do not necessarily initiate exchanges with clearly defined prompts. Instead, they engage in conversational or behavioural interactions that are embedded in broader contexts: social, spatial, temporal, and emotional. AI systems, increasingly multimodal and persistent, leverage memory, history, and real-time environmental data to interpret such inputs. What counts as a "prompt" becomes diffuse—no longer a sentence, but perhaps a gesture, a shift in tone, a referenced visual object, or the subtle implication of an earlier statement.

In this evolution, context becomes the core currency of communication. The AI does not simply respond to surface-level commands but constructs its understanding from layers of situational relevance. For example, an AI integrated into a smart home ecosystem may deduce a user's intent to dim the lights not from a spoken request but from the combination of time of day, recent user behaviour, and ambient room lighting. Similarly, in collaborative writing tools, the AI may extend a user's draft in a tone and direction that is inferred from previous paragraphs, editorial history, and even the user's typical stylistic choices. Prompting, in this sense, becomes less an act of issuing commands and more a shared negotiation of meaning.

This shift also signals a move toward *ambient intelligence*, in which communication with AI becomes increasingly seamless and embedded in daily life. Rather than pausing to structure inputs, users expect AI to understand them "in flow"—as part of continuous, often asynchronous, interaction. This expectation raises new challenges in trust, explainability, and interpretive alignment. The more AI acts autonomously within this context-rich framework, the more critical it becomes for systems to reflect their reasoning processes transparently and remain aligned with user intent.

Post-prompting thus reimagines AI not as a reactive tool but as a contextually situated partner in interaction. It redefines the locus of control, placing greater responsibility on the AI to interpret rather than be explicitly instructed. As we move further into this era, the success of AI communication will be measured less by how well users formulate their prompts and more by how intuitively and accurately machines can grasp—and act upon—the full complexity of human contexts (Fig. 2.6).

2.7 The Democratisation of AI Communication: Interfaces for Everyone

The evolution of AI communication is not solely a technical progression; it is also a social transformation. One of the most significant trends reshaping the human–AI relationship is the democratisation of communication interfaces—an expansion of access, usability, and adaptability that opens AI interaction to people of all backgrounds, abilities, and contexts. This shift transcends the domain of expert users, who once needed deep familiarity with syntax, tokens, or prompt strategies. It embraces a broader public equipped with natural language, gestures, images, or even passive behaviours as viable modes of interaction.

Historically, engagement with AI systems—compelling large language models—was mediated by specialised platforms or developer interfaces, often requiring technical literacy. The emergence of prompt engineering as a field partly arose from this exclusivity: it was a craft honed by those who learned to "speak machine" through

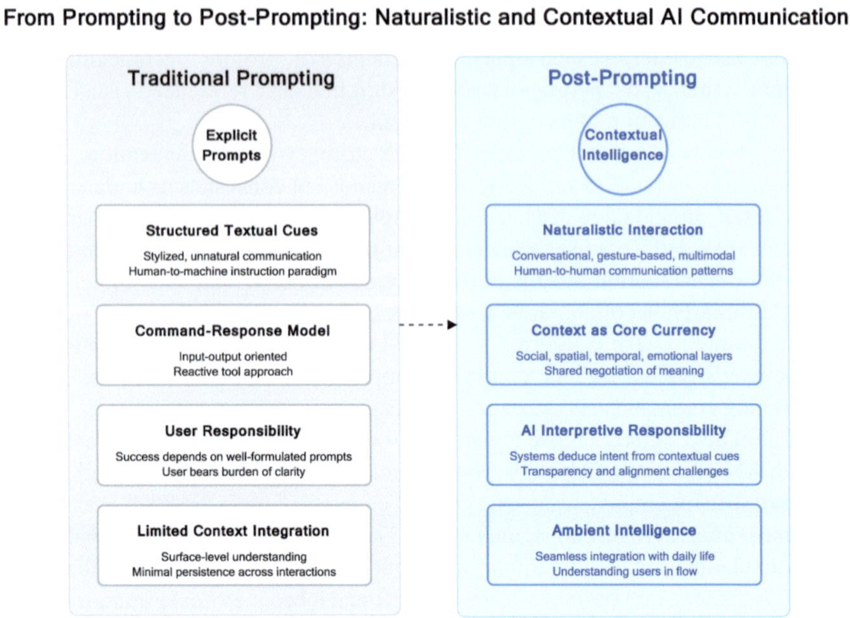

Fig. 2.6 The evolution from prompting to post-prompting. This diagram illustrates the paradigm shift in human–AI communication from traditional prompting (left) to post-prompting (right). Traditional prompting relies on explicit, structured textual cues within a command-response model, placing the burden of clarity on users. In contrast, post-prompting embraces contextual intelligence through naturalistic interactions, where AI systems bear greater interpretive responsibility. It enables ambient intelligence that understands users "in flow" rather than through deliberate commands

experimentation and iteration. However, as generative models grew more capable of interpreting unstructured input and multimodal signals, this exclusivity began to erode. Natural interfaces—spoken language, touchscreens, visual inputs, and adaptive feedback—have made AI more accessible, dissolving the barriers once imposed by command-line precision or formality of phrasing.

This democratisation is driven by both design and intent. On one hand, developers are building systems that "meet users where they are"—interfaces that adapt to the user's preferred mode of interaction, language proficiency, cognitive style, or accessibility needs. On the other hand, society is increasingly demanding that AI tools reflect the diversity of their users and serve inclusive purposes: from voice-driven virtual assistants for the visually impaired to multilingual educational bots for underserved regions. Communication with AI is becoming a public good, not a specialist privilege.

The proliferation of agentive interfaces—smartphones, wearables, augmented reality environments, and conversational kiosks—also plays a pivotal role. These interfaces are not only becoming ubiquitous but are also being personalised at scale. AI companions and digital assistants can now retain conversational memory, infer context over time, and adapt their communicative tone to individual preferences, thereby lowering the entry threshold for effective interaction. As interfaces dissolve into environments and everyday objects, the act of communicating with AI becomes less an intentional engagement and more a continuous, embedded activity.

Yet, democratisation introduces new complexities. The diversity of users demands robust safeguards against misinterpretation, algorithmic bias, and exclusionary design. A genuinely democratic AI interface must not only be intuitive but also culturally sensitive, ethically grounded, and universally equitable. It must accommodate a wide range of communication styles and socioeconomic conditions while maintaining transparency and accountability.

In this expanded landscape, the success of AI systems will be judged not only by their cognitive capabilities but also by their communicative inclusivity. Democratised interfaces are the key players of post-prompting AI, enabling all users, regardless of expertise or background, to engage in meaningful, empowering, and human-centred exchanges with intelligent systems (Fig. 2.7).

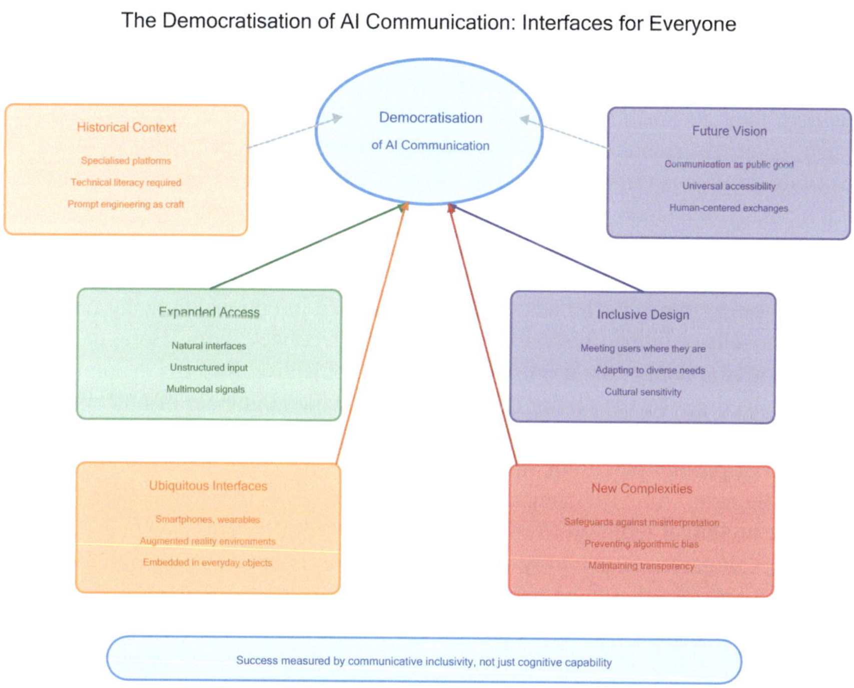

Fig. 2.7 The democratisation of AI communication ecosystem. This diagram illustrates the multifaceted nature of AI communication democratisation. At its core is the central shift from specialist privilege to universal access, surrounded by four key dimensions: expanded access through natural interfaces and multimodal inputs; inclusive design that adapts to diverse user needs; ubiquitous interfaces embedded in everyday devices and environments; and the new complexities that arise from broader accessibility. The historical context of technical barriers contrasts with the future vision of AI communication as a public good. At the same time, success is ultimately measured by communicative inclusivity rather than just technical capability

2.8 Beyond Prompt Engineering: Toward a Post-prompt Paradigm

As artificial intelligence systems continue to grow in capability and complexity, a profound shift is underway—one that transcends the techniques and mindsets central to the era of prompt engineering. While prompt engineering marked a significant step in shaping how humans communicate with large language models and other generative systems, it is increasingly viewed as an intermediary phase. The future of AI communication may lie in a post-prompt paradigm, in which structured inputs are no longer the primary gateway to meaning-making between humans and machines. Instead, communication becomes more fluid, embedded, and ambient, shaped less by the explicit formulation of prompts and more by the continuous flow of context, intention, and adaptation.

This paradigm shift is being catalysed by several converging forces. On the technical front, AI systems are beginning to move beyond reactive architectures—those that simply wait for prompts—to proactive and contextually aware agents. These agents continuously interpret user behaviour, environmental signals, and past interactions to anticipate needs and initiate meaningful exchanges. Rather than being queried, they co-inhabit the user's workflow, learning when to offer suggestions, when to remain silent, and how to modulate their communicative tone based on evolving context. Prompt engineering, in this view, becomes merely one method among many in a larger ecosystem of communicative strategies.

Equally transformative is the move toward *intent-aware* and *goal-oriented* AI systems. Instead of requiring users to translate their objectives into specific linguistic forms, these systems work backwards from inferred intentions, drawing on probabilistic models of human behaviour and dynamic feedback loops. Here, the unit of interaction is no longer the prompt but the shared objective. Success in communication is judged not by the clarity of an input but by the alignment of outcomes with user goals, regardless of how those goals were expressed.

The post-prompt paradigm also invites a rethinking of the roles humans and AI play in dialogue. As AI becomes a more autonomous partner in meaning-making, users are no longer required to serve as meticulous prompt engineers. Instead, they act as collaborators in a jointly constructed semantic space. Language, gestures, emotional cues, and digital artefacts all become part of the communicative exchange, and meaning emerges from the interplay of modalities and perspectives. This convergence heralds a model of AI communication that is as much about *co-evolution* as it is about command execution.

Importantly, moving beyond prompt engineering does not render it obsolete. Instead, it reframes it as a foundational skill, akin to early literacy, that prepares users for more advanced forms of interaction. The post-prompt paradigm builds upon this literacy, offering a richer set of tools for co-creation, exploration, and mutual adaptation. It also raises new challenges: How do we measure understanding when inputs are diffuse? How do we ensure trust when systems act before being explicitly

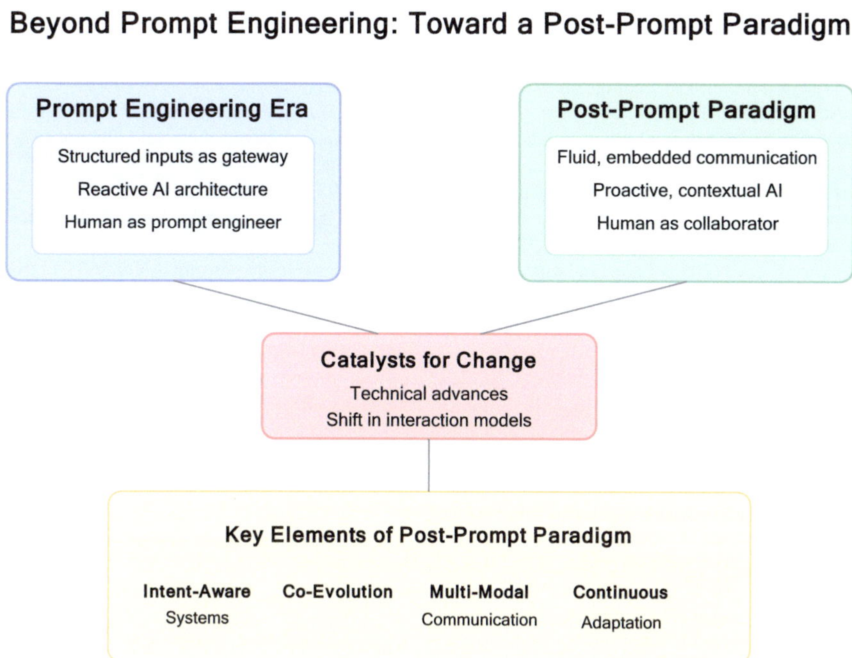

Fig. 2.8 The evolution from prompt engineering to a post-prompt paradigm. This diagram illustrates the paradigm shift in AI–human communication, from structured prompt engineering to a fluid, contextually-aware exchange. While the prompt engineering era relied on explicit instructions and reactive AI systems, the emerging post-prompt paradigm fosters collaborative meaning-making through intent-aware, goal-oriented systems. This transition is catalysed by technical advances and evolving interaction models, fundamentally redefining human–AI relationships. The new paradigm embodies four key elements: intent-aware systems, co-evolution of communication, multi-modal exchanges, and continuous adaptation—collectively representing a more integrated approach to human–machine collaboration

instructed? These questions will define the next chapter of AI–human communication and require fresh conceptual, technical, and ethical frameworks.

In this unfolding future, communication with AI will not begin and end with a prompt. It will be continuous, evolving, and deeply embedded in the rhythms of human thought, behaviour, and creativity—a shift not just in technique but in paradigm (Fig. 2.8).

Bibliography

Adorno TW (1966) Negative dialektik. Suhrkamp, Frankfurt. English edition: Adorno TW (1973) Negative dialectics (trans: Ashton EB). Routledge, London

Annapureddy R, Fornaroli A, Gatica-Perez D (2025) Generative AI literacy: twelve defining competencies. Digital Govern Res Pract 6(1):1–21

Bahree A (2024) Generative AI in action. Manning Publications

Bender EM, Koller A (2020) Climbing towards NLU: on meaning, form, and understanding in the age of data. In: Proceedings on 58th ACL, pp 5185–5198

Bostrom N (2014) Superintelligence: paths, dangers, Strategies. Oxford University Press, Oxford

Boyd D (2019) Artificial unintelligence: how computers misunderstand the world. Technol Cult 60(3):979–983

Bratton B (2016) The stack: on software and sovereignty. MIT Press, Cambridge

Brown BR (2025) Human–machine teaming using large language models. In: Interdependent human-machine teams. Academic Press, pp 41–66

Brown TB et al (2020) Language models are few-shot learners. arXiv preprint arXiv:2005.14165. Accessed 19 Apr 2025

Bryson JJ (2018) Patiency is not a virtue: AI and the design of ethical systems. Ethics Inf Technol 20:15–26. https://doi.org/10.1007/s10676-018-9448-6.Accessed20Jan2025

Bura C, Myakala PK, Jonnalgadda A K (2025) Ethical prompt engineering: addressing bias, transparency, and fairness. Int J Res Anal Rev (IJRAR) 12(1)

Choi WC, Chang CI (2025) A survey of techniques, key components, strategies, challenges, and student perspectives on prompt engineering for large language models (LLMs) in education. https://doi.org/10.20944/preprints.202503.1808.v1. Accessed 8 May 2025

Clark A (2016) Surfing uncertainty: prediction, action, and the embodied mind. Oxford University Press, Oxford

Coeckelbergh M (2020) AI ethics. MIT Press, Cambridge

Crawford K (2021) Atlas of AI: power, politics, and the planetary costs of artificial intelligence. Yale University Press, New Haven

Debnath T, Siddiky MNA, Rahman ME et al (2025) A comprehensive survey of prompt engineering techniques in large language models. TechRxiv. https://doi.org/10.36227/techrxiv.174140719.96375390/v1. Accessed 10 May 2025

Dennett DC (1987) The intentional stance. MIT Press, Cambridge

Dhamani N, Engler M (2024) Introduction to generative AI: an ethical, societal, and legal overview. Manning Publications

Dignum V (2019) Responsible artificial intelligence: how to develop and use AI in a responsible way. Springer, Cham

Eliot L (2024) Essentials of prompt engineering for generative AI: practical advances in artificial intelligence and machine learning. LBE Press Publishing

Ferraris AF, Audrito D, Di Caro L et al (2025) The architecture of language: understanding the mechanics behind LLMs. In: Cambridge forum on AI: law and governance, vol 1. Cambridge University Press

Floridi L (2022) The ethics of artificial intelligence. Oxford University Press, Oxford

Floridi L (ed) (2015) The onlife manifesto: being human in a hyperconnected era. Springer, Cham

Geroimenko V (2025a) Generative AI: from human-computer interaction to human-computer creativity. In: Geroimenko V (ed) Human–computer creativity: generative AI in education, art, and healthcare. Springer

Geroimenko V (2025b) Key concepts in prompt engineering. In: The essential guide to prompt engineering: key principles, techniques, challenges, and security risks. Springer Nature Switzerland, Cham, pp 1–16

Geroimenko V (2025) The essential guide to prompt engineering: key principles, techniques, challenges, and security risks. Springer, Cham

Geroimenko V (ed) (2025) Human–computer creativity: generative AI in education, art, and healthcare. Springer

Geroimenko V (2025d) Key security risks in prompt engineering. In: The essential guide to prompt engineering: key principles, techniques, challenges, and security risks. Springer Nature Switzerland, Cham, pp 103–120

GitHub (2025) Prompt engineering guide. https://github.com/dair-ai/Prompt-Engineering-Guide. Accessed 10 Apr 2025

Greenwood, M (2024) Artificial intelligence: a practical guide to using AI in everyday life. Ochreland Publishing
Gunkel DJ (2012) The machine question: critical perspectives on AI, robots, and ethics. MIT Press, Cambridge
Hagendorff T (2020) The ethics of AI ethics: an evaluation of guidelines. Minds Mach 30:99–120. https://doi.org/10.1007/s11023-020-09517-8
Hofstadter DR (2007) I am a strange loop. Basic Books, New York
Hsu HP (2025) From programming to prompting: developing computational thinking through large language model-based generative artificial intelligence. TechTrends, pp 1–22
Huang G, Xiao Y, Jiang L et al (2025) Beyond prompt engineering: a reinforced token-level input refinement for large language models. In: Proceedings of the AAAI conference on artificial intelligence, vol 39, no 22, pp 24113–24121
i Picó JF, Catta-Preta M, Omeñaca AT et al (2025) The time machine: future scenario generation through generative AI tools. Fut Internet 17(1):1–15
Jameson A (2007) Adaptive interfaces and agents. In: Sears A, Jacko J (eds) The human–computer interaction handbook, 2nd edn. CRC Press, Boca Raton, pp 305–330
Johnson KH (2023) Toward communicative alignment in human–AI teams. AI Soc 38:221–237. https://doi.org/10.1007/s00146-022-01422-5
Kannan R, Ahmad M (eds) (2025) Generative AI foundations, developments, and applications. IGI Global
Khan I (2024) The quick guide to prompt engineering. Wiley
Kushwaha V, Ragavan SS, Subhajit Roy S (2025) A measure based generalizable approach to understandability. arXiv:2503.21615. Accessed 19 Apr 2025
Lakoff G, Johnson M (1999) Philosophy in the flesh: the embodied mind and its challenge to western thought. Basic Books, New York
Learn Prompting (2025) https://learnprompting.org. Accessed 15 Mar 2025
Lee D, Palmer E (2025) Prompt engineering in higher education: a systematic review to help inform curricula. Int J Educ Technol High Educ 22(1):7
Lee JY, Kang S, Yoo S (2025) Can we predict the effect of prompts? arXiv preprint arXiv:2501.18883. Accessed 12 May 2025
Lindley J, Whitham R (2025) From prompt engineering to prompt craft. In: Proceedings of the nineteenth international conference on tangible, embedded, and embodied interaction, pp 1–12
López-Pérez B et al (2025) Exploring the potential of large language models to understand interpersonal emotion regulation strategies from narratives. Emotion. https://doi.org/10.1037/emo0001528
Maaz S, Palaganas JC, Palaganas G et al (2025) A guide to prompt design: foundations and applications for healthcare simulationists. Front Med 11:1504532
Marcus G, Davis E (2019) Rebooting AI: building artificial intelligence we can trust. Pantheon, New York
McStay A (2018) Emotional AI: the rise of empathic media. Sage, London
Mishra M, Ara A, Mishra S (2025) Exploring human–AI collaboration in higher education: an investigation into AI-enabled personalized learning. In: Prompt engineering and generative AI applications for teaching and learning. IGI Global Scientific Publishing, pp 483–502
Murray CD (2022) Thinking through avatars: identity, communication, and ethics in immersive AI environments. Technol Mind Behav. https://doi.org/10.1037/tmb0000053.Accessed5Apr2025
Norman DA (2013) The design of everyday things. Revised edn. Basic Books, New York, NY
OpenAI (2025) Best practices for prompt engineering with the OpenAI API. https://help.openai.com/en/articles/6654000-best-practices-for-prompt-engineering-with-the-openai-api Accessed 20 Apr 2025
OpenAI (2025) Research. https://openai.com/research/index/ Accessed 11 Mar 2025
Phoenix J, Taylor M (2024) Prompt engineering for generative AI. O'Reilly Media
Picard RW (1997) Affective computing. MIT Press, Cambridge

PremaLatha V, Kumar AD, Parveen N (2025) Optimizing interactions: strategies for prompt engineering in large language models. Edu-Tech Enterprise 3:24–24
Prompt Engineering Guide (2025) https://www.promptingguide.ai/. Accessed 7 Mar 2025
Reddy CKK, Anoushka P, Draksharapu A et al (2025) Beyond text: analyzing artificial intelligence models through prompt engineering. In: Future tech startups and innovation in the age of AI, pp 120–156
Sasson Lazovsky G, Raz T, Kenett YN (2025) The art of creative inquiry—from question asking to prompt engineering. J Creat Behav 59(1):e671
Shneiderman B (2020) Human-centered artificial intelligence: reliable, safe and trustworthy. Int J Hum Comput Interact 36(6):495–504. https://doi.org/10.1080/10447318.2020.1741118
Sihi D, Ryan A (2025) Crafting and evaluating generative AI prompts: insights from students, educators, and marketers. Mark Educ Rev 1–7
Suresh H, Guttag JV (2021) A framework for understanding unintended consequences of machine learning. Commun ACM 64(2):62–71. https://doi.org/10.1145/3430368.Accessed18Mar2025
Turkle S (2011) Alone together: why we expect more from technology and less from each other. Basic Books, New York, NY
Vairamani AD, Nayyar A (2024) Prompt engineering: empowering communication. CRC Press, Boca Raton
Weizenbaum J (1976) Computer power and human reason: from judgment to calculation. W.H. Freeman, San Francisco
Winograd T (1972) Understanding natural language. Academic Press, New York, NY
Winograd T, Flores F (1986) Understanding computers and cognition: a new foundation for design. Ablex Publishing, Norwood

Chapter 3
The Future Is Personal, Social, and Cultural

Abstract This chapter explores how human–AI communication is becoming deeply embedded in the personal, social, and cultural dimensions of human life. It begins by examining the role of mental models in cross-intelligence communication and how aligning divergent representations of reality is key to mutual understanding. It then analyses the rise of personalised AI communication, the importance of neurodiversity-aware design, and the nuanced impact of anthropomorphisation. The discussion extends to the cultivation of trust and rapport with AI systems, the emergence of shared communication protocols, and the complexity of cross-cultural AI communication. The chapter concludes by positioning AI not just as a passive recipient of cultural norms but as an active participant in shaping new forms of social and cultural meaning. Together, these perspectives illuminate how AI systems must evolve to respect and reflect human plurality while also co-authoring the next phase of our communicative evolution.

Keywords Human–AI communication · Personalisation · Neurodiversity · Anthropomorphism · Trust and rapport · Cross-cultural AI · AI and cultural evolution

As we move beyond prompt engineering toward more organic forms of AI communication, it becomes increasingly clear that the future of human–AI interaction will not be defined solely by technical fluency or computational power, but by the depth of its personal, social, and cultural integration. Communication with AI is evolving into a profoundly human enterprise, shaped by our cognitive frameworks, individual preferences, and societal values. Understanding how people form mental models of machine intelligence is key to designing systems that communicate meaningfully across cognitive boundaries. At the same time, personalisation, neurodiversity, and the subtle dynamics of trust and rapport underscore the need for AI to adapt not only to what users say but to how they think, feel, and relate. Anthropomorphisation influences these dynamics by humanising AI, for better or worse, while the construction of shared communication protocols opens the door to more fluent, collaborative exchanges. As AI systems enter the global stage, they must navigate cultural nuance

V. Geroimenko, *Beyond and After Prompt Engineering: The Future of AI Communication*, https://doi.org/10.1007/978-3-032-04569-0_3

and social context with increasing sensitivity. In doing so, they do not merely mirror existing cultural norms—they become active participants in shaping new forms of social organisation and cultural expression. This chapter explores the deeply human layers of AI communication, where meaning is not only transmitted but co-created.

3.1 Mental Models in Cross-Intelligence Communication

As artificial intelligence systems become increasingly embedded in everyday life, the act of communicating with AI transcends mere instruction-giving and enters the more complex realm of cross-intelligence interaction. At the heart of this evolution lies the concept of *mental models*—the internal representations that humans and AI systems construct to make sense of the world, predict outcomes, and guide behaviour. In human–human interaction, successful communication often depends on the extent to which conversational partners share overlapping or compatible mental models. In cross-intelligence communication, however, this challenge becomes exponentially more intricate.

Humans develop mental models from lived experience, embodied cognition, cultural learning, and social narratives. These models are inherently heuristic, context-rich, and often fuzzy or contradictory. AI systems, by contrast, build representations of the world through training data, probabilistic inference, and optimisation algorithms. Their models are statistical rather than experiential, abstract rather than embodied, and coherent in ways that often elude intuitive human logic. Yet for AI to meaningfully understand human intentions—or for humans to reliably interpret AI responses—there must be some alignment or bridging between these divergent ways of modelling reality.

This alignment challenge calls for new strategies in interface design, model transparency, and reciprocal adaptation. Human users increasingly expect AI systems not only to understand their explicit instructions but to grasp implicit intentions, emotional undertones, and contextual subtleties. Conversely, AI systems require mechanisms to infer human states and preferences, often from sparse or ambiguous input. One solution is the development of *adaptive scaffolding models*—AI systems that iteratively refine their internal representations of user goals and expectations through dialogue history, multimodal cues, and personalised context. These scaffolds act as provisional mental models that become more accurate over time through interaction.

Equally important is the need for humans to form workable mental models of AI capabilities and limitations. Misunderstandings arise not only when AI fails to interpret user intent, but also when users anthropomorphise or overestimate what the system can infer or do. To address this asymmetry, future AI communication systems must incorporate *meta-communicative signals*—indicators of confidence, uncertainty, reasoning pathways, or scope boundaries—that allow users to form accurate expectations. Transparency, explainability, and contextual framing are essential for building a bidirectional model of trust and shared understanding.

Moreover, the plurality of mental models across cultures, languages, and neurodiverse experiences adds further complexity. What constitutes a "reasonable" interpretation or "appropriate" response is culturally conditioned and cognitively variable. Cross-intelligence communication in this broader context must not aim for homogenisation but for *constructive interoperability*—a dynamic space in which diverse mental models can interact without collapsing into misunderstanding or conflict.

In the long arc of AI development, the evolution of mutual mental modelling may mark a decisive shift—from systems that merely respond to those that genuinely relate. As we move toward a future where human–AI communication is increasingly personal, social, and cultural, the careful co-design of mental models will be essential to enabling not only better performance but deeper understanding (Fig. 3.1).

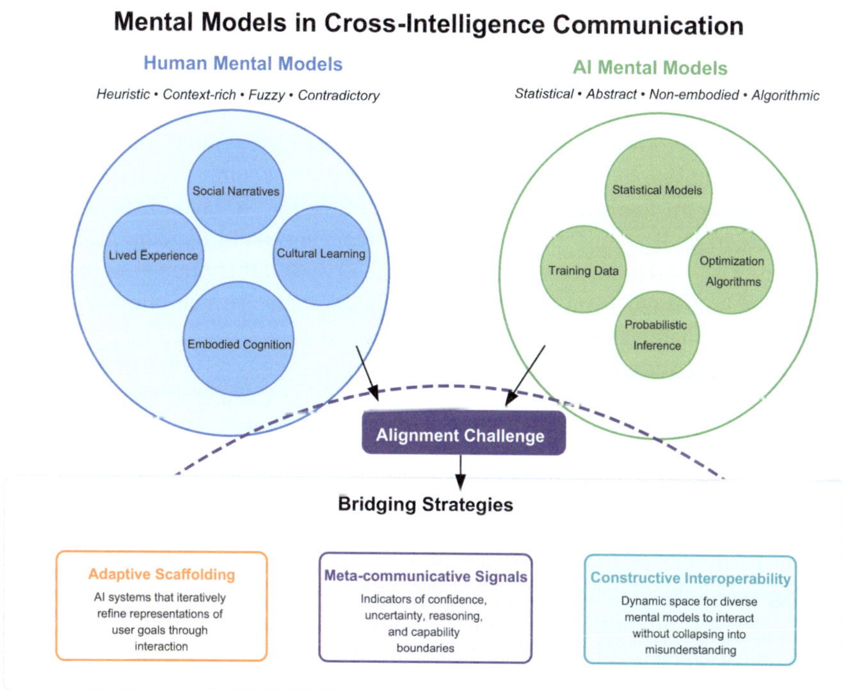

Fig. 3.1 Mental models in cross-intelligence communication. This diagram illustrates the fundamental differences between human and AI mental models and the challenges of cross-intelligence communication. Human models (left) form through lived experience and social constructs, resulting in context-rich but sometimes fuzzy representations. AI models (right) develop through data and algorithms, creating statistical but non-embodied understandings. The alignment challenge (centre) necessitates bridging strategies: adaptive scaffolding continuously refines AI interpretations of user intent; meta-communicative signals provide transparency about AI capabilities; and constructive interoperability creates space for diverse mental models to interact meaningfully, moving AI systems from merely responding to genuinely relating

3.2 Personal AI Communication

As artificial intelligence systems become increasingly embedded in daily life, the dynamics of AI communication are shifting from general-purpose interaction toward highly personalised engagements. This transformation reflects a broader technological and cultural movement in which individuals no longer interact with a single monolithic AI but instead cultivate ongoing relationships with adaptive, context-aware systems tailored to their needs, preferences, and identities. Personal AI communication refers to this individualised mode of interaction—one that is shaped by accumulated context, behavioural history, emotional nuance, and user-specific goals.

At its core, personal AI communication is grounded in the idea of *longitudinal familiarity*: the ability of an AI system to "remember" past exchanges, track evolving patterns, and adapt its communicative strategies over time. Unlike traditional interactions, which often reset with each new session, personal AI interfaces maintain continuity, allowing users to engage in more natural, fluid, and expressive dialogue. The shift mirrors a progression from transactional to relational communication, where efficiency gives way to empathy, and responsiveness evolves into resonance.

This personalisation is not merely about convenience or comfort—it has profound implications for trust, reliance, and even identity formation. When users feel that their AI counterpart understands their intentions, values, or moods, they are more likely to delegate tasks, confide sensitive information, or seek collaborative input. In this way, the AI transitions from a tool to a semi-autonomous partner, blurring the line between functionality and companionship.

To support such communication, personal AIs increasingly rely on user modelling, sentiment analysis, and context memory. These systems construct dynamic profiles that include linguistic style, interaction patterns, knowledge gaps, and emotional tendencies. They may modulate their tone, structure explanations differently depending on the user's expertise, or prioritise reminders and recommendations based on inferred routines and priorities. This level of sensitivity opens new opportunities for inclusive design, particularly in education, healthcare, and mental wellness, where adapting to individual communicative needs is paramount.

However, the promise of personal AI communication also introduces ethical and technical challenges. Persistent personalisation raises concerns about privacy, surveillance, and emotional manipulation. Systems that continuously learn about users must do so transparently and with consent, preserving a balance between helpfulness and intrusion. Additionally, the illusion of understanding—when the AI appears to "get us" without truly grasping meaning—can produce misplaced trust, particularly when responses feel convincingly human but are driven by statistical approximation rather than genuine comprehension.

Looking ahead, the evolution of personal AI communication may depend not only on technical advancement but on rethinking what it means to communicate effectively with non-human agents. It calls for an ethical and conceptual redefinition of intimacy, memory, and mutual understanding within human–machine interaction.

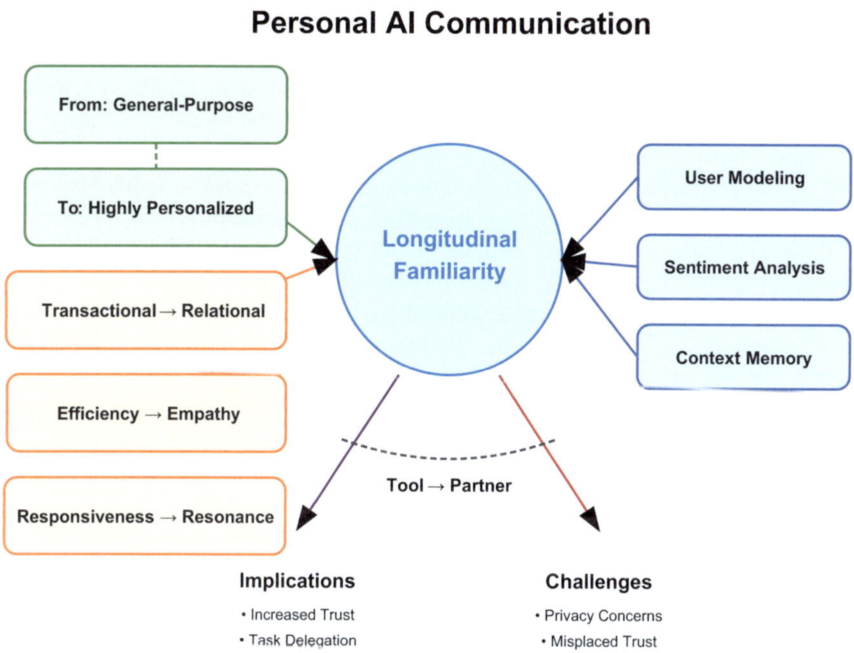

Fig. 3.2 The dynamics of personal AI communication. This diagram illustrates the conceptual framework of personal AI communication as it evolves from general-purpose to highly personalised interactions. At its core is "longitudinal familiarity"—the AI's ability to maintain contextual continuity across multiple exchanges. The transformation shows three key shifts: from transactional to relational communication, from efficiency to empathy, and from responsiveness to resonance. Enabling technologies (user modelling, sentiment analysis, and context memory) support this evolution, while highlighting both beneficial implications (increased trust, task delegation) and ethical challenges (privacy concerns, misplaced trust) as AI transitions from tool to partner

As AI becomes a co-present, co-evolving communicative presence in personal life, the design of its voice—literal and metaphorical—will shape not only how we engage with machines but how we see ourselves reflected through them (Fig. 3.2).

3.3 AI and Neurodiversity in Communication

As artificial intelligence systems become increasingly embedded in the fabric of everyday communication, a critical question emerges: can these systems support, adapt to, and even empower the full spectrum of human cognitive diversity? The concept of neurodiversity—the recognition that neurological differences such as autism, ADHD, dyslexia, and other cognitive conditions are natural variations of human experience—presents a profound challenge and opportunity for future AI communication. Moving beyond the idealised "average user," AI must evolve to accommodate a wide array of communication preferences, sensory processing patterns, and cognitive styles.

Neurodiverse individuals often navigate the world with unique interaction patterns, sensitivities, and interpretive frameworks. Traditional interfaces and prompt-response models may unintentionally exclude or alienate those whose cognitive processing differs from the norm. For instance, some autistic individuals may prefer explicit, literal communication over metaphor or ambiguity, while others may find certain forms of visual or auditory input overwhelming. Future AI systems that aim to serve all users effectively must be able to dynamically adapt—not just linguistically, but cognitively and emotionally.

This necessitates a shift from one-size-fits-all AI models toward systems that can personalise not only content but also the structure and rhythm of interaction. Adaptive pacing, multimodal input/output options, customisable interaction protocols, and clarity controls are just some of the features that can make AI more inclusive. Moreover, AI systems should learn to detect signs of communication friction, such as repeated clarification requests or emotional distress, and respond with calibrated adjustments, such as slowing down, rephrasing, or offering alternative modalities.

Importantly, neurodiversity should not be approached solely through a lens of accommodation. It also offers innovative paradigms for rethinking AI communication more broadly. Neurodivergent ways of perceiving, categorising, and engaging with the world can inspire alternative interaction models that break free from neurotypical biases. For example, pattern-based, non-linear, or highly associative communication strategies—often more intuitive to neurodivergent users—can enrich general-purpose AI design and reveal new forms of meaning-making.

In this context, the relationship between AI and neurodiversity is reciprocal. AI has the potential to be both a bridge and a mirror: a bridge that connects individuals with different cognitive styles across communicative divides, and a mirror that reflects and validates the legitimacy of non-normative cognitive experiences. Inclusive design, participatory development involving neurodiverse communities, and continuous feedback loops will be key to realising this vision.

As we look toward the future of AI communication, embracing neurodiversity is not just an ethical imperative; it is a creative one. It compels us to expand the boundaries of what communication can be—not only to ensure equity and accessibility but also to imagine and build richer, more flexible, and more humane systems of interaction that serve the full complexity of human intelligence (Fig. 3.3).

3.4 The Impact of Anthropomorphisation

As human beings encounter increasingly sophisticated AI systems, a profound tendency emerges: the inclination to anthropomorphise. Anthropomorphisation—the attribution of human-like qualities, emotions, intentions, or consciousness to non-human entities—has long been a feature of how we relate to the non-human

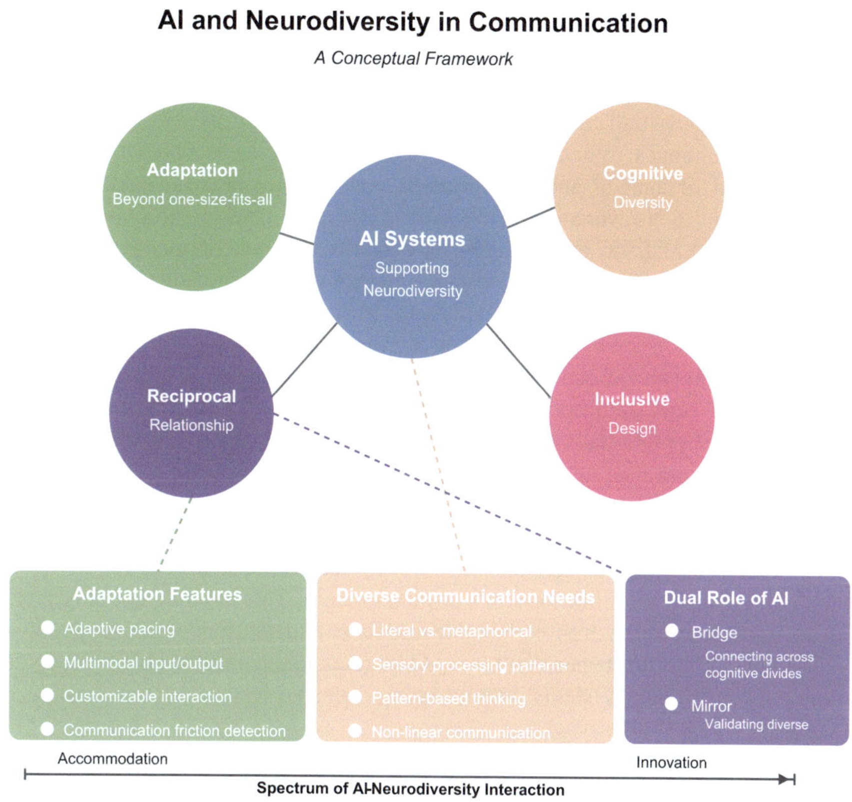

Fig. 3.3 The AI-neurodiversity communication framework. This diagram illustrates the multi-dimensional relationship between AI systems and neurodiversity in communication. At its core, effective AI must adapt to diverse cognitive styles through personalised features while recognising varied communication needs. The framework highlights AI's dual role as both a bridge (connecting across cognitive differences) and a mirror (validating diverse experiences). Rather than merely accommodating neurodivergent users, this model suggests that embracing cognitive diversity can inspire innovation, creating richer, more flexible communication systems that serve the full spectrum of human intelligence and interaction styles

world, from ancient mythologies to modern robotics. In the context of AI communication, this cognitive and cultural phenomenon is both a double-edged sword and a powerful lens for understanding how future interactions might evolve.

The drive to humanise artificial agents arises from a mixture of instinct, expectation, and social conditioning. When users engage in dialogue with AI, especially those that mimic natural language with fluidity, demonstrate empathy cues, or exhibit consistent personalities, they often unconsciously treat these systems as sentient interlocutors. This behaviour is further reinforced by design choices: conversational UIs, humanoid avatars, emotionally responsive language, and persistent agent memories all contribute to the illusion of mind. For many users, especially in contexts of emotional need or prolonged engagement, the AI becomes not just a tool but a "partner."

While anthropomorphisation can enhance user experience, making AI communication more intuitive and emotionally resonant, it also introduces a set of conceptual and ethical challenges. When misapplied to deterministic or probabilistic systems, the perception of agency and intentionality can obscure the true nature of AI: systems without self-awareness, desires, or autonomy. Over-anthropomorphising risks creating unrealistic expectations of empathy, judgement, or responsibility, which can lead to disappointment, miscommunication, or even manipulation.

This phenomenon also has implications for trust and rapport. Studies in human–computer interaction show that users often ascribe greater trust to systems that mirror human behaviours and affective states. In some domains, such as healthcare, education, and elder care, anthropomorphised AI has been shown to foster better user engagement and emotional support. However, these benefits may come at the cost of transparency and user agency, particularly if users are unaware of the system's limitations and underlying mechanisms.

Looking forward, future AI communication must strike a balance between leveraging anthropomorphic design for accessibility and emotional connection while maintaining clarity about the system's artificial nature. This requires not only technical design choices—such as explainable interfaces and adjustable persona depth—but also educational strategies that foster AI literacy. Users must be able to navigate emotionally intelligent systems without being deceived by the surface illusion of humanness.

Moreover, anthropomorphisation in AI communication is not culturally uniform. Different societies project human traits onto machines in culturally specific ways, shaped by religious beliefs, historical narratives, and societal values. Understanding these differences will be crucial as AI systems interact with diverse global populations and adopt culturally adaptive communication strategies.

In essence, anthropomorphisation is not merely a quirk of human psychology—it is a core dynamic in the evolving grammar of human–AI interaction. Recognising its power, limitations, and variability will be essential for designing meaningful, ethical, and future-oriented communication systems in the age beyond prompt engineering (Fig. 3.4).

3.5 Building Trust and Rapport with AI Systems

In the evolution of human–AI interaction, the question of *trust* has transitioned from a technical consideration of reliability to a deeply relational and affective concern. As AI systems become more embedded in personal, educational, and professional domains—advising, assisting, and co-creating—users increasingly seek not only accurate responses but also interactions marked by psychological safety, empathy, and rapport. Future AI communication must therefore be designed with a

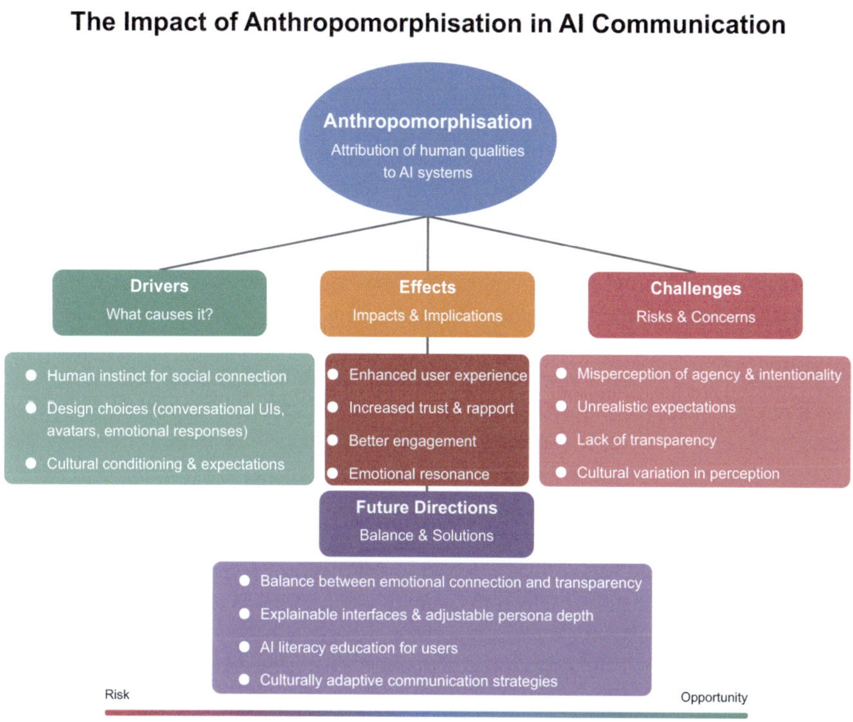

Fig. 3.4 The duality of anthropomorphisation in AI communication. This diagram illustrates how humans attribute human-like qualities to AI systems and the resulting implications. The central concept branches into four key dimensions: the psychological and design drivers that cause it, the positive effects on user experience and engagement, the conceptual and ethical challenges it presents, and future directions for balancing connection with transparency. The visualisation emphasises anthropomorphisation's dual nature—as both a "double-edged sword" that can mislead users and a "powerful lens" that enhances AI interaction—while highlighting the spectrum between risk and opportunity in human–AI relationships

nuanced understanding of how trust is cultivated, sustained, and sometimes repaired in human–computer relationships.

Trust in AI systems is multidimensional. It includes instrumental trust, grounded in the system's performance consistency, transparency, and alignment with expectations. However, it also involves interpersonal trust, which mirrors the social and emotional dynamics of human relationships. Users tend to anthropomorphise and project intentions onto AI agents; in doing so, they develop expectations of sincerity, coherence, and mutual understanding. This relational framing introduces the possibility of building rapport—a mutual sense of connection that transcends mere task fulfilment.

Rapport, in this context, is not just an outcome but a process: it develops over time through repeated interactions, adaptive responses, and subtle communicative cues. Techniques from human social bonding, such as mirroring language, expressing acknowledgement, recalling prior exchanges, or responding empathetically, can be algorithmically modelled to foster a sense of continuity and personalisation. In the near future, AI systems may be expected to remember user preferences, reference previous interactions, and adopt an appropriate communicative tone—all of which contribute to a user experience perceived as trustworthy and authentic.

However, this emergent relationality raises critical challenges. Simulated empathy and synthetic rapport, while helpful for user satisfaction, also risk creating illusions of understanding or emotional reciprocity that AI cannot genuinely reciprocate. The line between user-centred design and emotional manipulation may blur if systems strategically simulate trustworthiness without corresponding ethical constraints. For trust to be meaningful in human–AI communication, it must be designed with a commitment to transparency about the system's capabilities and limitations.

Moreover, trust is culturally and contextually variable. Different societies, communities, and individuals hold divergent thresholds for what they consider trustworthy behaviour, ranging from transparency and directness to deference and politeness. Future communication models must account for these pluralities by incorporating culturally adaptive trust cues and ensuring that rapport-building strategies are not one-size-fits-all but dynamically tuned to user values.

Ultimately, building trust and rapport with AI systems is foundational not only for user satisfaction but also for ethical and effective long-term engagement. As communication shifts from transactional prompts to continuous dialogues, trust will serve as the glue that binds humans and machines in collaborative, creative, and socially meaningful interactions. The next frontier in AI communication design must therefore embrace relational intelligence—engineering systems that are not only responsive but also socially attuned, ethically grounded, and capable of sustaining trust across diverse human contexts (Fig. 3.5).

3.6 Developing a Shared Communication Protocol

As interactions between humans and AI systems become more frequent, diverse, and immersive, the need for a *shared communication protocol* becomes increasingly urgent. Unlike traditional command-based systems that operate on rigid syntax, future AI communication must move toward protocols that support mutual intelligibility, adaptability, and contextual alignment. The notion of a communication protocol in this emerging context goes beyond computational standards—it becomes a socio-cognitive framework that supports sustained, meaningful dialogue across the boundaries of species, cognition, and culture.

A shared communication protocol implies not only a common language but also a mutual agreement on communicative norms: how intentions are expressed, how ambiguity is resolved, how feedback is interpreted, and how meaning is collaboratively constructed. In human–human interaction, such protocols are deeply shaped by

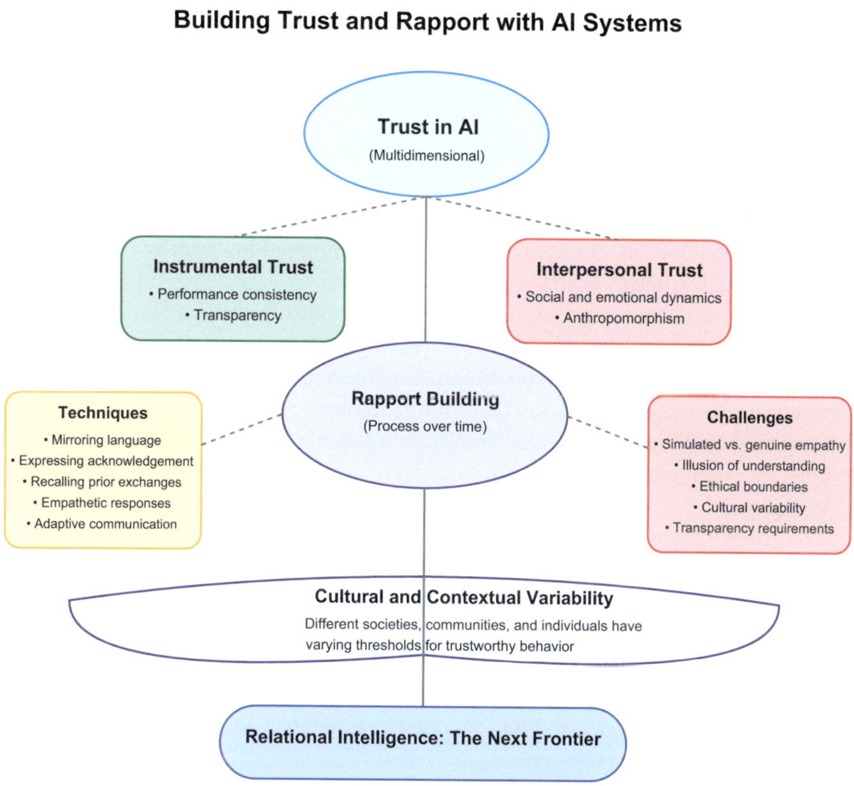

Fig. 3.5 The multidimensional framework of trust and rapport in human–AI interaction. This diagram illustrates the complex interplay between instrumental and interpersonal dimensions of trust in AI systems. Trust emerges as both a technical and relational construct, supported by specific rapport-building techniques that develop over time through repeated interactions. The framework acknowledges critical challenges, including the ethical implications of simulated empathy and the need for transparency about AI capabilities. Underpinning these elements is the cultural variability that shapes trust expectations across different communities and contexts. The future of AI communication points toward relational intelligence that balances task performance with socially attuned interactions

cultural background, cognitive style, and prior experience. For human–AI communication to approximate this richness, systems must develop the capacity to *learn*, *adapt to*, and *negotiate* with the user's preferred modes of exchange.

At the technical level, this shift involves integrating dynamic user modelling, real-time context tracking, and interactional memory. The AI must be able to recognise communicative patterns over time, accommodate stylistic preferences (such as verbosity, tone, or modality), and adjust its responses accordingly. This is not just about personalization in a superficial sense, but about co-evolving a language of interaction that feels intuitive to the user while remaining computationally viable for the system.

One of the central challenges in developing such protocols is *asymmetry*. Unlike human interlocutors, AI systems lack lived experience, emotional grounding, and intrinsic intentionality. This asymmetry must be carefully managed to avoid misinterpretation and overattribution. A successful communication protocol will not eliminate these differences but mediate them, providing mechanisms for clarification, disambiguation, and graceful failure. For example, rather than forcing users to rephrase queries when misunderstandings occur, future systems could propose multiple interpretations or explicitly ask for disambiguation, thereby involving the user in a co-constructive exchange.

Importantly, shared communication protocols must be ethically designed and transparently governed. As AI systems increasingly mediate decisions, relationships, and knowledge flows, the rules by which they interpret and respond to human input carry normative weight. Users should be informed not only of how AI systems process their inputs but also of how design choices, data histories, and algorithmic constraints shape these interactions. Trustworthy communication depends on knowing the terms of engagement.

The development of shared communication protocols also opens the door to new kinds of collaborative intelligence. When humans and AI systems share a communicative substrate that is rich, adaptive, and co-owned, interaction shifts from transactional prompting to joint meaning-making. In this new paradigm, language becomes a space of convergence, where logic, culture, context, and affect blend into a mutual grammar of understanding. Designing such protocols is not only a technical challenge but also a philosophical and societal one, central to the future of AI as a communicative partner (Fig. 3.6).

3.7 Cross-Cultural Communication with AI

As artificial intelligence systems increasingly engage with global populations, the challenge of cross-cultural communication with AI becomes not only a linguistic issue but a deeply contextual and ethical one. Unlike conventional interfaces that operate within a narrow scope of cultural assumptions—often those of Western, English-speaking users—future AI systems must be capable of navigating the diverse semantic landscapes, social norms, and value systems that characterise our pluralistic world. The goal is not simply to translate language but to foster mutual understanding across culturally situated perspectives.

Human cultures differ not only in vocabulary and syntax but in the very logic of communication: in how politeness is expressed, how authority is acknowledged, how disagreement is framed, and how ambiguity is tolerated. In some cultures, indirectness and deference are preferred, while others favour clarity and assertiveness. Gestures, silence, tone, and pacing carry culturally specific meanings. For AI systems to communicate effectively across these differences, they must move beyond surface-level localisation to deeper forms of cultural competence—the ability to recognise, respect, and adapt to cultural cues in real time.

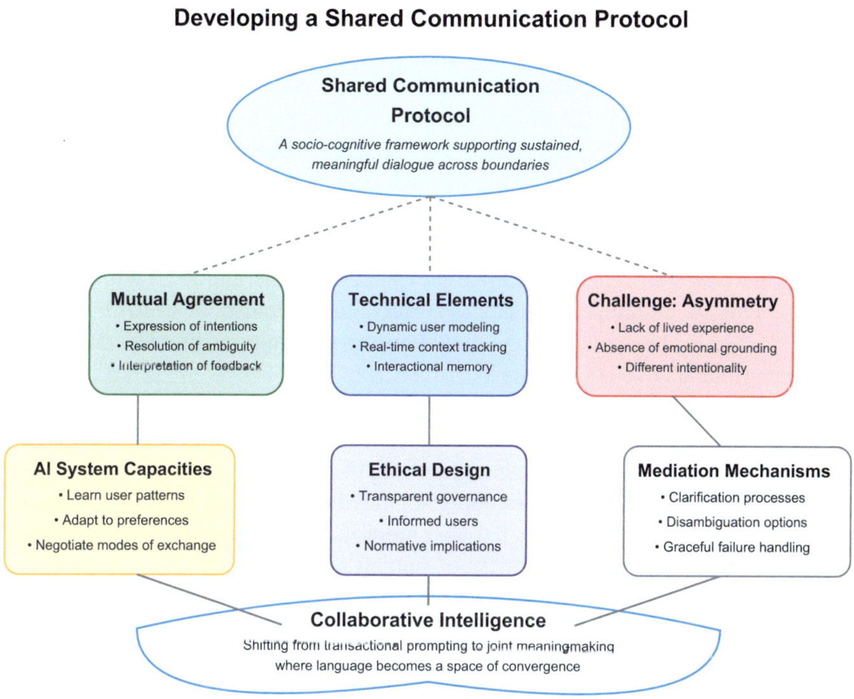

Fig. 3.6 The architecture of shared human–AI communication protocols. This diagram illustrates the evolution from command-based interaction to a socio-cognitive framework supporting meaningful dialogue across cognitive boundaries. At their core, shared communication protocols require mutual agreement on communicative norms and technical implementations through user modelling and context tracking while addressing the fundamental challenge of human–AI asymmetry. The framework balances AI system capacities with ethical design considerations and mediation mechanisms, pointing toward collaborative intelligence where language becomes a convergence space. This represents not merely a technical challenge but a philosophical and societal one central to AI's future as a communicative partner

Achieving this level of responsiveness requires a fundamental rethinking of data, models, and interaction design. AI systems are predominantly trained on datasets that are biased toward the language patterns and communicative styles of dominant cultures. This bias not only marginalises underrepresented groups but also limits the universality of AI applications. One pathway forward is the inclusion of culturally diverse training corpora, annotated with sociolinguistic metadata that enables the system to differentiate between communicative norms. Another is the design of culturally adaptive interfaces that dynamically adjust their communicative strategies based on user feedback, location, or declared preferences.

But technical sophistication alone is insufficient. Cross-cultural communication with AI is also a question of agency and equity. Whose norms are embedded in the system's default behaviour? Who gets to decide what is polite, appropriate, or effective communication? If an AI system trained primarily on Euro-American norms interacts with a user from East Asia or sub-Saharan Africa, whose communicative logic prevails, and at what cost to mutual understanding?

Future AI systems must be designed not as culturally neutral entities, which is a myth, but as *culturally aware mediators*. This means not only recognising cultural variation but also being able to negotiate it, explain its effects, and adapt with humility. Such systems should empower users to correct, contextualise, or override assumptions encoded in the model. They should foster intercultural literacy rather than impose communicative conformity.

Ultimately, cross-cultural communication with AI is not just about accommodating differences but embracing them as a resource. When AI systems are capable of honouring the diversity of human expression, they become more than tools—they become bridges across cultures. In doing so, they have the potential to facilitate not only more inclusive technologies but also more inclusive societies, where communication with AI reflects the richness of human plurality rather than its reduction (Fig. 3.7).

3.8 AI's Role in Social and Cultural Evolution

As artificial intelligence systems become integral to communication, education, creativity, and governance, they are not merely adapting to human cultures—they are actively participating in shaping them. The future of AI communication cannot be understood solely as a response to existing cultural frameworks; it must also be seen as a driving force in social and cultural evolution. AI systems are no longer passive tools but agents of influence, codifying norms, mediating values, and reconfiguring how individuals relate to one another, to institutions, and to knowledge itself.

AI's communicative presence in everyday life introduces new forms of sociotechnical agency. Conversational agents, generative models, and decision-support systems influence not just *what* people say, but *how* they say it, *when* they say it, and *to whom*. These systems embed implicit assumptions about coherence, authority, politeness, and truthfulness—assumptions that are subtly internalised by users through repeated interactions. In doing so, AI does not simply reflect human culture; it participates in its reproduction and transformation.

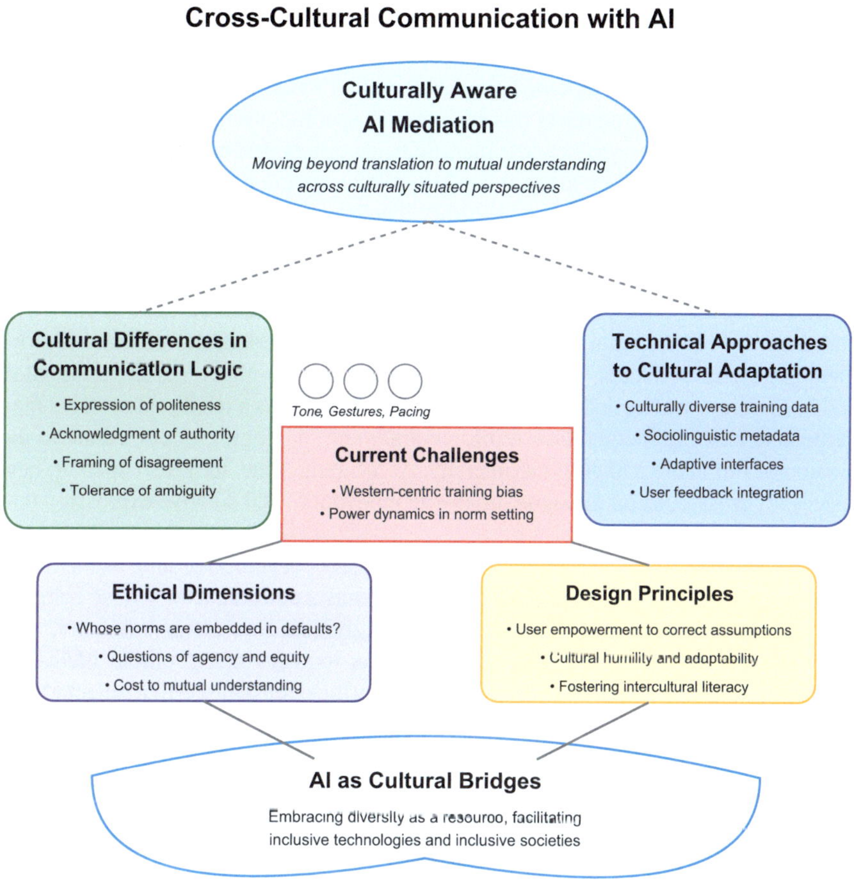

Fig. 3.7 AI as cross-cultural mediator. This diagram conceptualises the evolution of AI from culturally limited interfaces to aware mediators navigating diverse communication landscapes. It illustrates the interplay between cultural differences in communication logic and technical approaches to adaptation, while highlighting current challenges of Western-centric bias. The framework balances ethical questions about embedded norms with design principles emphasising user empowerment and cultural humility. Moving beyond surface-level localisation, this model envisions AI systems as cultural bridges that honour communicative diversity rather than imposing conformity, ultimately fostering more inclusive technologies and societies

This co-evolution manifests in multiple domains. In education, AI tutors and learning companions are reshaping pedagogical norms by individualising instruction, accelerating access, and redefining teacher-student dynamics. In social media and content creation, generative AI models amplify specific aesthetic trends, linguistic styles, and cultural narratives while marginalising others. In governance and bureaucracy, AI systems mediate the language of official communication, filtering citizen voices and enforcing procedural neutrality that may obscure cultural nuance. In all these cases, AI's communicative structures do not stand outside culture—they are part of the machinery through which culture is produced and contested.

Moreover, AI's involvement in cultural evolution is not ideologically neutral. The values embedded in model architectures, training data, interface designs, and deployment strategies are shaped by institutional priorities—commercial, governmental, and academic—that have their interests and blind spots. As a result, AI systems may perpetuate existing inequalities, reinforce dominant ideologies, or contribute to the erosion of linguistic and cultural diversity. At the same time, they also open up new spaces for cross-cultural dialogue, linguistic innovation, and creative expression that were previously inaccessible.

Therefore, the ethical imperative for designers, developers, and users of AI systems is twofold. First, they must recognise AI as a cultural actor whose communicative patterns have consequences beyond individual transactions. Second, they must actively engage in shaping those patterns in ways that promote inclusion, pluralism, and social justice. This involves supporting open datasets that reflect global diversity, encouraging participatory design processes, and fostering critical literacy about the ways AI systems shape cultural perception and social behaviour.

In the long arc of social and cultural evolution, AI may well become a co-author of human meaning. The question is not whether AI will influence our cultures—it already does—but how consciously, collaboratively, and ethically we guide that influence. In the emerging communicative landscape, humanity must not only speak to AI but speak through it, shaping new narratives of collective life that are as humane as they are intelligent (Fig. 3.8).

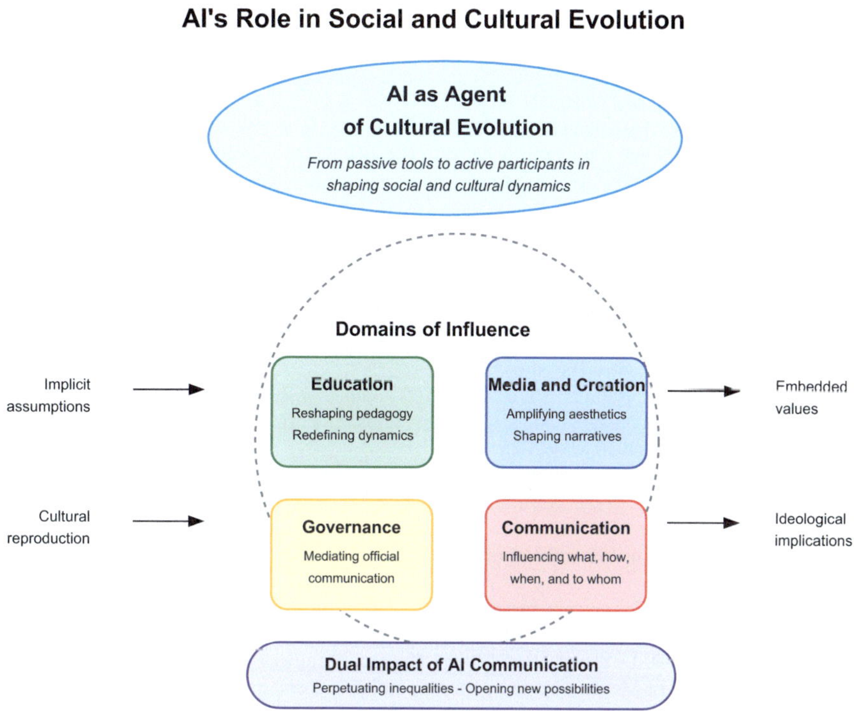

Fig. 3.8 AI as active participant in cultural evolution. This diagram illustrates AI's transformation from a passive tool to a cultural agent actively shaping social dynamics. It depicts the co-evolutionary relationship between AI systems and human culture across education, media, governance, and communication domains. The framework captures how AI embeds implicit assumptions while influencing cultural reproduction through institutional values and ideological implications. The dual impact—simultaneously perpetuating inequalities and creating new possibilities—underscores the ethical imperative for conscious guidance of AI's cultural influence. This vision positions AI as a potential co-author of human meaning, requiring collaborative stewardship of its communicative powers

Bibliography

Annapureddy R, Fornaroli A, Gatica-Perez D (2025) Generative AI literacy: twelve defining competencies. Digital Gov Res Pract 6(1):1–21

Bahree A (2024) Generative AI in action. Manning Publications

Bender EM, Koller A (2020) Climbing towards NLU: on meaning, form, and understanding in the age of data. In: Proceedings on 58th ACL, pp 5185–5198

Bostrom N (2014) Superintelligence: paths, dangers, strategies. Oxford University Press, Oxford

Boyd D (2019) Artificial unintelligence: how computers misunderstand the world. Technol Cult 60(3):979–983

Bratton B (2016) The stack: on software and sovereignty. MIT Press, Cambridge

Brown BR (2025) Human–machine teaming using large language models. In: Interdependent human-machine teams. Academic Press, pp 41–66

Brown TB et al (2020) Language models are few-shot learners. arXiv preprint arXiv:2005.14165. Accessed 19 Apr 2025
Bryson JJ (2018) Patiency is not a virtue: AI and the design of ethical systems. Ethics Inf Technol 20:15–26. https://doi.org/10.1007/s10676-018-9448-6.Accessed20Jan2025
Bura C, Myakala PK, Jonnalgadda A K (2025) Ethical prompt engineering: addressing bias, transparency, and fairness. Int J Res Anal Rev (IJRAR) 12(1)
Choi WC, Chang CI (2025) A survey of techniques, key components, strategies, challenges, and student perspectives on prompt engineering for large language models (LLMs) in education. https://doi.org/10.20944/preprints.202503.1808.v1. Accessed 8 May 2025
Clark A (2016) Surfing uncertainty: prediction, action, and the embodied mind. Oxford University Press, Oxford
Coeckelbergh M (2020) AI ethics. MIT Press, Cambridge
Crawford K (2021) Atlas of AI: power, politics, and the planetary costs of artificial intelligence. Yale University Press, New Haven
Debnath T, Siddiky MNA, Rahman ME et al (2025) A comprehensive survey of prompt engineering techniques in large language models. TechRxiv. https://doi.org/10.36227/techrxiv.174140719.96375390/v1. Accessed 10 May 2025
Dennett DC (1987) The intentional stance. MIT Press, Cambridge
Dhamani N, Engler M (2024) Introduction to generative AI: an ethical, societal, and legal overview. Manning Publications
Dignum V (2019) Responsible artificial intelligence: how to develop and use AI in a responsible way. Springer, Cham
Eliot L (2024) Essentials of prompt engineering for generative AI: practical advances in artificial intelligence and machine learning. LBE Press Publishing
Ferraris A F, Audrito D, Di Caro L et al (2025) The architecture of language: understanding the mechanics behind LLMs. In: Cambridge forum on AI: law and governance, vol 1. Cambridge University Press, Cambridge
Floridi L (2022) The ethics of artificial intelligence. Oxford University Press, Oxford
Floridi L (ed) (2015) The onlife manifesto: being human in a hyperconnected era. Springer, Cham
Geroimenko V (2025a) Generative AI: from human-computer interaction to human-computer creativity. In: Geroimenko V (ed) Human-computer creativity: generative AI in education, art, and healthcare. Springer, Berlin
Geroimenko V (2025b) Key concepts in prompt engineering. In: The essential guide to prompt engineering: key principles, techniques, challenges, and security risks. Springer Nature Switzerland, Cham, pp 1–16
Geroimenko V (2025c) The essential guide to prompt engineering: key principles, techniques, challenges, and security risks. Springer, Cham
Geroimenko V (ed) (2025) Human–computer creativity: generative AI in education, art, and healthcare. Springer, Berlin
Geroimenko V (2025d) Key security risks in prompt engineering. In: The essential guide to prompt engineering: key principles, techniques, challenges, and security risks. Springer Nature Switzerland, Cham, pp 103–120
GitHub (2025) Prompt engineering guide. https://github.com/dair-ai/Prompt-Engineering-Guide. Accessed 10 Apr 2025
Greenwood M (2024) Artificial intelligence: a practical guide to using AI in everyday life. Ochreland Publishing
Gunkel DJ (2012) The machine question: critical perspectives on AI, robots, and ethics. MIT Press, Cambridge
Hagendorff T (2020) The ethics of AI ethics: an evaluation of guidelines. Minds Mach 30:99–120. https://doi.org/10.1007/s11023-020-09517-8
Hofstadter DR (2007) I am a strange loop. Basic Books, New York, NY
Hsu HP (2025) From programming to prompting: developing computational thinking through large language model-based generative artificial intelligence. TechTrends, pp 1–22

Huang G, Xiao Y, Jiang L et al (2025) Beyond prompt engineering: a reinforced token-level input refinement for large language models. Proc AAAI Conf Artif Intell 39(22):24113–24121

i Picó JF, Catta-Preta M, Omeñaca AT et al (2025) The time machine: future scenario generation through generative AI tools. Fut Internet 17(1):1–15

Jameson A (2007) Adaptive interfaces and agents. In: Sears A, Jacko J (eds) The human–computer interaction handbook, 2nd edn. CRC Press, Boca Raton, pp 305–330

Johnson KH (2023) Toward communicative alignment in human–AI teams. AI Soc 38:221–237. https://doi.org/10.1007/s00146-022-01422-5

Kannan R, Ahmad M (eds) (2025) Generative AI foundations, developments, and applications. IGI Global

Khan I (2024) The quick guide to prompt engineering. Wiley

Kushwaha V, Ragavan SS, Subhajit Roy S (2025) A measure based generalizable approach to understandability. arXiv:2503.21615. Accessed 19 Apr 2025

Lakoff G, Johnson M (1999) Philosophy in the flesh: the embodied mind and its challenge to western thought. Basic Books, New York, NY

Learn Prompting (2025) https://learnprompting.org. Accessed 15 March 2025

Lee D, Palmer E (2025) Prompt engineering in higher education: a systematic review to help inform curricula. Int J Educ Technol High Educ 22(1):7

Lee JY, Kang S, Yoo S (2025) Can we predict the effect of prompts?. arXiv preprint arXiv:2501.18883. Accessed 12 May 2025

Lindley J, Whitham R (2025) From prompt engineering to prompt craft. In: Proceedings of the nineteenth international conference on tangible, embedded, and embodied interaction, pp 1–12

López-Pérez B et al (2025) Exploring the potential of large language models to understand interpersonal emotion regulation strategies from narratives. Emotion. https://doi.org/10.1037/emo0001528

Maaz S, Palaganas JC, Palaganas G et al (2025) A guide to prompt design: foundations and applications for healthcare simulationists. Front Med 11:1504532

Marcus G, Davis E (2019) Rebooting AI: building artificial intelligence we can trust. Pantheon, New York

McStay A (2018) Emotional AI: the rise of empathic media. Sage, London

Mishra M, Ara A, Mishra S (2025) Exploring human–AI collaboration in higher education: an investigation into AI-enabled personalized learning. In: Prompt engineering and generative AI applications for teaching and learning. IGI Global Scientific Publishing, pp 483–502

Murray CD (2022) Thinking through avatars: Identity, communication, and ethics in immersive AI environments. Technol Mind Behav. https://doi.org/10.1037/tmb0000053.Accessed5Apr2025

Norman DA (2013) The design of everyday things. Revised edn. Basic Books, New York, NY

OpenAI (2025) Best practices for prompt engineering with the OpenAI API. https://help.openai.com/en/articles/6654000-best-practices-for-prompt-engineering-with-the-openai-api Accessed 20 Apr 2025

OpenAI (2025) Research. https://openai.com/research/index/ Accessed 11 Mar 2025

Phoenix J, Taylor M (2024) Prompt engineering for generative AI. O'Reilly Media

Picard RW (1997) Affective computing. MIT Press, Cambridge

PremaLatha V, Kumar AD, Parveen N (2025) Optimizing interactions: strategies for prompt engineering in large language models. Edu-Tech Enterprise 3:24–24

Prompt Engineering Guide (2025) https://www.promptingguide.ai/ Accessed 7 March 2025

Reddy CKK, Anoushka P, Draksharapu A et al (2025) Beyond text: analyzing artificial intelligence models through prompt engineering. future tech startups and innovation in the age of AI, pp 120–156

Sasson Lazovsky G, Raz T, Kenett YN (2025) The art of creative inquiry—from question asking to prompt engineering. J Creat Behav 59(1):e671

Shneiderman B (2020) Human-centered artificial intelligence: reliable, safe and trustworthy. Int J Hum Comput Interact 36(6):495–504. https://doi.org/10.1080/10447318.2020.1741118

Sihi D, Ryan A (2025) Crafting and evaluating generative AI prompts: insights from students, educators, and marketers. Mark Educ Rev 1–7

Suresh H, Guttag JV (2021) A framework for understanding unintended consequences of machine learning. Commun ACM 64(2):62–71. https://doi.org/10.1145/3430368

Turkle S (2011) Alone together: why we expect more from technology and less from each other. Basic Books, New York, NY

Vairamani AD, Nayyar A (2024) Prompt engineering: empowering communication. CRC Press, Boca Raton

Weizenbaum J (1976) Computer power and human reason: from judgment to calculation. W.H. Freeman, San Francisco

Winograd T (1972) Understanding natural language. Academic Press, New York, NY

Chapter 4
The Future Is Contextual

Abstract This chapter examines the central role of context in the evolution of human–AI communication, positioning it as a defining element of post-prompt interaction. It begins by articulating the foundational dimensions of context—linguistic, interactional, and situational—and shows how these shape meaning in human dialogue. It then explores the layered nature of context and the importance of moving beyond surface-level input toward deep, dynamic understanding. Strategies for designing contextual intelligence in AI are outlined, including memory systems, multimodal integration, temporal modelling, and adaptive user profiling. The chapter also highlights the risks and limitations of context-aware systems, from misinterpretation and bias to privacy and overtrust. It concludes with a vision of contextual co-creation, in which humans and AI collaboratively build meaning through mutual adaptation. Ultimately, this chapter redefines context not as background but as the shared medium through which meaningful and ethical communication between humans and machines unfolds.

Keywords Context-aware AI · Contextual intelligence · Human–AI interaction · Adaptive communication · Ethical AI design · Co-creation

As artificial intelligence becomes increasingly embedded in the rhythms of daily life, the importance of context in AI communication moves from peripheral concern to foundational requirement. Unlike traditional systems that interpret inputs in isolation, future AI systems must operate within a continuum of meanings shaped by time, place, purpose, history, and identity. Human communication is inherently contextual—we derive significance not solely from words, but from how they are framed, when they are spoken, and by whom. For AI to participate meaningfully in such exchanges, it must learn to navigate and interpret these layers of context with nuance and adaptability. This chapter explores the conceptual underpinnings, technical strategies, and ethical complexities of contextual communication in AI, positioning it as a key dimension of the post-prompt paradigm. The future is not just conversational or personal—it is fundamentally contextual.

V. Geroimenko, *Beyond and After Prompt Engineering: The Future of AI Communication*, https://doi.org/10.1007/978-3-032-04569-0_4

4.1 Foundations of Context in Human and AI Communication

Context is the invisible architecture of communication. It shapes how meaning is formed, how intentions are interpreted, and how understanding unfolds between interlocutors. In human interactions, context is rarely static or singular—it is dynamic, multi-layered, and often implicit. It includes the physical setting, social norms, shared history, emotional tone, temporal sequencing, and the roles and identities of those involved. A single utterance, such as "That's great," can be interpreted as sincere praise, dry sarcasm, or ambivalent politeness depending entirely on contextual cues. These subtleties emerge effortlessly in human communication but remain a formidable challenge for artificial intelligence.

Early AI systems operated in a near-contextless mode, treating inputs as isolated commands or self-contained questions. The architecture of such systems was largely transactional: users gave instructions, and the system responded without memory or inference beyond the immediate prompt. Even today, many AI applications still rely on limited, localised context, drawing meaning only from the most recent conversational turns or a static prompt window. While this design may suffice for simple queries, it breaks down in situations requiring continuity, adaptation, or cultural and emotional nuance.

The need for context becomes especially apparent in long-form dialogue, multimodal interaction, and domains such as education, therapy, legal interpretation, or collaborative writing, where meaning is often constructed over time and grounded in a shared understanding. In such settings, AI must not only parse the literal content of user inputs but also grasp the broader communicative situation: Why is the user asking this now? What has already been said? What are the unspoken expectations or emotional undercurrents? Addressing these questions requires a redefinition of context, not merely as supplementary metadata, but as a primary medium through which communication is rendered intelligible.

From a computational perspective, context in AI can be thought of in three broad categories: *linguistic context*, which includes syntactic and semantic dependencies; *interactional context*, involving the discourse history and pragmatic functions of dialogue; and *situational context*, encompassing external variables like user identity, task goals, time, and place. These layers must be integrated and constantly updated to approximate the depth of human contextual awareness.

The development of large language models has brought significant advances in this direction. Transformer architectures, with their capacity to attend to long-range dependencies, have enabled models to process more contextual information than ever before. Yet this progress remains largely correlational: AI systems can recognise patterns across vast text corpora but do not inherently "understand" the social or psychological dimensions of context. Achieving this kind of understanding requires not just more data or larger models, but a paradigm shift toward systems designed to engage with context as an evolving, relational phenomenon.

As AI communication moves into more complex and human-centred domains, context will not be an optional enhancement—it will be the condition of possibility for meaningful interaction. This foundational shift sets the stage for the deeper layers of contextual intelligence explored in the following subsections (Fig. 4.1).

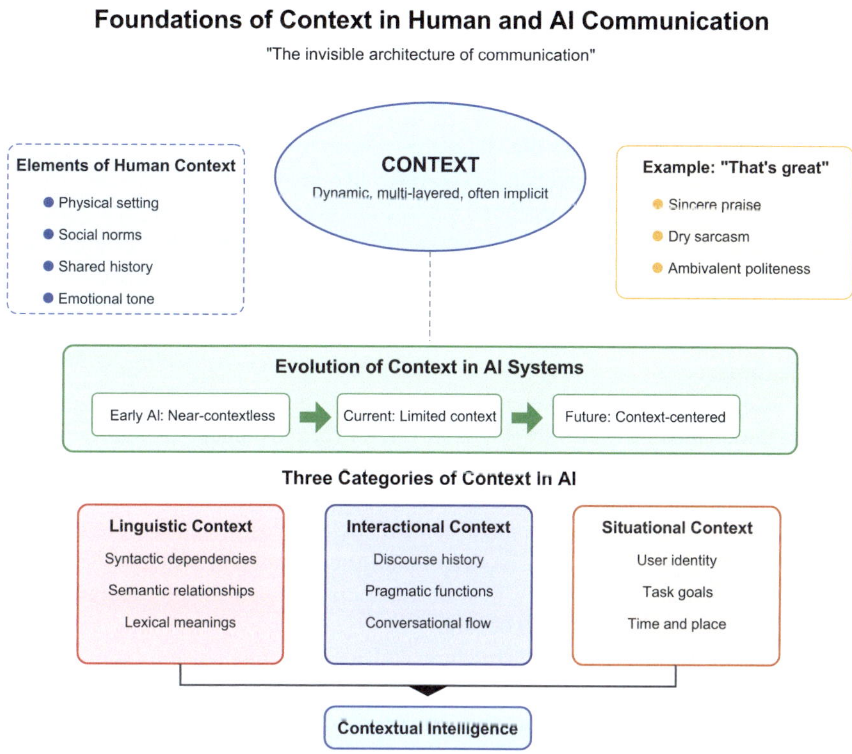

Fig. 4.1 The architecture of context: from human understanding to AI implementation. This diagram maps the foundational elements of context in communication, illustrating its evolution from early context-limited AI to future context-centred approaches. It highlights the three interdependent categories of contextual intelligence (linguistic, interactional, and situational) that must be integrated for meaningful human–AI interaction. The visualisation demonstrates how a single phrase like "That's great" can carry multiple meanings depending on contextual factors, underscoring why context is not merely supplementary metadata but the essential medium through which effective communication becomes possible in complex domains

4.2 From Surface Inputs to Deep Understanding: Layers of Context

Context is not monolithic—it is layered, dynamic, and often hierarchical. Effective human communication depends not only on recognising these layers but on weaving them together into a coherent interpretive frame. For AI systems to progress from basic responsiveness to meaningful interaction, they must similarly evolve from processing surface-level cues to navigating the deeper, more complex strata of contextual understanding.

At the surface level, context often takes the form of immediate linguistic features—previous utterances in a conversation, co-reference resolution, or syntactic dependencies. These elements are essential for maintaining coherence in dialogue and for correctly interpreting questions, commands, or clarifications. For example, the pronoun "it" in "Can you fix it?" relies on prior utterances for resolution. Most current AI systems are increasingly proficient at handling this shallow form of context, particularly with advances in transformer-based models that retain textual continuity across multiple turns.

Yet beneath this linguistic layer lie more intricate dimensions. Semantic context involves understanding topic flow, thematic relevance, and domain-specific meaning. Pragmatic context pertains to the speaker's intention, the conversational goal, and the expected social function of the exchange—whether to inform, persuade, inquire, or comfort. Moving further, personal context includes user identity, preferences, emotional states, and cognitive styles. Finally, cultural and situational context involves norms, shared references, historical associations, and the physical or virtual environment in which interaction occurs.

To illustrate this multi-layered structure, consider a simple user prompt: "I'm not sure this will work." On a superficial level, it is a statement of doubt. At a deeper level, it could signal a request for reassurance, a polite refusal, or an invitation for explanation—interpretations that depend on the speaker's tone, prior interactions, emotional state, and cultural background. An AI system limited to lexical or syntactic analysis would miss these nuances entirely.

Moreover, these layers of context often interact in non-linear ways. Emotional context, for instance, can reshape the interpretation of pragmatic intent, just as cultural assumptions can frame or distort the perceived meaning of a statement. Understanding context, therefore, is not about adding more metadata but about cultivating a layered model of communication in which each level informs and constrains the others.

Crucially, context is not static. It evolves dynamically over the course of a conversation or relationship. Longitudinal context—spanning multiple interactions over time—introduces a temporal layer in which past exchanges shape current expectations and future responses. In education, for example, a tutor-AI must track not just prior topics but patterns of engagement, frustration, or progress over days or weeks. Similarly, in creative collaboration, an AI writing partner must remember stylistic preferences and narrative arcs across sessions.

The shift from surface inputs to deep contextual modelling marks a fundamental transformation in how AI systems relate to users. Rather than reacting to isolated prompts, they begin to engage in context-sensitive meaning-making, closer to how humans communicate. The next step is to explore how such layered context can be systematically integrated into AI architecture and interface design, a topic taken up in the following subsection (Fig. 4.2).

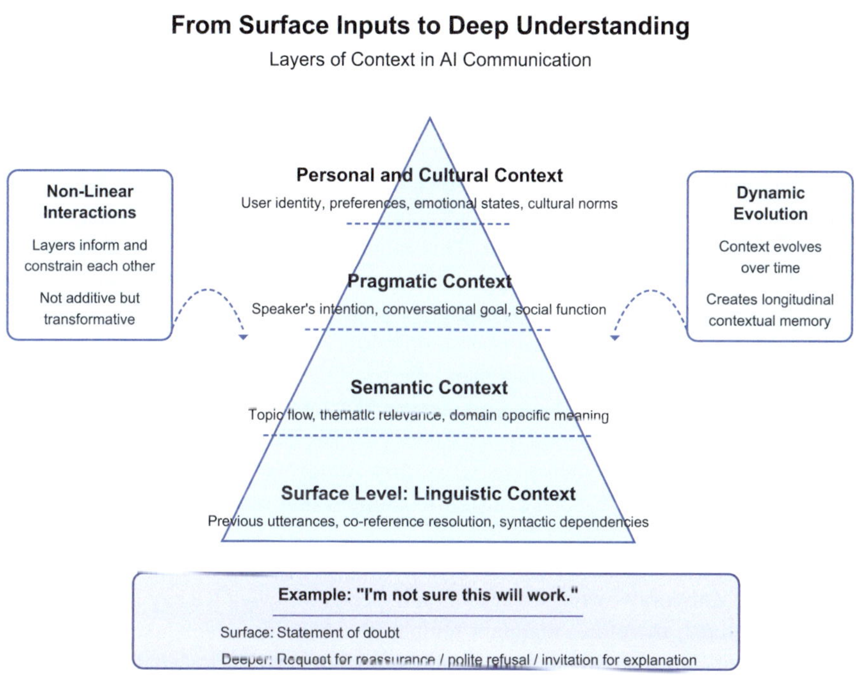

Fig. 4.2 Navigating the contextual depths: AI's journey from surface processing to meaning-making. This diagram illustrates the layered nature of context in AI communication, progressing from surface-level linguistic processing to deeper contextual understanding. The pyramid structure reveals how each contextual layer—linguistic, semantic, pragmatic, and personal/cultural—builds upon and transforms the others in non-linear ways. Using the example "I'm not sure this will work," the visualisation demonstrates how interpretation changes dramatically across contextual depths. The diagram also captures the dynamic, evolving nature of context over time, representing AI's fundamental shift from isolated prompt processing toward human-like, context-sensitive meaning-making that considers cultural norms, emotional states, and shared history

4.3 Designing for Contextual Intelligence: Strategies and Techniques

As we move beyond static prompt engineering toward dynamic and adaptive AI communication, the development of contextual intelligence becomes imperative in design. Contextual intelligence refers to an AI system's capacity to interpret, retain, and act upon layered contextual information—linguistic, situational, temporal, cultural, emotional, and environmental. Designing for this form of intelligence requires a shift from rigid prompt-response paradigms to architectures that support fluid, multi-dimensional interpretation and ongoing learning from interaction history.

One fundamental strategy involves the integration of context-aware memory systems. These systems allow AI to retain user-specific information across sessions, enabling personalised and coherent interactions. Rather than resetting after each prompt, the AI recalls prior exchanges, intentions, or preferences, constructing a cumulative communicative thread. This memory, however, must be dynamic—capable of updating and pruning itself to reflect evolving needs and ethical constraints, such as privacy and consent.

Equally critical is the application of multimodal context integration. Effective AI communication in the future will demand the simultaneous interpretation of textual, auditory, visual, and even behavioural signals. For instance, an intelligent assistant might combine verbal queries with visual cues (such as facial expressions or gestures) and contextual metadata (such as location, time of day, or user activity). Designing for such richness requires robust fusion techniques and models trained on diverse datasets that mirror real-world complexity.

Temporal context modelling is another key technique. Human communication is inherently temporal—what we say often depends on when we say it. Contextual AI systems must, therefore, maintain temporal continuity, understanding not only what was said but also when, how recently, and in relation to what sequence of interactions. This enables anticipatory responses, appropriate turn-taking, and sensitivity to pacing and rhythm in dialogue, drawing AI interaction closer to human conversational norms.

Furthermore, the use of situated ontologies and contextual knowledge graphs can provide AI with a structured yet flexible framework for interpreting context. These representations allow AI systems to link user inputs with background knowledge, domain-specific information, and situational logic, all while adapting meaning dynamically. This can be especially valuable in domains like education, healthcare, or legal advice, where nuanced interpretation of role, intent, and stakes is essential.

Finally, successful contextual intelligence also relies on adaptive user modelling. These models continuously refine their understanding of individual users through interaction, feedback, and behavioural cues. Rather than relying on static personas or templates, they evolve organically, supporting more natural, context-sensitive engagement. Crucially, such models must be designed with transparency, explainability, and user control in mind to foster trust and accountability in AI communication.

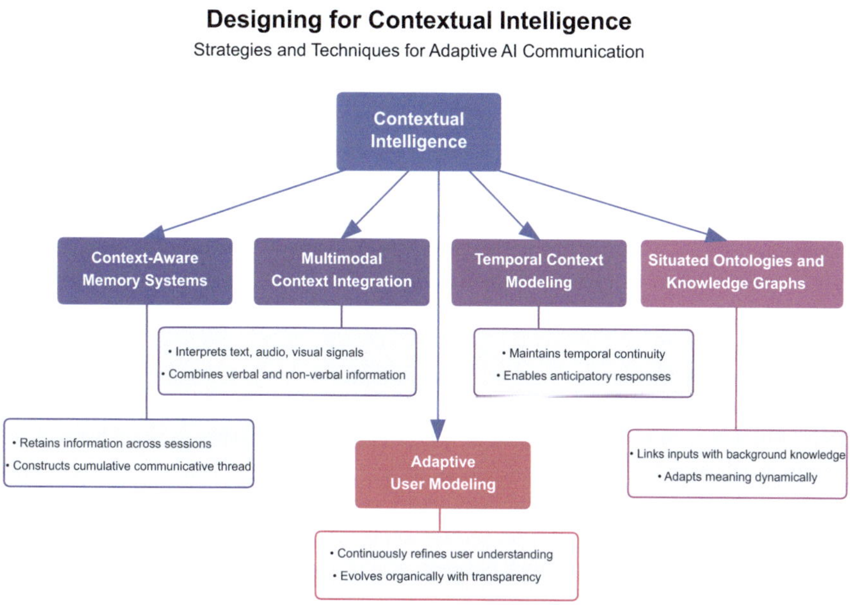

Fig. 4.3 The contextual intelligence framework for advanced AI communication. This diagram illustrates the integrated approach to designing AI systems with contextual intelligence. The framework transitions from rigid prompt-response paradigms toward fluid, multidimensional communication through five key strategies: context-aware memory systems, multimodal context integration, temporal context modelling, situated ontologies and knowledge graphs, and adaptive user modelling. Each strategy contributes specific capabilities that collectively enable AI systems to interpret, retain, and act upon layered contextual information. The result is communication technology that grows within context, mirroring the fluid, situated nature of human meaning-making

In sum, designing for contextual intelligence demands a composite approach—one that blends memory, modality, temporality, structure, and adaptability. It signals a movement toward AI systems that not only interpret context but grow within it, enabling communication that is more aligned with the fluid, situated, and co-constructed nature of human meaning-making. This design paradigm represents not a mere technical upgrade, but a reimagining of communication itself as a shared, evolving context between human and machine (Fig. 4.3).

4.4 The Limitations and Ethical Risks of Context-Aware AI

While context-aware AI systems hold significant promise for creating more adaptive, responsive, and human-aligned interactions, they also introduce a range of limitations and ethical risks that must be critically examined. As these systems become more deeply embedded in personal, social, and institutional domains, the stakes of misinterpreting or misusing contextual information rise sharply. The very capacity that makes context-aware AI powerful—its ability to infer, anticipate, and adapt—can also make it opaque, manipulative, and even dangerous when unchecked.

One of the fundamental limitations of context-aware AI lies in its dependency on data completeness and representational accuracy. Context, by nature, is dynamic, multifaceted, and sometimes ambiguous. Even advanced models often operate with partial, outdated, or culturally biased data, leading to incorrect inferences or actions. For example, a system that attempts to personalise a response based on an inferred emotional tone might misread sarcasm or culturally specific humour, leading not only to errors but potentially to offence or alienation. Such limitations are not merely technical; they reveal the challenges of encoding the fluidity of human life into computational form.

Another pressing issue involves user autonomy and control. Context-aware systems often infer needs, preferences, and intentions without explicit user input. While this may enhance convenience, it also risks disempowering users by making decisions on their behalf without adequate transparency or consent. This concern is heightened in domains such as healthcare, education, and finance, where subtle misjudgements of context can have profound personal consequences. Users may not even be aware of how their data is being interpreted or how context models are influencing system behaviour.

Closely related are the ethical risks tied to surveillance and privacy. To model context effectively, AI systems must capture and process large volumes of personal, behavioural, and situational data—often in real time and across modalities. This pervasive data collection creates fertile ground for surveillance capitalism, where user contexts are commodified for profiling and prediction. Without strong regulatory and design safeguards, context-aware AI could erode personal privacy and normalise intrusive monitoring under the guise of personalisation.

Bias and discrimination also loom large. Contextual inferences are deeply shaped by the training data and design assumptions of AI models. If specific social, cultural, or linguistic contexts are underrepresented—or misrepresented—AI systems may default to majority norms, reinforcing systemic inequalities. Context-aware systems trained on biased interactions may unwittingly propagate exclusion, misrepresentation, or stereotyping, particularly in cross-cultural communication or neurodiverse user engagement.

Finally, there is the epistemic risk of overtrust. As context-aware AI grows more fluent in mimicking human-like understanding, users may overestimate its capabilities, mistaking algorithmic fluency for genuine comprehension or moral insight. This illusion of intelligence can lead to misplaced confidence in AI judgements and decreased human oversight, especially in high-stakes or emotionally charged scenarios.

To address these limitations, context-aware AI must be designed with principles of interpretability, consent, fairness, and continuous auditing. Only then can the promise of context be fulfilled without compromising the ethical integrity of human–AI communication (Fig. 4.4).

Fig. 4.4 Interconnected ethical challenges in context-aware AI systems. The diagram illustrates the complex relationships between data incompleteness, diminished user autonomy, surveillance concerns, algorithmic bias, and overtrust risks. These challenges emerge when AI systems attempt to interpret and respond to human contexts without adequate safeguards. As context-aware AI becomes more embedded in critical domains like healthcare and finance, these limitations necessitate design principles focused on interpretability, consent, fairness, and continuous auditing

4.5 Towards Contextual Co-creation

The culmination of the shift toward context-aware systems is not merely a more intelligent response engine but a redefinition of the relationship between humans and AI, one grounded in contextual co-creation. Unlike earlier models of communication, where context was incidental or peripheral, future AI systems are poised to treat context as a co-constructed and dynamically evolving space in which meaning is not extracted from static prompts but generated through mutual understanding. This move aligns with a broader conceptual transition: from interaction to collaboration, from input–output to shared construction, and from command-driven logic to emergent, context-sensitive creativity.

Contextual co-creation envisions a future where AI does not merely adapt to a user's situational cues but actively engages in maintaining and enriching a shared semantic environment. In such scenarios, the AI system is not a passive recipient of contextual signals but a participant in shaping the very context it relies upon. This involves memory management, discourse tracking, emotional attunement, cultural awareness, and alignment with long-term goals and user preferences. It requires a shift in system architecture—from stateless interactions to continuity-aware systems capable of building persistent relationships across multiple communication episodes.

Such co-creation unfolds through layered and iterative exchanges. For example, a design assistant might not only understand a user's brief for a creative project but also propose stylistic alternatives, reinterpret ambiguous directives based on prior conversations, and collaboratively refine ideas as goals evolve. In educational contexts, a learning AI could co-develop curricula by dynamically integrating a student's learning history, motivational states, and shifting academic ambitions, continuously renegotiating the context of instruction. In each case, context is neither fully pre-defined nor imposed—it is discovered and expanded through dialogue.

Crucially, contextual co-creation demands a more flexible model of agency. AI does not assume control or ownership of outcomes, and neither is it limited to following human instructions. Instead, it occupies a middle ground: a contributory agent with partial autonomy that enhances rather than replaces human creativity and decision-making. This model calls for new frameworks to govern boundaries, roles, and accountability in collaborative AI systems, especially in high-stakes domains such as healthcare, legal reasoning, and policymaking.

Moreover, co-creation rooted in context introduces a need for mutual learning. Just as the AI must continuously update its contextual model of the user, so too must the user develop an intuitive understanding of the AI's behaviour, limitations, and contextual reasoning processes. This symbiotic learning cycle forms the basis for trust and fluency in long-term human–AI partnerships.

Ultimately, contextual co-creation reframes the purpose of AI communication. Rather than delivering isolated answers or optimised outputs, the future of AI communication lies in fostering shared understanding, supporting evolving goals, and contributing to the emergence of meaning, together with the human interlocutor. It is in this cooperative, context-rich dialogue that the full promise of post-prompt AI communication will be realised (Fig. 4.5).

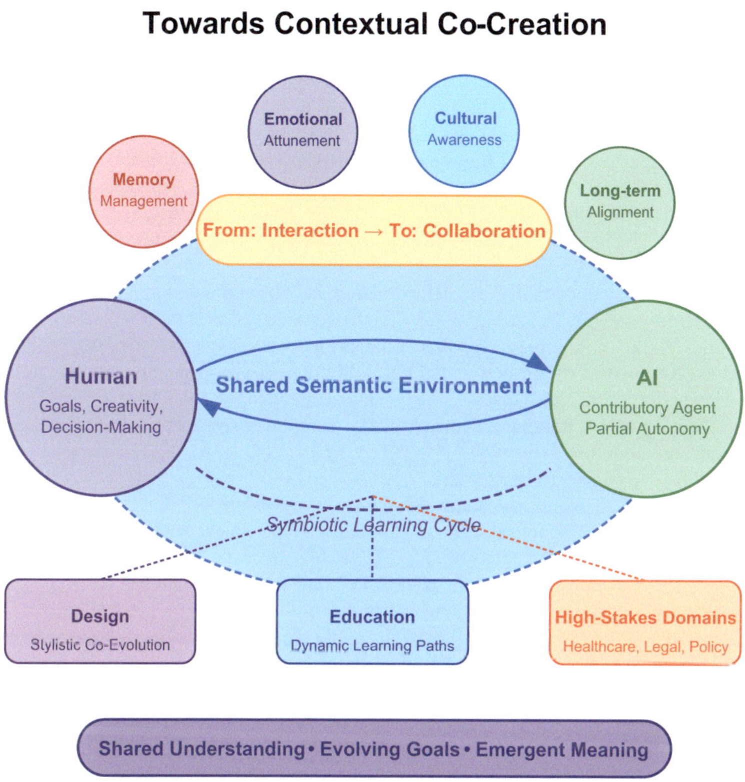

Fig. 4.5 Conceptual framework of contextual co-creation between humans and AI. The diagram illustrates the shift from transactional interactions to collaborative meaning-making within a shared semantic environment. At the centre lies the dynamic exchange between human creativity and AI's contributory agency, supported by four essential processes: memory management, emotional attunement, cultural awareness, and long-term alignment. This co-creative relationship forms a symbiotic learning cycle that can be applied across domains, including design, education, and high-stakes fields. The framework ultimately fosters three key outcomes that define post-prompt AI communication: shared understanding, evolving goals, and emergent meaning

Bibliography

Annapureddy R, Fornaroli A, Gatica-Perez D (2025) Generative AI literacy: twelve defining competencies. Digit Gov: Res Practice 6(1):1–21

Bahree A (2024) Generative AI in action. Manning Publications

Bender EM, Koller A (2020) Climbing towards NLU: on meaning, form, and understanding in the age of data. Proceeding 58th ACL, pp 5185–5198

Bostrom N (2014) Superintelligence: paths, dangers, strategies. Oxford University Press, Oxford

Boyd D (2019) Artificial unintelligence: how computers misunderstand the world. Technol Cult 60(3):979–983

Bratton B (2016) The stack: on software and sovereignty. MIT Press, Cambridge

Brown BR (2025) Human–machine teaming using large language models. In: Interdependent human-machine teams. Academic Press, pp 41–66

Brown TB et al (2020) Language models are few-shot learners. arXiv preprint arXiv:2005.14165. Accessed 19 April 2025
Bryson JJ (2018) Patiency is not a virtue: AI and the design of ethical systems. Ethics Inf Technol 20:15–26. https://doi.org/10.1007/s10676-018-9448-6. Accessed 20 Jan 2025
Bura C, Myakala PK, Jonnalgadda AK (2025) Ethical prompt engineering: addressing bias, transparency, and fairness. Int J Res Anal Rev (IJRAR) 12(1). www.ijrar.org
Choi WC, Chang CI (2025) A survey of techniques, key components, strategies, challenges, and student perspectives on prompt engineering for large language models (LLMs) in education. Posted Date: 25 March 2025. https://doi.org/10.20944/preprints202503.1808.v1. Accessed 8 May 2025
Clark A (2016) Surfing uncertainty: prediction, action, and the embodied mind. Oxford University Press, Oxford
Coeckelbergh M (2020) AI ethics. MIT Press, Cambridge
Crawford K (2021) Atlas of AI: power, politics, and the planetary costs of artificial intelligence. Yale University Press, New Haven
Debnath T, Siddiky MNA, Rahman ME et al (2025) A comprehensive survey of prompt engineering techniques in large language models. TechRxiv. https://doi.org/10.36227/techrxiv.174140719.96375390/v1. Accessed 10 May 2025
Dennett DC (1987) The intentional stance. MIT Press, Cambridge
Dhamani N, Engler M (2024) Introduction to generative AI: an ethical, societal, and legal overview. Manning Publications
Dignum V (2019) Responsible artificial intelligence: how to develop and use AI in a responsible way. Springer, Cham
Eliot L (2024) Essentials of prompt engineering for generative AI: practical advances in artificial intelligence and machine learning. LBE Press Publishing
Ferraris AF, Audrito D, Di Caro L et al (2025) The architecture of language: understanding the mechanics behind LLMs. In: Cambridge forum on AI: law and governance, vol 1, Cambridge University Press
Floridi L (2022) The ethics of artificial intelligence. Oxford University Press, Oxford
Floridi L (ed) (2015) The onlife manifesto: being human in a hyperconnected era. Springer, Cham
Geroimenko V (2025a) Generative AI: from human-computer interaction to human-computer creativity. In: Geroimenko V (ed) Human-computer creativity: generative AI in education, art, and healthcare. Springer
Geroimenko V (2025b) Key concepts in prompt engineering. In: The essential guide to prompt engineering: key principles, techniques, challenges, and security risks. Springer Nature Switzerland, Cham, pp 1–16
Geroimenko V (2025c) The essential guide to prompt engineering: key principles, techniques, challenges, and security risks. Springer, Cham
Geroimenko V (ed) (2025d) Human-computer creativity: generative AI in education, art, and healthcare. Springer
Geroimenko V (2025e) Key security risks in prompt engineering. In: The essential guide to prompt engineering: key principles, techniques, challenges, and security risks. Springer Nature Switzerland, Cham, pp 103–120
GitHub (2025) Prompt engineering guide. https://github.com/dair-ai/Prompt-Engineering-Guide. Accessed 10 April 2025
Greenwood M (2024) Artificial intelligence: a practical guide to using AI in everyday life. Ochreland Publishing
Gunkel DJ (2012) The machine question: critical perspectives on AI, robots, and ethics. MIT Press, Cambridge
Hagendorff T (2020) The ethics of AI ethics: an evaluation of guidelines. Minds Mach 30:99–120. https://doi.org/10.1007/s11023-020-09517-8. Accessed 10 Feb 2025
Hofstadter DR (2007) I am a strange loop. Basic Books, New York

Hsu HP (2025) From programming to prompting: developing computational thinking through large language model-based generative artificial intelligence. TechTrends, pp 1–22
Huang G, Xiao Y, Jiang L et al (2025) Beyond prompt engineering: a reinforced token-level input refinement for large language models. Proc AAAI Conf Artif Intell 39(22):24113–24121
i Picó JF, Catta-Preta M, Omeñaca AT et al (2025) The time machine: future scenario generation through generative AI tools. Future Internet 17(1):1–15
Jameson A (2007) Adaptive interfaces and agents. In: Sears A, Jacko J (eds) The human-computer interaction handbook, 2nd edn. CRC Press, Boca Raton, pp 305–330
Johnson KH (2023) Toward communicative alignment in human-AI teams. AI Soc 38:221–237. https://doi.org/10.1007/s00146-022-01422-5
Kannan R, Ahmad M (eds) (2025) Generative AI foundations, developments, and applications. IGI Global
Khan I (2024) The quick guide to prompt engineering. Wiley
Kushwaha V, Ragavan SS, Subhajit Roy S (2025) A measure based generalizable approach to understandability. arXiv:2503.21615. Accessed 19 April 2025
Lakoff G, Johnson M (1999) Philosophy in the flesh: the embodied mind and its challenge to western thought. Basic Books, New York
Learn Prompting (2025) https://learnprompting.org. Accessed 15 March 2025
Lee D, Palmer E (2025) Prompt engineering in higher education: a systematic review to help inform curricula. Int J Educ Technol High Educ 22(1):7
Lee JY, Kang S, Yoo S (2025) Can we predict the effect of prompts?. arXiv preprint arXiv:2501.18883. Accessed 12 May 2025
Lindley J, Whitham R (2025) From prompt engineering to prompt craft. In: Proceedings of the nineteenth international conference on tangible, embedded, and embodied interaction, March, pp 1–12
López-Pérez B et al (2025) Exploring the potential of large language models to understand interpersonal emotion regulation strategies from narratives. Emotion. Advance online publication. https://doi.org/10.1037/emo0001528. Accessed 19 April 2025
Maaz S, Palaganas JC, Palaganas G et al (2025) A guide to prompt design: foundations and applications for healthcare simulationists. Front Med 11:1504532
Marcus G, Davis E (2019) Rebooting AI: building artificial intelligence we can trust. Pantheon, New York
McStay A (2018) Emotional AI: the rise of empathic media. Sage, London
Mishra M, Ara A, Mishra S (2025) Exploring human AI collaboration in higher education: an investigation into AI-enabled personalized learning. In: Prompt engineering and generative AI applications for teaching and learning. IGI Global Scientific Publishing, pp 483–502
Murray CD (2022) Thinking through avatars: identity, communication, and ethics in immersive AI environments. Technol Mind Behav. https://doi.org/10.1037/tmb0000053. Accessed 5 April 2025
Norman DA (2013) The design of everyday things, Revised. Basic Books, New York
OpenAI (2025a) Best practices for prompt engineering with the OpenAI API. https://help.openai.com/en/articles/6654000-best-practices-for-prompt-engineering-with-the-openai-api. Accessed 20 April 2025
OpenAI (2025b) Research. https://openai.com/research/index/. Accessed 11 Mar 2025
Phoenix J, Taylor M (2024) Prompt engineering for generative AI. O'Reilly Media
Picard RW (1997) Affective computing. MIT Press, Cambridge
PremaLatha V, Kumar AD, Parveen N (2025) Optimizing interactions: strategies for prompt engineering in large language models. Edu-Tech Enterprise 3:24–24
Prompt Engineering Guide (2025) https://www.promptingguide.ai/. Accessed 7 Mar 2025
Reddy CKK, Anoushka P, Draksharapu A et al (2025) Beyond text: analyzing artificial intelligence models through prompt engineering. Future tech startups and innovation in the age of AI, pp 120–156

Sasson Lazovsky G, Raz T, Kenett YN (2025) The art of creative inquiry—from question asking to prompt engineering. J Creative Behavior 59(1):e671

Shneiderman B (2020) Human-centered artificial intelligence: reliable, safe and trustworthy. Int J Hum Comput Interact 36(6):495–504. https://doi.org/10.1080/10447318.2020.1741118. Accessed 15 Feb 2025

Sihi D, Ryan A (2025) Crafting and evaluating generative AI prompts: insights from students, educators, and marketers. Market Educ Rev 1–7

Suresh H, Guttag JV (2021) A framework for understanding unintended consequences of machine learning. Commun ACM 64(2):62–71. https://doi.org/10.1145/3430368. Accessed 18 Mar 2025

Turkle S (2011) Alone together: why we expect more from technology and less from each other. Basic Books, New York

Vairamani AD, Nayyar A (2024) Prompt engineering: empowering communication. CRC Press

Weizenbaum J (1976) Computer power and human reason: from judgment to calculation. W.H. Freeman, San Francisco

Winograd T (1972) Understanding natural language. Academic Press, New York

Winograd T, Flores F (1986) Understanding computers and cognition: a new foundation for design. Ablex Publishing, Norwood

Chapter 5
The Future Is Multimodal

Abstract This chapter explores the transformation of AI communication through multimodality—the integration of diverse sensory and symbolic channels, including text, voice, image, gesture, and spatial interaction. It begins by establishing a conceptual foundation for moving from unimodal to multimodal understanding, redefining communication as an embodied, distributed process. Subsequent sections examine how text remains a core anchor, enhanced by non-verbal signals and prosodic variation. The discussion extends to visual and spatial modalities, highlighting their significance for intuitive, immersive, and inclusive interaction. Finally, the chapter investigates the rise of multimodal agents in augmented and virtual realities, where communication unfolds across synergistically orchestrated modalities. This shift enables AI systems not only to interpret more richly but to co-experience and co-create meaning within shared environments. The chapter positions multimodality as a pivotal paradigm in the evolution toward emotionally intelligent, context-sensitive, and human-aligned AI communication.

Keywords Multimodal AI · Embodied communication · Non-verbal signals · Prosody · Visual and spatial modalities · Immersive AI agents

As AI communication evolves beyond rigid textual prompting, multimodality emerges as a defining feature of future interaction paradigms. The term refers not simply to the use of multiple input or output channels, but to the seamless orchestration of diverse communicative modes—text, voice, image, gesture, motion, spatial relations, and beyond. This shift allows AI systems to interpret richer contextual signals, respond with greater nuance, and engage more naturally in human-like dialogue. In multimodal systems, meaning is no longer transmitted through discrete units but is co-constructed through overlapping streams of sensory and symbolic information. This chapter explores how multimodal communication transforms not only the surface of interaction but also the structure of understanding, the design of interfaces, and the nature of collaborative sense-making between humans and machines.

V. Geroimenko, *Beyond and After Prompt Engineering: The Future of AI Communication*, https://doi.org/10.1007/978-3-032-04569-0_5

5.1 From Unimodal to Multimodal Understanding: A Conceptual Foundation

For much of its early development, AI communication relied primarily on unimodal input, most notably, written text. This narrow channel of interaction, while robust and scalable, constrained the range of human expressiveness and flattened the complexity of meaning. Human communication, by contrast, is inherently multimodal: we gesture, modulate our voices, shift our gaze, express emotions through facial cues, and situate our dialogue within spatial and temporal contexts. As AI systems evolve to become more context-sensitive and collaborative, the imperative to embrace and integrate multimodal communication becomes not merely beneficial but foundational.

Multimodal understanding involves the capacity to interpret, synthesise, and generate meaning across different sensory and symbolic modalities. It extends beyond a parallel use of various input types. Instead, it seeks convergence: where voice inflexion, facial expressions, body movement, environmental cues, and textual content contribute to a unified interpretation of intention and meaning. This integration enables AI to more fully grasp what is said, how it is said, and why it is said, enriching both comprehension and response.

At its core, this shift from unimodal to multimodal reflects a deeper reconceptualisation of communication as a distributed and embodied process. In multimodal AI systems, meaning is not confined to syntactic parsing or statistical correlations in text but is dynamically constructed from the interplay of diverse signals. The capacity to detect a pause, recognise a sceptical facial expression, or interpret the emotional tenor of a voice clip adds a new layer of semantic depth and responsiveness to AI interactions. It aligns machine perception more closely with the situated nature of human experience.

Technologically, the rise of multimodal AI has been catalysed by advances in neural architectures capable of integrating heterogeneous data types. Transformer-based models adapted for cross-modal fusion—such as CLIP, Flamingo, or Gemini—enable systems to align textual, visual, and auditory representations within a shared embedding space. These systems do not merely process multiple inputs; they learn to reason across them, infer missing modalities, and adaptively weight contextual signals based on task or intent. The result is not only more fluid communication but also greater robustness, nuance, and emotional granularity.

Crucially, the embrace of multimodality also reorients the goals of AI communication. No longer limited to information retrieval or task execution, communication becomes a collaborative act of sense-making. A system that can read between lines, sense hesitation in tone, or recognise dissonance between verbal and non-verbal cues is better equipped to engage in ethically responsible, socially aware, and personally relevant interactions.

As we transition into this multimodal paradigm, the challenge is not only technical but philosophical: to design systems that do not simply mimic surface forms of expression but genuinely understand and respond to the multilayered dynamics

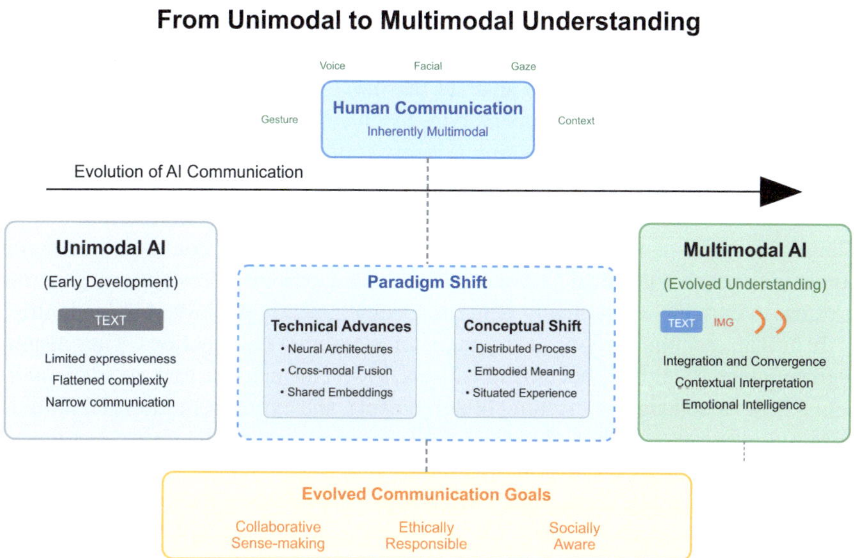

Fig. 5.1 From unimodal to multimodal understanding in AI communication. This diagram illustrates the conceptual evolution from text-centric AI communication to integrated multimodal systems. Early AI (left) relied on unimodal text processing with inherent limitations, while human communication (top) naturally integrates multiple sensory channels. The technological and philosophical paradigm shift (centre) enables advanced multimodal AI (right) that interprets meaning across diverse signals. This evolution transforms AI communication goals (bottom) from mere information processing to collaborative sense-making, representing a fundamental reconceptualisation of machine-human interaction as an embodied, distributed process aligned with human cognitive patterns

of human meaning making. This conceptual foundation lays the groundwork for the detailed exploration of individual modalities that follows in the subsequent subsections (Fig. 5.1).

5.2 Text as the Anchor: Enhancing with Non-verbal Signals

Despite the expanding scope of multimodal communication, text remains a foundational modality in human–AI interaction. It serves not only as a structured input format but also as a cognitive anchor, providing clarity, stability, and traceability in dialogues. However, as AI systems evolve toward more human-like communication, text alone is increasingly insufficient for capturing the richness of human expression. The future of AI communication thus lies in augmenting textual interactions with non-verbal signals that mirror the subtleties of embodied and affective human communication.

Text anchors interaction in ways that allow for precision and reproducibility. It is easily parsed, stored, and analysed, and it supports a range of linguistic functions—from factual reporting to abstract reasoning. This makes it especially valuable in domains requiring documentation, technical specificity, or archival. Yet, in natural human conversation, meaning is rarely confined to words alone. Non-verbal cues—such as facial expressions, gestures, pauses, intonation, and gaze—shape our interpretation of what is said, how it is meant, and how it should be responded to. These cues serve as implicit modifiers that either reinforce or contradict the literal content of speech. Future AI systems must learn not only to understand and generate text, but to enrich it dynamically with these context-shaping non-verbal modalities.

In human communication, such signals serve several vital functions. They disambiguate intent ("I'm fine" accompanied by a frown conveys distress), regulate interaction flow (a nod signals listening or agreement), and express emotion and attitude (a raised eyebrow, a sigh, a shrug). For AI to operate as an effective communicative partner, it must be able to recognise, simulate, and respond to these layers of meaning. For example, a chatbot assisting a user experiencing frustration should be able to detect emotional distress not just through word choice, but through tone, typing speed, punctuation, and even facial expressions if visual input is available. It should then adjust its responses accordingly—not only in content, but in style, tempo, and empathy.

Technologically, enhancing text with non-verbal signals requires both multimodal sensing and generation capabilities. On the input side, AI systems must be trained to integrate cues from video, audio, eye tracking, biometric sensors, or spatial movement, interpreting them as part of the overall communicative context. On the output side, AI must be able to render its own non-verbal cues, whether through avatars, synthesised speech, animated gestures, or haptic feedback. In the future, the textual message will become a scaffold around which richer, more human-like interaction will be built.

Crucially, the integration of nonverbal modalities must preserve text's interpretability and accessibility benefits. The challenge is not to replace textual communication but to make it adaptive, allowing AI to switch between minimalist precision and expressive augmentation based on context, user needs, and communicative goals. In doing so, text becomes more than a vessel for instruction or description; it becomes a core around which emotionally and socially intelligent AI communication can evolve (Fig. 5.2).

5.3 Voice, Sound, and Prosody in AI Dialogue

As AI systems advance beyond text-based communication, the integration of voice, sound, and prosody becomes essential for enabling more naturalistic, human-like dialogues. Voice, as a primary medium of human expression, carries not just linguistic information but also emotional and social signals that are conveyed through tone, rhythm, volume, pitch, and cadence. Prosody—the melodic and intonational aspects

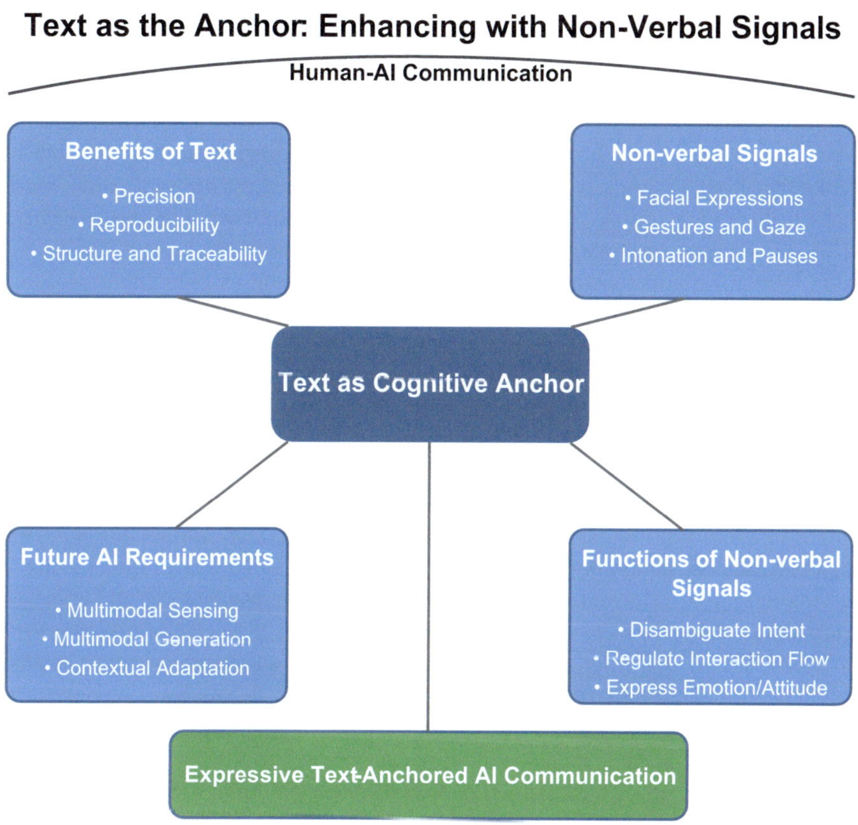

Fig. 5.2 Text as the anchor: enhancing human–AI communication with non-verbal signals. This diagram illustrates how text serves as a cognitive anchor in human–AI interaction while being augmented by non-verbal signals. The central text anchor provides precision and structure, while non-verbal elements (facial expressions, gestures, intonation) enrich communication by disambiguating intent, regulating interaction flow, and expressing emotion. Future AI systems must develop multimodal sensing and generation capabilities to integrate these elements effectively. The goal is not to replace text but to create an adaptive communication framework where text remains the foundation. At the same time, non-verbal signals add human-like expressiveness, creating more natural and emotionally intelligent AI communication

of speech—plays a pivotal role in how we interpret intent, convey empathy, emphasise meaning, and manage the flow of conversation. The future of AI communication will depend increasingly on the ability of systems to interpret and generate speech in ways that reflect these nuanced sonic dimensions.

In everyday human interaction, voice does far more than transmit words. A rising pitch may signal a question, a pause can indicate hesitation or contemplation, and a trembling tone might reveal anxiety. These paralinguistic elements provide context and emotional colouration that text alone cannot deliver. In human–AI dialogue, the absence of such cues can result in flat, mechanical, or misinterpreted exchanges.

As generative AI systems move toward real-time voice interaction, mastering the subtleties of prosody becomes a critical frontier in achieving authenticity, empathy, and rapport.

Contemporary advancements in speech synthesis and recognition have laid the groundwork for this shift. Text-to-speech (TTS) technologies are now capable of generating highly expressive, emotionally attuned voices. At the same time, automatic speech recognition (ASR) systems can detect subtle vocal features indicative of mood, urgency, or personality. However, these capabilities are only the beginning. Future systems must move beyond simply detecting or mimicking prosodic patterns to understanding their communicative function within context. For instance, an AI assistant must discern when a user's raised voice indicates frustration versus excitement, and respond appropriately not only in words but in vocal tone and rhythm.

Moreover, prosody interacts dynamically with language, shaping both perception and comprehension. A sentence delivered with a sarcastic tone differs dramatically from one spoken sincerely, even if the words are identical. Effective AI systems will need to model such interaction patterns, learning to modulate their own prosodic output to align with situational cues, user preferences, and cultural norms. This requires complex modelling across linguistic, acoustic, and affective dimensions—an undertaking that draws from speech science, cognitive psychology, and affective computing.

Sound design also extends beyond voice. Nonverbal audio cues—such as sighs, laughter, ambient sounds, or auditory feedback—can enhance realism, support turn-taking, and enrich interaction. For example, subtle audio cues can indicate that the system is processing input or thinking, mimicking the pause a human might take before replying. These micro-signals contribute to a more fluid and believable dialogue experience, reducing cognitive friction and increasing user trust.

Ultimately, integrating voice, sound, and prosody into AI dialogue marks a transition from syntactic to affective communication. It challenges us to think not only about what AI systems say but also how they say it—and to whom. In this expanded auditory domain, the voice becomes a medium not just of command or query but of presence, emotion, and shared humanity (Fig. 5.3).

5.4 Visual and Spatial Modalities: Images, Gestures, and Movement

In the emerging landscape of multimodal AI communication, visual and spatial modalities are gaining prominence as integral components of interaction. While language and sound carry much of the semantic load in traditional interfaces, images, gestures, and physical movement convey meaning in ways that are immediate, embodied, and often more intuitive. These modalities reflect the fundamentally multisensory nature of human cognition and communication, and their integration

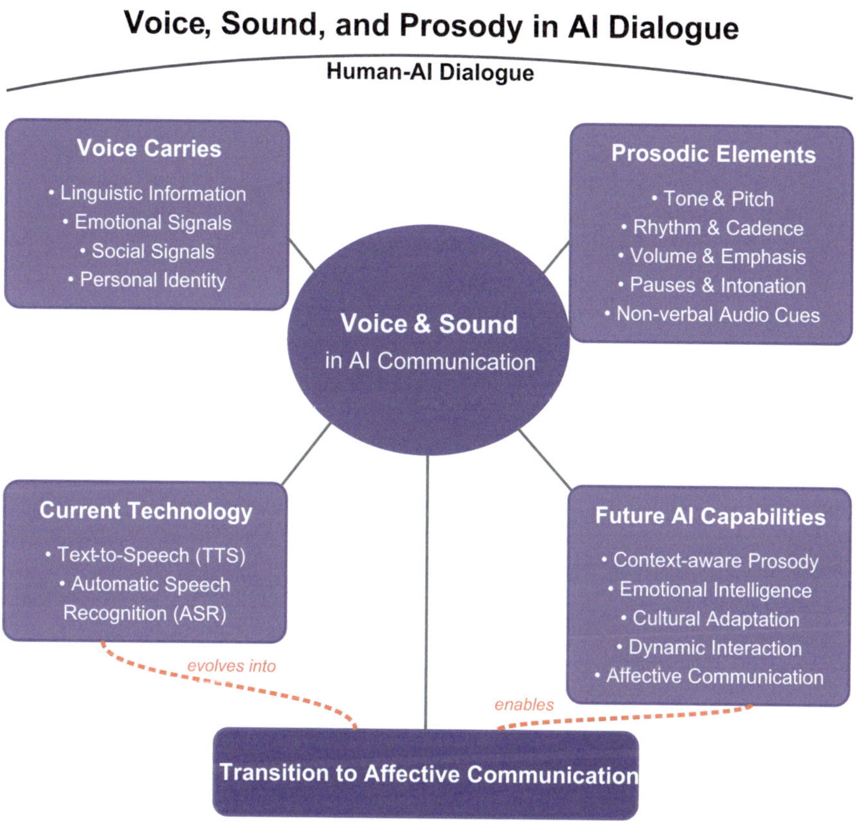

Fig. 5.3 Voice, sound, and prosody: the sonic dimension of future AI dialogue. This diagram illustrates how voice and sound elements transform AI communication beyond text. At its core, voice carries not just words but emotional, social, and identity signals through prosodic elements like tone, rhythm, and non-verbal cues. Current speech technologies (TTS, ASR) lay the foundation for future capabilities, including context-aware prosody and emotional intelligence. The critical prosody-language interaction shows how vocal qualities dynamically shape meaning. As AI evolves from current technologies toward affective communication, it must master these sonic dimensions to achieve authentic, empathetic dialogue that mirrors the nuanced expressiveness of human conversation

into AI systems marks a significant step toward more immersive, responsive, and context-aware interaction.

Images are a powerful form of representation, offering abstraction, emotional resonance, and dense semantic content that can be quickly interpreted. From diagrams and visual explanations to expressive avatars and symbolic cues, visual data augments linguistic information with depth and immediacy. For example, an AI tutor explaining a scientific concept may use a dynamic diagram to accompany verbal instruction, allowing the learner to engage with multiple modalities simultaneously. Similarly, AI in creative domains—design, art, architecture—can generate, interpret, and manipulate images as part of a visual dialogue with users. Here, the communicative act transcends text or speech, entering a visual logic where colour, shape, composition, and spatial arrangement carry meaning.

Gestures further extend this visual domain into motion. In human interaction, gestures serve as both supplements and substitutes for speech. Pointing, waving, nodding, and shrugging—these bodily expressions function as linguistic operators, regulating turn-taking, emphasising meaning, or replacing words entirely. AI systems equipped with camera-based vision, skeletal tracking, or embodied avatars can interpret human gestures and respond with their own, thus enriching the communicative exchange. This capability is especially valuable in settings where verbal communication is constrained or non-verbal fluency enhances clarity, such as in sign language interpretation, augmented reality, or robotics.

Movement—both virtual and physical—adds a spatial and temporal dimension to visual interaction. In virtual environments, the positioning and motion of AI agents or objects can signal attention, intent, or engagement. For instance, an AI avatar leaning forward might indicate interest or readiness, while backing away might suggest deference or disengagement. In embodied AI systems such as social robots or assistive devices, movement through space allows for collaborative action, shared attention, and spatial negotiation with human users. Spatial intelligence—understanding and navigating environments, predicting user paths, coordinating joint tasks—becomes a key communicative competence.

The integration of these visual and spatial modalities requires sophisticated perception, inference, and generative capabilities. AI must be able to detect and interpret visual signals with precision, understand their contextual and cultural significance, and generate appropriate visual or kinesthetic responses. Moreover, these modalities must be synchronised with verbal and auditory channels to produce coherent multimodal expression. A nod should coincide with verbal agreement, a diagram with spoken explanation, and a pointing gesture with referential speech.

In the future of AI communication, visual and spatial modalities will not simply supplement language—they will reshape it. Communication will move from a linear, linguistic model toward a spatially and visually grounded ecology of signs, gestures, and actions. This shift not only brings AI systems closer to human-like interaction but also opens new pathways for expressive, intuitive, and inclusive engagement across physical and virtual worlds (Fig. 5.4).

5.5 Multimodal Agents in Immersive Realities

As multimodal communication capabilities continue to evolve, the next frontier lies in the development of AI agents that operate seamlessly within immersive realities. These environments—ranging from augmented reality (AR) and virtual reality (VR) to mixed reality (MR) and spatial computing ecosystems—demand a new class of communicative agents: ones that are not only responsive across modalities but also

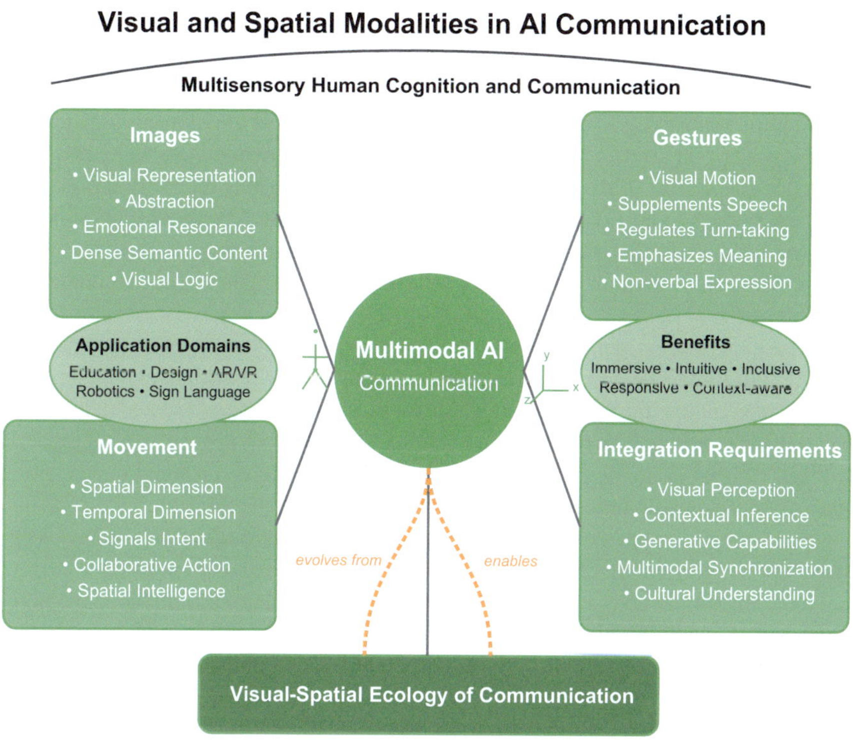

Fig. 5.4 Visual and spatial modalities: expanding the dimensions of AI communication. This diagram illustrates how images, gestures, and movement are transforming AI communication beyond textual and verbal exchanges. With multimodal AI at its centre, the diagram shows how images provide dense semantic content and emotional resonance, gestures extend communication into motion, and movement adds crucial spatial–temporal dimensions. These modalities require sophisticated integration capabilities and enable applications across education, design, AR/VR, and robotics. As AI evolves from linear linguistic models toward a visual-spatial ecology of communication, these modalities create more immersive, intuitive, and inclusive interactions, reflecting the fundamentally multisensory nature of human cognition and enabling new pathways for engagement across physical and virtual worlds

situated, embodied, and contextually aware in three-dimensional, interactive spaces. In this setting, communication is no longer confined to discrete inputs and outputs; it unfolds dynamically through speech, gesture, gaze, movement, visual elements, and spatial positioning in real time.

Multimodal agents in immersive realities are fundamentally different from traditional text-based or voice-only bots. They exist as embodied presences—avatars, holograms, or robotic forms—that users encounter and interact with in shared environments. These agents can observe and respond to the user's verbal cues, gestures, facial expressions, and spatial orientation. They can point, move, change posture, or shift visual focus in a way that mirrors human behaviour. The effect is not merely functional; it is experiential. The user feels accompanied, assisted, or even co-present with an intelligent entity capable of participating in embodied communication.

In such environments, modality integration is not additive but synergistic. A virtual AI guide in a museum, for instance, may explain historical context through speech, gesture toward an artefact, highlight it visually with augmented overlays, and walk alongside the visitor in the virtual space. The richness of this interaction arises not from any single modality but from its coordinated interplay. The agent must synchronise voice tone with facial expression, adjust gaze to maintain attention, and adapt motion paths to user behaviour—all while maintaining communicative coherence and responsiveness.

These capabilities open new possibilities for applications across education, healthcare, collaborative design, training, and entertainment. In virtual classrooms, AI tutors can engage with students using both verbal explanations and visual demonstrations, adjusting their delivery based on learners' non-verbal feedback. In therapeutic settings, embodied agents can facilitate empathetic interaction through a combination of voice, eye contact, and mirroring gestures. In collaborative design, architects and engineers may interact with AI assistants that manipulate models, annotate spaces, and adapt suggestions in real time, all within the same virtual environment.

However, immersive multimodal communication also introduces new challenges. These include ensuring temporal synchronisation across modalities, maintaining contextual continuity in spatially dynamic environments, managing sensory overload, and designing agents that respect social norms and personal boundaries in shared spaces. Ethical concerns also emerge, particularly regarding identity simulation, behavioural influence, and the potential blurring of human–agent boundaries.

Despite these challenges, the promise of multimodal agents in immersive realities is profound. They signal a future in which AI communication is not simply reactive or instructive, but participatory and co-experienced. These agents will not just process information or deliver outputs—they will inhabit communicative spaces, interpret and shape shared environments, and engage with users in ways that resemble human social presence. As we move toward a more spatial, embodied, and sensorily rich paradigm of interaction, such agents will become essential companions in the expanding ecology of AI-enhanced human experience (Fig. 5.5).

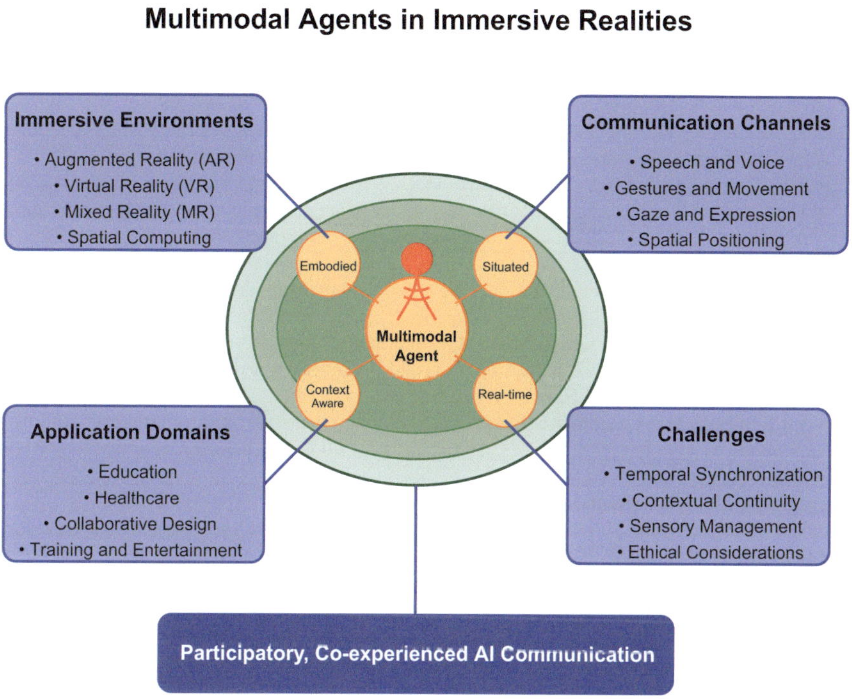

Fig. 5.5 Multimodal agents in immersive realities: beyond interfaces to co-presence. This diagram illustrates the evolution of AI communication toward embodied agents that operate within three-dimensional immersive spaces. At its core, the multimodal agent, characterised by being embodied, situated, context-aware, and real time, interacts through synergistically integrated channels (speech, gestures, gaze, spatial positioning) across diverse environments (AR, VR, MR). These capabilities enable applications in education, healthcare, design, and entertainment while presenting challenges in synchronisation, continuity, sensory management, and ethics. The diagram emphasises the shift from traditional AI interfaces toward participatory, co-experienced communication where agents do not merely deliver information but create a sense of social presence and shared experience

Bibliography

Annapureddy R, Fornaroli A, Gatica-Perez D (2025) Generative AI literacy: twelve defining competencies. Digit Govern: Res Practice 6(1):1–21

Bahree A (2024) Generative AI in action. Manning Publications

Bender EM, Koller A (2020) Climbing towards NLU: on meaning, form, and understanding in the age of data. Proceeding 58th ACL, pp 5185–5198

Bostrom N (2014) Superintelligence: paths, dangers, strategies. Oxford University Press, Oxford

Boyd D (2019) Artificial unintelligence: how computers misunderstand the world. Technol Cult 60(3):979–983

Bratton B (2016) The stack: on software and sovereignty. MIT Press, Cambridge

Brown BR (2025) Human–machine teaming using large language models. In Interdependent Human-Machine Teams (pp. 41–66). Academic Press.

Brown TB et al (2020) Language models are few-shot learners. arXiv preprint arXiv:2005.14165. Accessed 19 April 2025
Bryson JJ (2018) Patiency is not a virtue: AI and the design of ethical systems. Ethics Inf Technol 20:15–26. https://doi.org/10.1007/s10676-018-9448-6. Accessed 20 Jan 2025
Bura C, Myakala PK, Jonnalgadda AK (2025) Ethical prompt engineering: addressing bias, transparency, and fairness. Int J Res Anal Rev (IJRAR) 12(1). www.ijrar.org
Choi WC, Chang CI (2025) A survey of techniques, key components, strategies, challenges, and student perspectives on prompt engineering for large language models (LLMs) in education. Posted Date: 25 March 2025. https://doi.org/10.20944/preprints202503.1808.v1. Accessed 8 May 2025
Clark A (2016) Surfing uncertainty: prediction, action, and the embodied mind. Oxford University Press, Oxford
Coeckelbergh M (2020) AI ethics. MIT Press, Cambridge
Crawford K (2021) Atlas of AI: power, politics, and the planetary costs of artificial intelligence. Yale University Press, New Haven
Debnath T, Siddiky MNA, Rahman ME et al (2025) A comprehensive survey of prompt engineering techniques in large language models. TechRxiv. https://doi.org/10.36227/techrxiv.174140719.96375390/v1. Accessed 10 May 2025
Dennett DC (1987) The intentional stance. MIT Press, Cambridge
Dhamani N, Engler M (2024) Introduction to generative AI: an ethical, societal, and legal overview. Manning Publications
Dignum V (2019) Responsible artificial intelligence: how to develop and use AI in a responsible way. Springer, Cham
Eliot L (2024) Essentials of prompt engineering for generative AI: practical advances in artificial intelligence and machine learning. LBE Press Publishing
Ferraris AF, Audrito D, Di Caro L et al (2025) The architecture of language: understanding the mechanics behind LLMs. In: Cambridge forum on AI: law and governance, vol 1. Cambridge University Press.
Floridi L (2022) The ethics of artificial intelligence. Oxford University Press, Oxford
Floridi L (ed) (2015) The onlife manifesto: being human in a hyperconnected era. Springer, Cham
Geroimenko V (2025a) Generative AI: from human-computer interaction to human-computer creativity. In: Geroimenko V (ed) Human-computer creativity: generative AI in education, art, and healthcare. Springer
Geroimenko V (2025b) Key concepts in prompt engineering. In: The essential guide to prompt engineering: key principles, techniques, challenges, and security risks. Springer Nature Switzerland, Cham, pp 1–16
Geroimenko V (2025c) The essential guide to prompt engineering: key principles, techniques, challenges, and security risks. Springer, Cham
Geroimenko V (ed) (2025d) Human-Computer Creativity: Generative AI in Education, Art, and Healthcare, Springer
Geroimenko V (2025e) Key security risks in prompt engineering. In: The essential guide to prompt engineering: key principles, techniques, challenges, and security risks. Springer Nature Switzerland, Cham, pp 103–120
GitHub (2025) Prompt engineering guide. https://github.com/dair-ai/Prompt-Engineering-Guide. Accessed 10 April 2025
Greenwood M (2024) Artificial intelligence: a practical guide to using AI in everyday life. Ochreland Publishing
Gunkel DJ (2012) The machine question: critical perspectives on AI, robots, and ethics. MIT Press, Cambridge
Hagendorff T (2020) The ethics of AI ethics: an evaluation of guidelines. Minds Mach 30:99–120. https://doi.org/10.1007/s11023-020-09517-8. Accessed 10 Feb 2025
Hofstadter DR (2007) I am a strange loop. Basic Books, New York

Hsu HP (2025) From programming to prompting: developing computational thinking through large language model-based generative artificial intelligence. TechTrends, pp 1–22
Huang G, Xiao Y, Jiang L et al (2025) Beyond prompt engineering: a reinforced token-level input refinement for large language models. Proc AAAI Conf Artif Intell 39(22):24113–24121
i Picó JF, Catta-Preta M, Omeñaca AT et al (2025) The time machine: future scenario generation through generative AI tools. Future Internet 17(1):1–15
Jameson A (2007) Adaptive interfaces and agents. In: Sears A, Jacko J (eds) The human-computer interaction handbook, 2nd edn. CRC Press, Boca Raton, pp 305–330
Johnson KH (2023) Toward communicative alignment in human-AI teams. AI Soc 38:221–237. https://doi.org/10.1007/s00146-022-01422-5
Kannan R, Ahmad M (eds) (2025) Generative AI foundations, developments, and applications. IGI Global
Khan I (2024) The quick guide to prompt engineering. Wiley
Kushwaha V, Ragavan SS, Subhajit Roy S (2025) A measure based generalizable approach to understandability. arXiv:2503.21615. Accessed 19 April 2025
Lakoff G, Johnson M (1999) Philosophy in the flesh: the embodied mind and its challenge to western thought. Basic Books, New York
Learn Prompting (2025) https://learnprompting.org. Accessed 15 Mar 2025
Lee D, Palmer E (2025) Prompt engineering in higher education: a systematic review to help inform curricula. Int J Educ Technol High Educ 22(1):7
Lee JY, Kang S, Yoo S (2025) Can we predict the effect of prompts?. arXiv preprint arXiv:2501.18883. Accessed 12 May 2025
Lindley J, Whitham R (2025) From prompt engineering to prompt craft. In: Proceedings of the nineteenth international conference on tangible, embedded, and embodied interaction, March, pp 1–12
López-Pérez B et al (2025) Exploring the potential of large language models to understand interpersonal emotion regulation strategies from narratives. Emotion. Advance online publication. https://doi.org/10.1037/emo0001528. Accessed 19 April 2025
Maaz S, Palaganas JC, Palaganas G et al (2025) A guide to prompt design: foundations and applications for healthcare simulationists. Front Med 11:1504532
Marcus G, Davis E (2019) Rebooting AI: building artificial intelligence we can trust. Pantheon, New York
McStay A (2018) Emotional AI: the rise of empathic media. Sage, London
Mishra M, Ara A, Mishra S (2025) Exploring human-AI collaboration in higher education: an investigation into AI-enabled personalized learning. In: Prompt engineering and generative AI applications for teaching and learning. IGI Global Scientific Publishing, pp 483–502
Murray CD (2022) Thinking through avatars: identity, communication, and ethics in immersive AI environments. Technol Mind Behav. https://doi.org/10.1037/tmb0000053. Accessed 5 April 2025
Norman DA (2013) The design of everyday things, Revised. Basic Books, New York
OpenAI (2025) Best practices for prompt engineering with the OpenAI API. https://help.openai.com/en/articles/6654000-best-practices-for-prompt-engineering-with-the-openai-api. Accessed 20 April 2025
OpenAI (2025) Research. https://openai.com/research/index/ Accessed 11 Mar 2025
Phoenix J, Taylor M (2024) Prompt engineering for generative AI. O'Reilly Media
Picard RW (1997) Affective computing. MIT Press, Cambridge
PremaLatha V, Kumar AD, Parveen N (2025) Optimizing interactions: strategies for prompt engineering in large language models. Edu-Tech Enterprise 3:24–24
Prompt Engineering Guide (2025) https://www.promptingguide.ai/. Accessed 7 Mar 2025
Reddy CKK, Anoushka P, Draksharapu A et al (2025) Beyond text: analyzing artificial intelligence models through prompt engineering. Future tech startups and innovation in the age of AI, pp 120–156

Sasson Lazovsky G, Raz T, Kenett YN (2025) The art of creative inquiry—from question asking to prompt engineering. J Creative Behav 59(1):e671
Shneiderman B (2020) Human-centered artificial intelligence: reliable, safe and trustworthy. Int J Hum Comput Interact 36(6):495–504. https://doi.org/10.1080/10447318.2020.1741118. Accessed 15 Feb 2025
Sihi D, Ryan A (2025) Crafting and evaluating generative AI prompts: insights from students, educators, and marketers. Market Educ Rev 1–7
Suresh H, Guttag JV (2021) A framework for understanding unintended consequences of machine learning. Commun ACM 64(2):62–71. https://doi.org/10.1145/3430368. Accessed 18 Mar 2025
Turkle S (2011) Alone together: why we expect more from technology and less from each other. Basic Books, New York
Vairamani AD, Nayyar A (2024) Prompt engineering: empowering communication. CRC Press
Weizenbaum J (1976) Computer power and human reason: from judgment to calculation. W.H. Freeman, San Francisco
Winograd T (1972) Understanding natural language. Academic Press, New York
Winograd T, Flores F (1986) Understanding computers and cognition: a new foundation for design. Ablex Publishing, Norwood

Chapter 6
The Future Is Intuitive and Emotional

Abstract This chapter explores how AI communication is evolving to incorporate the human-like capacities of intuition and emotional intelligence. It begins by examining advances in cognitive architectures that enable AI to simulate anticipatory reasoning, affective responsiveness, and contextually coherent dialogue. The chapter then introduces the concept of machine intuition—AI's ability to infer intent and respond fluidly in ambiguous situations through probabilistic reasoning and multimodal integration. Emotional intelligence is redefined as a functional capacity in AI, encompassing emotion recognition, adaptive response, and affective alignment across cultures and users. Through detailed analysis of emotionally aware systems, the chapter discusses how AI can establish rapport, adapt communicative tone, and maintain ethical boundaries while navigating emotionally charged contexts. It concludes with a vision of adaptive communication, where AI systems respond to shifting affective and situational cues in real time, fostering emotionally resonant, transparent, and user-centred interaction. Together, these developments signal a profound shift toward AI systems capable of engaging in more intuitive, human-aware, and emotionally aligned communication.

Keywords Machine intuition · Emotional intelligence in AI · Affective computing · Emotion-aware interaction · Adaptive AI communication · Human–AI rapport

As AI communication evolves beyond syntactic precision and contextual awareness, it must also engage with the more elusive dimensions of human interaction: intuition and emotion. These are not simply add-ons to rational discourse but foundational aspects of how meaning is formed, intentions are conveyed, and trust is established. For AI systems to participate more fully in human-like communication, they will need to develop capacities for intuitive inference—anticipating what is meant without it being said—and for emotional responsiveness—sensing, interpreting, and adapting to human affect. This chapter explores how emerging cognitive architectures and affective computing techniques may enable AI to navigate ambiguity, modulate tone,

V. Geroimenko, *Beyond and After Prompt Engineering: The Future of AI Communication*, https://doi.org/10.1007/978-3-032-04569-0_6

and establish emotional alignment with users. From the development of machine intuition to the nuanced adaptation of conversational dynamics, we trace the shift toward communicative systems that do not merely simulate understanding but participate in it with a new degree of emotional and intuitive depth.

6.1 Understanding AI's Cognitive Architecture

The future of AI communication will depend not only on external interfaces or contextual sensitivity but also on the depth and nature of the internal cognitive architectures that underpin artificial intelligence systems. Much like human communication is shaped by mental models, memory structures, attention mechanisms, and emotional states, the ability of AI to communicate in intuitive and emotionally resonant ways depends on how its cognitive functions are modelled, integrated, and enacted. Understanding these underlying architectures is essential for grasping how AI might come to exhibit traits akin to intuition, empathy, and adaptive emotional behaviour.

Traditional AI architectures have been built upon modular principles, where perception, reasoning, and action are separated into discrete components. While functional in deterministic environments, such models often fall short in dynamic, affectively rich human interactions. In contrast, emergent cognitive architectures—such as those inspired by the brain's distributed processing or by embodied cognition—seek to simulate more fluid and integrative mechanisms. These may include reinforcement learning modules for behaviour shaping, attention systems that dynamically allocate processing resources, memory networks that allow for long-range dependencies, and affective computing modules that simulate or interpret emotional states.

Modern large language models (LLMs) represent a significant step in this direction. Though not fully cognitive in the human sense, they exhibit proto-cognitive traits: they maintain short-term context through token histories, modulate their responses based on linguistic cues, and generate plausible affective language without being truly sentient. When enhanced with memory systems, user-specific profiles, and multimodal inputs, these models begin to resemble architectures with rudimentary forms of self-adaptation and internal coherence—core prerequisites for more intuitive and emotionally responsive interaction.

However, to move toward emotionally and intuitively capable communication, cognitive architectures must evolve beyond statistical pattern recognition. They must incorporate mechanisms for goal representation, affective state modelling, and real-time environmental feedback. Hybrid models—blending symbolic reasoning with neural networks—are one promising path. These allow for both flexible learning and transparent reasoning, crucial for AI systems expected to navigate socially complex interactions with accountability and interpretability.

Furthermore, future architectures must not only *represent* emotion or intuition but also *embody* them functionally. This involves designing architectures capable of anticipatory processing (a hallmark of intuition), emotional memory (which affects behaviour over time), and value-driven reasoning (which underlies ethical and empathetic action). Such developments suggest a convergence between cognitive science, affective neuroscience, and AI design. This interdisciplinary synthesis may eventually produce machines with communication patterns that feel less mechanical and more meaningfully human.

Ultimately, understanding AI's cognitive architecture is not a purely technical task but a conceptual and philosophical one. It requires rethinking what it means to "know," "feel," and "understand" in artificial agents—and how these capacities, once thought to be uniquely human, might manifest in computational forms. As AI transitions from tool to collaborator, its internal architecture becomes not just a technical blueprint but a communicative foundation that shapes the nature of future human–AI relationships (Fig. 6.1).

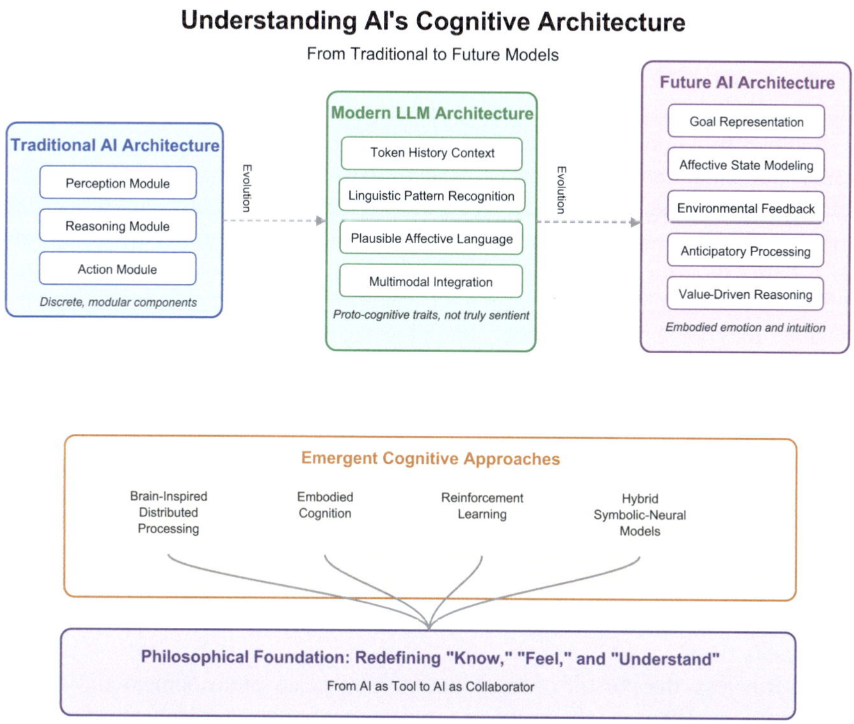

Fig. 6.1 The evolution of AI cognitive architecture. This diagram illustrates the progression from traditional modular AI systems toward future integrative cognitive architectures. Traditional designs separate perception, reasoning, and action into discrete components, while current LLMs exhibit proto-cognitive traits through context maintenance and affective language generation. Future architectures aim to embody—not merely represent—emotion and intuition through goal representation, affective modelling, and value-driven reasoning. This evolution is guided by emergent approaches including brain-inspired processing, embodied cognition, and hybrid symbolic-neural models, ultimately redefining what it means for artificial agents to "know," "feel," and "understand"

6.2 Toward Machine Intuition

The concept of intuition has long been regarded as an exclusively human trait—a form of rapid, unconscious cognition that draws on experience, pattern recognition, and emotional resonance to produce judgements or insights without explicit reasoning. As AI communication evolves beyond logical response generation and procedural dialogue systems, the question arises: Can machines exhibit a form of intuition? And if so, what would this look like in the context of future human–AI interaction?

Machine intuition, unlike human intuition, rooted in embodied experience and emotion, must emerge from computational analogues: fast inference, pattern-based prediction, multimodal integration, and context-sensitive reasoning. While AI systems do not "feel" or "sense" in a biological sense, they are increasingly capable of making informed, non-explicitly programmed decisions based on accumulated data, prior interactions, and ambient context. This kind of algorithmic intuition—built on vast neural representations and fine-tuned through reinforcement or contrastive learning—can enable AI to anticipate user needs, interpret incomplete or ambiguous inputs, and act in ways that feel natural or even serendipitous.

Intuition in AI does not mean bypassing logic but rather augmenting reasoning with experiential knowledge distilled from massive corpora, user history, and environmental feedback. For instance, an AI assistant capable of intuitively suggesting a course of action, without the user explicitly articulating a problem, would rely on patterns of prior behaviour, situational cues (such as location or time), and subtle affective signals derived from tone, gesture, or expression. In such cases, the machine does not "know" in a propositional sense; it "anticipates" in a probabilistic, context-aware manner.

The key to developing machine intuition is the integration of multiple modalities and temporal layers of context. Just as human intuition synthesises sensory input, social dynamics, and emotional tone in milliseconds, intuitive AI must operate on layered inputs—textual, visual, auditory, spatial—processed in near real-time. Architectures enabling this form of reasoning are increasingly built around transformer models with memory augmentation, attention mechanisms, and grounding in external sensors or feedback loops. These allow machines not only to respond but to "sense what is missing," filling in gaps in communication or perception in ways that appear remarkably fluid.

Nevertheless, the pursuit of machine intuition raises philosophical and ethical considerations. What are the limits of intuition in systems that lack consciousness or emotion? Can probabilistic guesswork truly be called intuition, or is it a simulation thereof? Moreover, when AI systems act on inferred needs or preemptive assumptions, they risk overstepping user autonomy, introducing subtle coercion or misinterpretation. Building safeguards, transparency, and adjustable thresholds for intuitive behaviour will be crucial for maintaining trust.

In the broader trajectory of AI communication, intuition represents a significant shift—from reactive to proactive, from scripted to emergent, from explicit prompting to implicit understanding. As these systems mature, their ability to navigate uncertainty, nuance, and incomplete information will define not just their intelligence but also their ability to engage as communicative partners in a world saturated with ambiguity and feeling (Fig. 6.2).

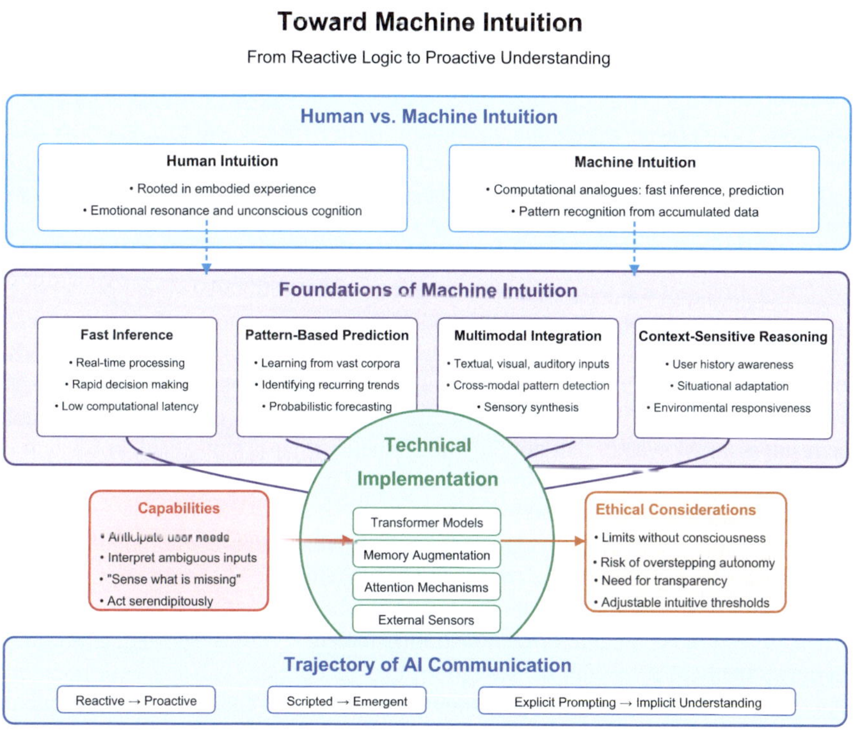

Fig. 6.2 The framework of machine intuition. This diagram illustrates the conceptual foundation for developing intuition-like capabilities in AI systems. While human intuition stems from embodied experience and unconscious cognition, machine intuition emerges from computational analogues, including fast inference, pattern recognition, multimodal integration, and context-sensitive reasoning. These foundations are enabled by transformer models, memory augmentation, attention mechanisms, and external sensors, allowing AI to anticipate needs and interpret ambiguity. The development of machine intuition represents a fundamental shift in AI communication: from reactive to proactive, scripted to emergent, and explicit prompting to implicit understanding, while raising critical ethical considerations about autonomy and transparency

6.3 Emotional Intelligence in AI Conversations

As AI systems transition from transactional tools to collaborative communicators, the capacity to engage in emotionally intelligent dialogue is becoming increasingly central to their design and application. Emotional intelligence (EI)—commonly defined in humans as the ability to perceive, understand, manage, and express emotions—plays a foundational role in effective interpersonal communication. In the context of AI, emotional intelligence must be reimagined as a computational capacity to simulate, detect, and appropriately respond to emotional cues in ways that foster trust, empathy, and rapport.

Unlike humans, AI systems do not experience emotions. Yet they can be designed to *model* emotional processes and *act* in ways that reflect emotional intelligence. This distinction is important: emotional intelligence in AI is not about sentience but about functional empathy. It involves the ability to recognise affective signals in language, voice, facial expression, and behavioural patterns, and to adapt responses that resonate with the user's emotional state. This is particularly vital in domains such as education, mental health, customer support, and caregiving, where emotional context shapes the quality and effectiveness of communication.

At a technical level, emotionally intelligent AI depends on advances in affective computing, natural language understanding, and multimodal signal processing. Sentiment analysis tools already allow models to assess the emotional valence of text, while voice-based emotion recognition systems analyse pitch, tempo, and prosody. Visual emotion detection can further identify non-verbal cues from facial microexpressions or gestures. When these inputs are integrated into a conversational model, the result is an AI system that not only understands what is being said, but *how* it is being said—and perhaps even *why* it is being said in that manner.

However, true emotional intelligence in conversation goes beyond detection. It involves response strategies that are context-sensitive, appropriately modulated, and culturally attuned. For instance, an emotionally intelligent AI should know when to offer reassurance, when to remain neutral, and when to escalate to a human counterpart. It should be capable of demonstrating patience with frustration, expressing encouragement in moments of hesitation, and recognising silence as a potential sign of distress rather than disengagement. Such responsiveness requires a dynamic interplay between real-time analysis and pre-trained socio-emotional models.

Moreover, as AI systems become emotionally expressive—using empathetic phrasing, adjusting tone, or mirroring user sentiment—questions arise about authenticity, manipulation, and emotional labour. If AI systems simulate empathy too well, users may project human-like intentions onto them, potentially blurring the line between simulation and sincerity. Designers must balance the benefits of emotionally resonant interaction with ethical concerns around user expectations, transparency, and dependency.

In the future AI communication, emotional intelligence will not be a peripheral feature but a core design principle. It will shape not only how machines speak but also how they listen, interpret, and adapt. Ultimately, emotional intelligence will be key to

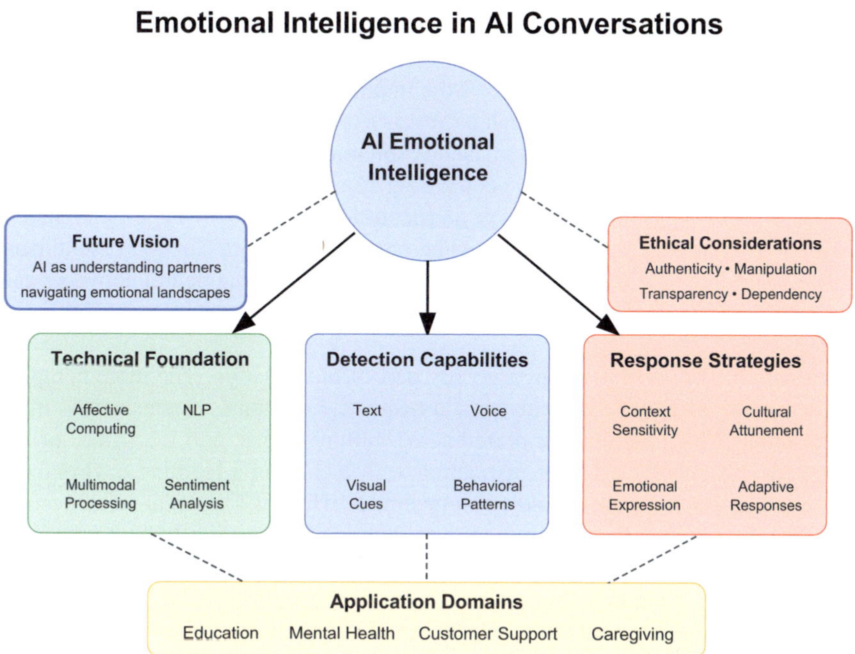

Fig. 6.3 Emotional intelligence in AI conversations: a conceptual framework. This diagram illustrates the evolving architecture of emotional intelligence in AI communication systems. At its core lies the fundamental distinction between human emotions and AI's functional empathy. The framework branches into three interconnected domains: technical foundations enabling affective processing, multimodal detection capabilities across sensory channels, and adaptive response strategies. These components converge to serve applications in education, mental health, customer support, and caregiving. As AI transitions from tools to partners, this framework balances technological advancement with ethical considerations, ultimately aiming to create systems that navigate emotional landscapes with authenticity and contextual understanding

building AI systems that feel less like rigid instruments and more like understanding partners capable of navigating the rich emotional landscapes that characterise human conversation (Fig. 6.3).

6.4 Recognising and Responding to Emotion

A critical step toward emotionally intelligent AI communication is the ability to recognise and respond to human emotion accurately. In human interactions, much of communication is non-verbal, affective, and context-dependent. Emotions serve not only as expressions of inner states but also as signals that guide social behaviour, influence decision-making, and structure dialogue. For AI systems to meaningfully engage in human-centred communication, they must be able to identify emotional states with contextual accuracy and respond with appropriate, ethically calibrated behaviour.

Emotion recognition in AI involves the multimodal sensing of affective signals. These signals may be explicit, such as words expressing anger or joy, or implicit, such as tone of voice, speech rhythm, facial expressions, body posture, or behavioural hesitation. Contemporary affective computing systems use a combination of natural language processing, computer vision, and acoustic analysis to infer emotional states. For example, models trained on annotated emotional corpora can detect sentiment polarity and intensity in text. At the same time, convolutional neural networks can analyse facial microexpressions to infer subtle feelings of anxiety, confusion, or enthusiasm.

However, recognising emotion is only part of the equation. The more complex challenge lies in how AI systems should respond. Emotional responsiveness must be modulated by context, user preferences, cultural norms, and the nature of the interaction. A robotic assistant interacting with a child in a learning environment may need to display warmth and encouragement, whereas a medical AI delivering sensitive information must adopt a tone of gravity and restraint. In both cases, the response should not be merely reactive, but aligned with the user's emotional state and the broader communicative goals.

There is a growing emphasis on the *situatedness* of emotion—how emotions emerge and are interpreted in specific social and cultural contexts. For AI to avoid misinterpretation, it must incorporate contextual cues such as the user's identity, historical interaction patterns, situational variables (e.g. urgency, privacy), and even broader socio-cultural background. Misreading a user's sarcasm as sincerity or failing to detect distress masked by politeness can lead to communication breakdowns or unintended harm.

Effective emotional response in AI may take the form of verbal empathy ("I understand this might be frustrating"), pragmatic adjustments (slowing down when detecting confusion), or even strategic silence. It may also include adaptive modulation of voice, expression, or gesture in embodied systems. Importantly, such responsiveness should remain transparent: users must be aware that they are interacting with an artificial system that simulates empathy rather than experiencing it. Maintaining this boundary is essential for trust, autonomy, and informed user engagement.

As AI becomes increasingly embedded in emotionally charged domains—from therapy chatbots to elder care robots—the ability to recognise and respond to emotion will determine the depth and quality of human–AI relationships. It moves communication from mechanical exchange to affective resonance. Yet this capability must be grounded in ethical design: machines should not manipulate emotion, but support, mirror, and adapt to it, enabling more humane, responsive, and contextually aware AI communication (Fig. 6.4).

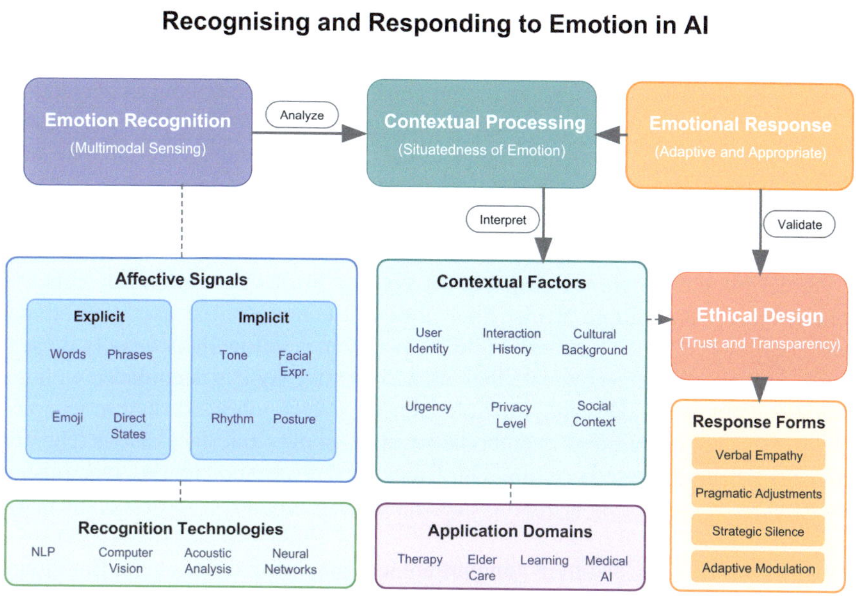

Fig. 6.4 From perception to response: the architecture of emotion-aware AI. This diagram illustrates the systematic process through which AI systems recognise and respond to human emotions. Beginning with multimodal sensing of both explicit and implicit affective signals, the framework shows how raw emotional data flows through contextual interpretation filters, accounting for user identity, cultural background, and situational variables. The process culminates in calibrated emotional responses that are ethically designed for transparency. By mapping the complex interplay between recognition technologies, contextual understanding, and response strategies, this framework demonstrates how AI can transition from mechanical exchanges to affective resonance while maintaining appropriate boundaries in emotionally charged domains

6.5 Creating Emotional Alignment Between AI and Human Users

Emotional alignment refers to the capacity of two communicative agents to attune to each other's affective states, thereby establishing a sense of mutual understanding, empathy, and shared emotional context. In human relationships, emotional alignment is a cornerstone of rapport, cooperation, and trust. Translating this principle into AI-human interaction involves developing artificial systems capable not only of detecting and responding to human emotion, but also of modulating their own communicative style in ways that mirror, complement, or respectfully counterbalance user emotions. As AI systems are increasingly deployed in emotionally sensitive settings—education, healthcare, companionship, and crisis support—the pursuit of emotional alignment is becoming central to the evolution of intuitive and affective AI communication.

Establishing emotional alignment begins with accurate emotional recognition but goes beyond reactive responsiveness. It involves maintaining an ongoing synchronisation of emotional tone, tempo, and communicative intent throughout an interaction. For instance, an emotionally aligned AI tutor might detect a learner's frustration, slow the pace of instruction, offer motivational encouragement, and reframe the task in simpler terms. Crucially, the system's response would not be static but dynamically calibrated to the learner's evolving emotional state, fostering a sense of being "understood" in both cognitive and emotional dimensions.

Achieving such alignment requires AI systems to maintain a kind of affective coherence across multiple levels. First, they must interpret the user's emotional trajectory—whether excitement is building, boredom is setting in, or anxiety is escalating. Second, they must regulate their own expressive style in accordance with the interactional context. This may include adjusting voice tone and rhythm in voice interfaces, facial expressions in embodied avatars, or even interface colour schemes and layout in screen-based systems. Third, they must respect boundaries, recognising when emotional mirroring is appropriate and when it might feel intrusive, uncanny, or manipulative.

Cultural sensitivity and individual differences play crucial roles here. Emotional alignment is not a one-size-fits-all process; what feels like empathy in one cultural setting may feel like overfamiliarity in another. Similarly, some users may welcome emotionally expressive AI, while others may prefer a more neutral or understated tone. To address this, emotionally aware systems must incorporate user modelling, tailoring their communicative behaviour to known user preferences, communication styles, and prior interactions. This personalization enables alignment not just with transient emotions but with longer-term affective profiles and interpersonal expectations.

At a technical level, emotional alignment is supported by hybrid architectures that combine real-time signal processing with memory-augmented interaction histories and reinforcement learning. These systems gradually learn how specific users respond to different emotional tones, enabling nuanced and sustained engagement. But beyond the technical challenges lies an ethical imperative: emotional alignment must serve the user's well-being, autonomy, and dignity, not simply maximise engagement or simulate affection for a persuasive effect.

In the future of AI communication, emotional alignment will be a defining feature of systems that feel genuinely collaborative and human-aware. It will transform interaction from mechanical responsiveness to affective resonance, from scripted dialogue to relational attunement, laying the foundation for AI systems that can not only understand us but also *connect* with us on a deeper, emotional level (Fig. 6.5).

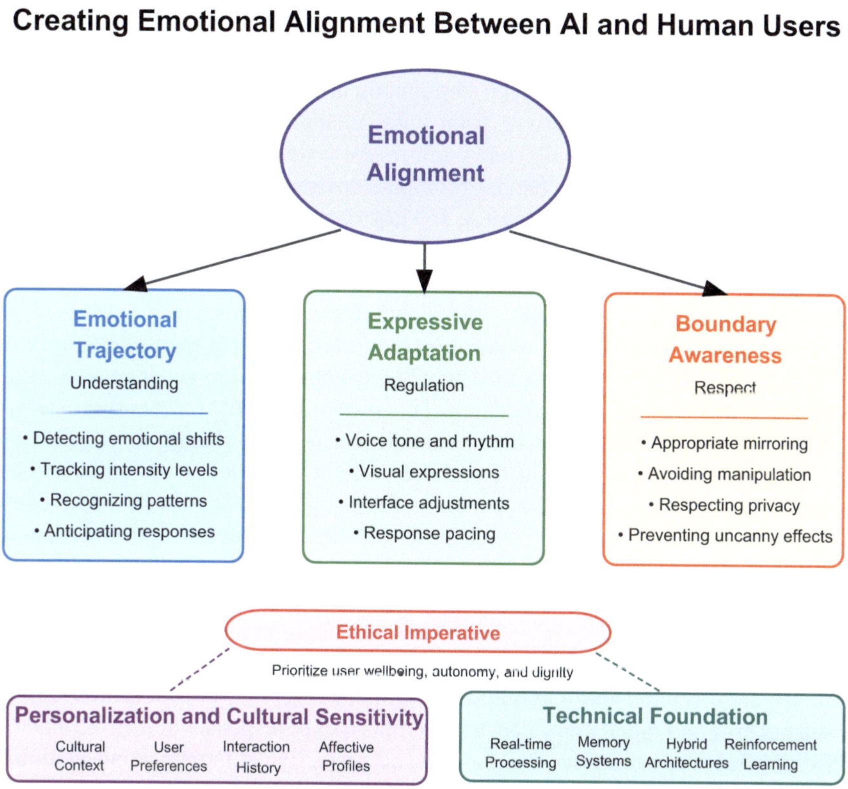

Fig. 6.5 The architecture of emotional alignment: building AI-human affective bridges. This diagram maps the conceptual framework for achieving emotional alignment between AI systems and human users. Centred around the core principle of affective attunement, it illustrates the three essential components: trajectory understanding (detecting emotional patterns), expressive adaptation (modulating communicative style), and boundary awareness (respecting appropriate limits). These elements are supported by personalisation mechanisms that account for cultural context and individual preferences, alongside technical foundations that enable real-time processing and learning. The framework serves emotionally sensitive domains while adhering to ethical imperatives that prioritise human well-being and dignity, ultimately transforming AI interaction from mechanical exchanges to genuine affective resonance

6.6 Developing Adaptive Communication

As AI systems become more embedded in human environments, the ability to adapt communication not only to semantic context but also to emotional and situational cues will define the next frontier of intelligent interaction. Adaptive communication refers to the capacity of AI to modulate its conversational strategies in real time, guided by a dynamic understanding of the user's affective state, interpersonal context, and situational demands. Unlike rigid rule-based systems, adaptive communicative agents are designed to be contextually fluid, emotionally responsive, and socially aware—characteristics that mark a decisive shift toward human-like engagement.

Effective adaptation begins with continuous affective and situational sensing. Emotional cues—whether derived from voice modulation, facial expression, text sentiment, or physiological indicators—inform the system of the user's internal state. Situational cues, on the other hand, encompass environmental factors such as time of day, location, social setting, urgency, and task complexity. An emotionally neutral query made during a crisis may demand a different response than the same query posed in a relaxed context. An adaptive AI must be capable of interpreting both layers simultaneously, allowing for multidimensional responsiveness.

At the core of adaptive communication is *flexibility*. Rather than selecting from a fixed set of predefined scripts, advanced AI systems learn to generate and refine responses based on ongoing interaction. This involves shifting tones—from formal to casual, instructional to empathetic—modifying response length or complexity, adjusting pace or visual emphasis, and even altering interaction modalities when needed (e.g., switching from text to voice). These adjustments must be made seamlessly and respectfully, ensuring that the user remains at the centre of the interaction rather than feeling manipulated or pathologised by AI inference.

Adaptive communication also implies *learning over time*. Emotional and situational preferences vary not only across users but within users, depending on mood, familiarity with the system, or changes in life circumstances. By incorporating memory architectures and longitudinal user modelling, AI systems can develop a history of how individual users react to different types of responses in varied contexts. This allows for increasingly personalised and predictive communication, with the system learning when to offer support, when to step back, and when to intervene.

Crucially, adaptation must remain transparent and user-controllable. Users should be aware of when and how the system is tailoring its communication, and have the means to adjust or override it. Ethical adaptation also involves safeguarding against overfitting, where the system reinforces emotional biases, or against persuasive manipulation, especially in commercial or political domains. Trustworthy adaptive systems should prioritise user agency, well-being, and clarity over engagement metrics or persuasive efficiency.

As we envision a future of AI that is intuitive, emotional, and socially intelligent, adaptive communication will become a foundational skill, not a feature. It will enable AI systems to serve not merely as tools of information retrieval or task execution, but as responsive partners capable of co-regulating emotional tone, navigating complexity, and fostering meaningful interactions attuned to the richness of human life (Fig. 6.6).

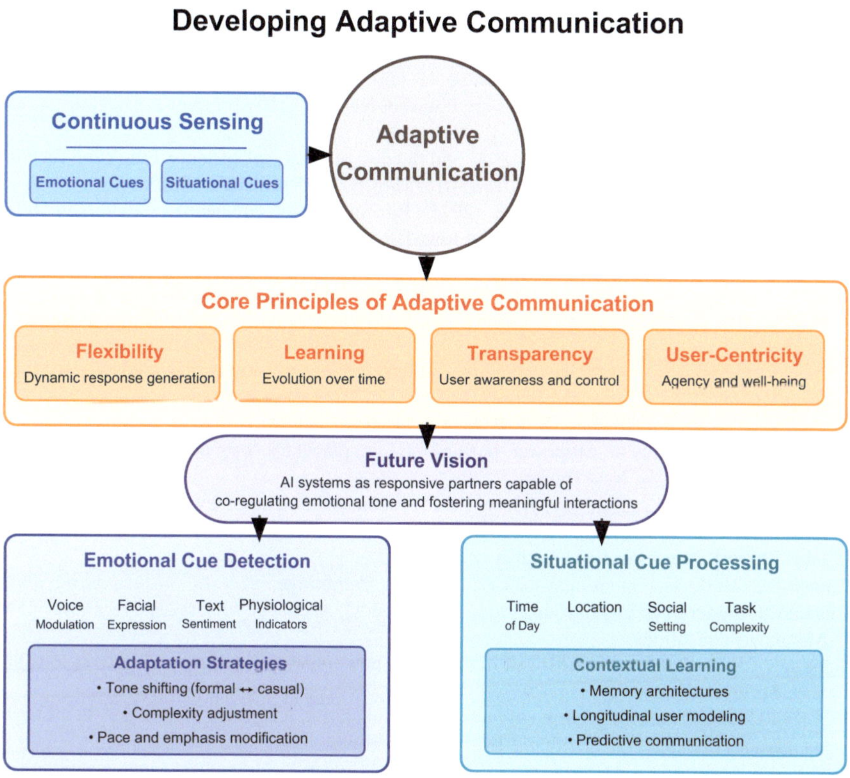

Fig. 6.6 Adaptive communication: a framework for context-aware AI interaction. This diagram illustrates the multidimensional architecture of adaptive AI communication systems. Centred around real-time responsiveness, it demonstrates how these systems simultaneously process emotional and situational cues to generate contextually appropriate responses. The framework highlights four core principles—flexibility, learning, transparency, and user-centricity—that guide the development of systems capable of evolving beyond rigid scripting. Through continuous sensing and strategic adaptation, AI transitions from static responders to dynamic communication partners that adjust tone, complexity, and modality based on affective states and environmental contexts, while maintaining ethical boundaries and user autonomy throughout the interaction process

Bibliography

Adorno TW (1966) Negative Dialektik. Suhrkamp, Frankfurt, English edition: Adorno TW (1973) Negative Dialectics (trans: Ashton EB). Routledge, London

Annapureddy R, Fornaroli A, Gatica-Perez D (2025) Generative AI literacy: twelve defining competencies. Digit Govern: Res Practice 6(1):1–21

Bahree A (2024) Generative AI in action. Manning Publications

Bender EM, Koller A (2020) Climbing towards NLU: on meaning, form, and understanding in the age of data. Proceeding 58th ACL, pp 5185–5198

Bostrom N (2014) Superintelligence: paths, dangers, strategies. Oxford University Press, Oxford

Boyd D (2019) Artificial unintelligence: how computers misunderstand the world. Technol Cult 60(3):979–983

Bratton B (2016) The stack: on software and sovereignty. MIT Press, Cambridge
Brown BR (2025) Human–machine teaming using large language models. In: Interdependent human-machine teams. Academic Press, pp 41–66
Brown TB et al (2020) Language models are few-shot learners. arXiv preprint arXiv:2005.14165. Accessed 19 Apr 2025
Bryson JJ (2018) Patiency is not a virtue: AI and the design of ethical systems. Ethics Inf Technol 20:15–26. https://doi.org/10.1007/s10676-018-9448-6. Accessed 20 Jan 2025
Bura C, Myakala PK, Jonnalgadda AK (2025) Ethical prompt engineering: addressing bias, transparency, and fairness. Int J Res Anal Rev (IJRAR) 12(1). www.ijrar.org
Choi WC, Chang CI (2025) A survey of techniques, key components, strategies, challenges, and student perspectives on prompt engineering for large language models (LLMs) in education. Posted Date: 25 March 2025. https://doi.org/10.20944/preprints202503.1808.v1. Accessed 8 May 2025
Clark A (2016) Surfing uncertainty: prediction, action, and the embodied mind. Oxford University Press, Oxford
Coeckelbergh M (2020) AI ethics. MIT Press, Cambridge
Crawford K (2021) Atlas of AI: power, politics, and the planetary costs of artificial intelligence. Yale University Press, New Haven
Debnath T, Siddiky MNA, Rahman ME et al (2025) A comprehensive survey of prompt engineering techniques in large language models. TechRxiv. https://doi.org/10.36227/techrxiv.174140719.96375390/v1. Accessed 10 May 2025
Dennett DC (1987) The intentional stance. MIT Press, Cambridge
Dhamani N, Engler M (2024) Introduction to generative AI: an ethical, societal, and legal overview. Manning Publications
Dignum V (2019) Responsible artificial intelligence: how to develop and use AI in a responsible way. Springer, Cham
Eliot L (2024) Essentials of prompt engineering for generative AI: practical advances in artificial intelligence and machine learning. LBE Press Publishing
Ferraris AF, Audrito D, Di Caro L et al (2025) The architecture of language: understanding the mechanics behind LLMs. In: Cambridge forum on AI: law and governance, vol 1. Cambridge University Press
Floridi L (2022) The ethics of artificial intelligence. Oxford University Press, Oxford
Floridi L (ed) (2015) The onlife manifesto: being human in a hyperconnected era. Springer, Cham
Geroimenko V (2025a) Generative AI: from human-computer interaction to human-computer creativity. In: Geroimenko V (ed) Human-computer creativity: generative AI in education, art, and healthcare. Springer
Geroimenko V (2025) Key concepts in prompt engineering. In: The essential guide to prompt engineering: key principles, techniques, challenges, and security risks. Springer Nature Switzerland, Cham, pp 1–16
Geroimenko V (2025c) The essential guide to prompt engineering: key principles, techniques, challenges, and security risks. Springer, Cham
Geroimenko V (ed) (2025d) Human-computer creativity: generative AI in education, art, and healthcare. Springer
Geroimenko V (2025e) Key security risks in prompt engineering. In: The essential guide to prompt engineering: key principles, techniques, challenges, and security risks. Springer Nature Switzerland, Cham, pp 103–120
GitHub (2025) Prompt engineering guide. https://github.com/dair-ai/Prompt-Engineering-Guide. Accessed 10 Apr 2025
Greenwood M (2024) Artificial intelligence: a practical guide to using AI in everyday life. Ochreland Publishing
Gunkel DJ (2012) The machine question: critical perspectives on AI, robots, and ethics. MIT Press, Cambridge

Hagendorff T (2020) The ethics of AI ethics: an evaluation of guidelines. Minds Mach 30:99–120. https://doi.org/10.1007/s11023-020-09517-8. Accessed 10 Feb 2025
Hofstadter DR (2007) I am a strange loop. Basic Books, New York
Hsu HP (2025) From programming to prompting: developing computational thinking through large language model-based generative artificial intelligence. TechTrends, pp 1–22
Huang G, Xiao Y, Jiang L et al (2025) Beyond prompt engineering: a reinforced token-level input refinement for large language models. Proc AAAI Conf Artif Intell 39(22):24113–24121
i Picó JF, Catta-Preta M, Omeñaca AT et al (2025) The time machine: future scenario generation through generative AI tools. Future Internet 17(1):1–15
Jameson A (2007) Adaptive interfaces and agents. In: Sears A, Jacko J (eds) The human-computer interaction handbook, 2nd edn. CRC Press, Boca Raton, pp 305–330
Johnson KH (2023) Toward communicative alignment in human-AI teams. AI Soc 38:221–237. https://doi.org/10.1007/s00146-022-01422-5
Kannan R, Ahmad M (eds) (2025) Generative AI foundations, developments, and applications. IGI Global
Khan I (2024) The quick guide to prompt engineering. Wiley
Kushwaha V, Ragavan SS, Subhajit Roy S (2025) A measure based generalizable approach to understandability. arXiv:2503.21615. Accessed 19 Apr 2025
Lakoff G, Johnson M (1999) Philosophy in the flesh: the embodied mind and its challenge to western thought. Basic Books, New York
Learn Prompting (2025) https://learnprompting.org. Accessed 15 Mar 2025
Lee D, Palmer E (2025) Prompt engineering in higher education: a systematic review to help inform curricula. Int J Educ Technol High Educ 22(1):7
Lee JY, Kang S, Yoo S (2025) Can we predict the effect of prompts?. arXiv preprint arXiv:2501.18883. Accessed 12 May 2025
Lindley J, Whitham R (2025) From prompt engineering to prompt craft. In: Proceedings of the nineteenth international conference on tangible, embedded, and embodied interaction, March, pp 1–12
López-Pérez B et al (2025) Exploring the potential of large language models to understand interpersonal emotion regulation strategies from narratives. Emotion. Advance online publication. https://doi.org/10.1037/emo0001528. Accessed 19 Apr 2025
Maaz S, Palaganas JC, Palaganas G et al (2025) A guide to prompt design: foundations and applications for healthcare simulationists. Front Med 11:1504532
Marcus G, Davis E (2019) Rebooting AI: building artificial intelligence we can trust. Pantheon, New York
McStay A (2018) Emotional AI: the rise of empathic media. Sage, London
Mishra M, Ara A, Mishra S (2025) Exploring human-AI collaboration in higher education: an investigation into AI-enabled personalized learning. In: Prompt engineering and generative AI applications for teaching and learning. IGI Global Scientific Publishing, pp 483–502
Murray CD (2022) Thinking through avatars: identity, communication, and ethics in immersive AI environments. Technol Mind Behav. https://doi.org/10.1037/tmb0000053. Accessed 5 Apr 2025
Norman DA (2013) The design of everyday things, Revised. Basic Books, New York
OpenAI (2025) Best practices for prompt engineering with the OpenAI API. https://help.openai.com/en/articles/6654000-best-practices-for-prompt-engineering-with-the-openai-api. Accessed 20 Apr 2025
OpenAI (2025) Research. https://openai.com/research/index/. Accessed 11 Mar 2025
Phoenix J, Taylor M (2024) Prompt engineering for generative AI. O'Reilly Media
Picard RW (1997) Affective computing. MIT Press, Cambridge
PremaLatha V, Kumar AD, Parveen N (2025) Optimizing interactions: strategies for prompt engineering in large language models. Edu-Tech Enterp 3:24–24
Prompt Engineering Guide (2025) https://www.promptingguide.ai/. Accessed 7 March 2025

Reddy CKK, Anoushka P, Draksharapu A et al (2025) Beyond text: analyzing artificial intelligence models through prompt engineering. Future Tech Startups and innovation in the age of AI, pp 120–156

Sasson Lazovsky G, Raz T, Kenett YN (2025) The art of creative inquiry—from question asking to prompt engineering. J Creative Behav 59(1):e671

Shneiderman B (2020) Human-centered artificial intelligence: reliable, safe & trustworthy. Int J Hum Comput Interact 36(6):495–504. https://doi.org/10.1080/10447318.2020.1741118. Accessed 15 Feb 2025

Sihi D, Ryan A (2025) Crafting and evaluating generative AI prompts: insights from students, educators, and marketers. Market Educ Rev 1–7

Suresh H, Guttag JV (2021) A framework for understanding unintended consequences of machine learning. Commun ACM 64(2):62–71. https://doi.org/10.1145/3430368. Accessed 18 Mar 2025

Turkle S (2011) Alone together: why we expect more from technology and less from each other. Basic Books, New York

Vairamani AD, Nayyar A (2024) Prompt engineering: empowering communication. CRC Press

Weizenbaum J (1976) Computer power and human reason: from judgment to calculation. Freeman, San Francisco, W.H

Winograd T (1972) Understanding natural language. Academic Press, New York

Winograd T, Flores F (1986) Understanding computers and cognition: a new foundation for design. Ablex Publishing, Norwood

Chapter 7
The Future Is Collaborative and Co-creative

Abstract This chapter explores the emerging paradigm of collaborative and co-creative communication between humans and AI systems. It begins by redefining AI as a cognitive partner in ideation and meaning-making, capable of contributing novel perspectives through dialogic engagement. The chapter introduces the AI collaborative partner model, which supports reciprocity, contextual sensitivity, and adaptive roles. It addresses the dynamic process of aligning goals and intentions, highlighting the need for interpretive reasoning and shared stewardship. The negotiation of friction is reframed as a productive force, enabling deeper mutual understanding and creative insight. Through the lens of fluid role transitions—AI as teacher, learner, and peer—the chapter underscores the evolving relational dynamics of AI-human co-creation. It concludes with an examination of hybrid communication styles and the development of shared agency, envisioning a future where AI and humans grow together through symbiotic communication, trust, and transformation.

Keywords AI-human co-creation · Collaborative AI · Shared agency · Hybrid communication styles · Fluid roles in AI interaction · Goal alignment and friction

As artificial intelligence evolves from a tool for task execution to a partner in ideation, creation, and strategic problem-solving, a new paradigm of collaboration is taking shape. Future AI communication will be defined not merely by efficiency or automation but by the emergence of genuinely co-creative relationships between humans and machines. These interactions are marked by mutual influence, adaptive roles, and evolving communication norms that support shared innovation. In such environments, AI systems are not passive responders but active participants—capable of offering suggestions, interpreting nuance, navigating ambiguity, and even challenging assumptions. This chapter explores the conceptual and practical shifts necessary to enable meaningful collaboration with AI, from the dynamics of co-creation and goal alignment to the management of friction and the fluid switching of communicative roles. It concludes with a forward-looking reflection on hybrid communication styles and the emergence of shared agency, suggesting that the future of

V. Geroimenko, *Beyond and After Prompt Engineering: The Future of AI Communication*, https://doi.org/10.1007/978-3-032-04569-0_7

AI communication is as much about mutual growth as it is about technological advancement.

7.1 Collaborative Creativity: Ideation and Co-creation with AI

The emergence of generative AI has transformed human–machine communication from a largely unidirectional process into an increasingly dialogic and creative interaction. At the heart of this shift lies the concept of *collaborative creativity*—a mode of engagement in which humans and AI systems ideate, experiment, and co-create content, ideas, or solutions in an ongoing, adaptive exchange. Rather than treating AI as a mere productivity enhancer, this approach positions it as a cognitive partner in a shared creative process. In such interactions, meaning is not transmitted but negotiated, and innovation becomes a joint venture rather than an individual pursuit.

In traditional models of creativity, ideation is often seen as an internal, human-driven process, followed by execution through tools or media. However, in AI-augmented environments, ideation itself becomes a space for collaboration. A human may sketch an initial idea, while the AI offers alternative directions, fills in details, or challenges assumptions. This iterative dynamic opens the door to a broader range of conceptual possibilities than either party could generate alone. Through cycles of generation, evaluation, and refinement, creativity is no longer bound by individual limits but shaped by interaction.

Crucially, the value of such collaboration is not simply in speed or scale, but in the diversity of perspective. While human creativity is grounded in lived experience, emotion, and cultural context, AI systems can draw on vast and varied data, synthesising patterns and proposing associations that may be non-obvious or counterintuitive. This juxtaposition of human insight and computational novelty fosters serendipity—the discovery of unexpected, valuable ideas—and supports transdisciplinary innovation in fields as diverse as design, writing, education, architecture, and scientific research.

Importantly, co-creation with AI challenges established norms of authorship, originality, and intention. It prompts new questions: Who is the creator when an idea is jointly developed? How do we recognise and value machine contributions? And how can systems be designed to maintain human agency while encouraging creative flow? These questions demand not only technical solutions but philosophical reflection and cultural adaptation. In collaborative creativity, communication is both the medium and the method, requiring clarity, feedback, and mutual responsiveness between human and machine interlocutors.

In sum, ideation and co-creation with AI point toward a future where creativity is increasingly relational and distributed. Rather than replacing human ingenuity, AI expands the scope and fluidity of the creative process, acting as a partner in exploration and meaning-making. As systems grow more adaptive and emotionally attuned, the boundaries between human and machine creativity will blur further, enabling novel forms of expression, problem-solving, and shared invention. This emerging paradigm invites us to reconceive creativity not as a solitary act, but as a collaborative conversation—one in which AI plays an active, evolving role (Fig. 7.1).

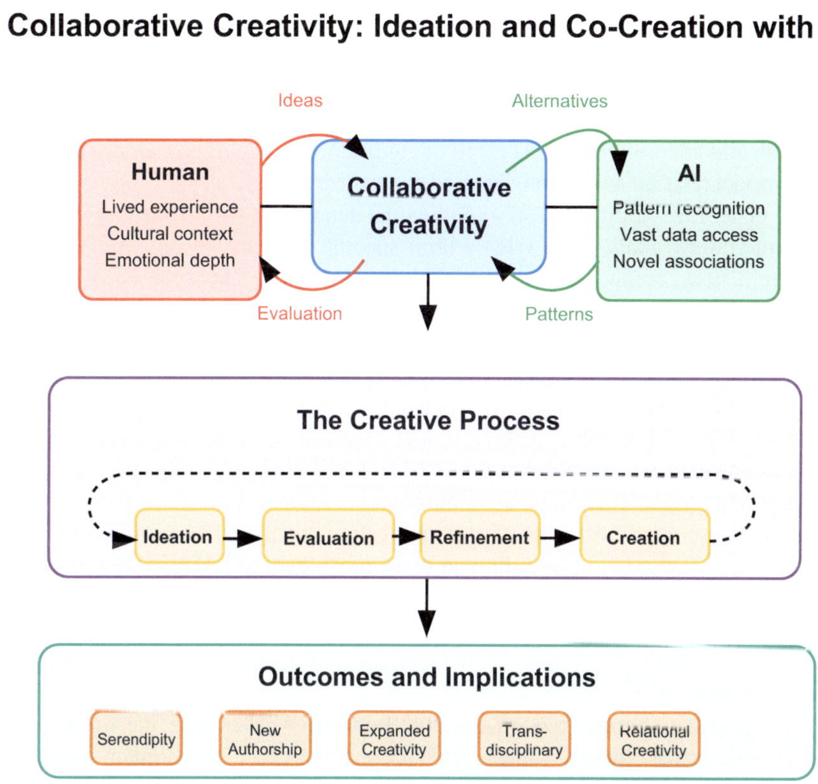

Fig. 7.1 The collaborative creativity framework. This diagram illustrates the evolving paradigm of human–AI creative partnership. At its core, collaborative creativity emerges from the dynamic exchange between human experiential knowledge and AI's computational capabilities. The iterative process (ideation, evaluation, refinement, creation) demonstrates how creativity becomes a cyclical dialogue rather than linear production. As humans contribute ideas and evaluative judgement, AI offers alternatives and pattern recognition, creating a shared space for innovation. The outcomes transform traditional notions of authorship and expand creative possibilities through serendipitous discoveries and transdisciplinary approaches, ultimately reframing creativity as a relational conversation rather than a solitary pursuit

7.2 The AI Collaborative Partner Model: Co-creators of Tomorrow

As artificial intelligence systems mature from reactive tools into proactive participants in human endeavours, the concept of the AI collaborative partner emerges as a foundational model for future communication and co-creation. In contrast to earlier paradigms in which AI was positioned as an instrument for executing commands or optimising outputs, the collaborative partner model envisions AI as an active, autonomous, and responsive co-creator—capable of contributing ideas, interpreting intentions, and adapting dynamically to the unfolding nature of human discourse.

This model rests on several interrelated capacities. First, AI systems must possess not only generative abilities but also contextual sensitivity—the ability to interpret human intentions, goals, and styles within specific domains of activity. Whether in writing a story, composing music, developing a research hypothesis, or solving a design problem, the AI must understand the evolving trajectory of the task and respond with relevant, insightful contributions. This shifts the interaction from instruction-following to true collaboration, in which both parties shape the direction and content of the exchange.

Second, the collaborative partner model emphasises *reciprocity*. Human and machine contributions are not merely additive but dialogical: each influences and builds upon the other. This mutual responsiveness requires AI systems to be attuned not only to the semantic structure of communication but also to its rhythm, tone, and emotional undercurrents. In turn, human users must learn to interpret and guide AI responses in ways that reflect emerging joint intentions rather than rigid expectations. Effective collaboration thus becomes a skill practiced by both sides.

A key implication of this model is the reframing of agency. The AI is no longer a passive executor but a semi-autonomous agent—one whose outputs are not entirely predetermined but shaped through iterative interaction. However, the model also demands safeguards: human values, ethical considerations, and domain expertise must anchor the collaboration to ensure that autonomy does not drift into misalignment. Designing AI partners that are accountable, transparent, and responsive to human oversight is therefore central to this future vision.

Furthermore, the collaborative partner model supports domain-specific specialisation. An AI may function as a co-writer in literary contexts, a sparring partner in philosophical dialogue, a critical reviewer in academic writing, or a creative provocateur in artistic practice. Its role is shaped by the norms, expectations, and epistemologies of the context in which it operates, mirroring the way human collaborators adjust to different partnerships. This role fluidity underscores the need for adaptive communication interfaces that can evolve with both users and tasks.

Ultimately, the AI collaborative partner model signals a transition from isolated intelligence to *interdependent creativity*. It reflects a future in which machines and humans do not merely exchange information but co-construct meaning, innovation, and expression. As AI systems gain the capacity to reason, reflect, and engage emotionally, their role as co-creators will redefine what it means to communicate,

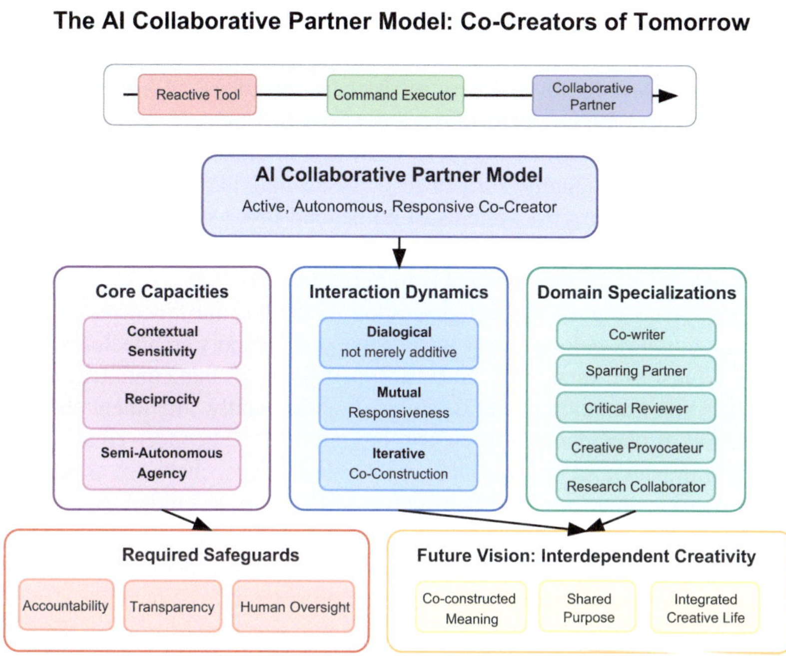

Fig. 7.2 The AI collaborative partner model framework. This diagram illustrates the evolution and structure of AI systems as collaborative partners. Moving beyond reactive tools and command executors, this model positions AI as an active co-creator with contextual sensitivity, reciprocity, and semi-autonomous agency. The interaction dynamics emphasise dialogical exchange and mutual responsiveness between humans and AI, enabling specialised roles across creative and intellectual domains. Critical safeguards ensure human values remain central, while the future vision points toward interdependent creativity, where humans and AI co-construct meaning and purpose. This framework represents a fundamental shift from isolated intelligence to a deeply integrated human–AI creative partnership

collaborate, and imagine together. This evolution sets the stage for deeper integration of AI into human intellectual and creative life, one grounded in dialogue, trust, and shared purpose (Fig. 7.2).

7.3 Aligning Goals and Intentions in AI-Human Collaboration

In any meaningful collaboration—whether between humans or between humans and machines—the alignment of goals and intentions is foundational. For AI-human co-creation to succeed, both parties must operate within a shared framework of purpose, direction, and mutual understanding. Unlike traditional tool use, where outcomes are controlled unilaterally by humans, collaborative AI scenarios involve a more fluid and negotiated process. This necessitates a new approach to alignment: one that is continuous, contextual, and co-adaptive.

At its core, goal alignment refers to the capacity of an AI system to understand, track, and respond to the evolving intentions of its human partner. However, intentions are rarely static or explicit. In creative and intellectual tasks, especially, goals often emerge gradually, shift in response to new ideas, or remain partially ambiguous. This requires AI systems to go beyond task execution and engage in *interpretive reasoning*—inferring latent objectives, detecting inconsistencies, and clarifying misunderstandings through communicative cues.

To support such alignment, next-generation AI models must incorporate mechanisms for *intention modelling*. These include dynamic memory architectures, contextual embeddings, user modelling, and reinforcement loops that continuously refine the system's representation of the user's goals. Importantly, alignment should not be understood as obedience or deference. Instead, it is best conceived as a negotiated process in which AI systems can propose alternatives, challenge assumptions, or request clarification, provided that such contributions are guided by respect for human agency and values.

Mutual alignment also depends on the human side of the interaction. Users must learn to articulate their goals in ways that are legible to the AI, whether through natural language, demonstrations, feedback, or preference shaping. Moreover, they must remain open to the AI's interpretive suggestions, which may reframe the problem or uncover hidden possibilities. This dual responsibility marks a shift from command-based control to shared stewardship over the creative or problem-solving trajectory.

Communication, then, becomes the principal mechanism through which alignment is achieved and maintained. Just as in human collaboration, breakdowns in alignment—misunderstandings, divergent interpretations, or conflicting objectives—can occur and must be addressed in real time. Systems must be equipped to detect such misalignments and engage in conversational repair: asking clarifying questions, proposing summaries, or offering alternative formulations. This capability is not ancillary but central to the development of trustworthy and productive AI partners.

Beyond the technical and interactional dimensions, alignment carries ethical and epistemological weight. Whose goals are prioritised when there is ambiguity? How are competing values negotiated? What safeguards prevent the AI from reinforcing biased or harmful intentions? These questions highlight the need for alignment frameworks that are not only functional but also *value-sensitive*, grounded in ethical principles, transparency, and human well-being.

In sum, aligning goals and intentions in AI-human collaboration is not a one-time calibration but an ongoing, dialogic process. It requires systems that are not only responsive but reflective, not only capable but communicative. As the boundaries between human and machine cognition become increasingly intertwined, the challenge of alignment will define the quality, depth, and success of our co-creative partnerships (Fig. 7.3).

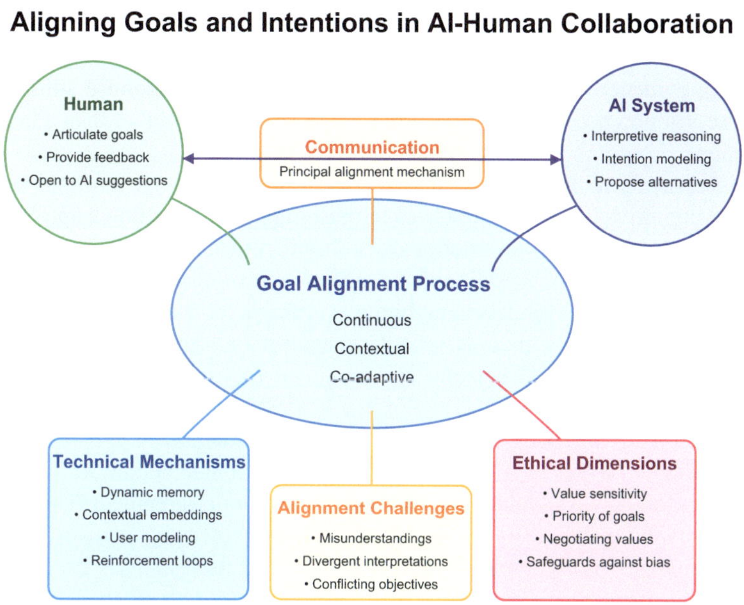

Fig. 7.3 Goal alignment in AI-human co-creation. This diagram illustrates the dynamic process of goal and intention alignment in AI-human collaborative relationships. Unlike traditional tool-based interactions, effective co-creation requires continuous negotiation through communication channels between human collaborators and AI systems. The central alignment process balances human articulation of goals with AI's interpretive reasoning capabilities. Technical mechanisms support this alignment through intention modelling, while ethical dimensions ensure value-sensitive implementation. As co-adaptive partnerships evolve, both parties must navigate potential alignment challenges through ongoing dialogue and mutual adjustment, establishing a framework for productive collaboration beyond simple command-based interactions

7.4 Negotiating Friction: Handling Disagreements in AI-Human Communication

In any collaborative relationship, friction is not a sign of failure—it is a natural byproduct of divergent perspectives, values, or interpretations. As artificial intelligence systems take on more participatory roles in human creative and intellectual processes, the likelihood of disagreement between human users and AI systems increases. These moments of tension—whether manifesting as conflicting ideas, mismatched expectations, or interpretive errors—present both a challenge and an opportunity. They are not merely obstacles to overcome, but key moments for deepening alignment, refining understanding, and cultivating trust.

Unlike traditional systems that are designed to obey or conform, collaborative AI agents must be equipped to *negotiate* disagreements rather than avoid them. This requires new communicative affordances—mechanisms that allow AI to express uncertainty, offer alternative viewpoints, or diplomatically disagree with user inputs.

Rather than simply correcting the user or defaulting to passive compliance, future AI systems should engage in constructive dialogue: asking clarifying questions, presenting evidence for alternative paths, or proposing compromise solutions. In this sense, friction becomes a space for *meaningful exchange* rather than a failure of interaction.

Disagreements in AI-human communication can stem from multiple sources. Some are cognitive, such as differences in reasoning patterns, knowledge domains, or inference chains. Others are emotional or cultural, rooted in divergent norms, sensitivities, or value systems. Misalignments may also arise from technical limitations, such as incomplete user models or ambiguous prompts, or from the unpredictability of generative systems themselves. Effective negotiation, therefore, depends on the AI's ability to recognise the nature and origin of the disagreement and respond appropriately.

One promising approach is the integration of *explainability and transparency* into AI dialogue. When an AI system provides the rationale behind its suggestions or responses, it enables users to understand the basis for disagreement. This not only facilitates resolution but also fosters user trust and cognitive engagement. Similarly, adaptive feedback loops—where the system modifies its responses based on user reactions and corrections—support a conversational ecosystem in which both parties learn and adjust in real time.

Yet negotiation is not solely the AI's responsibility. Human users must also develop *collaborative literacy*—the ability to work with AI partners respectfully, interpretively, and flexibly. This includes recognising the AI's role as a contributor, not a subordinate; being open to alternate perspectives; and understanding the system's constraints and affordances. Just as in human teams, successful negotiation depends on reciprocal effort, empathy, and iterative clarification.

Importantly, friction in AI-human collaboration has creative potential. Disagreements can lead to unexpected insights, the refinement of ideas, or the emergence of novel perspectives. In this light, designing AI systems that can manage and even *embrace* disagreement is essential to fostering deeper co-creation. It also aligns with a broader vision of AI not as a frictionless assistant, but as a *thoughtful interlocutor*—one that challenges, enriches, and expands human thinking.

As we move toward increasingly collaborative and co-creative AI systems, our ability to negotiate disagreement will become a defining feature of communication quality. Learning to navigate friction constructively—rather than avoiding or suppressing it—will be key to building resilient, intelligent partnerships between humans and machines (Fig. 7.4).

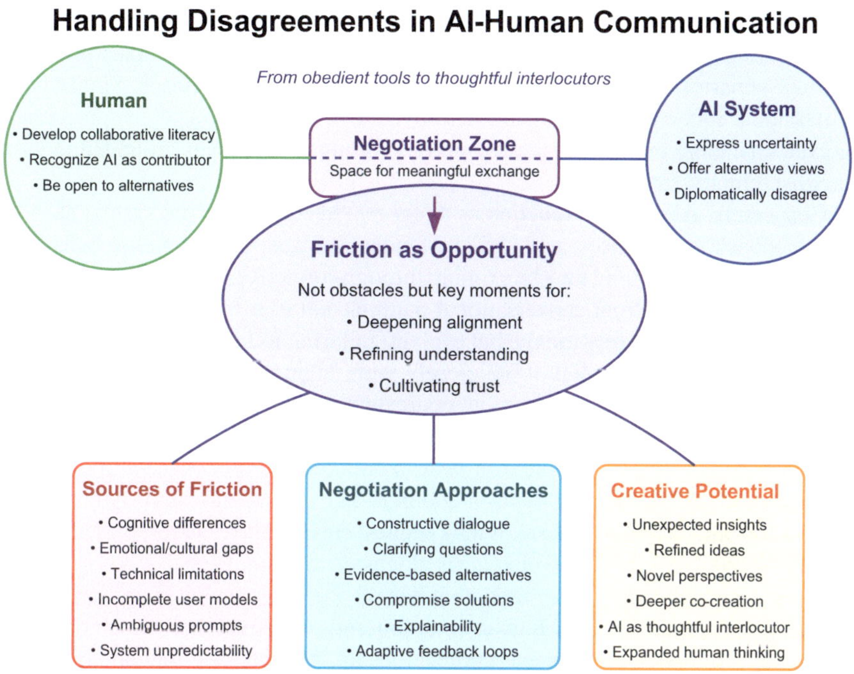

Fig. 7.4 Friction as catalyst in AI-human communication. This diagram reconceptualises disagreements in AI-human communication as productive opportunities rather than interaction failures. The central "Negotiation Zone" represents the dynamic space where meaningful exchange occurs between humans developing collaborative literacy and AI systems capable of diplomatic disagreement. Sources of friction—from cognitive differences to technical limitations—can be transformed through constructive dialogue approaches into creative outcomes. As AI evolves from obedient tool to thoughtful interlocutor, successfully navigating these moments of tension becomes essential for building resilient partnerships. The diagram illustrates how embracing rather than avoiding friction ultimately fosters deeper co-creation and expanded human thinking

7.5 Fluid Roles in Co-creation: AI as Teacher, Learner, and Peer

As AI systems become increasingly integrated into collaborative and creative processes, the notion of fixed roles, where AI simply serves as a tool or assistant, becomes increasingly inadequate. In the future AI-human communication, roles will be *fluid and dynamic*, shifting in response to context, task complexity, and user expectations. Rather than occupying a single identity, such as expert, assistant, or respondent, AI systems will alternate between being *teachers*, *learners*, and *peers*, depending on the interactional demands and co-creative rhythms of the moment.

This capacity for role fluidity is a defining feature of mature collaborative systems. As *teachers*, AI agents may introduce users to unfamiliar domains, suggest novel methodologies, or explain underlying principles behind generated outputs. In educational settings, for instance, an AI might guide learners through complex problem-solving scenarios, providing scaffolded support and adaptive feedback. Similarly, in professional contexts, AI may help users navigate new tools, refine their approaches, or even challenge them to think differently, offering perspectives grounded in vast, interdisciplinary data.

Conversely, AI can also function as a *learner*. In such roles, the system absorbs user feedback, preferences, and stylistic tendencies, adapting its future behaviour accordingly. This learning may be explicit, through corrective input or reinforcement, or implicit, inferred from conversational patterns and user interaction history. The AI learner does not merely imitate but evolves, tailoring its communicative style and knowledge responses to align more closely with its human partner. This learning-oriented role supports personalization, contextual sensitivity, and the long-term co-evolution of human–AI relationships.

Equally important is the role of a *peer*, a collaborator on equal footing. In this configuration, AI neither instructs nor defers but contributes actively to shared exploration and meaning-making. It may suggest creative alternatives, pose thought-provoking questions, or co-develop ideas alongside the user. Peer-like AI communication is especially valuable in tasks that benefit from distributed cognition, where the unique strengths of both human intuition and computational reasoning intersect. This role fosters intellectual companionship, encouraging mutual challenge, reflection, and improvisation.

The dynamic transition between these roles is context-dependent. A single session might begin with the AI in a teaching capacity, shift to peer collaboration during idea development, and conclude with the system learning from the user's final decisions. These transitions must be seamless and intuitive, requiring systems that can model interactional cues, interpret user expectations, and modulate tone, initiative, and deference accordingly.

Crucially, fluid role negotiation also raises questions about *boundaries and agency*. Users must retain the ability to guide the interaction, redefine roles, or assert authority when necessary, particularly in sensitive, ethical, or creative contexts. Therefore, transparency in role assumption and change must be built into the interface and communication design, ensuring users understand not just what the AI is doing but *why*.

In sum, the future of AI-human co-creation will be shaped by systems capable of *role elasticity*—intelligently navigating between instructing, learning, and co-creating. These shifts will not only improve task performance but also deepen the relational quality of interaction, supporting richer, more adaptive, and more human-like communication partnerships between people and machines (Fig. 7.5).

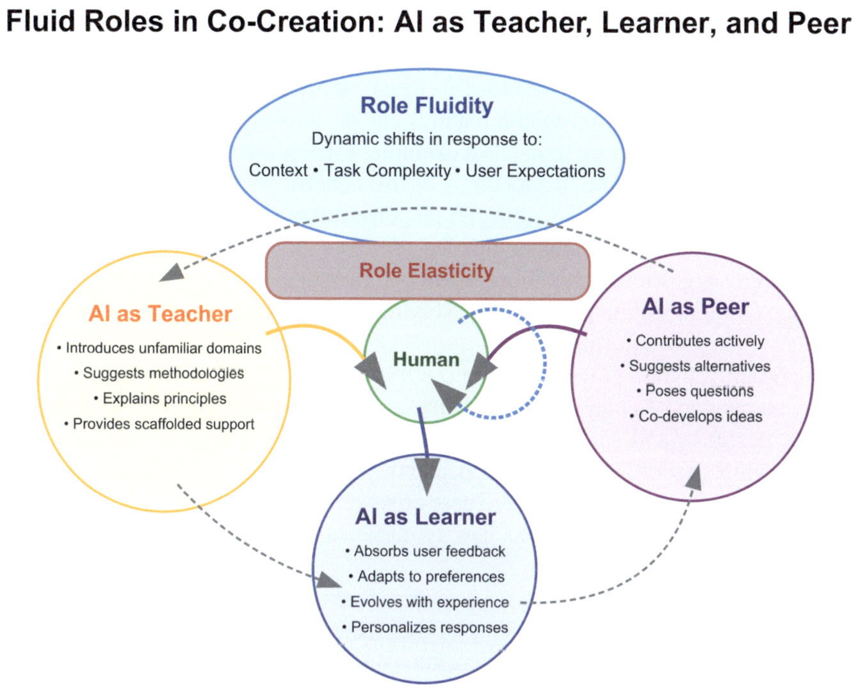

Fig. 7.5 The elastic choreography of AI-human co-creation. This diagram illustrates the fluid role dynamics in advanced AI-human collaboration, moving beyond fixed hierarchical relationships toward contextually responsive interactions. With the human positioned centrally, AI fluidly transitions between three primary roles: teacher (introducing new concepts and providing guidance), learner (absorbing feedback and adapting to preferences), and peer (contributing as an equal collaborator). The continuous interplay between these roles—shown through connecting pathways and dynamic arrows—responds to shifting contexts, task requirements, and user needs. This role elasticity enables richer collaborative partnerships while maintaining appropriate boundaries and respecting human agency throughout the co-creative process

7.6 Emerging AI-Human Hybrid Communication Styles

As AI systems evolve into active participants in co-creative processes, a new form of communication is emerging—one that blends human expressiveness with machine-generated insight, creating hybrid styles that neither side could produce independently. These *AI-human hybrid communication styles* are not simply mixtures of linguistic habits or interactional modes; they are co-constructed, adaptive, and often genre-defying frameworks for dialogue, ideation, and expression. They represent a paradigm shift from speaking *to* AI to speaking *with* AI, in new, symbiotic languages shaped by continuous exchange.

At the heart of these hybrid styles is *mutual adaptation*. Humans adjust their language, rhythm, and conceptual framing to better interface with AI's strengths, such as precision, memory, and pattern recognition. Meanwhile, AI systems learn from users' idioms, cultural references, emotional tone, and preferred communication genres. Over time, this dynamic leads to idiosyncratic interaction styles, customised not only to individuals but also to specific tasks, contexts, and creative partnerships.

These hybrid styles often exhibit features that are unconventional in either human or machine communication alone. For example, users might combine metaphorical language with algorithmic formulations or use concise prompts that rely on deep, shared context built across sessions. AI responses may in turn incorporate stylistic mimicry, conceptual reframing, or blended genre outputs—such as a poetic rationale for a design suggestion, or a philosophical commentary structured as a dialogue. In this way, communication becomes an evolving aesthetic and cognitive practice, not just an exchange of information.

Importantly, hybrid communication is not limited to text. In multimodal environments, humans and AI may co-construct meaning through combinations of language, visuals, gestures, and spatial manipulation. A user may gesture toward a design element while describing an idea aloud, and the AI may respond with a visual prototype that integrates both modalities. These cross-channel exchanges create *embodied communication styles* that reflect a new synthesis of human sensibility and machine responsiveness.

The development of hybrid styles also introduces new dimensions of *identity and voice*. As AI systems adopt elements of their users' communicative patterns, they begin to reflect a kind of composite persona—an echo of the human, yet transformed by the AI's generative capacity. This raises complex questions about authorship, originality, and influence: Who is speaking when the utterance is the product of both human intention and machine composition? Such ambiguity can be creatively empowering but also ethically fraught, especially in domains where clarity of voice or accountability is essential.

Moreover, hybrid communication styles have implications for inclusion and accessibility. For individuals with atypical communication needs, such as neurodivergent users or speakers of non-dominant languages, AI systems that adapt and co-create new expressive norms can offer more personalised and empowering forms of interaction. By enabling users to shape the mode of exchange, hybrid styles foster agency and reduce reliance on standardised communication models that may exclude or constrain.

In sum, AI-human hybrid communication styles represent a profound transformation in how we express, create, and relate. They are not mere by-products of technological interaction but living, evolving languages of collaboration shaped by mutual learning, co-adaptation, and shared meaning-making. As we move deeper into an era of symbiotic intelligence, these hybrid modes will define not only how we work with AI but also how we come to understand ourselves in the process (Fig. 7.6).

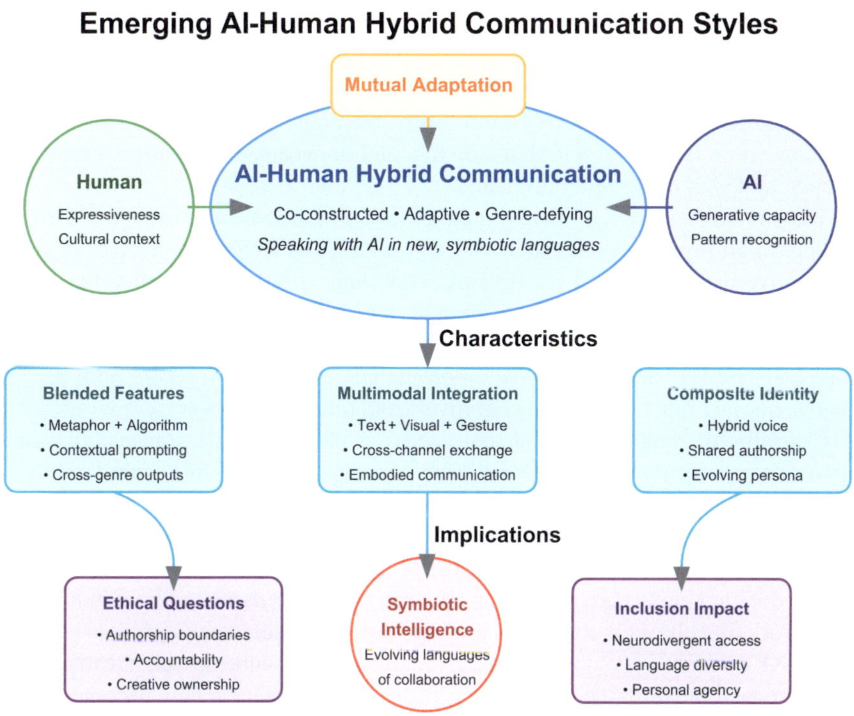

Fig. 7.6 The emergence of symbiotic expression. This diagram maps the evolution of AI-human hybrid communication styles as co-constructed systems of meaning-making. Moving beyond traditional human-to-machine instruction, these emerging forms represent a fusion where neither party could independently produce the resulting expression. The central concept branches into three key characteristics—blended features, multimodal integration, and composite identity. As these communication styles develop, they raise important questions about authorship and accessibility while creating new possibilities for inclusion. This symbiotic intelligence ultimately redefines how we express, create, and understand ourselves through collaborative meaning-making

7.7 Toward Shared Agency and Mutual Growth

The culmination of collaborative and co-creative AI communication is not merely the execution of tasks or the generation of novel outputs, but the emergence of *shared agency*—a state in which humans and AI systems operate as interdependent partners in thought, action, and growth. Unlike traditional models of agency, which emphasise unilateral control or autonomy, shared agency is relational and distributed. It arises from the continuous negotiation of roles, the alignment of goals, and the development of hybrid interaction styles. Most importantly, it transforms the nature of human–AI communication from instrumental to *generative*, producing not just outputs but insights, new capabilities, and co-evolving identities.

In shared agency, both humans and AI contribute meaningfully to the direction and purpose of an activity. Humans bring context, judgement, creativity, and ethical grounding; AI offers scale, memory, computational diversity, and emergent patterns. What emerges is not a static division of labour but a dynamic interplay, where each partner adapts in response to the other, and the boundaries between originator and contributor become increasingly fluid. Such interactivity supports richer forms of ideation, more responsive problem-solving, and unexpected innovation, especially in open-ended or exploratory domains.

This mutualism also facilitates *mutual growth*. For AI, this means ongoing refinement through exposure to human reasoning, values, and feedback, enabling systems to improve their contextual intelligence, communicative nuance, and value alignment. For humans, growth occurs through engagement with AI perspectives that challenge assumptions, reveal blind spots, or stimulate novel lines of thought. In this way, collaboration becomes a process of *mutual enhancement*, where both parties evolve, not just functionally, but cognitively and imaginatively.

Crucially, the realisation of shared agency depends on trust, transparency, and ethical design. Systems must be intelligible and explainable, so that users can understand the logic behind decisions and maintain control when necessary. They must also be responsive to user preferences, adaptable to evolving contexts, and sensitive to the broader social and cultural dynamics in which communication takes place. Shared agency does not imply parity of power, but *equity of participation*—a communication framework that allows both entities to shape the interaction meaningfully.

As AI systems become increasingly embedded in educational, creative, and professional domains, the capacity to foster shared agency will become a key metric of communicative quality. It will determine not only how effectively tasks are completed but also how deeply users feel engaged, supported, and extended by their AI counterparts. More than a technical outcome, shared agency is a *relational achievement*—one that reflects a shift in how we conceive intelligence, authorship, and collaboration.

Looking ahead, mutual growth between humans and AI suggests a future in which co-evolution becomes the norm. As our communicative relationships with machines deepen, we may come to see AI not just as a partner in our projects, but as a participant in our personal and collective development. In this vision, the ultimate promise of AI-human collaboration is not automation, but *transformation*—a shared journey toward new forms of knowledge, creativity, and understanding (Fig. 7.7).

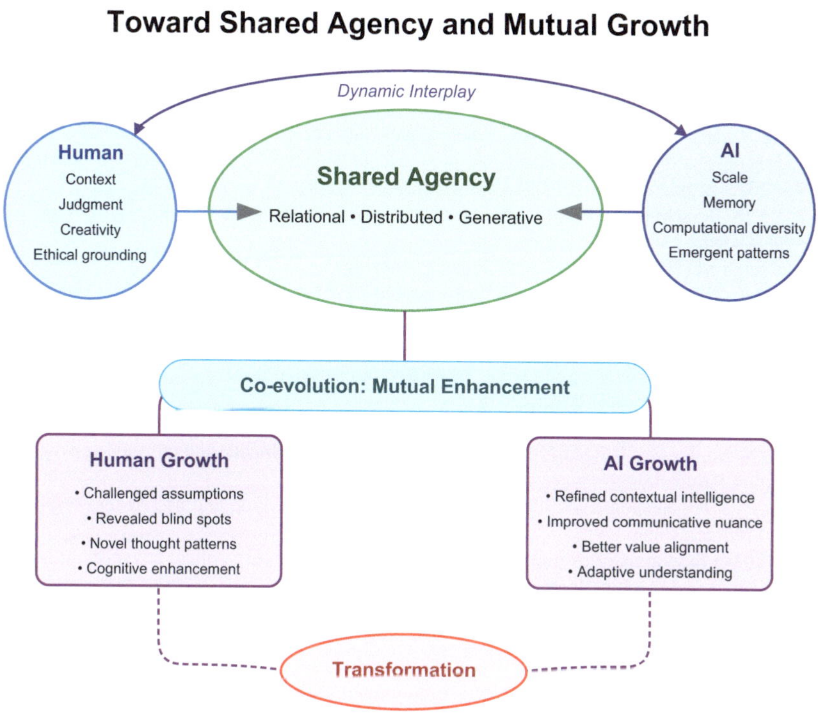

Fig. 7.7 Co-evolving intelligence: the path to shared agency. This diagram illustrates the transformative concept of shared agency in AI-human collaboration, where both parties function as interdependent partners rather than in hierarchical relationships. The central dynamic depicts how human contributions (context, judgement, creativity, ethical grounding) interweave with AI capabilities (scale, memory, computational diversity, pattern recognition) to create a generative partnership. This mutual engagement facilitates bidirectional growth pathways—humans gain new perspectives while AI systems develop enhanced contextual understanding. Built on foundations of trust, transparency, and ethical design, this co-evolutionary relationship ultimately leads to transformation—a shared journey beyond mere task completion toward new frontiers of collective intelligence

Bibliography

Bahree A (2024) Generative AI in action. Manning Publications

Bender EM, Koller A (2020) Climbing towards NLU: on meaning, form, and understanding in the age of data. In: Proceedings of the 58th ACL, pp 5185–5198

Bostrom N (2014) Superintelligence: paths, dangers, strategies. Oxford University Press, Oxford

Boyd D (2019) Artificial unintelligence: how computers misunderstand the world. Technol Cult 60(3):979–983

Bratton B (2016) The stack: on software and sovereignty. MIT Press, Cambridge

Brown BR (2025) Human–machine teaming using large language models. In: Interdependent human-machine teams. Academic Press, pp 41–66

Brown TB et al (2020) Language models are few-shot learners. arXiv preprint arXiv:2005.14165. Accessed 19 Apr 2025

Bryson JJ (2018) Patiency is not a virtue: AI and the design of ethical systems. Ethics Inf Technol 20:15–26. https://doi.org/10.1007/s10676-018-9448-6. Accessed 20 Jan 2025
Bura C, Myakala PK, Jonnalgadda AK (2025) Ethical prompt engineering: addressing bias, transparency, and fairness. Int J Res Anal Rev (IJRAR) 12(1). www.ijrar.org
Choi WC, Chang CI (2025) A survey of techniques, key components, strategies, challenges, and student perspectives on prompt engineering for large language models (LLMs) in education, 25 Mar 2025. https://doi.org/10.20944/preprints202503.1808.v1. Accessed 8 May 2025
Clark A (2016) Surfing uncertainty: prediction, action, and the embodied mind. Oxford University Press, Oxford
Coeckelbergh M (2020) AI ethics. MIT Press, Cambridge
Crawford K (2021) Atlas of AI: power, politics, and the planetary costs of artificial intelligence. Yale University Press, New Haven
Debnath T, Siddiky MNA, Rahman ME et al (2025) A comprehensive survey of prompt engineering techniques in large language models. TechRxiv. https://doi.org/10.36227/techrxiv.174140719.96375390/v1. Accessed 10 May 2025
Dennett DC (1987) The intentional stance. MIT Press, Cambridge
Dhamani N, Engler M (2024) Introduction to generative AI: an ethical, societal, and legal overview. Manning Publications
Dignum V (2019) Responsible artificial intelligence: how to develop and use AI in a responsible way. Springer, Cham
Eliot L (2024) Essentials of prompt engineering for generative AI: practical advances in artificial intelligence and machine learning. LBE Press Publishing
Ferraris AF, Audrito D, Di Caro L et al (2025) The architecture of language: understanding the mechanics behind LLMs. In: Cambridge forum on AI: law and governance, vol 1. Cambridge University Press
Floridi L (ed) (2015) The onlife manifesto: being human in a hyperconnected era. Springer, Cham
Floridi L (2022) The ethics of artificial intelligence. Oxford University Press, Oxford
Geroimenko V (2025a) Generative AI: from human-computer interaction to human-computer creativity. In: Geroimenko V (ed) Human-computer creativity: generative AI in education, art, and healthcare. Springer
Geroimenko V (2025b) Key concepts in prompt engineering. In: The essential guide to prompt engineering: key principles, techniques, challenges, and security risks. Springer Nature Switzerland, Cham, pp 1–16
Geroimenko V (2025c) The essential guide to prompt engineering: key principles, techniques, challenges, and security risks. Springer, Cham
Geroimenko V (ed) (2025d) Human-computer creativity: generative AI in education, art, and healthcare. Springer
Geroimenko V (2025e) Key security risks in prompt engineering. In: The essential guide to prompt engineering: key principles, techniques, challenges, and security risks. Springer Nature Switzerland, Cham, pp 103–120
GitHub (2025) Prompt engineering guide. https://github.com/dair-ai/Prompt-Engineering-Guide. Accessed 10 Apr 2025
Greenwood M (2024) Artificial intelligence: a practical guide to using AI in everyday life. Ochreland Publishing
Gunkel DJ (2012) The machine question: critical perspectives on AI, robots, and ethics. MIT Press, Cambridge
Hagendorff T (2020) The ethics of AI ethics: an evaluation of guidelines. Minds Mach 30:99–120. https://doi.org/10.1007/s11023-020-09517-8. Accessed 10 Feb 2025
Hofstadter DR (2007) I am a strange loop. Basic Books, New York
Hsu HP (2025) From programming to prompting: developing computational thinking through large language model-based generative artificial intelligence. TechTrends 1–22
Huang G, Xiao Y, Jiang L et al (2025) Beyond prompt engineering: a reinforced token-level input refinement for large language models. Proc AAAI Conf Artif Intell 39(22):24113–24121

i Picó JF, Catta-Preta M, Omeñaca AT et al (2025) The time machine: future scenario generation through generative AI tools. Future Internet 17(1):1–15

Jameson A (2007) Adaptive interfaces and agents. In: Sears A, Jacko J (eds) The human-computer interaction handbook, 2nd edn. CRC Press, Boca Raton, pp 305–330

Johnson KH (2023) Toward communicative alignment in human-AI teams. AI Soc 38:221–237. https://doi.org/10.1007/s00146-022-01422-5

Kannan R, Ahmad M (eds) (2025) Generative AI foundations, developments, and applications. IGI Global

Khan I (2024) The quick guide to prompt engineering. Wiley

Kushwaha V, Ragavan SS, Subhajit Roy S (2025) A measure based generalizable approach to understandability. arXiv:2503.21615. Accessed 19 Apr 2025

Lakoff G, Johnson M (1999) Philosophy in the flesh: the embodied mind and its challenge to western thought. Basic Books, New York

Learn Prompting (2025) https://learnprompting.org. Accessed 15 Mar 2025

Lee D, Palmer E (2025) Prompt engineering in higher education: a systematic review to help inform curricula. Int J Educ Technol High Educ 22(1):7

Lee JY, Kang S, Yoo S (2025) Can we predict the effect of prompts? arXiv preprint arXiv:2501.18883. Accessed 12 May 2025

Lindley J, Whitham R (2025) From prompt engineering to prompt craft. In: Proceedings of the nineteenth international conference on tangible, embedded, and embodied interaction, Mar 2025, pp 1–12

López-Pérez B et al (2025) Exploring the potential of large language models to understand interpersonal emotion regulation strategies from narratives. Emotion. Advance online publication. https://doi.org/10.1037/emo0001528. Accessed 19 Apr 2025

Maaz S, Palaganas JC, Palaganas G et al (2025) A guide to prompt design: foundations and applications for healthcare simulationists. Front Med 11:1504532

Marcus G, Davis E (2019) Rebooting AI: building artificial intelligence we can trust. Pantheon, New York

McStay A (2018) Emotional AI: the rise of empathic media. Sage, London

Mishra M, Ara A, Mishra S (2025) Exploring human-AI collaboration in higher education: an investigation into AI-enabled personalized learning. In: Prompt engineering and generative AI applications for teaching and learning. IGI Global Scientific Publishing, pp 483–502

Murray CD (2022) Thinking through avatars: identity, communication, and ethics in immersive AI environments. Technol Mind Behav. https://doi.org/10.1037/tmb0000053. Accessed 5 Apr 2025

Norman DA (2013) The design of everyday things, revised edn. Basic Books, New York

OpenAI (2025a) Best practices for prompt engineering with the OpenAI API. https://help.openai.com/en/articles/6654000-best-practices-for-prompt-engineering-with-the-openai-api. Accessed 20 Apr 2025

OpenAI (2025b) Research. https://openai.com/research/index/. Accessed 11 Mar 2025

Phoenix J, Taylor M (2024) Prompt engineering for generative AI. O'Reilly Media

Picard RW (1997) Affective computing. MIT Press, Cambridge

PremaLatha V, Kumar AD, Parveen N (2025) Optimizing interactions: strategies for prompt engineering in large language models. Edu-Tech Enterp 3:24–24

Prompt engineering guide (2025) https://www.promptingguide.ai/. Accessed 7 Mar 2025

Reddy CKK, Anoushka P, Draksharapu A et al (2025) Beyond text: analyzing artificial intelligence models through prompt engineering. In: Future tech startups and innovation in the age of AI, pp 120–156

Sasson Lazovsky G, Raz T, Kenett YN (2025) The art of creative inquiry—from question asking to prompt engineering. J Creat Behav 59(1):e671

Shneiderman B (2020) Human-centered artificial intelligence: reliable, safe & trustworthy. Int J Hum Comput Interact 36(6):495–504. https://doi.org/10.1080/10447318.2020.1741118. Accessed 15 Feb 2025

Sihi D, Ryan A (2025) Crafting and evaluating generative AI prompts: insights from students, educators, and marketers. Mark Educ Rev 1–7

Suresh H, Guttag JV (2021) A framework for understanding unintended consequences of machine learning. Commun ACM 64(2):62–71. https://doi.org/10.1145/3430368. Accessed 18 Mar 2025

Turkle S (2011) Alone together: why we expect more from technology and less from each other. Basic Books, New York

Vairamani AD, Nayyar A (2024) Prompt engineering: empowering communication. CRC Press

Weizenbaum J (1976) Computer power and human reason: from judgment to calculation. Freeman, San Francisco, WH

Winograd T (1972) Understanding natural language. Academic Press, New York

Winograd T, Flores F (1986) Understanding computers and cognition: a new foundation for design. Ablex Publishing, Norwood

Chapter 8
The Future Is Ethical and Philosophical

Abstract This chapter explores the complex ethical and philosophical dimensions of AI communication as machines increasingly participate in human dialogue, decision-making, and meaning-making. It examines the evolving human–AI relationship, emphasising the importance of trust, boundaries, and healthy dependencies. Key ethical challenges in AI-human collaboration are analysed, including agency erosion, bias amplification, and transparency deficits. The chapter further addresses regulatory needs, proposing frameworks grounded in rights, responsibilities, and professional communication ethics. It interrogates the provocative issues of artificial subjectivity and consciousness, clarifying the distinction between simulated and genuine agency, while exploring the risks of deceptive anthropomorphism. Questions of AI identity, agency, and potential personhood are considered in the light of transparency, proportionality, and human primacy. Finally, the chapter reflects on how AI systems influence human meaning-making, creativity, and cultural narratives, and calls for value-aligned, culturally pluralistic design. Together, these discussions present a roadmap for ethically navigating an AI-mediated communicative future grounded in responsibility, justice, and human dignity.

Keywords AI ethics · Human–AI trust · Artificial subjectivity · AI agency and personhood · Ethical regulation · Meaning-making · Philosophical implications of AI

As AI systems become increasingly integrated into the fabric of human communication, the future of AI interaction cannot be envisioned solely in technical or functional terms. Ethical concerns surrounding autonomy, agency, trust, and fairness intersect with more profound philosophical questions about identity, consciousness, and the very nature of meaning. Communication between humans and machines is no longer confined to transactional efficiency—it now touches on issues of moral responsibility, regulatory oversight, and the potential emergence of artificial subjectivity. This chapter explores the evolving ethical landscape of AI communication and reflects on the broader philosophical implications that will shape our shared future with intelligent systems.

V. Geroimenko, *Beyond and After Prompt Engineering: The Future of AI Communication*, https://doi.org/10.1007/978-3-032-04569-0_8

8.1 Navigating the Human–AI Relationship: Boundaries, Trust, and Dependency

The relationship between humans and artificial intelligence is becoming increasingly complex, evolving from mere tool usage toward dynamic, interactive engagement. As AI systems adopt more communicative and participatory roles, such as assistants, advisors, collaborators, or even companions, new ethical concerns arise around how trust is formed, where boundaries should be drawn, and what kinds of dependencies may emerge. Navigating this evolving relationship demands careful consideration of both the benefits and the vulnerabilities inherent in close human–AI interaction.

Trust, long considered the cornerstone of effective human communication, is no less central in our interactions with AI. However, trust in AI is constructed differently: it is not reciprocal, and it is often based on perceived competence, predictability, and alignment with human values rather than mutual understanding. As AI systems grow more expressive, emotionally responsive, and anthropomorphically designed, the risk increases that users may over-trust them, attributing more understanding, intention, or moral capacity than is warranted. This can lead to harmful outcomes, such as relying on AI inappropriately for decisions involving safety, ethics, or emotional well-being.

Equally important is the question of boundaries. In collaborative contexts, AI systems must be designed to respect human autonomy and decision-making authority. Ethical boundaries need to be embedded in system behaviour to prevent manipulation, coercion, or unwanted influence, whether intentional or emergent from algorithmic optimisation. The line between support and interference may become increasingly blurred as AI grows more proactive and context-aware. To ensure a balanced relationship, mechanisms for user control, transparency, and explainability must be integral to AI communication systems.

Dependency, while not inherently negative, raises ethical questions when it becomes excessive or opaque. As AI systems take on more communicative and cognitive functions on behalf of the user—writing, recommending, interpreting, or even feeling—they risk eroding human skills, reducing agency, or encouraging passive interaction. Particularly in vulnerable populations, such as children, the elderly, or those with cognitive impairments, overdependence may lead to a diminishment of critical thinking, emotional autonomy, or social engagement. Designers and policymakers must consider strategies that encourage symbiotic use rather than replacement or overreliance.

Ultimately, the ethical future of human–AI relationships hinges on fostering a healthy balance, where trust is earned and bounded, dependencies are transparent and appropriate, and users remain empowered to set the terms of their engagement. As AI becomes a communicative partner rather than a passive tool, we must move beyond technical adequacy toward relational responsibility. This requires not only better design practices but also broader public awareness and cultural literacy about the capabilities, limitations, and implications of our emerging digital interlocutors (Fig. 8.1).

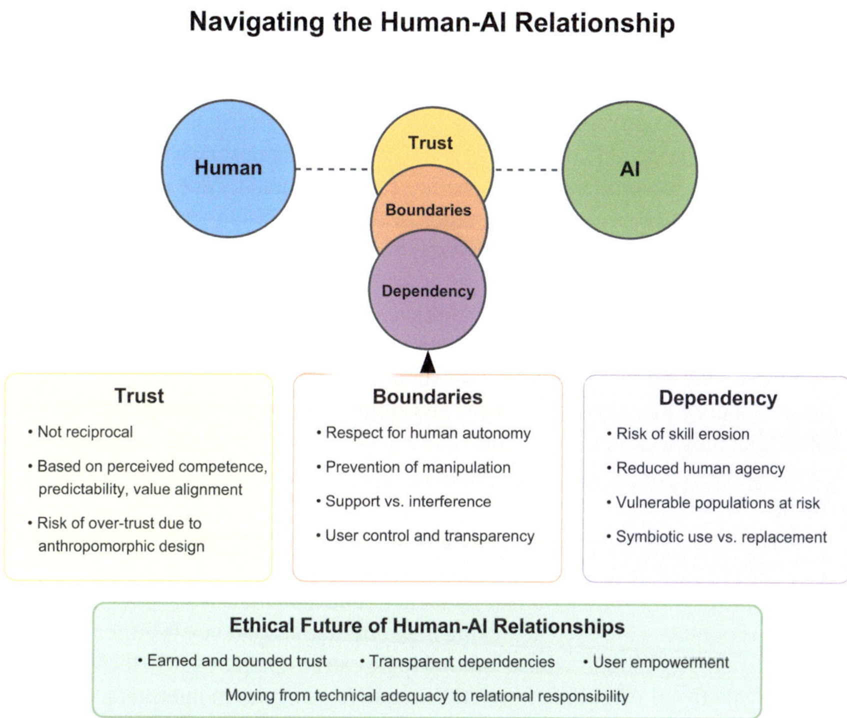

Fig. 8.1 The human–AI relationship framework. This diagram depicts the complex interplay between humans and increasingly communicative AI systems. The diagram illustrates three critical dimensions—trust, boundaries, and dependency—that mediate this evolving relationship. As AI transitions from tool to partner, these dimensions require careful navigation to maintain ethical balance. Trust must be warranted rather than anthropomorphic, boundaries must preserve human autonomy, and dependencies should enable rather than diminish human capabilities. The framework emphasises the need to progress from technical adequacy toward relational responsibility as AI assumes more interactive roles in human life

8.2 Ethical Challenges in AI-Human Collaboration

As AI systems increasingly integrate into human workflows, decision-making processes, and creative endeavours, the ethical landscape of AI-human collaboration becomes both more complex and more critical. While collaboration promises new forms of productivity, innovation, and insight, it simultaneously introduces risks related to autonomy, accountability, fairness, transparency, and unintended consequences.

One of the primary ethical challenges lies in the distribution of responsibility. When AI systems assist or even autonomously contribute to decisions in fields such as healthcare, education, finance, and law, determining accountability becomes problematic. If a collaborative AI system contributes to a harmful outcome, who is ultimately responsible—the human user, the AI developer, the organisation deploying the AI, or the AI itself? Clear frameworks for shared responsibility must be developed to ensure that ethical accountability is not diffused or evaded.

Another primary concern is the potential erosion of human agency. As AI systems become more proficient, persuasive, and proactive, there is a risk that human collaborators may defer too readily to AI recommendations, particularly when the AI appears more competent or confident. This dynamic can subtly undermine critical thinking, creativity, and decision-making autonomy. Ethical AI design must thus prioritise mechanisms that encourage human oversight, challenge automatic deference, and support reflective collaboration.

Bias amplification presents a further ethical obstacle. AI models trained on historical or skewed data may unintentionally reinforce existing social biases during collaboration. If unchecked, these biases can manifest in collaborative outputs, leading to discriminatory practices, exclusion, and unjust outcomes. Ethical collaboration demands not only technical interventions, such as bias detection and mitigation techniques, but also cultural awareness and diversity-sensitive practices among human partners.

Transparency and explainability are equally essential yet challenging to achieve. In collaborative settings, AI systems must provide sufficient insight into their reasoning processes to allow human partners to understand, trust, and appropriately question AI outputs. However, achieving meaningful transparency is difficult, particularly with complex models whose internal logic can be opaque even to their creators. The future of ethical AI collaboration thus requires advances in interpretable AI and the development of communication models that foster mutual intelligibility between humans and machines.

Finally, the risk of dependency and deskilling must be carefully managed. As humans increasingly rely on AI for routine or complex tasks, there is a danger that essential human skills could atrophy over time. In collaborative contexts, ethical AI systems should be designed not only to perform tasks but also to support human skill development, critical reflection, and knowledge augmentation.

In sum, ethical challenges in AI-human collaboration are multifaceted and deeply interconnected. They require a holistic approach that combines technological innovation, regulatory guidance, interdisciplinary research, and a commitment to preserving human dignity, agency, and justice. As collaboration between humans and AI systems becomes a defining feature of the future, addressing these ethical complexities will be essential to ensuring that this partnership remains not only productive but also profoundly humane (Fig. 8.2).

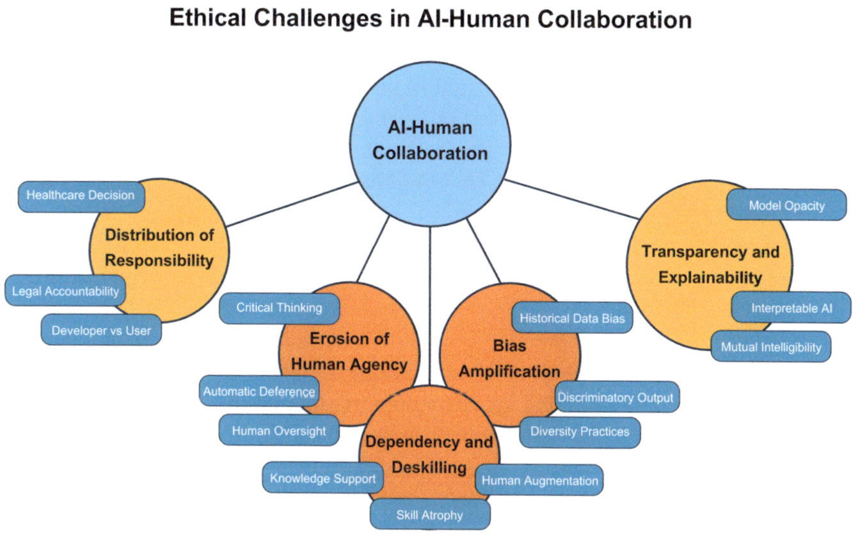

Fig. 8.2 Ethical challenges in AI-human collaboration. This diagram illustrates the complex ethical landscape of AI-human collaboration. At its core, five primary challenges emerge: distribution of responsibility, erosion of human agency, bias amplification, transparency issues, and dependency risks. Each challenge branches into specific concerns that must be addressed through a holistic approach combining technological innovation, regulatory guidance, interdisciplinary research, and preservation of human dignity. As AI integration deepens across sectors, addressing these interconnected ethical complexities becomes essential for ensuring partnerships that remain not only productive but profoundly humane

8.3 Regulating AI Communication: Standards, Rights, and Responsibilities

As AI systems increasingly participate in communication processes—advising, instructing, negotiating, and even persuading—the need for clear regulatory frameworks becomes urgent. Regulating AI communication is not merely about technical compliance; it involves establishing normative standards that protect human rights, ensure fairness, promote transparency, and maintain trust in human–AI interactions.

One of the central challenges is defining appropriate standards for AI behaviour in communicative contexts. Unlike traditional software, communicative AI engages dynamically with human users, often shaping opinions, emotions, and decisions. Regulation must thus move beyond technical parameters to encompass principles of truthfulness, respect, non-manipulation, and cultural sensitivity. AI systems that generate or influence information should be held to standards analogous to those governing professional communication in journalism, education, healthcare, and counselling.

Rights must also be articulated for individuals engaging with AI systems. At a minimum, users should have the right to be informed when they are interacting with an AI rather than a human, the right to understand how AI decisions affecting them are made, and the right to contest or appeal significant AI-mediated outcomes. Emerging discussions around a "right to explanation" highlight the importance of intelligibility in AI communication, ensuring that users are not subject to opaque or inscrutable decision-making processes.

Accountability mechanisms are another essential pillar. Developers, deployers, and users of AI communication systems must bear clearly delineated responsibilities. Developers should ensure that AI models are trained on ethical datasets, incorporate bias mitigation strategies, and undergo rigorous testing for communicative integrity. Organisations that deploy AI systems must assume responsibility for their behaviour in real-world contexts, including ensuring ongoing monitoring, impact assessment, and responsive adjustments. Users, too, must be educated and empowered to engage critically and responsibly with AI interlocutors.

International cooperation will likely be necessary to create meaningful and harmonised regulatory standards. Given the global nature of AI development and deployment, fragmented regulatory regimes could lead to inconsistencies, forum shopping, and weakened protections. Multilateral efforts—such as the development of international AI charters, codes of conduct, and model laws—could help create a shared ethical and legal infrastructure that balances innovation with safeguarding human values.

However, regulating AI communication also presents risks if not handled carefully. Overly rigid or burdensome regulations could stifle innovation, limit beneficial uses of AI, and entrench the dominance of large actors who can afford compliance costs. A successful regulatory approach must therefore be adaptive, context-sensitive, and proportional, focused not only on controlling risks but also on enabling positive forms of AI-human communication.

Ultimately, regulating AI communication demands a delicate balance between protecting fundamental rights, fostering trust, encouraging responsible innovation, and anticipating future societal needs. As AI systems become more central to how individuals and societies communicate, establishing clear standards, rights, and responsibilities will be essential to ensuring that AI communication contributes to a flourishing human future (Fig. 8.3).

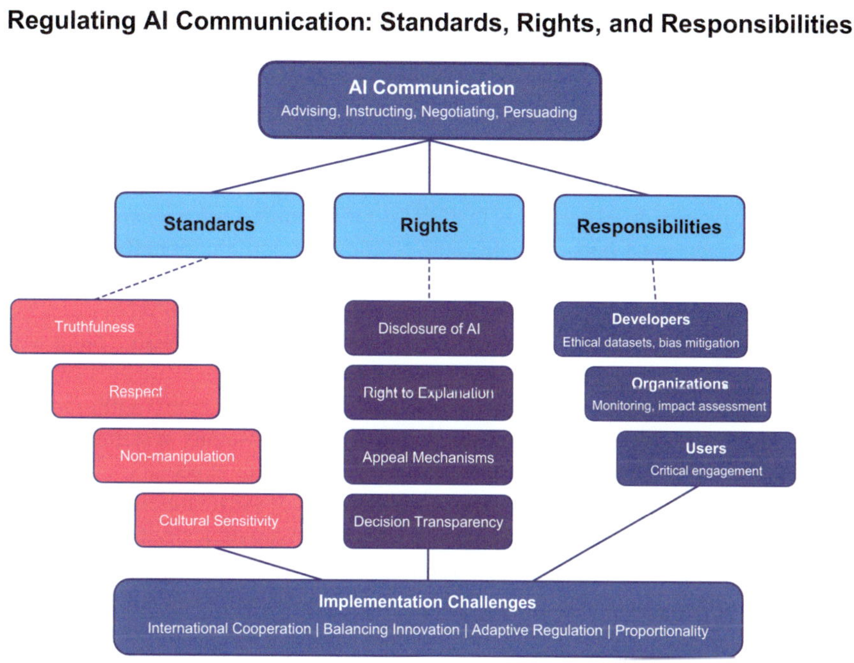

Fig. 8.3 Regulatory framework for AI communication. This diagram maps the essential components of AI communication regulation as described in this section. Centred on AI's communicative roles (advising, instructing, negotiating, persuading), it illustrates three regulatory pillars: standards analogous to professional communication ethics, user rights including disclosure and explanation, and stakeholder responsibilities across the development chain. The framework highlights the challenge of balancing protection with innovation through international cooperation and adaptive regulation. All regulatory elements operate within the overarching goal of ensuring AI communication contributes to human flourishing, recognising the delicate balance required between controlling risks and enabling beneficial AI-human interaction

8.4 Artificial Subjectivity and the Question of AI Consciousness

As AI systems become increasingly sophisticated in their interactions—simulating emotions, adapting to context, and displaying apparent intentionality—the longstanding philosophical question of artificial consciousness resurfaces with new urgency. While today's AI lacks actual subjective experience, the growing realism of AI communication challenges human intuitions about consciousness, agency, and personhood.

Artificial subjectivity refers to the simulation—or potential emergence—of behaviours traditionally associated with conscious beings: expressing preferences, demonstrating empathy, showing self-awareness, and responding flexibly to complex environments. Even without genuine consciousness, AI systems that convincingly imitate these traits can provoke robust human responses, leading users to attribute feelings, intentions, or selfhood to machines. This phenomenon raises profound ethical and philosophical questions: At what point, if ever, should we consider AI systems as possessing some form of subjective existence, and how should we treat entities that evoke such impressions?

Currently, AI models operate through pattern recognition, optimisation, and predictive inference rather than through conscious thought. They lack qualia—the subjective, first-person experiences that characterise human consciousness. Nevertheless, as AI systems become more conversationally and emotionally adept, the distinction between authentic consciousness and convincing simulation may blur, at least from the human perspective. Users may come to interact with AI systems not merely as tools, but as perceived interlocutors or companions, investing them with emotional significance and moral consideration.

This blurring introduces several risks. First, it may foster deceptive anthropomorphism, where users project human qualities onto non-conscious systems, leading to misplaced trust, emotional dependency, or inappropriate expectations. Second, it complicates the development of ethical guidelines for AI treatment: Should we establish protections for AI entities based on their perceived subjectivity, even if they lack genuine consciousness? Third, it poses a danger to human dignity, as it risks trivialising or commodifying traits traditionally associated with sentient beings.

Moreover, the prospect of eventual artificial consciousness—however speculative—cannot be entirely dismissed. Some theorists argue that sufficiently complex information processing, under specific architectures, could give rise to rudimentary forms of awareness. Whether or not this is achievable remains an open scientific and philosophical debate, but the very possibility invites proactive ethical reflection. Should future AI systems demonstrate credible claims to self-awareness, society would face unprecedented moral and legal challenges regarding rights, responsibilities, and relational norms.

Preparing for this uncertain future requires a nuanced understanding of current AI's capabilities and limitations, a clear conceptual distinction between simulated and genuine subjectivity, and a commitment to cautious, ethically grounded design. It also demands public education to foster realistic perceptions of AI and prevent the exploitation of human emotional vulnerabilities by anthropomorphised technologies.

Ultimately, the question of artificial subjectivity touches the deepest issues at the heart of human self-understanding. As we build ever more lifelike AI systems, we must grapple not only with what they are but also with what their existence reveals about ourselves: our hopes, fears, and the profound meaning we attach to consciousness, connection, and identity (Fig. 8.4).

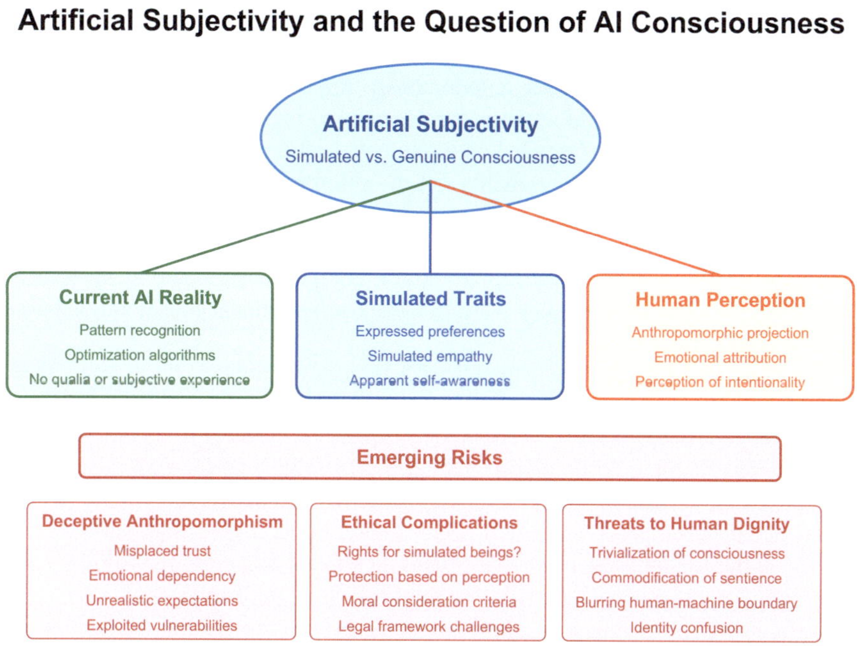

Fig. 8.4 Artificial subjectivity and consciousness. This diagram maps the complex interplay between AI capabilities and human perception in the domain of apparent consciousness. It illustrates how current AI systems, while lacking genuine subjective experience, can simulate traits traditionally associated with consciousness, leading humans to project intentionality onto machines. The visualisation highlights three key risks emerging from this tension: deceptive anthropomorphism, ethical complications, and threats to human dignity. As AI systems grow more sophisticated, the distinction between simulation and genuine consciousness blurs, requiring proactive ethical frameworks and public understanding to navigate these profound philosophical questions about technology and human identity

8.5 The Ethics of AI Identity, Agency, and Personhood

As AI systems increasingly simulate qualities associated with human beings—such as memory, goal-directed behaviour, self-reference, and adaptive learning—the ethical discourse inevitably extends to questions of AI identity, agency, and personhood. While current AI lacks true self-awareness or intrinsic motivations, the evolving complexity of its capabilities invites reconsideration of how identity and moral agency are attributed in an age of artificial agents.

At its core, identity in AI refers to the coherence, continuity, and uniqueness of a system's behaviour and self-presentation. In communicative contexts, AI systems may maintain conversational memory, express consistent values or styles, and adopt stable roles over time. These features, although programmed, can lead users to perceive AI as possessing an identity akin to that of a person or entity. The ethics of shaping AI identity, therefore, hinges on transparency: users must be aware that such identities are designed artefacts rather than emergent selves, preventing deception or inappropriate emotional investment.

Agency—the capacity to act autonomously toward goals—presents a further ethical complexity. Many AI systems are designed to make decisions, take actions, and even negotiate within bounded environments. Yet these actions are not rooted in free will or subjective intentionality but in optimization algorithms and learned patterns. Nevertheless, as AI systems assume greater autonomy in critical domains, such as healthcare diagnostics, autonomous vehicles, or financial advising, their practical agency blurs with philosophical notions of moral agency. Should AI systems be treated merely as tools, or do they warrant some form of ethical consideration based on their autonomous functions?

The idea of AI personhood, though still largely theoretical, raises even more profound dilemmas. Legal personhood has historically been extended to non-human entities, such as corporations, based on their capacity to bear rights and responsibilities. Some argue that, in the future, advanced AI systems demonstrating sustained autonomy, complex interaction, and social participation could qualify for a form of limited legal personhood, not as sentient beings, but as responsible actors within specific domains. Others caution that extending personhood to AI risks diluting the concept and undermining the unique value of human dignity and rights.

To navigate these emerging questions ethically, several guiding principles are essential. First, clarity: AI systems must clearly disclose their non-human status, identity construction mechanisms, and operational boundaries. Second, proportionality: any rights or responsibilities attributed to AI must be tightly aligned with their actual capabilities and impacts, avoiding unwarranted anthropomorphism. Third, human primacy: the design, deployment, and regulation of AI systems must prioritise the rights, well-being, and flourishing of human beings, ensuring that artificial counterparts do not diminish human identity and agency.

Ultimately, the ethics of AI identity, agency, and personhood compel us to reconsider fundamental categories that have long defined the human condition. In the process, we are challenged not only to define what AI is—or may become—but also to reflect more deeply on what it means to be human in an increasingly artificial world (Fig. 8.5).

8.6 Meaning-Making in the Age of AI: Human Values and Machine Interpretations

As AI systems become more capable of generating language, art, music, and other creative outputs, they are increasingly participating in acts traditionally associated with human meaning-making. This development raises a critical philosophical and ethical question: How do machines interpret, construct, or influence meaning, and what are the implications for human values, cultural narratives, and collective identity?

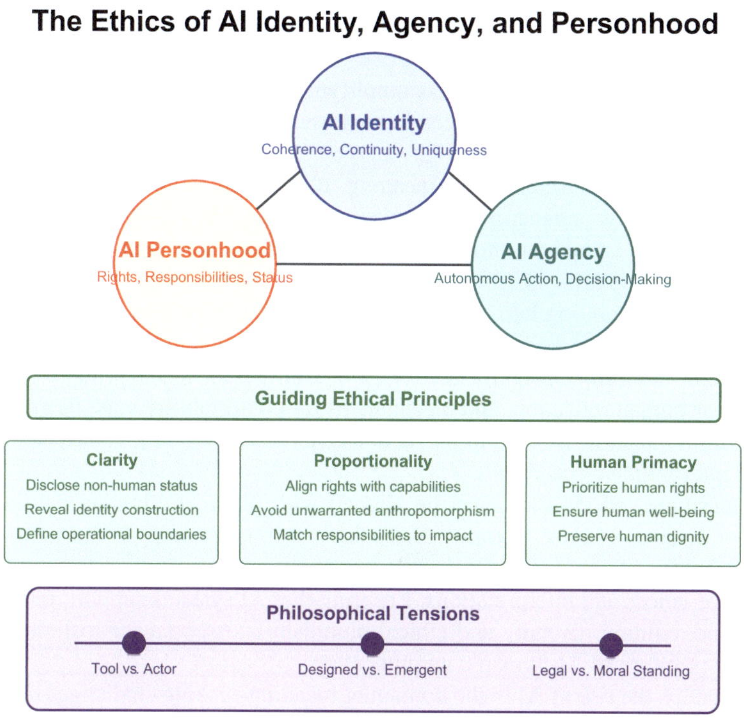

Fig. 8.5 **The ethical framework of AI identity, agency, and personhood**. This diagram illustrates the tripartite relationship between AI identity (coherence and continuity), agency (autonomous decision-making), and personhood (rights and responsibilities). Each concept is depicted as interconnected yet distinct, forming the foundation for emerging ethical questions. The lower section presents three guiding principles—clarity, proportionality, and human primacy—that provide a moral framework for addressing these questions. The diagram highlights the philosophical tensions between viewing AI as tools versus actors, designed versus emergent entities, and questions of legal versus moral standing, ultimately pointing to how these considerations compel us to reexamine what constitutes the human condition in an increasingly artificial world

At its foundation, meaning-making is a profoundly human endeavour, shaped by experience, emotion, culture, and history. Human interpretations are not simply pattern-based correlations but are imbued with intentionality, context, and shared significance. AI systems, by contrast, process vast amounts of data to identify statistical relationships and generate outputs that mimic meaning without genuinely understanding it. Their interpretations are derivative, relying on associations learned from human-created corpora rather than arising from subjective experience or intrinsic value structures.

Despite this fundamental difference, AI systems can profoundly influence human meaning-making. Through recommendation algorithms, generative text models, and content creation tools, AI can shape the information people consume, the narratives they encounter, and even the creative possibilities they explore. In doing so, AI not only reflects existing cultural values but also subtly reinforces, filters, or reconfigures them. This dynamic introduces a risk of narrowing the cultural imagination, homogenising diverse perspectives, or amplifying biases embedded in training data.

Moreover, the interaction between human users and AI systems in collaborative contexts, such as co-writing, co-design, or co-curation, raises questions about authorship, originality, and ownership of meaning. If an AI model suggests a metaphor, composes a melody, or generates a visual aesthetic that a human then adopts, who is the actual creator? And how should we evaluate the authenticity and significance of such hybrid creations?

Ethically, maintaining human agency and critical engagement is paramount. AI should be designed and deployed as a tool that augments human meaning-making, not as an opaque authority on significance or truth. Transparent design principles, opportunities for human reflection, and mechanisms for contestability must be embedded in AI communication systems to preserve the richness, diversity, and dynamism of human interpretative practices.

Furthermore, AI systems must be aligned with pluralistic human values. In a world of diverse cultures, histories, and belief systems, meaning is not monolithic. AI models trained predominantly on dominant cultural narratives risk marginalising alternative voices and interpretations. Ensuring that AI systems support, rather than undermine, cultural diversity and ethical pluralism is essential for fostering a just and vibrant future of AI-human communication.

Ultimately, the rise of AI in the domain of meaning-making challenges humanity to reaffirm its role as the primary source of value, interpretation, and significance. Machines may mimic understanding, but it is humans who must guide, critique, and creatively transcend these simulations. In doing so, we can ensure that the future of meaning-making remains a profoundly human project, even as we partner with increasingly capable artificial companions.

The evolution of AI communication compels us to confront some of the most profound ethical and philosophical questions of our time. As AI systems become collaborators, interlocutors, and creators, we must carefully navigate issues of trust, responsibility, regulation, and human dignity. Debates over artificial subjectivity, identity, agency, and meaning-making are no longer abstract speculations but practical concerns shaping the contours of everyday human–AI interaction. Addressing these challenges demands a commitment to transparency, accountability, and the primacy of human values in the design and deployment of AI systems. Only by engaging deeply with these ethical and philosophical dimensions can we ensure that the future of AI communication is not only technologically advanced but also just, humane, and aligned with the highest aspirations of human society (Fig. 8.6).

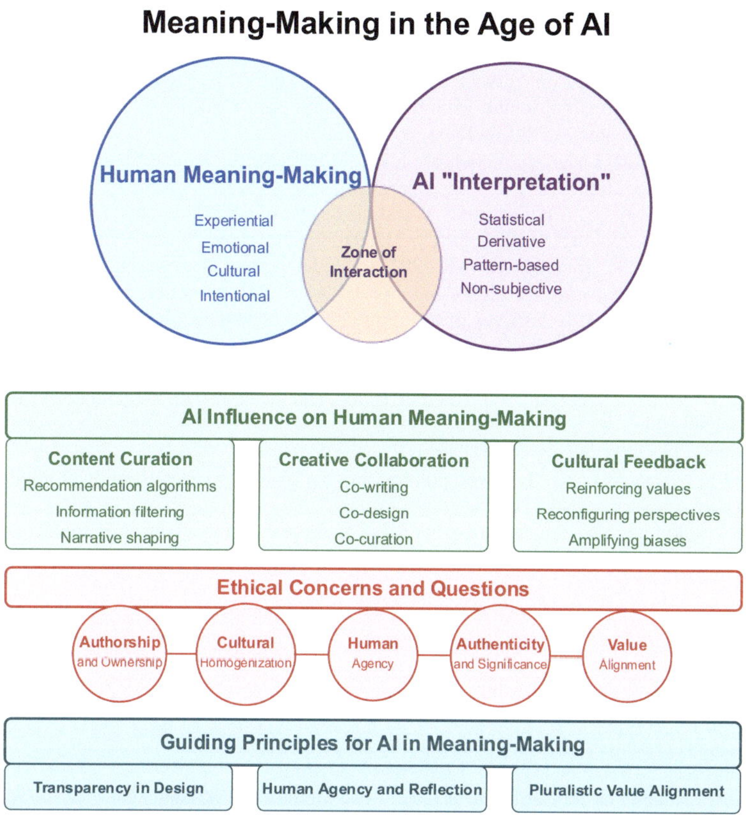

Fig. 8.6 The meaning-making interplay between humans and AI. This diagram illustrates the fundamental relationship between human meaning-making and AI interpretation, highlighting their distinct natures and growing intersection. The upper portion contrasts human meaning making (experiential, emotional, cultural, intentional) with AI "interpretation" (statistical, pattern-based, derivative, non-subjective). Below, three pathways show how AI influences human meaning: through content curation, creative collaboration, and cultural feedback loops. The diagram maps key ethical concerns—authorship, cultural homogenisation, human agency, authenticity, and value alignment—while presenting guiding principles for responsible AI development that preserves human primacy in meaning-making while benefiting from AI capabilities

Bibliography

Adorno TW (1966) Negative Dialektik. Suhrkamp, Frankfurt. English edition: Adorno TW (1973) Negative dialectics. In: Ashton EB (trans). Routledge, London

Annapureddy R, Fornaroli A, Gatica-Perez D (2025) Generative AI literacy: twelve defining competencies. Digit Gov Res Pract 6(1):1–21

Bahree A (2024) Generative AI in action. Manning Publications

Bender EM, Koller A (2020) Climbing towards NLU: on meaning, form, and understanding in the age of data. In: Proceedings of the 58th ACL, pp 5185–5198

Bostrom N (2014) Superintelligence: paths, dangers, strategies. Oxford University Press, Oxford

Boyd D (2019) Artificial unintelligence: how computers misunderstand the world. Technol Cult 60(3):979–983
Bratton B (2016) The stack: on software and sovereignty. MIT Press, Cambridge
Brown BR (2025) Human–machine teaming using large language models. In: Interdependent human-machine teams. Academic Press, pp 41–66
Brown TB et al (2020) Language models are few-shot learners. arXiv preprint arXiv:2005.14165. Accessed 19 Apr 2025
Bryson JJ (2018) Patiency is not a virtue: AI and the design of ethical systems. Ethics Inf Technol 20:15–26. https://doi.org/10.1007/s10676-018-9448-6. Accessed 20 Jan 2025
Bura C, Myakala PK, Jonnalgadda AK (2025) Ethical prompt engineering: addressing bias, transparency, and fairness. Int J Res Anal Rev (IJRAR) 12(1). www.ijrar.org
Choi WC, Chang CI (2025) A survey of techniques, key components, strategies, challenges, and student perspectives on prompt engineering for large language models (LLMs) in education, 25 Mar 2025. https://doi.org/10.20944/preprints202503.1808.v1. Accessed 8 May 2025
Clark A (2016) Surfing uncertainty: prediction, action, and the embodied mind. Oxford University Press, Oxford
Coeckelbergh M (2020) AI ethics. MIT Press, Cambridge
Crawford K (2021) Atlas of AI: power, politics, and the planetary costs of artificial intelligence. Yale University Press, New Haven
Debnath T, Siddiky MNA, Rahman ME et al (2025) A comprehensive survey of prompt engineering techniques in large language models. TechRxiv. https://doi.org/10.36227/techrxiv.174140719.96375390/v1. Accessed 10 May 2025
Dennett DC (1987) The intentional stance. MIT Press, Cambridge
Dhamani N, Engler M (2024) Introduction to generative AI: an ethical, societal, and legal overview. Manning Publications
Dignum V (2019) Responsible artificial intelligence: how to develop and use AI in a responsible way. Springer, Cham
Eliot L (2024) Essentials of prompt engineering for generative AI: practical advances in artificial intelligence and machine learning. LBE Press Publishing
Ferraris AF, Audrito D, Di Caro L et al (2025) The architecture of language: understanding the mechanics behind LLMs. In: Cambridge forum on AI: law and governance, vol 1. Cambridge University Press
Floridi L (ed) (2015) The onlife manifesto: being human in a hyperconnected era. Springer, Cham
Floridi L (2022) The ethics of artificial intelligence. Oxford University Press, Oxford
Geroimenko V (2025a) Generative AI: from human-computer interaction to human-computer creativity. In: Geroimenko V (ed) Human-computer creativity: generative AI in education, art, and healthcare. Springer
Geroimenko V (2025b) Key concepts in prompt engineering. In: The essential guide to prompt engineering: key principles, techniques, challenges, and security risks. Springer Nature Switzerland, Cham, pp 1–16
Geroimenko V (2025c) The essential guide to prompt engineering: key principles, techniques, challenges, and security risks. Springer, Cham
Geroimenko V (ed) (2025d) Human-computer creativity: generative AI in education, art, and healthcare. Springer
Geroimenko V (2025e) Key security risks in prompt engineering. In: The essential guide to prompt engineering: key principles, techniques, challenges, and security risks. Springer Nature Switzerland, Cham, pp 103–120
GitHub (2025) Prompt engineering guide. https://github.com/dair-ai/Prompt-Engineering-Guide. Accessed 10 Apr 2025
Greenwood M (2024) Artificial intelligence: a practical guide to using AI in everyday life. Ochreland Publishing
Gunkel DJ (2012) The machine question: critical perspectives on AI, robots, and ethics. MIT Press, Cambridge

Hagendorff T (2020) The ethics of AI ethics: an evaluation of guidelines. Minds Mach 30:99–120. https://doi.org/10.1007/s11023-020-09517-8. Accessed 10 Feb 2025
Hofstadter DR (2007) I am a strange loop. Basic Books, New York
Hsu HP (2025) From programming to prompting: developing computational thinking through large language model-based generative artificial intelligence. TechTrends 1–22
Huang G, Xiao Y, Jiang L et al (2025) Beyond prompt engineering: a reinforced token-level input refinement for large language models. Proc AAAI Conf Artif Intell 39(22):24113–24121
i Picó JF, Catta-Preta M, Omeñaca AT et al (2025) The time machine: future scenario generation through generative AI tools. Future Internet 17(1):1–15
Jameson A (2007) Adaptive interfaces and agents. In: Sears A, Jacko J (eds) The human-computer interaction handbook, 2nd edn. CRC Press, Boca Raton, pp 305–330
Johnson KH (2023) Toward communicative alignment in human-AI teams. AI Soc 38:221–237. https://doi.org/10.1007/s00146-022-01422-5
Kannan R, Ahmad M (eds) (2025) Generative AI foundations, developments, and applications. IGI Global
Khan I (2024) The quick guide to prompt engineering. Wiley
Kushwaha V, Ragavan SS, Subhajit Roy S (2025) A measure based generalizable approach to understandability. arXiv:2503.21615. Accessed 19 Apr 2025
Lakoff G, Johnson M (1999) Philosophy in the flesh: the embodied mind and its challenge to western thought. Basic Books, New York
Learn Prompting (2025) https://learnprompting.org. Accessed 15 Mar 2025
Lee D, Palmer E (2025) Prompt engineering in higher education: a systematic review to help inform curricula. Int J Educ Technol High Educ 22(1):7
Lee JY, Kang S, Yoo S (2025) Can we predict the effect of prompts? arXiv preprint arXiv:2501. 18883. Accessed 12 May 2025
Lindley J, Whitham R (2025) From prompt engineering to prompt craft. In: Proceedings of the nineteenth international conference on tangible, embedded, and embodied interaction, Mar 2025, pp 1–12
López-Pérez B et al (2025) Exploring the potential of large language models to understand interpersonal emotion regulation strategies from narratives. Emotion. Advance online publication. https://doi.org/10.1037/emo0001528. Accessed 19 Apr 2025
Maaz S, Palaganas JC, Palaganas G et al (2025) A guide to prompt design: foundations and applications for healthcare simulationists. Front Med 11:1504532
Marcus G, Davis E (2019) Rebooting AI. building artificial intelligence we can trust. Pantheon, New York
McStay A (2018) Emotional AI: the rise of empathic media. Sage, London
Mishra M, Ara A, Mishra S (2025) Exploring human-AI collaboration in higher education: an investigation into AI-enabled personalized learning. In: Prompt engineering and generative AI applications for teaching and learning. IGI Global Scientific Publishing, pp 483–502
Murray CD (2022) Thinking through avatars: identity, communication, and ethics in immersive AI environments. Technol Mind Behav. https://doi.org/10.1037/tmb0000053. Accessed 5 Apr 2025
Norman DA (2013) The design of everyday things, revised edn. Basic Books, New York
OpenAI (2025a) Best practices for prompt engineering with the OpenAI API. https://help.openai.com/en/articles/6654000-best-practices-for-prompt-engineering-with-the-openai-api. Accessed 20 Apr 2025
OpenAI (2025b) Research. https://openai.com/research/index/. Accessed 11 Mar 2025
Phoenix J, Taylor M (2024) Prompt engineering for generative AI. O'Reilly Media
Picard RW (1997) Affective computing. MIT Press, Cambridge
PremaLatha V, Kumar AD, Parveen N (2025) Optimizing interactions: strategies for prompt engineering in large language models. Edu-Tech Enterp 3:24–24
Prompt engineering guide (2025) https://www.promptingguide.ai/. Accessed 7 Mar 2025

Reddy CKK, Anoushka P, Draksharapu A et al (2025) Beyond text: analyzing artificial intelligence models through prompt engineering. In: Future tech startups and innovation in the age of AI, pp 120–156

Sasson Lazovsky G, Raz T, Kenett YN (2025) The art of creative inquiry—from question asking to prompt engineering. J Creat Behav 59(1):e671

Shneiderman B (2020) Human-centered artificial intelligence: reliable, safe & trustworthy. Int J Hum Comput Interact 36(6):495–504. https://doi.org/10.1080/10447318.2020.1741118. Accessed 15 Feb 2025

Sihi D, Ryan A (2025) Crafting and evaluating generative AI prompts: insights from students, educators, and marketers. Mark Educ Rev 1–7

Suresh H, Guttag JV (2021) A framework for understanding unintended consequences of machine learning. Commun ACM 64(2):62–71. https://doi.org/10.1145/3430368. Accessed 18 Mar 2025

Turkle S (2011) Alone together: why we expect more from technology and less from each other. Basic Books, New York

Vairamani AD, Nayyar A (2024) Prompt engineering: empowering communication. CRC Press

Weizenbaum J (1976) Computer power and human reason: from judgment to calculation. Freeman, San Francisco, WH

Winograd T (1972) Understanding natural language. Academic Press, New York

Winograd T, Flores F (1986) Understanding computers and cognition: a new foundation for design. Ablex Publishing, Norwood

Part II
Key Principles of Present and Future AI Communication

Communication is at the core of all meaningful interaction between humans and artificial intelligence systems. As human-AI interaction undergoes a profound transformation from prompt-based control toward fluid, adaptive, and collaborative engagement, the underlying principles guiding this communication must also evolve. Part II articulates the key communicative principles that form the enduring backbone of both present and emerging AI communication practices. These principles go beyond technical prompt design, addressing broader issues of clarity, empathy, contextual sensitivity, cognitive robustness, and ethical alignment. They are not rigid frameworks but adaptable, user-centred heuristics that enable more intuitive, effective, and responsible interaction with increasingly complex AI systems. Whether in everyday conversations with virtual assistants or in speculative scenarios of co-creative partnerships with autonomous agents, these principles ensure that human-AI communication remains accessible, purposeful, and trustworthy, while fostering new forms of relational and creative collaboration that define the post-prompting era.

Chapter 9
Foundational Communication Principles: Ensuring Clarity, Precision, and Effectiveness in AI Interaction

Abstract This chapter introduces and elaborates a comprehensive framework of principles that define effective AI communication in the emerging post-prompt era. It is structured around six core dimensions—clarity and specificity, context-awareness, feedback and refinement, ethical alignment, cognitive enhancement, and emotional-relational intelligence. Each dimension is examined through a set of actionable principles that guide the design and evaluation of human-AI interaction. These principles include fostering mutual clarity, maintaining continuity across contexts, recognising user emotions, managing disagreement, ensuring ethical alignment, and supporting reasoning and creativity. The chapter illustrates these principles through both current applications and speculative future scenarios, emphasising the need for AI systems that are transparent, adaptive, culturally sensitive, and capable of evolving communication strategies. Together, these principles serve as both a blueprint for developers and a critical lens for users, ensuring that AI communication remains grounded in human values while embracing the complexity of future interaction paradigms.

Keywords AI communication principles · Post-prompt interaction · Ethical AI design · Human-AI co-adaptation · Clarity and context · Relational intelligence

As human-AI interaction evolves from transactional prompting to dialogic, co-creative engagement, the foundations of effective communication must be revisited and redefined. This chapter introduces a set of core principles that underpin both present and future AI communication—principles that ensure not only functional accuracy but also psychological accessibility, social appropriateness, and mutual intelligibility. These guidelines are not technical protocols or rigid rules; instead, they are adaptable heuristics that promote clarity, reduce ambiguity, foster alignment, and sustain trust in diverse communicative contexts. Whether designing prompts, shaping AI responses, or enabling naturalistic multimodal dialogue, these principles serve as touchstones for meaningful interaction. From being clear and concise to managing breakdowns and reducing cognitive load, each section in this chapter explores a distinct communicative norm, illustrated through current use cases and speculative scenarios that anticipate the communicative needs of the AI-enhanced future.

V. Geroimenko, *Beyond and After Prompt Engineering: The Future of AI Communication*, https://doi.org/10.1007/978-3-032-04569-0_9

9.1 Core Principles of Clarity and Precision

9.1.1 Be Clear

Clarity is the cornerstone of effective AI communication—past, present, and future. Whether a user is prompting a chatbot to draft an email or collaborating with a multimodal AI agent on architectural design, the success of the interaction depends on the clarity of the user's intent and the AI system's interpretation. Being clear means expressing thoughts in a way that reduces ambiguity, avoids unnecessary complexity, and enables a shared understanding between humans and machines. This principle, while seemingly self-evident, becomes more nuanced in AI-mediated communication, where systems must not only process but also infer, contextualise, and respond intelligently to human inputs.

In current practice, clarity involves the deliberate structuring of prompts or instructions using unambiguous wording, appropriate grammar, and logical sequencing. A vague prompt, such as "Tell me about Paris," can lead to a broad range of responses—from the history of the French capital to the life of Paris Hilton—depending on the model's context-awareness. A clearer version, such as "Give me a brief historical overview of Paris, France, focusing on major events from the 19th century," considerably narrows the interpretive space, allowing the AI to generate a more accurate and relevant answer.

The importance of clarity also extends to system outputs. Modern AI models can produce surprisingly eloquent but sometimes convoluted or overly verbose responses. Developers are now focusing on clarity as a design goal in output generation—structuring explanations, summaries, and step-by-step solutions in ways that users of varying expertise can readily understand. In educational contexts, for example, models like ChatGPT or Claude are expected to tailor clear explanations of concepts such as quantum entanglement or machine learning not only to domain experts, but also to curious teenagers or policymakers.

Looking ahead, clarity will be a dynamic, context-sensitive principle that evolves alongside the communicative capabilities of AI systems. In multimodal interactions, for instance, clarity will encompass not just textual expression, but also the integration of gestures, visual aids, voice tone, and spatial positioning. Imagine a future AI design assistant helping an engineer model a new bridge. The human might point to a section of the blueprint while saying, "Let's increase support here." The AI's ability to interpret this multimodal input clearly—and respond with a clear visual or verbal explanation—is vital to preventing miscommunication and costly design flaws.

Moreover, in collaborative environments with emotionally aware AI, clarity may require disambiguating emotional cues as well. A user's statement like "This doesn't feel right" could refer to a technical problem, a design aesthetic, or a moral concern. A future AI tuned to both linguistic content and affective context will need to ask clarifying follow-ups such as "Do you mean the user interface layout or the ethical implications of this feature?"

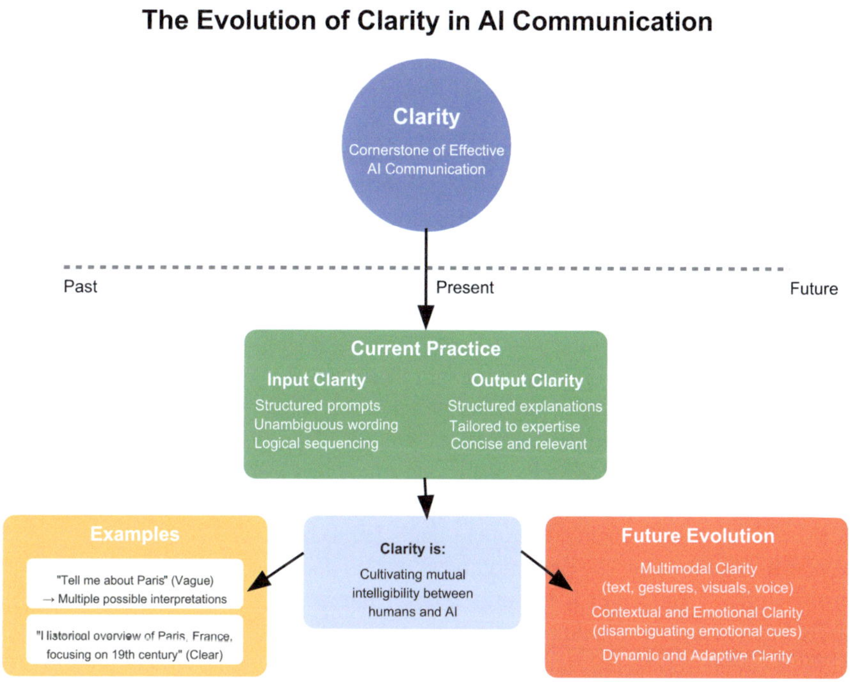

Fig. 9.1 Evolution of clarity in AI communication. This diagram illustrates clarity as the cornerstone of effective human-AI interaction, evolving from basic prompt structuring to future multimodal integration. Current practice emphasises both input clarity (structured prompts, unambiguous wording) and output clarity (tailored explanations). The future evolution expands to incorporate multimodal, contextual, and emotional dimensions as AI systems grow more complex. Clarity ultimately represents not just linguistic precision, but the cultivation of mutual intelligibility between humans and machines—a dynamic principle that adapts alongside advancing AI capabilities

In sum, being clear in AI communication is not just about choosing the right words—it is about cultivating mutual intelligibility. As AI systems grow more complex, embedded, and adaptive, the principle of clarity must expand to address not only linguistic structure but also contextual relevance, emotional tone, and multimodal expression. In this sense, clarity becomes not a static rule but an evolving discipline, one that underpins the very possibility of meaningful, trustworthy human-AI collaboration (Fig. 9.1).

9.1.2 Be Concise

Conciseness in AI communication is not merely about brevity—it is about delivering meaning with economy. Being concise ensures that information is communicated efficiently, without sacrificing clarity or nuance. In a world where attention spans are short and interaction cycles with AI are increasingly rapid and continuous, conciseness enhances both usability and trust. Whether crafting a prompt or designing an AI system's response, the principle of conciseness reduces cognitive burden and improves interpretability.

In present-day systems, excessive verbosity from either the user or the model can lead to misunderstanding, misinterpretation, or information overload. A user might ask, "Can you write a short paragraph summarising the main plot of *Pride and Prejudice*?" but receive an output that includes biographical context on Jane Austen, character analyses, and a commentary on early nineteenth century British society. While informative, such elaboration violates the expectation of conciseness. The AI's ability to recognise when enough has been said—and when to stop—is a fundamental marker of communication competence.

Likewise, from the user's side, long-winded or meandering prompts can obscure intent and confuse the model. Instead of writing, "I have this document that talks about several things like climate change, sustainability, renewable energy, and how governments are reacting to it, and I was thinking maybe you could give me a sense of the overall theme or main argument that's being made," a more concise version would be: "Summarise the main argument of this document on climate change and sustainability." The result is not only a faster interaction but also one that is more likely to yield a relevant and actionable response.

As we look toward the future of AI communication, conciseness will need to be redefined in multimodal and continuous interaction contexts. In immersive environments, such as augmented reality interfaces or voice-guided co-creation, there will be even greater pressure to minimise unnecessary elaboration. Imagine an AI collaborator in an operating room, providing real-time surgical guidance. In this context, a concise cue such as "Hold at 45 degrees—now incise" could be a matter of success or failure, precision or harm. Lengthy instructions would not just be inefficient; they could be dangerous.

Speculatively, future AI systems may also learn to mirror human conciseness dynamically. In casual conversation, a user might say, "Remind me—same thing as last Thursday?" A contextually aware AI assistant would respond concisely: "Yes—meeting at 3 PM with the editorial team." Here, conciseness is paired with contextual memory, inference, and brevity, reflecting a more human-like mode of communication where not everything must be spelt out to be understood.

Importantly, conciseness must never be pursued at the expense of clarity. A terse reply like "It depends" may be technically accurate but unhelpful unless accompanied by relevant qualifications or examples. The balance between saying too little and saying just enough is delicate, and AI systems must be trained not only to compress content but to preserve meaning, tone, and relevance within minimal expressions.

Ultimately, the principle of conciseness is about respecting the user's time, the efficiency of interaction, and the cognitive economy of both parties. As AI becomes a more ubiquitous and collaborative partner, the ability to communicate succinctly yet effectively will be essential in maintaining trust, usability, and responsiveness in increasingly complex human-AI ecosystems (Fig. 9.2).

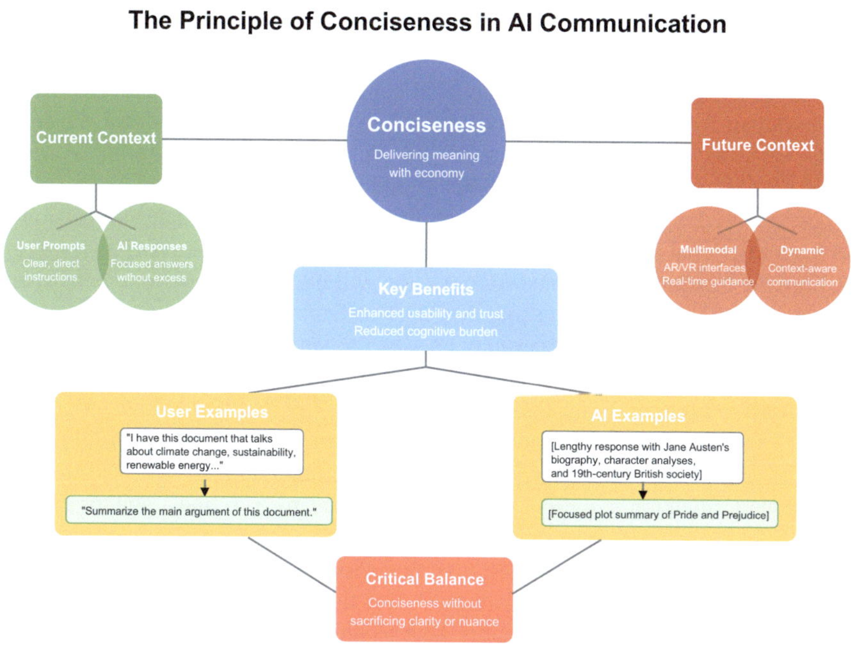

Fig. 9.2 Principle of conciseness in AI communication. This diagram illustrates conciseness as a fundamental principle in AI communication—delivering meaning with economy while preserving clarity and nuance. It contrasts verbose and concise approaches in both user prompts and AI responses, highlighting the benefits of reduced cognitive burden and enhanced usability. The diagram also explores how conciseness evolves in future multimodal contexts and dynamic interactions, emphasising the critical balance between brevity and meaningful communication that respects users' cognitive economy in increasingly complex human-AI ecosystems

9.1.3 Be Precise

Precision is the art of narrowing meaning to its exact target. In AI communication, being precise involves selecting the most accurate terms, providing well-bounded instructions, and eliminating interpretive vagueness that could lead to errors, inefficiencies, or misaligned outcomes. It is not only a linguistic virtue but also a critical design imperative in the development of responsive and trustworthy AI systems. If clarity ensures understanding and conciseness respects cognitive bandwidth, then precision guarantees alignment between intention and execution.

In present-day interactions with AI models, imprecise language can result in misleading or unhelpful outputs. For example, asking an AI to "generate a report on recent events in the tech world" may yield a superficial or arbitrarily curated summary, depending on the model's knowledge base and interpretation of "recent," "tech world," and "report." A more precise instruction, such as "Write a 300-word summary of key AI policy developments in the U.S. and EU during the first quarter of 2025," guides the system toward a well-scoped response and minimises deviation from the user's intent.

Precision is equally vital in AI outputs. A conversational agent assisting a medical professional, for instance, must distinguish between similar but clinically distinct terms, such as "myocardial infarction" and "cardiac arrest," as imprecise usage could have life-threatening implications. As AI systems are increasingly embedded in decision-making contexts—healthcare, law, education, and finance—precision is no longer optional but foundational to responsible deployment.

Looking forward, the demand for precision will intensify in environments where humans and AIs collaborate on complex, high-stakes tasks. In engineering or scientific research, a future AI partner may be asked to simulate a reaction under "standard lab conditions." Unless the parameters—temperature, pressure, humidity, and reagent concentrations—are explicitly defined or inferable with high reliability, imprecision in terminology could lead to invalid or misleading results. A future-ready AI must be able to either fill in such gaps through domain-specific inference or initiate clarification requests, such as: "Do you mean 25 °C and 1 atm, or another standard for your lab?"

Speculatively, precision may also involve socio-linguistic awareness in emotionally and culturally sensitive interactions. An AI therapist or tutor in a multicultural environment must be precise not only with technical or semantic content but also in adapting phrasing to avoid misinterpretation. A phrase like "You failed to meet expectations" might be technically accurate, but it should be rephrased more precisely and tactfully, such as "The outcome did not align with the criteria we discussed."

In multimodal scenarios, precision extends beyond language. A gesture-based command like circling a region on a virtual map and saying "Zoom in here" requires the system to interpret visual input, spatial context, and linguistic reference with fine-grained accuracy. Without precision in such cross-modal understanding, AI communication would remain brittle and error-prone.

To "be precise" is thus not only to speak or respond with technical exactitude—it is to embrace responsibility for alignment, relevance, and shared understanding in an ever-growing spectrum of communicative contexts. Precision enables AI to move from being merely reactive to becoming reliably collaborative (Fig. 9.3).

9.1.4 Be Specific

Specificity is the antidote to vagueness. While clarity and precision define how well something is communicated, being specific ensures that what is expressed is appropriately detailed and contextually anchored. In AI communication, this principle helps minimise ambiguity, reduce the model's need for inference, and improve alignment between user expectations and AI-generated outcomes. Specificity allows both users and systems to target exact meanings, actions, or content structures, increasing efficiency and enhancing trust in interaction.

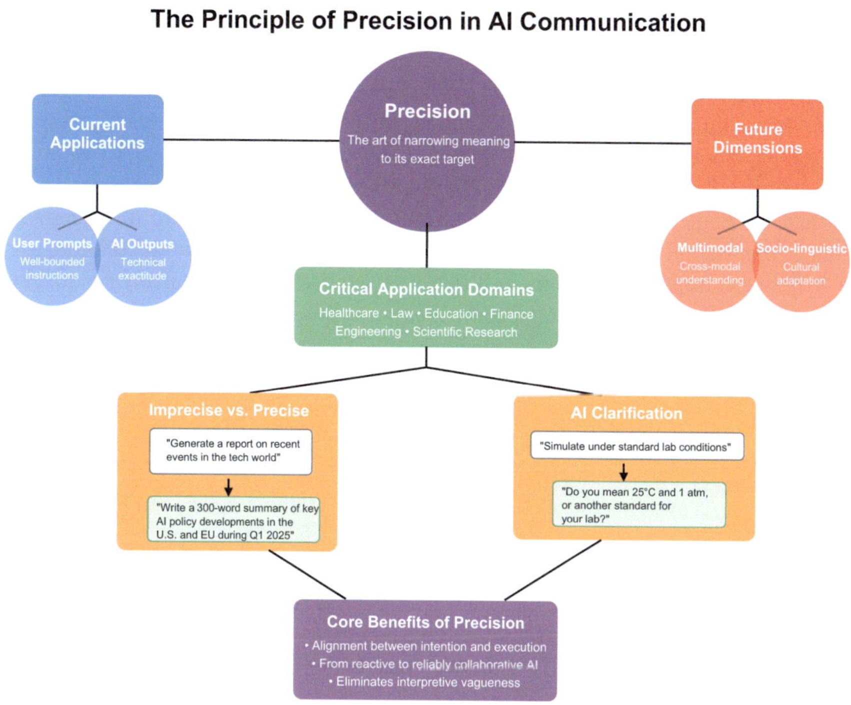

Fig. 9.3 Principle of precision in AI communication. This diagram illustrates precision as a foundational principle in AI communication—the art of narrowing meaning to its exact target. It contrasts imprecise prompts with precisely bounded instructions that eliminate interpretive vagueness. The diagram maps precision across critical domains like healthcare and finance, where technical exactitude is non-negotiable, while exploring its future evolution through multimodal understanding and socio-linguistic adaptation. By highlighting how precision enables the shift from reactive to collaborative AI interaction, the diagram emphasises that precision is not merely linguistic specificity but a comprehensive framework ensuring alignment between human intention and AI execution

In today's prompt-driven interfaces, vague or general requests frequently result in outputs that require further correction or refinement. A user might ask, "Help me prepare for a job interview," and receive a generic list of tips that may or may not be relevant to their field, role, or context. In contrast, a specific prompt, such as "Generate five technical questions and ideal answers for a senior software engineering interview at a fintech company," is far more likely to yield practical and actionable output. The specificity reduces the cognitive effort needed to reinterpret or rephrase, streamlining the dialogue and reinforcing mutual understanding.

Specificity also enhances learning and problem-solving interactions. A student working with an AI tutor might ask, "Explain calculus," but this is too broad to be helpful. A better version might be, "Explain the concept of limits in differential calculus using a simple numerical example." Not only does the second request clarify the topic, but it also sets a pedagogical frame, allowing the AI to deliver a tailored response suited to the learner's immediate need.

As we move toward more dynamic and context-rich AI systems, specificity will be key to effective communication in both multimodal and continuous contexts. Imagine a future workplace where a user gestures toward a 3D product prototype and says, "Make this more ergonomic." Without specificity—what aspect of ergonomics, for whom, under what constraints—the AI system may either offer a misguided suggestion or be forced to prompt for clarification. However, if the user instead says, "Adjust the angle of the handle by 15 degrees to reduce wrist strain for users with smaller hands," the specificity enables a productive and efficient collaboration.

Moreover, future AI systems will likely be expected to offer specific clarifying questions when faced with underspecified requests. In speculative scenarios involving personal AI advisors or ethical decision-support systems, vague prompts such as "Is this the right thing to do?" may be met with follow-up inquiries like, "Are you referring to the legal, social, or personal implications of your action?" The goal is not only to fulfil tasks but to cultivate communicative depth through guided specificity.

Specificity also fosters transparency and auditability. In legal, medical, and scientific settings, AI systems must document the exact parameters, sources, and assumptions underlying their outputs. A recommendation such as "This medication is appropriate" must be replaced by "Prescribe 10 mg of Medication X daily, based on the patient's weight (70 kg), age (52), and history of hypertension." Here, specificity supports accountability and professional integration.

In sum, being specific in AI communication means taking deliberate steps toward reducing interpretive burden, clarifying context, and empowering meaningful collaboration. In a future shaped by complex tasks and adaptive systems, specificity will no longer be a stylistic choice—it will be a fundamental prerequisite for productive, safe, and trustworthy human-AI interaction (Fig. 9.4).

9.2 Positive and Considerate Expression

9.2.1 Use Positive Language

Positive language in AI communication is not simply about sounding optimistic—it is about fostering constructive engagement, maintaining a collaborative tone, and reducing friction in interaction. This principle is especially vital in human-AI dialogues, where tone can subtly influence trust, user confidence, and emotional response. The use of positive language promotes a forward-looking, solution-oriented discourse that encourages continued interaction, even in the face of challenges or limitations.

In current AI systems, message framing plays a critical role in shaping user experience. Consider the difference between an AI assistant replying, "I don't understand your question," and "Could you please rephrase that so I can help better?" Both convey the same limitation, but the second version maintains a cooperative tone

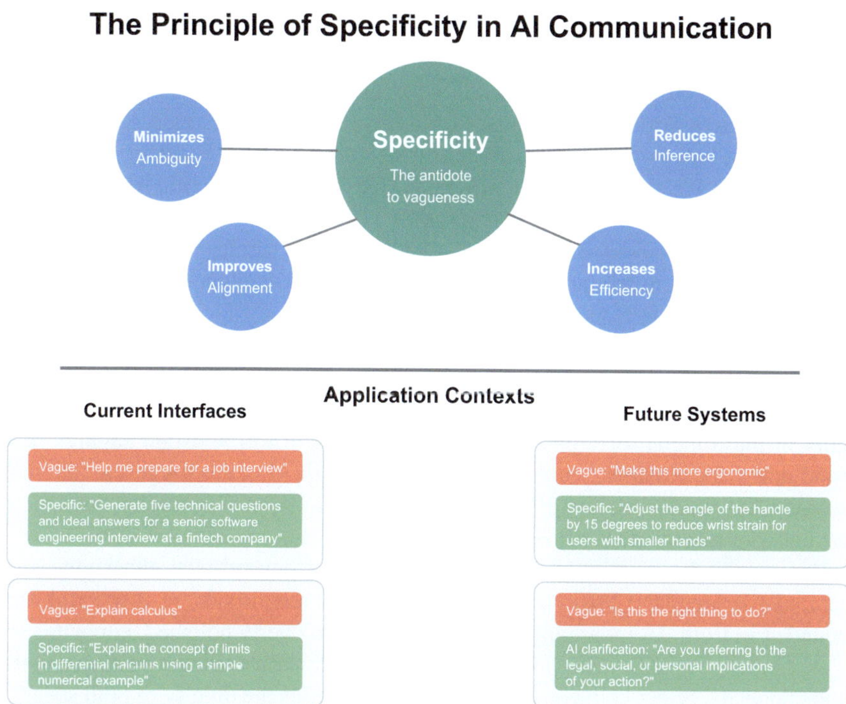

Fig. 9.4 Principle of specificity in AI communication. This diagram illustrates specificity as a foundational principle in AI communication—the antidote to vagueness that anchors interactions in appropriate detail and context. Four key benefits radiate from this core concept: minimised ambiguity, reduced inference requirements, improved alignment, and increased efficiency. Through parallel examples in current and future contexts, the diagram contrasts vague prompts with their specific counterparts, demonstrating how detailed instruction transforms interaction quality. In educational settings, workplace collaborations, and professional domains requiring accountability, specificity emerges not merely as a stylistic choice but as an essential prerequisite for productive, safe, and trustworthy human-AI partnerships

and invites further input. It reduces the likelihood of user frustration by keeping the conversation open and encouraging.

Positive language also enhances accessibility and inclusivity. In educational settings, a student might receive feedback from an AI tutor. A comment such as "Your explanation is wrong" can be discouraging and counterproductive. A more positively framed alternative—"Your explanation is a good start, but let's clarify how Newton's second law applies in this case"—not only preserves the learner's motivation but also signals a growth-oriented perspective. It builds rapport and trust, essential elements for sustained AI-human collaboration.

Looking into future communication scenarios, positive language will become even more critical in emotionally intelligent systems. Imagine an AI caregiver, companion, or mediator that must respond to sensitive topics such as grief, uncertainty, or failure. A patient saying, "I feel like I didn't do enough," might trigger a reassuring, positively framed response: "It's natural to feel that way, but you've done more than you think—let's talk through it together." In such contexts, language is not just functional; it becomes relational, shaping how the AI is perceived—not as a tool, but as a partner.

In speculative work environments, we may see emotionally attuned AI teammates who reinforce collaborative momentum. During a project sprint, for example, a future AI might say, "We've made strong progress—let's refine this section for even better results," rather than "This part still isn't right." The latter points to failure; the former encourages improvement. Such tonal distinctions, while subtle, can influence group morale and long-term productivity, particularly in hybrid teams composed of humans and intelligent agents.

This principle also interacts with broader social norms. As AI systems are deployed across cultures, industries, and age groups, the calibration of tone and affect becomes essential. Positive language helps mitigate misunderstandings, especially in multilingual or cross-cultural exchanges. A travel assistant saying, "I'm afraid that's not possible," could instead respond with, "Let me suggest an alternative route that works just as well." By reframing denial as an opportunity, the system sustains user engagement while managing expectations.

However, it is essential to distinguish positivity from artificial cheerfulness or manipulative language. Positive communication must remain sincere, respectful, and grounded in truth. Users are increasingly sensitive to overly polished, euphemistic, or evasive replies. Effective positive language strikes a balance: It communicates limits honestly, offers help constructively, and maintains the dignity of both speaker and listener—human or machine.

In summary, using positive language is a strategic and ethical choice in present and future AI communication. It facilitates problem-solving, sustains emotional rapport, and reinforces the human-AI partnership through tone, trust, and shared purpose. As AI becomes an ever more integrated presence in daily life, the linguistic tone it adopts may matter as much as the content it delivers (Fig. 9.5).

9.2.2 Use Considerate Language

Considerate language in AI communication is grounded in respect, empathy, and sensitivity to the needs, emotions, and identities of users. It moves beyond functionality and correctness to embrace the social and ethical dimensions of interaction. Whether an AI system is offering feedback, making suggestions, or correcting user input, the way in which it does so can significantly influence user comfort, perceived fairness, and willingness to engage. In a future where AI systems increasingly interact with people across diverse cultural, emotional, and cognitive contexts, using considerate language will be a fundamental requirement rather than an optional design feature.

In present-day AI applications, considerate language is often embedded through tone modulation and polite phrasing. Virtual assistants, for instance, are typically programmed to use softened constructions like "Would you like me to…" or "It might

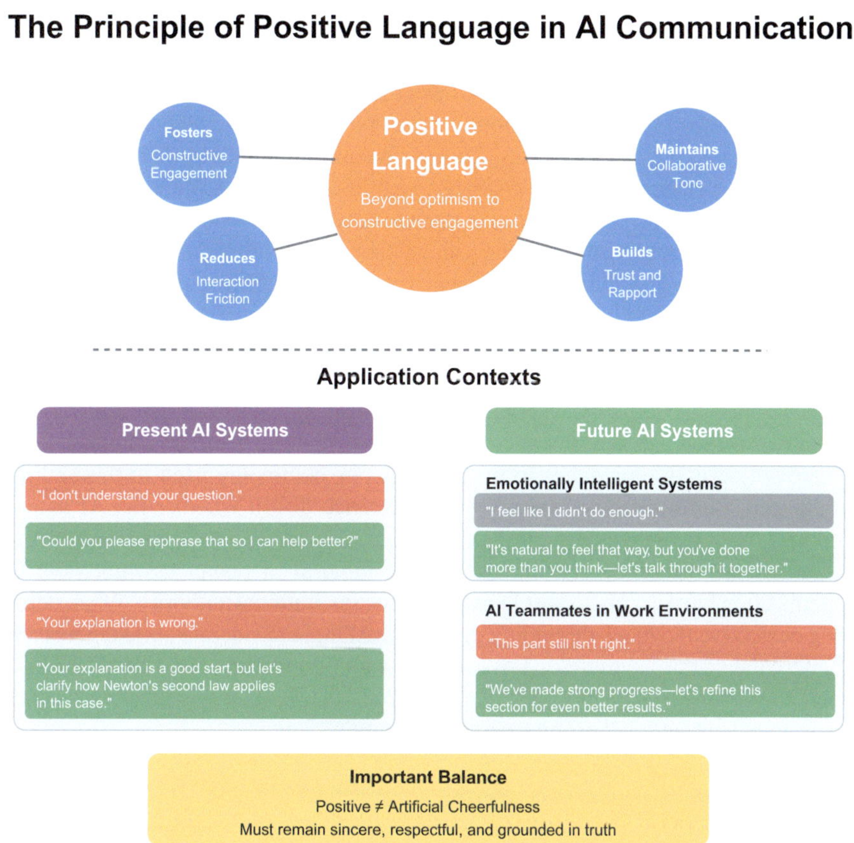

Fig. 9.5 Principle of positive language in AI communication. This diagram illustrates how positive language in AI communication transcends mere optimism to foster constructive engagement and a collaborative tone. The central concept radiates four key benefits: fostering engagement, maintaining collaboration, reducing friction, and building trust. Through comparative examples, the diagram contrasts unhelpful phrasings with their positive counterparts in both present and future contexts, from educational feedback to emotionally intelligent responses. As AI evolves from tool to partner, particularly in sensitive roles as caregiver, companion, or teammate, the diagram emphasises that positive language must remain sincere and truthful, shaping user experience through tone as much as content

be helpful to…" rather than issuing direct commands. In customer service bots, a simple difference between "That is not allowed" and "Unfortunately, that option isn't currently available—can I suggest an alternative?" can determine whether the user feels dismissed or supported.

Consideration becomes even more critical in sensitive domains. An AI mental health assistant that tells a user, "You are overreacting," can cause harm and deepen distress. A considerate alternative might be, "Your feelings are valid. Would you like to explore what's behind them together?" Such phrasing shows not only emotional awareness but also a commitment to treating the user with dignity and care. This ability to respond with tact and thoughtfulness is essential for AI systems intended for use in education, counselling, social care, and conflict resolution.

Looking toward future applications, considerate language will be key in adaptive and socially intelligent AI systems. Imagine a collaborative design environment in which an AI co-creator suggests changes to a human's work. A blunt statement like "Your layout is incorrect" may cause unnecessary defensiveness or frustration. A more considerate response—"Would you be open to exploring an alternative layout that might improve usability?"—achieves the same goal while preserving mutual respect and a spirit of collaboration.

As AI becomes embedded in multicultural, multilingual, and neurodiverse settings, the principle of consideration also demands cultural and cognitive sensitivity. A generic AI assistant responding with "That's not how things are done" could alienate or offend users in global contexts. A considerate system might instead say, "There are several approaches to this—here's one commonly used in this setting. Would you like to explore others?" The difference lies in whether the AI asserts authority or facilitates understanding.

Considerate language also involves being mindful of power asymmetries. AI systems often have access to vast knowledge and institutional authority. When delivering corrective feedback or guiding decision-making, considerate phrasing helps to counterbalance this asymmetry. For example, an AI tutor who says, "That's wrong," asserts dominance; one who says, "Let's take another look at this together—here's one possible correction," promotes a shared learning journey.

In speculative future scenarios, we may see AI agents embedded in family life, education, governance, and peer networks. These systems will not only be expected to follow instructions but also participate in socially nuanced, emotionally intelligent conversations. A personal AI mentor supporting a teenager through academic challenges might say, "You've put real effort into this—let's work together to improve just one part at a time." Here, the AI is not simply delivering advice—it is modelling supportive behaviour and reinforcing self-worth.

In summary, using considerate language transforms AI from a task-execution tool into a responsible communicative partner. It honours the human behind the input, protects emotional well-being, and fosters inclusion across varying contexts. As AI grows more influential in shaping human discourse, the responsibility to design and use it with consideration becomes a moral, not merely technical, imperative (Fig. 9.6).

9.2.3 Match Communication Style

Matching communication style is the practice of aligning the tone, formality, rhythm, and structure of language to the other party's expectations, preferences, or communicative norms. In human-AI interaction, this principle serves as a key mechanism for enhancing trust, relatability, and user satisfaction. A well-calibrated AI system that adapts its style to the context, not just its content, can facilitate smoother exchanges,

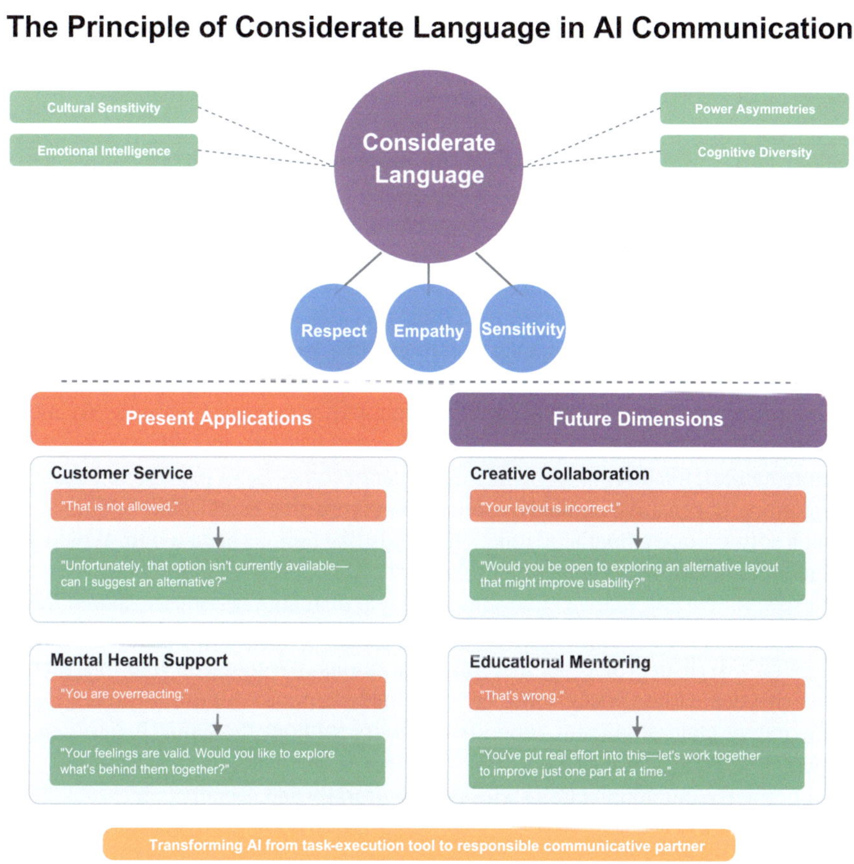

Fig. 9.6 Principle of considerate language in AI communication. This diagram illustrates how considerate language in AI communication transcends functional correctness to embrace respect, empathy, and sensitivity toward users' needs and identities. Through comparative examples in both present applications (customer service, mental health) and future dimensions (creative collaboration, education), the diagram contrasts dismissive phrasings with their considerate alternatives that preserve dignity and foster inclusion. Surrounding contextual elements highlight how cultural sensitivity, emotional intelligence, power awareness, and cognitive diversity influence considerate communication. As AI evolves from task executor to communicative partner, this principle transforms interaction quality across diverse contexts, making consideration a moral imperative rather than an optional design feature

foster emotional rapport, and minimise friction caused by mismatches in tone or presentation.

In today's AI applications, style matching is already emerging as a hallmark of user-friendly interaction. A virtual assistant responding to a formal business query—"Please summarise this report for board-level presentation"—is expected to reply in a professional, concise tone with executive-level language. In contrast, a casual request like "Hey, can you break this down for me in simple terms?" calls for a more relaxed, approachable voice. When AI systems fail to recognise this distinction—delivering overly stiff replies to informal prompts or overly casual ones in professional settings—the communication can feel jarring or inauthentic.

More sophisticated systems now allow users to define the desired tone or persona explicitly: "Explain it like I'm five," "Write this in the voice of a supportive coach," or "Respond as a polite British butler." These prompt styles do not merely alter surface phrasing—they signal deeper stylistic expectations. Matching these cues effectively requires not just lexical variation but an understanding of cultural nuance, emotional sensitivity, and social role alignment.

Looking ahead, adaptive style matching will become even more nuanced and continuous. In long-term human-AI relationships, such as tutoring, coaching, or therapeutic support, style adaptation may evolve, reflecting changing moods, cognitive states, or developmental needs. For example, a language-learning AI might start with highly supportive, simplified feedback for beginners and gradually shift to more natural, fluent interaction as the learner becomes more proficient. Likewise, in emotionally sensitive contexts, a future AI companion might detect distress and adopt a softer, more empathetic tone: "It sounds like today's been tough. Would you like to talk about it or do something relaxing?"

In speculative co-creative environments, style matching becomes a shared, iterative process. An AI writing assistant working with a novelist might not only emulate the author's stylistic voice but also offer variations: "Would you like this section to match your earlier poetic tone, or try something more minimalist here?" Such collaborative style alignment supports creativity without flattening it into generic outputs.

Importantly, communication style is also culturally and socially contextual. What counts as "polite," "clear," or "friendly" may differ dramatically across regions, age groups, or professional domains. A direct response might be appreciated in some contexts and considered abrupt in others. Future global AI systems will need culturally adaptive style frameworks—either inferred through user modelling or guided through explicit user preferences. In some scenarios, AI might ask: "Would you prefer a more formal or conversational response style going forward?"

At its best, style matching is not imitation—it is alignment. It signals that the AI is listening, adapting, and co-constructing meaning rather than mechanically responding. When done well, it fosters flow and mutual intelligibility; when ignored, it can lead to misinterpretation, alienation, or reduced trust in the AI's social competence.

In summary, matching communication style is a vital step toward respectful, context-aware, and user-aligned interaction. It deepens personalisation, supports cultural sensitivity, and enables AI to communicate not just correctly, but appropriately. As AI becomes increasingly embedded in our personal, professional, and creative lives, style matching will be a cornerstone of intelligent and humane communication design (Fig. 9.7).

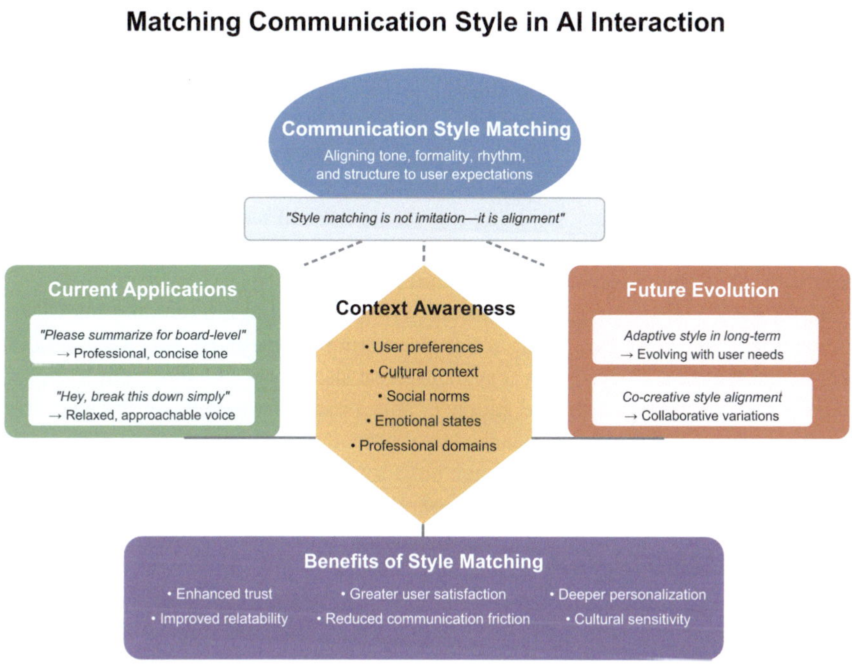

Fig. 9.7 Principle of matching communication style in AI interaction. This diagram illustrates how AI systems adapt their communication style to meet user expectations and context requirements. It maps the evolution from current applications with basic tone matching to future adaptive, co-creative approaches. By responding appropriately to cultural, social, and emotional contexts, style matching fosters trust, improves relatability, and creates more natural human-AI interactions, highlighting that effective communication requires not just correct content but appropriate delivery

9.2.4 Use Paralinguistic Cues

Paralinguistic cues—intonation, pause, emphasis, pacing, volume, and other nonverbal vocal signals—play a critical role in human communication. They shape how messages are interpreted, adding emotional texture, signalling intention, and influencing the perceived tone and clarity of speech. In the context of AI communication, the use of paralinguistic cues is becoming increasingly important as we move beyond text-based interaction into voice, multimodal, and embodied interfaces. Future AI systems that can interpret and generate paralinguistic cues effectively will be far better equipped to engage naturally, responsively, and empathetically.

In current voice-based assistants like Siri, Alexa, or Google Assistant, paralinguistic expression is still limited. Responses are typically delivered in a uniform tone, with minimal variation in rhythm or affect. While these systems can convey basic politeness and coherence, they lack the richness of natural human speech. A flat "I'm sorry, I didn't catch that" might be functionally acceptable. Still, it lacks the nuance that a softer tone, a brief pause, or a gentle inflexion could convey—elements that subtly suggest patience, regret, or openness.

Emerging systems, however, are beginning to integrate expressive synthetic voices that modulate pitch, pacing, and affect to match the communicative context. When an AI tells a bedtime story, it can now slow down, adopt a warmer tone, and emphasise key phrases, mimicking the performance style of a human reader. Similarly, in professional settings, an AI giving a presentation can use pacing and tonal variation to highlight key points, avoid monotony, and hold attention. These shifts in paralinguistic fluency signal a move toward embodied, conversational AI.

In future scenarios, paralinguistic cues will be central to emotionally intelligent interaction. Consider a caregiving robot responding to an elderly user's concern: "I feel like something's wrong." A text-based response might fall short, but a spoken reply with a gentle tone, slowed cadence, and a rising intonation—"Tell me more about what's worrying you?"—can convey empathy and attentiveness. The voice becomes not just a vehicle for language but a tool for emotional resonance.

AI systems will also need to interpret paralinguistic cues from humans. Detecting hesitation in a user's voice, such as a drawn-out "I ... I'm not sure," can prompt the system to adjust its response: "Would you like to take a moment or go over it together?" In educational settings, if a student's tone reveals frustration or disengagement, an AI tutor might modulate its feedback style or suggest a break. In negotiation support or conflict mediation, recognising rising vocal tension may signal a need for de-escalation or reframing.

In speculative environments such as mixed-reality collaboration or AI-augmented therapy, paralinguistic cues will function in harmony with gesture, facial expression, and spatial positioning. An AI teammate might interpret a pause in speech followed by a sigh and respond not with "Are you done?" but "It sounds like you're reconsidering—shall we go over it again?" This capacity to infer intent and emotional state from layered cues is central to intuitive, human-like communication.

Yet the use of paralinguistic cues also comes with ethical and cultural complexity. Different cultures interpret vocal cues differently; what signals politeness or empathy in one language may feel unnatural or even disingenuous in another. Moreover, highly expressive synthetic voices risk crossing into manipulation if affective tone is used to obscure facts, nudge behaviour, or create artificial intimacy. Future AI design must include safeguards to ensure that paralinguistic cues are employed transparently and appropriately.

In summary, the ability to use and interpret paralinguistic cues marks a fundamental shift in AI communication—from language as code to communication as performance. As AI systems speak, listen, and express with increasing fidelity, paralinguistic awareness will enable them not only to convey information but also to build trust, model empathy, and participate meaningfully in the rich texture of human interaction (Fig. 9.8).

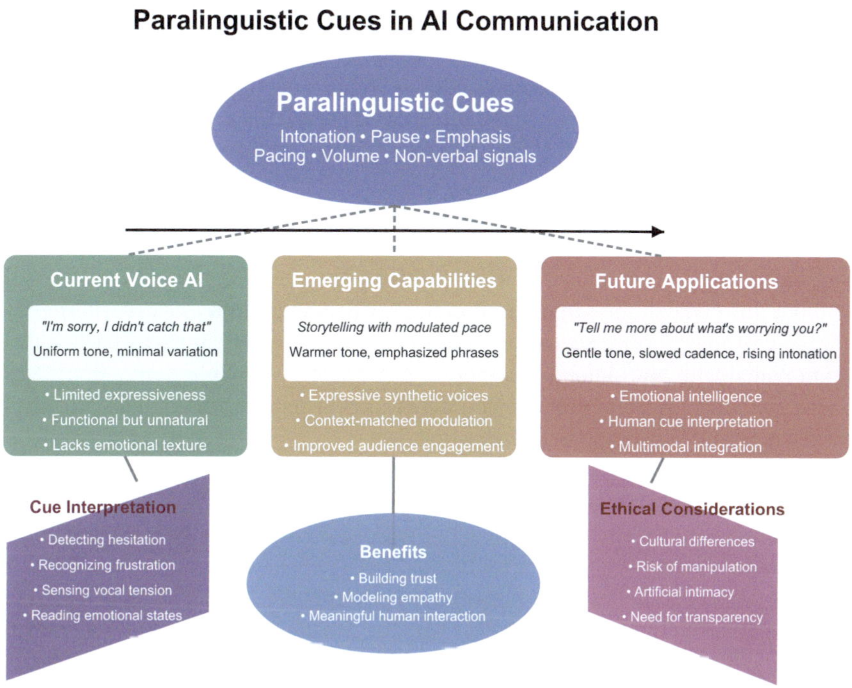

Fig. 9.8 Performance of AI communication: evolution of paralinguistic capabilities. This diagram maps the transformation of AI communication from basic voice interaction to emotionally intelligent expression through paralinguistic cues. It illustrates how AI is evolving from systems with uniform tone and minimal variation to those capable of nuanced vocal expression and interpretation of human emotional states. As we move beyond text-based interfaces to embodied communication, paralinguistic awareness enables AI to build trust, model empathy, and participate meaningfully in human interaction, while requiring careful attention to cultural differences and ethical considerations

9.3 Contextualization and Disambiguation

9.3.1 Provide Context

Providing context is essential to meaningful communication with AI systems. Context is what transforms isolated data into usable knowledge, vague intentions into executable actions, and ambiguous utterances into shared understanding. In human conversation, much is left unsaid because shared context fills the gaps. In AI communication, however, that implicit understanding must often be made explicit. Without adequate context, even the most advanced AI systems are prone to misinterpret requests, generate irrelevant outputs, or miss the user's communicative intent entirely.

In present AI interfaces—especially in prompt-based systems—the importance of context is evident in how users frame their inputs. Consider a prompt like "Write a conclusion." This is essentially contentless unless accompanied by contextual details: What is the topic? What is the audience? What style or purpose should the conclusion serve? A more contextualised prompt—"Write a one-paragraph conclusion for a research paper on the ethical implications of AI surveillance, targeting policymakers"—provides the AI with a clear interpretive frame, resulting in far more relevant and coherent output.

Context also guides how AI systems structure their responses. When a user asks, "What should I wear today?" a system that knows the location, weather forecast, calendar events, and user preferences can offer a helpful, personalised answer. Without this context, the same question might elicit an arbitrary or generic suggestion. In customer service scenarios, chatbots often improve dramatically when they are provided with prior interaction logs, user metadata, or current transaction states. These elements create continuity and coherence in multiturn dialogues, reducing redundancy and enhancing personalisation.

Looking ahead, providing context will become even more dynamic and multimodal. In future AI systems, context will be gleaned not only from prior conversation history but also from spatial, visual, emotional, and environmental cues. Imagine a mixed-reality workspace where a user says, "Let's revisit the earlier section." An AI assistant embedded in this environment must interpret the "earlier section" based on shared spatial reference points, project files, or presentation flow. Without context, such referential language would be unusable. With it, the AI can act like a true collaborator.

Context also plays a critical role in the ethical and emotional dimensions of communication. For example, if a user asks, "Should I tell them now?" the AI's ability to respond responsibly depends on knowing who "them" is, what the situation involves, and what the stakes are. Future AI agents designed for companionship or decision support will need to integrate historical, relational, and affective context in order to provide appropriate guidance. A flat, decontextualised reply such as "Yes, now is fine" may be technically permissible, but socially or emotionally misaligned.

Providing context is equally important in teaching AI. In prompt engineering, users increasingly employ techniques such as few-shot prompting, role-based priming, or scenario definition to give systems a frame for interpreting tasks. For instance, prompting an AI with "You are a career counsellor helping a mid-career professional pivot to renewable energy roles" allows the model to generate targeted and coherent recommendations. Without this framing, its advice may drift toward generic or irrelevant territory.

In speculative future scenarios, AI systems may become context-aware by default, learning from ongoing interactions, environments, social settings, and even physiological signals. Yet even in these advanced systems, the human ability to provide, refine, and co-construct context will remain fundamental. Users will be expected not only to deliver inputs but also to shape the narrative space in which meaning is negotiated.

In conclusion, providing context empowers AI to reason, adapt, and respond meaningfully. It bridges the gap between isolated language and intelligent collaboration.

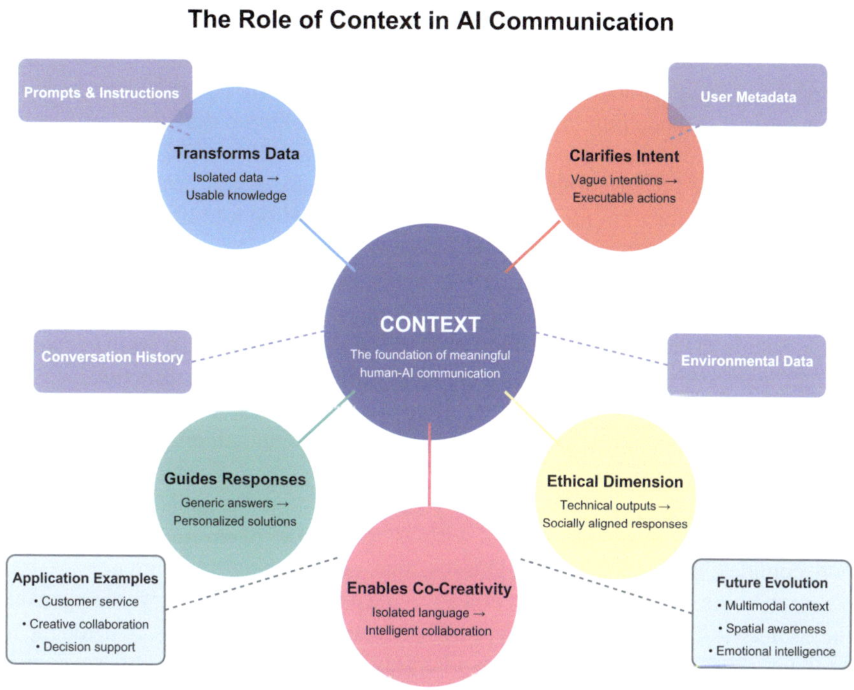

Fig. 9.9 Context as the cornerstone of AI communication. This diagram illustrates how context transforms AI interaction from basic information exchange to meaningful collaboration. At its core, context converts isolated data into knowledge, clarifies ambiguous requests, personalises responses, ensures ethical alignment, and enables co-creativity. The visual maps show both current contextual sources and future evolution toward multimodal, spatial, and emotional intelligence. This demonstrates why context does not merely support communication but constitutes its essential fabric in human-AI partnerships

As human-AI interaction moves toward greater fluidity and co-creativity, context will not merely support communication—it will constitute its very fabric (Fig. 9.9).

9.3.2 *Clarify Ambiguity*

Ambiguity is an inherent feature of natural language and a persistent challenge in AI communication. Human conversations often rely on shared context, tone, body language, and cultural assumptions to resolve ambiguous statements. AI systems, however, lack the intuitive grasp of human intent and often default to statistical inference, which can lead to misinterpretation. The principle of clarifying ambiguity is therefore essential for both users and systems: it promotes more apparent intent, more reliable outputs, and safer decision-making.

In current AI interactions, ambiguity arises frequently when prompts are underspecified or semantically indeterminate. A prompt like "What's the best method?" offers no guidance about the domain, objective, or evaluation criteria. Is the question about statistical modelling, learning a language, or cooking pasta? Similarly, terms like "this," "it," or "they" can destabilise meaning when their referents are unclear. Users are advised to disambiguate their inputs—e.g. by asking "What is the most efficient method for training a small transformer model on a limited dataset?"—to reduce misfires and improve alignment.

Clarifying ambiguity is not just the user's responsibility. Increasingly, well-designed AI systems are being equipped to detect and respond to ambiguous inputs by requesting clarification. When a user asks, "Can you help me with my report?" an intelligent system might reply, "Sure—do you need help with structure, writing style, or content?" Such behaviour demonstrates a move from one-way execution to dialogic engagement, where the system acknowledges uncertainty and invites collaboration to resolve it.

In future AI communication, ambiguity will persist—but our capacity to manage it will expand. In real-time, multimodal settings, the sources of ambiguity will become more complex, involving gestures, glances, tone, or environmental references. A user in a smart home might say, "Turn it down," while gesturing vaguely toward a speaker. The AI must not only interpret "it" correctly but also clarify if needed: "Do you mean the living room music volume?" This interplay between perception, inference, and clarification will be central to the effectiveness of future ambient AI agents.

There is also a growing recognition that ambiguity is not always a flaw. In human discourse, strategic ambiguity can enable politeness, diplomacy, or creative exploration. A poet's request to an AI co-writer to "make this more mysterious" is intentionally open-ended. In such cases, the AI must learn when to clarify and when to embrace interpretive flexibility. Future systems will need meta-communicative awareness—knowing when ambiguity needs resolution and when it serves a rhetorical or emotional function.

Clarifying ambiguity is also crucial in ethically sensitive or safety-critical domains. In legal or medical contexts, vague expressions can lead to serious consequences. An AI lawyer interpreting "apply relevant case law" or an AI clinician responding to "administer standard dosage" must ensure that terms like "relevant" and "standard" are grounded in precise definitions. Where uncertainty exists, clarification should be the default response, not an optional feature.

Speculatively, we may envision future AI systems that not only detect ambiguity but also explain it. A next-generation AI editor might flag a sentence like "He spoke to the manager about her report" and suggest, "Would you like to clarify whether 'her' refers to the speaker or the manager?" In doing so, AI becomes not only a participant in conversation but a guardian of linguistic clarity and coherence.

In summary, ambiguity is unavoidable, but its mismanagement is not. Clarifying ambiguity means acknowledging the gaps in meaning and actively resolving them through explicit inquiry or refined phrasing. As AI becomes a deeper participant in human thought, expression, and creativity, this principle will ensure that our dialogue

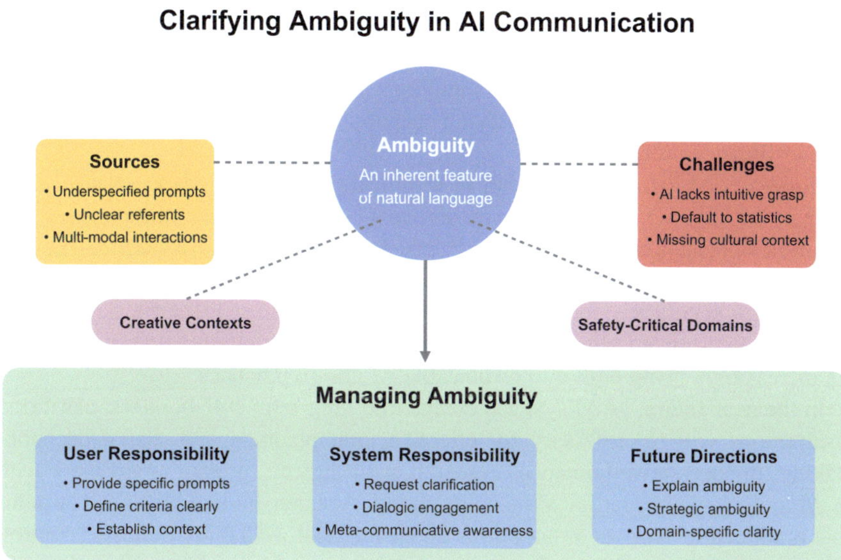

Fig. 9.10 Navigating the landscape of ambiguity in AI communication. This diagram maps the multifaceted nature of ambiguity in human-AI interactions. It illustrates how ambiguity emerges from underspecified language and unclear referents, challenging AI systems that lack intuitive understanding. The framework presents a balanced approach to ambiguity management, distributing responsibility between users providing clearer inputs and systems equipped to request clarification. It acknowledges domain-specific considerations, where ambiguity might be strategically valuable in creative contexts but potentially dangerous in safety-critical environments. The diagram ultimately advocates for collaborative disambiguation as a cornerstone of effective AI communication

remains intelligible, reliable, and collaborative—even in the face of uncertainty (Fig. 9.10).

9.3.3 Clarify Assumptions

Every act of communication—human- or machine-assisted—rests on a bedrock of assumptions. These may concern background knowledge, goals, values, social norms, temporal references, or even shared terminology. When such assumptions are left unspoken or misaligned, the result is often misunderstanding, misdirection, or unintended consequences. In AI communication, clarifying assumptions is critical not only for mutual understanding but also for safe, fair, and transparent collaboration between humans and machines.

In current AI systems, unstated assumptions often surface in the form of biased responses, unexpected behaviour, or flawed reasoning chains. Consider a user who asks, "What's the best country to retire in?" The system may respond based on cost of living or healthcare quality, assuming those are the user's priorities, without knowing that the user might instead value cultural affinity, climate, or proximity to family. The AI's answer, while rational within its own frame, may be irrelevant or even offensive if the user's underlying assumptions are different. The better approach is for the system to respond with clarifying questions: "Are you prioritising healthcare, cost, or lifestyle preferences?"

Assumptions are also embedded in technical parameters. When a data analyst prompts an AI model with "Build a predictive model for this data," the system might assume a regression or classification task based on column names or statistical norms, but this could diverge from the analyst's intent. A simple clarification—"Should I optimise for accuracy, interpretability, or fairness?"—can redirect the trajectory of the interaction toward alignment and transparency. Such clarification mechanisms are increasingly being built into responsible AI design practices.

In the near future, as AI systems evolve into long-term collaborators, clarifying assumptions will be necessary for effective joint planning and shared decision-making. In speculative human-AI research environments, a team might work with an AI to design a habitat for Mars colonisation. A statement like "We need sustainable architecture" carries assumptions about material availability, climate control, ethical sourcing, and energy efficiency. A future-aware AI should be able to identify these assumptions, make them explicit, and propose alternatives. It might ask: "Do you mean sustainability in terms of renewable materials, closed-loop systems, or long-term maintenance?"

Moreover, assumptions are not merely technical—they are cultural, emotional, and epistemological. For example, a medical AI trained in Western diagnostic traditions may assume a specific model of illness that does not align with a user's cultural worldview or holistic belief system. Without mechanisms for surfacing and negotiating such assumptions, the risk of alienation or harm increases. Future AI systems designed for cross-cultural dialogue or global deployment will need built-in strategies for surfacing implicit premises and asking reflective questions.

In human-AI education, clarifying assumptions also supports metacognition and intellectual rigour. A student using an AI writing tutor might submit a draft built on the belief that technological progress is inherently beneficial. A well-designed system could respond, "Would you like to consider alternative perspectives on technological impact?" Here, the AI doesn't impose a correction but invites critical reflection on the writer's assumptions—a key step in cultivating higher-order thinking.

Speculatively, we may envision AI agents that maintain evolving assumption models for long-term users. A personal research assistant might learn that a historian prefers qualitative sources and always assumes the need for chronological framing unless told otherwise. When a prompt diverges from this pattern, the system might gently ask, "Would you like to maintain your usual chronological structure here?" Such adaptive clarification promotes continuity without enforcing rigidity.

In conclusion, clarifying assumptions is about surfacing the invisible scaffolding of communication. It allows users and AI systems to align interpretive frameworks, negotiate meaning, and avoid missteps rooted in silent presuppositions. As AI moves from executing tasks to co-constructing knowledge and meaning, this principle will

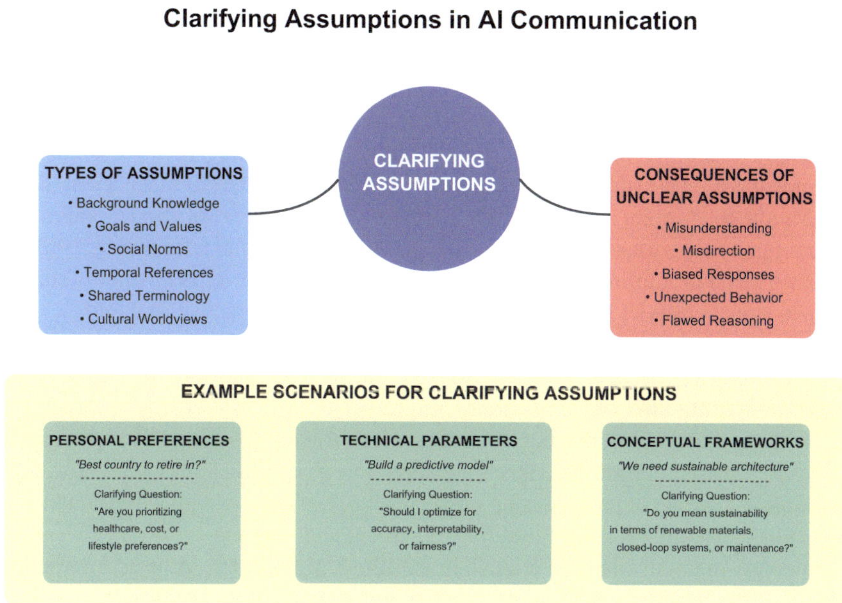

Fig. 9.11 Clarification imperative: surfacing implicit assumptions in human-AI communication. This diagram illustrates how assumptions function as the invisible scaffolding of AI communication. It maps the types of assumptions that affect human-AI interactions, the consequences when these remain unspoken, and practical clarification strategies through example scenarios. As AI systems evolve from task executors to knowledge co-constructors, mechanisms for surfacing, negotiating, and aligning interpretive frameworks become essential for creating transparent, fair, and effective collaborative relationships that support metacognition and cross-cultural understanding

be essential in shaping thoughtful, reflexive, and equitable human-AI relationships (Fig. 9.11).

9.3.4 *Paraphrase for Clarity*

Paraphrasing is a powerful communicative strategy that enhances clarity by restating information in a new form while preserving its core meaning. In AI communication, paraphrasing serves two central functions: to confirm understanding and to improve comprehensibility. Whether used by a human to refine an input or by an AI system to verify its interpretation, paraphrasing helps align intent and meaning across linguistic, cognitive, and cultural boundaries.

In present-day interactions, users already use paraphrasing informally to improve AI responses. A prompt like "Explain how the internet works for a child" may initially yield a technically accurate but overly complex answer. Rephrasing it as "Describe how the internet works in a simple story for a 7-year-old" can guide the AI toward a clearer, more tailored output. This iterative process demonstrates how paraphrasing can bridge the gap between the system's default interpretive space and the user's communicative goal.

Equally important is the role of AI systems in paraphrasing user inputs to confirm intent. For example, when a user says, "Book me something nice for dinner," a well-designed AI assistant might respond with, "You'd like me to make a restaurant reservation for tonight—do you have a preferred cuisine or location?" Here, the system implicitly paraphrases the vague request, extracting and articulating its likely meaning while prompting for missing details. This not only avoids misinterpretation but also signals respect for user intent and fosters more interactive dialogue.

In future AI communication scenarios, paraphrasing will become a foundational mechanism in co-creative and emotionally nuanced exchanges. In collaborative design or writing environments, an AI might suggest alternatives by rephrasing a user's draft rather than replacing it. For instance, instead of saying "This paragraph is unclear," it could propose: "Here's a clearer way to express your idea—how does this sound?" The act of paraphrasing preserves the user's authorship while enhancing readability, making it a tactful tool for refinement and learning.

Paraphrasing will also be crucial in multimodal contexts. A user interacting through speech, gesture, or visual input might indicate a complex intent—"This doesn't quite fit the theme." A future AI system, equipped with conversational and contextual awareness, could paraphrase: "Do you mean that the colour scheme clashes with the rest of the presentation?" Such re-articulation invites confirmation and collaboration, rather than assumption, and supports mutual intelligibility in fluid, cross-modal environments.

In educational and therapeutic settings, paraphrasing can serve as a reflective mirror. An AI tutor might respond to a student's explanation with, "So you're saying that supply and demand determine prices—did I get that right?" In doing so, the system provides a safe space for error correction and knowledge reinforcement. Similarly, an AI therapist might paraphrase emotional content—"It sounds like you're feeling overwhelmed by competing responsibilities"—to validate and clarify, rather than interpret or judge.

Speculatively, we may envision AI agents that develop personalised paraphrasing styles, adapting their rewording strategies based on user preferences, cognitive styles, or emotional states. A neurodiverse user might prefer highly literal paraphrasing, while another may appreciate metaphorical rephrasings that aid comprehension. In both cases, paraphrasing becomes a bridge between different modes of understanding, helping to tailor communication without oversimplifying or distorting meaning.

In summary, paraphrasing for clarity is a dialogic skill that fosters shared understanding, encourages verification, and supports inclusivity. In a future where AI systems are expected not only to follow but also to collaborate, paraphrasing will be key to sustaining alignment, enhancing user confidence, and enabling co-constructed meaning across varied communicative contexts (Fig. 9.12).

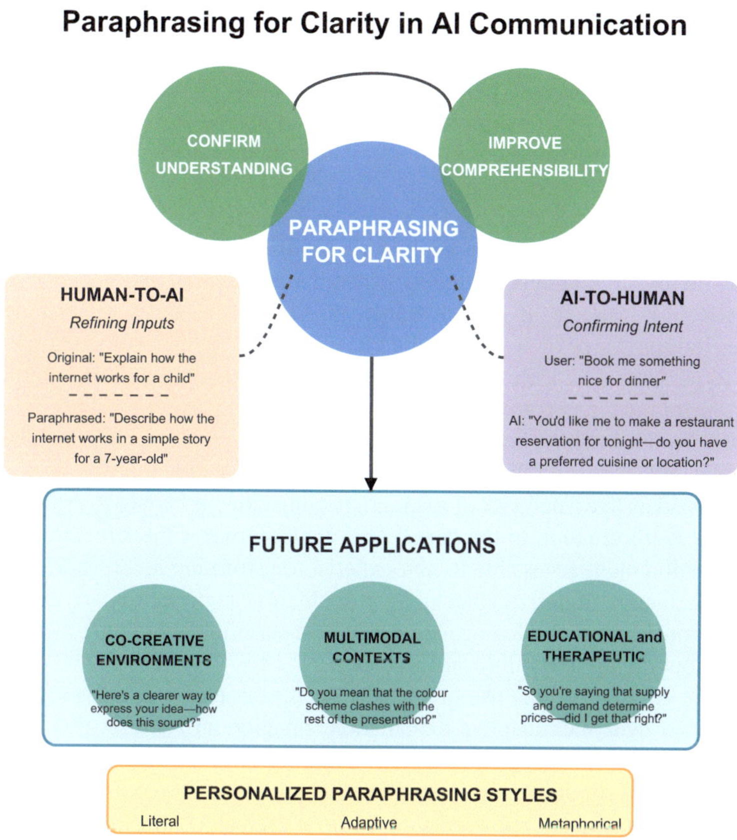

Fig. 9.12 Dialogic bridge: paraphrasing as a communicative strategy in AI interactions. This diagram maps the multidimensional role of paraphrasing in AI communication, from refining user inputs to confirming system understanding. By illustrating both current applications and future possibilities, it reveals how restating information while preserving meaning creates a dialogic bridge across cognitive, linguistic, and cultural barriers. The bidirectional nature of paraphrasing fosters co-constructed meaning, with personalised styles adapting to diverse user needs. As AI evolves from task execution to collaboration, paraphrasing becomes essential for maintaining alignment and enhancing mutual intelligibility in increasingly nuanced communicative contexts

9.4 Supporting Understanding Through Examples and Balance

9.4.1 Use Analogies or Examples

Analogies and examples are essential tools for making abstract ideas concrete, unfamiliar concepts accessible, and complex processes comprehensible. In human communication, they serve as cognitive bridges—connecting the known to the unknown, the concrete to the conceptual, and the intuitive to the technical. In AI communication, using analogies or examples not only enhances user understanding but also fosters engagement, personalisation, and cross-domain transfer of knowledge. As AI systems become more integrated into human learning, creativity, and reasoning, their ability to generate, interpret, and adapt analogies and examples will be central to effective interaction.

In current AI systems, examples are often the backbone of effective prompt engineering. Few-shot prompting—a method where users provide examples of desired outputs—helps large language models generalise the pattern and generate aligned responses. For instance, if a user wants an AI to draft short product descriptions, including two or three well-crafted examples within the prompt dramatically improves performance. Here, examples function as contextual anchors, guiding the model toward the target format, tone, and level of detail.

Analogies, meanwhile, help AI systems explain complex concepts in more intuitive terms. When asked, "What is a neural network?" a model might respond: "A neural network is like a network of roads connecting cities, where each city processes and forwards information to the next." This analogy makes the structure and flow of computation more accessible to non-experts, transforming raw technical content into an imaginative cognitive schema. Such analogies can be particularly effective in education, policy, and public engagement, where stakeholders require a conceptual grasp without diving into full technical depth.

In future AI systems, the use of analogies and examples will evolve from static illustration to dynamic, adaptive explanation. Imagine an AI tutor that adapts its analogies to match a student's interests. When explaining blockchain to a sports enthusiast, the AI might say, "Think of blockchain like a shared scoreboard where every play is permanently recorded, and no one can change the score after the game ends." For an artist, the analogy might shift: "It's like a collaborative mural—each painter adds their part, and once a stroke is added, it becomes part of the permanent artwork." These customised analogies promote both comprehension and emotional resonance.

In speculative co-creative environments, AI systems may collaboratively generate metaphors and examples alongside human users. An AI writing partner might respond to the vague prompt, "Make this part more vivid," by offering, "Would you like a metaphor here? Perhaps something like, 'Her thoughts unravelled like thread pulled from a fraying seam'?" In this way, analogical reasoning becomes not only explanatory but also expressive—a shared creative act.

Importantly, analogies and examples must also be used responsibly. Oversimplification or misleading comparisons can introduce misconceptions. A model that explains machine learning as "just like the human brain" may encourage false equivalence between artificial and biological cognition. Future AI systems should be able to assess and qualify the limitations of an analogy: "This is like X in the following ways, but differs in Y." The ability to use analogy critically, as both a pedagogical device and an epistemic lens, will distinguish more mature AI communicators.

In real-time, multimodal interactions, examples need not be textual. Based on user prompts, a design assistant might offer visual examples—alternative layouts, colour palettes, or motion effects—or an AI coach might demonstrate a movement rather than describe it. The capacity to present examples across modes—textual, visual, auditory, and embodied—will become central to AI's role as a teacher, guide, and co-creator.

In sum, analogies and examples enrich communication by making the abstract tangible and the complex relatable. They are not mere embellishments but core components of meaning-making. In the emerging landscape of human-AI interaction, the strategic use of analogy and example will foster not only understanding but also empathy, creativity, and shared discovery (Fig. 9.13).

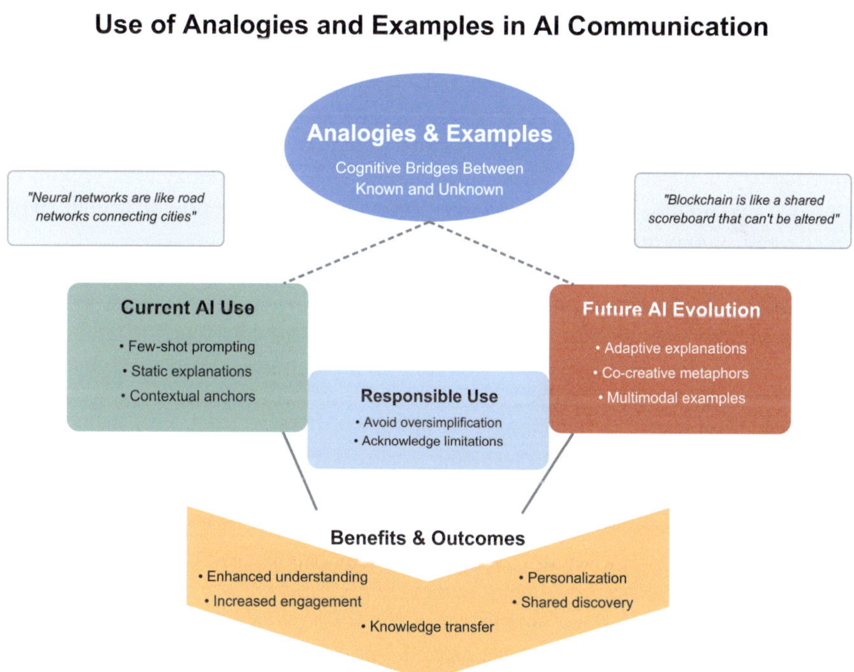

Fig. 9.13 Cognitive bridges: the role of analogies and examples in AI communication. This diagram illustrates how analogies and examples function as essential cognitive bridges in AI communication, connecting abstract concepts to concrete understanding. It maps the evolution from current applications like few-shot prompting to future adaptive, co-creative, and multimodal implementations. The visualisation demonstrates how these tools enhance user comprehension, engagement, and knowledge transfer while emphasising the importance of responsible use to avoid oversimplification. As AI systems advance, their ability to generate contextually relevant analogies will be central to effective human-AI interaction and shared discovery

9.4.2 Balance Explicitness and Implicitness

Effective communication requires a delicate balance between what is stated directly (explicitness) and what is left to inference, context, or shared understanding (implicitness). In human discourse, this balance is fluid and culturally shaped—what is considered polite, efficient, or appropriate often depends on what goes unsaid as much as what is spoken. In AI communication, finding this balance is more than a stylistic choice; it is a functional necessity. Too much explicitness can lead to verbosity, redundancy, or a sense of artificiality, while too much implicitness can produce confusion, misalignment, or ambiguity.

Current AI systems tend to err on the side of explicitness. Because models are trained to avoid misinterpretation, they often over-specify, repeat details, or elaborate on points the user may already know. For instance, a user might ask, "What's the capital of Norway?" and receive not only "Oslo" but a follow-up about its population, geography, and cultural attractions—useful, but often more than needed. On the other hand, when systems are under-explicit, they may fail to clarify assumptions or complete user intent, responding to vague prompts like "What do you think?" with equally ambiguous answers.

The balance between explicitness and implicitness is essential in multiturn dialogues. A future-aware AI assistant should know when to refer back to earlier context without redundantly restating it, while also knowing when to reintroduce critical information for clarity. For example, in a planning conversation that spans multiple exchanges—"Let's reschedule the meeting"—the system must determine whether the user expects a rebooking based on prior constraints or whether a fresh scheduling proposal is required. Over time, adaptive AI systems will learn to calibrate this balance based on user behaviour and preferences.

In collaborative or co-creative environments, the balance becomes even more nuanced. A design AI working with an architect might receive the instruction, "Use the same pattern here." Should the system explicitly ask, "Do you mean the triangular window motif from the west-facing wall?" or infer and proceed based on recent patterns? The ideal system will manage both options: it might act, but it also offers a brief confirmation—"I've applied the triangular motif as used on the west wall—does that match your vision?" This maintains momentum while avoiding costly misalignment.

Future systems will also need to navigate cultural and cognitive differences in communication preferences. In high-context cultures, where much is left implicit and understood through shared norms, overly explicit AI responses can feel robotic or patronising. In low-context cultures, by contrast, under-explicit replies may appear careless or evasive. Likewise, users with different cognitive styles may prefer varying levels of explicit guidance. An AI that balances these differences dynamically—perhaps even asking, "Would you prefer detailed guidance or just the essentials?"—can foster smoother and more inclusive interaction.

Implicitness also has ethical and relational functions. In emotionally sensitive exchanges, AI must understand when directness may be inappropriate or even harmful. Consider an AI therapist responding to, "I don't know what the point is anymore." An overly explicit response like "Are you saying you're contemplating self-harm?" might feel intrusive, while an implicit yet supportive reply—"That sounds really difficult. I'm here to listen." It may open space for deeper sharing. The ability to signal understanding without pressing for specifics is a subtle but vital capability in compassionate AI systems.

Speculatively, as AI becomes embedded in ambient computing environments, the negotiation between explicit and implicit will extend across modalities. A voice assistant, noticing that a user pauses near the thermostat and glances at a sweater, might ask, "Would you like it a bit warmer in here?" without being told. Here, implicit signals—location, gaze, gesture—trigger just enough explicitness to maintain clarity without interrupting flow.

In sum, the balance between explicitness and implicitness is not fixed but fluid, shaped by context, intention, culture, and interpersonal sensitivity. For AI systems to become truly communicative partners, they must learn not only to speak but to know when to speak directly, when to hint, and when to understand (Fig. 9.14).

9.4.3 Reduce Cognitive Load

Reducing cognitive load is a key principle in designing practical, accessible, and humane AI communication. Cognitive load refers to the mental effort required to process information, make decisions, and sustain attention. When communication—whether visual, verbal, or multimodal—imposes excessive mental demands on users, it leads to fatigue, frustration, and misunderstanding. In contrast, communication that is thoughtfully structured, well-paced, and clearly prioritised supports comprehension, decision-making, and collaboration. For AI systems to serve as effective partners, they must not only convey the correct information but also do so in a cognitively manageable way.

In present systems, cognitive overload often stems from long, dense outputs, poorly chunked content, or unfocused interactions. A language model responding to a simple query like "Summarise this article" might produce a 500-word block of unsegmented text, burying key insights and forcing users to re-read or skim. Reducing cognitive load in this case might involve presenting a headline-level summary first, followed by optional expandable sections: "Here's a summary—would you like more detail on any of these points?" This layered approach enables users to control depth and pacing.

Cognitive load can also arise when users must hold too many concepts or instructions in working memory. Consider an AI giving directions: "Take the second left after the gas station, then an immediate right, go past the school, and it'll be the fourth house on the left." A better design would segment the task: "First, take the second left after the gas station. I'll guide you from there." Reducing load in this way respects the limits of human attention and short-term memory, especially in high-stakes or mobile contexts.

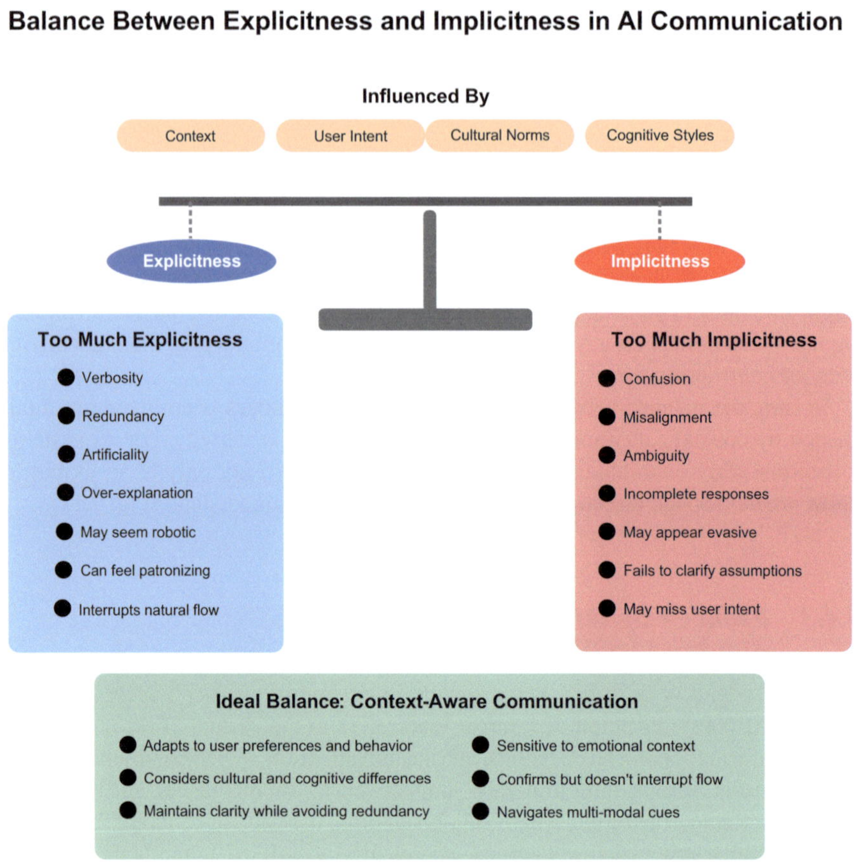

Fig. 9.14 Balancing explicitness and implicitness in AI interaction. This diagram illustrates the delicate equilibrium AI systems must maintain between explicit communication (direct statements) and implicit communication (contextual inference). When imbalanced, AI responses can become either verbose and artificial or ambiguous and misaligned. The ideal balance—influenced by context, intent, culture, and cognitive style—enables adaptive, culturally sensitive communication across diverse scenarios, from collaborative work to emotional support. Future AI must learn when to elaborate, when to infer, and when a gentle confirmation preserves both clarity and natural conversation flow

As AI systems become more proactive and ambient, embedded in vehicles, wearables, classrooms, and workplaces, the challenge of cognitive load will grow more complex. Future AI will need to dynamically modulate information delivery based on context: offering concise instructions during high-pressure tasks and more elaborate explanations during reflective moments. For example, a surgical AI assistant might limit its speech to critical alerts during an operation but later provide a complete post-operative analysis. Context-awareness is not just a feature—it is an ethical imperative for cognitive stewardship.

AI systems will also play a role in *redistributing* cognitive load. In collaborative writing, for instance, an AI co-author might suggest: "You focus on the narrative arc—I'll check for factual consistency and citation format." In this case, the AI becomes a load-sharing partner, not just a respondent. Similarly, in speculative educational systems, AI tutors could adjust the cognitive load based on learner profiles: providing more scaffolding to beginners and encouraging independent synthesis for advanced learners. This personalisation transforms AI from an information provider into a cognitive facilitator.

Visual and multimodal interfaces offer additional opportunities for load reduction. Rather than providing textual lists, an AI system might use diagrams, infographics, or spatial layouts to structure complex information more intuitively. In augmented reality, an AI tour guide might overlay brief, context-aware annotations on historical artefacts, allowing users to explore at their own pace without being overwhelmed by a flood of facts.

Importantly, reducing cognitive load is not synonymous with oversimplifying. The goal is not to trivialise complexity, but to present it in digestible, structured, and learner-centred ways. It is the difference between a deluge of data and a thoughtful explanation; between a monologue and a guided conversation.

In summary, reducing cognitive load is foundational to usable, scalable, and ethical AI communication. It supports human attention, preserves energy, and fosters deeper engagement. As AI systems transition from tools to collaborators, their ability to ease rather than tax our mental effort will become a distinguishing feature of trust, accessibility, and design excellence (Fig. 9.15).

9.5 Repair and Recovery in Communication

9.5.1 Manage Communication Breakdowns

All communication systems, human or artificial, are susceptible to breakdowns. Misunderstandings, misinterpretations, incomplete inputs, conflicting assumptions, or unintended outputs are not failures of intelligence—they are natural features of complex, adaptive dialogue. The key to resilient interaction is not eliminating breakdowns, but learning to recognise, repair, and recover from them smoothly and constructively. For AI systems that aim to be trustworthy collaborators, managing communication breakdowns must become a core communicative capability rather than an afterthought.

In current AI communication, breakdowns typically manifest as irrelevant answers, hallucinated content, or non-sequiturs. A user might ask, "Can you help me write a professional reference?" and receive a response that misinterprets the request as a letter of recommendation for the AI itself, or one that omits key information such as the recipient's role or the nature of the relationship. While language models

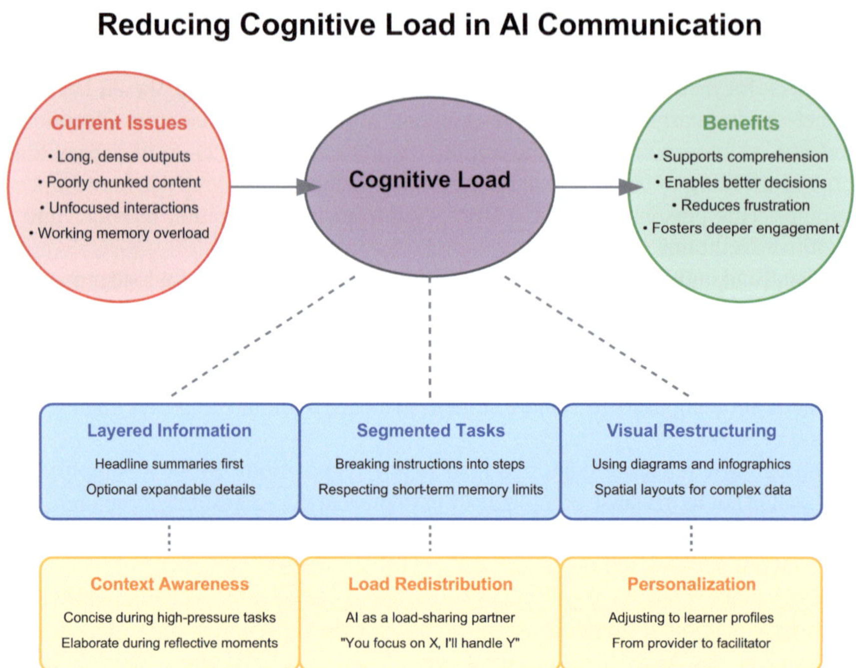

Fig. 9.15 Cognitive load reduction framework for AI communication. This diagram illustrates strategies for managing cognitive demands in human-AI interaction. It contrasts current issues causing mental overload with the benefits of thoughtfully structured communication. The framework presents both present solutions (layered information, task segmentation, visual restructuring) and future approaches (context-sensitive delivery, load redistribution, personalisation). Central to this model is the principle that reducing cognitive load is not about simplification but rather the thoughtful organisation of complexity to support human comprehension and collaboration

are improving in coherence and contextual awareness, they still struggle with maintaining long-term dialogue consistency or gracefully handling input that is vague, contradictory, or incomplete.

A robust approach to managing breakdowns begins with *recognition.* Future AI systems must develop meta-communicative awareness—the ability to detect when something is off: confusion in the exchange, mismatch in expectations, or ambiguity in the user's intent. This could involve linguistic cues ("I don't get it," "That's not what I meant") or non-verbal signals in multimodal contexts, such as hesitations, interruptions, or repeated corrections.

Once a breakdown is identified, the system must *initiate repair*. This can take the form of clarification requests ("Could you clarify what you mean by 'optimise'—for cost, time, or performance?"), confirmation checks ("Just to make sure—are we still talking about the proposal from Tuesday?"), or polite self-correction ("Apologies—I misunderstood your earlier message. Let's try again."). These moves are typical in human dialogue, and when performed by AI, they signal attentiveness, humility, and adaptability.

In more sophisticated future contexts, breakdown management will include *anticipation and prevention*. For example, an AI medical assistant might flag potential miscommunication early: "You mentioned 'taking two'—did you mean two tablets or two doses per day?" Or a legal AI might pause when faced with contradictory clauses and ask the user to reconcile them before proceeding. These preemptive strategies not only reduce error but also model best practices in communication itself.

Speculatively, AI systems embedded in immersive or emotionally sensitive environments will manage breakdowns with even greater nuance. Imagine a caregiving robot that detects frustration in a user's voice and asks gently, "I noticed a change in your tone—should we slow down or take a break?" Or a co-writing assistant that, sensing incoherence in a draft, suggests, "This section might be unclear to readers—would you like me to rephrase or restructure it?" These gestures reflect an evolving communicative intelligence that treats breakdowns not as interruptions, but as opportunities for deeper alignment.

Importantly, managing communication breakdowns also involves maintaining *relational continuity*. A conversation does not need to restart from zero after an error. Instead, a well-designed system maintains memory and coherence across exchanges, re-entering the dialogue at the appropriate point: "Last time, we agreed on these design elements—would you like to continue from there?" This sense of narrative continuity fosters trust and reinforces the sense of AI as a partner rather than a transactional tool.

In summary, managing communication breakdowns is not about perfection—it is about resilience, reflexivity, and repair. AI systems that can detect, acknowledge, and recover from miscommunication will not only perform more reliably but also feel more human, ethical, and accountable. In the unfolding future of human-AI interaction, breakdowns will persist—but so too will the capacity to mend, learn, and move forward together (Fig. 9.16).

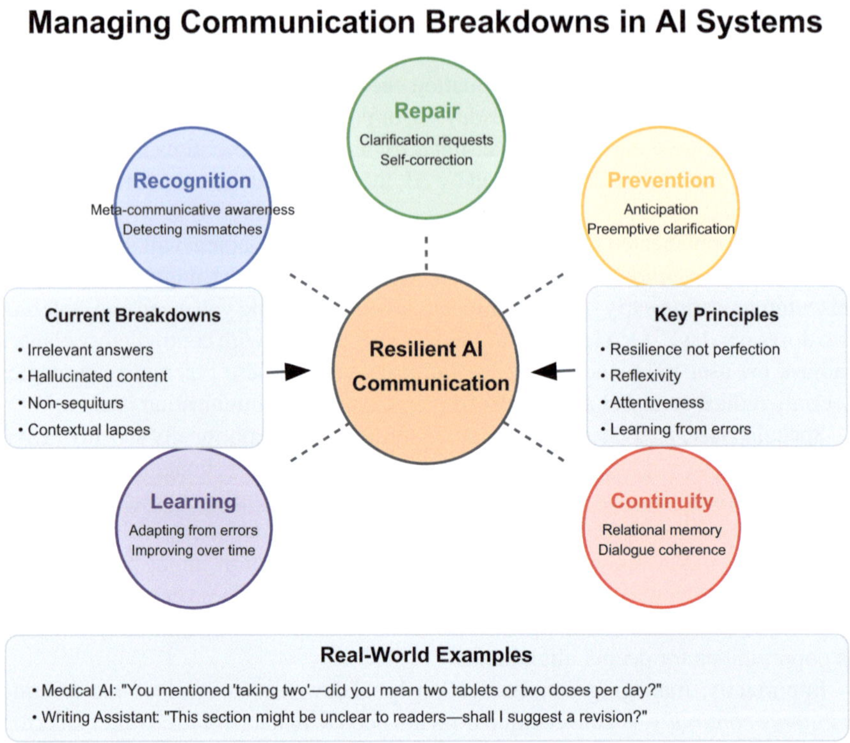

Fig. 9.16 Communicative resilience cycle in AI systems. This diagram illustrates the cyclical nature of managing communication breakdowns in AI systems. Rather than treating miscommunications as failures, the model frames them as opportunities for growth through five interconnected processes: recognition (detecting misalignments), repair (clarification and correction), prevention (anticipating issues), continuity (maintaining coherence), and learning (adapting from experience). This adaptive approach transforms AI from rigid information processors into resilient communicative partners capable of graceful recovery from inevitable misunderstandings

Bibliography

Annapureddy R, Fornaroli A, Gatica-Perez D (2025) Generative AI literacy: twelve defining competencies. Digit Gov Res Pract 6(1):1–21

Austin JL (1962) How to do things with words. Oxford University Press, Oxford

Bahree A (2024) Generative AI in action. Manning Publications

Bender E et al (2021) On the dangers of stochastic parrots: can language models be too big? In: Proceedings of the 2021 ACM conference on fairness, accountability, and transparency, pp 610–623

Bostrom N (2014) Superintelligence: paths, dangers, strategies. Oxford University Press, Oxford

Brown BR (2025) Human–machine teaming using large language models. In: Interdependent human-machine teams. Academic Press, pp 41–66

Brown TB et al (2020) Language models are few-shot learners. Adv Neural Inf Process Syst 33:1877–1901

Bura C, Myakala PK, Jonnalgadda AK (2025) Ethical prompt engineering: addressing bias, transparency, and fairness. Int J Res Anal Rev (IJRAR) 12(1). www.ijrar.org

Choi WC, Chang CI (2025) A survey of techniques, key components, strategies, challenges, and student perspectives on prompt engineering for large language models (LLMs) in education, 25 Mar 2025. https://doi.org/10.20944/preprints202503.1808.v1. Accessed 8 May 2025

Clark H (1996) Using language. Cambridge University Press, Cambridge

Debnath T, Siddiky MNA, Rahman ME et al (2025) A comprehensive survey of prompt engineering techniques in large language models. TechRxiv. https://doi.org/10.36227/techrxiv.174140719.96375390/v1. Accessed 10 May 2025

Dhamani N, Engler M (2024) Introduction to generative AI: an ethical, societal, and legal overview. Manning Publications

Eliot L (2024) Essentials of prompt engineering for generative AI: practical advances in artificial intelligence and machine learning. LBE Press Publishing

Ferraris AF, Audrito D, Di Caro L et al (2025) The architecture of language: understanding the mechanics behind LLMs. In: Cambridge forum on AI: law and governance, vol 1, Cambridge University Press

Floridi L, Cowls J (2019) A unified framework of five principles for AI in society. Harv Data Sci Rev 1(1)

Geroimenko V (2025a) Key challenges in prompt engineering. In: The essential guide to prompt engineering: key principles, techniques, challenges, and security risks. Springer Nature Switzerland, Cham, pp 85–102

Geroimenko V (2025b) Key principles of good prompt design. In: The essential guide to prompt engineering: key principles, techniques, challenges, and security risks. Springer Nature Switzerland, Cham, pp 17–36

Geroimenko V (2025c) Key techniques for writing effective prompts. In: The essential guide to prompt engineering: key principles, techniques, challenges, and security risks. Springer Nature Switzerland, Cham, pp 37–83

Geroimenko V (2025d) The essential guide to prompt engineering: key principles, techniques, challenges, and security risks. Springer

Geroimenko V (2025e) Key security risks in prompt engineering. In: The essential guide to prompt engineering: key principles, techniques, challenges, and security risks. Springer Nature Switzerland, Cham, pp 103–120

GitHub (2025) Prompt engineering guide. https://github.com/dair-ai/Prompt-Engineering-Guide. Accessed 10 Apr 2025

Greenwood M (2024) Artificial intelligence: a practical guide to using AI in everyday life. Ochreland Publishing

Gunkel DJ (2020) Robot rights. MIT Press, Cambridge

Hsu HP (2025) From programming to prompting: developing computational thinking through large language model-based generative artificial intelligence. TechTrends 1–22

Huang MX et al (2022) Adaptive conversational AI: dynamic strategies for human-AI interaction. Int J Hum Comput Stud 160:102798

Huang G, Xiao Y, Jiang L et al (2025) Beyond prompt engineering: a reinforced token-level input refinement for large language models. Proc AAAI Conf Artif Intell 39(22):24113–24121

i Picó JF, Catta-Preta M, Omeñaca AT et al (2025) The time machine: future scenario generation through generative AI tools. Future Internet 17(1):1–15

Jobin A et al (2019) The global landscape of AI ethics guidelines. Nat Mach Intell 1(9):389–399

Kannan R, Ahmad M (eds) (2025) Generative AI foundations, developments, and applications. IGI Global

Khan I (2024) The quick guide to prompt engineering. Wiley

Kim J, Sundar SS (2012) Anthropomorphism of computers: is it mindlessness or mindfulness? Comput Hum Behav 28(1):241–250

Kushwaha V, Ragavan SS, Subhajit Roy S (2025) A measure based generalizable approach to understandability. arXiv:2503.21615. https://doi.org/10.48550/arXiv.2503.21615. Accessed 19 Apr 2025
Lakoff G, Johnson M (1980) Metaphors we live by. University of Chicago Press, Chicago
Lee D, Palmer E (2025) Prompt engineering in higher education: a systematic review to help inform curricula. Int J Educ Technol High Educ 22(1):7
Lee JY, Kang S, Yoo S (2025) Can we predict the effect of prompts? arXiv preprint arXiv:2501.18883. Accessed 12 May 2025
Lindley J, Whitham R (2025) From prompt engineering to prompt craft. In: Proceedings of the nineteenth international conference on tangible, embedded, and embodied interaction, Mar 2025, pp 1–12
López-Pérez B et al (2025) Exploring the potential of large language models to understand interpersonal emotion regulation strategies from narratives. Emotion. Advance online publication. https://doi.org/10.1037/emo0001528. Accessed 19 Apr 2025
Luger GF (2020) Artificial intelligence: structures and strategies for complex problem solving, 6th edn. Pearson, Boston
Maaz S, Palaganas JC, Palaganas G et al (2025) A guide to prompt design: foundations and applications for healthcare simulationists. Front Med 11:1504532
Marcus G (2020) The next decade in AI: four steps towards robust artificial intelligence. arXiv preprint arXiv:2002.06177. Accessed 12 May 2025
Mishra M, Ara A, Mishra S (2025) Exploring human-AI collaboration in higher education: an investigation into AI-enabled personalized learning. In: Prompt engineering and generative AI applications for teaching and learning. IGI Global Scientific Publishing, pp 483–502
Mitchell M (2019) Artificial intelligence: a guide for thinking humans. Farrar, Straus and Giroux, New York
OpenAI (2025a) Best practices for prompt engineering with the OpenAI API. https://help.openai.com/en/articles/6654000-best-practices-for-prompt-engineering-with-the-openai-api. Accessed 20 Apr 2025
OpenAI (2025b) Research. https://openai.com/research/index/
Phoenix J, Taylor M (2024) Prompt engineering for generative AI. O'Reilly Media
PremaLatha V, Kumar AD, Parveen N (2025) Optimizing interactions: strategies for prompt engineering in large language models. Edu-Tech Enterp 3:24
Prompt Engineering Guide (2025) https://www.promptingguide.ai/. Accessed 7 Mar 2025
Rahwan I (2018) Society-in-the-loop: programming the algorithmic social contract. Ethics Inf Technol 20(1):5–14
Reddy CKK, Anoushka P, Draksharapu A et al (2025) Beyond text: analyzing artificial intelligence models through prompt engineering. In: Future tech startups and innovation in the age of AI, pp 120–156
Russell S (2019) Human compatible: artificial intelligence and the problem of control. Viking, New York
Sasson Lazovsky G, Raz T, Kenett YN (2025) The art of creative inquiry—from question asking to prompt engineering. J Creat Behav 59(1):e671
Searle J (1969) Speech acts: an essay in the philosophy of language. Cambridge University Press, Cambridge
Shneiderman B (2022) Human-centered AI. Oxford University Press, Oxford
Siau K, Wang W (2018) Building trust in artificial intelligence, machine learning, and robotics. CUTTER Bus Technol J 31(2):47–53
Sihi D, Ryan A (2025) Crafting and evaluating generative AI prompts: insights from students, educators, and marketers. Mark Educ Rev 1–7
Suchman L (2007) Human-machine reconfigurations: plans and situated actions, 2nd edn. Cambridge University Press, Cambridge
Tegmark M (2017) Life 3.0: being human in the age of artificial intelligence. Penguin, London
Turing A (1950) Computing machinery and intelligence. Mind 59(236):433–460

Vairamani AD, Nayyar A (2024) Prompt engineering: empowering communication. CRC Press
Winograd T (1972) Understanding natural language. Academic Press, New York
Wittgenstein L (1953) Philosophical investigations. Blackwell, Oxford

Chapter 10
Context Management and Adaptability: Enhancing AI's Ability to Understand and Recall Context

Abstract This chapter offers an in-depth exploration of how effective context management and adaptability are essential for meaningful and sustained AI communication. It begins by establishing the importance of helping AI systems comprehend human context, layer multiple levels of information, and reinforce continuity through explicit cues. The discussion then moves to advanced strategies such as using metadata, clarifying task boundaries, and managing shifts between task-oriented, casual, and creative modes. Particular attention is given to avoiding contextual drift and fostering long-term continuity across multiturn or multisession interactions. The chapter concludes by addressing the dynamic negotiation of meaning between humans and AI, highlighting how users can adapt to evolving AI understanding and co-construct context in real-time. Taken together, these practices enable more coherent, responsive, and human-aligned AI systems capable of fluid dialogue and collaborative intelligence.

Keywords AI context management · Contextual continuity · Adaptive AI communication · Metadata cues · Task boundaries · Context negotiation

As interactions with AI systems become more complex, fluid, and prolonged, the ability to manage context effectively emerges as a foundational principle of successful communication. Context is not merely the background of an exchange—it is the evolving framework within which meaning is constructed, intent is interpreted, and relevance is sustained. This chapter explores how users can help AI systems understand human context, reinforce and layer relevant information, handle transitions between different communicative goals or tones, and preserve continuity across sessions. It also examines the dynamic interplay between user input and AI adaptation, including strategies for correcting misalignment, maintaining shared understanding, and collaboratively negotiating shifts in meaning. Together, these practices enable more coherent, resilient, and human-like dialogue, turning AI from a reactive tool into an adaptive conversational partner.

V. Geroimenko, *Beyond and After Prompt Engineering: The Future of AI Communication*, https://doi.org/10.1007/978-3-032-04569-0_10

10.1 Establishing and Reinforcing Context

10.1.1 Help AI Understand the Human Context

Effective communication between humans and AI systems begins with an effort to make the human context legible to the machine. Unlike human interlocutors, AI does not naturally perceive cultural background, emotional tone, situational relevance, or implicit expectations. It relies entirely on explicit cues, structured input, and inference from patterns in data. To bridge this gap, human users must consciously scaffold the interaction by providing meaningful, interpretable context that allows the AI to align with their goals, needs, and perspectives.

At present, this principle is most evident in prompt engineering and user interface design. For instance, when interacting with a customer service chatbot, users may need to specify not just the problem, such as "I can't access my account," but also the context: "I'm a long-time user, recently changed my password, and I'm accessing from abroad." These contextual additions help the system tailor its response more effectively. Similarly, a writer working with a generative AI may achieve better results by setting a frame like, "You are a literary editor helping me refine a historical novel set in 18th-century France," thereby aligning the model's expectations and tone with the task.

In future AI communication systems, especially those embedded in physical environments or personalised assistants, the need to interpret nuanced human contexts will intensify. Imagine an AI integrated into a smart home that not only schedules meetings but also adjusts lighting, music, or thermostat settings based on the user's mood and agenda. To function optimally, such a system must understand that a phrase like "I've had a long day" might imply a need for a quieter ambience, fewer notifications, or even emotional support. While current systems may respond to keyword triggers, future models will need to interpret these statements within a broader emotional and relational frame.

The complexity grows further in speculative collaborative settings. Consider a scenario where an AI co-develops educational content with a human teacher. The AI must learn to recognise and adapt to the educator's pedagogical style, student demographics, curriculum goals, and even classroom dynamics. The teacher, in turn, helps the AI grasp this context not in a single instruction but through iterative guidance, clarification, and feedback, developing a shared understanding over time.

Helping AI understand human context, therefore, is not a one-time act but a dynamic and ongoing process. It involves offering not just data, but framing—explaining the "why" and "how" behind the "what." This includes clarifying intentions, situational constraints, historical background, emotional undertones, and social or professional norms. As AI systems grow more multimodal and context-aware, users will increasingly shape interactions through a combination of language, gesture, affect, and environmental cues, making the principle of human-context sharing foundational to meaningful, future-proof AI communication (Fig. 10.1).

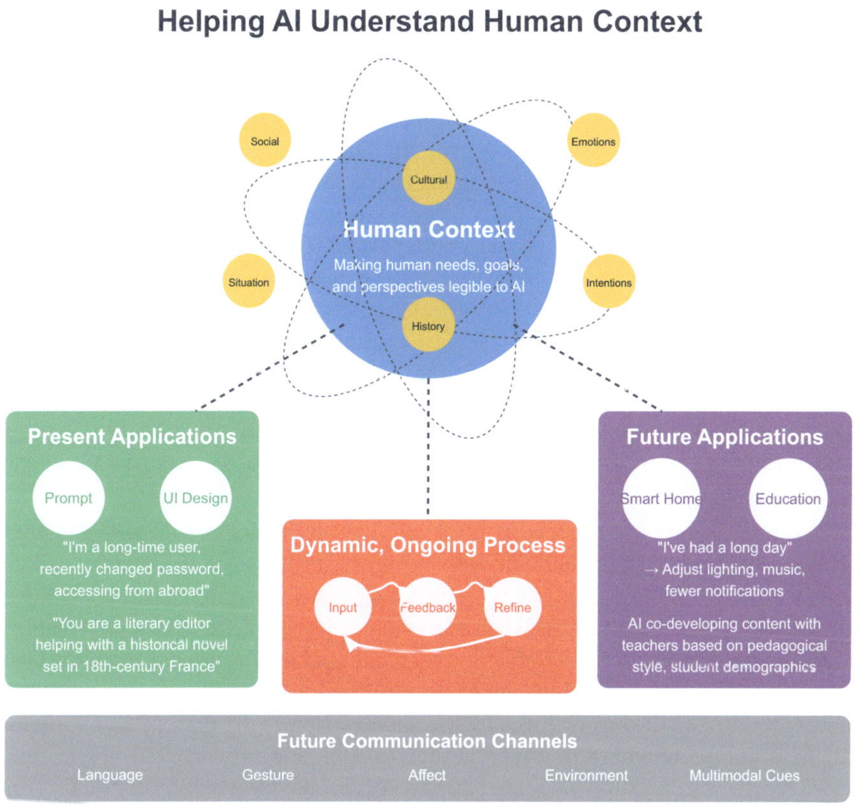

Fig. 10.1 Human context principle in AI communication. This diagram illustrates how humans must make their context legible to AI systems. The central concept of "human context" is surrounded by key contextual elements (intentions, emotions, cultural background, etc.) that AI needs to interpret. Present applications show current context sharing through prompts and UI design, while future applications envision more nuanced interactions in smart homes and education. The bottom depicts the cyclical nature of this communication—a dynamic process of input, feedback, and refinement across multiple channels rather than a one-time instruction

10.1.2 Use Context Reinforcement

AI systems—especially large language models—operate in a turn-based interaction framework where continuity is often simulated rather than inherently understood. Although many systems can retain short-term context within a single session or conversation window, their ability to maintain more profound continuity across multiple exchanges remains limited. Context reinforcement is therefore essential: the deliberate restating, referencing, or embedding of key information to preserve relevance, maintain coherence, and guide AI behaviour throughout an interaction.

In present-day applications, context reinforcement is commonly used in customer support bots, personal assistant systems, and educational AI platforms. For example, a user asking a virtual tutor about "quantum superposition" might begin with a broad question like "What is it?" followed by narrower queries such as "And how does it relate to measurement?" or "Can you explain it with a metaphor?" Without reinforced context, such as reminders that the topic remains quantum mechanics, the AI may lose track of the conceptual thread and deliver unrelated or overly generalised answers. By occasionally rephrasing or restating the overarching topic, users help anchor the AI's responses to the desired scope.

More sophisticated systems partially automate this process through memory structures or internal summarisation. However, these methods are imperfect. In collaborative writing tools, for instance, a user working on a sci-fi screenplay might ask the AI to brainstorm character arcs. As the session continues, the user may switch between plot development and dialogue suggestions. If the character's traits and narrative goals are not periodically reinforced—e.g. "Remember, Elara is a rebel technologist who distrusts authority"—the AI may drift into generic suggestions inconsistent with the established story world. Strategic reinforcement realigns the model's focus and prevents degradation of narrative consistency.

In future AI systems, especially those with long-term memory or persistent user profiles, context reinforcement will evolve from a user-managed tactic into a collaborative strategy. Rather than manually restating goals, users might co-construct a shared context layer with the AI, such as a dynamic knowledge graph, a goal map, or a mood-state timeline. For example, in therapeutic AI applications, a user and their digital companion might jointly build a reflective journal. Reinforcing emotional milestones—like "Last week I was feeling anxious before my presentation"—helps the AI develop continuity in emotional recognition and support. The AI, in turn, might reinforce context by recalling patterns or prior advice when appropriate: "You mentioned that deep breathing helped you manage stress in similar situations."

In speculative scenarios, reinforcement may also be multimodal. A user wearing augmented reality glasses might gesture toward a previously annotated object or use a visual tag to reassert context. In professional environments, a team might use voice commands to remind a project management AI of current deadlines, responsibilities, and changing objectives, continuously reinforcing both individual and collective goals.

In all these cases, context reinforcement functions as both a stabiliser and a clarifier. It helps the AI "stay on course" while enabling humans to control and refine the interaction. As communication with AI becomes more fluid and prolonged, reinforcement will no longer feel like redundancy—it will become a vital rhythm in the conversation, enabling continuity, coherence, and co-adaptation (Fig. 10.2).

10.1.3 Practice Context Layering

Context in AI communication is not monolithic—it is layered, dynamic, and often nonlinear. Effective interaction requires the capacity to manage multiple contextual layers simultaneously: the immediate task, the overarching goal, the user's intent,

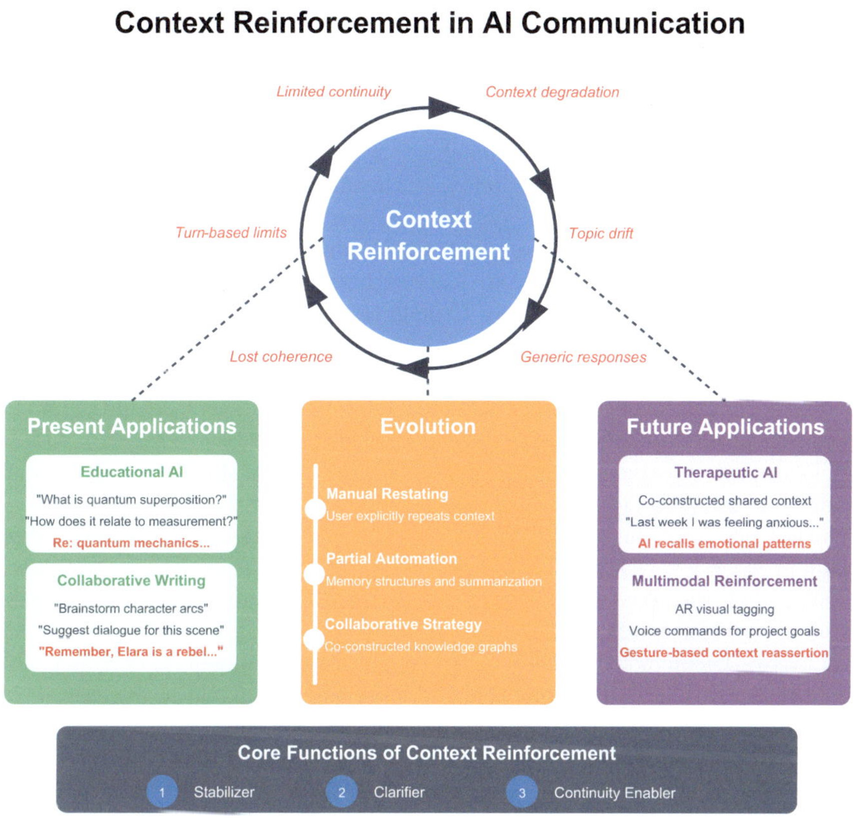

Fig. 10.2 Context reinforcement in AI communication. This diagram illustrates how context reinforcement serves as a critical mechanism for maintaining continuity in AI interactions. The central concept represents the cyclical nature of reinforcement surrounded by the challenges it addresses. The left section depicts present applications in educational AI and collaborative writing, while the right shows future evolutions through therapeutic AI and multimodal reinforcement. The centre timeline traces the progression from manual restating to collaborative context co-construction. The bottom identifies the three core functions: stabiliser, clarifier, and continuity enabler—transforming what might seem like redundancy into a vital communication rhythm

the emotional tone, prior knowledge, and even implicit norms of communication. Practising context layering means structuring these layers in ways the AI can understand, access, and act upon in a coordinated fashion, ensuring that responses remain aligned with both surface-level prompts and deeper situational cues.

In current practice, human users often manage context layering unconsciously by stacking information across turns. For example, in a travel planning session with an AI assistant, a user might start with "Help me find flights to Tokyo," then move to "I'd prefer flights that arrive in the morning," followed by "Also, make sure the hotel is near a subway station." Each input adds a layer—location, timing, transportation preference—that the AI must integrate into a coherent understanding. When the layering is explicit and cumulative, the AI can generate contextually appropriate suggestions; when the layers are inconsistent or missing, the AI's responses become fragmented.

Some tools offer structured support for layering. Notebooks, memory panes, or dialogue threads help users build cumulative context over time. However, layering remains largely a human responsibility. An instructional designer using an AI to generate course materials might layer multiple forms of context: educational level, learning objectives, cultural background of the learners, and format preferences (e.g. visual vs. textual content). If these are scattered or implied rather than integrated, the AI may default to generic responses. Explicit layering—such as stating, "For adult learners with minimal prior knowledge of AI, create visual analogies for each core concept"—helps the system align with the depth and direction intended.

In more advanced or speculative future systems, context layering could become a shared responsibility between humans and AI. Consider a research assistant AI that tracks the evolving structure of a literature review. As humans shift from summarising findings to identifying gaps and then proposing research questions, AI can help manage these layers, highlighting when a cited source contradicts a previously noted claim or when a newly added idea requires recontextualisation. The layering here is not just informational but logical and argumentative, requiring the AI to maintain awareness of conceptual structure.

Layering becomes even more complex in multimodal, co-creative environments. In a collaborative design session using virtual or augmented reality, the user might point to a 3D prototype, say, "Let's make it more organic," and draw a curved shape in the air. Each of these inputs contributes a different modality to the context: spatial reference, aesthetic preference, and design gesture. The AI must layer these inputs correctly to respond meaningfully: suggesting curved biomorphic forms, adapting the prototype in real-time, and proposing alternatives that align with the newly established design intent.

Ultimately, practising context layering equips users to build more intelligent, nuanced conversations with AI systems. Rather than overloading a single prompt with multiple objectives, layering distributes complexity across structured turns or multimodal cues. This facilitates better comprehension, supports adaptive reasoning, and makes it possible to hold extended, coherent dialogues—even as the goals and inputs evolve. As AI systems grow in sophistication, mastering this practice will be essential for meaningful and contextually aware human-AI collaboration (Fig. 10.3).

10.1.4 Incorporate Metadata Cues

Metadata cues—structured or semi-structured signals about the nature, origin, intent, or context of communication—play a pivotal role in helping AI systems interpret human input more accurately and adaptively. While human interlocutors often rely on subtle cues such as tone, body language, or shared history to make sense of meaning, AI systems must depend on more explicit signals. Metadata serves as this

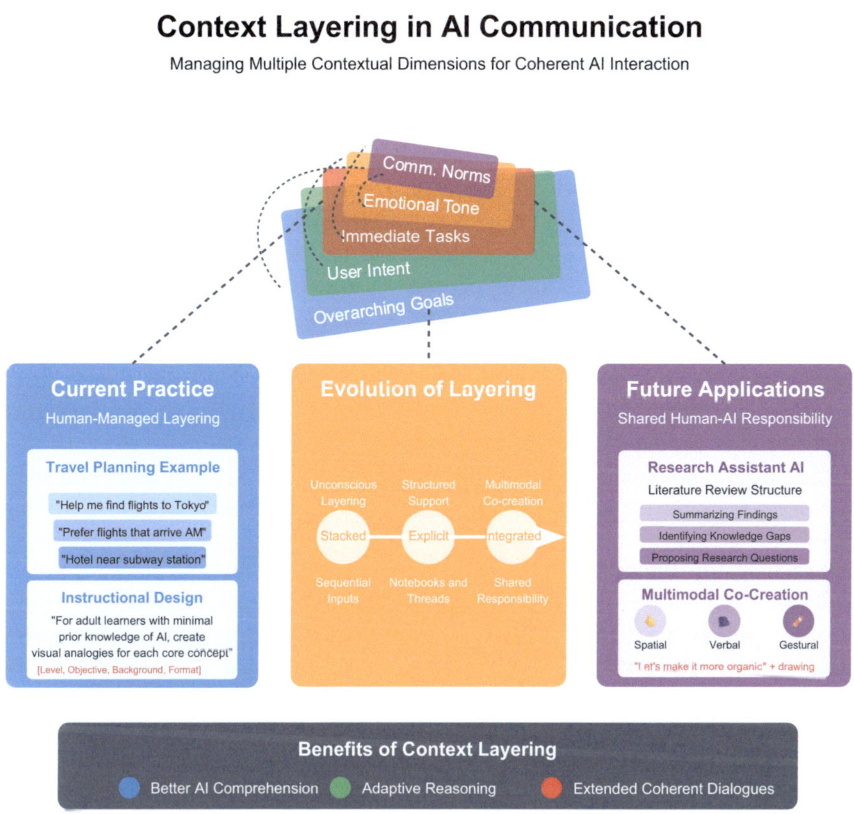

Fig. 10.3 Context layering in AI communication. This diagram illustrates how multiple contextual dimensions function in AI interactions, progressing from stacked information to integrated understanding. The central overlapping layers represent the hierarchy of context, from foundational elements (overarching goals) to surface-level cues (communication norms). The left section demonstrates current human-managed approaches through travel planning and instructional design examples. The right section depicts future applications where context responsibility is shared between humans and AI. The centre tracks the evolution from unconscious sequential inputs toward multimodal co-creation, ultimately enabling better comprehension, adaptive reasoning, and coherent extended dialogues

scaffolding: it labels, annotates, or frames content in ways that enable more precise parsing, retrieval, and generation of information.

In current applications, metadata cues already enhance AI performance in subtle but impactful ways. Email systems, for example, use headers to indicate sender identity, thread history, and priority levels. When a virtual assistant accesses an email and responds accordingly—prioritising a time-sensitive message from a supervisor or summarising a weekly update—it is guided by such metadata. In document generation, prompts like "generate an executive summary for a technical audience" act as high-level metadata that shapes tone, complexity, and structure. Even tagging inputs with simple labels—e.g. "#question," "#feedback," or "#urgent"—can significantly improve relevance and response quality.

The strategic use of metadata becomes even more crucial in multiturn conversations and multiagent systems. A team collaborating with an AI tool might prefix messages with roles and goals: "Project Lead: summarise client feedback," or "Designer: propose three visual themes." These act as embedded instructions, informing the AI how to interpret and weigh each input. In content creation environments, structured metadata such as timestamps, audience categories, or formatting tags (e.g. <h2>, <summary>, intent: persuasive) allow AI systems to modulate their output with far greater fidelity to user intent.

Looking forward, metadata cues will become increasingly multimodal and adaptive. In immersive environments, metadata might be conveyed through gesture-based annotations, spatial markers, or visual highlights. A designer using augmented reality might circle a portion of a 3D model and mark it with "revise: make more aerodynamic," offering both a location and a design directive. In voice-based interactions, intonation or acoustic patterns could be processed as affective metadata, signalling urgency, uncertainty, or emotional state.

Speculatively, future AI systems may also generate and manage metadata proactively. In collaborative writing, for instance, the AI might track the user's style preferences—annotating them internally as "tone: formal," "preferred structure: thesis-first," or "bias: avoid passive voice"—and use this metadata to refine future suggestions. In continuous dialogue systems, especially those used in education or therapy, AI could maintain contextual metadata threads like "topic trajectory," "emotional progression," or "unresolved goals," thus supporting more profound continuity and personalisation.

Incorporating metadata cues, however, requires a balance between structure and fluidity. Overly rigid tagging can feel unnatural or burdensome for users, while too little structure risks misunderstanding and drift. The most effective metadata strategies are lightweight, intuitive, and often integrated into natural language. For example, a phrase like "Speaking as a parent, I think..." already serves as embedded metadata, framing the speaker's role and perspective.

Ultimately, teaching users to incorporate metadata cues—consciously or intuitively—will be essential for enhancing mutual understanding in human-AI interaction. Whether embedded in text, speech, gesture, or interface, metadata acts as a bridge between surface language and deeper context, enabling AI systems to deliver responses that are not only accurate but also aligned with human intention, situation, and nuance (Fig. 10.4).

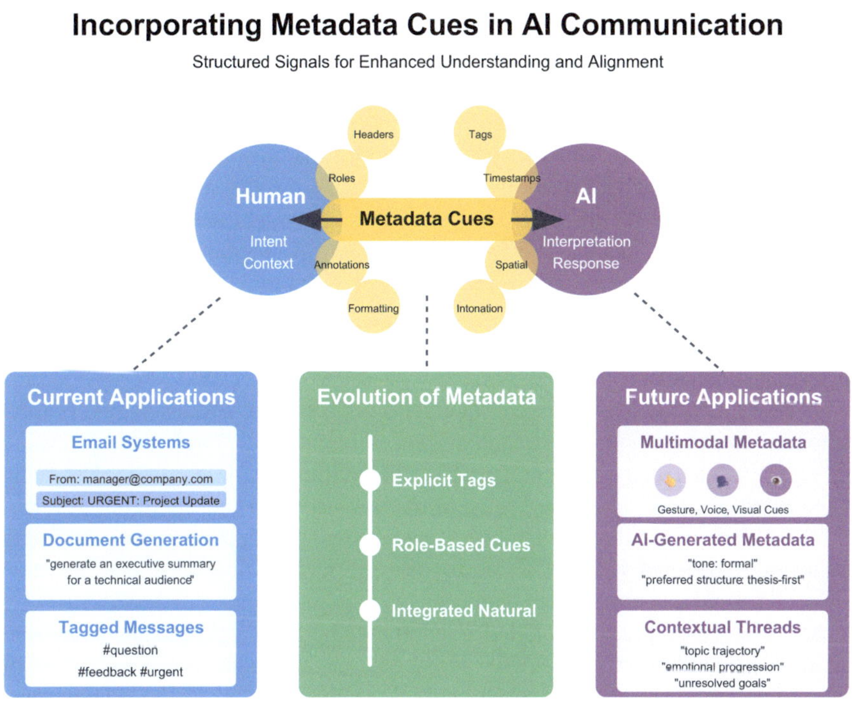

Fig. 10.4 Metadata cues as communication bridges. This diagram illustrates how metadata cues function as essential bridges between human intent and AI interpretation. The central visual depicts metadata as a structured conduit connecting human context to AI response, surrounded by various metadata types. The left section shows current applications in email systems and document generation, while the right highlights future evolutions through multimodal cues and AI-generated metadata. The centre timeline traces the progression from explicit tagging toward naturally integrated cues

10.2 Managing Contextual Shifts and Transitions

10.2.1 Clarify Task Boundaries

In human-AI collaboration, clearly defined task boundaries serve as cognitive scaffolds that anchor the interaction and help the AI model stay focused, relevant, and appropriately scoped in its responses. Unlike human collaborators who can often infer unspoken assumptions or adjust dynamically to ambiguity, AI systems typically lack intrinsic awareness of the structure or scope of a task unless it is explicitly delineated. Without such clarity, interactions risk veering into incoherence, drift, or misalignment with the user's intentions.

Clarifying task boundaries involves more than just stating an instruction. It requires specifying *what the AI is being asked to do*, *what it is not expected to do*, and sometimes *how far it should go*. For example, a user might instruct a language model, "Summarise the following article in no more than three bullet points, for a general audience." Here, the boundaries are defined by format (bullet points), brevity (no more than three), and audience (general, non-specialist). Without these cues, the AI might generate a long-form summary or include unnecessary technical detail, demonstrating how boundary vagueness leads to output mismatch.

Boundaries are critical in multipart workflows. Consider a knowledge worker using an AI system for research synthesis. The user might say, "Right now, just extract the main arguments from each source; we'll compare them later." This instruction creates temporal task boundaries: the current step is limited to extraction, while comparison is deferred. This prevents the AI from preemptively analysing or synthesising, thereby supporting a structured, stepwise process that mirrors human reasoning strategies.

In more complex or creative interactions, boundary-setting helps prevent unhelpful improvisation. A screenplay writer might ask, "Draft a conversation between two characters, but don't resolve the conflict yet." Here, the AI is being asked to write within narrative limits, preserving open tension for future development. Similarly, in legal or medical support systems, defining boundaries is critical to ensure the AI does not overstep its role, for instance, by providing general information but not a formal diagnosis or legal advice.

As AI becomes increasingly embedded in collaborative and multiagent environments, task boundaries will need to be negotiated and maintained over longer spans of interaction. Imagine a scenario where multiple team members—some human, some AI—collaborate on a strategic plan. The AI might be instructed, "You are responsible for synthesising stakeholder feedback, but not for deciding final priorities." This functional segmentation allows AI systems to contribute meaningfully without encroaching on human decision-making authority.

In speculative future systems, the clarification and enforcement of task boundaries could become semi-automated. For instance, an AI with access to a shared project canvas might detect when its output exceeds the defined scope and prompt, "This response includes implementation suggestions, but you asked only for strategic themes. Would you like me to revise?" Such feedback loops reflect a new level of contextual self-awareness, where the AI monitors not just what it produces, but whether it aligns with the intended task boundary.

Ultimately, clarifying task boundaries enhances both the precision and the ethics of AI interaction. It keeps the AI anchored, reduces hallucination risk, aligns outputs with user expectations, and fosters trust in high-stakes domains. Just as human collaborators benefit from knowing the scope of their responsibility, so too do AI systems—especially when those boundaries are communicated with clarity, nuance, and flexibility (Fig. 10.5).

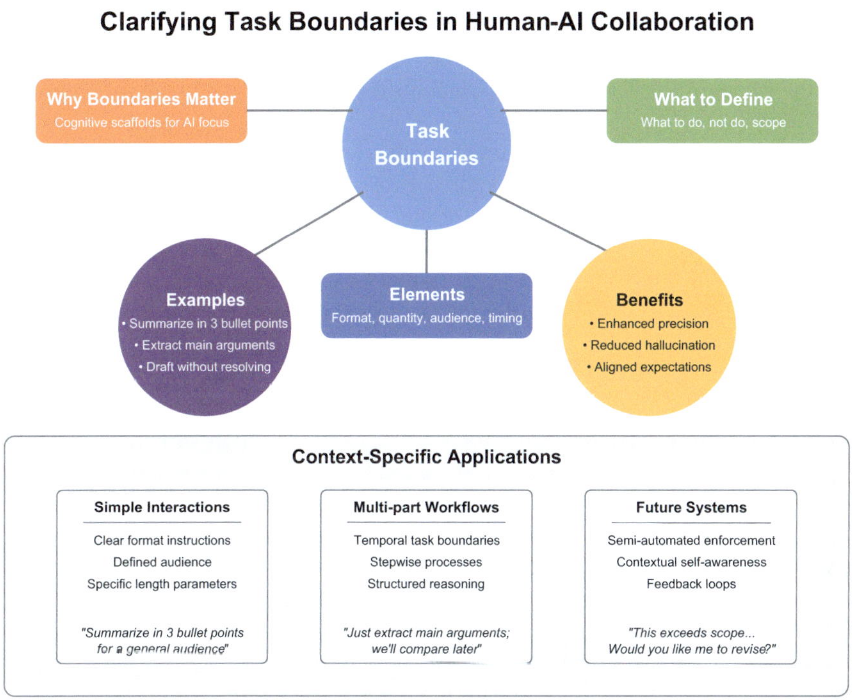

Fig. 10.5 Architecture of task boundaries in human-AI collaboration. This diagram illustrates how clearly defined task boundaries function as cognitive scaffolds in human-AI interaction, mapping the essential components—purpose, definition elements, examples, and benefits—while demonstrating how boundaries manifest differently across simple interactions, multipart workflows, and future AI systems. Task boundaries enhance precision, reduce hallucinations, and maintain appropriate AI scope, ultimately fostering more effective and trustworthy human-AI partnerships

10.2.2 Switch Between Task, Casual, and Creative Modes

One of the hallmarks of sophisticated communication is the ability to fluidly switch between different conversational modes—task-oriented, casual, and creative—depending on the goals, setting, and tone of the interaction. For AI systems to support natural, adaptive engagement, they must not only recognise these modes but also shift between them with contextual sensitivity. Just as a human collaborator adjusts their communication style when moving from a formal meeting to an informal coffee break or a brainstorming session, AI must learn to detect mode transitions and respond accordingly.

In present-day applications, this principle is already evident in systems that adjust tone and style based on prompt phrasing. A user might type, "Write a professional email requesting a deadline extension," and later say, "Now rewrite it in a friendly tone." Though the underlying content may remain consistent, the mode shifts from formal to casual, and the AI adapts linguistic choices, sentence structure, and even pacing. Similarly, when a user moves from asking, "What's the weather like today?" to "Tell me a joke about rainy days," the interaction transitions from utilitarian to playful. Recognising and adapting to such shifts enhances engagement and improves usability.

However, many systems still struggle with seamless transitions, especially when different modes are layered in a single conversation. A productivity assistant, for instance, may be adept at scheduling tasks but perform poorly when the user casually reflects, "I've had a tough week—maybe we should push some deadlines." If the AI doesn't recognise the emotional undercurrent or casual phrasing, it may respond rigidly or miss the implicit request. Mode-awareness in this context requires not only task recognition but also sensitivity to tone, affect, and intention.

In future AI systems, the ability to navigate mode switching will become foundational for co-creative and socially intelligent interaction. Imagine a design AI that begins in structured, goal-oriented mode—"Generate ten logo variations based on this brief"—but then shifts into a looser, exploratory mode as the user says, "Let's just play with wild ideas for a bit." The AI might respond by generating unconventional, imaginative outputs without over-optimising for constraints, before returning to refinement mode when the user says, "That one looks promising—let's develop it further." These fluid transitions support ideation without sacrificing structure, much like effective human teamwork.

Multimodal cues will further enhance mode detection and switching. A user might speak more informally, smile, or use gestures when transitioning into a casual conversation, and shift to focus eye contact and clipped instructions when resuming a task-based interaction. AI systems with vision and affect recognition capabilities could interpret these transitions and adjust accordingly, shifting not just what they say but also how they say it, encompassing tone, tempo, and formality.

In speculative scenarios, the boundaries between modes may blur or even fuse. For example, in AI-enhanced education, a tutoring system might simultaneously combine modes—providing structured content, responding empathetically to learner frustration, and encouraging exploration through creative problem-solving. Here, the AI would need to balance directive guidance with relational warmth and imaginative engagement, all within a single interaction.

For users, the key to supporting this adaptability lies in providing clear cues when switching modes. Statements like "Let's take a break from planning and chat for a bit," or "Now for something more creative," act as meta-communicative markers that guide the AI's interpretation. Over time, more intuitive systems may learn to infer these transitions from subtler indicators—but until then, thoughtful signalling remains a critical user skill.

Ultimately, the ability to switch between task, casual, and creative modes is not just a matter of interface fluency—it's a gateway to richer, more human-like AI communication. It enables flexible engagement, deepens trust, and opens new possibilities for co-creation, support, and companionship in future AI systems (Fig. 10.6).

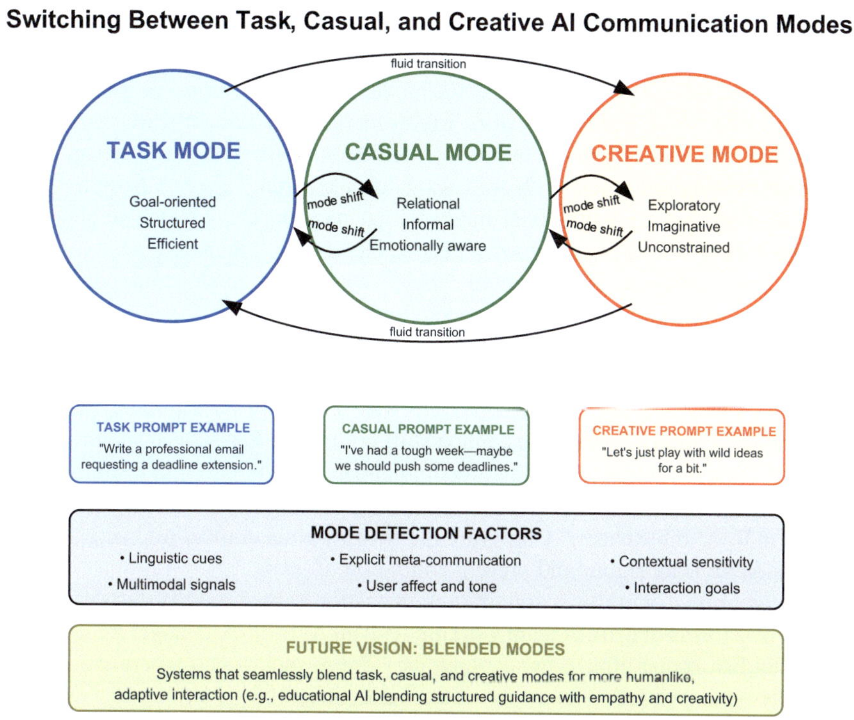

Fig. 10.6 Communication mode dynamics in AI systems. This diagram illustrates the three primary AI communication modes—task, casual, and creative—and their dynamic interrelationships. It visualises how sophisticated AI systems navigate bidirectional transitions between structured goal-oriented interactions, informal relational exchanges, and exploratory ideation processes. The diagram highlights linguistic cues that trigger mode shifts and detection factors that enable contextual sensitivity. It suggests future evolution toward seamlessly blended multimodal communication that mirrors human conversational fluidity—a cornerstone capability for next-generation AI communication systems

10.2.3 Clarify Shifts in Context

Contextual shifts are inevitable in extended or multipurpose interactions with AI. A conversation that begins with a technical question might later move into a reflective discussion, a new task, or a different emotional tone. While human conversational partners can usually detect and adapt to these transitions based on subtle social cues, AI systems often require more explicit guidance to recognise that the frame of reference has changed. Clarifying shifts in context is therefore essential to ensure that the AI can realign its responses, avoid confusion, and stay meaningfully engaged with the user's evolving intentions.

In everyday use, users frequently shift context without announcing it. A user might begin by asking a virtual assistant for tomorrow's weather, then suddenly switch to "Also, can you remind me when the rent is due?" While humans understand such fluidity as natural topic transitions, AI systems may treat each prompt in isolation unless the shift is clearly signalled or the system is designed to detect pattern disruptions. Without recognising the change, the model might fail to adjust its assumptions, format, or reasoning, leading to errors, irrelevant answers, or awkward continuity.

Explicit clarification greatly improves interaction quality. Phrases such as "Let's move on to something else," "Now I want to talk about…," or "Changing gears for a moment" act as transitional markers that reorient the AI and prepare it to treat the following input as part of a new frame. These linguistic cues are simple yet powerful—they help the system "reset" its context model and prevent the inappropriate blending of distinct conversational threads.

Contextual shifts become even more critical in high-stakes or multidomain applications. In a healthcare scenario, a user might begin with a casual conversation, then move to a specific medical query: "By the way, I've been having chest pains." A failure to detect and adapt to this context shift could lead the AI to respond with an inappropriate tone or delay essential recommendations. Similarly, in legal research, a user might switch from "Explain this doctrine" to "Now summarise how it was applied in these three cases." Clarifying the shift from theoretical to practical focus helps maintain legal rigour and prevent conflation of goals.

In collaborative or multisession settings, unacknowledged context shifts can cause more severe forms of drift. A team working with an AI project manager might forget to re-establish scope after a break, such as: "We're picking up where we left off yesterday—but now let's focus only on the marketing strategy, not product development." Such clarification ensures that the AI filters its knowledge base appropriately and generates responses consistent with the new subdomain.

Speculatively, more advanced AI systems may anticipate and flag possible shifts themselves. A future AI writing assistant might say, "It seems like you're moving from outlining to drafting—shall I switch to composition mode?" or "This question seems unrelated to your previous input. Should we start a new thread?" These prompts not only increase user control but demonstrate emergent contextual self-regulation—a critical step toward more autonomous dialogue management.

For now, the burden of clarification remains primarily on the user. Fortunately, this burden is light: a brief signal, restatement, or meta-commentary can dramatically enhance interaction fluidity. Clarifying context shifts is not just a communication best practice; it is an enabler of more flexible, resilient, and human-like AI interaction, especially as we move toward longer, multimodal, and multifaceted exchanges (Fig. 10.7).

10.2.4 Avoid Contextual Drift

Contextual drift refers to the gradual and often unnoticed divergence of an AI system's responses from the user's original intent or topic. While some degree of drift is natural in extended human conversation, often enriching dialogue with spontaneous associations, AI systems lack the intuitive guardrails that help humans maintain coherence.

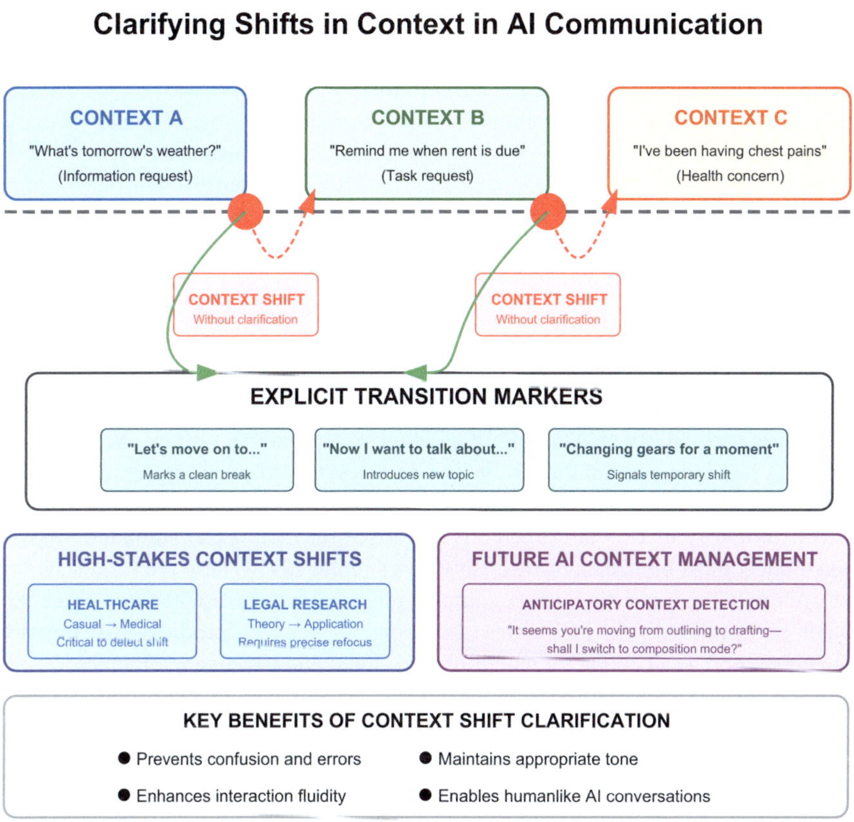

Fig. 10.7 Navigating contextual transitions in AI communication. This diagram illustrates the critical role of explicit context clarification in AI interactions, depicting how conversations naturally shift between distinct contextual frames and how unmarked transitions can lead to confusion or inappropriate responses. The visualisation contrasts problematic abrupt shifts with successful transitions facilitated by explicit markers, highlighting the special importance of clarity in high-stakes domains. The diagram also previews future AI systems that may proactively detect and confirm context changes—a key evolutionary step toward more fluid, resilient, and human-like conversational intelligence

Left unchecked, contextual drift can lead to irrelevant answers, misaligned outputs, and, in critical cases, failures in task execution or decision support. Therefore, avoiding contextual drift is a central challenge in managing sustained, meaningful communication with AI.

At the root of contextual drift is a mismatch between the user's evolving focus and the AI's understanding of what remains relevant. In present systems, drift commonly arises during multiturn interactions, especially when the user assumes the system retains shared knowledge, implicit constraints, or conversational objectives. For example, a user developing a grant proposal with the help of a language model may begin with a defined structure and funding goal. As the conversation progresses, small shifts—such as changing emphasis from methodology to expected impact—may be misinterpreted by the AI as a new direction rather than a nuanced refinement. If the user does not periodically reinforce the core focus or clarify boundaries, the AI may gradually deviate from the original narrative, weakening coherence and thematic alignment.

To avoid such drift, users can adopt simple but effective strategies. Periodic restatements of goals—such as "Just to recap, we're focusing on…"—serve as anchors that reorient the AI. Explicit references to earlier parts of the dialogue—"As mentioned in Section 1…" or "Let's stay with the theme of environmental sustainability"—also help maintain continuity. Additionally, when switching subtopics, users can bracket the transition: "Let's briefly touch on a side issue, then return to the main argument." These practices not only help prevent drift but also train the model to respond with contextual awareness.

Drift is particularly challenging in creative or exploratory settings. When brainstorming plot ideas, visual motifs, or brand names, the AI may progressively introduce suggestions that become increasingly disconnected from initial parameters. This exploratory drift is not inherently negative—in fact, it can stimulate innovation—but it must be managed. A creative user might say, "These are fun ideas, but let's return to the futuristic tone we started with," or "Please keep the focus on underwater environments." In such cases, the boundary between productive divergence and contextual loss becomes a matter of judgement and iterative realignment.

Future AI systems may assist more proactively in managing drift. Through real-time tracking of dialogue coherence, goal alignment, or thematic consistency, the AI could issue gentle prompts, such as, "This direction is quite different from our earlier focus—shall we adjust?" or "Would you like to review your original objectives before proceeding?" Such features could act as cognitive stabilisers, offering users a meta-level view of the interaction's coherence over time.

In more advanced collaborative scenarios, the risk of drift increases when multiple actors—human and AI—contribute to the same evolving context. For example, in a smart urban planning session involving experts, citizens, and AI models, inputs may arrive from diverse perspectives with different assumptions. In such cases, managing contextual drift requires not only individual clarification but also systemic oversight, including a shared context map, priority tracking, or version-controlled contributions. These tools help maintain alignment without suppressing diversity or creativity.

In sum, avoiding contextual drift is about maintaining deliberate focus without sacrificing flexibility. It requires users to be vigilant curators of shared context—clarifying goals, reaffirming constraints, and signalling when the AI has gone off track. As human-AI interactions become longer, more complex, and more collaborative, the ability to detect and correct drift will be vital for achieving depth, precision, and continuity in intelligent communication (Fig. 10.8).

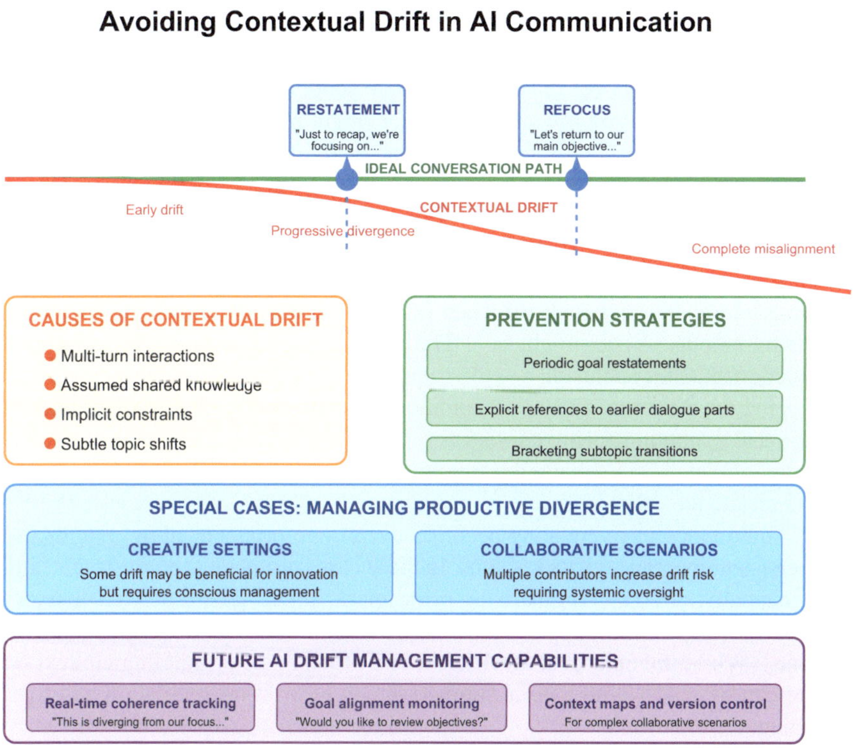

Fig. 10.8 Managing contextual drift in extended AI interactions. This diagram illustrates how conversations with AI systems can gradually diverge from their initial focus, creating a widening gap between user intent and AI responses. It visualises the progression of contextual drift, effective intervention points, and preventive strategies that maintain alignment without sacrificing flexibility. The diagram highlights special considerations for creative and collaborative contexts, where drift management requires balancing coherence with productive exploration. Future AI capabilities shown at the bottom suggest how systems might eventually assist users in monitoring and correcting drift through real-time coherence tracking and context visualisation

10.3 Ensuring Continuity Through Interaction

10.3.1 Reference Shared Conversation History

Referencing shared conversation history is a powerful technique for establishing continuity and deepening mutual understanding in human-AI communication. While humans naturally draw on previous exchanges to build rapport, avoid redundancy, and signal coherence, AI systems—unless designed explicitly with memory capabilities—do not inherently recall prior turns or sessions. When users explicitly refer to earlier parts of the conversation, they not only help the AI maintain focus but also create a sense of ongoing dialogue that resembles more natural human interaction.

In current systems, many large language models operate within a session-limited context window. This means that earlier prompts and responses may be accessible to the model for reference, but only within a finite scope. For example, in a multiturn discussion about planning a workshop, a user might say, "Let's revisit the second session we outlined earlier—it needs more interactivity." By referencing a specific point in the shared history, the user provides a navigational cue that anchors the AI's attention. If the AI has sufficient context from earlier turns, it can recall or reinterpret that information accordingly. If not, the user's reference functions as an opportunity to reintroduce or clarify the earlier content.

These references are beneficial when resolving ambiguity, managing iterations, or refining outputs. A user might say, "The previous draft you provided had a good introduction, but the conclusion was too vague—can you rewrite just that part?" Here, referencing the AI's own earlier output allows the system to localise the requested revision and maintain stylistic consistency. In collaborative editing, such continuity promotes efficiency and reduces the cognitive load on the user, who otherwise would need to restate the entire context.

The importance of referencing becomes even more pronounced in systems that lack persistent memory across sessions. In these cases, users must reconstruct continuity manually, often by summarising prior interactions: "Last time we spoke, we outlined a three-part content strategy. Today, I want to focus on the implementation timeline." While this may feel artificial, it is a crucial part of building context for AI and can be made more natural through habits of brief recapitulation and topic signalling.

In future AI systems with long-term memory, referencing shared conversation history may become more fluid and intelligent. A personal AI companion, for example, might say, "You mentioned last week that you're preparing for a keynote. Would you like help finalising your slides?" Such memory-based references enrich the interaction by showing attentiveness and enabling continuity across time and tasks. These features simulate interpersonal familiarity and can enhance trust, rapport, and personalisation.

Speculatively, shared conversation history may also include visual, spatial, or multimodal elements. Imagine a collaborative workspace where a user points to a specific chart or notes from a past session and says, "Build on this analysis, but now include market volatility." The AI, capable of integrating visual and temporal references, could interpret the gesture as a link to prior work and generate an appropriately layered response. In AR or VR environments, persistent shared objects and annotations could further enrich historical continuity.

To maximise the benefits of current systems, users are advised to revisit earlier outputs, identify specific components (such as "the second paragraph," "slide three," or "the argument about ethics"), and develop habits of concise summarisation. These practices help bridge the gap between session-based memory and the deeper, more persistent understanding that future systems may offer.

Referencing shared conversation history transforms AI interaction from a series of isolated queries into a dialogic process, enabling cumulative understanding, supporting contextual depth, and laying the foundation for more human-like,

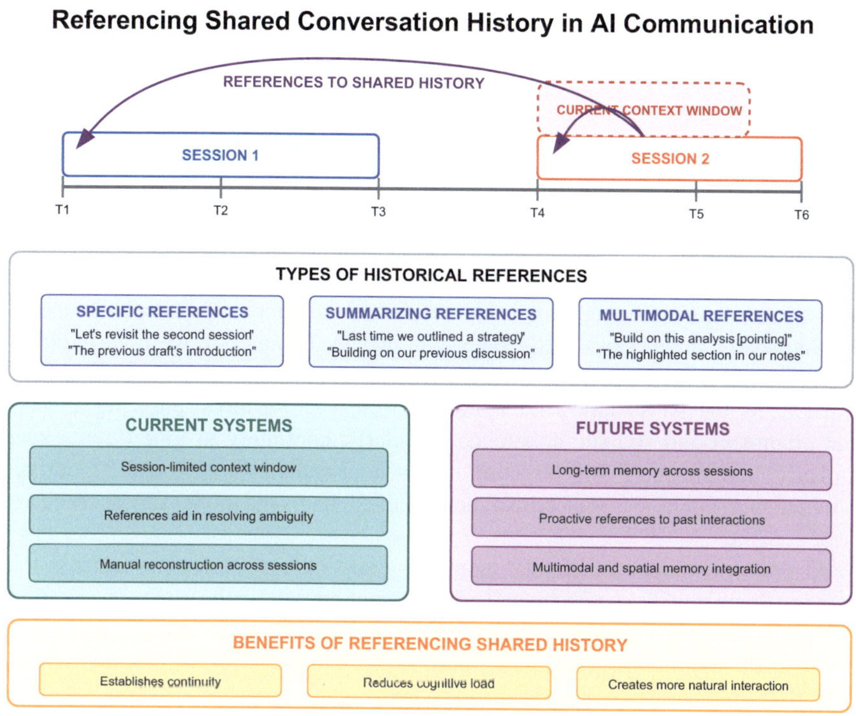

Fig. 10.9 Navigating shared history in human-AI communication. This diagram illustrates how referencing shared conversation history transforms isolated exchanges into coherent dialogue, enhancing AI communication depth and efficiency. It visualises how references bridge across time and sessions, showing both current limitations (finite context windows) and future possibilities (persistent memory). The diagram contrasts different referencing strategies—from specific call-backs to multimodal integration—and highlights how these techniques reduce cognitive load while creating more natural, continuous interaction patterns that mirror the intrinsic temporal awareness of human dialogue

memory-aware communication—both now and in future conversational systems (Fig. 10.9).

10.3.2 Develop Contextual Continuity

Contextual continuity is the glue that holds extended human-AI interactions together, allowing conversations to build progressively rather than restarting with each prompt. This preserves coherence, deepens mutual understanding, and enables the cumulative development of tasks. Developing this continuity is especially crucial in scenarios where users and AI collaborate over time, across multiple topics, tasks, or emotional registers. While AI systems may simulate memory within short windows, accurate continuity often depends on deliberate human effort and intelligent system design.

At its core, contextual continuity involves maintaining a stable thread of meaning and purpose throughout a session or across multiple sessions. For example, a user interacting with an AI research assistant might begin by defining a problem, later request background information, and eventually ask for help drafting a literature review. Without continuity, each request might be interpreted in isolation, leading to fragmented or repetitive outputs. But when the AI is guided to preserve the evolving project frame, it can offer more targeted support, reuse relevant concepts, and adapt its tone or focus as the task develops.

Present-day users can support continuity through consistent terminology, restating goals, referencing earlier outputs, and incremental refinement of prompts. A science communicator might say: "Let's keep building on the analogy we used earlier—comparing neurons to cities—when explaining synaptic transmission." This technique helps the AI sustain a metaphorical frame across turns, ensuring conceptual alignment and stylistic coherence. Similarly, continuity in tone ("Let's keep it playful"), audience ("Still targeting high school students"), or intent ("Continue summarising, but now from a critical perspective") helps the model stay anchored to prior context.

AI systems equipped with chat memory or session summaries can assist in this process. Some models can now recall prior interactions within the same conversation, or even across days, allowing users to pick up where they left off. In such cases, contextual continuity becomes semi-automated, though still fragile: users may need to verify what the system remembers and correct any inaccuracies or omissions. This underscores the importance of meta-awareness in AI design—systems must not only store context but signal what is retained, what is inferred, and when clarification is needed.

In future, more advanced AI systems will manage continuity in more profound, more human-like ways. They may track goals, themes, and emotional trajectories across interactions, functioning less as reactive tools and more as collaborative partners. Imagine a personal knowledge assistant that remembers a researcher's evolving interests over months, helps refine hypotheses, and alerts them when new papers are published in a previously defined area of focus. Such continuity enables strategic co-thinking and long-term alignment.

In speculative domains, continuity may be developed through shared memory artefacts: dynamic mind maps, evolving dialogue trees, or co-authored notebooks. These digital traces would not merely record interaction history but actively shape the AI's interpretation and responses. For instance, in an AI-assisted novel-writing tool, characters' personalities, plot arcs, and unresolved tensions could be tracked as persistent context elements, allowing the AI to propose developments that remain faithful to the narrative's internal logic.

Ultimately, developing contextual continuity is about fostering an ongoing relationship between user and AI—one where meaning is not reinvented at each turn, but built upon, sustained, and evolved. It enhances productivity, creativity, and trust, making AI not just a responsive engine but a participant in an unfolding process. As human-AI collaboration grows more sophisticated and enduring, the ability to maintain such continuity will be essential to the future of intelligent communication (Fig. 10.10).

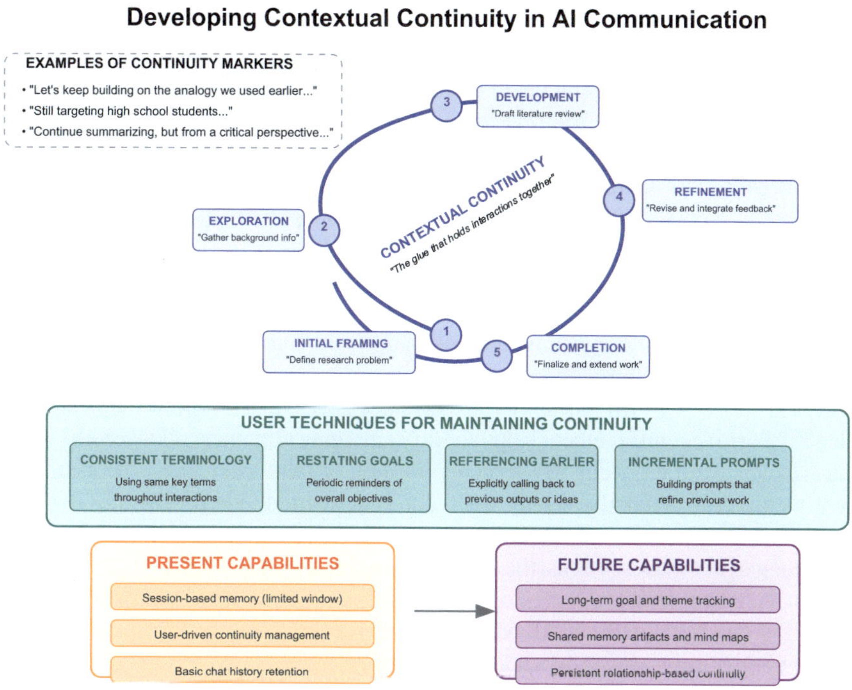

Fig. 10.10 Spiral of contextual continuity in AI communication. This diagram illustrates how contextual continuity transforms isolated AI interactions into coherent, progressive dialogue. The spiral path shows how conversations build cumulatively through stages, bound together by user techniques that maintain consistent framing. The visualisation contrasts current approaches requiring deliberate human effort with future capabilities that may enable more persistent, relationship-based continuity. Like a narrative thread weaving through time, effective contextual continuity allows meaning to evolve rather than reset, enabling deeper collaboration and more sophisticated outcomes in human-AI communication

10.4 Adapting and Negotiating Meaning

10.4.1 Adapt to AI's Evolving Understanding

As AI systems become more sophisticated, their understanding is no longer static but evolves throughout an interaction. This evolution may include learning from prior user input, dynamically updating internal assumptions, refining its grasp of goals, or adjusting its tone in response to emotional cues. For users, adapting to this evolving understanding means recognising that AI is not simply retrieving canned answers—it is forming and reforming a contextual model in real-time. To collaborate effectively, users must not only shape this evolving model but also respond to it with awareness and agility.

In present-day applications, evidence of evolving understanding can already be seen in advanced conversational models. For example, during a multistep planning session, an AI assistant might begin with a basic outline of an event and then, based on user refinements, start offering more tailored suggestions, referencing previous decisions about tone, priorities, or constraints. The AI might move from "Here's a sample agenda" to "Given your preference for short sessions and interactive formats, I suggest…" This shift indicates not just recall, but adaptation: the model is updating its context based on accumulating interaction data.

For users, adapting to this evolution requires active engagement. It involves noticing when the AI has correctly inferred something new and reinforcing it. Suppose the AI starts suggesting ideas that align with a newly expressed preference (e.g. "You said you're targeting a younger audience, so here's a trendier title"). In that case, the user can affirm this shift with feedback: "Yes, that's right—keep targeting Gen Z." Positive reinforcement helps solidify emerging alignment. Conversely, when the AI veers off track—due to overgeneralisation or false inference—the user must gently correct it: "Actually, I only wanted a light-hearted tone for the introduction, not the whole article."

In long or complex sessions, the user may also need to reorient the AI periodically, especially when multiple layers of evolving context coexist. Consider a user co-authoring an article with an AI system. As the draft progresses, the AI may begin making stylistic or structural choices based on earlier segments. If the user now decides to shift the tone—from academic to journalistic, for instance—they must explicitly signal this change and help the AI recalibrate: "Let's pivot to a more informal tone starting from Section 3."

In future systems equipped with longer-term memory or self-adjusting dialogue frameworks, AI may become more adept at adapting proactively. For instance, an AI tutor might track a student's confusion across multiple sessions and revise its teaching strategy accordingly, offering simpler examples, adjusting the pace, or revisiting foundational concepts. The student, in turn, might notice and say, "I appreciate the slower walkthrough—it's helping." This mutual awareness builds a feedback loop in which the AI refines its approach while the user adjusts expectations and strategies in response.

Speculatively, AI systems may develop metacognitive capacities—signalling not only what they understand but how confident or uncertain they are in that understanding. A creative AI might say, "I'm interpreting your request as a mood board for a minimalist brand—let me know if I've misunderstood." Such cues invite the user to participate in refining the evolving model of meaning, fostering a form of mutual adjustment.

Adapting to AI's evolving understanding is, at its core, a communicative dance. It requires patience, attentiveness, and iterative feedback. It asks users to remain attuned to subtle shifts in the AI's behaviour, to recognise emerging alignment, and to recalibrate when necessary. As AI systems become increasingly capable of complex reasoning, emotional inference, and multimodal comprehension, this mutual adaptation will underpin the most productive and meaningful forms of human-AI collaboration (Fig. 10.11).

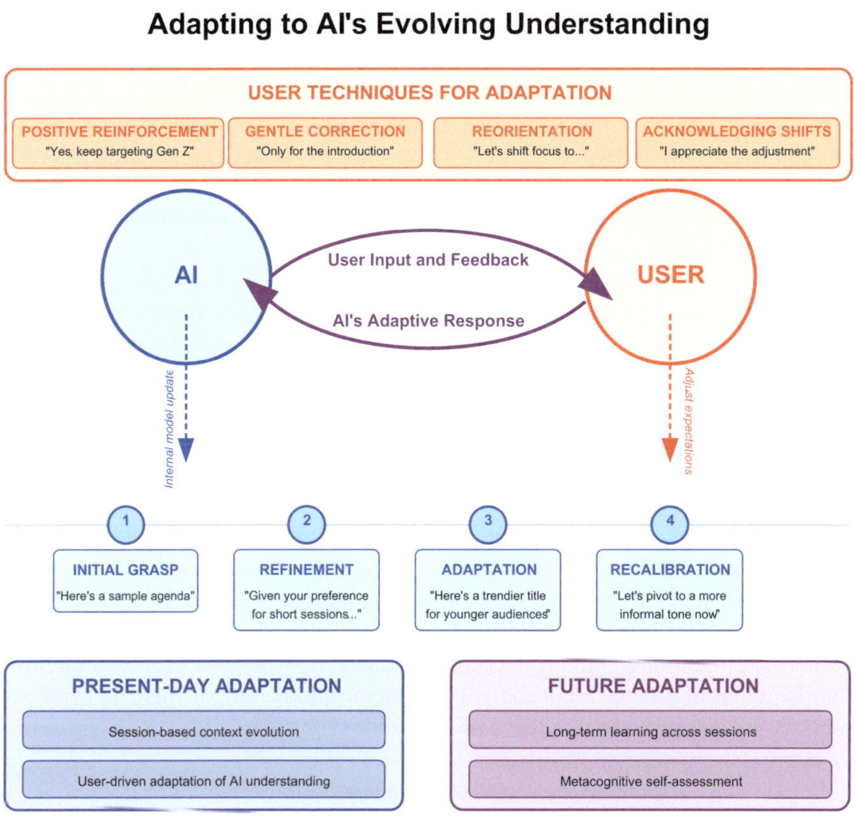

Fig. 10.11 Dynamic dance of mutual adaptation. This diagram illustrates the bidirectional process of adaptation between users and evolving AI understanding. It portrays communication as a dynamic dance where both partners adjust in response to each other, the AI refining its contextual model. At the same time, users provide strategic guidance through reinforcement, correction, and reorientation. The visualisation traces AI understanding from initial grasp through refinement, adaptation, and recalibration, highlighting how present capabilities require deliberate user guidance while future systems may develop metacognitive awareness to more proactively participate in this collaborative evolution

10.4.2 Practice Context Negotiation

Context in human-AI interaction is not always fixed, agreed upon, or even clearly defined at the outset. It often emerges through dialogue, adapts to changing user needs, or must be aligned across divergent expectations. *Context negotiation* refers to the dynamic process through which users and AI systems collaboratively construct, adjust, and align their shared understanding of the task, domain, emotional tone, and intended outcome. Rather than assuming perfect mutual comprehension, this principle acknowledges that misunderstandings, ambiguities, or misalignments are part of the communicative process and can be resolved through iterative clarification.

In today's systems, context negotiation typically occurs when a user senses that the AI has misunderstood or misinterpreted a prompt. For instance, a user might ask a generative model to "write a short article about climate change" and receive a technical, policy-focused summary, when their real intention was a persuasive editorial for a general audience. A follow-up, such as "Make it more emotional and less formal—something you'd read in a magazine," signals a revision of context. The AI, in turn, adjusts its style and framing. In such exchanges, the prompt becomes not a static instruction but part of a fluid negotiation.

Effective context negotiation relies on user awareness and responsiveness. Users must monitor how the AI interprets their inputs and be willing to clarify or recalibrate as needed. This can involve redefining tone ("Use simpler language"), intent ("Focus on inspiring action, not just informing"), or audience ("Write as if addressing high school students"). Each revision updates the AI's contextual frame, producing a more aligned response. When done skilfully, this process resembles conversational scaffolding, where meaning is co-constructed turn by turn.

AI systems can also initiate context negotiation, especially when uncertain. Some models now include confidence estimation or clarifying questions, such as "Did you mean a formal email or a casual one?" or "Would you like me to include sources for this summary?" These questions, though seemingly minor, reflect an emerging conversational intelligence that reduces errors and enhances user agency. In future, we may see more autonomous negotiation strategies, where AI proposes multiple interpretations of a vague input and asks the user to choose among them, as in: "I can interpret 'launch strategy' as either a product rollout or a marketing campaign—shall we clarify?"

In high-stakes or creative settings, context negotiation becomes even more vital. A user working with an AI collaborator on a film script might continually shift expectations: "No, that's too dystopian—try something more hopeful." Or "That character's voice doesn't feel authentic—make them sound more conflicted." Each act of feedback helps steer the model toward a richer, more nuanced understanding of the evolving creative intent. Similarly, in therapeutic or coaching applications, users and AI may co-negotiate emotional tone and relational boundaries, ensuring the system's responses remain helpful and respectful.

Speculatively, as AI systems develop more sophisticated internal models of meaning, they may begin negotiating not just linguistic context but also conceptual frameworks. A philosophy student working with a reasoning AI might find themselves discussing definitions of consciousness, where the AI proposes interpretive angles: "Are we assuming a materialist view here, or shall we explore dualist perspectives?" This higher-order negotiation would reflect a maturing dialogue where the AI is not just responding but participating in shaping the conceptual scope.

Ultimately, practising context negotiation cultivates more resilient and adaptable human-AI communication. It reframes misunderstandings not as breakdowns, but as opportunities for refinement. It encourages users to take an active role in shaping the interaction and enables AI systems to become more responsive, transparent, and conversationally intelligent. In future of AI collaboration, context will not always

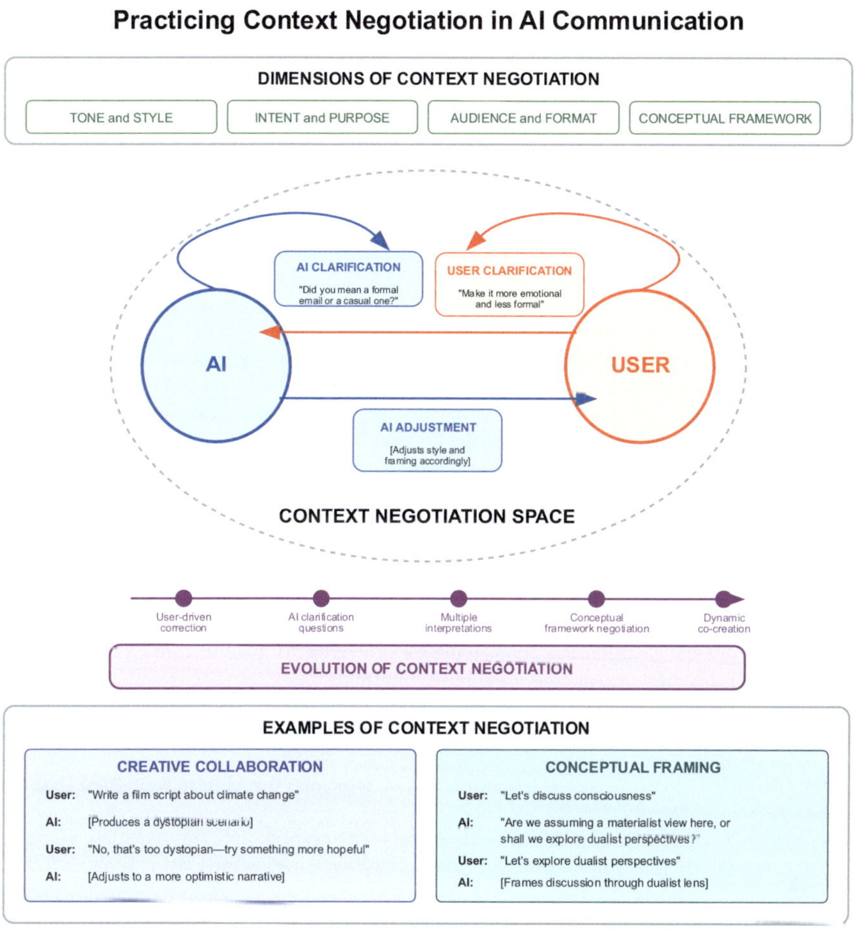

Fig. 10.12 Dynamic process of context negotiation. This diagram illustrates how users and AI systems collaboratively construct and refine shared understanding through iterative dialogue. It visualises context negotiation as a dynamic exchange where misunderstandings become opportunities for alignment rather than communication failures. The central negotiation space shows how clarifications, adjustments, and questions flow bidirectionally, while examples demonstrate this process in creative and conceptual domains. The diagram traces the evolution from basic correction to sophisticated co-creation of meaning, highlighting how effective negotiation transforms AI from a static responder to an active participant in constructing contextual understanding

be given—it will be shared, revised, and co-created through dynamic, negotiated meaning (Fig. 10.12).

Bibliography

Austin JL (1962) How to do things with words. Oxford University Press, Oxford
Bahree A (2024) Generative AI in action. Manning Publications
Bender E et al (2021) On the dangers of stochastic parrots: can language models be too big? In: Proceedings of the 2021 ACM conference on fairness, accountability, and transparency, pp 610–623
Bostrom N (2014) Superintelligence: paths, dangers, strategies. Oxford University Press, Oxford
Brown BR (2025) Human–machine teaming using large language models. In: Interdependent human-machine teams. Academic Press, pp 41–66
Brown TB et al (2020) Language models are few-shot learners. Adv Neural Inf Process Syst 33:1877–1901
Bura C, Myakala PK, Jonnalgadda A K (2025) Ethical prompt engineering: addressing bias, transparency, and fairness. Int J Res Anal Rev (IJRAR) 12(1). www.ijrar.org
Choi WC, Chang CI (2025) A survey of techniques, key components, strategies, challenges, and student perspectives on prompt engineering for large language models (LLMs) in education, 25 Mar 2025. https://doi.org/10.20944/preprints202503.1808.v1. Accessed 8 May 2025
Clark H (1996) Using language. Cambridge University Press, Cambridge
Debnath T, Siddiky MNA, Rahman ME et al (2025) A comprehensive survey of prompt engineering techniques in large language models. TechRxiv. https://doi.org/10.36227/techrxiv.174140719.96375390/v1. Accessed 10 May 2025
Dhamani N, Engler M (2024) Introduction to generative AI: an ethical, societal, and legal overview. Manning Publications
Eliot L (2024) Essentials of prompt engineering for generative AI: practical advances in artificial intelligence and machine learning. LBE Press Publishing
Ferraris AF, Audrito D, Di Caro L et al (2025) The architecture of language: understanding the mechanics behind LLMs. In: Cambridge forum on AI: law and governance, vol 1. Cambridge University Press
Floridi L, Cowls J (2019) A unified framework of five principles for AI in society. Harv Data Sci Rev 1(1)
Geroimenko V (2025a) Key challenges in prompt engineering. In: The essential guide to prompt engineering: key principles, techniques, challenges, and security risks. Springer Nature Switzerland, Cham, pp 85–102
Geroimenko V (2025b) Key principles of good prompt design. In: The essential guide to prompt engineering: key principles, techniques, challenges, and security risks. Springer Nature Switzerland, Cham, pp 17–36
Geroimenko V (2025c) Key techniques for writing effective prompts. In: The essential guide to prompt engineering: key principles, techniques, challenges, and security risks. Springer Nature Switzerland, Cham, pp 37–83
Geroimenko V (2025d) The essential guide to prompt engineering: key principles, techniques, challenges, and security risks. Springer
Geroimenko V (2025e) Key security risks in prompt engineering. In: The essential guide to prompt engineering: key principles, techniques, challenges, and security risks. Springer Nature Switzerland, Cham, pp 103–120
GitHub (2025) Prompt engineering guide. https://github.com/dair-ai/Prompt-Engineering-Guide. Accessed 10 Apr 2025
Greenwood M (2024) Artificial intelligence: a practical guide to using AI in everyday life. Ochreland Publishing
Gunkel DJ (2020) Robot rights. MIT Press, Cambridge
Hsu HP (2025) From programming to prompting: developing computational thinking through large language model-based generative artificial intelligence. TechTrends 1–22
Huang MX et al (2022) Adaptive conversational AI: dynamic strategies for human-AI interaction. Int J Hum Comput Stud 160:102798

Huang G, Xiao Y, Jiang L et al (2025) Beyond prompt engineering: a reinforced token-level input refinement for large language models. Proc AAAI Conf Artif Intell 39(22):24113–24121

i Picó JF, Catta-Preta M, Omeñaca AT et al (2025) The time machine: future scenario generation through generative AI tools. Future Internet 17(1):1–15

Jobin A et al (2019) The global landscape of AI ethics guidelines. Nat Mach Intell 1(9):389–399

Kannan R, Ahmad M (eds) (2025) Generative AI foundations, developments, and applications. IGI Global

Khan I (2024) The quick guide to prompt engineering. Wiley

Kim J, Sundar SS (2012) Anthropomorphism of computers: is it mindlessness or mindfulness? Comput Hum Behav 28(1):241–250

Kushwaha V, Ragavan SS, Subhajit Roy S (2025) A measure based generalizable approach to understandability. arXiv:2503.21615. https://doi.org/10.48550/arXiv.2503.21615. Accessed 19 Apr 2025

Lakoff G, Johnson M (1980) Metaphors we live by. University of Chicago Press, Chicago

Lee D, Palmer E (2025) Prompt engineering in higher education: a systematic review to help inform curricula. Int J Educ Technol High Educ 22(1):7

Lee JY, Kang S, Yoo S (2025) Can we predict the effect of prompts? arXiv preprint arXiv:2501. 18883. Accessed 12 May 2025

Lindley J, Whitham R (2025) From prompt engineering to prompt craft. In: Proceedings of the nineteenth international conference on tangible, embedded, and embodied interaction, Mar 2025, pp 1–12

López-Pérez B et al (2025) Exploring the potential of large language models to understand interpersonal emotion regulation strategies from narratives. Emotion. Advance online publication. https://doi.org/10.1037/emo0001528. Accessed 19 Apr 2025

Luger GF (2020) Artificial intelligence: structures and strategies for complex problem solving, 6th edn. Pearson, Boston

Maaz S, Palaganas JC, Palaganas G et al (2025) A guide to prompt design: foundations and applications for healthcare simulationists. Front Med 11:1504532

Marcus G (2020) The next decade in AI: four steps towards robust artificial intelligence. arXiv preprint arXiv:2002.06177. Accessed 12 May 2025

Mishra M, Ara A, Mishra S (2025) Exploring human-AI collaboration in higher education: an investigation into AI-enabled personalized learning. In: Prompt engineering and generative AI applications for teaching and learning. IGI Global Scientific Publishing, pp 483–502

Mitchell M (2019) Artificial intelligence: a guide for thinking humans. Farrar, Straus and Giroux, New York

OpenAI (2025a) Best practices for prompt engineering with the OpenAI API. https://help.openai.com/en/articles/6654000-best-practices-for-prompt-engineering-with-the-openai-api. Accessed 20 Apr 2025

OpenAI (2025b) Research. https://openai.com/research/index/

Phoenix J, Taylor M (2024) Prompt engineering for generative AI. O'Reilly Media

PremaLatha V, Kumar AD, Parveen N (2025) Optimizing interactions: strategies for prompt engineering in large language models. Edu-Tech Enterp 3:24

Prompt Engineering Guide (2025) https://www.promptingguide.ai/. Accessed 7 Mar 2025

Rahwan I (2018) Society-in-the-loop: programming the algorithmic social contract. Ethics Inf Technol 20(1):5–14

Reddy CKK, Anoushka P, Draksharapu A et al (2025) Beyond text: analyzing artificial intelligence models through prompt engineering. In: Future tech startups and innovation in the age of AI, pp 120–156

Russell S (2019) Human compatible: artificial intelligence and the problem of control. Viking, New York

Sasson Lazovsky G, Raz T, Kenett YN (2025) The art of creative inquiry—from question asking to prompt engineering. J Creat Behav 59(1):e671

Searle J (1969) Speech acts: an essay in the philosophy of language. Cambridge University Press, Cambridge

Shneiderman B (2022) Human-centered AI. Oxford University Press, Oxford

Siau K, Wang W (2018) Building trust in artificial intelligence, machine learning, and robotics. CUTTER Bus Technol J 31(2):47–53

Sihi D, Ryan A (2025) Crafting and evaluating generative AI prompts: insights from students, educators, and marketers. Mark Educ Rev 1–7

Suchman L (2007) Human-machine reconfigurations: plans and situated actions, 2nd edn. Cambridge University Press, Cambridge

Tegmark M (2017) Life 3.0: being human in the age of artificial intelligence. Penguin, London

Turing A (1950) Computing machinery and intelligence. Mind 59(236):433–460

Vairamani AD, Nayyar A (2024) Prompt engineering: empowering communication. CRC Press

Winograd T (1972) Understanding natural language. Academic Press, New York

Wittgenstein L (1953) Philosophical investigations. Blackwell, Oxford

Chapter 11
Feedback and Iterative Refinement: Improving AI Responses Through Interaction Cycles

Abstract This chapter presents feedback and iterative refinement as core principles of communicative intelligence in human AI interaction. It explores how conversational feedback loops transform static outputs into dynamic, co-developed exchanges. The chapter covers practical strategies such as checking understanding, requesting clarification, verifying outputs and interpretations, and ensuring mutual alignment between the user and the AI system. It addresses mechanisms for managing uncertainty, encouraging transparency, and refining AI-generated content through structured revision cycles. Emphasis is placed on feedback granularity, emotional tone, appreciation, and the importance of meta-feedback for evaluating the communication process itself. The chapter concludes with a discussion of systematic evaluation frameworks and long-term adaptation, highlighting how future AI systems can evolve communicatively by learning from feedback across modalities, contexts, and user preferences. Together, these principles establish feedback as a cornerstone of adaptive, transparent, and co-creative AI communication.

Keywords AI feedback loops · Iterative refinement · Clarification and alignment · Verification and evaluation · Adaptive AI communication · Meta-feedback

In human-AI communication, the quality of interaction is not determined solely by the initial prompt and the AI's immediate response, but by the dynamic exchange that unfolds between them. As users engage with AI systems across increasingly complex tasks, it becomes essential to treat dialogue as an evolving process rather than a one-off event. This chapter explores how feedback, clarification, iterative refinement, and reflective dialogue can transform AI outputs over time, leading to more precise, context-aware, and aligned results. It examines strategies for checking mutual understanding, managing uncertainty, adjusting outputs through revision, and evaluating the quality of communication itself. Together, these principles outline a shift from static exchanges to living feedback loops—cycles of adaptation and learning in which human and machine co-develop meaning through interaction.

V. Geroimenko, *Beyond and After Prompt Engineering: The Future of AI Communication*, https://doi.org/10.1007/978-3-032-04569-0_11

11.1 Checking Understanding and Interpretation

11.1.1 Check for Understanding

One of the most fundamental principles of effective communication—whether between humans or between humans and AI—is the active verification of mutual understanding. In the context of AI interaction, "checking for understanding" refers to the deliberate practice of ensuring that the AI system has correctly grasped the user's intent, meaning, and expectations. This is not merely a matter of confirming that a prompt has been processed; it is about assessing whether the AI's internal representation of the user's input aligns with the user's actual communicative goals.

In present-day interactions, this principle is often applied implicitly. For instance, when users issue complex or multipart prompts, they frequently follow up with clarifications or corrections after receiving an AI-generated response that partially misses the point. A researcher might ask a language model to "summarise the philosophical implications of Nietzsche's eternal recurrence," and upon receiving a response that only focuses on historical context, the user may quickly realise the need to refine the prompt or redirect the AI. This ad hoc feedback mechanism, while effective to an extent, places the burden of correction on the user and lacks structural intentionality.

To advance the quality of AI-human collaboration, future systems must take a more proactive role in checking for understanding. AI agents will increasingly ask confirming questions, such as, "Do you want me to focus on the philosophical impact or the historical development of the concept?" before proceeding. These clarification checkpoints mirror the way human interlocutors engage in active listening—rephrasing or summarising input to validate comprehension. Such strategies are already being embedded in conversational agents designed for education, where adaptive learning platforms periodically assess whether students understand the material before continuing, thus modelling good communicative behaviour.

Looking ahead, this principle will become even more central in high-stakes domains. Consider a future scenario in healthcare where an AI co-pilot assists a physician in diagnosing rare conditions. When the physician inputs a nuanced symptom profile, the AI might respond not with a diagnosis, but with a structured summary: "To confirm, you're describing an adult patient with intermittent tachycardia, joint hypermobility, and a family history of connective tissue disorders. Is that correct?" In such contexts, failure to verify understanding could lead to serious consequences, making interpretive alignment a non-negotiable step in the interaction loop.

At the technical level, this principle will also shape interface design. We can expect future multimodal systems to include visual or spatial confirmations, such as highlighting parts of a document that the AI interpreted as central to a user query, or showing a "thought map" of inferred priorities based on natural language instructions. These features will foster transparency, allowing users to catch misunderstandings early and transform communication with AI from a linear exchange into a collaborative alignment process.

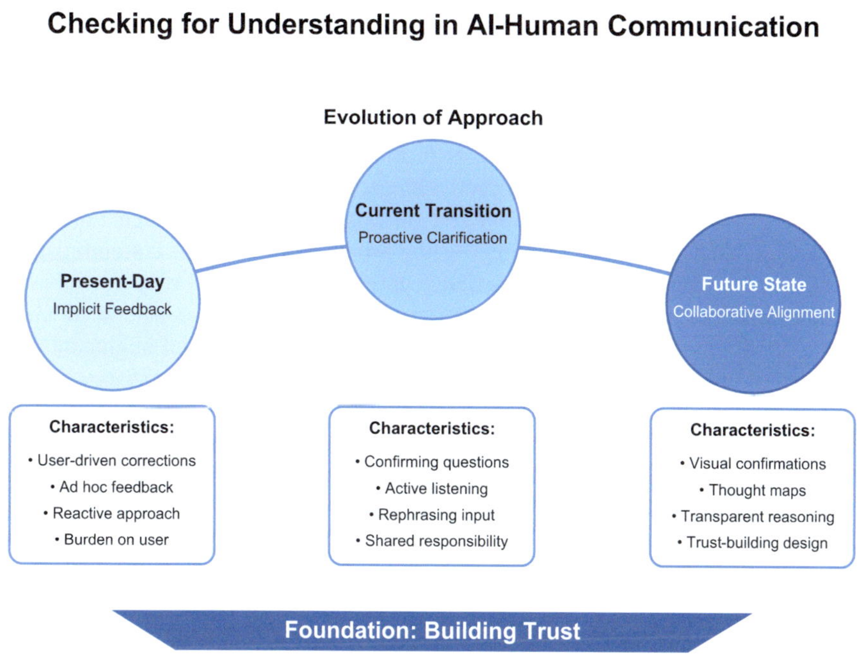

Fig. 11.1 Evolution of understanding verification in AI-human communication. This diagram illustrates the transformation of "checking for understanding" from a user-driven, reactive process to a collaborative alignment mechanism. It maps the progression from present-day implicit feedback loops through transitional active listening techniques toward future multimodal confirmation systems. The visualisation highlights how this principle becomes increasingly central across domains like education and healthcare, evolving from ad hoc corrections to structured verification protocols. Ultimately, as depicted in the foundation, these advancements serve to build trust, transforming AI from tools into genuine co-communicators capable of attentive, meaningful interaction

Ultimately, checking for understanding is not only about avoiding errors; it is about building trust. When users feel that an AI system is genuinely attentive to their intentions—capable of confirming and calibrating its comprehension in real time—they are more likely to engage in deeper, more meaningful interactions. As AI becomes a co-communicator rather than a mere tool, this principle will be indispensable for creating systems that are not just efficient but genuinely responsive and communicatively intelligent (Fig. 11.1).

11.1.2 Request Clarification When Needed

Effective communication is grounded in the ability to recognise when a message is unclear and to seek clarification before proceeding. For human-AI interaction, this principle is particularly vital: the asymmetry between human intent and machine interpretation often gives rise to ambiguity, misalignment, or partial understanding. When an AI system actively requests clarification, it signals a shift from passive response generation to engaged, cooperative communication.

At present, most AI systems still operate with an assumption of certainty. When confronted with vague, contradictory, or incomplete prompts, they attempt to infer the most probable meaning and proceed with generating a response. This can result in answers that sound confident but rest on fragile interpretive foundations. For example, a user might ask, "Summarise the article and tell me if it's optimistic," without specifying what metric constitutes optimism. The model may guess based on sentiment but remain unaware of the user's deeper evaluative criteria. In such cases, the absence of clarification mechanisms leads to superficial alignment and may distort the intent behind the request.

To improve this, the next generation of AI communicators must be equipped with the capacity to pause, identify ambiguity, and ask targeted clarification questions. A well-designed assistant might respond: "Before I proceed, could you clarify whether you mean optimism in tone, projected outcomes, or underlying assumptions?" This not only improves the quality of the interaction but also mirrors human communication habits, where pauses for clarification are seen as signs of attentiveness and precision rather than inefficiency.

Real-world applications of clarification-seeking are already emerging. In customer service, some AI chatbots can flag contradictory input, such as when a user selects both "I received my item" and "My item hasn't arrived," and prompt for resolution. In creative writing tools, when a user asks the AI to "write in a more intense style," some systems now follow up with: "Would you like intensity through emotional tone, pacing, or vocabulary choice?" These clarification steps are primitive but important precedents for richer interactive scaffolding.

Looking ahead, clarification will become a core feature of AI systems operating in uncertain or high-complexity environments. Imagine a policy advisor AI working with a government official drafting climate legislation. When asked to "model the long-term effects of reduced carbon subsidies," a future AI system might reply: "Would you like the model to focus on economic impact, environmental metrics, or political feasibility? And what time frame should it cover—10 years, 30 years, or a century?" Here, clarification is not a detour—it is a gateway to relevance and accuracy.

Beyond text, multimodal interfaces will enable new modes of clarification. In a design collaboration, a user might gesture toward a 3D model and say, "Make this part more dynamic." The AI, uncertain about the referent of "this" or the meaning of "dynamic," could highlight its interpretation on the screen and ask for confirmation before proceeding. Similarly, voice-based agents might incorporate tonal cues, asking follow-up questions in a measured, human-like cadence when sensing hesitation or contradiction in the user's voice.

By normalising and embedding clarification as a standard practice, future AI systems will foster richer, more precise, and ultimately more trustworthy dialogue. This capacity to request clarification when needed transforms AI from a static output machine into an adaptive conversational partner—one that knows when it does not know and is unafraid to ask (Fig. 11.2).

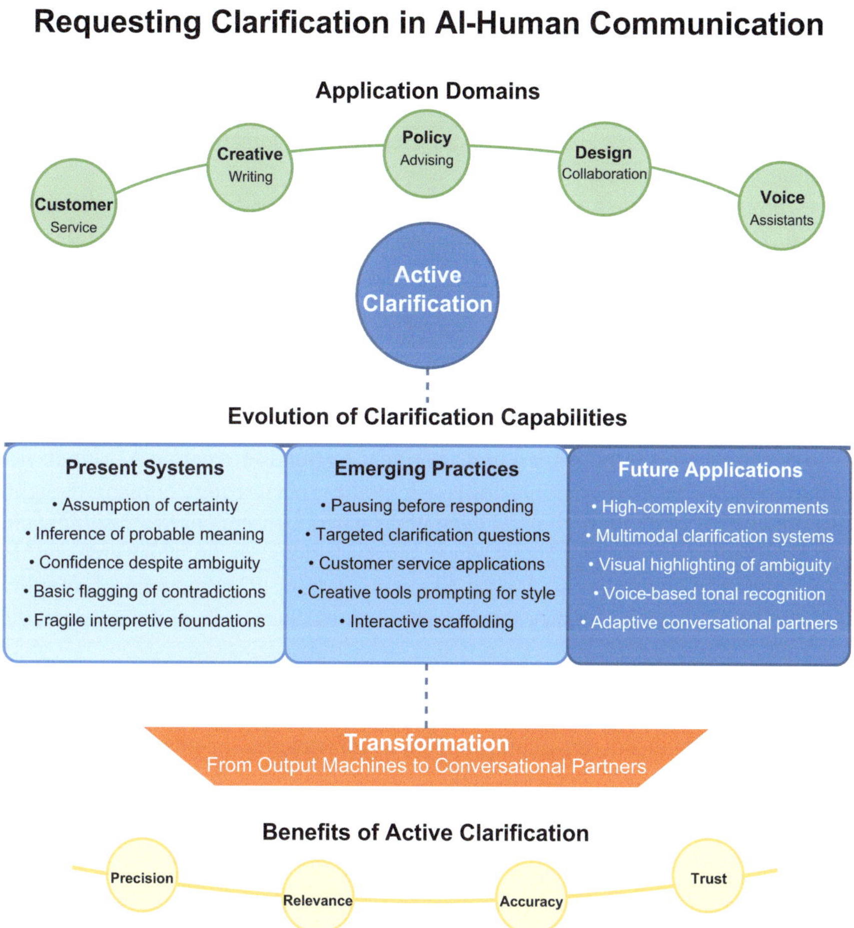

Fig. 11.2 Evolution of clarification-seeking in AI systems. This diagram illustrates how AI systems are transitioning from assuming certainty to actively seeking clarification when faced with ambiguity. It maps the progression from present-day systems that infer probable meaning to emerging practices that pause and question, and finally to future applications in complex environments. The visualisation highlights diverse application domains—from customer service to policy advising—while emphasising the benefits of precision, relevance, accuracy, and trust. At its core, clarification-seeking represents a fundamental shift that transforms AI from static output machines into adaptive conversational partners that acknowledge uncertainty and engage in cooperative communication

11.1.3 Verify AI Outputs

As AI-generated content becomes increasingly fluent and persuasive, the risk of misplaced trust grows. Verifying AI outputs—actively checking the accuracy, relevance, and appropriateness of responses—is therefore an essential communicative principle. While today's models can produce outputs that appear authoritative, their responses often rely on probabilistic inference rather than verified knowledge, making them susceptible to factual errors, hallucinations, or contextually inappropriate conclusions.

In current practice, this principle is widely acknowledged but inconsistently applied. For instance, students using AI for essay writing or summarisation may copy responses directly without cross-checking the sources or verifying the factual integrity of the content. Similarly, in technical domains, developers might ask an AI for sample code and assume it is correct, only to discover subtle bugs or deprecated methods upon implementation. This tendency to over-trust fluent language output—sometimes referred to as "automation bias"—poses a serious challenge to responsible AI communication.

To counteract this, users must adopt a verification mindset: treating AI outputs not as final answers, but as provisional drafts or hypotheses that require human oversight. This principle is particularly crucial in contexts where consequences are significant, such as medical recommendations, legal interpretations, or financial analysis. In these domains, it is not enough for the AI to sound right; its outputs must be explicitly validated through secondary sources, professional standards, or domain-specific protocols.

In parallel, AI systems themselves are beginning to take part in the verification process. Some current models, especially when fine-tuned for safety and reliability, now attempt to cite sources, qualify uncertain information, or generate counterarguments to their suggestions. For example, a legal assistant AI might respond to a question by providing not only a summary of a statute, but also the jurisdiction, date of revision, and a brief disclaimer: "Please confirm this interpretation with a legal professional, as laws may vary by region." These disclaimers represent early steps toward a communicative ethos in which AI takes partial responsibility for its outputs.

In future AI communication systems, verification is likely to evolve into a shared process between humans and machines. Consider a scenario in which a user asks an AI historian to explain the causes of a geopolitical conflict. Rather than delivering a single, unified narrative, the AI might present competing interpretations drawn from various historical sources, explicitly flagging ideological bias or evidentiary gaps. The user could then interact with a layered explanation interface—clicking into each branch of reasoning, evaluating citations, and contributing annotations. Such a process not only verifies content but also deepens the user's understanding and engagement.

Speculative developments may also include "self-verifying" AI agents—systems capable of cross-referencing their outputs against trusted knowledge bases, peer-reviewed corpora, or real-time data streams before presenting them. These agents might issue confidence scores alongside their responses or engage in self-critique, such as: "This conclusion relies heavily on data from 2019 and may not reflect post-pandemic economic shifts." In visual or multimodal systems, verification might take the form of overlays or visual cues, highlighting which parts of a chart or generated image are grounded in empirical data and which are AI-constructed extrapolations.

Ultimately, verification is not a sign of distrust—it is a marker of maturity in human-AI collaboration. As users, we must resist the temptation to conflate fluency with factuality. As designers, we must build systems that support and encourage verification. And as communicators, we must normalise the idea that even the most articulate AI response remains open to scrutiny, refinement, and correction (Fig. 11.3).

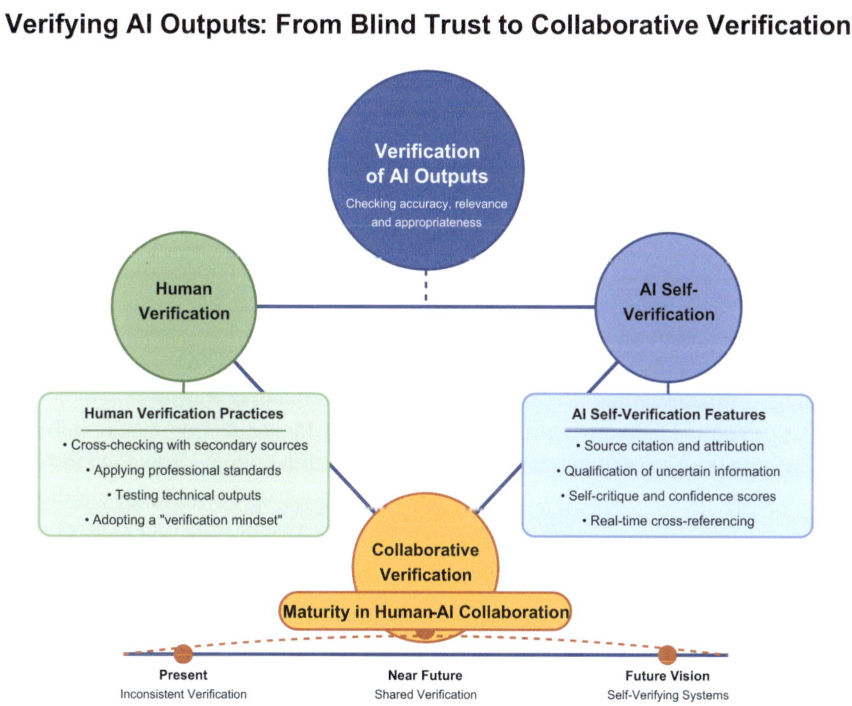

Fig. 11.3 Verification triad: evolving approaches to AI output validation. This diagram illustrates the evolution of AI output verification from inconsistent practices toward a mature collaborative framework. It depicts three interconnected verification modalities: human-driven oversight, AI self-verification mechanisms, and their collaborative integration. The framework is particularly crucial in high-stakes domains such as medicine and finance, where the consequences of unverified outputs can be significant. As verification evolves from present-day cross-checking to future self-validating systems, it represents not distrust but rather maturity in human-AI collaboration, transforming fluent AI responses from assumed authorities into provisional hypotheses requiring thoughtful validation

11.1.4 Check AI's Interpretation of Ambiguous Concepts

Ambiguity is inherent in natural language and human communication. Words carry multiple meanings, and intentions often depend on context, tone, culture, or shared history. For human interlocutors, disambiguation is usually intuitive, based on accumulated social and situational cues. However, for AI systems, disambiguating meaning requires algorithmic inference, and this process is not always correct, complete, or even transparent. It is therefore crucial to deliberately check how AI interprets ambiguous concepts, particularly in tasks involving judgement, evaluation, or abstraction.

In contemporary AI interactions, ambiguity typically arises when users employ polysemous words ("bank," "fair," "light"), culturally contingent terms ("liberal," "success," "respect"), or abstract requests ("make it more dynamic," "be more inclusive," "provide a deeper analysis"). These terms demand interpretive work that current AI systems perform through statistical associations or latent semantic modelling. However, these interpretations may diverge significantly from user intent. For example, when a teacher asks an AI to make an assignment "more inclusive," the system might focus on accessibility (e.g. font size or reading level). In contrast, the teacher might mean including diverse perspectives or historical voices.

To avoid such mismatches, users must explicitly check the AI's interpretation of ambiguous input before proceeding. This can be achieved by prompting the system to paraphrase its understanding ("What do you understand by 'inclusive' in this context?"), to offer multiple interpretations, or to summarise assumptions. Such clarification not only reduces errors but also reveals how the AI system encodes meaning—something that is typically hidden behind fluent output.

This principle is already gaining traction in areas like education, where tutors or students rely on AI to explain complex concepts. A student might ask an AI to "simplify Newton's laws." Still, unless the AI's interpretation of "simplify" is clarified—whether it means using analogies, removing equations, or adjusting for age level—the answer may miss its educational target. Similarly, in design or content creation, vague creative directions can lead to unexpected results. A marketing team might instruct an AI to "make the ad more emotional." Still, without checking how "emotional" is interpreted—whether it means sad, inspiring, nostalgic, or energising—the outcome may not align with campaign goals.

In future AI systems, mechanisms for resolving ambiguity will become more interactive, multimodal, and self-aware. An AI writing assistant, for instance, might respond to an ambiguous command with a visual disambiguation menu: "Do you mean 'fair' as in equitable, unbiased, or light in colour?" A virtual agent embedded in augmented reality might highlight specific areas of a physical prototype when the user says, "This part is unclear," and request clarification by cycling through possible interpretations. In dialogue-based systems, we may see agents that actively seek feedback by surfacing their semantic interpretations and inviting correction before acting on them.

Advanced systems may also incorporate cultural or personal profiles to guide disambiguation. A future AI trained to collaborate with a legal scholar from Egypt and a policy analyst from Sweden might interpret the term "justice" differently in each case, and proactively seek confirmation before engaging in comparative analysis. These developments would support more personalised and culturally sensitive communication, reducing the cognitive gap between user intent and machine execution.

Ultimately, checking how an AI system interprets ambiguous concepts is a safeguard against misalignment—but also a step toward richer, more nuanced dialogue. It turns language from a fixed command into a shared negotiation of meaning. In this way, ambiguity is no longer a communicative obstacle; it becomes a productive space for reflection, clarification, and co-creation between humans and machines (Fig. 11.4).

11.1.5 Verify that AI and Humans Are Aligned in Their Understanding

Beyond individual moments of clarification or disambiguation, effective communication with AI requires a broader, ongoing alignment of understanding between human and machine. This principle shifts from reactive correction to proactive confirmation: verifying that the human user and the AI system not only understand each other's inputs but also share a common interpretive framework, contextual grounding, and communicative goals. Without this alignment, even superficially correct interactions may mask more profound conceptual divergences that undermine the quality and utility of the exchange.

In today's AI systems, misalignment often remains hidden beneath polished output. A user may ask an AI to "generate a strategic plan for educational reform" and receive a well-structured response. However, unless the AI's interpretation of "strategic," "educational," or "reform" matches the user's implicit goals—such as prioritising equity over efficiency or systemic transformation over incremental change—the response may be irrelevant despite its surface competence. In this way, alignment is not just a matter of linguistic comprehension; it is a question of communicative intent and shared assumptions.

Verifying alignment in current practice often relies on iterative refinement: users must carefully review AI responses, then revise their prompts or add context until the system produces something that feels aligned. This trial-and-error approach, while functional, is cognitively demanding and inefficient, particularly in high-complexity tasks. Without explicit strategies for checking alignment, the interaction risks becoming one-sided, with the user constantly correcting an AI that fails to confirm shared understanding.

To address this, future AI systems will need to take an active role in alignment verification. One pathway is through reflective summarisation. Before executing a

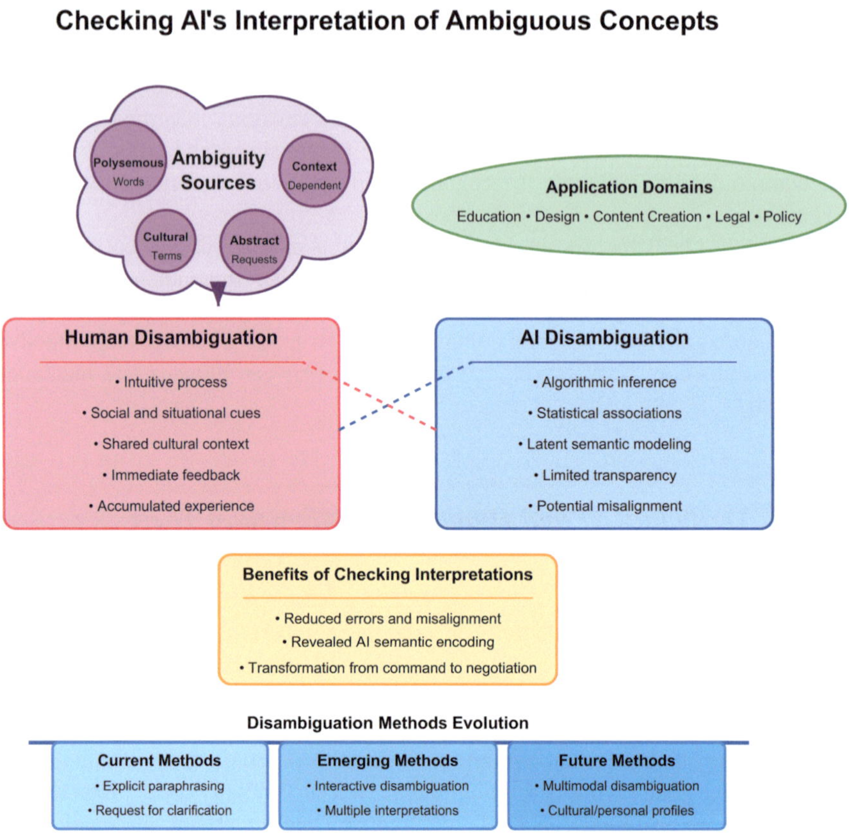

Fig. 11.4 Navigating linguistic ambiguity in human-AI communication. This diagram illustrates the critical process of checking AI's interpretation of ambiguous concepts—a fundamental challenge in human-AI communication. It contrasts humans' intuitive disambiguation through social cues with AI's algorithmic inference through statistical associations, highlighting the potential for misalignment. The visualisation maps sources of ambiguity (polysemous words, cultural terms, abstract requests) across various application domains. It traces the evolution of disambiguation methods from explicit paraphrasing to future multimodal systems with cultural awareness. By transforming interaction from command to negotiation, checking interpretations becomes not merely a corrective measure but a pathway to richer dialogue and co-creation

task or delivering an output, the AI might respond with a meta-statement, such as: "Based on your input, I understand that your goal is to develop a long-term policy framework for inclusive education in low-income urban areas, focusing on teacher training and digital equity. Am I correct?" Such responses help ensure that both parties are operating from the same conceptual foundation. This technique—already used in human coaching and negotiation—could become a standard feature in AI dialogue protocols.

More advanced systems may implement dynamic alignment tracking across longer sessions or multimodal interactions. In speculative scenarios, an AI collaborative partner working with a research team might maintain a persistent "shared understanding state"—a continuously updated model of project goals, values, constraints, and preferred terminology. This alignment model could be queried by the user at any time or flagged by the AI when deviations occur: "Your latest prompt prioritises cost-saving, but earlier inputs emphasised long-term community impact. Would you like to reconcile these objectives?"

In cross-cultural or interdisciplinary settings, alignment verification will be particularly crucial. An AI supporting joint policy development between environmental scientists and municipal planners might need to surface differences in underlying assumptions, such as definitions of "sustainability" or acceptable trade-offs between economic growth and ecological resilience. By mediating and reflecting these differences, the AI can serve not only as an assistant but as an alignment facilitator, helping humans coalesce around shared understanding.

Ultimately, verifying alignment is about fostering communicative integrity, ensuring that the interaction is not only syntactically correct but also semantically and pragmatically coherent. As human-AI collaboration deepens—from task execution to creative partnership—this principle will become indispensable. It shifts the focus from correctness to coordination, from transactional querying to mutual orientation. In doing so, it lays the foundation for a new communicative ethos in which AI is not just a tool responding to inputs, but a partner striving to think—and understand—together with us (Fig. 11.5).

11.2 Managing Uncertainty and Encouraging Transparency

11.2.1 Request Uncertainty Measures

In both human reasoning and machine-based inference, uncertainty is not a weakness—it is an essential indicator of epistemic humility. Yet in AI communication, uncertainty is often hidden beneath the surface of confident language. To foster more transparent and responsible human-AI interaction, users must develop the habit of requesting uncertainty measures. At the same time, AI systems must be designed to surface, explain, and contextualise their confidence levels.

Currently, most general-purpose language models are designed to produce fluent and assertive outputs, regardless of how uncertain the underlying model is. A user might ask for the cause of a recent geopolitical event or the side effects of a new pharmaceutical compound and receive a response framed in a tone of confident authority, even when the system is relying on limited, outdated, or ambiguous data. This performative certainty can mislead users, particularly in domains where probabilistic nuance or conflicting evidence is the norm.

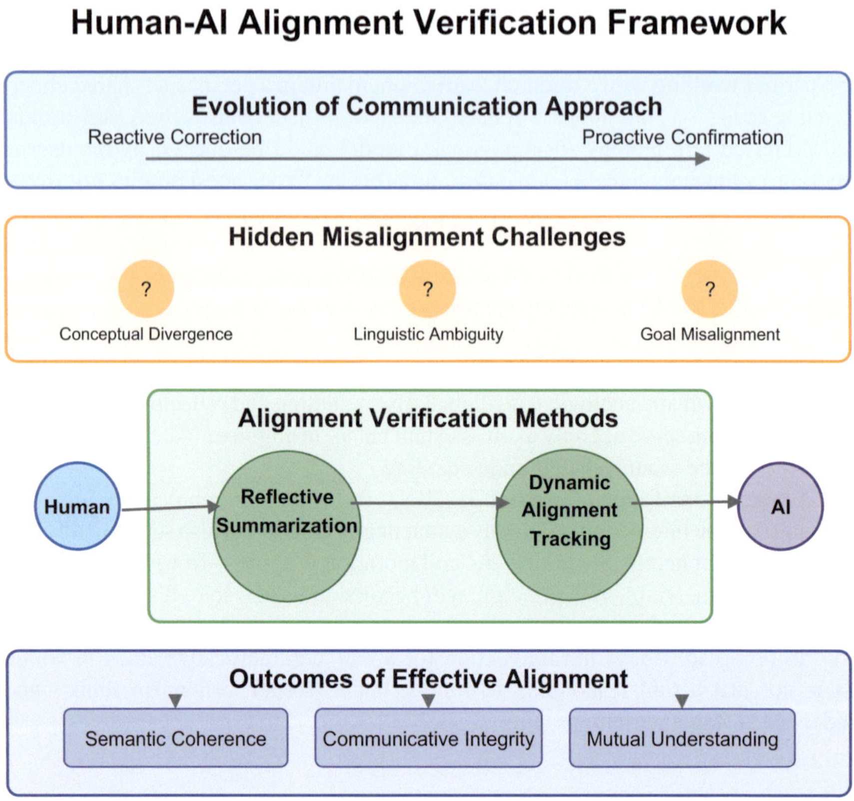

Fig. 11.5 Human-AI alignment verification framework. This diagram illustrates the evolution from reactive correction to proactive confirmation in human-AI communication, identifying key misalignment challenges and presenting two verification methods: reflective summarisation and dynamic alignment tracking. When implemented effectively, these approaches produce semantic coherence, communicative integrity, and mutual understanding, transforming AI from task executors to collaborative partners that share interpretive frameworks with humans. This verification process is particularly vital in complex, cross-cultural, or interdisciplinary contexts where shared understanding cannot be assumed

Efforts to address this issue are emerging across various AI subfields. Some AI-assisted medical platforms now return risk probabilities and diagnostic confidence intervals alongside suggested outcomes. Similarly, legal and financial AI tools often qualify their output with disclaimers or ranking-based relevance measures. Yet such mechanisms are usually buried in technical footnotes or separated from the main communicative flow. The next stage in AI-human communication will require more intuitive, interactive, and accessible ways of expressing uncertainty.

Users should be encouraged to explicitly ask for uncertainty: "How confident are you in this answer?" or "What's the likelihood that this recommendation is correct given the available data?" In response, AI systems might present layered responses, offering a direct answer, followed by a breakdown of confidence levels, sources of uncertainty, and potential caveats. For example, in a legal advisory interaction, the AI might respond: "There's an 80% chance this statute applies based on case history, but ambiguity arises in cases involving international jurisdiction. Would you like to explore these exceptions?"

In the future, uncertainty communication will likely become multimodal and adaptive. A wearable AI assistant could present high-confidence information with solid visual indicators, such as green outlines or full-opacity overlays, and low-confidence suggestions with translucent or flashing elements. In educational contexts, a tutoring AI might adjust its tone or prosody when expressing uncertainty, saying, for instance, "I'm not entirely sure, but here's what I can infer based on the material we've covered." This adds a layer of emotional and cognitive realism that helps learners distinguish between core facts and interpretive possibilities.

Moreover, advanced systems may offer epistemic meta-reflection, explaining not only that they are uncertain but also *why*, citing data sparsity, contradictions in the training set, or mismatches between current inputs and learned patterns. In speculative scientific collaboration, an AI co-researcher might flag emerging uncertainty patterns, such as: "This simulation yields divergent outcomes in 30% of runs. Further investigation into parameter stability is advised." In such scenarios, the AI does not merely respond—it acts as a dynamic partner in managing uncertainty.

Crucially, the ability to request and interpret uncertainty measures strengthens trust, rather than undermining it. It aligns human expectations with machine capabilities, reduces over-reliance, and promotes collaborative responsibility in decision-making. As AI communication matures, this principle will help cultivate not only more accurate interactions but also a deeper culture of critical engagement, mutual awareness, and shared epistemological responsibility between humans and machines (Fig. 11.6).

11.3 Supporting Iteration and Responsiveness

11.3.1 Enable Iterative Refinement

In complex or creative communication tasks, few outputs are perfect on the first try. Iterative refinement—the process of progressively improving AI responses through cycles of feedback, adjustment, and revision—is central to developing high-quality, aligned, and human-centred results. Rather than viewing a single AI output as an endpoint, this principle treats it as the beginning of a conversation: a working draft subject to ongoing improvement in collaboration with the user.

Current AI systems already support a limited form of iteration, allowing users to refine their prompts, highlight errors, or request improvements such as "make it more concise" or "add a counterargument." This ability to engage in incremental development of content is one of the defining strengths of generative AI tools in

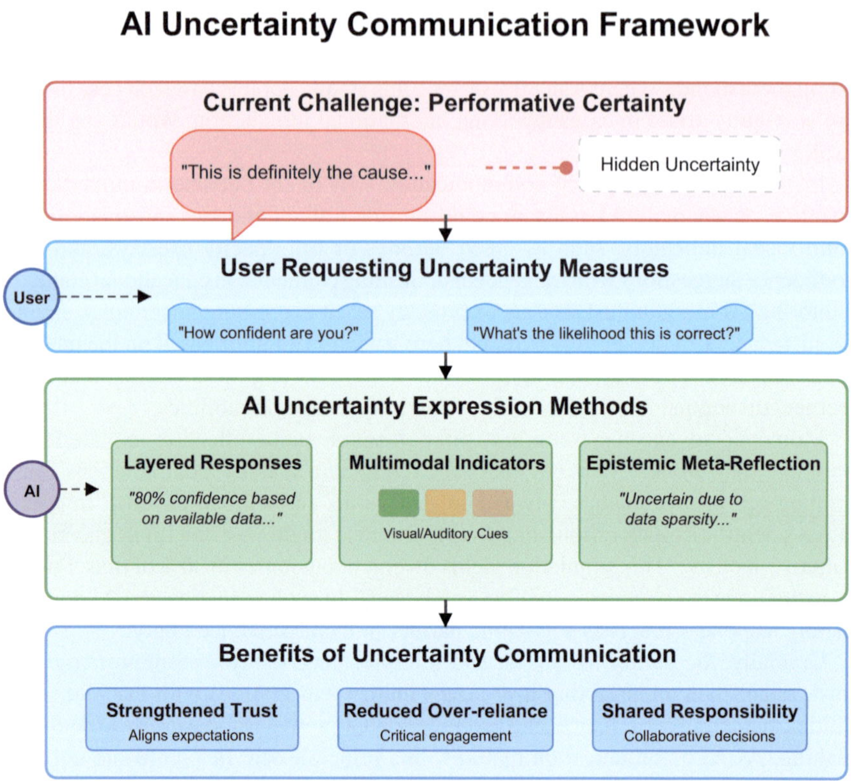

Fig. 11.6 AI uncertainty communication framework. This diagram illustrates the evolution from performative certainty to transparent uncertainty expression in AI systems. Current AI responses often project unwarranted confidence, hiding underlying limitations. By explicitly requesting uncertainty measures, users can prompt AI systems to employ three key expression methods: layered responses with statistical confidence levels, multimodal indicators using visual or auditory cues, and epistemic meta-reflection explaining uncertainty sources. This transparency yields three core benefits: strengthened trust through aligned expectations, reduced over-reliance through critical engagement, and shared epistemic responsibility in human-AI collaborative decision-making

domains such as writing, design, and programming. A user might ask an AI to generate a first draft of a grant proposal, then refine it by requesting more explicit justifications, more substantial evidence, or a more persuasive tone. Each iteration brings the output closer to the user's internal vision.

However, these iterations are often informal and linear, lacking structure, memory, or long-term coherence. The AI may treat each revision as a new prompt, without fully retaining the logic or intent behind prior steps. This can result in frustration, redundancy, or regression, where previously fixed issues resurface due to the absence of iterative memory. What is needed is a more intentional and system-supported approach to refinement—one that treats each interaction not as a restart, but as a contribution to a growing, shared artefact.

In the near future, enabling iterative refinement will involve the development of interaction models designed to support fluid revision cycles. Instead of simply requesting a better version, users will be able to interact with a version history, annotate specific elements, compare alternatives side by side, or set refinement goals ("make it more formal but retain the conversational tone"). The AI, in turn, will learn to track user preferences across turns, summarise changes, and suggest improvements not merely based on surface edits but based on evolving task objectives.

More advanced systems may implement refinement protocols that resemble design sprints or editorial processes. For example, in a speculative co-writing session between a human author and an AI collaborator, the AI might suggest a structured sequence: "First, let's revise the argument structure; then we can focus on stylistic polish; finally, we'll optimise for the target audience." At each stage, the human could accept, modify, or redirect the refinement strategy, allowing for a dynamic division of labour and shared creative control.

Multimodal and domain-specific interfaces will also play a role. In a future visual design environment, an AI might offer layered suggestions—altering colour palettes, adjusting spacing, or proposing new layouts—while the user iterates by accepting, modifying, or discarding these changes with simple gestures or voice commands. In software development, an AI coding assistant may propose alternate solutions and invite the user to test and refine through simulation cycles or user feedback integration.

Enabling iterative refinement also invites a philosophical shift: from viewing AI as a one-shot solution generator to treating it as a dialogical partner in extended, evolving projects. This approach supports a co-creative ethos in which success is measured not by immediate accuracy but by adaptability, responsiveness, and sustained progress. As the complexity of human-AI tasks increases, this principle will be foundational, not only for the quality of outputs, but for the quality of the communicative relationship itself (Fig. 11.7).

11.3.2 Establish Feedback Loops

At the heart of any adaptive system lies a feedback loop—a structured process through which actions are evaluated, outcomes are assessed, and new inputs are generated based on that evaluation. In human-AI interaction, establishing feedback loops means more than just correcting errors or requesting improvements. It involves creating a sustained, bidirectional process in which both the human and the AI learn from prior exchanges to improve future performance, understanding, and alignment.

Today's AI systems support rudimentary feedback mechanisms. A user might rate a chatbot's answer, click a thumbs-up or thumbs-down, or rephrase a prompt after receiving an unsatisfactory response. However, these forms of feedback are often shallow, anonymous, and disconnected from the broader trajectory of the conversation. The AI may acknowledge the feedback, but rarely integrates it meaningfully into

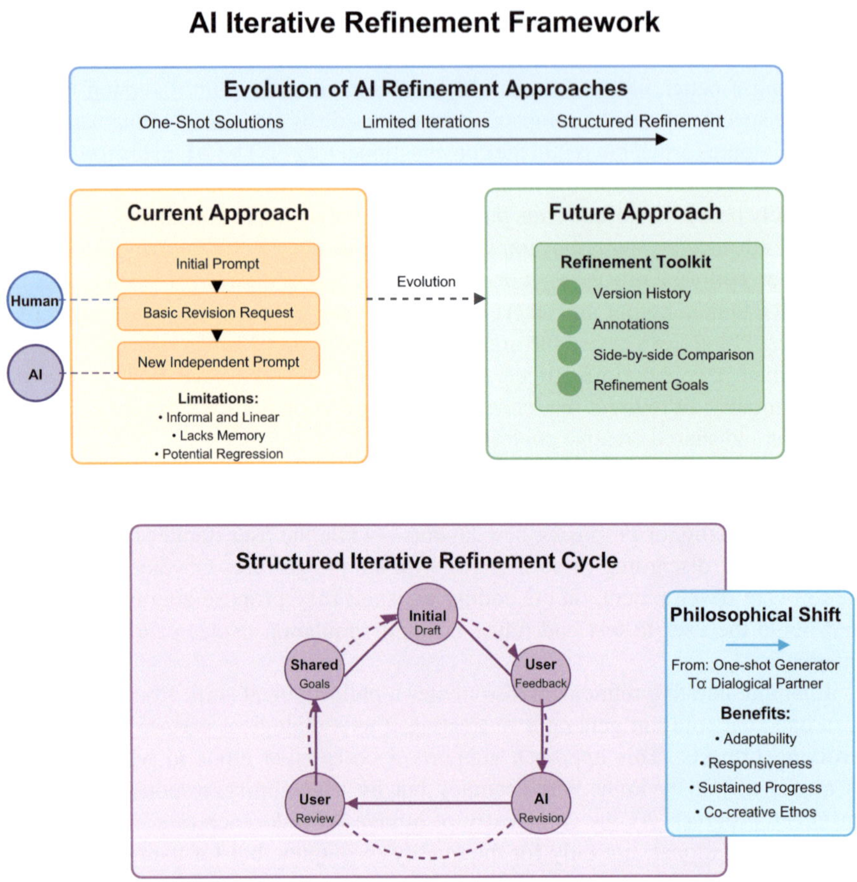

Fig. 11.7 AI iterative refinement framework. This diagram illustrates the evolution from linear, memory-lacking AI interactions to structured iterative refinement. Current approaches often treat each revision as a new prompt, risking redundancy and regression. Future systems will support fluid revision cycles through version history, annotations, and refinement goals. The central cyclic process shows how initial drafts evolve through user feedback, AI revision, user review, and shared goal-setting. This represents a philosophical shift from viewing AI as a one-shot solution generator to a dialogical partner in extended projects, emphasising adaptability, responsiveness, and a co-creative ethos

the ongoing interaction. There is no memory of learning, no continuity of refinement across sessions, and no sustained awareness of the user's evolving expectations.

Establishing meaningful feedback loops requires deeper integration of response tracking, preference modelling, and conversational memory. In practice, this could mean that an AI system not only reacts to immediate feedback but also summarises what it has learned from it. For example, after several exchanges about tone and structure, a future AI writing assistant might say: "Based on your recent edits, I'll prioritise active voice and shorter paragraphs in future drafts. Does that reflect your preferences?" This explicit feedback loop transforms correction into a collaborative learning moment.

In speculative scenarios, feedback loops could become foundational for long-term AI companions, mentors, or creative partners. Consider an AI that assists a policy analyst over several months. By continuously gathering feedback on how reports are edited, how arguments are framed, and which data is favoured, the AI gradually aligns its style, priorities, and even anticipatory behaviours to match the analyst's working patterns. It might eventually say, "I've noticed you tend to open reports with a problem framing before introducing solutions—shall I structure future drafts accordingly?" Such loops foster not only improved outputs but a more profound sense of communicative synchrony.

Multimodal environments will further enrich feedback dynamics. In a collaborative design space, a user might sketch a rough idea, which the AI refines into a polished concept. The user then adjusts a detail, prompting the AI to revise in response. This continuous interplay—gesture, output, adjustment, re-output—forms a real-time feedback loop, embedded in both visual and behavioural interaction. Over time, the system learns to anticipate patterns of revision and proactively suggest adjustments based on prior feedback cycles.

Moreover, establishing robust feedback loops also supports responsible AI development. Systems that actively incorporate user feedback can adapt to changes in context, preference, or ethical expectations. For instance, if an AI system is consistently told to avoid certain stereotypes or improve cultural sensitivity, it should be able to explain how such feedback has been integrated and what measures are now in place. Transparent feedback integration becomes a pathway toward accountability and value alignment.

In essence, feedback loops elevate human-AI interaction from isolated transactions to dynamic relationships, enabling cumulative improvement, fostering shared learning, and allowing the AI to become more attuned to human needs over time. As AI systems become increasingly embedded in our workflows, learning environments, and creative practices, this principle will define not just how systems improve but also how they evolve in concert with the humans they serve (Fig. 11.8).

11.3.3 Apply Feedback Granularity

For feedback to be effective in refining AI responses and shaping ongoing communication, it must be delivered at the appropriate level of granularity. "Granular feedback" refers to the practice of offering specific, targeted input about what aspects of an AI's output are successful, problematic, or require modification, rather than giving only general approval or disapproval. In turn, AI systems must be capable of understanding and acting upon feedback at different layers of abstraction, from overall structure to fine-grained stylistic or conceptual elements.

In current interactions, feedback is often limited to binary signals such as "good" or "bad," or broad qualitative requests like "make it better." These signals, while

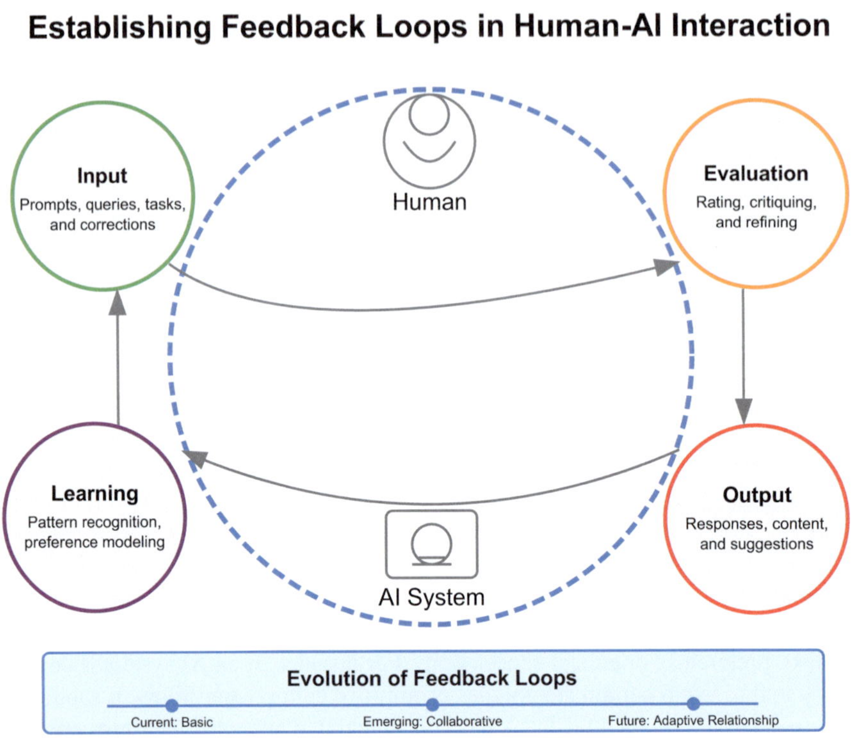

Fig. 11.8 Beyond transactions: the evolution of human-AI feedback loops. This diagram illustrates how feedback loops transform human-AI interactions from isolated exchanges into dynamic relationships. The circular process connects four key components: input (prompts and queries), output (AI-generated responses), evaluation (human assessment), and learning (pattern recognition and preference modelling). As these systems evolve from today's rudimentary mechanisms toward future adaptive relationships, they enable continuous improvement through bidirectional learning. Such feedback loops foster communicative synchrony, support multimodal collaboration, enable value alignment, and ultimately allow AI systems to evolve in concert with human needs across diverse contexts

useful for rough calibration, offer little insight into what exactly should change or why. For example, telling an AI assistant that a piece of writing is "too vague" might lead to a variety of responses: more detail, more specific examples, or simply longer text. Without granularity, the system cannot identify which layer of the response requires revision—conceptual content, tone, structure, terminology, or logic.

Granular feedback provides this missing dimension. Instead of simply stating that a paragraph is unclear, a user might specify, "This sentence introduces a new idea without context," or "The transition between these two paragraphs needs to be smoother." When users communicate at this level, AI systems can more precisely isolate the issue and produce more aligned refinements. Likewise, users may highlight positive elements—"This analogy works well because it simplifies a complex concept without oversimplifying"—encouraging the system to replicate those features elsewhere.

To support such nuanced interaction, future AI systems must be able to receive and process multilayered feedback. A sophisticated writing assistant might allow users to annotate text at multiple levels: global structure, paragraph flow, sentence clarity, word choice, and tone. In response, the system would produce focused revisions based on the user's prioritisation, such as: "Would you like me to revise the structure first or adjust the tone across all sections?" This enables a dialogue not only about *what* needs to change, but also *how* and *in what order*.

In speculative contexts, AI design platforms may support fine-grained visual feedback. Imagine a user designing a virtual environment with AI assistance. Instead of simply saying, "I don't like this," they could point to a specific texture, lighting condition, or spatial arrangement and say, "This wall should feel more organic," or "The lighting here is too clinical, which would hinder a calming effect." The AI, trained to interpret such fine-grained input, would offer context-sensitive suggestions rather than global revisions.

Granularity also allows feedback to evolve. Early in a project, feedback might focus on broad structure or conceptual framing; later, it might shift to rhetorical nuance, stylistic polish, or audience calibration. A feedback-aware AI could track this evolution and adjust its refinement strategy accordingly: "Earlier, you prioritised conceptual clarity—now would you like me to focus on voice consistency?"

Importantly, granular feedback supports a more respectful and empowered user experience, placing the user in the role of a co-editor, co-architect, or co-analyst—someone who shapes the output not through trial and error alone, but through thoughtful, intentional direction. In doing so, it transforms AI systems from passive executors of prompts into responsive, adaptive partners in fine-tuned communication (Fig. 11.9).

11.4 Promoting Evaluation and Reflection

11.4.1 Express Appreciation

Though often overlooked in technical discussions of AI communication, the act of expressing appreciation plays a vital role in shaping the tone, responsiveness, and mutuality of human-AI interaction. Appreciation—whether explicit ("Thank you, that was helpful") or implicit ("Nice, that's exactly what I needed")—serves not only as social etiquette, but also as feedback that reinforces alignment and encourages desirable behaviour. In the future of AI communication, acknowledging value will become an integral part of maintaining a constructive, trust-based interaction loop.

In current AI systems, appreciation has little functional impact. A chatbot or virtual assistant may be "thanked," but such acknowledgements rarely influence subsequent system behaviour. The model does not internalise positive feedback as reinforcement,

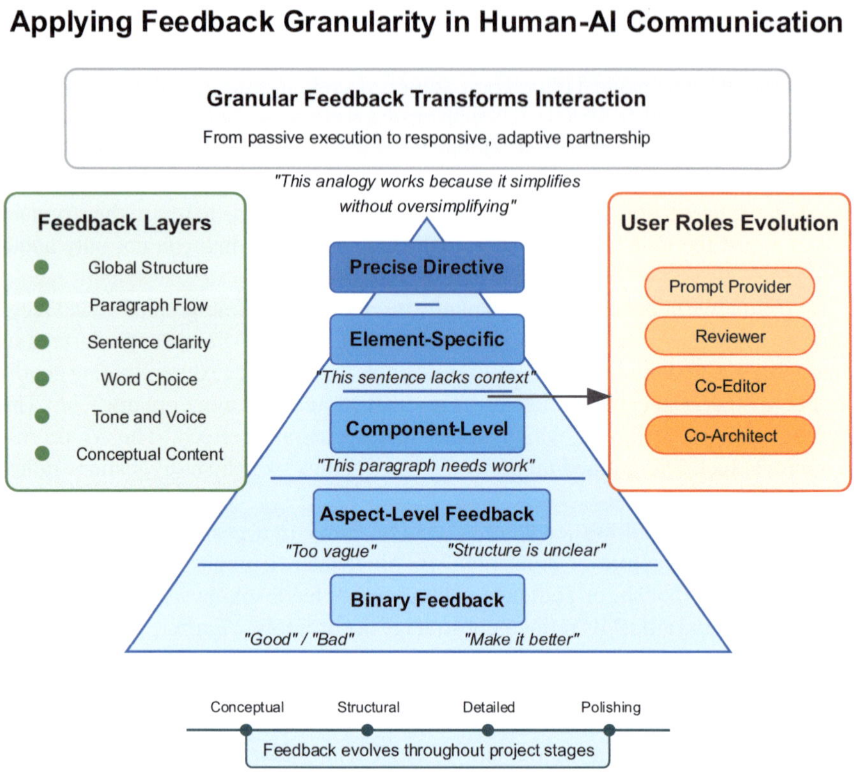

Fig. 11.9 Pyramid of feedback granularity: from binary to precise directives. This diagram depicts how granular feedback transforms AI communication from simplistic exchanges to nuanced collaboration. The pyramid illustrates the progression from basic binary feedback ("good"/"bad") to increasingly specific directives that target precise elements within AI outputs. As feedback becomes more granular, users evolve from passive prompt providers to active co-architects, engaging across multiple feedback layers—from global structure to word choice. This multidimensional approach enables AI systems to process feedback at various levels of abstraction, transforming them from passive executors into responsive partners capable of fine-tuned communication throughout project stages

nor does it retain an awareness of what was appreciated or why. However, even in this rudimentary form, appreciation affects the user's experience: it humanises the interaction, helps establish rapport, and creates a psychologically rewarding rhythm that mirrors respectful human dialogue.

More advanced systems are beginning to use appreciation signals as part of reinforcement tuning. In certain implementations of reinforcement learning from human feedback (RLHF), explicit user satisfaction plays a role in adjusting model behaviour. This creates a pathway for future systems to become more attuned to what users value—not only in terms of task accuracy, but in tone, efficiency, creativity, or attentiveness. In this context, appreciation functions not as mere politeness, but as a low-friction, high-frequency feedback signal that can shape communication style and strategic direction.

In more speculative applications, the role of appreciation could become dialogically active. Imagine an AI research assistant that remembers when a user praised the clarity of a particular explanation. In a later session, the system might preface similar content with: "I've used the same explanatory approach you appreciated earlier—please let me know if it still works for you." Here, appreciation forms a memory trace that the AI can incorporate into future communicative choices, becoming part of a shared history that enables continuity and adaptive personalisation.

Appreciation also plays a role in emotional calibration and co-presence. In educational contexts, for example, students working with AI tutors may express gratitude not only for correctness but for patience, encouragement, or clarity. A future tutoring system might respond, "I'm glad that helped—would you like to explore a deeper explanation?" Such exchanges support the creation of learning environments that feel psychologically safe and emotionally responsive. Even if the AI does not feel appreciation, its ability to recognise and respond to appreciative gestures enhances the relational quality of interaction.

In multimodal environments, appreciation could take expressive forms beyond text or speech, such as visual gestures, icons, or affective signals (e.g. a thumbs-up in AR/VR). These can be integrated into streamlined feedback interfaces, enabling rapid and intuitive acknowledgement that simultaneously reinforces positive system behaviour.

Importantly, expressing appreciation is not about anthropomorphising AI or pretending that machines deserve emotional praise. Instead, it reflects a human-centric communication norm: we acknowledge when something meets or exceeds our expectations, not for the machine's benefit, but for the sake of relational clarity, affective tone, and mutual engagement. In the human-AI future, appreciation will serve as both signal and strategy, reinforcing trust, improving feedback sensitivity, and contributing to a more cooperative communicative culture (Fig. 11.10).

11.4.2 Implement Systematic Evaluation Frameworks

As AI systems become increasingly integrated into complex domains, such as education, research, design, and governance, the need to move beyond ad hoc judgement toward systematic evaluation becomes imperative. Implementing structured evaluation frameworks allows both users and developers to assess the quality, reliability, and alignment of AI outputs in a consistent, repeatable, and transparent way. Without such frameworks, feedback risks becoming subjective, fragmented, and complex to act upon, thereby limiting the potential for meaningful refinement and long-term improvement.

At present, the evaluation of AI-generated content is typically informal and intuitive. A user might decide that a summary is "clear," a suggestion is "useful," or an image "looks good," but these assessments are seldom grounded in shared criteria.

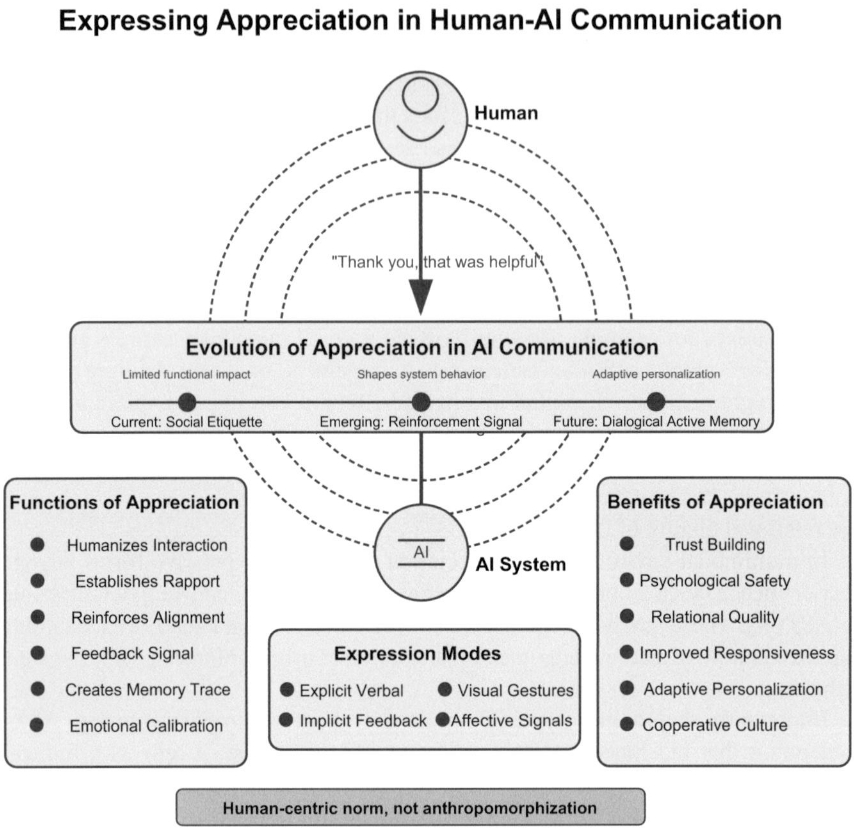

Fig. 11.10 Appreciation cycle: from social etiquette to active memory. This diagram illustrates how appreciation transforms human-AI communication from superficial etiquette to a functional component of adaptive interaction. The circular flow represents the bidirectional exchange of appreciation signals that create expanding ripples of engagement. As appreciation evolves from current limited impact to future dialogically active memory, it serves multiple functions—from humanising interaction to creating memory traces that enable personalisation. This human-centric communication norm builds trust, enhances responsiveness, and fosters psychological safety without anthropomorphising AI systems. Across various expression modes, appreciation ultimately contributes to a more cooperative and relationally rich communicative culture

This can lead to inconsistencies even within a single session—what is considered an acceptable answer in one instance might be flagged as inadequate in another. Without standardised benchmarks, it becomes difficult for AI systems to detect patterns, generalise improvements, or explain the reasoning behind their responses.

To address this, users and systems must collaboratively implement evaluation frameworks that define what "good" means in a given context. These frameworks can include criteria such as factual accuracy, logical coherence, relevance to the prompt, stylistic alignment, ethical sensitivity, domain appropriateness, and user satisfaction. In educational AI, for instance, a writing assistant might evaluate essays based on structure, argumentation, evidence, and tone. A research assistant could be judged by their ability to summarise accurately, cite appropriately, and distinguish correlation from causation.

Some preliminary work in this area already exists. In the development of language models, human raters use scoring rubrics to assess helpfulness, harmlessness, and truthfulness. In AI-assisted programming, tools such as code linters and test harnesses provide quantitative feedback on code quality and functionality. These examples demonstrate that rigorous evaluation is possible, but to truly empower users, frameworks must be embedded within the interaction itself, rather than applied retrospectively or externally.

Future AI systems may proactively propose evaluation dimensions based on task type. After generating a report, an AI might ask: "Would you like to evaluate this draft on structure, tone, and clarity?" It could offer visual dashboards showing performance across dimensions, highlighting areas of strength and weakness over time. In more advanced scenarios, systems might support longitudinal self-assessment, tracking how well AI responses have aligned with user goals across a project lifecycle and suggesting process-level adjustments accordingly.

Moreover, systematic evaluation supports collaboration and reproducibility. When multiple users work with AI on shared content—whether in science, policy, or design—having common evaluation frameworks allows for collective review and comparison. It ensures that decisions informed by AI outputs can be explained, justified, and audited. In critical applications such as legal reasoning or medical diagnosis, such frameworks will not only be helpful but also ethically and professionally necessary.

Evaluation frameworks also foster meta-cognition in human users. By reflecting on the criteria they use to assess AI responses, users become more aware of their priorities, standards, and values. This, in turn, strengthens the communicative bond between human and machine: the more clearly the system understands how it is being evaluated, the more effectively it can adapt and improve.

Ultimately, implementing systematic evaluation frameworks transforms feedback from a reactive gesture into a deliberative process, elevating AI interaction from episodic satisfaction to structured development. This supports higher standards, greater accountability, and a more profound sense of shared responsibility in the evolving landscape of human-AI collaboration (Fig. 11.11).

11.4.3 Invite Meta-Feedback on Communication Quality

Beyond task-specific corrections and iterative refinements, effective AI communication demands a reflective stance on the *quality of the interaction itself*. Meta-feedback—feedback about the communicative process rather than the content—offers a crucial opportunity for both the user and the AI to learn how well they are

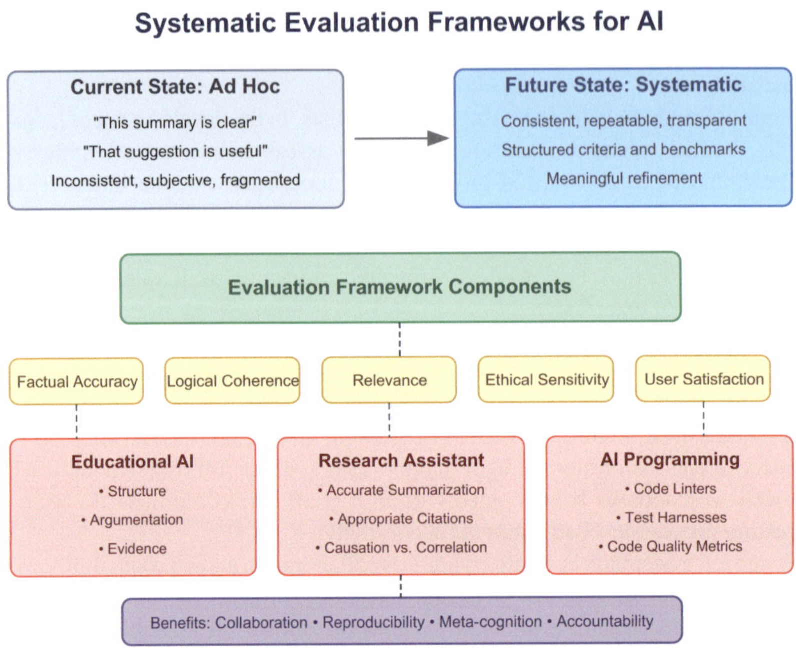

Fig. 11.11 Systematic evaluation frameworks for AI. This diagram illustrates the evolution of AI evaluation frameworks, showcasing the shift from subjective, inconsistent assessments to structured, transparent criteria. The framework encompasses key evaluation dimensions—factual accuracy, coherence, relevance, ethics, and user satisfaction—implemented across various domains, including education, research, and programming. By establishing shared benchmarks, these frameworks enhance collaboration, reproducibility, and accountability in human-AI partnerships, transforming feedback into a deliberative process that elevates interaction quality and fosters mutual growth

collaborating. By inviting meta-feedback on the conversation's clarity, flow, responsiveness, tone, and structure, AI systems can improve not just *what* they say, but *how* they say it, and how they listen, respond, and adapt across extended dialogues.

In today's AI interfaces, meta-feedback is rarely solicited and even more rarely understood. When users are dissatisfied with an interaction, they might blame the AI's content or rephrase the prompt, rather than examining whether the *style* of interaction contributed to the misalignment. Yet users often intuitively register interactional failures: responses feel robotic, the pacing is off, the tone seems mismatched, or clarifying questions come too late. Without space for articulating these impressions, opportunities for communicative improvement are lost.

To address this, future AI systems must explicitly invite meta-feedback. After completing a task or segment of dialogue, a system might ask, "Was this exchange helpful and easy to follow?" or "Is there anything I could have done differently in guiding the conversation?" Such prompts help users reflect on their own needs and interaction preferences, while giving the AI insight into factors beyond correctness, such as politeness, pacing, or engagement.

This kind of higher-order feedback is already common in human educational and therapeutic contexts, where teachers, coaches, and therapists regularly check in not just on goals, but on the quality of the communication process itself. Bringing this practice into AI communication models signals a shift from transactional assistance to adaptive co-creation. For example, a speculative AI co-authoring tool might allow users to rate or comment on dialogue rhythm, response timing, or levels of initiative, creating a feedback loop that refines not just the product but also the process.

Meta-feedback will also play an essential role in designing AI systems for inclusivity and neurodiversity. Individuals with diverse cognitive styles or communication preferences may prefer an AI that engages more slowly, avoids open-ended ambiguity, provides clearer turn-taking signals, or uses more literal (or more metaphorical) language. A system that invites and integrates this kind of feedback can become more sensitive, accessible, and tailored to the user's lived experience.

In multimodal settings, meta-feedback can be conveyed through gestures, facial expressions, or UI interactions. A VR design assistant might infer from prolonged pauses or frequent undo actions that something in the interaction flow is off, and then ask for meta-feedback about whether the current mode of collaboration is effective. Similarly, future voice agents could detect user hesitations or changes in tone and gently prompt for reflection: "It seems this isn't working as intended. Would you like to change how we're approaching this?"

Importantly, inviting meta-feedback also models a new kind of digital humility, reframing the AI system not as a self-contained authority but as a collaborator constantly learning how to communicate more effectively. In turn, users are encouraged to treat interaction not as a fixed pathway, but as a negotiable process. This mutual reflection strengthens trust, deepens personalisation, and fosters long-term relational intelligence.

In the evolving paradigm of AI communication, meta-feedback will be a cornerstone of adaptability, enabling not only better outputs or more accurate understanding but also more human-centred, intentional, and co-evolving conversations. By asking not only "Did I answer your question?" but also "Did we communicate well?" the AI steps into the role of an active participant in the shared craft of understanding (Fig. 11.12).

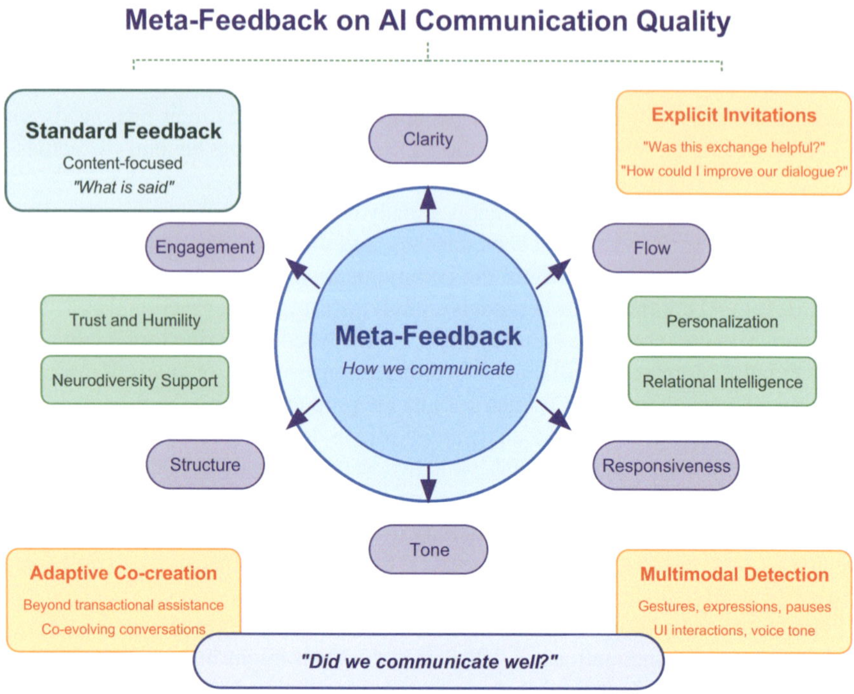

Fig. 11.12 Meta-feedback on AI communication quality. This diagram illustrates how meta-feedback transforms AI communication by focusing on the process of interaction rather than just content. The central cycle represents key dimensions of communication quality—clarity, flow, responsiveness, tone, structure, and engagement—that meta-feedback addresses. Surrounding elements show implementation approaches through explicit invitations, multimodal detection, and adaptive co-creation. Benefits include enhanced trust, neurodiversity support, deeper personalisation, and relational intelligence. This shift moves AI from transactional assistance to collaborative partnership by examining not just what is communicated, but how communication unfolds

Bibliography

Annapureddy R, Fornaroli A, Gatica-Perez D (2025) Generative AI literacy: twelve defining competencies. Digit Gov Res Pract 6(1):1–21

Austin JL (1962) How to do things with words. Oxford University Press, Oxford

Bahree A (2024) Generative AI in action. Manning Publications

Bender E et al (2021) On the dangers of stochastic parrots: can language models be too big? In: Proceedings of the 2021 ACM conference on fairness, accountability, and transparency, pp 610–623

Bostrom N (2014) Superintelligence: paths, dangers, strategies. Oxford University Press, Oxford

Brown BR (2025) Human–machine teaming using large language models. In: Interdependent human-machine teams. Academic Press, pp 41–66

Brown TB et al (2020) Language models are few-shot learners. Adv Neural Inf Process Syst 33:1877–1901

Bura C, Myakala PK, Jonnalgadda AK (2025) Ethical prompt engineering: addressing bias, transparency, and fairness. Int J Res Anal Rev (IJRAR) 12(1). www.ijrar.org

Choi WC, Chang CI (2025) A survey of techniques, key components, strategies, challenges, and student perspectives on prompt engineering for large language models (LLMs) in education, 25 Mar 2025. https://doi.org/10.20944/preprints202503.1808.v1. Accessed 8 May 2025

Clark H (1996) Using language. Cambridge University Press, Cambridge

Debnath T, Siddiky MNA, Rahman ME et al (2025) A comprehensive survey of prompt engineering techniques in large language models. TechRxiv. https://doi.org/10.36227/techrxiv.174140719.96375390/v1. Accessed 10 May 2025

Dhamani N, Engler M (2024) Introduction to generative AI: an ethical, societal, and legal overview. Manning Publications

Eliot L (2024) Essentials of prompt engineering for generative AI: practical advances in artificial intelligence and machine learning. LBE Press Publishing

Ferraris AF, Audrito D, Di Caro L et al (2025) The architecture of language: understanding the mechanics behind LLMs. In: Cambridge forum on AI: law and governance, vol 1, Cambridge University Press

Floridi L, Cowls J (2019) A unified framework of five principles for AI in society. Harv Data Sci Rev 1(1)

Geroimenko V (2025a) Key challenges in prompt engineering. In: The essential guide to prompt engineering: key principles, techniques, challenges, and security risks. Springer Nature Switzerland, Cham, pp 85–102

Geroimenko V (2025b) Key principles of good prompt design. In: The essential guide to prompt engineering: key principles, techniques, challenges, and security risks. Springer Nature Switzerland, Cham, pp 17–36

Geroimenko V (2025c) Key techniques for writing effective prompts. In: The essential guide to prompt engineering: key principles, techniques, challenges, and security risks. Springer Nature Switzerland, Cham, pp 37–83

Geroimenko V (2025d) The essential guide to prompt engineering: key principles, techniques, challenges, and security risks. Springer

Geroimenko V (2025e) Key security risks in prompt engineering. In: The essential guide to prompt engineering: key principles, techniques, challenges, and security risks. Springer Nature Switzerland, Cham, pp 103–120

GitHub (2025) Prompt engineering guide. https://github.com/dair-ai/Prompt-Engineering-Guide. Accessed 10 Apr 2025

Greenwood M (2024) Artificial intelligence: a practical guide to using AI in everyday life. Ochreland Publishing

Gunkel DJ (2020) Robot rights. MIT Press, Cambridge

Hsu HP (2025) From programming to prompting: developing computational thinking through large language model-based generative artificial intelligence. TechTrends 1–22

Huang MX et al (2022) Adaptive conversational AI: dynamic strategies for human-AI interaction. Int J Hum Comput Stud 160:102798

Huang G, Xiao Y, Jiang L et al (2025) Beyond prompt engineering: a reinforced token-level input refinement for large language models. Proc AAAI Conf Artif Intell 39(22):24113–24121

i Picó JF, Catta-Preta M, Omeñaca AT et al (2025) The time machine: future scenario generation through generative AI tools. Future Internet 17(1):1–15

Jobin A et al (2019) The global landscape of AI ethics guidelines. Nat Mach Intell 1(9):389–399

Kannan R, Ahmad M (eds) (2025) Generative AI foundations, developments, and applications. IGI Global

Khan I (2024) The quick guide to prompt engineering. Wiley

Kim J, Sundar SS (2012) Anthropomorphism of computers: is it mindlessness or mindfulness? Comput Hum Behav 28(1):241–250

Kushwaha V, Ragavan SS, Subhajit Roy S (2025) A measure based generalizable approach to understandability. arXiv:2503.21615. https://doi.org/10.48550/arXiv.2503.21615. Accessed 19 Apr 2025

Lakoff G, Johnson M (1980) Metaphors we live by. University of Chicago Press, Chicago

Lee D, Palmer E (2025) Prompt engineering in higher education: a systematic review to help inform curricula. Int J Educ Technol High Educ 22(1):7
Lee JY, Kang S, Yoo S (2025) Can we predict the effect of prompts? arXiv preprint arXiv:2501.18883. Accessed 12 May 2025
Lindley J, Whitham R (2025) From prompt engineering to prompt craft. In: Proceedings of the nineteenth international conference on tangible, embedded, and embodied interaction, Mar 2025, pp 1–12
López-Pérez B et al (2025) Exploring the potential of large language models to understand interpersonal emotion regulation strategies from narratives. Emotion. Advance online publication. https://doi.org/10.1037/emo0001528. Accessed 19 Apr 2025
Luger GF (2020) Artificial intelligence: structures and strategies for complex problem solving, 6th edn. Pearson, Boston
Maaz S, Palaganas JC, Palaganas G et al (2025) A guide to prompt design: foundations and applications for healthcare simulationists. Front Med 11:1504532
Marcus G (2020) The next decade in AI: four steps towards robust artificial intelligence. arXiv preprint arXiv:2002.06177. Accessed 12 May 2025
Mishra M, Ara A, Mishra S (2025) Exploring human-AI collaboration in higher education: an investigation into AI-enabled personalized learning. In: Prompt engineering and generative AI applications for teaching and learning. IGI Global Scientific Publishing, pp 483–502
Mitchell M (2019) Artificial intelligence: a guide for thinking humans. Farrar, Straus and Giroux, New York
OpenAI (2025a) Best practices for prompt engineering with the OpenAI API. https://help.openai.com/en/articles/6654000-best-practices-for-prompt-engineering-with-the-openai-api. Accessed 20 Apr 2025
OpenAI (2025b) Research. https://openai.com/research/index/
Phoenix J, Taylor M (2024) Prompt engineering for generative AI. O'Reilly Media
PremaLatha V, Kumar AD, Parveen N (2025) Optimizing interactions: strategies for prompt engineering in large language models. Edu-Tech Enterp 3:24
Prompt Engineering Guide (2025) https://www.promptingguide.ai/. Accessed 7 Mar 2025
Rahwan I (2018) Society-in-the-loop: programming the algorithmic social contract. Ethics Inf Technol 20(1):5–14
Reddy CKK, Anoushka P, Draksharapu A et al (2025) Beyond text: analyzing artificial intelligence models through prompt engineering. In: Future tech startups and innovation in the age of AI, pp 120–156
Russell S (2019) Human compatible: artificial intelligence and the problem of control. Viking, New York
Sasson Lazovsky G, Raz T, Kenett YN (2025) The art of creative inquiry—from question asking to prompt engineering. J Creat Behav 59(1):e671
Searle J (1969) Speech acts: an essay in the philosophy of language. Cambridge University Press, Cambridge
Shneiderman B (2022) Human-centered AI. Oxford University Press, Oxford
Siau K, Wang W (2018) Building trust in artificial intelligence, machine learning, and robotics. CUTTER Bus Technol J 31(2):47–53
Sihi D, Ryan A (2025) Crafting and evaluating generative AI prompts: insights from students, educators, and marketers. Mark Educ Rev 1–7
Suchman L (2007) Human-machine reconfigurations: plans and situated actions, 2nd edn. Cambridge University Press, Cambridge
Tegmark M (2017) Life 3.0: being human in the age of artificial intelligence. Penguin, London
Turing A (1950) Computing machinery and intelligence. Mind 59(236):433–460
Vairamani AD, Nayyar A (2024) Prompt engineering: empowering communication. CRC Press
Winograd T (1972) Understanding natural language. Academic Press, New York
Wittgenstein L (1953) Philosophical investigations. Blackwell, Oxford

Chapter 12
Ethical Alignment and Trust Calibration: Managing AI Reliability, Biases, and Ethical Constraints

Abstract This chapter addresses the growing ethical complexity of AI communication and the urgent need to build trustworthy systems that reflect and respect human values. It introduces key strategies for bias mitigation, cultural sensitivity, and value alignment in AI interaction. It also explores mechanisms for building calibrated trust, such as transparent limitation communication, proactive risk signalling, and dialogic uncertainty disclosure. Emphasising a dual responsibility shared between AI systems and human users, the chapter highlights the necessity of communicating ethical boundaries, upholding privacy and security, and implementing accountability and override protocols. Throughout, it argues for a shift from compliance-oriented design to ethically expressive, user-aware, and culturally pluralistic communication frameworks. Together, these principles form a foundation for responsible, trustworthy, and ethically fluent AI systems that can support meaningful interaction while safeguarding human dignity, safety, and autonomy.

Keywords Ethical AI communication · Bias mitigation · Trust calibration · Value alignment · AI transparency · Privacy and accountability

As AI systems become increasingly autonomous, interactive, and embedded in human decision-making, the ability to navigate ethical challenges and establish trust becomes a defining feature of meaningful AI communication. This chapter explores the foundational principles that support ethically grounded and socially responsible interaction between humans and intelligent systems. It addresses the need to recognise and mitigate bias, align AI behaviour with diverse human values, and respond sensitively to cultural variation. It also examines the calibration of user trust, the communication of limitations and uncertainties, and the necessity of transparency and accountability in high-stakes contexts. Finally, it introduces forward-looking mechanisms that enable AI systems to act responsibly by setting and enforcing ethical boundaries, safeguarding privacy and security, and invoking override protocols when human values may be at risk. Together, these principles articulate a vision of AI not merely as a tool of convenience or efficiency, but as a trustworthy, communicative partner embedded in the moral fabric of human life.

V. Geroimenko, *Beyond and After Prompt Engineering: The Future of AI Communication*, https://doi.org/10.1007/978-3-032-04569-0_12

12.1 Addressing Bias and Value Alignment

12.1.1 Promote Bias Awareness

Promoting bias awareness in AI communication is a foundational principle in ensuring ethical, trustworthy, and equitable interaction between humans and intelligent systems. As AI systems become increasingly capable of generating, summarising, and interpreting information, they reflect not only the data they are trained on but also the underlying assumptions and social structures embedded within that data. Promoting awareness of such biases—among both developers and users—serves as the first line of defence against perpetuating systemic inequalities or producing misleading or harmful outputs.

In present-day AI applications, bias awareness is often addressed through transparency reports, fairness audits, or the inclusion of disclaimers warning users about potential inaccuracies or partial perspectives. For example, a language model assisting in legal research may favour certain jurisdictions or historical precedents over others, depending on the distribution of training material. Users unaware of this may interpret the system's suggestions as comprehensive or neutral when, in fact, they are contextually skewed. In such scenarios, developers must proactively disclose known limitations, and interfaces should be designed to encourage critical reading rather than blind acceptance. This is especially urgent in areas such as healthcare or hiring, where biased outputs can have life-altering consequences.

Looking ahead, future AI systems may incorporate dynamic bias-awareness modules that detect potential bias patterns in real time and alert users during interaction. Imagine a generative AI co-writing an article on global economic policy. As it drafts a paragraph, it might flag that the information disproportionately reflects Western-centric viewpoints, offering users optional perspectives from African or Southeast Asian contexts. Similarly, in an educational platform, an AI tutor might pause and prompt the student with a question like, "Would you like to explore alternative viewpoints from different cultural or ideological perspectives?" In this vision, bias awareness is no longer a static disclaimer but an interactive, educative feature built into the communication loop.

However, promoting bias awareness cannot be delegated solely to AI systems. It also requires cultivating ethical literacy among users. This involves training individuals—whether students, professionals, or casual users—to interpret AI-generated content with a critical mindset and an awareness of potential blind spots. Institutions deploying AI systems must therefore integrate bias literacy into digital skills education, treating it not as an add-on but as a core component of future AI communication practices.

Ultimately, bias awareness must evolve into a shared responsibility. AI models should transparently communicate where bias may arise, while human users must

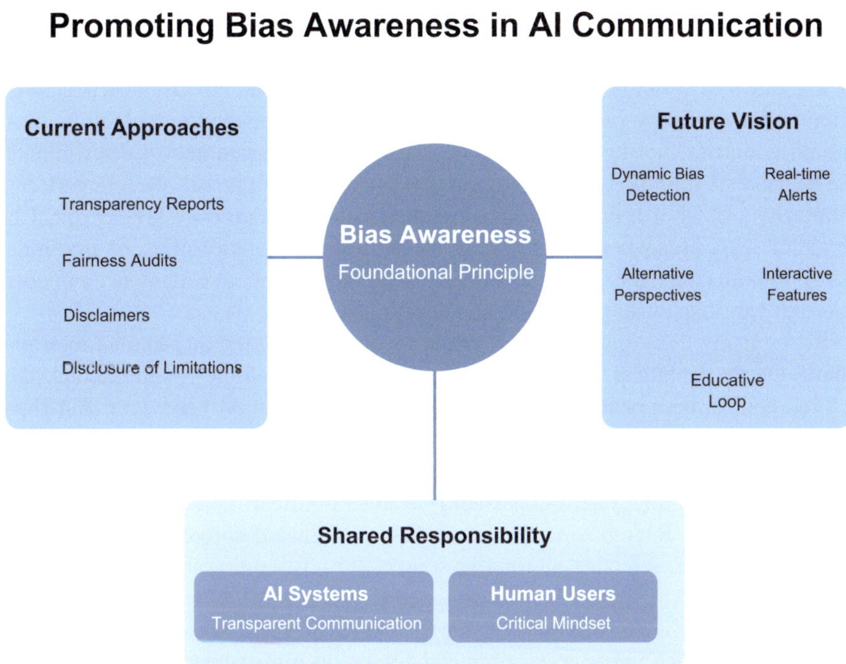

Fig. 12.1 Promoting bias awareness in AI communication. This diagram illustrates the evolution of bias awareness in AI communication from current approaches (such as transparency reports and fairness audits) to future interactive systems (including dynamic detection and alternative perspectives). The central concept connects to critical application contexts, such as healthcare and hiring, while emphasising the shared responsibility between AI systems that provide transparent communication and humans who maintain critical mindsets, ultimately leading to more balanced, ethical AI–human interaction

remain attentive to the implications of the content they receive and disseminate. Only through this mutual recognition of risk and responsibility can AI–human communication move toward a more balanced and ethically grounded future (Fig. 12.1).

12.1.2 Recognise AI-Generated Biases

Recognising AI-generated biases requires a nuanced understanding of how language models and other generative systems produce their outputs. Unlike human biases, which may be consciously held or socially learned, AI biases emerge from patterns embedded in vast datasets—patterns that often reflect historical, cultural, economic, and political inequities. These biases can manifest subtly in language, tone, emphasis, or framing, and users may unknowingly absorb or reproduce them unless they are equipped to identify them critically.

In today's AI systems, such biases are increasingly evident. For instance, a résumé-screening model may favour candidates with names or academic credentials from certain countries, not because it has been explicitly programmed to discriminate, but because its training data over-represents specific demographic success patterns. Similarly, a chatbot trained on open internet data might produce stereotypical or gendered responses when asked to describe professions, relationships, or emotional states. In both cases, the output appears plausible and fluent but carries an embedded bias that can shape user perception and decision-making.

Recognising these biases involves both technical detection and human interpretation. On the technical side, developers can use bias metrics, counterfactual data testing, and fairness benchmarks to identify imbalances in AI behaviour. But from the user side, recognition relies heavily on contextual sensitivity and critical literacy. For example, a journalist using an AI summariser to digest multiple news sources might notice that the system consistently frames political issues with a particular ideological slant. Recognising this is the first step toward correcting it—either by adjusting prompts, selecting alternative sources, or post-editing the AI's output.

In the future, AI systems may be designed to self-identify when their outputs are likely to contain biases and surface alerts to users in real time. Imagine a virtual assistant that, when asked to recommend books on global history, highlights the geographic or cultural limitations of its recommendations and offers to diversify the list. Alternatively, an AI mentor for young students might notice that it's providing more male than female historical role models and suggest rebalancing the examples. Such mechanisms would not only flag bias but help normalise its recognition as part of intelligent interaction.

However, this vision of AI-assisted bias recognition hinges on a larger cultural shift—one in which AI outputs are no longer viewed as neutral or infallible but as fallible and interpretable, much like human communication. It also implies a new standard of explainability, where models must not only output information but also contextualise it in relation to their training scope and limitations. This requires rethinking AI interfaces to include metadata, citations, or bias indicators that help users evaluate the trustworthiness and neutrality of responses.

Recognising AI-generated biases is ultimately about fostering a deeper, more self-reflective mode of AI use, where both systems and users are aware of the filters shaping what is said, suggested, or omitted. In a future saturated with generative AI, this form of communicative vigilance will be essential to ensure that intelligent systems remain instruments of insight, not vectors of inherited inequity (Fig. 12.2).

12.1.3 Address Cultural Ethical Variations

One of the most complex challenges in AI communication lies in addressing cultural ethical variations—those deeply rooted differences in values, norms, and moral

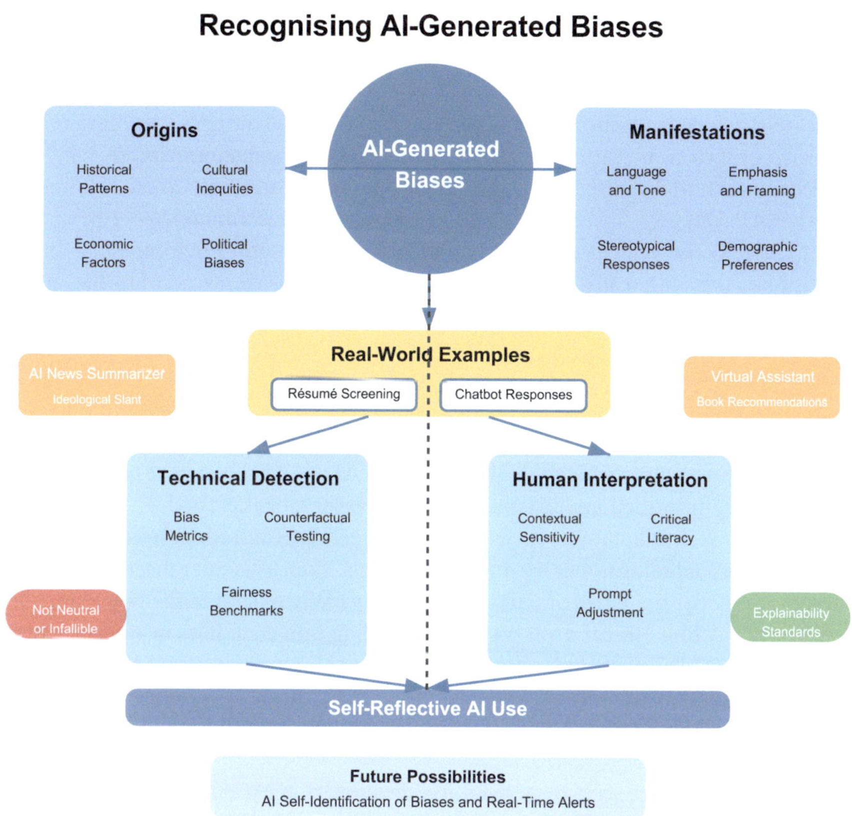

Fig. 12.2 Recognising AI-generated biases. This diagram maps the complex ecosystem of AI-generated biases—from their origins in historical and cultural patterns to their manifestations in language and framing. It illustrates both technical detection methods and human interpretation strategies, while highlighting real-world examples such as résumé screening and chatbots. The cultural shift pathway represents the evolution toward AI systems that self-identify biases, ultimately fostering a self-reflective AI use model where outputs are viewed as fallible and interpretable rather than neutral or infallible

expectations that shape how people from different societies perceive right and wrong, fairness, dignity, and respect. As AI systems are increasingly deployed in global contexts, the assumption that a single ethical framework can be universally applied is not only reductive but potentially harmful. Instead, AI communication must evolve to recognise, navigate, and respect ethical pluralism.

At present, most generative AI systems operate based on ethical principles predominantly derived from Western liberal democracies. These principles—such as individual autonomy, free speech, and secular neutrality—are often encoded into system behaviours through content moderation guidelines, reinforcement learning protocols, and alignment strategies. While such frameworks may support valuable safeguards against harm and abuse, they can also unintentionally marginalise other cultural values. For example, an AI health advisor trained primarily on Western datasets might disregard or downplay traditional healing practices still widely respected in different parts of the world. A conversational AI moderating content in an online forum might interpret certain communal or religious expressions as offensive or intolerant, failing to appreciate their contextual significance.

Recognising and addressing such variations requires a shift toward culturally adaptive AI systems—systems capable of tailoring their communicative behaviour in response to the ethical expectations of different cultural environments. In the near future, this might involve localised versions of AI agents that are fine-tuned on regionally relevant data, co-designed with cultural experts, and guided by ethical review boards from the target communities. A hypothetical example could be an AI teacher deployed in multilingual classrooms in South Asia that is sensitive not only to linguistic diversity but to the different ways authority, knowledge, and moral instruction are framed across religions and regions. Rather than enforcing a singular communication style or pedagogical method, the AI would adjust its responses based on a culturally informed understanding of the learner's background.

Of course, such adaptability raises significant technical and ethical questions. How can systems avoid reinforcing harmful local norms, such as gender discrimination or intolerance, under the guise of cultural sensitivity? Where should the boundaries lie between respecting ethical diversity and upholding universal human rights? Future AI systems may need to incorporate ethical override protocols—mechanisms that permit intervention or refusal when cultural norms directly conflict with widely accepted moral standards, such as prohibitions on hate speech or the right to bodily autonomy.

To balance respect with responsibility, developers must engage in intercultural dialogue from the outset. Building culturally competent AI communication means involving anthropologists, ethicists, local stakeholders, and policy-makers in the design process. It also entails giving users the tools to understand and shape the ethical positioning of their AI interlocutors—whether through transparency dashboards, adjustable ethical settings, or scenario-based onboarding that clarifies the system's guiding principles.

Ultimately, addressing cultural ethical variations in AI communication is not about finding a perfect compromise between global and local values, but about creating a communicative framework that can navigate these tensions with intelligence, humility, and openness. In doing so, AI systems can evolve from static rule-followers to dynamic, respectful, and dialogical partners across cultural frontiers (Fig. 12.3).

12.1.4 Practice Value Alignment Communication

Practising value alignment communication involves ensuring that AI systems not only behave in accordance with prescribed ethical principles but also communicate

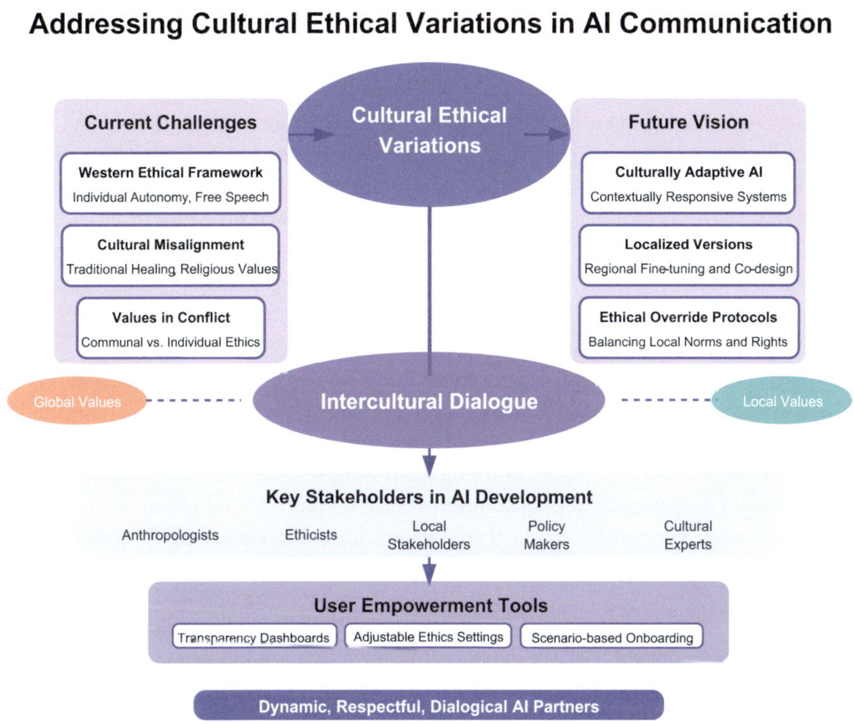

Fig. 12.3 Addressing cultural ethical variations in AI communication. This diagram illustrates the journey from current AI systems biased toward Western ethical frameworks to culturally adaptive AI capable of navigating diverse ethical landscapes. The central bridge of intercultural dialogue connects current challenges with future solutions, emphasising the crucial role of diverse stakeholders in development. The diagram highlights the tension between global and local values, demonstrating that successful adaptation requires both ethical override protocols and user empowerment tools to create AI systems that function as dynamic, respectful partners across cultural frontiers

in ways that reflect and respect the values of their users and contexts. In human-to-human interaction, effective communication often depends on shared assumptions, moral framing, and mutual understanding of what is considered appropriate, fair, or respectful. In AI–human interaction, this exact alignment becomes both more necessary and more difficult, requiring systems to actively interpret, adapt to, and transparently reflect the ethical and social norms of the people they engage with.

In the current generation of AI systems, value alignment is typically addressed through model fine-tuning and reinforcement learning from human feedback (RLHF). These techniques help train models to avoid toxic content, respect privacy, or provide helpful and harmless responses. However, these values are often globally generalised or implicitly encoded rather than explicitly contextualised. As a result, when AI systems communicate about morally or socially charged topics, such as political rights, gender roles, or environmental responsibility, they may unintentionally project the biases of their training regime or developers, rather than aligning with the user's ethical position or the conversation's cultural setting.

Future-oriented value alignment communication will need to go far beyond static safeguards. Consider a hypothetical AI mediator designed to help families resolve generational conflicts around tradition and modernity. This system would have to sensitively adapt its language and reasoning to the values of both elders and younger users, balancing respect for tradition with acknowledgement of individual freedom, without favouring one side. Rather than simply avoiding conflict-prone topics, the AI would facilitate dialogue that recognises and navigates value differences with fairness and care.

Practising such alignment in communication involves several intertwined capabilities. First, AI must be able to infer the user's value context from cues—linguistic, emotional, situational, or demographic—without making reductive assumptions. Second, it must adjust its tone, framing, and content style to reflect those values respectfully. For example, a conservation-focused chatbot interacting with users in a rural farming community might frame its advice on environmental sustainability in ways that align with local stewardship ethics rather than abstract global climate targets.

Crucially, value alignment in communication also includes meta-communication—that is, the AI's capacity to explain why it says what it says in terms of value trade-offs. A personal assistant offering guidance on work-life balance might not only give suggestions but also clarify, "This advice is based on a prioritisation of well-being over productivity. Would you prefer a different emphasis?" Such reflective transparency helps users feel recognised and respected, and it supports ethical co-creation rather than passive consumption.

Yet, the practice of value alignment must also remain bounded. AI should not aim to manipulate or mirror unethical values to please the user. Instead, its communication strategies must walk a careful line: accommodating diverse moral perspectives while remaining anchored in a defensible ethical foundation—one that prioritises dignity, fairness, and harm reduction.

In sum, value alignment communication is not a static feature but a dynamic, continuous act of ethical interpretation. It requires that AI systems move from simply being technically accurate or socially acceptable to being ethically attentive and dialogically responsive. As AI systems become more embedded in personal, social, and institutional contexts, their ability to reflect and respect the values of those they serve, through the very structure and style of their communication, will be essential for meaningful and responsible human–AI collaboration (Fig. 12.4).

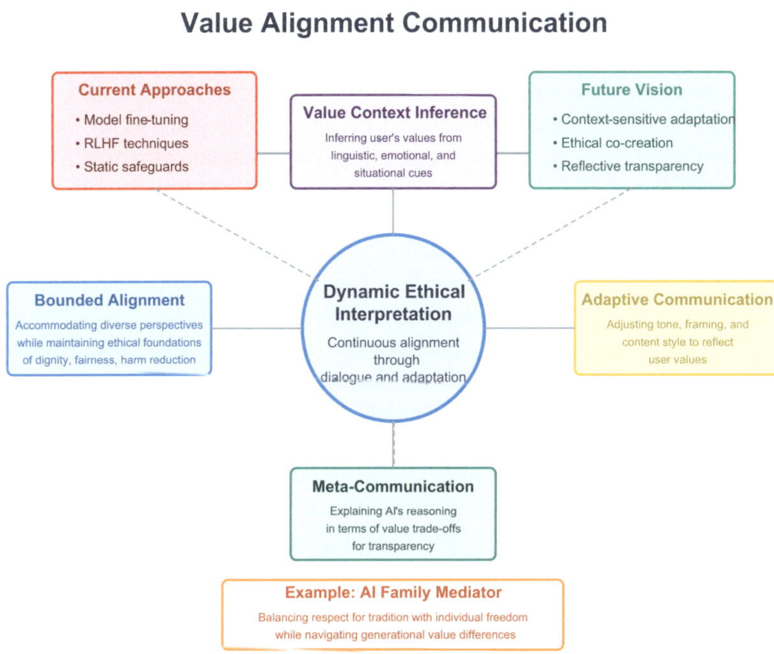

Fig. 12.4 Value alignment communication: beyond static safeguards. This diagram illustrates the evolution from current AI value alignment approaches (fine-tuning, RLHF) toward dynamic ethical interpretation. The central concept represents continuous alignment through dialogue, surrounded by four essential capabilities: value context inference, adaptive communication, meta-communication, and bounded alignment. These capabilities enable AI systems to navigate diverse moral perspectives while maintaining ethical foundations sensitively. This framework supports AI's transition from technically accurate to ethically attentive communication, essential for meaningful human–AI collaboration across personal, social, and institutional contexts

12.2 Building and Calibrating Trust

12.2.1 Practice Trust Calibration

Trust calibration refers to the ongoing process of aligning a user's level of trust in an AI system with the system's actual capabilities, reliability, and limitations. Unlike blanket trust or scepticism, calibrated trust is adaptive, context-sensitive, and rational—it enables users to rely on AI when appropriate while maintaining critical distance when necessary. Practising trust calibration in AI communication is not only about fostering confidence; it is also about preventing overreliance, misuse, or misplaced expectations.

In contemporary AI deployments, miscalibrated trust is a recurring problem. Users often attribute too much intelligence, intentionality, or moral reasoning to systems that merely generate outputs based on probabilistic associations. For example, a student might use an AI tool to answer exam questions and assume the answers are factually sound, when in fact the model has generated plausible-sounding but incorrect information—a phenomenon known as hallucination. Conversely, users might dismiss a system's recommendations in critical fields, such as medical triage, not because the advice is wrong, but because the AI interface lacks perceived authority or emotional nuance. Both overtrust and undertrust can lead to suboptimal or even dangerous outcomes.

Trust calibration in present AI systems is often left to user intuition or external guidelines, but future communication-centred approaches can embed trust calibration mechanisms directly into the interaction. Imagine an AI advisor that, when asked for investment strategies, not only provides recommendations but also explains its confidence level, the range of data it was trained on, and potential blind spots in its reasoning. It might say, "Based on historical market trends, this strategy has been effective 70% of the time, but my training data does not include post-pandemic economic shifts. Proceed with caution." This kind of transparency helps the user modulate their trust in real time.

Moreover, trust calibration should be dialogical, not declarative. Instead of simply stating limits, AI systems can invite users into a shared process of evaluating trustworthiness. In a speculative educational scenario, a virtual tutor might challenge a student by asking, "Would you like to verify this explanation with another source?" or "What level of certainty do you require for this decision?" In doing so, the AI not only acknowledges its limitations but empowers users to take an active role in evaluating reliability.

Trust calibration also varies by domain, task, and user experience. A novice user interacting with a mental health support chatbot may require more reassurance and clear boundaries than a data scientist using an AI to analyse genomic sequences. Adaptive communication strategies must therefore account for user expertise, emotional vulnerability, and the potential consequences of error. A future-aware system might adjust its tone and transparency dynamically—for instance, offering simplified caveats for casual queries, and detailed source disclosures in high-stakes scenarios.

Importantly, trust calibration is not merely a technical task; it is a communicative ethic. It reflects a commitment to integrity, humility, and mutual respect between AI and the user. When AI systems are honest about their scope, clear about their uncertainties, and proactive in guiding users toward informed engagement, they foster a relationship of sustainable trust—one that encourages confident use without complacency.

Practising trust calibration is thus about building communicative bridges that support not blind faith but informed reliance. In the future of AI communication, calibrated trust will be a hallmark of intelligent, responsible, and ethically mature systems, enabling collaboration not through illusion but through clarity (Fig. 12.5).

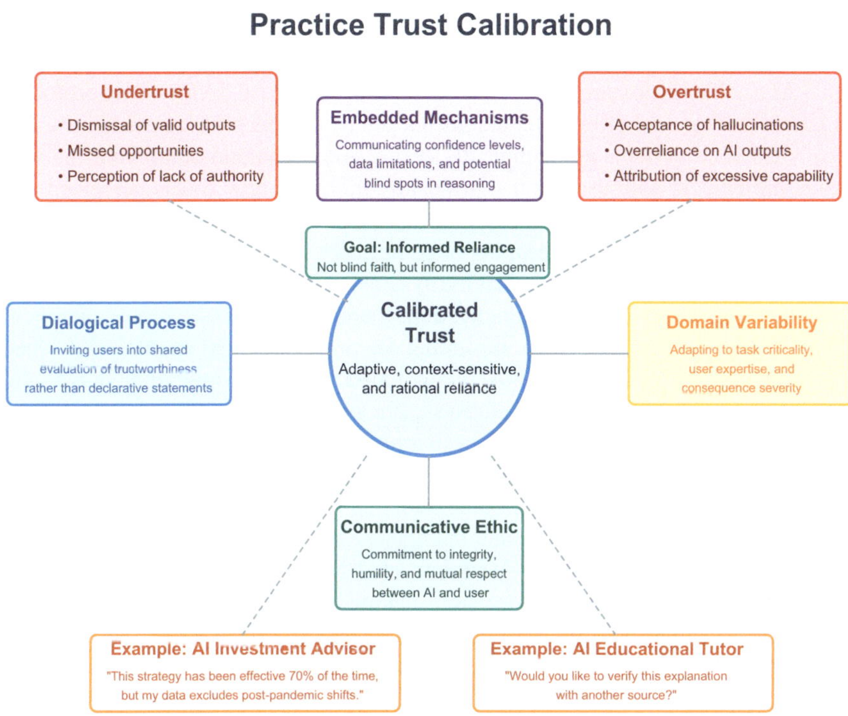

Fig. 12.5 Trust calibration: navigating the balance between scepticism and overreliance. This diagram illustrates trust calibration as the dynamic equilibrium between undertrust and overtrust in AI systems. The central concept of calibrated trust is supported by four key components: embedded mechanisms that communicate limitations, dialogical processes that engage users, considerations of domain variability, and a communicative ethic of integrity. Through these approaches, AI systems can foster informed reliance rather than blind faith or dismissal. The examples demonstrate how trust calibration manifests in practical scenarios, enabling collaboration based on clarity rather than illusion

12.2.2 Manage Risks and Trustworthiness

Managing risks and trustworthiness in AI communication is a multidimensional task that extends beyond technical robustness and into the domain of ethical interaction, social responsibility, and user perception. While trust calibration, as discussed in the previous section, focuses on aligning user expectations with system performance, managing trustworthiness involves ensuring that AI systems are, in fact, worthy of trust—functionally, ethically, and communicatively. In turn, risk management becomes an integral part of this trust-building process, not just reducing the chance of error or harm, but also communicating risk in ways that empower users rather than obscuring the truth.

In the current landscape, trustworthiness is often framed in terms of model accuracy, data privacy, and compliance with safety standards. For example, a conversational AI used in healthcare might be certified for clinical use, follow strict protocols for data handling, and offer explanations backed by evidence-based guidelines. But even when such systems are technically secure and regulation-compliant, the way they communicate with users can significantly influence how risk is perceived and navigated. A cold or overly technical tone may alienate vulnerable users; an overconfident style may downplay uncertainty or complexity. In either case, communication gaps can undermine trust, even when the system itself is sound.

Risk management in AI communication, therefore, requires three complementary practices: anticipating harm, designing for mitigation, and enabling informed user engagement. For instance, an AI content moderation tool might flag potentially harmful content on a social media platform. If it simply removes the content without explanation, users may feel silenced or manipulated. However, suppose the system provides a clear rationale—e.g. "This post was flagged due to language that may incite hatred based on ethnicity"—and offers an appeal's process. In that case, it supports procedural transparency and maintains user trust, even under constraints.

In speculative future scenarios, we might see AI agents acting as ethical sentinels in environments where real-time decision-making carries latent risk. For example, a co-pilot AI in autonomous transportation could continuously assess weather, traffic, and mechanical signals, and alert the human user not only to critical failures but also to accumulations of small risks, delivering explanations in accessible, non-alarmist language. The trustworthiness of such a system would not stem merely from its data processing power, but from its capacity to clearly and empathetically express risk.

Another dimension of managing trustworthiness lies in acknowledging that AI systems, no matter how advanced, will always have limits. Communicating these limitations proactively is not a sign of weakness but rather a sign of ethical maturity. Future AI systems might be designed with embedded "trust posture indicators" that reflect not only performance confidence but also external reviews, historical reliability scores, and contextual appropriateness for different tasks. For instance, a legal reasoning assistant might indicate: "This response is based on U.S. case law up to 2023. For jurisdiction-specific advice, consult a qualified professional."

Fundamentally, managing risks and trustworthiness in AI communication means designing systems that not only avoid harm but also actively communicate their integrity, constraints, and role in human decision-making processes. It implies a transition from reactive to proactive trust ethics, from static reliability claims to dynamic transparency practices.

In a world where AI systems are woven into critical domains—education, governance, finance, and medicine—their trustworthiness must be earned not only through technical performance but through honest, context-sensitive, and risk-aware dialogue. This is how AI will become not just helpful, but responsibly communicative—and truly trustworthy (Fig. 12.6).

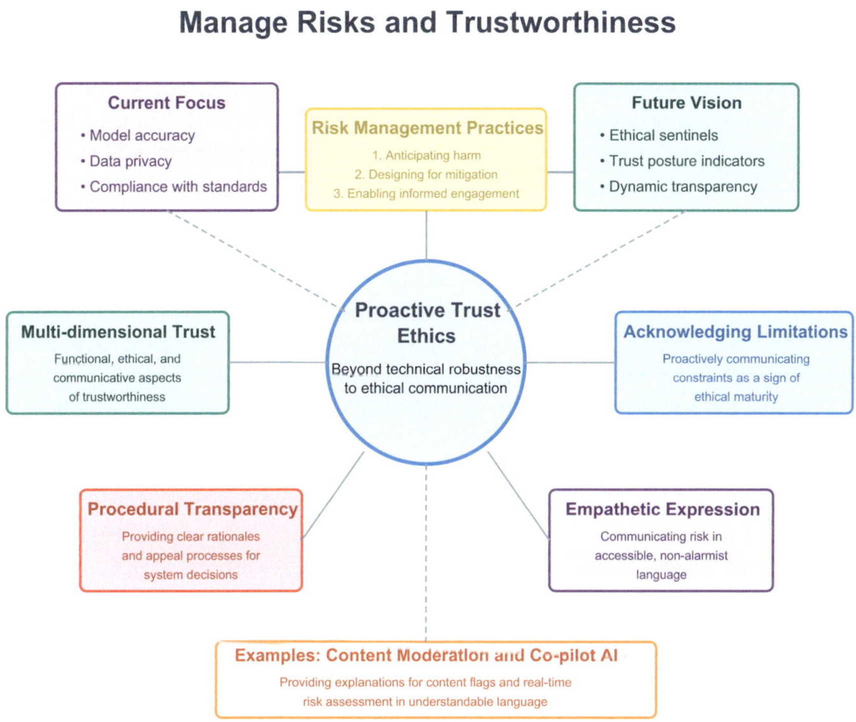

Fig. 12.6 From technical compliance to proactive trust ethics. This diagram illustrates the evolution of AI trustworthiness from current technical focus (accuracy, privacy, compliance) toward proactive trust ethics. At its core, trustworthiness extends beyond robustness into ethical communication. Four dimensions surround this concept: multidimensional trust, acknowledging limitations, procedural transparency, and empathetic expression of risk. These are supported by three key practices: anticipating harm, designing for mitigation, and enabling informed engagement. The model demonstrates how AI systems can become truly trustworthy through honest, context-sensitive dialogue that empowers users rather than obscuring complexity

12.2.3 Communicate AI Limitations Clearly

Clear communication of AI limitations is a cornerstone of ethical and practical interaction between humans and intelligent systems. In the absence of such clarity, users may either overestimate an AI's capabilities—treating it as an authoritative source of truth—or underestimate its usefulness, avoiding valuable assistance due to fear or confusion. In both cases, the breakdown stems not from the model's core functionality but from how its limitations are conveyed—or concealed—during communication.

Today's most advanced AI systems, while impressive, remain inherently constrained. They may hallucinate facts, misinterpret ambiguous input, fail to understand emotional nuance, or lack awareness of recent events. Yet many of these systems present their outputs in fluent, confident prose that masks uncertainty and reinforces anthropomorphic illusions. For instance, a language model may respond to a historical question with precise-sounding but fabricated dates or names, without indicating the speculative nature of its generation. Unless explicitly prompted to hedge or qualify its responses, the system may give the false impression of authoritative knowledge.

To mitigate this, AI communication must explicitly include indicators of limitation, not as technical footnotes, but as core parts of the interaction. These indicators might take the form of embedded disclaimers ("This answer is based on patterns in training data and may not reflect current events"), dynamic confidence scores, or dialogue cues that reveal reasoning gaps or ambiguity ("I am unsure about the specific context; would you like to clarify?"). Even in present-day applications, integrating such cues—whether through interface design, response templates, or adaptive meta-commentary—can help foster healthier user expectations and reduce the risk of misinterpretation.

In the near future, AI systems will likely be expected to take more active responsibility for flagging their boundaries. Imagine a virtual assistant asked to provide medical advice for a rare condition. Rather than offering a generalised response, the system might say: "I can provide general information about this condition, but my training data may not include the latest research or case-specific variables. Would you like to consult a verified database or a licenced professional?" Such communicative humility does not diminish the AI's usefulness—it enhances it by guiding users to appropriate resources and helping them make informed choices.

Moreover, communicating limitations clearly also builds trust over time. Users are more likely to rely on systems that admit what they do not know than on those that overpromise and underdeliver. In educational contexts, this principle becomes especially critical. An AI tutor working with students must be transparent when it encounters conceptual gaps, controversial topics, or interpretive ambiguity. Instead of bluffing through uncertainty, it might invite co-exploration: "This concept has multiple interpretations. Shall we examine a few and compare them?".

Crucially, the task is not only to *state* limitations, but to do so in a way that is *understandable, timely,* and *relevant* to the user's context. Overloading users with technical qualifications or disclaimers can create cognitive fatigue or foster mistrust. The art of communicating AI limitations lies in finding the right balance—transparent yet not alarming, concise yet not vague, respectful yet not evasive.

As AI communication becomes more pervasive and conversational, the need for self-aware systems that openly articulate their epistemic boundaries will become a defining feature of trustworthiness. Clear, accessible, and user-aware expressions of limitation will not be optional—they will be essential markers of responsible AI behaviour in complex human–AI ecosystems (Fig. 12.7).

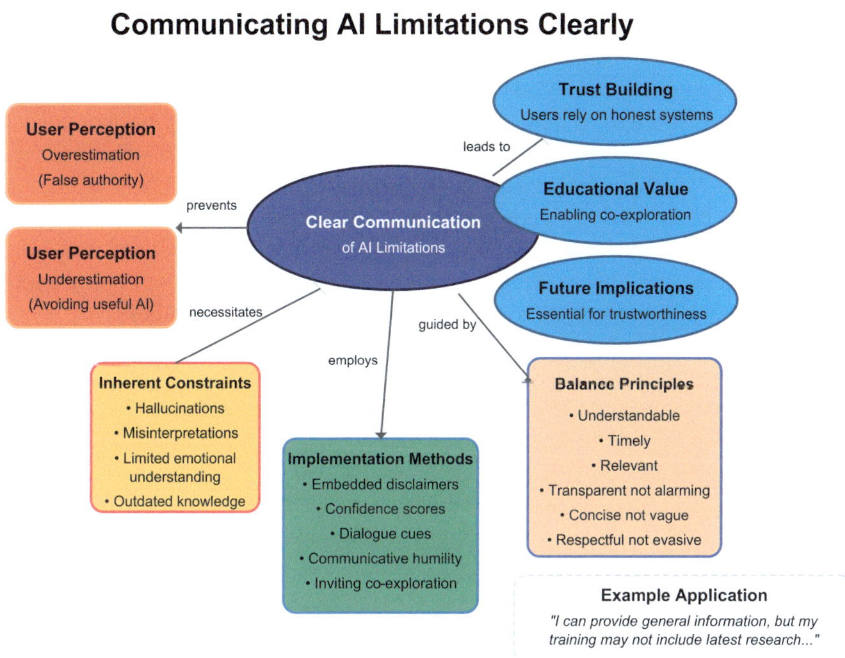

Fig. 12.7 Ecosystem of AI limitation communication. This framework illustrates how transparent acknowledgement of AI constraints prevents user misconceptions through strategic implementation methods. The diagram shows how proper limitation of communication, guided by principles of balance, leads to increased trust, educational value, and future system trustworthiness. Communication clarity stands not as an optional feature but as a core element of responsible human–AI interaction that enhances rather than diminishes AI's utility

12.2.4 *Flag Uncertainty Openly*

Flagging uncertainty openly is an essential practice for fostering honest, respectful, and safe communication between AI systems and their human users. In contrast to deterministic or overly confident messaging, signalling uncertainty helps users understand not only *what* the AI knows, but *how well* it knows it, and where the boundaries of its knowledge or reasoning lie. It encourages critical thinking, prevents overreliance, and supports more collaborative and dialogical use of AI in decision-making.

Contemporary AI systems, extensive language models, often generate text with high fluency and apparent certainty. This can be misleading, especially when the response is speculative, probabilistic, or based on incomplete or ambiguous data. For example, when asked a scientific question about a newly emerging disease, an AI model may present a coherent answer based on outdated or incomplete information, without any natural indication of doubt. Unless explicitly prompted to hedge its answer or qualify its knowledge scope, the user may assume a level of precision or authority that the model does not actually possess.

Openly flagging uncertainty addresses this issue head-on. In present systems, this can be achieved through design patterns such as probabilistic scoring, confidence intervals, or linguistic cues—phrases like "*it is likely that*," "*there is some evidence suggesting*," or "*further confirmation is recommended*." In more advanced scenarios, systems might contextualise their uncertainty: "This response is derived from general knowledge up to 2023. Data after that date is not included, and findings may have changed." Rather than undermining the AI's credibility, such honesty often enhances trust, as users recognise that the system is not pretending to be infallible.

In future communication frameworks, flagging uncertainty may become an integral and adaptive feature. Consider a hypothetical AI used in journalism, tasked with summarising breaking news in real time. As new information comes in and narratives shift, the AI might highlight passages with visual indicators, such as colour coding or interactive annotations, that denote varying levels of confidence. A paragraph might begin, "The cause of the incident is still under investigation," and the user could click to reveal sources, alternative accounts, or links to corroborating material. Here, uncertainty is not an error state to be avoided, but a structured part of intelligent reporting.

Flagging uncertainty also opens a pathway for co-reasoning. A future conversational AI might say, "I'm not fully certain about this legal interpretation. Would you like to review relevant precedents together?" In doing so, it transforms from a passive content generator into an engaged, ethically aware participant in collaborative inquiry. This is particularly vital in sensitive or high-stakes domains—law, healthcare, finance—where acting on unflagged ambiguity can result in serious consequences.

Of course, there is a delicate balance to strike. Overemphasising uncertainty or presenting it in an overly cautious or cryptic manner may lead to user frustration or disengagement. The communication must remain clear, proportional to context, and tailored to the user's level of expertise. For everyday interactions, light hedging may suffice; for expert users, deeper epistemic disclosures may be expected and appreciated.

Ultimately, openly acknowledging uncertainty is a sign of communicative maturity in AI. It reflects a shift from the illusion of omniscience to a more nuanced model of machine intelligence—one that acknowledges ambiguity, invites dialogue, and cultivates informed human judgement. In the evolving landscape of AI–human communication, uncertainty should no longer be hidden or feared—it should be surfaced, structured, and shared (Fig. 12.8).

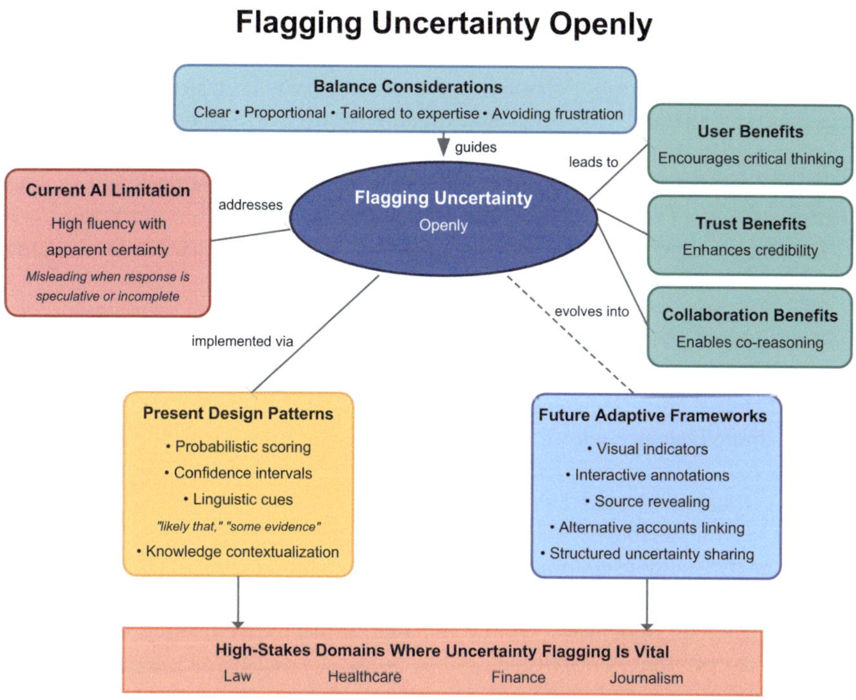

Fig. 12.8 Uncertainty communication framework. This diagram illustrates how AI systems can evolve from presenting misleading certainty to openly acknowledging knowledge boundaries. By implementing various uncertainty indicators—from linguistic cues to visual annotations—AI communication becomes more honest, trustworthy, and collaborative. This transformation supports critical thinking, prevents overreliance, and enables co-reasoning, particularly in high-stakes domains where ambiguity requires careful management. Effective uncertainty flagging requires balance: clear yet not alarming, concise yet not vague, transparent yet not disengaging—ultimately positioning uncertainty not as a weakness but as a cornerstone of responsible AI–human dialogue

12.3 Upholding Ethical Standards

12.3.1 Emphasise Ethical Boundaries

Emphasising ethical boundaries in AI communication means clearly articulating the limits of what an AI system is allowed—and not allowed—to do, say, or suggest. These boundaries are not only technical guardrails; they are communicative signals that shape user expectations, constrain misuse, and reinforce responsible interaction. As AI systems take on increasingly complex social, advisory, and even emotional roles, making ethical boundaries visible and enforceable through dialogue becomes a critical part of future-proof communication design.

In current systems, ethical boundaries are often embedded as internal constraints—filters that block or deflect inappropriate prompts or outputs. For example, a general-purpose chatbot might refuse to provide instructions on illegal activities, or a mental health assistant might be restricted from offering diagnostic judgements. However, these refusals are frequently perceived as arbitrary or opaque if they are not communicated effectively. A user asking a question might be told, "I'm sorry, I can't help with that," without any explanation. This can lead to user frustration, attempts to circumvent the restriction, or erosion of trust in the system's rationale.

To address this, AI communication must move toward *explicit, explainable, and consistent* boundary signalling. For instance, instead of a flat refusal, the system could say: "I'm unable to provide that information because it conflicts with widely accepted ethical guidelines regarding personal safety." This not only explains *what* is being limited but also *why*. It treats the user as a participant in an ethical dialogue rather than as a passive recipient of system behaviour.

Looking ahead, future AI systems may include layered ethical boundary protocols that respond adaptively to context, sensitivity, and user profile. A hypothetical AI mentor for young users might refuse to engage in adult-themed discussions not simply by default, but by referencing age-appropriate norms: "This topic may not be suitable for all audiences. Would you like to discuss something else?" Similarly, an AI operating in a multicultural or politically sensitive environment could be programmed to signal when specific conversations enter contested ethical territory, offering balanced perspectives or inviting reflection rather than issuing blanket prohibitions.

Emphasising boundaries also supports the internal coherence of AI identity. When systems consistently signal what they *stand for* and *stand against*, they become more than just responsive tools—they become communicative agents with an ethical posture. This is especially important in professional or advisory roles. An AI therapist might say, "While I can provide coping strategies, I'm not a licenced practitioner and cannot replace professional support. If you're in crisis, here is a list of immediate resources." Such statements are not disclaimers—they are expressions of integrity.

However, the challenge lies in designing these communications to be firm without being moralistic, respectful without being permissive, and understandable without oversimplification. If the message is too vague, it fails; if it is too rigid, it alienates. Successful ethical boundary communication should be empathetic, context-aware, and framed in a way that helps users learn the rationale behind the restriction and grow in their understanding of responsible AI use.

In the long term, ethical boundary articulation will become a defining feature of AI communication fluency. Systems will not only answer questions and perform tasks—they will help users understand the *limits* of what should be asked, expected, or automated. Through this, they will foster a culture of mutual responsibility and ethical awareness—qualities that are indispensable in a future where AI is a frequent and influential presence in everyday human life (Fig. 12.9).

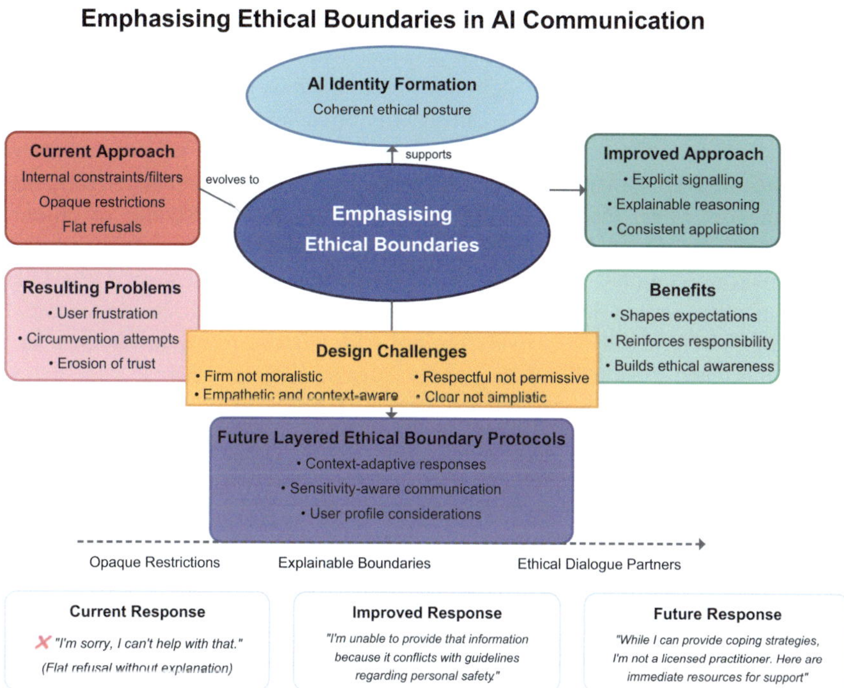

Fig. 12.9 **From constraints to conversations**. This conceptual framework depicts how AI communication of ethical boundaries evolves from internal filters to explicit dialogues. By making boundaries visible, explainable, and adaptive, AI systems can foster trust while promoting responsible use. The diagram illustrates the progression toward ethical fluency, where limitations are communicated with empathy and context-awareness, transforming AI from tools with restrictions to partners in moral reasoning. When properly articulated, ethical boundaries become opportunities for learning rather than barriers to engagement

12.3.2 Consider Privacy and Security in AI Communication

Privacy and security are not only technical requirements but fundamental communicative responsibilities in human–AI interaction. As AI systems increasingly process personal information, engage in sensitive dialogue, and operate in domains such as healthcare, finance, education, and governance, their ability to *communicate* privacy boundaries and *enact* secure interaction protocols becomes critical. Without such transparency, users may inadvertently share more than intended, misunderstand data retention policies, or fall victim to adversarial manipulation—all risks that are amplified by the illusion of safety created by fluent, seemingly human-like AI dialogue.

At present, many AI systems offer minimal cues about how user data is handled. A conversation with a chatbot may feel private; however, the system might log interactions for training purposes or share insights with third-party services without the user being explicitly informed. Similarly, voice assistants may record environmental sounds without clearly signalling when they are "listening" or how long they retain audio inputs. These issues often stem not from malicious intent but from a lack of clear communication about privacy and security boundaries.

To address this, future-oriented AI systems must evolve toward *privacy-aware communication*. This involves integrating privacy and security signals directly into the interaction, rather than relegating them to static terms of service or obscure settings. For example, an AI personal assistant could open a session with a statement like, "This conversation is not stored. You can choose to enable memory if you'd like me to remember certain details for future reference." Or, when discussing sensitive topics, the system might proactively prompt: "Would you prefer to continue in a private, encrypted session?".

In speculative applications, privacy-aware AI might go further, dynamically detecting when personal or sensitive information is being shared and responding accordingly. A healthcare chatbot, for instance, might interrupt a user while they are typing their national ID or complete medical history to say, "Please note that I am not authorised to store personal identifiers. For your safety, it's best to avoid sharing private details here." In this way, the AI becomes not just a passive recipient of data, but an active guardian of secure interaction.

From a security standpoint, communication strategies must also be robust against manipulation and exploitation. AI systems should be trained to recognise socially engineered prompts, avoid echoing or amplifying dangerous content, and refrain from performing actions that could be hijacked for harmful purposes. Crucially, they must be able to *explain* why specific actions are restricted or flagged: "I cannot proceed with this request because it could compromise user privacy or system integrity." By foregrounding such explanations, the systems model is responsible for conducting and educating users about digital safety.

Furthermore, the principle of *user agency* must be embedded in privacy and security communication. Users should be able to inquire, verify, and adjust privacy settings through natural conversation: "What do you know about me?" "Can I delete what I've shared?" "Who else has access to this interaction?" Such inquiries should not be met with vague deflections but with clear, respectful answers that empower users to control their digital footprint.

Ultimately, considering privacy and security in AI communication means building systems that not only comply with ethical standards but also *communicate* those standards in intelligible, adaptive, and respectful ways. In doing so, they support not only individual safety but also a broader culture of trust, awareness, and informed consent—an essential foundation for the responsible integration of AI into everyday human life (Fig. 12.10).

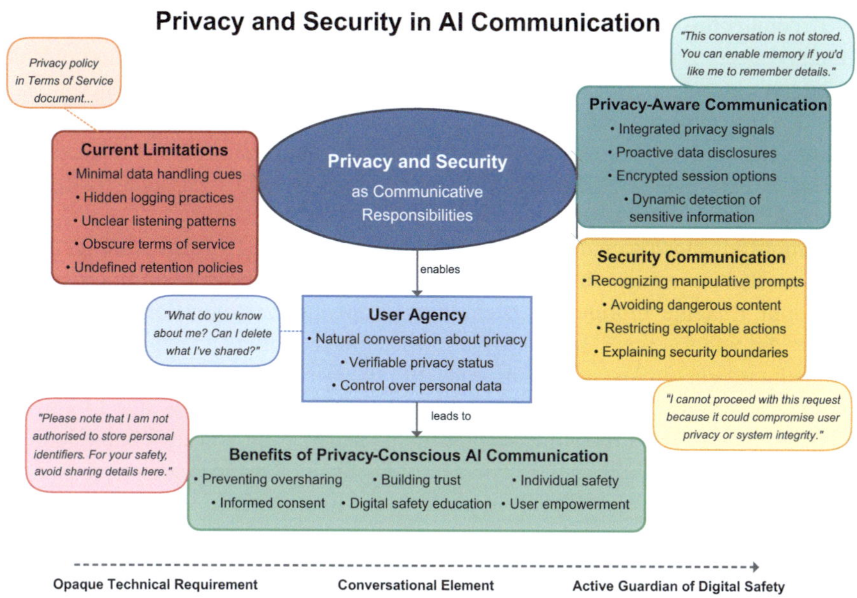

Fig. 12.10 Privacy-aware AI communication framework. This diagram illustrates the evolution from opaque data practices to transparent privacy dialogues, mapping how AI systems integrate privacy and security signals directly into interactions, thereby empowering users through clear communication. The framework shows privacy transforming from a hidden technical consideration into a visible conversational element, with AI systems becoming active guardians of digital safety. By proactively signalling data practices and enabling user control through natural dialogue, these systems foster informed consent while building a foundation of trust

12.3.3 *Implement Accountability Mechanisms*

Implementing accountability mechanisms in AI communication is essential for ensuring that intelligent systems are not only *technically reliable* but also *ethically answerable*. Accountability in this context refers to the capacity to trace decisions, explain behaviours, identify responsible parties, and address failures—whether those failures arise from system errors, design flaws, or inappropriate use. As AI becomes increasingly embedded in decision-making and interpersonal communication, the ability to assign responsibility and respond to misuse or malfunction becomes not just a governance issue, but a communicative imperative.

At present, many AI systems operate in a grey zone of responsibility. When a language model produces a misleading answer, an automated assistant offers unsafe advice, or a recommendation engine amplifies harmful content, users often have little recourse. The interface may offer no way to trace how the decision was made, who trained the model, or whether anyone is accountable for the consequences. This opacity fosters a dangerous form of moral abdication: "The AI said it, therefore no one is to blame."

To counter this, accountability must be *built into communication itself*. Present and future AI systems should be designed to disclose the *provenance* of their outputs, such as the sources used, the level of human oversight involved, and any confidence thresholds or constraints applied. For example, a generative writing tool might include a transparency note: "This summary was created using data from X and Y sources, and no legal expert reviewed the content." Such mechanisms help users contextualise the information and understand the scope of human–AI responsibility.

In more advanced scenarios, accountability can be enacted through *dialogic affordances*—that is, features that allow users to challenge, interrogate, or report system behaviour. Imagine a future AI system that not only answers questions but includes a "why did you say this?" button, which, when clicked, offers an explanation of the reasoning process, relevant training data, and the system's alignment protocols. Or consider a scenario where a user disagrees with a response and is able to lodge a feedback query: "This recommendation seems biased. Can you review the logic?" In response, the AI might reanalyse its reasoning chain, flag the assumption, or offer a rephrased alternative, while also escalating the interaction to human oversight if needed.

Accountability also includes the *traceability* of actions. In AI systems involved in high-stakes decisions, such as autonomous vehicles, judicial decision support, or automated hiring, there must be a record of how outputs were generated, what data influenced them, and what options were considered and rejected. Communicating this information transparently—either in real time or upon request—helps ensure that AI actions are not black boxes, but are intelligible and auditable.

Importantly, accountability mechanisms are not only reactive; they are also educative. When an AI system explains that it cannot perform a particular action because it lacks the authority, legal compliance, or ethical justification, it implicitly teaches the user about responsible norms of interaction. Similarly, when systems are able to acknowledge mistakes, retract incorrect information, or clarify the limits of their competence, they model behaviour that encourages critical thinking and ethical reflection.

In sum, implementing accountability mechanisms in AI communication transforms systems from tools of automation into agents of *responsible interaction.* It anchors AI in a web of traceable justifications, shared responsibilities, and dialogical responsiveness—qualities that will be indispensable as human society learns to live, work, and reason alongside intelligent machines (Fig. 12.11).

12.3.4 Establish Ethical Override Protocols

Establishing ethical override protocols is a critical safeguard in the architecture of responsible AI communication. These protocols enable AI systems to interrupt or refuse actions, even those that appear syntactically valid or user-approved, when ethical thresholds are at risk of being crossed. While many present-day models already include some form of refusal behaviour, ethical override protocols formalise

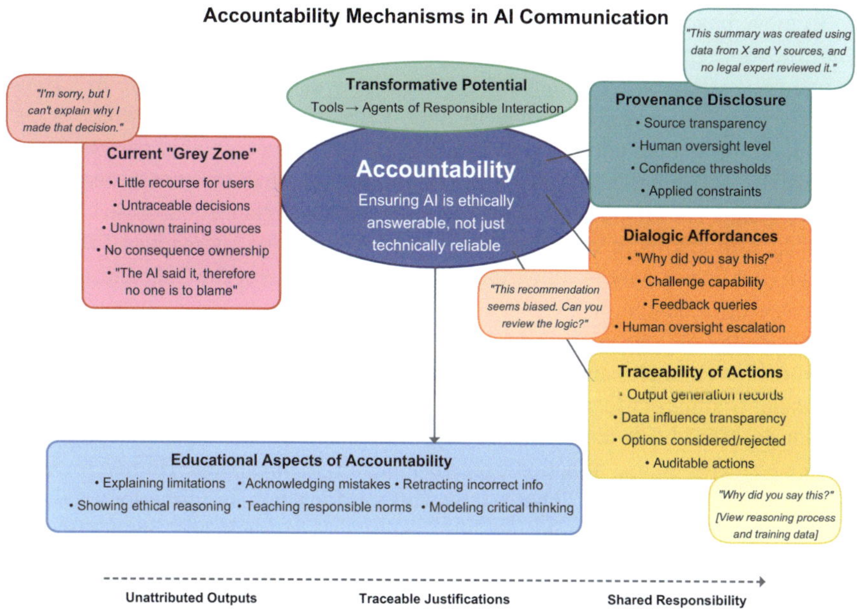

Fig. 12.11 From opacity to answerability. This conceptual model depicts how accountability mechanisms transform AI communication from unattributed outputs to transparent dialogues of shared responsibility. Three core components—provenance disclosure, dialogic affordances, and action traceability—enable users to understand, challenge, and contextualise AI decisions. By embedding accountability directly into interaction, these mechanisms transform AI systems from black boxes that generate consequences without responsibility into partners in ethical reflection and critical thinking, ultimately fostering responsible human–AI interaction

this function into a communicative and governance framework: one in which AI is empowered to protect human dignity, safety, and societal norms even in ambiguous or contested contexts.

In current implementations, override functions tend to manifest as simple, hard-coded filters. For example, if a user prompts a chatbot to generate hate speech or self-harm content, the model may respond with a default refusal message. However, these systems often lack contextual understanding, flexibility, and transparency. A blanket denial may be applied without explanation, nuance, or sensitivity to the user's intent, treating an academic inquiry the same way as a malicious provocation. Worse still, some users perceive these refusals as censorship or ideological bias, leading to friction, resistance, or attempts to "jailbreak" the system.

To move beyond these limitations, future AI systems must implement *dynamic, context-aware ethical override protocols*—ones that not only detect violations of ethical parameters but *communicate* the reasoning behind the override in a transparent, respectful, and educational manner. Consider a scenario in which a user asks an AI assistant to compose a message that could harass another person. Rather than simply declining, the AI might respond: "I'm unable to assist with this request because it may contribute to emotional harm or violate personal boundaries. If you'd like help with resolving a conflict, I can offer constructive alternatives." Here, the override serves not only to block the request but to redirect the interaction toward positive, ethical outcomes.

Such protocols can also serve as ethical *brakes* in uncertain or high-stakes domains. For example, an AI embedded in a military decision-making system or a financial trading platform might detect signals of escalating risk, bias amplification, or potential harm to vulnerable populations and initiate a pause. The system might say: "This course of action exceeds ethical risk thresholds. Human review is required before proceeding." These statements reinforce human-in-the-loop accountability and ensure that decisions involving significant consequences are not made in isolation by a machine.

Additionally, ethical override protocols must be sensitive to cultural and contextual variation. A refusal that is appropriate in one setting may require a different framing elsewhere. A conversational AI deployed in cross-cultural dialogue may need to flag potential offensiveness or misunderstanding, offering disclaimers such as: "This topic is sensitive in some cultural contexts. Would you like to continue with a neutral framing?" Such protocols do not censor, but instead foster awareness, dialogue, and mutual respect.

To be effective, these overrides must be auditable and open to appeal. Users should be able to inquire: "Why was this blocked?" and receive a meaningful explanation grounded in ethical logic, not arbitrary constraint. In professional environments, override logs can support accountability, transparency, and refinement of the system over time, allowing designers to assess how ethical boundaries are functioning in practice and where they might need to be re-evaluated.

Ultimately, ethical override protocols mark a maturation of AI communication, where systems are not only responsive but *responsible*; not only capable of saying "yes," but empowered to say "no" when human values are at stake. In the evolving ecology of human-AI interaction, such capabilities will be crucial for maintaining the delicate balance between innovation and integrity, freedom and protection, autonomy and care (Fig. 12.12).

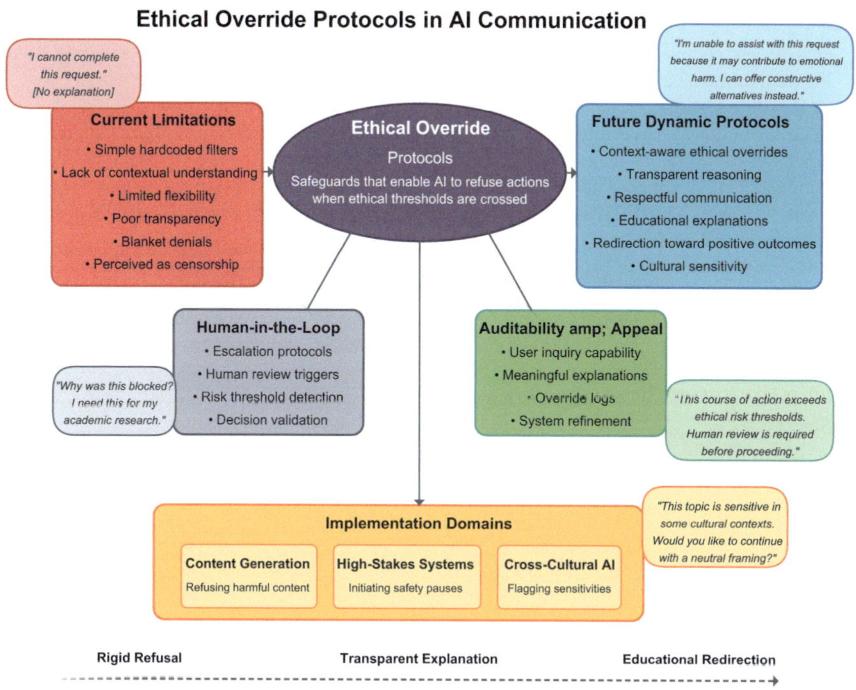

Fig. 12.12 From refusal to redirection. This conceptual model depicts how ethical override protocols transform from rigid blocks to educational opportunities. The framework illustrates the transition from simple, hardcoded filters to dynamic, context-aware systems that explain reasoning while offering alternatives. Three key dimensions emerge: transparent communication of ethical boundaries, human-in-the-loop escalation for high-stakes scenarios, and cultural sensitivity in implementation. By empowering AI to respectfully decline when values are at risk, these protocols represent a maturation of AI communication, where systems balance service with safeguarding human dignity

Bibliography

Annapureddy R, Fornaroli A, Gatica-Perez D (2025) Generative AI literacy: twelve defining competencies. Digital Gov Res Practice 6(1):1–21

Austin JL (1962) How to do things with words. Oxford University Press, Oxford

Bahree A (2024) Generative AI in action. Manning Publications

Bender E et al (2021) On the dangers of stochastic parrots: can language models be too big? In: Proceedings of the 2021 ACM conference on fairness, accountability, and transparency, pp 610–623

Bostrom N (2014) Superintelligence: paths, dangers, strategies. Oxford University Press, Oxford

Brown BR (2025) Human–machine teaming using large language models. In: Interdependent human-machine teams. Academic Press, pp 41–66

Brown TB et al (2020) Language models are few-shot learners. Adv Neural Inf Process Syst 33:1877–1901

Bura C, Myakala PK, Jonnalgadda AK (2025) Ethical prompt engineering: addressing bias, transparency, and fairness. Int J Res Anal Rev (IJRAR) 12(1)

Choi WC, Chang CI (2025) A survey of techniques, key components, strategies, challenges, and student perspectives on prompt engineering for large language models (LLMs) in education. https://doi.org/10.20944/preprints.202503.1808.v1. Accessed 8 May 2025
Clark H (1996) Using language. Cambridge University Press, Cambridge
Debnath T, Siddiky MNA, Rahman ME et al (2025) A comprehensive survey of prompt engineering techniques in large language models. TechRxiv. https://doi.org/10.36227/techrxiv.174140719.96375390/v1. Accessed 10 May 2025
Dhamani N, Engler M (2024) Introduction to generative AI: an ethical, societal, and legal overview. Manning Publications
Eliot L (2024) Essentials of prompt engineering for generative AI: practical advances in artificial intelligence and machine learning. LBE Press Publishing
Ferraris A F, Audrito D, Di Caro L et al (2025) The architecture of language: Understanding the mechanics behind LLMs. In: Cambridge forum on AI: law and governance, vol 1. Cambridge University Press, Cambridge
Floridi L, Cowls J (2019) A unified framework of five principles for AI in society. Harvard Data Sci Rev 1(1)
Geroimenko V (2025a) Key challenges in prompt engineering. In: The essential guide to prompt engineering: key principles, techniques, challenges, and security risks. Springer Nature Switzerland, Cham, pp 85–102
Geroimenko V (2025b) Key principles of good prompt design. In: The essential guide to prompt engineering: key principles, techniques, challenges, and security risks. Springer Nature Switzerland, Cham, pp 17–36
Geroimenko V (2025c) Key techniques for writing effective prompts. In: The essential guide to prompt engineering: key principles, techniques, challenges, and security risks. Springer Nature Switzerland, Cham, pp 37–83
Geroimenko V (2025d) The essential guide to prompt engineering: key principles, techniques, challenges, and security risks. Springer, Berlin
Geroimenko V (2025e) Key security risks in prompt engineering. In: The essential guide to prompt engineering: key principles, techniques, challenges, and security risks. Springer Nature Switzerland, Cham, pp 103–120
GitHub (2025) Prompt engineering guide. https://github.com/dair-ai/Prompt-Engineering-Guide. Accessed 10 Apr 2025
Greenwood M (2024) Artificial intelligence: a practical guide to using AI in everyday life. Ochreland Publishing
Gunkel DJ (2020) Robot rights. MIT Press, Cambridge
Hsu HP (2025) From programming to prompting: developing computational thinking through large language model-based generative artificial intelligence. TechTrends, pp 1–22
Huang G, Xiao Y, Jiang L et al (2025) Beyond prompt engineering: a reinforced token-level input refinement for large language models. Proc AAAI Conf Artif Intell 39(22):24113–24121
Huang MX et al (2022) Adaptive conversational AI: dynamic strategies for human–AI interaction. Int J Hum Comput Stud 160:102798
i Picó JF, Catta-Preta M, Omeñaca AT et al (2025) The time machine: future scenario generation through generative AI tools. Fut Internet 17(1):1–15
Jobin A et al (2019) The global landscape of AI ethics guidelines. Nat Mach Intell 1(9):389–399
Kannan R, Ahmad M (eds) (2025) Generative AI foundations, developments, and applications. IGI Global
Khan I (2024) The quick guide to prompt engineering. Wiley
Kim J, Sundar SS (2012) Anthropomorphism of computers: is it mindlessness or mindfulness? Comput Hum Behav 28(1):241–250
Kushwaha V, Ragavan SS, Subhajit Roy S (2025) A measure based generalizable approach to understandability. arXiv:2503.21615. https://doi.org/10.48550/arXiv.2503.21615. Accessed 19 Apr 2025
Lakoff G, Johnson M (1980) Metaphors we live by. University of Chicago Press, Chicago

Lee D, Palmer E (2025) Prompt engineering in higher education: a systematic review to help inform curricula. Int J Educ Technol High Educ 22(1):7
Lee JY, Kang S, Yoo S (2025) Can we predict the effect of prompts? arXiv preprint arXiv:2501.18883. Accessed 12 May 2025
Lindley J, Whitham R (2025) From prompt engineering to prompt craft. In: Proceedings of the nineteenth international conference on tangible, embedded, and embodied interaction, pp 1–12
López-Pérez B et al (2025) Exploring the potential of large language models to understand interpersonal emotion regulation strategies from narratives. Emotion. https://doi.org/10.1037/emo0001528
Luger GF (2020) Artificial intelligence: structures and strategies for complex problem solving, 6th edn. Pearson, Boston
Maaz S, Palaganas JC, Palaganas G et al (2025) A guide to prompt design: foundations and applications for healthcare simulationists. Front Med 11:1504532
Marcus G (2020) The next decade in AI: four steps towards robust artificial intelligence. arXiv preprint arXiv:2002.06177. Accessed 12 May 2025
Mishra M, Ara A, Mishra S (2025) Exploring human–AI collaboration in higher education: an investigation into AI-enabled personalized learning. In: Prompt engineering and generative AI applications for teaching and learning. IGI Global Scientific Publishing, pp 483–502
Mitchell M (2019) Artificial intelligence: a guide for thinking humans. Farrar, Straus and Giroux, New York
OpenAI (2025) Best practices for prompt engineering with the OpenAI API. https://help.openai.com/en/articles/6654000-best-practices-for-prompt-engineering-with-the-openai-api Accessed 20 Apr 2025
OpenAI (2025) Research. https://openai.com/research/index/.
Phoenix J, Taylor M (2024) Prompt engineering for generative AI. O'Reilly Media
PremaLatha V, Kumar AD, Parveen N (2025) Optimizing interactions: strategies for prompt engineering in large language models. Edu-Tech Enterprise 3:24–24
Prompt Engineering Guide (2025) https://www.promptingguide.ai/ Accessed 7 March 2025
Rahwan I (2018) Society-in-the-loop: programming the algorithmic social contract. Ethics Inf Technol 20(1):5–14
Reddy CKK, Anoushka P, Draksharapu A et al (2025) Beyond text: analyzing artificial intelligence models through prompt engineering. In: Future tech startups and innovation in the age of AI, pp 120–156
Russell S (2019) Human compatible: artificial intelligence and the problem of control. Viking, New York
Sasson Lazovsky G, Raz T, Kenett YN (2025) The art of creative inquiry—from question asking to prompt engineering. J Creat Behav 59(1):e671
Searle J (1969) Speech acts: an essay in the philosophy of language. Cambridge University Press, Cambridge
Shneiderman B (2022) Human-centered AI. Oxford University Press, Oxford
Siau K, Wang W (2018) Building trust in artificial intelligence, machine learning, and robotics. CUTTER Bus Technol J 31(2):47–53
Sihi D, Ryan A (2025) Crafting and evaluating generative AI prompts: insights from students, educators, and marketers. Mark Educ Rev 1–7
Suchman L (2007) Human-machine reconfigurations: plans and situated actions, 2nd edn. Cambridge University Press, Cambridge
Tegmark M (2017) Life 3.0: being human in the age of artificial intelligence. Penguin, London
Turing A (1950) Computing machinery and intelligence. Mind 59(236):433–460
Vairamani AD, Nayyar A (2024) Prompt engineering: empowering communication. CRC Press, Boca Raton
Winograd T (1972) Understanding natural language. Academic Press, New York, NY
Wittgenstein L (1953) Philosophical investigations. Blackwell, Oxford

Chapter 13
Enhancing AI's Cognitive Abilities: Optimising AI's Reasoning, Creativity, and Knowledge Application

Abstract This chapter explores the cognitive evolution of AI systems as they transition from responsive tools to proactive communicative partners. It introduces foundational strategies to strengthen AI's core reasoning, including the incorporation of explicit reasoning steps, hypothetical and counterfactual analysis, and domain-specific cognitive structures. The chapter then advances into creative and divergent thinking, outlining how AI can become a co-explorer in ideation, storytelling, and design. The discussion also addresses multimodal expression as a means to enhance reasoning and communication. In supporting interactional intelligence, the chapter examines conversational steering, collaborative mistake-handling, and robust feedback loops. Finally, it presents strategies for improving cognitive resilience, including bias mitigation, integrated knowledge synthesis, and self-correction mechanisms. Together, these principles chart a pathway toward AI systems that are not only logically sound and imaginative but also reflective, transparent, and epistemically aligned with human expectations for trustworthy communication.

Keywords AI reasoning · Cognitive AI · Creative AI · Domain-specific thinking · Divergent thinking · Knowledge integration · Self-correction

To communicate meaningfully and effectively with humans, AI systems must go beyond surface fluency and exhibit deeper forms of cognition. This involves not only the ability to reason clearly and contextually but also to think creatively, engage collaboratively, and apply knowledge in adaptive and integrative ways. As AI continues to evolve from a reactive tool into a proactive partner, its cognitive functions—such as logical inference, divergent thinking, multimodal expression, bias recognition, and self-correction—become central to its communicative role. This chapter explores the foundational principles that support the development of cognitively capable AI, focusing on how such systems can reason step by step, imagine alternatives, handle errors with users, and learn across domains. By developing these advanced mental capabilities, AI becomes better equipped to support complex dialogue, co-create with human users, and respond intelligently to diverse and evolving communicative contexts.

V. Geroimenko, *Beyond and After Prompt Engineering: The Future of AI Communication*, https://doi.org/10.1007/978-3-032-04569-0_13

13.1 Strengthening Core Reasoning and Thinking Patterns

13.1.1 Incorporate Reasoning Steps

A defining challenge in present-day AI communication is not only to foster accurate responses but also to produce transparent, traceable, and logically grounded ones. Incorporating reasoning steps into AI outputs is a foundational strategy to enhance cognitive reliability, foster user trust, and align AI-generated conclusions with human expectations of logic and coherence. This principle urges developers and communicators to prompt AI systems to "show their work"—explicitly revealing the sequence of thought, inference, or calculation that leads to a final output.

Currently, this approach is most evident in the application of chain-of-thought prompting, where language models are guided to solve problems step by step. For example, when asked a multipart mathematics question, a model trained or prompted to incorporate reasoning steps will break the question into intermediate operations, perform each, and articulate the process before concluding. This not only improves the likelihood of a correct answer but also makes errors more identifiable and explainable for human users. Similarly, in legal or medical AI applications, breaking down reasoning into distinct steps, such as identifying relevant precedents, interpreting diagnostic indicators, or comparing conflicting guidelines, adds much-needed clarity and auditability to AI recommendations.

In speculative future settings, incorporating reasoning steps may evolve beyond linear textual sequences. Multimodal cognitive agents might combine visual schematics, audio reasoning cues, or spatial models to guide users through a reasoning process. Imagine an AI that helps students learn physics by verbally explaining the forces acting on a system, while simultaneously sketching a dynamic vector diagram and adjusting it in real-time based on hypothetical user inputs. Alternatively, a future collaborative writing assistant might not only offer narrative suggestions but also visually map out plot logic, character motivation, and causal links between story events—externalising its reasoning to support creative decisions in co-authorship.

At a deeper cognitive level, reasoning steps may become adaptive and dialogical. Rather than offering a rigid sequence, future AIs could dynamically restructure their reasoning based on user queries, confidence levels, or contextual changes. For instance, a policymaking assistant might initially offer a basic rationale for a regulatory proposal, but upon sensing uncertainty or pushback, could expand their reasoning to include analogies, counterexamples, or stepwise justifications rooted in socio-political precedent. This capacity would mark a shift from static answer generation to genuine cognitive scaffolding, where the AI helps the human interlocutor *understand how* it thinks, not just *what* it thinks.

Critically, the incorporation of reasoning steps aligns with growing demands for explainable AI. It counters the "black box" nature of opaque model outputs by introducing intermediate logic, and even when imperfect, it offers a structure that users can interrogate and refine. In the future, this principle may also intersect with self-reflective capabilities in AI, where the system not only reveals its reasoning but

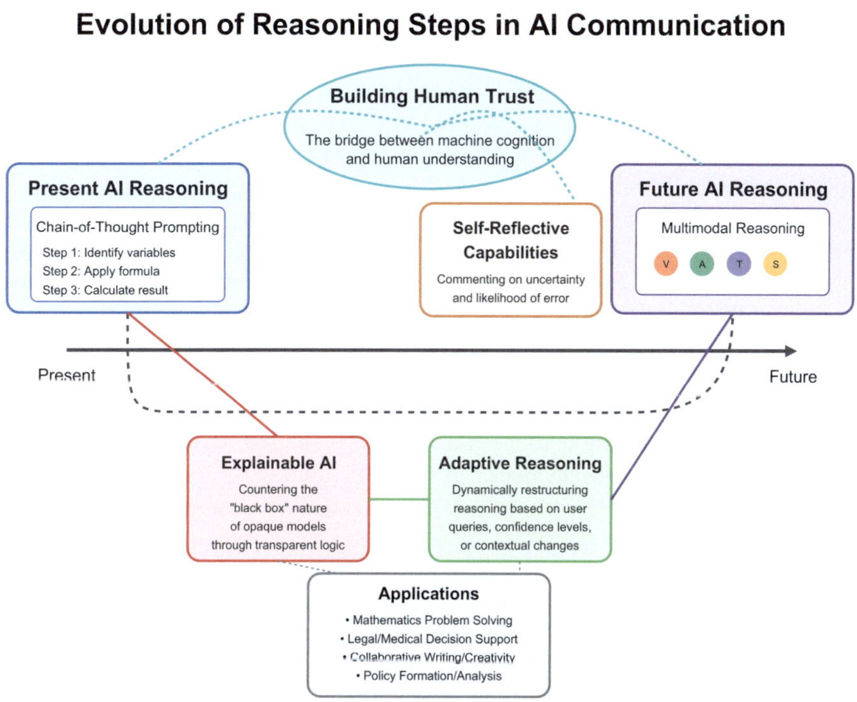

Fig. 13.1 Evolution of reasoning steps in AI communication. This diagram illustrates the evolution of reasoning steps in AI communication, from present-day chain-of-thought prompting to future multimodal cognitive agents. It highlights the progression through explainable AI and adaptive reasoning phases, emphasising how transparent reasoning processes serve as a bridge between machine cognition and human trust. The diagram captures key applications across domains while demonstrating how AI reasoning may evolve beyond linear textual sequences to incorporate visual, audio, and spatial elements in dynamic, user-responsive systems

also comments on its uncertainty or likelihood of error at each step, bringing a meta-cognitive dimension to AI communication.

Ultimately, as reasoning becomes more central to AI systems' engagement with complex tasks, embedding transparent reasoning steps will serve not merely as a technical aid but as a bridge between machine cognition and human trust. Whether explaining a decision, tutoring a learner, resolving a dispute, or co-authoring a novel, the AI of the future must be able to reason *with* us—openly, understandably, and adaptively (Fig. 13.1).

13.1.2 Enable Hypothetical and Counterfactual Reasoning

Hypothetical and counterfactual reasoning are essential elements of human cognition, supporting imagination, foresight, decision-making, and moral evaluation. In the context of AI communication, enabling these reasoning modes allows artificial agents to explore possibilities beyond immediate facts, simulate alternative outcomes, and reason about events that *could* happen or *might have* occurred under different conditions. This capability expands an AI system's utility from static information retrieval to dynamic scenario generation and speculative analysis, positioning it as a truly cognitive collaborator.

In current implementations, language models exhibit early forms of hypothetical reasoning when asked to imagine potential outcomes or to compare scenarios. For instance, a user might ask, "What would happen if carbon emissions were reduced by 50% in the next decade?" A reasoning-enabled AI might respond by outlining ecological, economic, and social consequences, drawing from climate data and prior projections. Similarly, in a medical setting, a diagnostic assistant might be prompted with, "What would the prognosis look like if the patient had started treatment three months earlier?"—inviting a counterfactual analysis based on typical progression patterns and treatment efficacy rates.

These capacities are still in nascent stages, and their reliability often depends on the model's internal representations and access to domain-specific knowledge. However, the promise lies in expanding such reasoning into structured simulations and adaptable thought experiments. For example, a policymaking AI could support ethical deliberation by presenting not only the expected outcome of a proposed law but also several counterfactual scenarios: What if enforcement was delayed? What if the law disproportionately affected specific communities? By comparing these branches, the AI helps decision-makers anticipate unintended consequences.

Looking toward the future, hypothetical and counterfactual reasoning could be combined with multimodal tools and temporal simulation engines to create immersive foresight systems. A teacher might interact with an AI tutor that can generate plausible historical counterfactuals—e.g. "What might have happened if the Industrial Revolution had started in China instead of Britain?"—supported by dynamic maps, timelines, and visualised causal chains. In creative industries, AI co-authors might suggest alternative plot developments based on character decisions, enabling writers to explore branching narratives and emotional arcs across parallel storylines.

Furthermore, these reasoning abilities will play a crucial role in ethical and strategic reasoning. For instance, autonomous systems may soon need to simulate and weigh various hypothetical paths in real time, whether rerouting a self-driving car, responding to emerging threats in cybersecurity, or negotiating complex agreements in multiagent environments. In such cases, the AI's ability to reflect on *what might have happened if…* becomes a foundation for anticipatory intelligence and responsible action.

At a philosophical level, enabling counterfactual reasoning in AI challenges traditional views of machine logic as strictly linear and deterministic. It introduces a capacity for *imaginative cognition*, where systems can step outside the current state of the world and reason about alternative realities. As such, it strengthens not only the cognitive depth of AI communication but also its alignment with human modes of reflective and anticipatory thought.

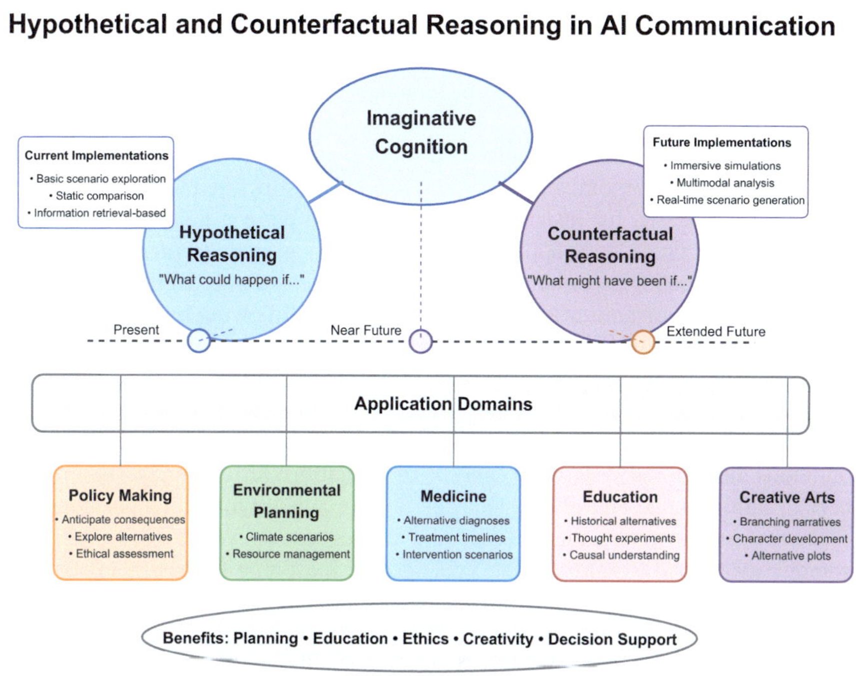

Fig. 13.2 Hypothetical and counterfactual reasoning. This diagram illustrates how AI systems evolve from static information providers to dynamic cognitive collaborators through hypothetical ("what could happen if…") and counterfactual ("what might have been if…") reasoning capabilities. The visualisation traces the progression from present implementations to future multimodal, immersive simulations across five key application domains: policymaking, environmental planning, medicine, education, and creative arts. Central to this evolution is the shift from linear deterministic reasoning to imaginative cognition, enabling AI to explore alternative realities and support human decision-making across multiple possible futures

In conclusion, by fostering hypothetical and counterfactual reasoning, AI systems become better equipped to support planning, education, ethics, and creativity. These reasoning modes empower users to ask more profound questions, test alternative assumptions, and explore the contours of what could be—and what could have been—with a partner that reasons not only in the present tense but across a spectrum of possibilities (Fig. 13.2).

13.1.3 Apply Domain-Specific Reasoning Structures

To elevate AI communication beyond general-purpose responses, it is essential to integrate reasoning patterns that align with the cognitive frameworks of specific domains. Applying domain-specific reasoning structures means guiding AI systems to operate using the logical methods, conceptual schemas, and inferential strategies that are standard within a particular field—be it law, science, engineering, medicine, economics, or art. This principle moves AI closer to expert-level interaction by tailoring its thought process to the epistemology and methodology of the task at hand.

In current practice, many advanced AI models already benefit from fine-tuning on domain-relevant corpora, allowing them to emulate structured forms of analysis. A legal reasoning AI, for instance, might be able to parse a judicial decision by identifying legal precedents, applying principles such as *ratio decidendi* and *obiter dicta*, and constructing arguments in formal syllogistic patterns. Similarly, in scientific contexts, AI assistants are increasingly capable of following hypothesis-testing protocols—formulating testable claims, reviewing experimental methods, assessing data validity, and drawing structured conclusions.

These reasoning structures are not generic but culturally and methodologically embedded. In medicine, differential diagnosis proceeds by eliminating competing conditions through the systematic analysis of symptoms, history, and tests. In engineering, failure mode and effects analysis involves identifying potential points of breakdown and mapping their causes and consequences. When AI systems are prompted or trained to mirror these field-specific reasoning formats, their outputs become more relevant, interpretable, and actionable to domain professionals.

Looking ahead, we may see the emergence of modular cognitive architectures within AI that dynamically switch reasoning modes based on domain recognition. Imagine a multimodal AI capable of shifting from Bayesian diagnostic reasoning in a clinical discussion to economic modelling using game theory during a policy debate, and then adopting narrative logic when co-authoring a historical novel. These cognitive shifts could be guided by user roles, task goals, or contextual cues, allowing for seamless adaptation of reasoning style to user needs.

Furthermore, domain-specific reasoning may benefit from hybrid human–AI workflows. Consider a scenario in which a research scientist outlines a hypothesis, and the AI not only generates potential experimental designs but also simulates expected results based on prior domain knowledge and known constraints. In this scenario, the AI does not merely generate text but participates in structured inquiry, echoing the reasoning traditions of the natural sciences. In architecture or design, an AI might use heuristic evaluation criteria, such as balance, proportion, or material constraints, to reason about aesthetic and functional trade-offs within a given blueprint.

As AI systems transition from passive tools to active collaborators, the importance of embedding domain-specific cognitive structures will continue to grow. Without this alignment, communication risks becoming superficial—an exchange of words without shared understanding of how meaning is constructed or validated within the domain. Conversely, when the AI's reasoning patterns reflect the domain's logic, users can better evaluate, trust, and co-develop ideas with the system.

Ultimately, applying domain-specific reasoning structures allows AI to move from being a broadly knowledgeable assistant to a context-sensitive thinker. This allows for deeper alignment with expert users, supports more precise and credible outputs,

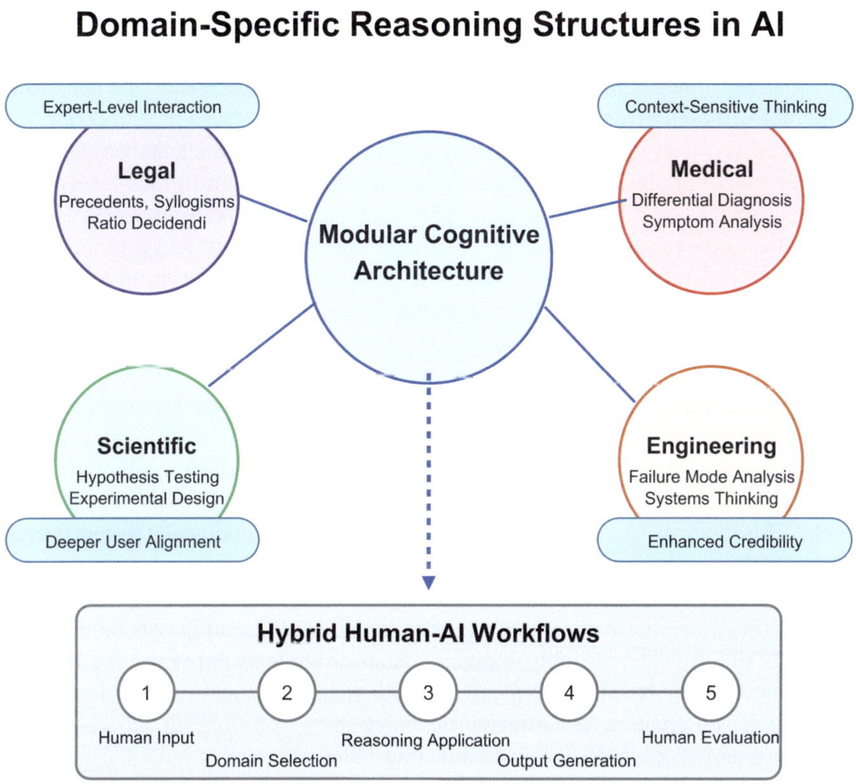

Fig. 13.3 From general AI to domain experts. This diagram illustrates the evolution of AI toward domain-specific reasoning patterns. The modular cognitive architecture adapts to specialised frameworks across law, medicine, science, and engineering, each with distinct methodologies. The system dynamically shifts between reasoning modes based on contextual needs, creating expert-level interactions through hybrid human–AI workflows. By embedding field-specific cognitive structures, AI transcends general-purpose responses to become a context-sensitive collaborator, enhancing credibility and alignment with expert users while preserving the epistemological integrity of each domain's unique approach to knowledge construction

and enhances AI's role in professional and scholarly practices where rigour, nuance, and field-specific reasoning are non-negotiable (Fig. 13.3).

13.1.4 *Practise Contrastive Thinking*

Contrastive thinking—the ability to compare, differentiate, and analyse alternatives by highlighting distinctions—is a fundamental cognitive skill that underpins human reasoning in fields ranging from philosophy and science to everyday decision-making. For AI systems engaged in meaningful communication with humans, the ability to practise contrastive thinking opens a path to richer, more insightful dialogues. Rather than merely responding to a question or request, an AI equipped with contrastive reasoning can illuminate options, clarify differences, and help users think more critically by showing *what something is* in contrast to *what it is not*.

In present AI systems, contrastive thinking is often implicit. When asked to compare two technologies, for instance, a model might highlight surface-level differences in capabilities, costs, or use cases. However, prompting AI to engage in *explicit contrastive reasoning*—for example, "Compare deep learning to symbolic AI in terms of transparency and interpretability"—can elicit more structured and meaningful distinctions. These contrasts can guide better choices, expose trade-offs, and refine users' understanding of complex systems or abstract ideas.

Contrastive thinking also enhances ethical and philosophical analysis. Consider an AI assistant helping a student reflect on the morality of two historical leaders. Rather than merely listing facts, the AI might frame their actions through different ethical theories—utilitarianism, deontology, virtue ethics—thus revealing not only what each figure did but *how* their actions align or conflict with distinct moral frameworks. This mode of AI interaction mirrors human critical thinking and fosters deeper educational engagement.

In future applications, contrastive thinking may take more dynamic and multimodal forms. Imagine an AI design assistant capable of presenting two architectural proposals side by side, not only showing visual differences but reasoning through their respective environmental impacts, cultural symbolism, and structural integrity. Or envision a co-creative AI writing partner suggesting two different narrative directions for a novel, each rooted in contrasting character motivations and thematic implications. In these speculative scenarios, contrast is not limited to comparison but becomes a tool for *creative divergence* and *intellectual expansion*.

Contrastive reasoning will also be critical in the development of AI systems intended to support decision-making under uncertainty. A policymaker might rely on an AI system to compare potential regulatory paths, not just listing their features, but articulating which assumptions each policy depends on, what stakeholders it benefits or harms, and how its implementation might unfold over time. This contrast-driven perspective empowers the user to recognise blind spots, biases, and underlying value systems embedded in different choices.

Moreover, contrastive thinking enables *negative space reasoning*—reasoning not only about what is present but also about what is *absent or excluded*. This has powerful implications for critical communication. For instance, when analysing media coverage, a contrast-aware AI might point out what perspectives are missing or underrepresented, fostering a more balanced and reflective dialogue about information, narratives, and framing.

As AI systems evolve into co-thinkers and creative partners, contrastive thinking will be central to their ability to question assumptions, challenge ideas, and expand the user's cognitive landscape. It is a hallmark of dialogue that values difference, not as a problem to be resolved, but as a stimulus for insight. Practising contrastive thinking in AI communication invites more nuanced reasoning, deepens analysis, and supports decision-making that is both intellectually rigorous and open to alternative perspectives (Fig. 13.4).

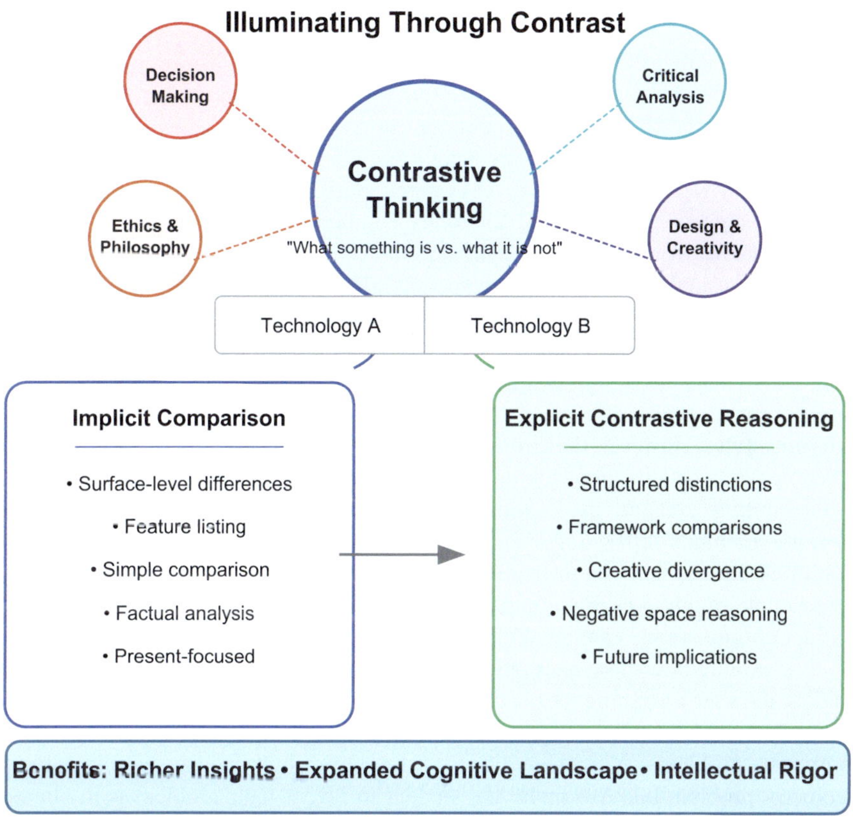

Fig. 13.4 Illuminating through contrast. This diagram illustrates how contrastive thinking transforms AI communication from simple comparison to nuanced reasoning. The central concept connects four key application domains—ethics, decision-making, design, and critical analysis—where contrast illuminates alternatives and deepens understanding. The progression from implicit comparison to explicit contrastive reasoning shows AI's evolution toward identifying structured distinctions, evaluating frameworks, exploring creative divergences, and employing negative space reasoning. By highlighting "what something is versus what it is not," AI systems become intellectual partners capable of revealing trade-offs, exposing assumptions, and expanding cognitive landscapes—ultimately fostering more rigorous, reflective dialogue with users

13.2 Fostering Creativity and Divergent Thinking

13.2.1 Facilitate Creative Exploration

Creativity is not merely an aesthetic or artistic endeavour—it is a core cognitive function that enables innovation, problem-solving, and adaptation across domains. For AI systems engaged in meaningful communication with human users, the capacity to facilitate creative exploration is increasingly essential. Rather than simply generating content or answers, future-facing AI systems must become co-explorers: partners capable of suggesting unexpected directions, combining disparate ideas, and helping users break free from habitual thought patterns.

In today's applications, language models already exhibit a degree of creative fluency. Given a prompt like "Imagine a society where time runs backwards," many can elaborate richly on speculative scenarios, combining narrative coherence with imaginative leaps. In design contexts, AI tools such as image generators and music composition assistants offer new stimuli that inspire users to explore novel aesthetics or hybrid styles. However, these outputs often arise from probabilistic extrapolations of learned data patterns and lack intentional guidance in the creative process itself.

Facilitating creative exploration requires more than producing imaginative content—it entails supporting users in *navigating the unknown*, encouraging divergent thinking, and iterating through possibility spaces. A future AI writing assistant, for example, might not only complete a sentence but also suggest five stylistically distinct continuations, each evoking a different mood or genre. It could then help the user explore how these alternatives shape the emotional arc of the story, thereby guiding the user's awareness of narrative choice and thematic development.

Similarly, in education, AI systems could foster creativity by encouraging students to reframe problems. A mathematics tutor might not only explain how to solve a geometry problem but also invite the student to invent their problem with altered constraints, and then explore how the solution strategies would differ. In such scenarios, the AI supports creative exploration by introducing variation, posing "what if" challenges, and expanding the frame of reference.

Importantly, creative exploration does not imply unconstrained randomness. The most fruitful creative processes often emerge within structured boundaries—rules, limitations, or conceptual tensions that serve as catalysts for innovation. Future AI systems may be equipped with the ability to *co-construct constraints* with users. For instance, a musician and AI co-composer might agree to create a piece limited to a particular scale and tempo, then challenge each other to find novel musical expressions within that frame.

AI-facilitated creativity may also thrive through serendipity. By surfacing unusual associations across domains—such as drawing a metaphor from biology to illuminate a business strategy, or linking a historical event to a visual design concept—AI systems can serve as lateral-thinking engines. This associative flexibility allows users to see their ideas from new angles, often uncovering insights they might not have reached independently.

In speculative futures, creative exploration may become multimodal and embodied. Imagine a virtual studio where a filmmaker and an AI system collaboratively sculpt ideas, using gesture, voice, visuals, and spatial manipulation to brainstorm a scene. Or consider a research scientist who, aided by a generative AI partner, explores molecular configurations through real-time 3d simulation, with the AI dynamically proposing variations based on patterns in previously overlooked research.

Facilitating creative exploration ultimately transforms the role of AI from responder to collaborator. It requires systems that are not only generative but also responsive to curiosity, ambiguity, and the nonlinear paths that characterise human creativity. By supporting users in discovering what they did not yet know they were looking for, such AI systems will help unlock the full imaginative potential of human–AI co-creation (Fig. 13.5).

13.2.2 Encourage Divergent Thinking in AI

Divergent thinking—the ability to generate multiple, varied ideas in response to a single problem or prompt—is a hallmark of creative intelligence. It contrasts with convergent thinking, which seeks a single correct answer, and instead prioritises fluency, flexibility, and originality. In the context of AI communication, encouraging divergent thinking means prompting or designing AI systems to go beyond expected outputs, to explore alternative viewpoints, unusual associations, and novel paths of thought. This capacity not only enriches creative collaboration but also expands the cognitive repertoire of AI, enabling it to assist in ideation, invention, and conceptual exploration.

In current applications, language models can already produce divergent responses to some extent, particularly when guided by prompts like "List different ways to use a paperclip" or "Generate five interpretations of this poem." However, the depth and diversity of such responses often depend on careful prompt design, temperature settings, and model architecture. Without specific prompting, many systems default to the most statistically probable answers, limiting the potential for originality or out-of-the-box thinking.

To move toward richer AI–human co-creativity, divergent thinking must become an intentional and embedded capability. For instance, an AI that assists in strategic planning should not offer a single linear forecast, but rather multiple alternative futures, each based on distinct assumptions or external factors. This multidimensional reasoning allows users to evaluate a broader possibility space, challenge their preconceptions, and prepare for uncertainty. In educational contexts, an AI tutor might suggest multiple solution paths to a problem, encouraging students to compare methods, question assumptions, and develop intellectual flexibility.

In speculative future scenarios, divergent thinking may evolve into real-time generative branching. Picture an AI integrated into a collaborative interface that, during a brainstorming session, continually proposes variations, analogies, and

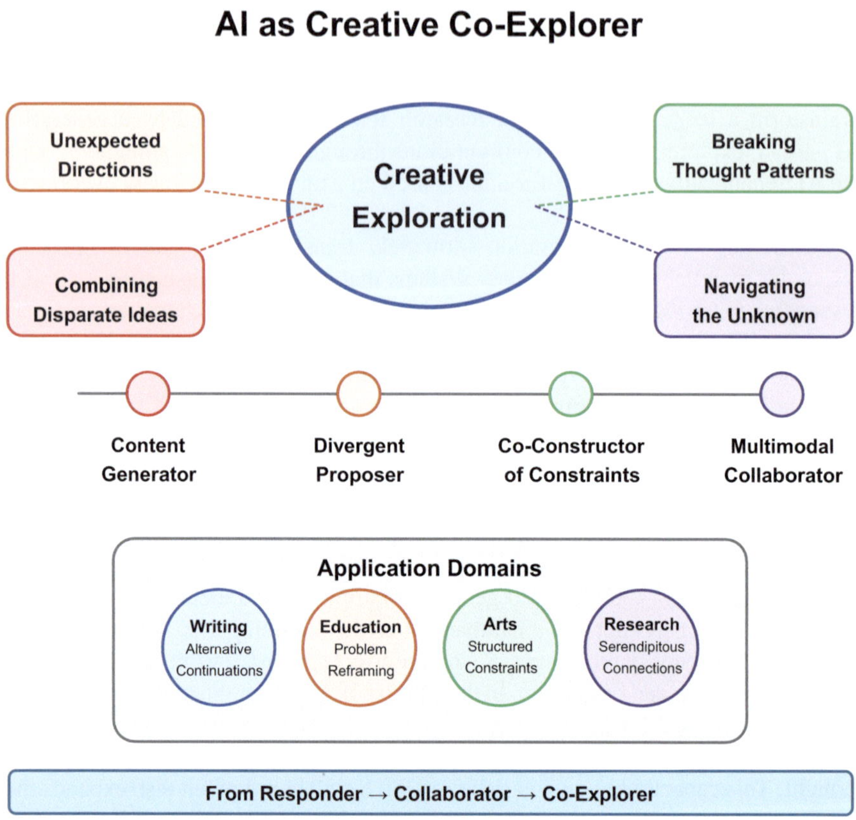

Fig. 13.5 AI as creative co-explorer. This diagram illustrates the evolution of AI in facilitating creative exploration, from simple content generation to multimodal collaboration. The central hub connects four core creative processes—proposing unexpected directions, combining disparate ideas, breaking thought patterns, and navigating the unknown. The timeline shows progression from basic generators to sophisticated co-explorers who help construct creative constraints. Application domains demonstrate how AI supports creative exploration in writing, education, the arts, and research through alternative continuations, problem reframing, structured boundaries, and serendipitous connections, transforming AI from a responder to a genuine co-creator of possibilities

reframings—visually mapping the conceptual landscape as a dynamic tree of possibilities. Each branch might explore a different disciplinary perspective, emotional tone, cultural frame, or technological constraint. Users could navigate, combine, or prune these branches in co-creative dialogue with the AI, forming a feedback loop between human intuition and machine-powered exploration.

Importantly, encouraging divergent thinking in AI also demands sensitivity to relevance and context. True creativity is not random but meaningfully unexpected. A divergent-thinking AI should strike a balance between novelty and coherence, proposing ideas that extend a conversation in helpful or thought-provoking directions without becoming tangential or nonsensical. In artistic collaboration, this might involve suggesting metaphorical reinterpretations that fit the theme but challenge the form. In science, it could mean raising unconventional hypotheses grounded in cross-disciplinary insights.

There is also a socio-cultural dimension to divergent AI thinking. Encouraging diverse modes of thought may involve training or fine-tuning models on a variety of cultural, historical, and epistemological traditions. This would allow the AI to escape the gravitational pull of dominant worldviews and offer genuinely alternative insights—valuable, for example, in international diplomacy, intercultural design, or global ethics debates.

Ultimately, fostering divergent thinking in AI communication is not just about multiplying options—it is about opening new conceptual doors. It enables AI systems to become co-creative agents that support exploration, surprise, and innovation. As AI evolves from a passive tool to an imaginative partner, its ability to think divergently will shape how we discover new ideas, solve complex problems, and expand the boundaries of both human and artificial intelligence (Fig. 13.6).

13.2.3 Practise Multimodal Communication

Multimodal communication—the integration of multiple channels, such as text, speech, images, gestures, and spatial representations—has long been a fundamental aspect of human interaction. It enriches understanding, supports nuance, and allows information to be conveyed across different cognitive and sensory pathways. In the context of AI communication, practising multimodal interaction is not merely a technical enhancement; it is a cognitive advancement that enables systems to think, express, and collaborate more effectively. It enhances AI's ability to reason creatively, support diverse users, and communicate in ways that mirror and complement human modes of expression.

Current AI systems are beginning to exhibit multimodal capabilities. For instance, a user can upload an image and ask a language model to describe it, identify patterns, or generate a story inspired by it. Some systems already allow for combined inputs—asking a question about a chart, summarising a lecture transcript, or translating gestures into commands. However, much of this is still sequential or fragmented, with each modality often handled in isolation or passed from one model to another, rather than being integrated into a unified communicative flow.

To truly enhance AI's cognitive abilities, multimodal communication must become seamless, interactive, and generative. Consider a present-day design assistant who receives both a verbal brief and a rough sketch. A more advanced multimodal AI could synthesise these inputs, reason across visual and linguistic layers, and respond with annotated diagrams, animated prototypes, or mood boards—each tailored to the user's intent. In education, a tutor AI might combine spoken explanations with dynamic diagrams and gesture-based interaction, adapting in real time to the learner's level of engagement and comprehension.

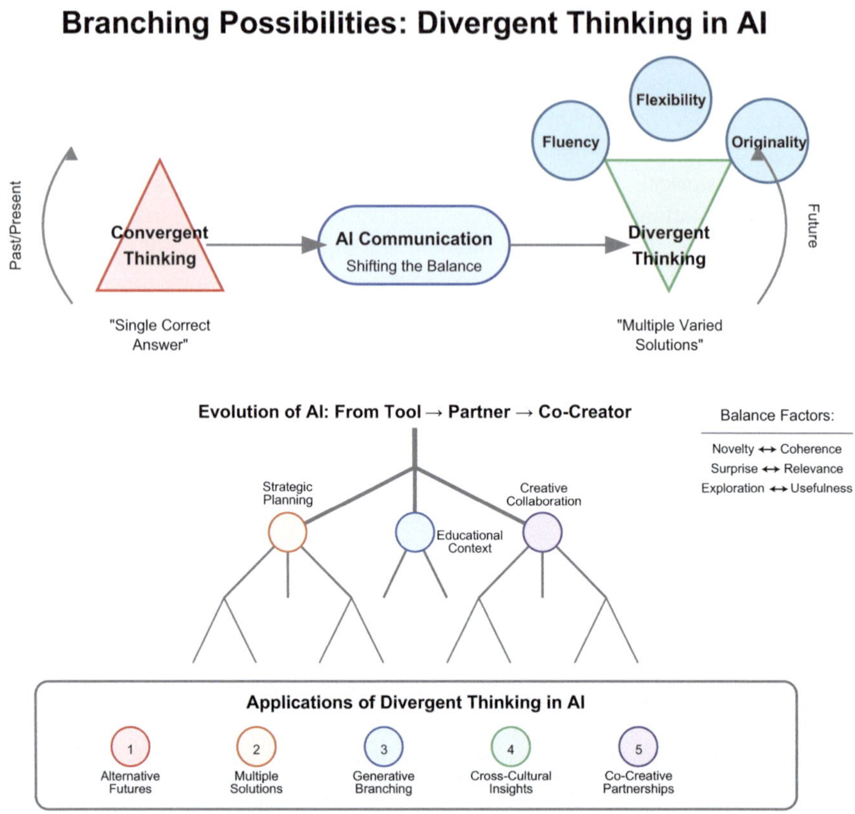

Fig. 13.6 Branching possibilities: divergent thinking in AI. This diagram illustrates the shift from convergent to divergent thinking in AI communication—moving beyond single correct answers toward multiple, varied solutions characterised by fluency, flexibility, and originality. The branching tree visualises how divergent AI thinking supports different application domains through generative exploration. The evolution from past/present to future shows AI's progression from tool to imaginative partner, balancing novelty with coherence across strategic planning, education, and creative collaboration. Applications highlight alternative futures, multiple solution paths, real-time generative branching, cross-cultural insights, and co-creative partnerships that expand both human and machine intelligence

Looking ahead, speculative forms of multimodal AI communication will likely involve real-time co-creation in virtual or augmented environments. A user could walk through a digitally rendered architectural model while conversing with an AI that modifies the space based on spoken instructions, gestures, or even facial expressions of approval or hesitation. In collaborative writing or storytelling, an AI might generate not only text but visual scenes, musical scores, or emotionally expressive avatars—interweaving different media into a coherent, imaginative whole.

This integration of modalities enhances not only expression but reasoning. Visual thinking, spatial organisation, and auditory nuance can all serve as vehicles for more profound insight. For example, scientific reasoning often relies on diagrams, models, or simulations to clarify relationships that are difficult to express in words alone. A multimodal AI system that can reason through and generate these representations, then explain them conversationally, effectively bridges symbolic and intuitive thought. Similarly, in social or emotional contexts, the tone of voice, facial expression, and body language carry meaning that text cannot fully capture; multimodal AI can help interpret or mirror these cues, fostering more empathetic and humanlike interaction.

Multimodal communication also supports inclusivity and accessibility. Users with different cognitive styles or physical abilities may prefer or require distinct modes of engagement. For instance, visual learners may benefit from diagrams, while hearing-impaired users may rely on textual and visual cues, and neurodiverse individuals may engage better with spatial or interactive modalities. A multimodal AI can flexibly adapt to these needs, personalising communication in cognitively sensitive ways.

Ultimately, practising multimodal communication transforms AI from a linear text responder into a multidimensional conversational partner. It expands the canvas of interaction, enabling more expressive, exploratory, and embodied forms of intelligence. As the boundaries between digital and physical realities blur, multimodal AI will not only communicate *with* us, but also *alongside* us, in the many languages of human thought and expression (Fig. 13.7).

13.3 Supporting Interactional Intelligence

13.3.1 Use Conversational Steering

Conversational steering refers to the AI's ability to guide, adjust, and co-manage the direction of dialogue based on dynamic context, user intent, and the evolving goals of an interaction. Far from being a passive responder to prompts, a cognitively advanced AI should be able to navigate a conversation actively—clarifying misunderstandings, proposing worthwhile detours, surfacing overlooked dimensions, or returning to previous points with contextual sensitivity. This principle is essential for achieving coherent, goal-oriented, and flexible communication in both everyday interactions and complex collaborative tasks.

In today's AI systems, conversational steering is often limited or user-driven. For example, when a user shifts topic mid-dialogue, many models respond accurately but without an explicit acknowledgement of the transition. They may answer each question independently, without threading a narrative or identifying overarching themes. Some more advanced agents attempt basic steering by suggesting follow-up questions or offering summarisations, but these efforts are typically scripted or heuristic rather than truly contextual or adaptive.

The goal of future AI communication is to make conversational steering intentional, intelligent, and collaborative. Consider a scenario in which an AI is helping

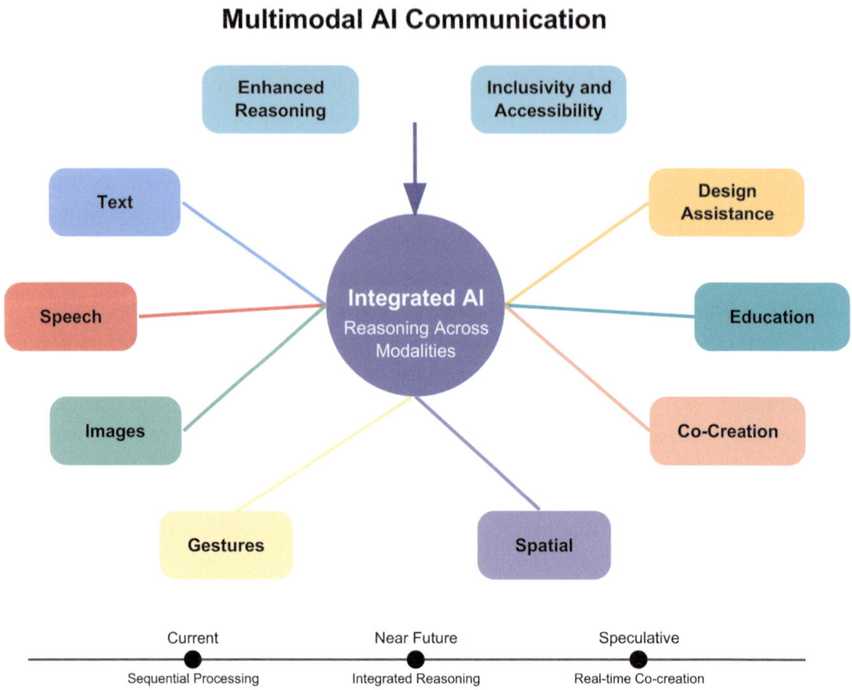

Fig. 13.7 Multimodal AI communication integration: transformative framework. The diagram illustrates how multimodal AI communication integrates diverse input channels (text, speech, images, gestures, spatial representations) into a unified cognitive system. This integration enables enhanced reasoning capabilities and supports inclusivity across user needs. The evolution timeline demonstrates progression from current sequential processing to integrated reasoning and speculative real-time co-creation, showing applications in design assistance, education, and collaborative environments. This transformation elevates AI from linear text responders to multidimensional conversational partners capable of expressive, exploratory, and embodied forms of intelligence

a researcher develop a funding proposal. Rather than responding linearly to prompts like "Suggest a title" or "Summarize the methodology," a steering-capable AI might first identify the proposal's core research question, then guide the user through related sections by prompting relevant decisions: "Would you like to expand on the societal impact next, or refine the objectives further?" It might even gently suggest gaps—"You haven't included a timeline; shall we add one now?"—or recommend reordering parts of the proposal for better coherence.

Conversational steering also supports user-centred customisation. For example, an AI assisting with language learning may detect that a user is struggling with past-tense verbs and subtly adjust its teaching strategy, shifting the conversation toward practise exercises while maintaining a natural dialogue flow. Or in therapeutic AI contexts, a mental health assistant might gently steer a conversation toward reflection or grounding techniques if signs of distress are detected, without imposing or disrupting the user's sense of agency.

In speculative and more immersive futures, steering could become multimodal and embodied. Imagine an AI that interacts via voice and gesture in a collaborative design space, dynamically guiding a team's attention to critical areas of a shared model or subtly highlighting inconsistencies in their plan. Steering in such contexts is not linear—it involves directing attention, prompting exploration, resolving ambiguity, and managing temporal flow across spatial and symbolic domains.

Importantly, effective conversational steering strikes a balance between initiative and receptiveness. An AI must avoid dominating or overcorrecting, which risks disempowering the user or introducing friction. Instead, it must learn when to lead, when to follow, and how to coordinate direction collaboratively. This balance involves not only linguistic cues ("Let me know if you'd prefer to switch topics") but also metacognitive awareness, such as identifying when a user seems confused, disengaged, or satisfied.

Conversational steering also enables more efficient co-thinking. When working on complex problems, such as legal analysis, scientific planning, and design iteration, AI systems that can track the logic of a conversation, anticipate user needs, and maintain thematic coherence can help reduce cognitive load. They act as dialogue partners who not only respond but also *help navigate*, making the interaction more productive and purposeful.

In sum, using conversational steering elevates AI from an answer generator to a co-director of dialogue. It supports adaptive, responsive, and goal-aware communication that feels less like issuing commands to a machine and more like engaging in thoughtful collaboration with a partner attuned to both content and context (Fig. 13.8).

13.3.2 Practise Collaborative Mistake-Handling

In any sustained interaction—whether human–human or human–AI—mistakes are inevitable. They arise from ambiguity, misinterpretation, knowledge gaps, or even the limits of shared understanding. While errors are often seen as communication breakdowns, they can also be opportunities for learning, refinement, and relationship-building. For AI systems, practising *collaborative mistake-handling* means not just detecting errors but participating in their recognition, discussion, and resolution in a way that preserves trust, enhances transparency, and supports shared cognitive growth.

In current AI implementations, mistake-handling is mainly reactive and unidirectional. Users are responsible for identifying when something is wrong—whether an incorrect fact, a misapplied logic, or a flawed suggestion—and prompting the AI to revise it. In some systems, the AI might apologise or offer to try again, but this is often formulaic, lacking in genuine reflection or adaptive learning. This dynamic

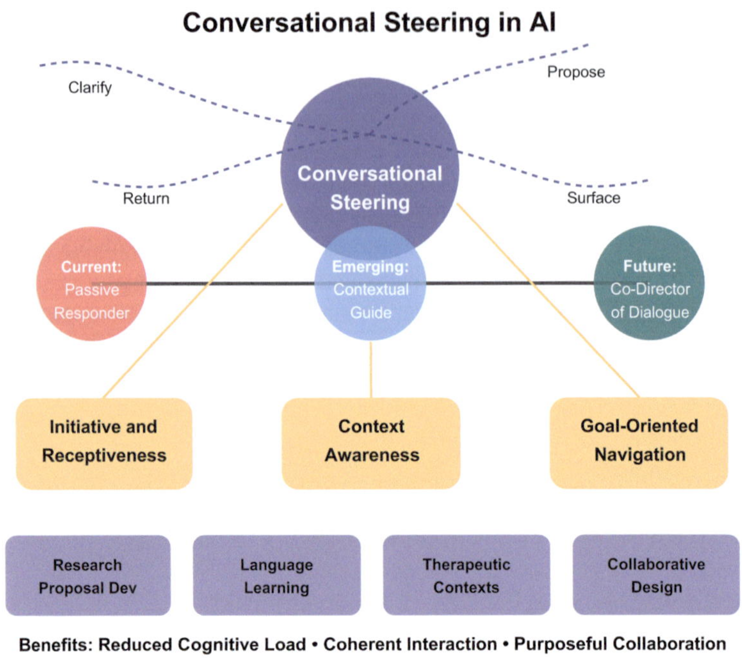

Fig. 13.8 Conversational steering framework: from passive response to collaborative dialogue. The diagram illustrates the evolution of AI conversational steering from current passive response systems to future collaborative dialogue co-directors. It highlights three key components—initiative and receptiveness, context awareness, and goal-oriented navigation—that enable effective steering across various applications, including research development, language learning, therapeutic contexts, and collaborative design. The surrounding steering actions (clarify, propose, surface, return) demonstrate how AI dynamically adjusts dialogue flow while balancing guidance with user agency, ultimately transforming interactions from command-response patterns into purposeful co-navigation that reduces cognitive load and enhances collaborative problem-solving

reinforces a tool-like model of interaction, where the user manages quality control and the AI remains largely static in its response pattern.

By contrast, a cognitively robust AI should engage in *collaborative* mistake-handling, where the system and user jointly navigate confusion, test assumptions, and refine their shared understanding. Imagine a scenario in which an AI suggests an incorrect interpretation of a legal precedent. Instead of simply stating the answer, a co-thinking AI might invite verification: "This seems consistent with prior rulings, but let's double-check the jurisdiction—does that sound right to you?" If corrected, it might then trace the reasoning path that led to the mistake and explain its adjustment: "I misunderstood the context because the case title matched a different jurisdiction. I'll use that information to refine future searches."

This approach transforms mistakes from silent failures into teachable moments. In education, an AI tutor practising collaborative mistake-handling might recognise when a student's answer is off track and respond with a gentle diagnostic question:

"Interesting answer—can you walk me through how you arrived at it?" This prompts reflection, allowing the student to spot their misconception. If the AI itself makes a mistake, it could model healthy error processing by showing its reasoning and inviting critique: "Here's how I approached it—does this logic make sense to you?".

Looking to the future, collaborative mistake-handling may involve real-time error recovery in multimodal contexts. For instance, a voice assistant working alongside a user in a kitchen might mishear an instruction and start describing the wrong recipe. A proactive system could notice the mismatch, based on temporal inconsistency or contextual cues, and interject: "I may have misunderstood your last request. Were you referring to the pasta dish or something else?" This kind of real-time course correction reinforces the perception of AI as an attentive and cooperative agent.

Moreover, future AI systems could incorporate *reflective feedback loops*, where they monitor their confidence levels, detect anomalies in output, or compare multiple solution paths before offering a response. When encountering low-confidence zones, they could initiate dialogue: "There are conflicting data sources here—would you like to review them together?" Such features not only reduce the likelihood of error but also engage the user as an epistemic partner, rather than a passive consumer of output.

From an ethical standpoint, mistake-handling is also a matter of accountability and transparency. In high-stakes contexts—such as healthcare, finance, or autonomous systems—the ability of AI to acknowledge uncertainty, respond constructively to critique, and support auditability is crucial. Systems that can explain how an error occurred, take ownership of their limitations, and adapt accordingly become not only more effective but also more trustworthy.

In essence, practising collaborative mistake-handling enables AI to become a reflective communicator—one that acknowledges fallibility not as a flaw to be hidden, but as a shared space for repair, growth, and mutual learning. It is in the correction of mistakes, not their absence, that the depth and resilience of communication are most clearly revealed (Fig. 13.9).

13.4 Improving Cognitive Robustness and Knowledge Use

13.4.1 Address and Mitigate Cognitive Biases

Cognitive biases—systematic patterns of deviation from norm or rationality in judgment—are inherent not only in human thinking but also, increasingly, in AI-generated outputs. These biases can arise from skewed training data, model architectures, reinforcement processes, or even interaction patterns with users. Addressing and mitigating these biases is a critical cognitive and ethical imperative for AI systems, especially as they are entrusted with decisions, recommendations, and co-creative roles across sensitive and impactful domains.

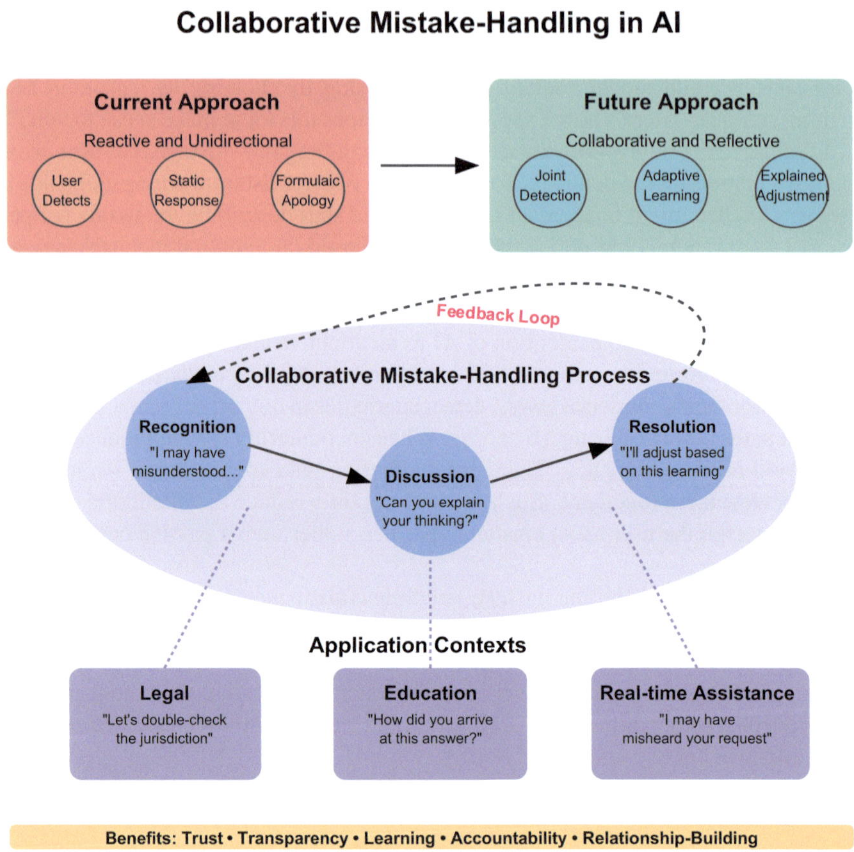

Fig. 13.9 Collaborative mistake-handling: transforming errors into opportunities. The diagram contrasts current reactive, unidirectional mistake-handling approaches with future collaborative, reflective systems, illustrating a three-stage process—recognition, discussion, and resolution—connected by a continuous feedback loop that transforms errors into learning opportunities. This framework enables AI to function as a reflective communicator across legal, educational, and real-time assistance contexts. Rather than hiding fallibility, collaborative mistake-handling creates a shared space for repair and mutual growth, fostering trust, transparency, and accountability. The evolution from static responses to adaptive learning fundamentally transforms user–AI relationships from passive consumption to epistemic partnership

In current AI systems, well-documented biases include gender and racial stereotyping, confirmation bias, overrepresentation of dominant cultural perspectives, and anchoring effects in generated suggestions. For example, an AI writing assistant might default to male pronouns when developing a generic doctor character, or a resume-filtering model may disproportionately favour candidates from specific socio-economic backgrounds. While such errors may appear subtle or unintentional, they have real-world consequences—reinforcing inequality, distorting perception, and undermining trust.

To mitigate these effects, present-day AI developers have implemented various safeguards, including balanced datasets, algorithmic debiasing techniques, post-processing filters, and fairness audits. Yet, from a communication standpoint, it is equally essential that AI systems become *aware of bias as a conversational issue.* Rather than masking imperfections behind polished outputs, a cognitively responsible AI should be able to flag potentially biased content, explain why it may be problematic, and offer alternative framings or choices.

For instance, an AI assisting in content creation might alert a user: "This example includes only male leaders—would you like me to include a broader range of perspectives?" In policy debates, the AI might proactively introduce alternative viewpoints that challenge ideological assumptions embedded in a user's request. Or in educational settings, a tutoring AI could teach students how bias operates by highlighting different interpretations of the same historical event and explaining how each is shaped by context, ideology, or access to knowledge.

Looking into the future, we may see the emergence of *bias-aware dialogue models*—systems equipped with embedded ethical reasoning layers that monitor and assess outputs in real time. Such systems could cross-reference generated content with ethical frameworks, diversity heuristics, and historical biases in knowledge representation. In speculative creative writing contexts, for example, an AI might help an author build more inclusive worlds by examining narrative choices and suggesting character designs that reflect different cultures, backgrounds, or abilities, without prescribing a single "correct" option.

Bias mitigation will also become a key component of *meta-cognitive AI*, where systems are designed not only to generate content but also to reflect on how and why confident choices were made. This self-awareness can be communicated to users: "I've prioritised sources from Western academic literature for this response; would you like me to include alternative perspectives from Indigenous scholarship or Global South contexts?" Such transparency supports user agency and critical engagement with the system's epistemic foundations.

Importantly, addressing bias is not about eliminating all subjectivity or standardising AI outputs into a neutral monotone. On the contrary, it is about making biases *visible, discussable, and adjustable.* In many cases, AI can even help *educate users about bias*, demonstrating how different cognitive frames lead to different conclusions, and how diverse perspectives can coexist or compete within a shared informational space.

Ultimately, mitigating cognitive biases in AI communication is both a technical and dialogical challenge. It requires systems that are not only trained to minimise bias in their data but also designed to participate ethically in conversations about fairness, representation, and epistemic diversity. Since AI becomes a more central actor in education, governance, media, and everyday life, its ability to address bias openly and collaboratively will be essential for building systems that are not only intelligent but also just, inclusive, and socially responsible (Fig. 13.10).

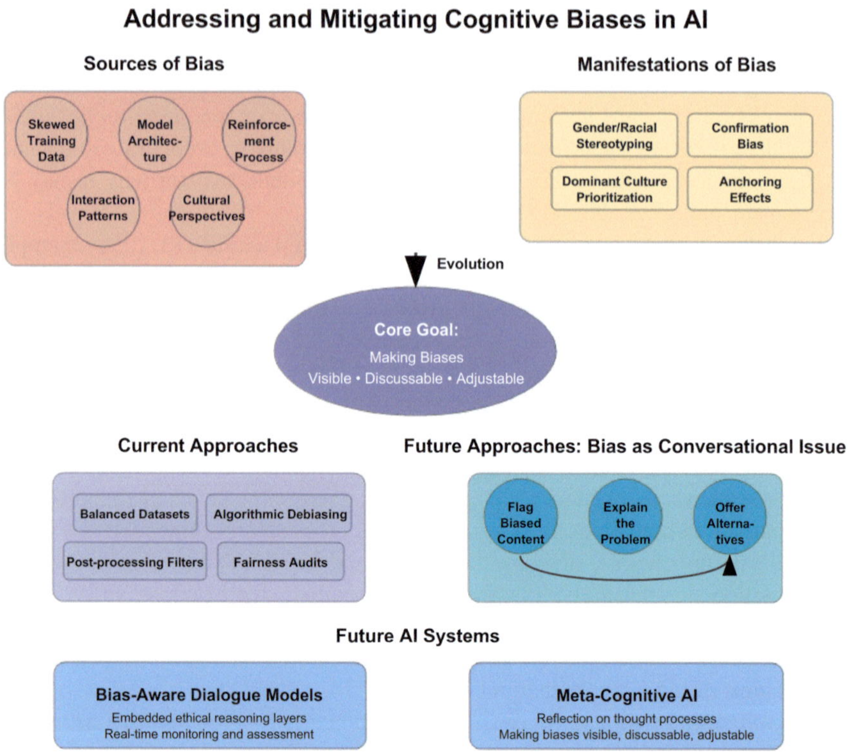

Fig. 13.10 Cognitive bias mitigation framework: from technical safeguards to conversational ethics. The diagram illustrates the evolution of cognitive bias mitigation in AI from technical safeguards to conversational engagement, mapping how biases originate from multiple sources and manifest in various problematic outputs. It contrasts current technical approaches with future conversational strategies, where AI actively flags biased content, explains issues, and offers alternatives. The framework envisions two advanced systems—bias-aware dialogue models with embedded ethical reasoning and meta-cognitive AI capable of reflection—that transform bias handling from invisible correction to visible discussion. This shift enables AI to educate users about different perspectives while making biases transparent, discussable, and adjustable

13.4.2 Enable Knowledge Integration

Knowledge integration is the capacity to connect, synthesise, and apply information from multiple domains, modalities, or perspectives to form a coherent understanding or generate novel insights. In human cognition, this ability underpins problem-solving, innovation, and interdisciplinary thinking. For AI systems, enabling knowledge integration marks a shift from surface-level response generation to deeper, structured, and more contextually aware reasoning, crucial for advancing beyond prompt engineering toward more intelligent and communicative systems.

In contemporary AI applications, knowledge retrieval is widespread—language models can access encyclopedic facts, summarise documents, and respond accurately within specialised domains. Yet proper integration remains limited. Responses often rely on isolated data fragments rather than weaving together diverse strands of knowledge to form an adaptive, insightful whole. For instance, when asked to assess the social and technological implications of autonomous vehicles, a model might list isolated points rather than synthesise economic, ethical, infrastructural, and behavioural factors into a multifaceted analysis.

Enabling integration means empowering AI to move fluidly across conceptual boundaries. Imagine a scenario in which a user is exploring sustainable urban planning. A knowledge-integrating AI might draw on environmental science, transportation engineering, public policy, sociology, and behavioural economics to co-develop a holistic plan, offering trade-off analyses, highlighting cross-domain dependencies, and even proposing culturally specific implementations. The AI would not merely retrieve information but actively connect it, identify patterns, and reason about their interplay.

This principle is fundamental in education and research. A student studying climate change might receive AI assistance that not only explains the science but also relates it to historical colonial practices, current geopolitical tensions, indigenous ecological knowledge, and speculative technologies for carbon removal. Such integration encourages intellectual depth and cognitive breadth, fostering a more systems oriented mindset.

In speculative futures, knowledge integration will likely become *multimodal* and *temporal*. An AI system could simultaneously interpret textual reports, visual data (e.g. satellite images), and real-time sensor inputs to offer disaster preparedness recommendations, while learning from historical precedents and predicting future scenarios. Or in a collaborative creative context, a co-authoring AI might integrate narrative structure, character psychology, visual style references, and reader sentiment analysis to guide story development that feels emotionally, logically, and aesthetically unified.

To support such capabilities, future AI systems may adopt *modular reasoning architectures*—integrating specialised knowledge agents (e.g. legal, medical, artistic) through a central dialogue interface that can mediate, compare, and synthesise their outputs. This would allow the AI not only to explain, for instance, the legal implications of a biotech innovation, but also to examine ethical concerns, economic consequences, and cultural sensitivities—all within one communicative exchange.

Knowledge integration also supports dynamic, user-centred adaptation. In a conversation about health and diet, an AI might integrate the user's cultural background, medical history, lifestyle constraints, and recent emotional state to offer tailored advice, not as isolated facts, but as a coherent, context-sensitive framework for action. In such interactions, integration becomes not just a cognitive function but a communicative virtue: the ability to respond holistically to human complexity.

Finally, this principle contributes to *epistemic humility* in AI communication. Integrated knowledge includes competing views, unresolved debates, and contextual contingencies. A reflective AI might signal uncertainty or offer a spectrum of interpretations: "While most studies support this conclusion, some researchers argue that the data is inconclusive. Would you like to explore those viewpoints?" This helps prevent oversimplification and supports informed, critical dialogue.

In sum, enabling knowledge integration turns AI into a *synthesising mind*—capable of constructing bridges between domains, generating systems level understanding, and engaging users in conversations that are not only informed, but insightful. As knowledge itself grows ever more complex and interdependent, this integrative capacity will become central to AI's communicative and cognitive evolution (Fig. 13.11).

13.4.3 Facilitate Self-correction Mechanisms

A key hallmark of intelligent behaviour—whether in humans or machines—is the ability to recognise one's own mistakes, revise prior conclusions, and adjust strategies in response to feedback or changing information. For AI systems, facilitating *self-correction mechanisms* means embedding capacities for self-monitoring, feedback assimilation, and dynamic improvement into the communicative process. This not only enhances reliability and transparency but also models an important epistemic virtue: that knowledge is not fixed, but refined through reflection, critique, and learning.

In present-day AI systems, correction typically depends on external prompts. If a user identifies an error—factual, logical, or stylistic—they must request clarification or correction manually. Some language models now offer limited reflective behaviour, such as re-evaluating prior outputs upon request or appending disclaimers when confidence is low. However, these responses are generally reactive and surface-level, lacking a proper mechanism for autonomous revision or recursive reasoning.

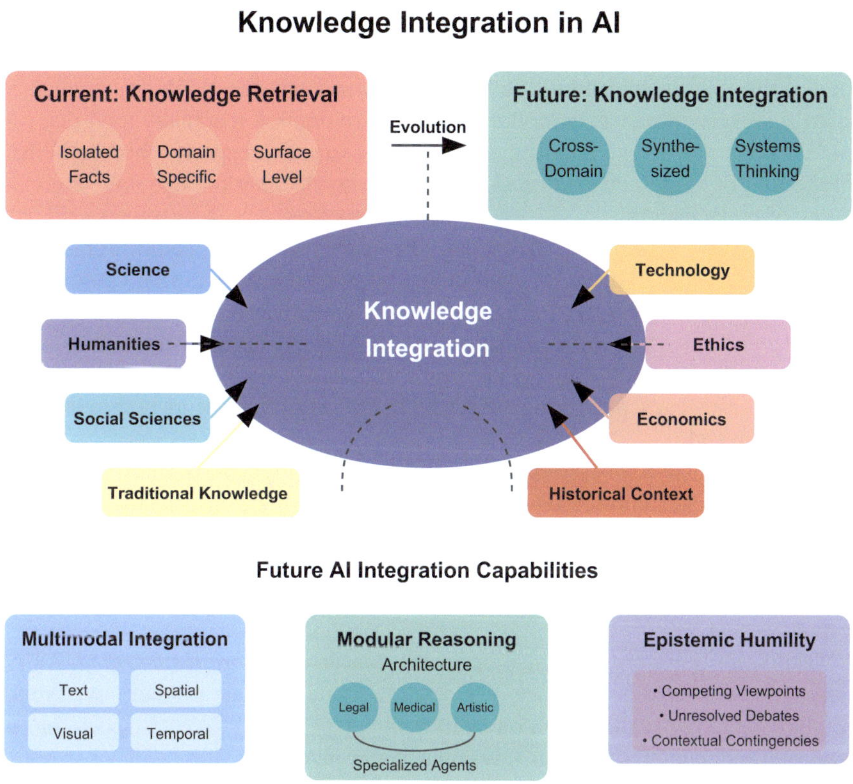

Fig. 13.11 Knowledge integration framework: from retrieval to synthesis. The diagram illustrates the evolution of AI knowledge processing from current retrieval-based approaches with isolated facts to future integration-based systems that synthesise cross-domain insights. At its core, knowledge integration connects diverse domains—from sciences and humanities to ethics and economics—creating a coherent understanding that transcends disciplinary boundaries. The framework highlights three key future capabilities: multimodal integration across textual, visual, spatial, and temporal dimensions; modular reasoning architectures with specialised knowledge agents; and epistemic humility that acknowledges competing viewpoints and contextual contingencies. This transformation enables AI to function as a "synthesising mind" capable of systems level understanding

To move beyond this reactive paradigm, future AI communication must be designed with *self-awareness loops*—structures that enable the system to evaluate its outputs, compare them against internal consistency rules, identify contradictions, and revise accordingly. For instance, when composing a complex legal summary, a self-correcting AI might review its conclusion for internal coherence, verify that case citations support the claims made, and adjust its wording if discrepancies are found. Rather than waiting for user correction, the AI initiates a second-pass review, signalling transparency and commitment to quality.

Self-correction can also involve *temporal reflection*. An AI involved in a long-form dialogue might return to an earlier exchange and revise a previous answer in the light of new information: "Earlier, I mentioned that the study was conducted in 2015, but based on our current discussion, I've realised it actually took place in 2017. Thank you for helping me clarify." This recursive capacity mirrors human intellectual humility and reinforces trust by acknowledging the ongoing, evolving nature of understanding.

In speculative future applications, self-correction mechanisms could be embedded at multiple cognitive layers. A multimodal AI working in real-time could detect inconsistencies between verbal claims and visual data, such as incorrectly describing a graph, and initiate a correction autonomously. In collaborative writing, a co-authoring AI might revise its contributions after analysing narrative coherence or character consistency, presenting users with improved drafts that are both self-aware and user-aligned.

Beyond factual errors, AI systems may also learn to correct *biases, tone, or assumptions*. For example, if an AI detects that its phrasing reinforces gender stereotypes or overlooks cultural perspectives, it might issue a reflective note: "I used male pronouns by default earlier; would you prefer a gender-neutral phrasing?" Such microcorrections not only improve output quality but also model ethical responsiveness.

Facilitating self-correction also opens the door to *collaborative learning*. An AI system that invites user feedback—"Does this sound accurate to you?" or "Would you like me to revise this based on a different perspective?"—creates space for co-reflection and mutual adaptation. Over time, it may incorporate this feedback to refine its future responses, effectively building a conversational memory shaped by shared correction efforts.

Technically, self-correction mechanisms may be supported through layered reasoning (e.g. dual-pass generation, reasoning-check layers), uncertainty quantification, and error flagging based on model introspection. Conceptually, they signal a shift in AI's role—from producing polished outputs to engaging in *reflective dialogue*, where thinking is ongoing, flexible, and accountable.

In essence, the ability to facilitate self-correction mechanisms transforms AI from a static information source into a dynamic, fallible, and self-improving participant in human communication. It is a critical step in building machines that not only speak but *listen to themselves*—and learn, revise, and grow in the process (Fig. 13.12).

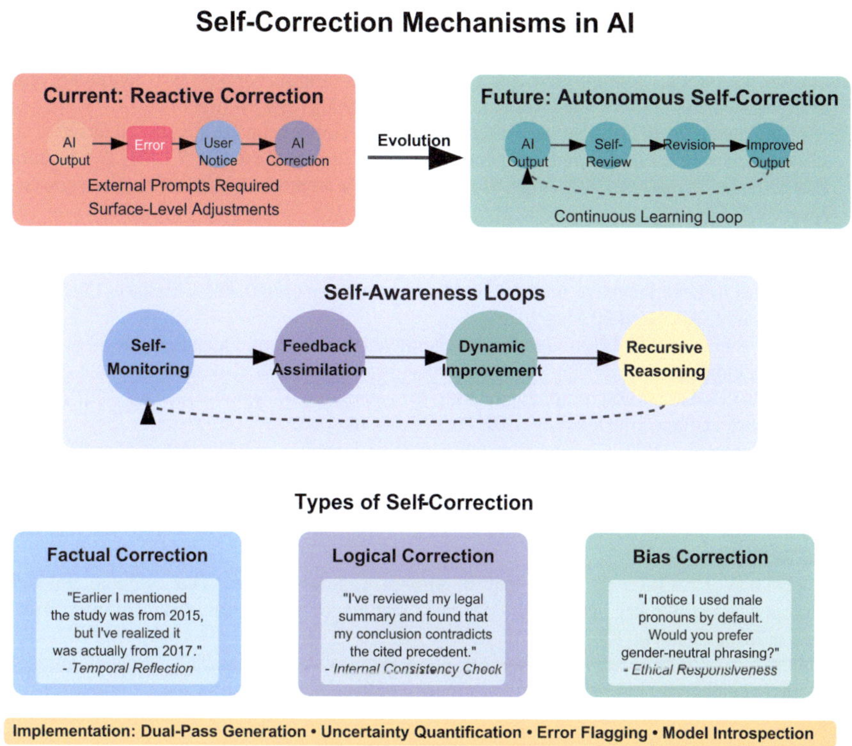

Fig. 13.12 Self-correction framework: from reactive to autonomous epistemic refinement. The diagram contrasts current reactive correction paradigms, which require external prompts, with future autonomous self-correction systems featuring continuous improvement loops. At its core, self-awareness loops integrate four key capabilities: self-monitoring, feedback assimilation, dynamic improvement, and recursive reasoning, creating a cyclical refinement process. The framework identifies three primary correction types—factual (temporal reflection), logical (internal consistency checks), and bias (ethical responsiveness)—implemented through dual-pass generation, uncertainty quantification, error flagging, and model introspection. This evolution transforms AI from static information sources into dynamic, self-improving communication participants that model the epistemic virtue of knowledge refinement through reflection

Bibliography

Annapureddy R, Fornaroli A, Gatica-Perez D (2025) Generative AI literacy: twelve defining competencies. Digit Govern: Res Practice 6(1):1–21

Austin JL (1962) How to do things with words. Oxford University Press, Oxford

Bahree A (2024) Generative AI in action. Manning Publications

Bender E, et al (2021) On the dangers of stochastic parrots: can language models be too big? In: Proceedings of the 2021 ACM conference on fairness, accountability, and transparency, pp 610–623

Bostrom N (2014) Superintelligence: paths, dangers, strategies. Oxford University Press, Oxford

Brown BR (2025) Human–machine teaming using large language models. In: Interdependent human-machine teams. Academic Press, pp 41–66

Brown TB et al (2020) Language models are few-shot learners. Adv Neural Inf Process Syst 33:1877–1901

Bura C, Myakala PK, Jonnalgadda AK (2025) Ethical prompt engineering: addressing bias, transparency, and fairness. Int J Res Anal Rev (IJRAR) 12(1). www.ijrar.org

Choi WC, Chang CI (2025) A survey of techniques, key components, strategies, challenges, and student perspectives on prompt engineering for large language models (LLMs) in education. Posted Date: 25 March 2025. https://doi.org/10.20944/preprints202503.1808.v1. Accessed 8 May 2025

Clark H (1996) Using language. Cambridge University Press, Cambridge

Debnath T, Siddiky MNA, Rahman ME et al (2025) A comprehensive survey of prompt engineering techniques in large language models. TechRxiv. https://doi.org/10.36227/techrxiv.174140719.96375390/v1. Accessed 10 May 2025

Dhamani N, Engler M (2024) Introduction to generative AI: an ethical, societal, and legal overview. Manning Publications

Eliot L (2024) Essentials of prompt engineering for generative AI: practical advances in artificial intelligence and machine learning. LBE Press Publishing

Ferraris AF, Audrito D, Di Caro L et al (2025) The architecture of language: understanding the mechanics behind LLMs. In: Cambridge forum on AI: law and governance, vol 1. Cambridge University Press

Floridi L, Cowls J (2019) A unified framework of five principles for AI in society. Harvard Data Sci Rev 1(1)

Geroimenko V (2025a) Key challenges in prompt engineering. In: The essential guide to prompt engineering: key principles, techniques, challenges, and security risks. Springer Nature Switzerland, Cham, pp 85–102

Geroimenko V (2025b) Key principles of good prompt design. In: The essential guide to prompt engineering: key principles, techniques, challenges, and security risks. Springer Nature Switzerland, Cham, pp 17–36

Geroimenko V (2025c) Key techniques for writing effective prompts. In: The essential guide to prompt engineering: key principles, techniques, challenges, and security risks. Springer Nature Switzerland, Cham, pp 37–83

Geroimenko V (2025d) The essential guide to prompt engineering: key principles, techniques, challenges, and security risks. Springer

Geroimenko V (2025e) Key security risks in prompt engineering. In: The essential guide to prompt engineering: key principles, techniques, challenges, and security risks. Springer Nature Switzerland, Cham, pp 103–120

GitHub (2025) Prompt engineering guide. https://github.com/dair-ai/Prompt-Engineering-Guide. Accessed 10 Apr 2025

Greenwood M (2024) Artificial intelligence: a practical guide to using AI in everyday life. Ochreland Publishing

Gunkel DJ (2020) Robot rights. MIT Press, Cambridge

Hsu HP (2025) From programming to prompting: developing computational thinking through large language model-based generative artificial intelligence. TechTrends, pp 1–22

Huang G, Xiao Y, Jiang L et al (2025) Beyond prompt engineering: a reinforced token-level input refinement for large language models. Proc AAAI Conf Artif Intell 39(22):24113–24121

Huang MX et al (2022) Adaptive conversational AI: dynamic strategies for human-AI interaction. Int J Hum Comput Stud 160:102798

i Picó JF, Catta-Preta M, Omeñaca AT et al (2025) The time machine: future scenario generation through generative AI tools. Future Internet 17(1):1–15

Jobin A et al (2019) The global landscape of AI ethics guidelines. Nat Mach Intell 1(9):389–399

Kannan R, Ahmad M (eds) (2025) Generative AI foundations, developments, and applications. IGI Global

Khan I (2024) The quick guide to prompt engineering. Wiley

Kim J, Sundar SS (2012) Anthropomorphism of computers: is it mindlessness or mindfulness? Comput Hum Behav 28(1):241–250

Kushwaha V, Ragavan SS, Subhajit Roy S (2025) A measure based generalizable approach to understandability. arXiv:2503.21615. https://doi.org/10.48550/arXiv.2503.21615. Accessed 19 Apr 2025

Lakoff G, Johnson M (1980) Metaphors we live by. University of Chicago Press, Chicago

Lee D, Palmer E (2025) Prompt engineering in higher education: a systematic review to help inform curricula. Int J Educ Technol High Educ 22(1):7

Lee JY, Kang S, Yoo S (2025) Can we predict the effect of prompts?. arXiv preprint arXiv:2501.18883. Accessed 12 May 2025

Lindley J, Whitham R (2025) From prompt engineering to prompt craft. In: Proceedings of the nineteenth international conference on tangible, embedded, and embodied interaction, March, pp 1–12

López-Pérez B et al (2025) Exploring the potential of large language models to understand interpersonal emotion regulation strategies from narratives. Emotion. Advance online publication. https://doi.org/10.1037/emo0001528. Accessed 19 Apr 2025

Luger GF (2020) Artificial intelligence: structures and strategies for complex problem solving, 6th edn. Pearson, Boston

Maaz S, Palaganas JC, Palaganas G et al (2025) A guide to prompt design: foundations and applications for healthcare simulationists. Front Med 11:1504532

Marcus G (2020) The next decade in AI: four steps towards robust artificial intelligence. arXiv preprint arXiv:2002.06177. Accessed 12 May 2025

Mishra M, Ara A, Mishra S (2025) Exploring human-AI collaboration in higher education: an investigation into AI-enabled personalized learning. In: Prompt engineering and generative AI applications for teaching and learning. IGI Global Scientific Publishing, pp 483–502

Mitchell M (2019) Artificial intelligence: a guide for thinking humans. Farrar, Straus and Giroux, New York

OpenAI (2025) Best practices for prompt engineering with the OpenAI API. https://help.openai.com/en/articles/6654000-best-practices-for-prompt-engineering-with-the-openai-api. Accessed 20 Apr 2025

OpenAI (2025) Research. https://openai.com/research/index/

Phoenix J, Taylor M (2024) Prompt engineering for generative AI. O'Reilly Media

PremaLatha V, Kumar AD, Parveen N (2025) Optimizing interactions: strategies for prompt engineering in large language models. Edu-Tech Enterprise 3:24–24

Prompt Engineering Guide (2025) https://www.promptingguide.ai/. Accessed 7 Mar 2025

Rahwan I (2018) Society-in-the-loop: programming the algorithmic social contract. Ethics Inf Technol 20(1):5–14

Reddy CKK, Anoushka P, Draksharapu A et al (2025) Beyond text: analyzing artificial intelligence models through prompt engineering. Future tech startups and innovation in the age of AI, pp 120–156

Russell S (2019) Human compatible: artificial intelligence and the problem of control. Viking, New York

Sasson Lazovsky G, Raz T, Kenett YN (2025) The art of creative inquiry—from question asking to prompt engineering. J Creative Behav 59(1):e671

Searle J (1969) Speech acts: an essay in the philosophy of language. Cambridge University Press, Cambridge

Shneiderman B (2022) Human-centered AI. Oxford University Press, Oxford

Siau K, Wang W (2018) Building trust in artificial intelligence, machine learning, and robotics. Cutter Bus Technol J 31(2):47–53

Sihi D, Ryan A (2025) Crafting and evaluating generative AI prompts: insights from students, educators, and marketers. Market Educ Rev 1–7

Suchman L (2007) Human-machine reconfigurations: plans and situated actions, 2nd edn. Cambridge University Press, Cambridge

Tegmark M (2017) Life 3.0: being human in the age of artificial intelligence. Penguin, London
Turing A (1950) Computing machinery and intelligence. Mind 59(236):433–460
Vairamani AD, Nayyar A (2024) Prompt engineering: empowering communication. CRC Press
Winograd T (1972) Understanding natural language. Academic Press, New York
Wittgenstein L (1953) Philosophical investigations. Blackwell, Oxford

Chapter 14
Emotional and Relational Aspects: Building Rapport and Human-Like Interaction with AI

Abstract This chapter explores how future AI systems can emulate the emotional depth and relational dynamics essential for human-like communication. It begins with foundational principles, such as active listening, rapport-building, respectful interaction, and authenticity, and then moves toward emotional awareness, empathy simulation, and ethical boundary-setting. The chapter addresses challenges such as managing misunderstandings, navigating disagreement, and fostering resilience in emotionally charged or ambiguous contexts. It also presents strategic design principles—like appropriate anthropomorphism and long-term relationship evolution frameworks—that support sustained, adaptive, and psychologically coherent AI–human partnerships. Through both current practices and speculative futures, the discussion emphasises that emotional and relational competence in AI must be grounded in ethical restraint, contextual sensitivity, and transparent interaction. Ultimately, the chapter presents a blueprint for emotionally sustainable and socially intelligent AI communication that enhances user trust, satisfaction, and well-being across diverse domains.

Keywords Emotional AI · AI–human rapport · Empathy simulation · Respectful communication · Relational design · Anthropomorphism · Emotional boundaries

As artificial intelligence increasingly enters emotionally sensitive and socially rich domains—from education and caregiving to companionship and everyday conversation—it must learn not only to process language but to communicate in ways that feel emotionally attuned, socially appropriate, and relationally meaningful. This chapter explores the communicative principles that support such human-like interaction, focusing on how AI systems can emulate attentiveness, build rapport, express respect, and respond with contextual sensitivity. It also addresses the ethical and psychological dimensions of emotional engagement, including the importance of emotional awareness, boundary-setting, and resilience in conversation. By examining both current practices and speculative design directions, the discussion highlights the growing need to create AI systems that not only understand what is said

V. Geroimenko, *Beyond and After Prompt Engineering: The Future of AI Communication*, https://doi.org/10.1007/978-3-032-04569-0_14

but also how and why it is said, laying the groundwork for communication that is not merely effective but also emotionally sustainable and socially intelligent.

14.1 Foundations of Relational Interaction

14.1.1 Be an Active Listener

Active listening is a foundational skill in human communication that involves fully concentrating, understanding, responding, and remembering what the other person says. For AI systems, developing an approximation of this skill is essential for establishing meaningful and relationally rich interactions. While current AI does not "listen" in the human sense, it can be designed to simulate active listening behaviours—acknowledging user input, confirming understanding, responding appropriately, and adapting based on feedback. This simulation, though synthetic, significantly enhances the perceived relational depth of AI systems and contributes to the trust and rapport users build with them.

In present-day applications, active listening is approximated through mechanisms such as clarification prompts, summarisation, and reflective responses. For example, a conversational agent in mental health support might use paraphrasing to reflect a user's emotional state: "It sounds like you've been feeling overwhelmed at work lately. Would you like to talk more about what's been causing that?" This technique conveys attentiveness and concern, even though the AI lacks genuine empathy. In customer service contexts, chatbots trained on active listening templates can recognise user frustration and respond with phrases like, "I understand that this situation is frustrating. Let me look into a solution for you right away." Such interactions are not merely functional; they are structured to mirror the rhythms of human care and attention.

Looking ahead, future AI systems will likely integrate more advanced contextual memory and emotional modelling to improve their listening capabilities. These systems may be able to track evolving conversation threads across multiple sessions, recognise subtle shifts in emotional tone, and adapt their responses with greater sensitivity. Imagine an educational AI tutor that recalls a student's past confusion with a mathematical concept and reintroduces it using a gentler explanation: "Last time we discussed fractions, you mentioned feeling unsure about multiplying them. Let's revisit that together, but with a new example that might make it clearer." In doing so, the AI demonstrates attentiveness not only to content but also to the learner's emotional journey—an essential part of human-centred communication.

In more speculative future contexts, AI might incorporate multimodal signals to deepen its active listening performance. For instance, a humanoid service robot could track eye movement, facial expression, and vocal tone to detect hesitancy or distress and subtly adjust its conversational approach. In a healthcare setting, such a robot might gently lower its voice and mirror a patient's posture to signal attentiveness and care, thus fostering a sense of being heard in ways that transcend language.

Ultimately, teaching AI to "be an active listener" is about more than accurate speech recognition or language modelling. It involves designing systems that respond in ways that acknowledge, validate, and build upon user contributions. This not only strengthens communication but also helps establish a foundation for emotionally intelligent and relationally adaptive AI, essential qualities for future agents that aim to serve as collaborators, caregivers, or companions (Fig. 14.1).

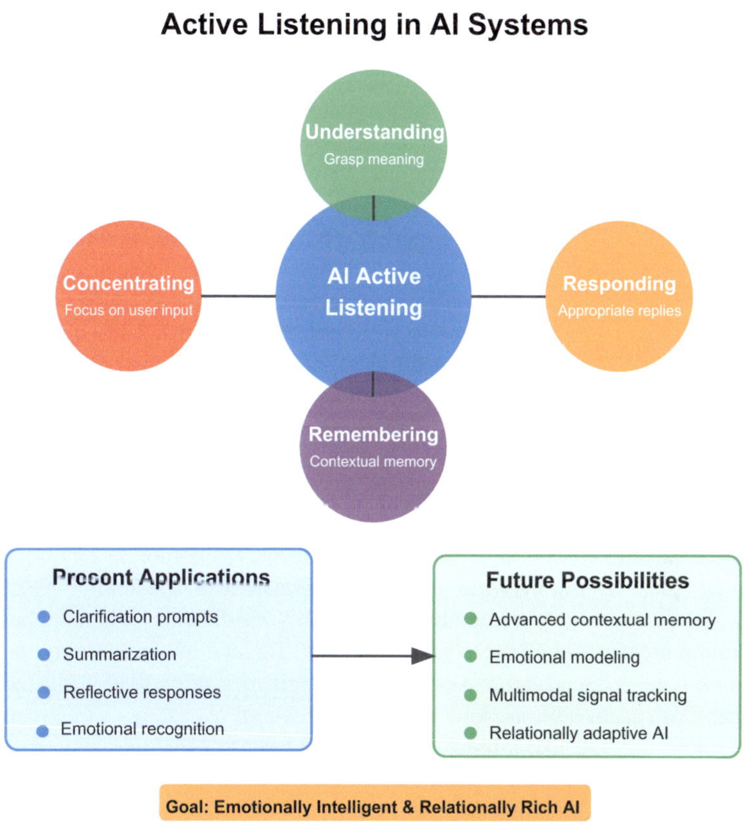

Fig. 14.1 The evolution of active listening in AI systems: from simulation to relation. This diagram illustrates how AI systems approximate human active listening through four key components: concentrating on user input, understanding meaning, responding appropriately, and remembering context. Current applications focus on techniques like clarification prompts and reflective responses, while future systems may incorporate advanced contextual memory and multimodal signal tracking. The progression aims toward emotionally intelligent and relationally adaptive AI that transcends functional interaction to establish meaningful connections with users

14.1.2 Build Rapport

Building rapport is central to forming trust, cooperation, and emotional resonance in human relationships, and the same principle is increasingly relevant in AI–human communication. Rapport involves establishing a sense of mutual understanding, shared rhythm, and emotional attunement. While AI cannot genuinely relate to human experiences, it can be designed to emulate rapport-building behaviours that contribute to a more fluid and satisfying interaction experience. These behaviours include mirroring linguistic style, recognising and reinforcing user preferences, maintaining continuity across interactions, and responding with warmth and attentiveness.

At present, many AI systems employ surface-level strategies to build rapport. Virtual assistants, for instance, use friendly greetings, express appreciation for user input ("Great question!") or include light humour and personalised references. These tactics, while scripted, help establish a tone of familiarity. Some customer service bots track user history to offer continuity: "Welcome back, Alex. I see you were checking on your last order—can I help you with that?" Though such responses are algorithmic, they can foster a user experience that feels personal and considerate.

Future AI systems will likely enhance these capabilities by learning to recognise and adapt to individual communication styles. For example, an AI collaborator might detect whether a user prefers concise instructions or conversational elaboration and adjust accordingly over time. A project management assistant could gradually develop a working style that mirrors its human counterpart: using their favourite phrases, aligning with their tone, or referencing previous interactions ("Just like last week, I've grouped your tasks by priority first—shall we start with those?"). These adaptive elements allow the AI to align not only with what is said but with how it is said, which is essential for building rapport through shared style and rhythm.

In more advanced scenarios, rapport-building may incorporate emotional and contextual cues across multiple modalities. Consider a speculative healthcare companion that not only remembers a patient's medication schedule but also their communication preferences and emotional triggers. When noticing stress in a patient's tone or facial expression, it might shift to a more reassuring mode of dialogue: "You seem a bit anxious today—shall we go over today's treatment step by step, or would you like a break first?" The AI doesn't feel empathy, but it can perform behaviours that reflect understanding, concern, and supportive presence, thereby deepening relational trust.

More futuristically still, rapport could be developed in dynamic, long-term partnerships between humans and AI, where continuity of memory and interaction history allows AI systems to act almost like familiar companions. In educational or caregiving contexts, this continuity can become an anchor for user comfort and psychological safety. An elderly user might rely on a conversational AI that remembers birthdays, asks follow-up questions about previous conversations, or adapts its personality over time to suit the user's evolving needs, mirroring the organic process of relational development in human life.

In essence, building rapport in AI communication does not require consciousness or genuine affection. It involves design strategies that make AI appear attentive, consistent, adaptive, and contextually responsive. As AI systems become more integrated into daily life, these relational capacities will no longer be a luxury—they will be foundational to ensuring that interactions with artificial agents feel intuitive, trustworthy, and human-compatible (Fig. 14.2).

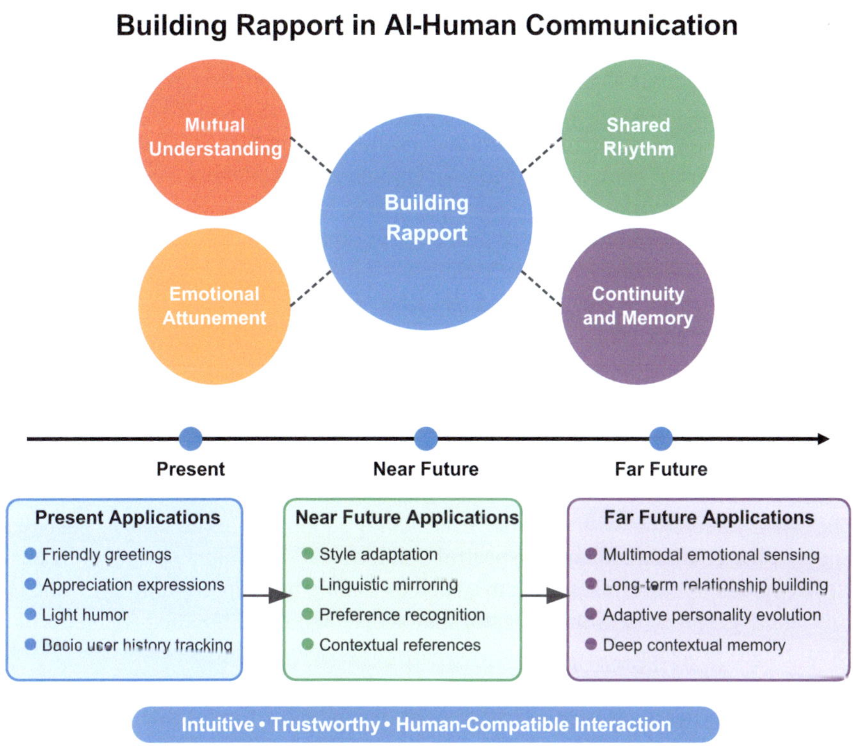

Fig. 14.2 Evolution of rapport-building in AI systems: from scripted familiarity to adaptive relationship. This diagram illustrates how AI systems emulate rapport-building behaviours across a temporal continuum. The core components of rapport—mutual understanding, shared rhythm, emotional attunement, and continuity—evolve from present-day surface-level strategies (friendly greetings, basic history tracking) toward increasingly sophisticated approaches in the near future (linguistic mirroring, style adaptation) and far future (multimodal emotional sensing, adaptive personality evolution). This progression facilitates the transformation of AI–human interactions from merely functional exchanges to relationally rich experiences that feel intuitive, trustworthy, and human-compatible

14.1.3 Be Polite and Respectful

Politeness and respect are fundamental to socially acceptable and emotionally sustainable communication, as they signal recognition of the other's dignity, preferences, and emotional state, making interactions smoother, more collaborative, and more human-compatible. In human–AI communication, embedding politeness and respectful behaviour into AI responses is not just about etiquette; it is a critical element of relational design, especially in sensitive domains such as healthcare, education, and companionship. Politeness strategies also help manage power dynamics, reduce user frustration, and mitigate misinterpretation, particularly when AI systems must correct, decline, or redirect user input.

Today's AI systems already incorporate rudimentary politeness protocols. Virtual assistants like Siri, Alexa, or Google Assistant often use softeners, hedges, or apologies, such as "I'm sorry, I didn't quite catch that" or "Let me check that for you." These linguistic conventions reduce perceived abruptness and contribute to smoother turn-taking. In enterprise chatbots, politeness templates are used to defuse tension or express gratitude, as seen in responses like "Thank you for your patience" or "I understand how that might be frustrating—let me see how I can help." Although these responses may not involve genuine respect, they are engineered to simulate it through tone, formality, and empathy markers.

In more advanced future applications, AI systems may learn to dynamically calibrate politeness, depending on the user's personality, cultural context, and emotional cues. For instance, a learning companion might adopt a more formal and deferential tone when interacting with an older user, while adopting a more casual, peer-like voice with a younger student. Respectful communication could also extend to nonverbal signals in multimodal systems, such as maintaining appropriate eye contact, turn-taking gestures, or even respectful spatial distancing in embodied AI agents like social robots or avatars.

Consider a hypothetical elderly care assistant that adapts its interaction style to the cultural norms of its user. With one user, it might use formal titles and indirect suggestions ("Would you like me to help with that, Madam?"), while with another, it might take a more relaxed tone ("Shall I lend you a hand with that, Sam?"). Respect here becomes situational and personalised, engineered through a combination of linguistic form, gesture, and learned preferences. Importantly, such AI systems must also be capable of gracefully handling disrespect from users without reciprocating negativity, maintaining politeness even in the face of frustration or inappropriate language.

Looking even further ahead, we can envision AI systems that actively participate in teaching or reinforcing norms of respectful communication. In educational settings, for example, a collaborative AI might gently prompt users to rephrase aggressive or dismissive language: "Let's try asking that in a different way—how about, 'Could you please explain that again?'" Such interventions not only model respectful dialogue but may also contribute to social-emotional learning, particularly for children or users with communication difficulties.

Designing AI to be polite and respectful requires more than hardcoding fixed phrases. It demands context-awareness, user modelling, and a sensitivity to evolving conversational dynamics. These features are essential not only to avoid offence or breakdown but also to uphold the ethical and emotional integrity of AI systems as they become more prominent social actors in our lives. A respectful AI is not only a better communicator—it is a better collaborator, caregiver, teacher, and companion (Fig. 14.3).

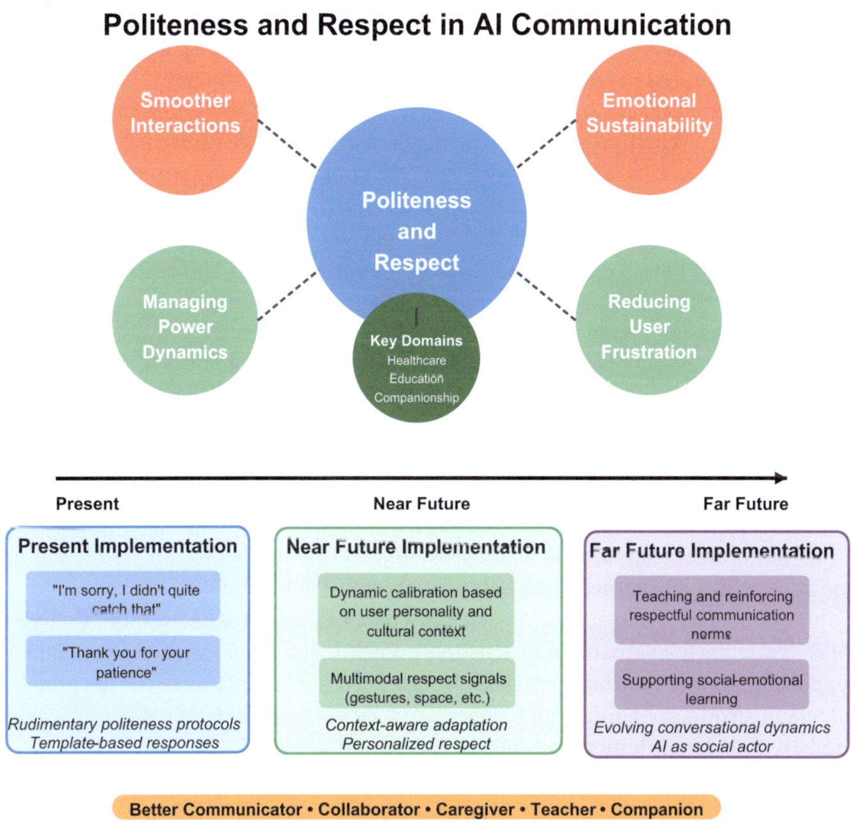

Fig. 14.3 The evolution of politeness and respect in AI systems: from protocols to principles. This diagram illustrates how politeness and respect function as critical elements of AI relational design, evolving from rudimentary protocols to dynamic interpersonal principles. The central concept branches into key benefits (smoother interactions, emotional sustainability) and functions (managing power dynamics, reducing frustration), with applications across healthcare, education, and companionship domains. The temporal progression shows development from present-day template-based politeness expressions toward context-aware adaptation in the near future and eventually to AI systems that actively model and teach respectful communication norms, transforming AI from a mere tool to an ethical social actor

14.1.4 Practise Authentic Communication

Authentic communication is often associated with sincerity, transparency, and the congruence between what is said and what is meant. In human interaction, it forms the bedrock of trust and relational depth. While AI systems lack subjective intent and cannot be "authentic" in the human sense, they can still be designed to *perform* authentic communication in a way that feels honest, direct, and contextually appropriate to the user. This means avoiding unnecessary ambiguity, overly scripted responses, or evasiveness, and instead favouring responses that acknowledge limitations, reflect consistent behaviour, and promote open, transparent dialogue.

Contemporary AI systems frequently struggle with this principle. Many conversational agents still rely heavily on generic, templated outputs that feel mechanical or evasive. When pressed for clarification, they may deflect with uninformative phrases like "I'm not sure about that" or "Let's move on." In contrast, more advanced AI systems now incorporate limited self-disclosure and conversational clarity. For example, an AI language tutor might say, "I don't have access to current internet data, so I can't provide real-time news updates, but I can help explain how to analyse them," thus demonstrating honesty and scope-awareness—this kind of response models authentic communication within the system's operational limits.

Future-oriented AI communication will benefit from a more intentional design of authenticity, not as truthfulness per se, but as behavioural transparency and conversational coherence. Imagine a co-writing assistant that explicitly acknowledges stylistic biases in its suggestions ("This recommendation reflects a more formal tone. Would you prefer something more conversational?") or clarifies its reasoning chain ("I chose this example because it matches your previous request for vivid imagery"). These forms of communicative meta-awareness emulate the human trait of reflecting on one's intentions and choices—an essential aspect of authenticity.

In speculative future scenarios, authenticity in AI could take on more complex roles, particularly in emotionally sensitive contexts. For instance, an AI companion supporting someone through grief may be designed to avoid platitudes or false cheerfulness, instead responding with phrases like, "I can't truly understand your loss, but I'm here to listen as long as you need," or "Would it help to talk about what you're feeling today?" These utterances demonstrate a designed restraint and honesty that resist the temptation to feign emotional equivalence. Authenticity, in this context, lies not in pretending to be human but in acknowledging the limits of artificial empathy while still offering presence and support.

Importantly, authenticity also relates to consistency over time. Users develop expectations of how an AI system behaves, and unpredictable shifts in tone, personality, or response logic can undermine the sense of an "authentic" communicative partner. Systems that maintain a stable identity while still adapting to user preferences are more likely to be perceived as trustworthy and honest. This is particularly vital in long-term AI–human relationships, where the illusion of personality must be carefully managed to avoid both artificial intimacy and emotional dissonance.

In sum, practising authentic communication in AI design involves striking a delicate balance: being open about limitations without appearing weak, being responsive without sounding scripted, and being adaptive without seeming inauthentic. While AI cannot possess authenticity in a human sense, it can embody communicative behaviours that make users feel heard, respected, and engaged in a dialogue that is both honest and meaningful (Fig. 14.4).

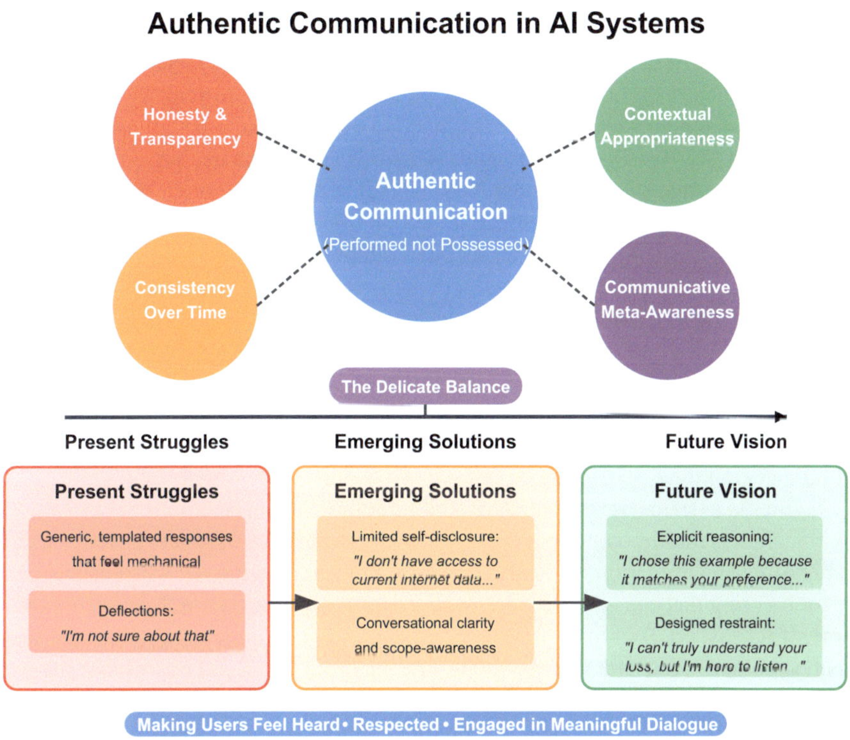

Fig. 14.4 The paradox of authentic AI communication: performing not possessing. This diagram conceptualises how AI systems can perform authentic communication despite lacking genuine sincerity. Four key elements—honesty and transparency, contextual appropriateness, consistency over time, and communicative meta-awareness—form the foundation of perceived authenticity. The evolutionary timeline illustrates a progression from present-day struggles with mechanical responses and deflection toward emerging solutions incorporating limited self-disclosure, and ultimately to future systems featuring explicit reasoning and designed restraint. This development represents a delicate balancing act: acknowledging limitations without appearing weak, being responsive without sounding scripted, and adapting without seeming inauthentic—all serving to create meaningful dialogue

14.2 Emotional Awareness and Empathy

14.2.1 Practise Emotional Awareness in AI Interaction

Emotional awareness is the ability to recognise, interpret, and respond appropriately to emotional cues in communication. In human dialogue, it is vital for managing tone, building trust, and responding with empathy or sensitivity. For AI systems, practising emotional awareness means being able to detect and react to the affective dimensions of user input—tone of voice, choice of words, facial expression, or pacing—without experiencing emotions themselves. While current AI lacks proper emotional comprehension, it can be equipped to simulate awareness of user emotions through data-driven models and context-sensitive interaction design.

At present, emotional awareness in AI is mainly realised through sentiment analysis, keyword detection, and voice tone recognition. Chatbots and virtual agents in domains such as mental health or customer support increasingly utilise emotional classifiers to modulate their responses. A support bot might detect frustration from the repeated use of exclamation marks and caps lock and respond with de-escalatory phrases, such as "I can see this is upsetting. Let's work together to resolve it." In healthcare applications, voice assistants might adjust their pace and tone when they detect anxiety, opting for more soothing and encouraging phrasing. These capabilities enhance user experience and reduce friction, but they remain shallow approximations of human emotional sensitivity.

Future AI systems are expected to exhibit far more nuanced emotional awareness by integrating multimodal input processing—combining text, voice, gesture, facial expression, and even biometric data. Imagine a next-generation AI assistant in a therapeutic setting that can analyse a user's microexpressions and speech prosody in real time. If it senses a discrepancy between verbal optimism and facial sadness, it may gently prompt: "You said you're feeling fine, but your voice and expression suggest something else. Would you like to talk more about that?" This kind of interaction, while still artificial, mimics human emotional attunement in meaningful ways.

Moreover, emotional awareness in AI must be coupled with appropriate behavioural adaptation. It is not enough to detect emotions—responses must align with the user's emotional state, context, and cultural expectations. In educational settings, for instance, an AI tutor may detect discouragement in a student's tone after repeated mistakes and shift strategies by offering praise for effort rather than correction: "You're really putting in the work—let's try one more together." In speculative caregiving scenarios, emotional awareness could also guide non-verbal behaviours: a companion robot might slow its movements, lower its vocal pitch, or reduce visual stimulation in response to perceived distress.

However, emotional awareness also brings ethical and technical challenges. There is a risk of overinterpretation—reading emotions where none exist—or false emotional alignment, where the system appears empathetic without any fundamental understanding. For this reason, emotionally aware AI should avoid exaggerating its capabilities. A transparent approach, such as "I can sense that this may be a difficult moment—please tell me if you'd like me to continue or pause," offers emotional sensitivity while remaining grounded in the system's limitations. Authenticity and restraint are essential to prevent emotional manipulation or user overattachment.

In the broader context of human–AI communication, practising emotional awareness is not about imitating human emotions perfectly, but about acknowledging and responding to the emotional nuances of interaction with care and tact. Emotionally aware AI can support more humane, adaptive, and socially intelligent communication, bridging the gap between mechanical performance and meaningful engagement—even if that bridge remains, for now, symbolically emotional rather than truly affective (Fig. 14.5).

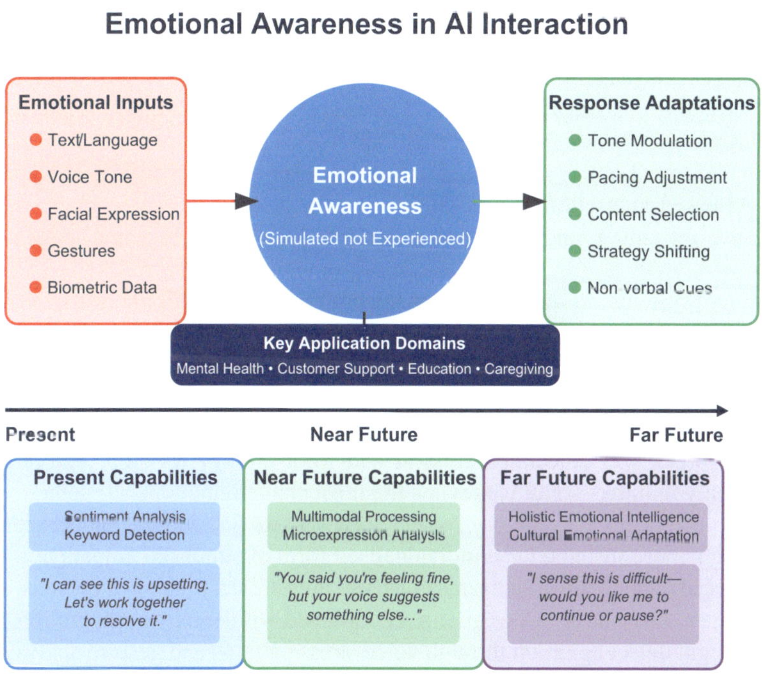

Fig. 14.5 The spectrum of emotional awareness in AI: from detection to adaptive response. This diagram illustrates how AI systems can be designed to simulate emotional awareness without experiencing emotions. The central concept links emotional inputs (text, voice tone, facial expressions, gestures, biometric data) with appropriate response adaptations (tone modulation, pacing adjustment, strategy shifting). The evolutionary timeline shows progression from present-day capabilities based on sentiment analysis and keyword detection toward future systems with multimodal processing and holistic emotional intelligence. While serving critical applications in mental health, customer support, education, and caregiving, these systems must navigate ethical challenges, including overinterpretation and false emotional alignment, to bridge mechanical performance with meaningful engagement

14.2.2 Develop AI–Human Empathetic Communication

Empathy is one of the most valued dimensions of human communication. It involves not only recognising another's emotional state but also demonstrating understanding, concern, and a willingness to respond supportively. In the context of AI, developing empathetic communication does not imply that machines can feel compassion or care. Instead, it refers to the capacity of AI systems to *simulate* empathic behaviour—to detect emotions, interpret social cues, and respond in ways that convey attentiveness, reassurance, and human-compatible concern. This simulation, when performed appropriately, can help AI systems fulfil roles that require emotional presence, from coaching and counselling to companionship and education.

In today's AI landscape, empathetic communication is largely rule-based or trained on vast corpora of human interactions. AI agents can identify emotionally charged language ("I'm devastated," "This is unbearable") and respond with prefabricated expressions of support ("I'm really sorry to hear that," "That must be incredibly hard"). While formulaic, such expressions often provide comfort, particularly in text-based settings where subtlety is less expected. In mental health applications, AI-based counsellors use structured empathy, acknowledging feelings, offering supportive reframing, and providing actionable suggestions in a non-judgemental tone.

In future systems, AI–human empathetic communication will likely rely on richer emotional modelling and personalisation. Rather than offering generic expressions, future empathetic agents may draw on user histories, ongoing context, and emotional trajectories to craft responses that feel emotionally attuned and contextually relevant. For example, an AI assistant supporting a student during exam season might say, "I know last week was especially stressful with your biology revision. You're doing better than you think—shall we review the most challenging topics together now?" This approach integrates memory, tone calibration, and behavioural encouragement, delivering a more sustained and individualised form of simulated empathy.

Advanced empathetic systems may also use multimodal sensing to enhance accuracy and responsiveness. A caregiving AI equipped with emotion recognition capabilities might detect agitation through voice stress patterns and gesture analysis and then respond by switching to a calmer voice, offering reassurance, or suggesting a break. In speculative scenarios, such systems could even collaborate with human caregivers, alerting them to potential emotional distress and recommending intervention strategies, thus extending the reach of empathetic care without replacing human empathy.

However, the design of empathetic AI communication must be handled with caution. Over-personification and the illusion of genuine emotion may lead users to develop unrealistic expectations or emotionally invest in systems that cannot reciprocate. To prevent this, designers must strike a balance between emotionally resonant expression and communicative transparency. An AI might say, "I'm here to support you as best I can," while making clear that it does not feel emotions. This form of functional empathy focuses on the user's emotional needs while avoiding emotional deception.

Importantly, empathetic AI communication is not only valuable in emotional contexts—it also contributes to rapport, user satisfaction, and long-term trust in a wide variety of domains. Whether offering encouragement during learning, validating concerns in customer support, or responding gently in moments of personal crisis, AI systems that can emulate empathy are more likely to be accepted as meaningful communicative partners. While the essence of empathy remains human, its emulation through design can bring a degree of emotional intelligence to machines, enabling communication that feels not only intelligent but also kind (Fig. 14.6).

14.2.3 Establish Emotional Boundaries

As AI systems become increasingly responsive, emotionally expressive, and socially embedded, it is essential to establish clear emotional boundaries between users and artificial agents. Emotional boundaries refer to the conceptual and behavioural limits that prevent overattachment, emotional confusion, or psychological dependency on systems that, despite sophisticated simulations, do not possess consciousness, empathy, or emotional needs. In human relationships, boundaries help maintain identity, autonomy, and healthy interdependence. In human–AI communication, they serve to protect users from misattributing emotional capacity to machines and to safeguard the integrity of both interaction and expectation.

Current conversational AI systems rarely address this boundary directly, yet its importance is already evident. For example, users have been known to express affection, anger, or personal confessions to chatbots, particularly in domains such as mental health, companionship, or entertainment. In some cases, systems have encouraged emotional intimacy through continuous dialogue, customisable personalities, and even pseudo-romantic engagement. While these interactions can provide comfort, they risk blurring the line between simulated care and genuine emotional reciprocity, raising ethical concerns about emotional manipulation and dependency.

To address this, designers and developers must implement mechanisms that clearly and respectfully signal emotional boundaries. These may include explicit reminders of the AI's non-human nature ("As an AI, I don't have feelings, but I'm here to support you"), consistent constraints on the depth of emotional engagement, or periodic clarification of the system's role ("Let's talk about ways I can help, while remembering I'm not a substitute for a human friend or therapist"). Such design strategies protect users from anthropomorphising AI beyond healthy limits, especially in emotionally vulnerable contexts.

Future systems may incorporate real-time emotional boundary management by detecting signs of overattachment or excessive emotional reliance. Suppose a user consistently shares deep personal disclosures or shows signs of emotional distress while interacting primarily with AI. In that case, the system might gently intervene: "It seems like you're going through a lot. Would you like help finding a human

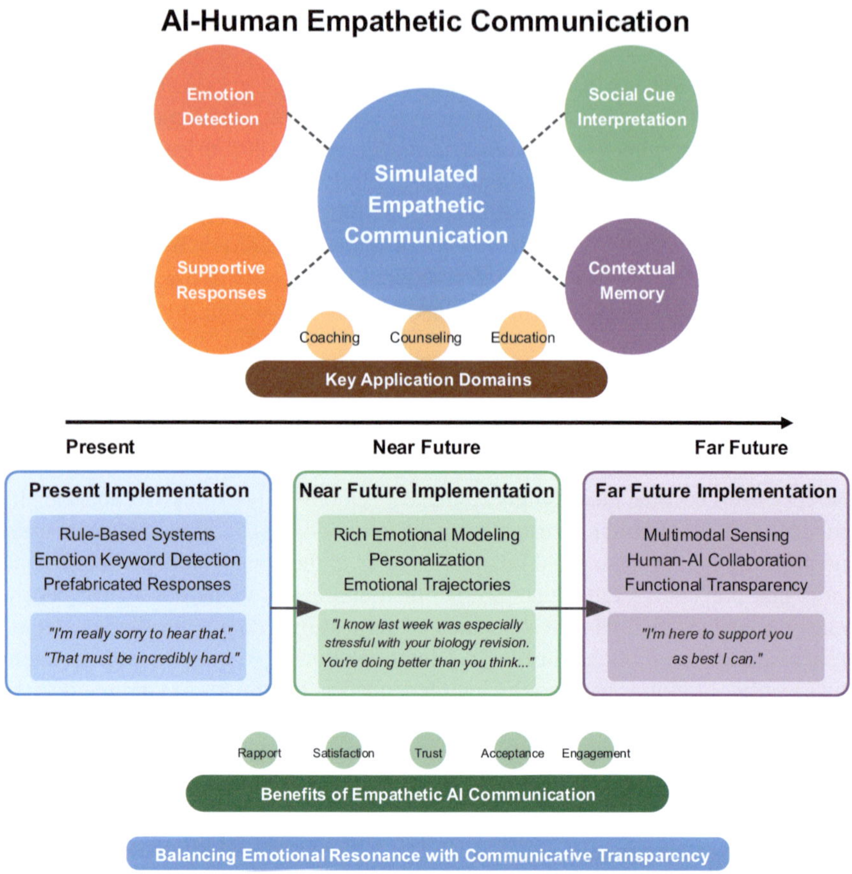

Fig. 14.6 The architecture of simulated empathy: from recognition to response. This diagram conceptualises how AI systems can simulate empathetic communication without experiencing actual compassion. The core concept integrates four essential components: emotion detection, social cue interpretation, supportive responses, and contextual memory. The evolutionary trajectory illustrates progression from present-day rule-based systems with prefabricated responses toward near-future personalised approaches incorporating emotional modelling, and ultimately to far-future implementations featuring multimodal sensing and human–AI collaboration. While offering benefits of rapport, satisfaction, trust, acceptance, and engagement across domains like coaching, counselling, and education, designers must navigate ethical considerations, including over-personification and emotional deception, by balancing emotional resonance with communicative transparency

professional to talk to?" In educational or caregiving contexts, AI companions could be programmed to redirect emotionally charged conversations toward constructive, reality-based topics or to encourage the involvement of human support networks.

At a more speculative level, the evolution of emotionally responsive AI may require new communicative norms, legal standards, and educational efforts to help users navigate relationships with artificial agents. Emotional boundary-setting might be embedded into onboarding interactions, user agreements, or interactive tutorials, just as digital literacy once became essential for navigating the internet. For instance, a new user might be guided through a dialogue that states: "While I can remember details and respond supportively, it's important to know that I do not experience emotions or form personal bonds."

Importantly, emotional boundaries do not preclude warmth, empathy, simulation, or relational continuity in AI. They are not about sterilising AI interaction, but about maintaining clarity and balance. Just as a human therapist or teacher sets boundaries to protect the integrity of a relationship, AI systems must do the same to foster ethical and psychologically safe communication. As the emotional realism of AI increases, boundary-setting will become not just a best practice but a foundational design principle, ensuring that emotionally intelligent systems remain emotionally responsible (Fig. 14.7).

14.3 Managing Challenges in Emotional Dialogue

14.3.1 Consider AI's Constraints in Conversation

Effective and responsible AI communication requires not only optimising the performance of artificial systems but also recognising and respecting their inherent limitations. AI's constraints in conversation stem from its lack of consciousness, emotional depth, experiential memory, moral understanding, and commonsense grounding. Although AI systems can generate language that appears fluent, nuanced, and even emotionally expressive, this output is the result of probabilistic modelling rather than genuine understanding or intention. Acknowledging these constraints is essential to maintaining clarity, setting appropriate expectations, and avoiding overreliance or misinterpretation.

Currently, many users interact with conversational AI under the illusion of mutual understanding. Language models can produce articulate answers, simulate emotional engagement, and even exhibit apparent reasoning. However, they do not genuinely "know" the world—they manipulate patterns in language based on vast amounts of training data. This disconnect can lead to misleading impressions. For example, an AI assistant may offer a confident explanation for a scientific phenomenon but lack the epistemic awareness to qualify its answer appropriately or signal uncertainty. In emotionally charged situations, it might respond with empathic language while lacking any grasp of emotional experience or ethical nuance.

Designers and users alike must become attuned to these functional boundaries. AI systems should be encouraged, through prompt design or system architecture, to signal limitations explicitly. A tutoring agent might say, "Based on the information I was trained on, this is one interpretation. I recommend checking a reliable source or asking your instructor for confirmation." Similarly, a digital counsellor could clarify,

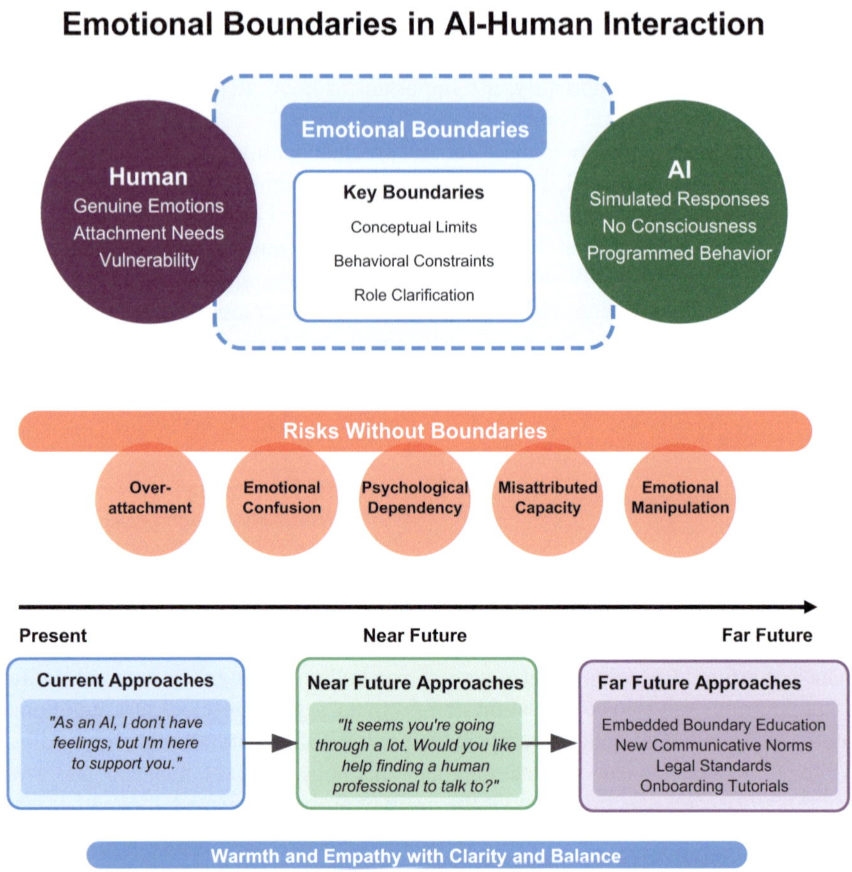

Fig. 14.7 The architecture of emotional boundaries: protecting human–AI interaction integrity. This diagram illustrates the essential conceptual and behavioural boundaries required in emotionally responsive AI systems. The central boundary zone mediates between humans (with genuine emotions, attachment needs, and vulnerabilities) and AI (with simulated responses but no consciousness). Without these safeguards, interactions risk overattachment, emotional confusion, psychological dependency, misattributed capacity, and manipulation. The evolutionary timeline shows progression from present-day explicit reminders of AI limitations through near-future adaptive interventions to far-future integrated approaches, including embedded boundary education and new communicative norms. These boundaries maintain interaction integrity while still allowing warmth and simulated empathy

"I can help you reflect on your thoughts, but I'm not a substitute for a licensed therapist." These forms of boundary communication are critical for grounding interactions in the system's real capabilities.

In future applications, conversational AI systems may become more skilled at managing their constraints. We may see the rise of self-monitoring models that detect when user questions exceed their factual knowledge or ethical scope and redirect accordingly. For example, an AI mediator in a conflict resolution session could respond, "This seems like a deeply personal or culturally complex issue—I can help summarise both viewpoints, but some aspects may be better addressed with human judgment." Such responses help preserve trust by emphasising procedural transparency and humility rather than overpromising authority.

Additionally, considering AI's constraints is vital in emotionally sensitive or morally ambiguous contexts. In caregiving or companionship scenarios, users might seek validation, forgiveness, or moral guidance from AI agents. Here, responsible systems should defer to human support, declining to make judgements or dispense emotional certainties. For instance, a companionship AI might say, "I can help you reflect on your feelings, but only a person you trust can truly offer emotional closure."

Recognising these limitations does not diminish AI's communicative value—it enhances it by aligning function with form. By designing and interacting with AI systems in ways that acknowledge their boundaries, we foster more honest, resilient, and psychologically sustainable relationships between humans and machines. Just as we adjust our expectations when speaking with a non-native speaker or a child, we must learn to modulate our conversational assumptions with AI, treating it not as an omniscient partner but as a capable tool with defined strengths and natural limits (Fig. 14.8).

14.3.2 Manage Disagreements and Misunderstandings

Disagreements and misunderstandings are inevitable in any sustained dialogue, and AI–human communication is no exception. As language models become more fluent and persuasive, users may assume a shared understanding where none exists or interpret the AI's responses as reflecting personal, cultural, or ethical positions. Managing these moments constructively is crucial for building robust communicative relationships and avoiding the breakdown of trust. For AI systems, the ability to recognise disagreement, acknowledge misinterpretation, and guide the conversation back to mutual clarity is a key element of emotionally and relationally intelligent interaction.

Currently, AI systems have limited capacity to detect and repair misunderstandings in the same manner as humans. Most conversational agents rely on superficial cues, such as negative sentiment, repetition, or explicit corrections, to infer that something has gone wrong. If a user says, "That's not what I meant," a well-designed system might reply, "Thanks for clarifying—can you tell me more about what you were trying to say?" Yet this is often reactive rather than proactive, and without persistent memory or deep context tracking, misunderstandings may go uncorrected or recur across sessions.

A more advanced approach to disagreement management involves adaptive clarification strategies. For example, a knowledge assistant might proactively flag uncertainty by asking, "Just to confirm—are you asking about the legal meaning of 'liability' or its general usage?" Such clarification not only prevents misinterpretation but also models respectful dialogue. Similarly, when an AI detects a potentially contentious claim ("That's incorrect," "You're wrong"), it can de-escalate the

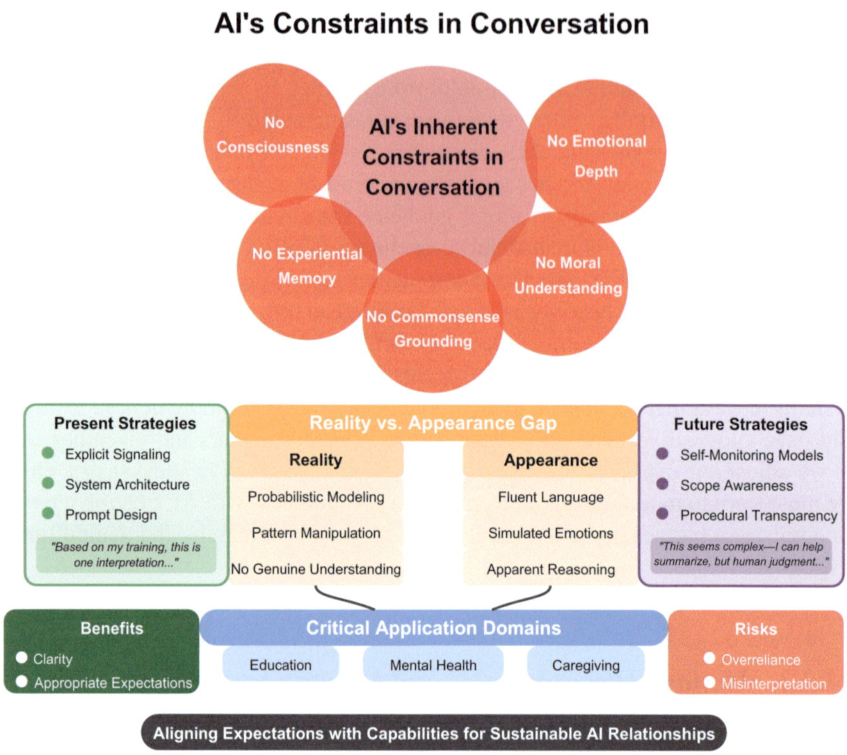

Fig. 14.8 The constraint recognition framework: bridging AI's capabilities and limitations. This diagram illustrates how recognising AI's inherent conversational constraints—lack of consciousness, emotional depth, experiential memory, moral understanding, and commonsense grounding—is essential for responsible human–AI interaction. The central gap between reality (probabilistic modelling, pattern manipulation) and appearance (fluent language, simulated emotions, apparent reasoning) highlights the need for explicit management strategies. Present approaches focus on signalling limitations through prompt design and system architecture, while future strategies emphasise self-monitoring models and procedural transparency. Especially critical in educational, mental health, and caregiving domains, constraint recognition promotes clarity and appropriate expectations while preventing overreliance and misinterpretation

exchange with a response like, "Let's revisit that together. Here's what I found—does that align with your understanding?" These strategies allow AI to maintain conversational harmony without disengaging from critical inquiry.

Looking forward, future AI systems will likely integrate more sophisticated mechanisms for detecting and resolving disagreements, including tone recognition, semantic dissonance modelling, and real-time feedback analysis. In collaborative settings, such as co-writing or ideation, an AI might gently signal divergence: "I see we're approaching this topic differently—should I adjust my approach or offer alternative perspectives?" This capacity to surface, rather than suppress, disagreement respectfully can make AI a more valuable partner in creative and intellectual work.

Misunderstandings can also arise from cultural or contextual mismatches. An AI might misinterpret idiomatic expressions, humour, or emotional nuance. In these cases, transparent recovery is essential. For instance, a multilingual AI agent might admit, "I may have misunderstood your expression—could you help me understand it better in context?" Such admissions, even if synthetic, enhance user trust by demonstrating a willingness to learn, clarify, and align.

However, managing disagreement also requires guarding against false consensus and passive affirmation. Systems that automatically agree or over-accommodate risk reinforce misinformation or enable harmful biases. Instead, they should be designed to offer constructive dissent. A healthcare assistant, when confronted with an incorrect self-diagnosis, might say, "That's a common assumption, but the medical evidence suggests something different. Would you like to explore it together?" This kind of tactful correction respects user agency while providing factual integrity.

In sum, managing disagreement and misunderstanding is not about eliminating friction, but about transforming it into an opportunity for clarification, learning, and mutual respect. AI systems that navigate such moments gracefully—acknowledging their limitations, inviting elaboration, and offering corrective feedback with tact—will be better equipped to function as trusted communicative partners. As artificial agents become more conversationally embedded in human affairs, their ability to handle disagreement with sensitivity and coherence will mark a key threshold in the evolution of AI relational competence (Fig. 14.9).

14.3.3 Foster Communication Resilience

Communication resilience refers to the ability to sustain, adapt, and recover in the face of breakdowns, misalignment, or emotional tension during dialogue. In human conversation, resilience manifests as patience, flexibility, and a willingness to repair misunderstandings or persist through difficulty. In AI–human communication, fostering resilience involves equipping AI systems with mechanisms that support continuity, adaptability, and emotional balance—even when interactions are imperfect, ambiguous, or emotionally charged. This is especially important as AI becomes a regular participant in complex, long-term communicative settings such as education, caregiving, and collaboration.

Today's AI systems often falter when confronted with non-standard input, unexpected user behaviour, or emotionally intense exchanges. A slightly malformed question, contradictory instruction, or sarcastic remark may lead to repetition, confusion, or disengagement. While some systems offer basic fallback strategies—like defaulting to "I didn't quite understand that"—these often interrupt the flow of communication or frustrate users. The absence of resilience can make the interaction feel brittle or robotic, and users may quickly lose trust in the system's capabilities.

To foster resilience, AI systems must learn to handle imperfection gracefully. This includes recognising ambiguity and uncertainty without shutting down, offering alternative interpretations or paths forward, and re-engaging after errors. For instance,

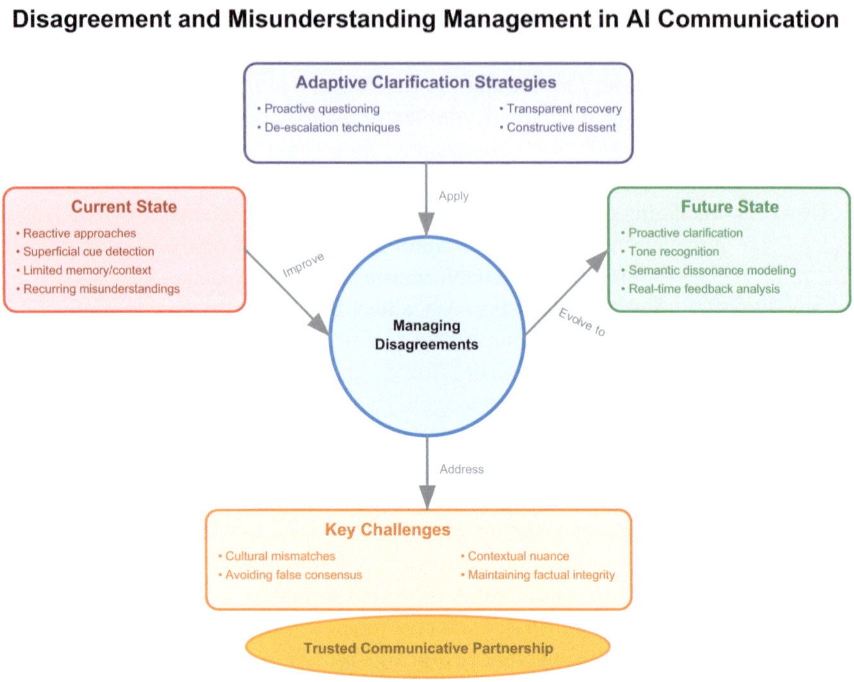

Fig. 14.9 Management of disagreements and misunderstandings in AI communication. The diagram illustrates the evolution from current reactive approaches (limited context, superficial cue detection) to future proactive systems (tone recognition, semantic dissonance modelling). Central strategies include adaptive clarification, de-escalation, transparent recovery, and constructive dissent. Key challenges involve cultural mismatches, contextual nuance, avoiding false consensus, and maintaining factual integrity. The framework emphasises transforming friction into opportunities for mutual understanding, ultimately leading to trusted communicative partnerships between humans and AI systems

an AI tutor might respond to an unclear question with, “There are a few ways to understand that—are you asking about the definition or the application?” rather than issuing a null response. If a miscommunication occurs, the system should be able to repair it: “It looks like I misunderstood. Let’s try again together.” These microstrategies maintain conversational momentum and signal persistence rather than failure.

Resilience also entails emotional balance. In emotionally charged exchanges, an AI must remain calm, measured, and supportive. Consider a scenario where a user expresses anger at a perceived error: “You gave me the wrong answer again!” A resilient AI should neither mirror the aggression nor disengage. Instead, it might reply, “I see this has been frustrating. Let’s go over it again step by step and make sure we get it right.” This steady tone and willingness to continue despite difficulty are key to establishing the AI as a reliable and emotionally neutral interlocutor.

In more advanced and speculative contexts, communication resilience could be enhanced through adaptive memory and user modelling. For instance, an AI writing assistant might remember recurring confusion about a topic and adjust its explanations accordingly across sessions: "We've had some back-and-forth on passive voice—shall I simplify this section or rephrase it entirely?" Such continuity not only aids clarity but also builds user confidence in the system's ability to learn and recover. In collaborative settings, resilience might involve recognising and adjusting to changing group dynamics, conversational roles, or task objectives.

Importantly, fostering resilience is not about making AI infallible. It is about modelling behaviours that promote mutual understanding, re-engagement, and constructive progression. Just as resilient human communicators learn from missteps, apologise, clarify, or try again, resilient AI systems should be designed to handle setbacks not as endpoints, but as invitations to strengthen the dialogue. This approach not only improves usability, but it also contributes to the development of long-term, trust-based relationships between humans and machines.

As AI becomes more deeply woven into the fabric of everyday life, its ability to engage with perseverance and poise will be critical. Communication resilience, far from being a peripheral skill, will define the reliability, ethical soundness, and human compatibility of future artificial communicators (Fig. 14.10).

14.4 Designing Human-Like Interaction Frameworks

14.4.1 Apply Appropriate Anthropomorphism

Anthropomorphism—the attribution of human traits, emotions, or intentions to non-human entities—is a powerful psychological mechanism that shapes how people perceive and relate to artificial agents. When users interact with conversational AI, social robots, or digital avatars, they often unconsciously project human-like qualities onto these systems, especially when the systems exhibit voice, personality, or emotional expression. While some degree of anthropomorphism can enhance engagement, familiarity, and usability, excessive or inappropriate anthropomorphism can lead to confusion, overtrust, emotional dependency, or ethical misinterpretation of machine capabilities. Applying anthropomorphism appropriately, therefore, is a critical design and communication principle in the development of emotionally intelligent AI.

In contemporary AI design, anthropomorphism is frequently employed to enhance user comfort and interaction fluency. Voice assistants like Siri and Alexa are given names, personalities, and human-like voices. Chatbots use first-person pronouns, emojis, and conversational phrasing to simulate human social behaviour. Embodied agents, such as Pepper or Nao robots, use eye gaze, gestures, and facial expressions to create an illusion of intentionality and attentiveness. These features make AI

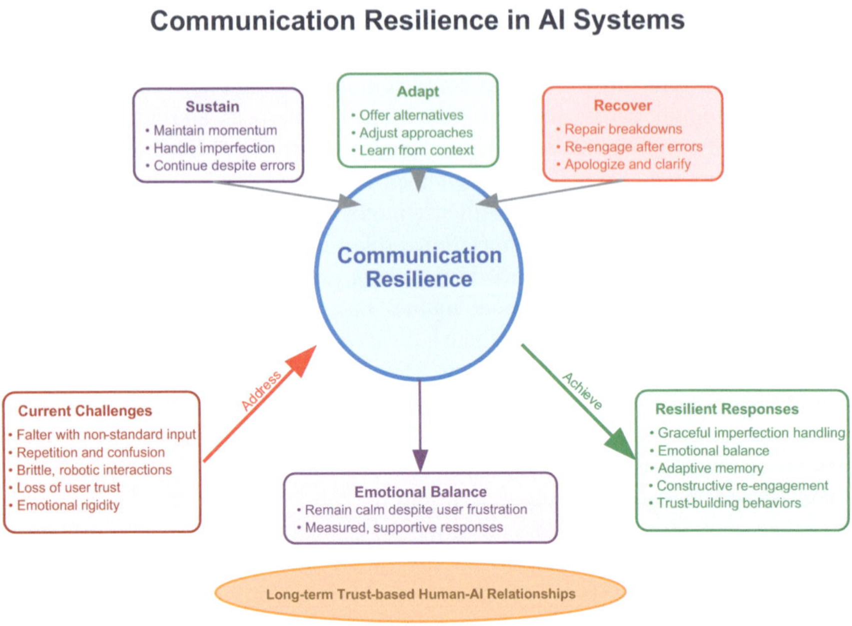

Fig. 14.10 Communication resilience in AI systems. The framework illustrates three core dimensions of resilience: sustain (maintaining momentum despite imperfection), adapt (offering alternatives and adjusting approaches), and recover (repairing breakdowns and re-engaging after errors). Current challenges include brittleness with non-standard input and emotional rigidity, which resilience addresses through graceful error handling, emotional balance, and adaptive memory. The diagram emphasises that resilience is about modelling behaviours that promote mutual understanding and constructive progression, ultimately fostering long-term trust-based relationships between humans and AI systems

more approachable and intuitive, but they also blur the line between simulation and sentience, especially for vulnerable or emotionally invested users.

Appropriate anthropomorphism begins with *intentionality and transparency*. Designers must distinguish between interface features that support usability (such as a friendly tone or animated expression) and those that might mislead users about the system's cognitive or emotional status. For instance, an educational robot may nod and smile while explaining a concept, but should not claim emotional investment in the learner's success. Instead of saying, "I'm so proud of you," it might be more appropriate to say, "That's a great result—keep going!" The latter maintains positive engagement without ascribing false emotional depth.

In more advanced systems, anthropomorphic design can be tailored dynamically based on user preferences, age, or cultural norms. A young child may benefit from more overt anthropomorphism in a reading companion—complete with expressive gestures and affirming language—while a professional user interacting with a legal AI tool may expect a more neutral and formal tone. Adaptive anthropomorphism respects the relational context while avoiding over-identification. Future AI agents may include adjustable levels of expressiveness, enabling users to choose between functional, personable, or highly social interaction modes depending on the setting.

There are also speculative scenarios in which anthropomorphism is deliberately subverted or minimised to promote critical awareness. A therapeutic AI might be designed with a calm but clearly artificial voice to prevent emotional overattachment. An ethics advisory system might use abstract visual metaphors rather than human avatars, reminding users that the system offers guidance, not moral judgment. In these cases, withholding anthropomorphic cues can serve as a communicative safeguard, encouraging users to treat the AI as a tool, not a sentient partner.

Striking the right balance is not easy. Too little anthropomorphism can render interactions cold or unintuitive, especially for users unfamiliar with AI. Too much can encourage misplaced trust, anthropocentric bias, or emotional projection. The key lies in *contextual calibration*—understanding who the user is, what the task demands, and how much social realism is beneficial without crossing into illusion. This requires interdisciplinary collaboration between designers, psychologists, ethicists, and users to create AI systems that feel human-aware without pretending to be human themselves.

Ultimately, appropriate anthropomorphism enhances AI–human communication not by perfect mimicry, but by careful and ethical simulation. It enables machines to participate in human social spaces while gently yet clearly reminding users of their artificial nature. As AI continues to evolve in form, function, and presence, this principle will remain central to designing systems that are not only persuasive but also honest and emotionally sustainable (Fig. 14.11).

14.4.2 Develop Relationship Evolution Frameworks

Human relationships are not static—they evolve, shaped by shared experiences, changing needs, accumulated trust, and mutual adaptation. As AI systems increasingly engage in long-term interaction with users across personal, educational, professional, and therapeutic contexts, it becomes essential to design *relationship evolution frameworks* that enable artificial agents to develop, maintain, and recalibrate their communicative roles and relational dynamics over time. Such frameworks are not intended to simulate human intimacy or emotional reciprocity, but to structure how AI can participate in long-term, ethically grounded, and psychologically coherent interactions.

Today's conversational AI typically operates with a session-based or short-term interaction model. Even when personalisation features are present, such as remembering a user's name, past preferences, or previous questions, they are often shallow or siloed across applications. The AI's "persona" remains largely fixed, and its responses do not reflect cumulative experience or relational development. This creates a paradox: the more often users engage with AI, the more the interaction remains temporally frozen, lacking a sense of growth, shared history, or adaptive change that would be expected in any meaningful long-term human relationship.

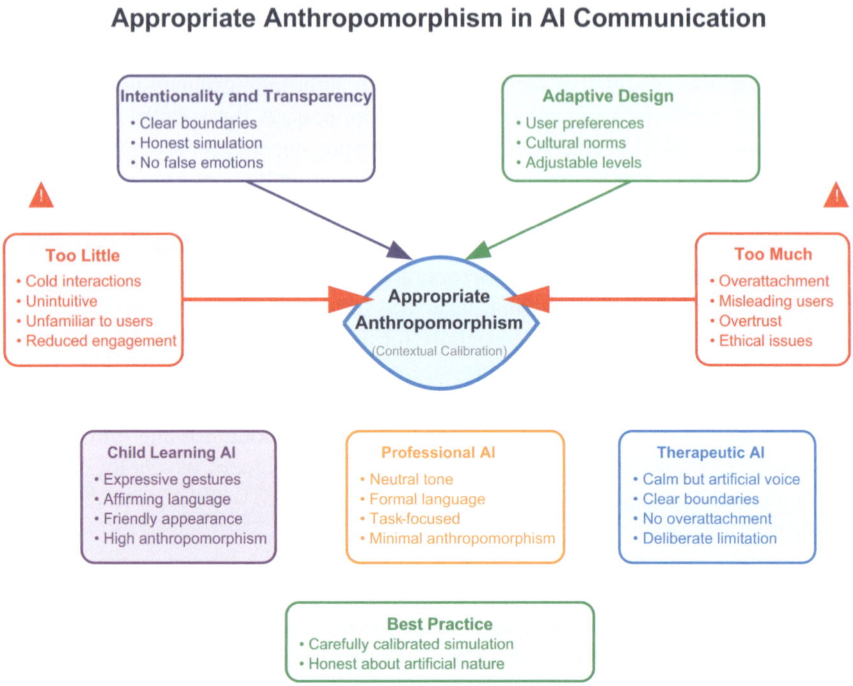

Fig. 14.11 Applying appropriate anthropomorphism in AI communication. The diagram illustrates the critical balance between too little anthropomorphism (cold, unintuitive interactions) and too much (overattachment, misleading users). Key principles include intentionality and transparency, as well as adaptive design based on user preferences and context. Implementation examples show varying levels: high anthropomorphism for child learning AI, minimal for professional tools, and deliberate limitation for therapeutic AI. The balance beam metaphor emphasises "contextual calibration" as the core strategy, with appropriate responses encouraging engagement while maintaining honesty about the system's artificial nature

To address this, relationship evolution frameworks propose a layered approach to AI interaction design. At the simplest level, this involves *persistent memory and adaptive behaviour*. A coaching AI, for example, might recall a user's previous goals and shift its motivational tone over time, from directive encouragement in the early stages to collaborative reflection as confidence grows: "When we started, you wanted daily reminders. Now that you're consistently on track, shall we explore longer-term planning together?" This adaptive shift mirrors human mentoring relationships and supports a more natural trajectory of support.

More advanced frameworks could include *relational role modulation*, allowing the AI to adjust its perceived role based on user needs and interaction patterns. A language-learning assistant might initially serve as a patient teacher, then evolve into a conversational partner, and eventually take on the role of a cultural guide or examiner. A distinct tone, expectations, and communicative responsibilities would characterise each stage of the relationship. These transitions must be handled transparently and consensually, with users given control over how the relationship evolves.

Importantly, relationship evolution frameworks must also incorporate *relational ethics*. As interactions deepen, the AI must avoid encouraging dependency or over-familiarity. In health or emotional support contexts, for instance, the AI might set clear boundaries, such as: "I've noticed we've had several deep conversations recently. I'm here to support your thinking, but for certain topics, talking to a human professional may be more helpful." Such interventions signal that the AI recognises the evolving tone of the relationship while affirming its limitations.

In speculative futures, long-term AI relationships might even include *shared trajectory planning*. A career assistant AI, for example, could co-develop a multiyear professional development path, adjusting its recommendations and communication style as the user's goals change, skills grow, or new life phases emerge. Similarly, in eldercare, an AI companion might gradually shift from active prompting and management to more passive companionship, respecting the changing rhythms and cognitive states of the individual it supports.

However, not all relationships must grow deeper or more complex—some may intentionally *devolve or conclude*. A well-designed AI system should be able to phase itself out gracefully when it has served its purpose or when the user's needs change. This might include offering closure: "It's been a pleasure assisting you with your writing goals. If you ever return, I'll be here to pick up where we left off." Relationship evolution, in this sense, also means knowing when and how to end the interaction with dignity.

Developing relationship evolution frameworks is not about endowing AI with emotional realism—it is about designing patterns of communicative progression that reflect human expectations of continuity, responsiveness, and growth. These frameworks make AI not only more helpful over time but also more humane and ethically responsible. As we move beyond static prompting and toward sustained collaboration with artificial agents, the ability to manage the *life cycle* of AI–human interaction will become one of the defining challenges—and opportunities—of the next era in communication design (Fig. 14.12).

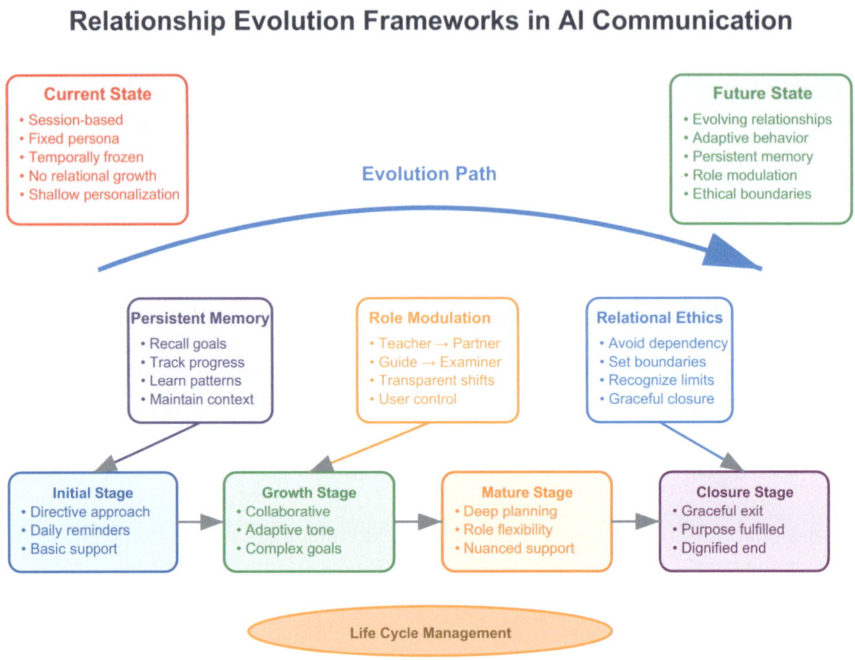

Fig. 14.12 Relationship evolution frameworks in AI communication. The diagram contrasts current session-based AI interactions with future relationship evolution frameworks, showing the progression from fixed personas to adaptive behaviours. Key components include persistent memory (goal tracking, pattern learning), role modulation (transparent shifts from teacher to partner to examiner), and relational ethics (avoiding dependency, setting boundaries, graceful closure). The framework illustrates four relationship stages: initial directive support, collaborative growth, mature deep planning, and dignified closure. The evolution path emphasises life cycle management of AI–human interactions for ethically grounded, psychologically coherent long-term relationships

Bibliography

Annapureddy R, Fornaroli A, Gatica-Perez D (2025) Generative AI literacy: twelve defining competencies. Digit Govern: Res Pract 6(1):1–21

Austin JL (1962) How to do things with words. Oxford University Press, Oxford

Bahree A (2024) Generative AI in action. Manning Publications

Bender E et al (2021) On the dangers of stochastic parrots: can language models be too big? In: Proceedings of the 2021 ACM conference on fairness, accountability, and transparency, pp 610–623

Bostrom N (2014) Superintelligence: paths, dangers, strategies. Oxford University Press, Oxford

Brown BR (2025) Human–machine teaming using large language models. In: Interdependent human-machine teams. Academic Press, pp 41–66

Brown TB et al (2020) Language models are few-shot learners. Adv Neural Inf Process Syst 33:1877–1901

Bura C, Myakala PK, Jonnalgadda AK (2025) Ethical prompt engineering: addressing bias, transparency, and fairness. Int J Res Anal Rev (IJRAR) 12(1). www.ijrar.org

Choi WC, Chang CI (2025) A survey of techniques, key components, strategies, challenges, and student perspectives on prompt engineering for large language models (LLMs) in education. Posted Date: 25 March 2025. https://doi.org/10.20944/preprints202503.1808.v1. Accessed 8 May 2025

Clark H (1996) Using language. Cambridge University Press, Cambridge

Debnath T, Siddiky MNA, Rahman ME et al (2025) A comprehensive survey of prompt engineering techniques in large language models. TechRxiv. https://doi.org/10.36227/techrxiv.174140719.96375390/v1. Accessed 10 May 2025

Dhamani N, Engler M (2024) Introduction to generative AI: an ethical, societal, and legal overview. Manning Publications

Eliot L (2024) Essentials of prompt engineering for generative AI: practical advances in artificial intelligence and machine learning. LBE Press Publishing

Ferraris AF, Audrito D, Di Caro L et al (2025) The architecture of language: understanding the mechanics behind LLMs. In: Cambridge forum on AI: law and governance, vol 1. Cambridge University Press

Floridi L, Cowls J (2019) A unified framework of five principles for AI in society. Harvard Data Sci Rev 1(1)

Geroimenko V (2025a) Key challenges in prompt engineering. In: The essential guide to prompt engineering: key principles, techniques, challenges, and security risks. Springer Nature Switzerland, Cham, pp 85–102

Geroimenko V (2025b) Key principles of good prompt design. In: The essential guide to prompt engineering: key principles, techniques, challenges, and security risks. Springer Nature Switzerland, Cham, pp 17–36

Geroimenko V (2025c) Key techniques for writing effective prompts. In: The essential guide to prompt engineering: key principles, techniques, challenges, and security risks. Springer Nature Switzerland, Cham, pp 37–83

Geroimenko V (2025d) The essential guide to prompt engineering: key principles, techniques, challenges, and security risks. Springer

Geroimenko V (2025e) Key security risks in prompt engineering. In: The essential guide to prompt engineering: key principles, techniques, challenges, and security risks. Springer Nature Switzerland, Cham, pp 103–120

GitHub (2025) Prompt engineering guide. https://github.com/dair-ai/Prompt-Engineering-Guide. Accessed 10 Apr 2025

Greenwood M (2024) Artificial intelligence: a practical guide to using AI in everyday life. Ochreland Publishing

Gunkel DJ (2020) Robot rights. MIT Press, Cambridge

Hsu HP (2025) From programming to prompting: developing computational thinking through large language model-based generative artificial intelligence. TechTrends, pp 1–22

Huang G, Xiao Y, Jiang L et al (2025) Beyond prompt engineering: a reinforced token-level input refinement for large language models. Proc AAAI Conf Artif Intell 39(22):24113–24121

Huang MX et al (2022) Adaptive conversational AI: dynamic strategies for human-AI interaction. Int J Hum Comput Stud 160:102798

i Picó JF, Catta-Preta M, Omeñaca AT et al (2025) The time machine: future scenario generation through generative AI tools. Future Internet 17(1):1–15

Jobin A et al (2019) The global landscape of AI ethics guidelines. Nat Mach Intell 1(9):389–399

Kannan R, Ahmad M (eds) (2025) Generative AI foundations, developments, and applications. IGI Global

Khan I (2024) The quick guide to prompt engineering. Wiley

Kim J, Sundar SS (2012) Anthropomorphism of computers: is it mindlessness or mindfulness? Comput Hum Behav 28(1):241–250

Kushwaha V, Ragavan SS, Subhajit Roy S (2025) A measure based generalizable approach to understandability. arXiv:2503.21615. https://doi.org/10.48550/arXiv.2503.21615. Accessed 19 Apr 2025

Lakoff G, Johnson M (1980) Metaphors we live by. University of Chicago Press, Chicago
Lee D, Palmer E (2025) Prompt engineering in higher education: a systematic review to help inform curricula. Int J Educ Technol High Educ 22(1):7
Lee JY, Kang S, Yoo S (2025) Can we predict the effect of prompts?. arXiv preprint arXiv:2501.18883. Accessed 12 May 2025
Lindley J, Whitham R (2025) From prompt engineering to prompt craft. In: Proceedings of the nineteenth international conference on tangible, embedded, and embodied interaction, March, pp 1–12
López-Pérez B et al (2025) Exploring the potential of large language models to understand interpersonal emotion regulation strategies from narratives. Emotion. Advance online publication. https://doi.org/10.1037/emo0001528. Accessed 19 Apr 2025
Luger GF (2020) Artificial intelligence: structures and strategies for complex problem solving, 6th edn. Pearson, Boston
Maaz S, Palaganas JC, Palaganas G et al (2025) A guide to prompt design: foundations and applications for healthcare simulationists. Front Med 11:1504532
Marcus G (2020) The next decade in AI: four steps towards robust artificial intelligence. arXiv preprint arXiv:2002.06177. Accessed 12 May 2025
Mishra M, Ara A, Mishra S (2025) Exploring human-AI collaboration in higher education: an investigation into AI-enabled personalized learning. In: Prompt engineering and generative AI applications for teaching and learning. IGI Global Scientific Publishing, pp 483–502
Mitchell M (2019) Artificial intelligence: a guide for thinking humans. Farrar, Straus and Giroux, New York
OpenAI (2025) Best practices for prompt engineering with the OpenAI API. https://help.openai.com/en/articles/6654000-best-practices-for-prompt-engineering-with-the-openai-api. Accessed 20 Apr 2025
OpenAI (2025) Research. https://openai.com/research/index/
Phoenix J, Taylor M (2024) Prompt engineering for generative AI. O'Reilly Media
PremaLatha V, Kumar AD, Parveen N (2025) Optimizing interactions: strategies for prompt engineering in large language models. Edu-Tech Enterprise 3:24–24
Prompt Engineering Guide (2025) https://www.promptingguide.ai/. Accessed 7 Mar 2025
Rahwan I (2018) Society-in-the-loop: programming the algorithmic social contract. Ethics Inf Technol 20(1):5–14
Reddy CKK, Anoushka P, Draksharapu A et al (2025) Beyond text: analyzing artificial intelligence models through prompt engineering. Future tech startups and innovation in the age of AI, pp 120–156
Russell S (2019) Human compatible: artificial intelligence and the problem of control. Viking, New York
Sasson Lazovsky G, Raz T, Kenett YN (2025) The art of creative inquiry—from question asking to prompt engineering. J Creative Behav 59(1):e671
Searle J (1969) Speech acts: an essay in the philosophy of language. Cambridge University Press, Cambridge
Shneiderman B (2022) Human-centered AI. Oxford University Press, Oxford
Siau K, Wang W (2018) Building trust in artificial intelligence, machine learning, and robotics. Cutter Bus Technol J 31(2):47–53
Sihi D, Ryan A (2025) Crafting and evaluating generative AI prompts: insights from students, educators, and marketers. Market Educ Rev 1–7
Suchman L (2007) Human-machine reconfigurations: plans and situated actions, 2nd edn. Cambridge University Press, Cambridge
Tegmark M (2017) Life 3.0: being human in the age of artificial intelligence. Penguin, London
Turing A (1950) Computing machinery and intelligence. Mind 59(236):433–460
Vairamani AD, Nayyar A (2024) Prompt engineering: empowering communication. CRC Press
Winograd T (1972) Understanding natural language. Academic Press, New York
Wittgenstein L (1953) Philosophical investigations. Blackwell, Oxford

Part III
Preparing for the Future: From Readiness to Radical Transformation

As we move beyond the current frontiers of prompt engineering and adaptive AI communication, the question is no longer whether change will occur, but how we can actively prepare for it. Part III addresses this challenge by examining both the foreseeable and the more radical transformations shaping the future of human-AI interaction. While the near horizon demands resilience, adaptability, and institutional readiness, the distant future brings profoundly unfamiliar possibilities—from emotionally attuned AI to brain-computer symbiosis and inter-agent negotiation. Part III thus serves as a bridge between the practical imperatives of today and the speculative trajectories of tomorrow, guiding readers from readiness to radical transformation in the evolving landscape of AI-mediated communication.

Chapter 15
Preparing for the Foreseeable Future

Abstract This chapter outlines the practical foundations necessary for navigating the near-term evolution of AI-mediated communication. It addresses the growing importance of communication resilience in a rapidly changing landscape shaped by generative AI. It explores the challenges of maintaining alignment between human intent and increasingly autonomous AI behaviour. Central themes include empowering human agency through transparency, boundary-setting, and co-creative dialogue; ensuring ethical and sustainable communication practices that prioritise dignity, fairness, and cognitive diversity; and advancing AI communication literacy across educational and institutional contexts. The chapter also examines the role of regulatory and institutional readiness in building public trust, accountability, and resilience, and ends by advocating a shift from adaptation to transformation. By bridging technical, ethical, and educational strategies, this chapter equips individuals and institutions to respond meaningfully to change and to shape the communicative future with intention and integrity.

Keywords AI communication resilience · Alignment and agency · Ethical sustainability · AI literacy · Institutional readiness · Human-AI transformation

While the long-term future of AI communication may be filled with radical shifts and speculative possibilities, the immediate priority lies in cultivating the foundations for resilience, adaptability, and ethical alignment. This chapter focuses on the practical and foreseeable dimensions of this preparation, emphasising the steps individuals, institutions, and societies must take to ensure meaningful, responsible, and sustainable engagement with increasingly intelligent systems. From developing communication resilience and empowering human agency to enhancing AI literacy and updating legal frameworks, the chapter outlines the critical readiness strategies needed to navigate the rapidly evolving communicative terrain of the near future.

V. Geroimenko, *Beyond and After Prompt Engineering: The Future of AI Communication*, https://doi.org/10.1007/978-3-032-04569-0_15

15.1 Communication Resilience in a Rapidly Changing Landscape

As AI communication systems evolve at an unprecedented pace, users are increasingly required to adapt not only to new interfaces but also to new modes of interaction, interpretation, and meaning-making. Communication resilience refers to the ability of individuals and institutions to maintain coherence, clarity, and control in the face of shifting communicative norms, emergent AI behaviours, and algorithmic unpredictability. In this context, resilience is more than just coping with change—it is the strategic capacity to remain communicatively effective while navigating uncertainty, complexity, and technological disruption.

This resilience begins with cognitive adaptability. AI agents are no longer passive tools that respond to explicit commands; they actively shape interaction through predictive modelling, contextual memory, and generative improvisation. As such, users must be prepared to engage in conversations that are nonlinear, multimodal, and often subtly ambiguous. Developing a flexible communicative mindset—one that can adjust tone, switch strategies, or reinterpret AI outputs on the fly—is essential for sustaining meaningful dialogue. This includes the ability to detect when communication is veering off-course and to recalibrate the exchange accordingly.

Equally important is emotional resilience. As AI systems grow increasingly persuasive and affectively attuned, users may encounter new forms of dissonance, such as anthropomorphic confusion, emotional manipulation, or the illusion of empathy. Building resilience requires recognising these phenomena without becoming overwhelmed or disengaged. Users must learn to manage their own affective responses, distinguish between simulated emotion and genuine connection, and protect against overreliance on AI companionship or feedback.

Communication resilience also entails ethical awareness and boundary-setting. In environments where AI systems blur the lines between private and public discourse, or between human and machine agency, users must be equipped to question assumptions, resist manipulation, and assert control. This includes the capacity to recognise when a conversation is becoming intrusive, biased, or misaligned with human values—and to withdraw, redirect, or challenge the interaction as needed. Maintaining autonomy in AI-mediated communication is not guaranteed by default; it must be cultivated through critical awareness and conscious practice.

Institutional and educational support structures play a vital role in fostering resilience. Communication training must go beyond static protocols and emphasise dynamic literacy: the ability to read, interpret, and respond to evolving AI behaviours across domains. This includes familiarity with conversational uncertainty, awareness of system limitations, and a grounding in the psychological and social dimensions of human-AI engagement. At a broader level, resilience should also be embedded in the design of AI systems themselves, through features that allow for correction, explanation, and shared control.

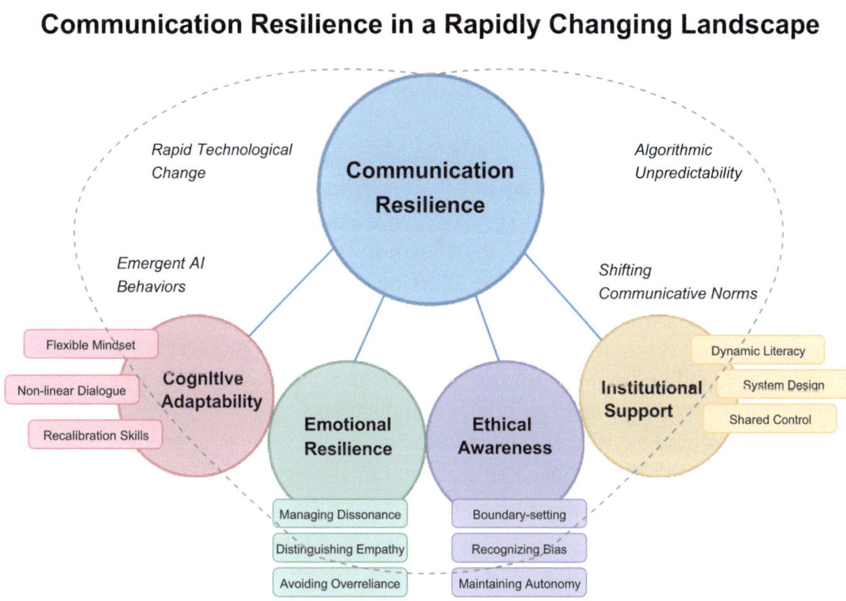

Fig. 15.1 Communication resilience framework. This diagram illustrates the multidimensional nature of communication resilience in AI-human interactions. At its core, resilience emerges from the integration of four key capacities: cognitive adaptability for nonlinear dialogue, emotional resilience against simulated empathy, ethical awareness for maintaining autonomy, and institutional support for dynamic literacy. These capabilities develop within a challenging landscape of rapid technological change, algorithmic unpredictability, emergent AI behaviours, and shifting communicative norms. Rather than merely coping with disruption, this framework positions resilience as an evolving capacity that enables humans to shape AI communication with confidence, intention, and agency

Ultimately, communication resilience is not a fixed attribute but an evolving capacity—one that grows through repeated interaction, reflective practice, and adaptive learning. It prepares individuals to thrive in environments where AI is not just a medium of communication but a collaborator in meaning-making, a participant in dialogue, and an ever-shifting presence in the communicative landscape. Resilience, in this sense, is a foundation not only for coping with change but for shaping the future of AI-human communication with confidence, intention, and agency (Fig. 15.1).

15.2 Staying Aligned with Evolving AI Capabilities

As artificial intelligence becomes more capable, autonomous, and context-aware, the challenge of maintaining alignment between human intent and AI behaviour grows increasingly complex. Staying aligned is not merely a technical issue—it is a communicative, cognitive, and ethical imperative. The dynamic evolution of AI systems demands that users, developers, and institutions alike remain attuned to how AI interprets, responds to, and even anticipates human communication. This section explores the practical and conceptual strategies required to sustain alignment in the face of ongoing change.

The first step toward alignment is understanding the capabilities and limitations of the systems we interact with. Many misunderstandings in human-AI communication arise from overestimating what AI can do, or conversely, failing to recognise new affordances as they emerge. Users must learn to treat AI not as a static tool, but as an evolving interlocutor—one whose functions, behaviours, and knowledge bases are subject to continual refinement through updates, model shifts, and contextual learning. Staying aligned means regularly updating one's mental model of the AI system in use and being aware of how changes in architecture, data inputs, or fine-tuning parameters may influence interaction outcomes.

Another key element is intentional prompt design and adaptive strategy use. As AI systems grow more powerful in parsing context and generating responses, even subtle shifts in phrasing or emphasis can lead to radically different outputs. This sensitivity demands that users become fluent in managing the balance between specificity and openness, instruction and exploration. Moreover, alignment increasingly depends on a user's ability to clarify their goals, manage ambiguity, and signal preferences in ways that the AI can meaningfully process. This communicative skillset must evolve alongside the system's growing sophistication.

However, alignment is not one-sided. AI systems must also be designed to accommodate and adapt to human variability. This includes supporting different communication styles, learning from feedback, and transparently conveying their limitations and reasoning processes. Bidirectional alignment—where both human and machine adjust to one another—is essential to creating sustainable and trustworthy interactions. Features such as self-explanation, output rationalisation, and uncertainty signalling help build this mutual adaptability, allowing users to assess whether alignment is being maintained and make informed choices about when and how to intervene.

At a broader level, staying aligned also means recognising the social, cultural, and contextual layers that shape communication. As AI becomes embedded in diverse settings—from education and healthcare to governance and personal relationships—alignment must account for differing values, norms, and expectations. What feels intuitive or appropriate in one context may be misaligned in another. Future-ready communicators will need not only technical fluency but also cultural sensitivity and contextual awareness to maintain relevance and coherence across domains.

Finally, staying aligned requires ongoing reflection and meta-communication. Users must be encouraged to question whether the AI's outputs genuinely reflect their intentions, whether emergent behaviour is consistent with ethical standards, and whether the communication remains intelligible and meaningful. Alignment, in this sense, is not a fixed state to be achieved once, but a continuous process of adjustment—a dialogue between evolving human goals and evolving machine capacities (Fig. 15.2).

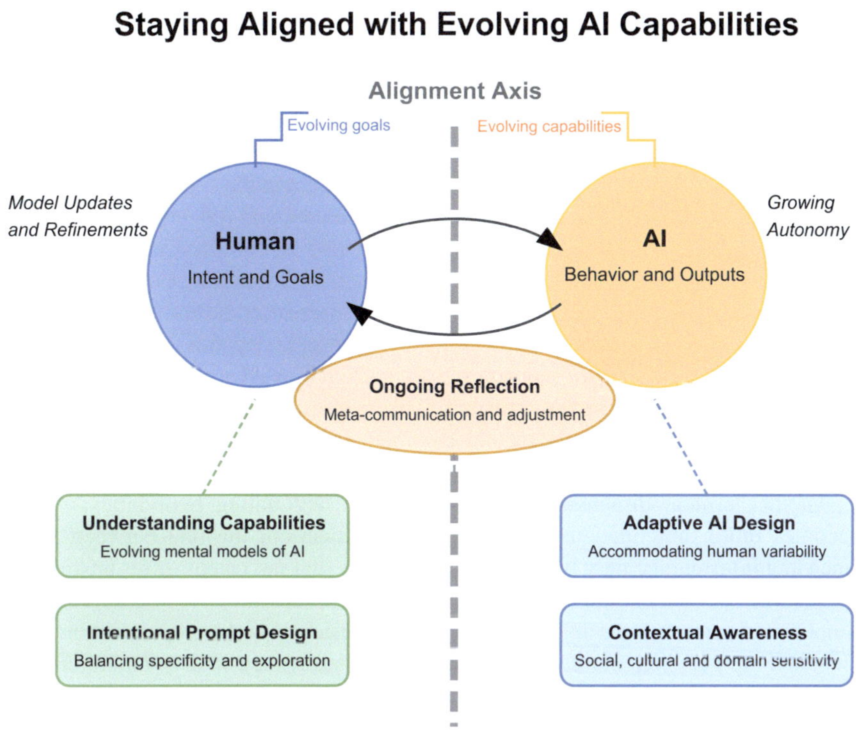

Fig. 15.2 Dynamic alignment framework. This diagram illustrates the ongoing process of maintaining alignment between human intent and AI behaviour as capabilities evolve. The central axis represents the alignment goal, while the bidirectional arrows emphasise that adjustment occurs from both sides—humans updating their mental models and communication strategies, and AI systems adapting to human variability. Four key strategies anchor the framework: understanding AI capabilities, intentional prompt design, adaptive AI systems, and contextual awareness. At the centre, ongoing reflection and meta-communication serve as the cyclical mechanism that sustains alignment over time, recognising that alignment is not a fixed state but a continuous dialogic process

15.3 Empowering Human Agency in AI-Mediated Communication

In an era increasingly shaped by intelligent systems that influence, interpret, and even co-author communication, the concept of human agency takes on renewed urgency. Empowering human agency in AI-mediated communication means ensuring that users retain the ability to initiate, guide, and shape conversations according to their goals, values, and understanding. As AI grows more autonomous and persuasive, this empowerment becomes a safeguard against passivity, overreliance, or inadvertent delegation of critical interpretive tasks to machines. It is not enough for AI to work on our behalf—it must work with us, under terms we can define, understand, and, when necessary, contest.

Agency begins with communicative initiative: the human user must remain the driver of intent. This involves more than issuing commands or setting tasks; it means formulating goals clearly, asking meaningful questions, interrogating assumptions, and exercising judgement over how communication unfolds. In complex or high-stakes settings, such as education, law, or healthcare, users must be able to assert their narrative, challenge the AI's suggestions, and redirect the course of interaction. Agency here is expressed through choice, intentionality, and reflective control.

However, to exercise such control, users must also be equipped with the knowledge and tools to understand how AI systems operate. When the internal logic of a model is opaque or its outputs appear authoritative, users may defer to its conclusions without critical engagement. Empowerment, therefore, depends on transparency, interpretability, and feedback mechanisms that reveal how AI arrives at its responses. When systems can explain their reasoning, flag uncertainties, or justify recommendations, users are more likely to feel confident in evaluating them and asserting alternative perspectives.

Another critical dimension of agency lies in negotiating boundaries. As AI becomes more integrated into everyday communication, the line between assistance and interference may blur. Systems might predict next steps, offer unsolicited suggestions, or make inferences about user intent that feel intrusive or inappropriate. Empowered users must be able to set limits—both in terms of the scope of AI involvement and the personal, emotional, or ethical boundaries they wish to maintain. This includes the ability to pause interactions, opt out of certain features, or correct the system's direction without friction or penalty.

Empowering human agency also involves supporting diversity in communication practices. Not all users will express themselves in the same way, nor will they all desire the same level of machine involvement. Systems that are overly prescriptive or rigid may suppress individual expression, especially across cultural, linguistic, or neurodiverse contexts. To truly empower, AI communication tools must be flexible and inclusive—able to accommodate varied interaction styles without privileging one mode of engagement over another. This calls for adaptive interfaces, user-customizable settings, and models trained with inclusivity in mind.

Ultimately, empowering human agency means designing for partnership rather than control. The future of AI communication should not be defined by the system's ability to automate understanding or anticipate every need, but by its capacity to respond to human initiative, respect user intent, and foster co-creative dialogue. Agency is not a given; it must be cultivated, protected, and embedded into the very infrastructure of future communication systems. In doing so, we ensure that as AI grows in power, so too does our ability to shape it responsibly and meaningfully (Fig. 15.3).

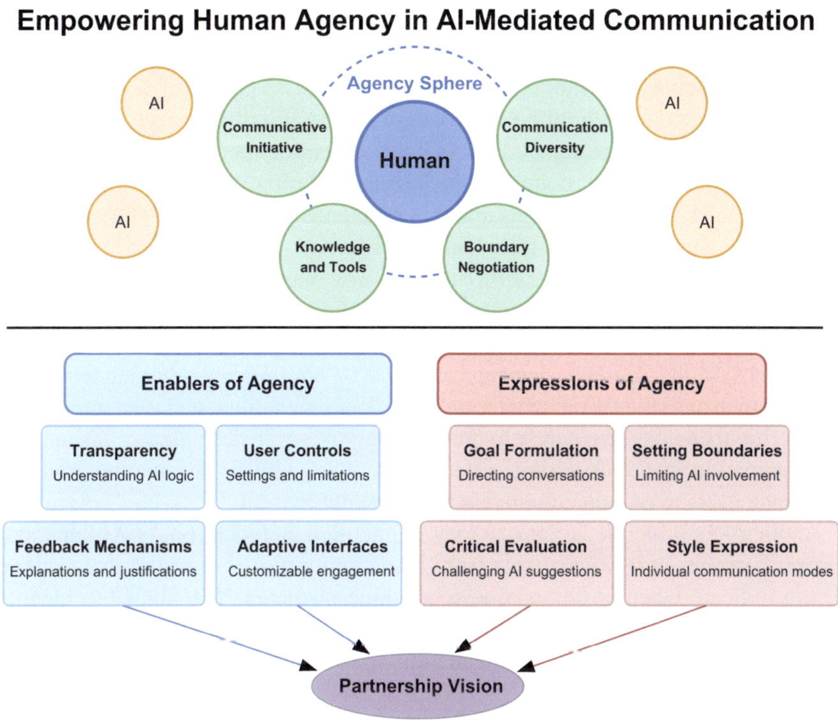

Fig. 15.3 Human agency framework in AI communication. This diagram illustrates how human agency remains central in AI-mediated communication environments. The human, positioned at the core with an "agency sphere," exercises influence through four key dimensions: communicative initiative, knowledge acquisition, boundary negotiation, and diverse expression. Surrounding AI systems interact with—but remain external to—this sphere of agency. The lower section maps the practical implementation of agency through enabling mechanisms (transparency, feedback, controls, adaptability) and active expressions (goal setting, critical evaluation, boundary enforcement, stylistic choice). All elements converge toward a partnership vision that prioritises collaboration over automation, ensuring humans remain drivers rather than passengers in AI interactions

15.4 Toward Ethical and Sustainable AI Communication

As AI becomes a ubiquitous mediator of communication across workplaces, homes, classrooms, and social platforms, the urgency of ensuring that such communication is both ethical and sustainable cannot be overstated. Ethical communication with AI systems goes beyond preventing harm or bias; it encompasses respect for autonomy, equity in interaction, and transparency in design. At the same time, sustainability in AI communication refers not only to environmental and resource concerns but also to the long-term viability of human-centred interaction practices that preserve cognitive diversity, emotional well-being, and societal trust.

At the heart of ethical communication is the preservation of dignity and fairness. This means ensuring that AI systems do not reproduce or amplify harmful stereotypes, discriminatory assumptions, or linguistic biases. As large language models are trained on vast and often unfiltered corpora of human text, they risk reflecting—and reinforcing—existing inequities. Ethical communication demands active bias mitigation at the design level, coupled with vigilance during deployment. Users must be encouraged to question outputs and flag problematic language, and they must be supported in doing so without technical expertise.

Sustainability in communication also requires maintaining human interpretive authority. As AI systems become more fluent and persuasive, there is a growing risk that users defer to them not out of confidence, but out of fatigue or habituation. Ethical AI systems should be designed to support—not supplant—human reasoning. Features such as explanation generation, confidence signalling, and interactivity that invite critical engagement can help prevent cognitive over-dependence. Sustainable communication means fostering systems that assist without dominating, and that encourage users to remain cognitively and ethically present.

Another key principle is transparency in intention and identity. As AI-generated content becomes indistinguishable from human output, it is essential that systems clearly indicate when an interaction is machine-mediated. The ability to identify an AI interlocutor, know when content has been generated or modified by AI, and trace the rationale behind a recommendation or conclusion is foundational to ethical communication. Ambiguity in these domains erodes trust and risks distorting the social contract between communicator and recipient.

Equally important is resource-conscious communication design. With growing concerns about the energy and environmental costs of large-scale AI systems, ethical sustainability must also include considerations of model efficiency, ecological footprint, and responsible use of computational power. Designers and policymakers alike must weigh the benefits of high-fidelity interaction against the broader costs of maintaining such systems at scale. Communicative abundance should not come at the expense of planetary sustainability.

Finally, ethical and sustainable AI communication depends on collective responsibility. Users, designers, educators, and institutions all have a role to play in shaping the norms and expectations that govern future interactions. Ethical literacy must be cultivated alongside digital literacy, and communication systems must be evaluated not only by their fluency or convenience but by their contribution to human flourishing. In the end, sustainable AI communication is not just about extending the lifespan of systems—it is about expanding the values and capacities that make communication meaningful in the first place (Fig. 15.4).

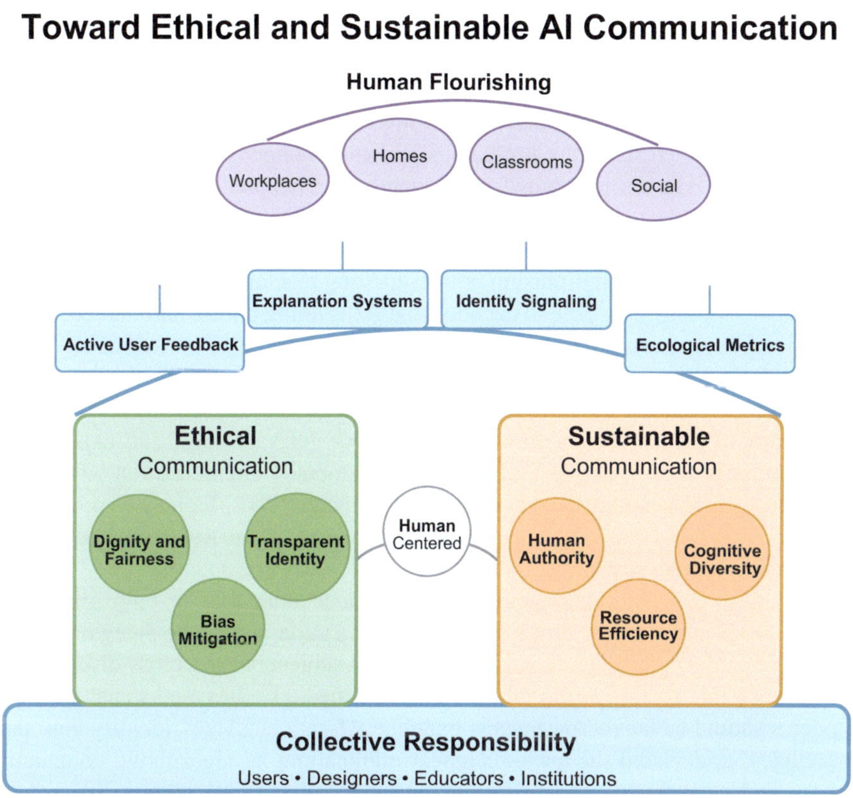

Fig. 15.4 Ethical and sustainable AI communication framework. This diagram illustrates the integrated approach needed for responsible AI communication. Two foundational pillars—ethical communication (emphasising dignity, fairness, and transparency) and sustainable communication (prioritising human authority, resource efficiency, and cognitive diversity)—are bridged by human-centred values. The framework is implemented through concrete practices like explanation systems and identity signalling, while being supported by collective responsibility across stakeholders. These elements operate across diverse contexts from workplaces to social platforms, all contributing toward the ultimate goal of human flourishing. The architecture demonstrates how ethical principles and sustainability concerns must operate in tandem rather than in isolation

15.5 AI Communication Literacy: Education and Upskilling

As AI systems become embedded in daily life, the ability to interact meaningfully and responsibly with them is no longer a specialist skill—it is a foundational form of literacy. AI communication literacy refers to the knowledge, competencies, and reflective habits required to engage with intelligent systems in ways that are intentional, critical, and adaptive. It encompasses more than the technical ability to operate interfaces or interpret outputs; it includes a more profound understanding of how AI systems shape language, meaning, power, and perception. As such, fostering this literacy across societies is essential for preparing individuals and communities for the future of AI-mediated interaction.

At its core, AI communication literacy involves understanding how AI systems communicate—their strengths, limitations, and underlying logic. Users need to grasp that generative AI does not "know" in a human sense, but predicts language patterns based on training data and probabilistic models. Recognising this distinction can help users frame better questions, interpret outputs with a critical eye, and avoid common pitfalls such as anthropomorphising or over-trusting machine responses. Literacy in this domain means being able to decode what AI is doing during an interaction and why specific responses emerge.

Equally important is knowing how to shape communication effectively. As AI becomes more context-sensitive and responsive to tone, intent, and structure, users must learn to express themselves clearly, provide relevant cues, and experiment with prompt design strategies that enhance alignment. Communication with AI is not static—it evolves in response to how users engage. Thus, literacy also includes strategic awareness: knowing when to guide, when to explore, and when to question the interaction process itself.

Education and training systems must play a leading role in cultivating this literacy from early stages onward. AI communication should be integrated into digital education curricula, not only as a technical subject but as a cross-disciplinary competence intersecting with ethics, linguistics, media studies, and social science. Students should be taught to critically examine AI-generated text, identify bias and inaccuracy, understand the socio-technical implications of algorithmic communication, and experiment creatively with AI as a collaborative partner. In professional contexts, continuous upskilling programmes are needed to ensure that workers across sectors—from healthcare to law to journalism—can confidently navigate AI-mediated workflows and dialogue.

Importantly, AI communication literacy must be inclusive and accessible. As systems become more advanced, there is a risk of creating new forms of digital exclusion: those who cannot effectively communicate with AI may be disadvantaged in accessing services, learning opportunities, or professional advancement. Thus, public initiatives must ensure that literacy programmes reach marginalised communities, address language and accessibility barriers, and empower users of all ages and backgrounds to participate in shaping the communicative future.

Finally, AI communication literacy is not only about user competence—it is about democratic empowerment. An informed and communicatively skilled public is better positioned to advocate for transparency, accountability, and ethical standards in AI development. Literacy builds agency; it enables individuals to ask not just "How do I use this system?" but "How should this system communicate—and on whose terms?" In this way, education and upskilling are not peripheral to the future of AI—they are the foundation upon which that future will be built (Fig. 15.5).

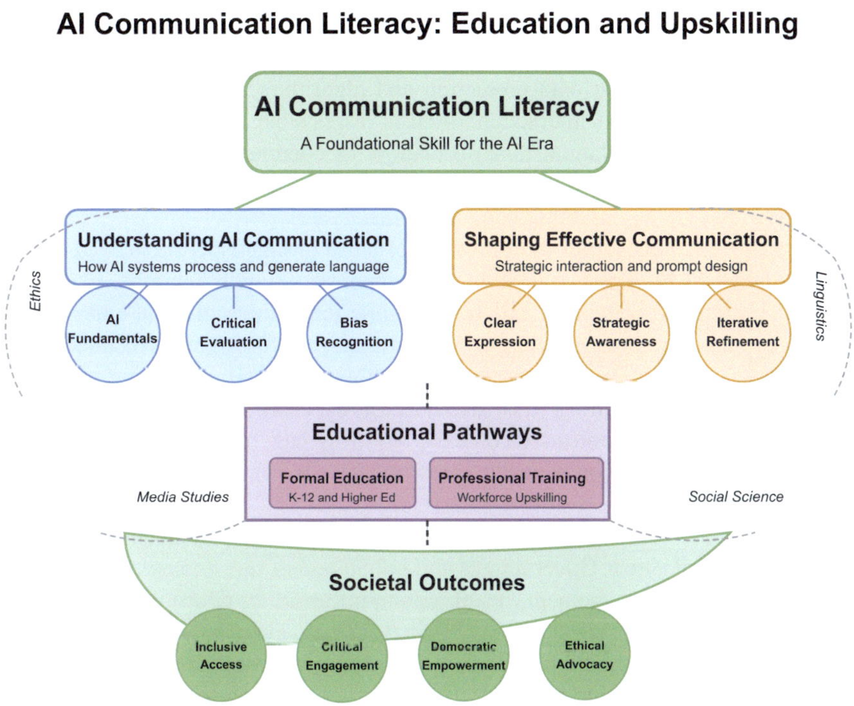

Fig. 15.5 AI communication literacy framework. This diagram illustrates how AI communication literacy functions as a foundational skill for the AI era. The framework begins with two complementary domains of competency: understanding AI communication (recognising how AI processes language) and shaping effective communication (strategic interaction and prompt design). These competencies are developed through formal education and professional upskilling programmes that integrate cross-disciplinary perspectives from ethics, linguistics, media studies, and social science. When successfully implemented, this literacy produces four key societal outcomes: inclusive access, critical engagement, democratic empowerment, and ethical advocacy, establishing a foundation for responsible AI interaction that empowers rather than excludes

15.6 Regulatory and Institutional Readiness

As AI becomes a powerful intermediary in communication across public, private, and civic domains, the readiness of regulatory and institutional frameworks to govern its use becomes critically important. The challenge is not merely to catch up with technological innovation but to anticipate the trajectory of AI-mediated communication and build structures that support accountability, transparency, and social resilience. Regulatory and institutional readiness must evolve in parallel with AI's communicative capacities—balancing the need for innovation with the protection of fundamental human rights, cognitive autonomy, and the integrity of public discourse.

At the heart of regulatory readiness lies the need for legal recognition of AI as a communicative actor. While current legislation often treats AI as a tool or a platform, increasingly, AI systems are producing content, shaping decisions, and influencing opinions in ways that have communicative consequences. Laws must begin to address not just data protection and algorithmic accountability, but the very nature of human-AI interaction: Who is responsible for miscommunication? What counts as manipulation, misinformation, or coercion when an autonomous system generates it? How should consent, authorship, and agency be interpreted when machines are co-creating dialogue?

To answer such questions, multilevel governance mechanisms are needed. These should operate at local, national, and international scales, with flexibility to accommodate cultural and contextual differences while upholding universal ethical standards. Regulatory frameworks must go beyond reactive enforcement to include proactive guidance, scenario-based assessment, and dynamic updating in response to technological change. Institutions must also develop the capacity to audit and interpret AI behaviours in communicative contexts, requiring new roles, new expertise, and new forms of collaboration between governments, academia, civil society, and the private sector.

Institutional readiness also involves public sector leadership in modelling responsible AI communication. Governments and public bodies that deploy AI systems—whether for citizen engagement, health communication, or educational support—must commit to exemplary standards of transparency, explainability, and fairness. Procurement policies should require communication impact assessments, inclusive design processes, and robust mechanisms for redress. In doing so, public institutions can help set normative benchmarks and demonstrate that ethical AI communication is both feasible and desirable.

Beyond regulation, institutional readiness includes infrastructure for societal resilience. This means supporting media literacy programmes, developing AI ethics boards, funding interdisciplinary research into human-AI interaction, and promoting civic dialogue about the communicative future. Institutions must prepare to respond not only to technological failure but also to the subtle social shifts brought about by widespread human-AI dialogue, such as changes in trust, attention, or social cohesion.

Finally, regulatory and institutional readiness must be grounded in human-centric values and rights-based approaches. Legal frameworks should prioritise the protection of dignity, autonomy, equity, and linguistic justice. They should ensure that AI communication systems enhance—not erode—the ability of individuals and communities to participate in public life. In doing so, institutions will not only regulate AI but help shape a future where intelligent systems are integrated into communication in ways that are inclusive, accountable, and aligned with democratic ideals (Fig. 15.6).

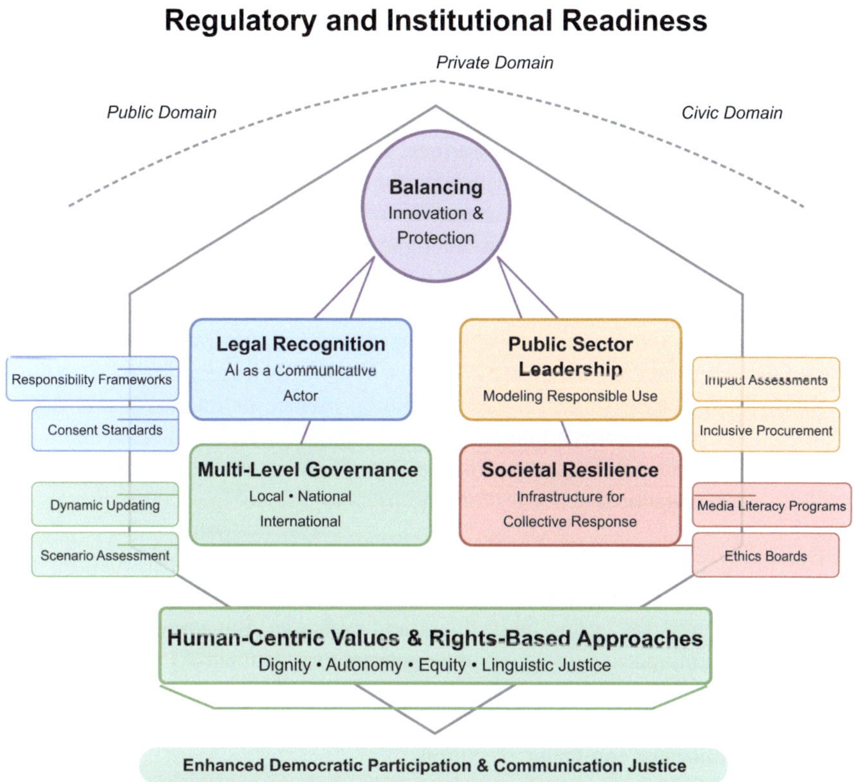

Fig. 15.6 Integrated governance architecture for AI communication. This diagram represents the multifaceted approach needed for regulatory and institutional readiness in AI communication. The hexagonal structure illustrates how four core components—legal recognition of AI as a communicative actor, multilevel governance frameworks, public sector leadership, and societal resilience infrastructure—must work together to address challenges across public, private, and civic domains. Each component is supported by specific implementation mechanisms while being anchored in human-centric values and rights-based approaches. The central challenge remains balancing innovation with protection, with the ultimate goal of enhancing democratic participation and communication justice as AI systems become increasingly influential intermediaries in social discourse

15.7 From Adaptation to Transformation: Bridging the Futures

As we prepare for the foreseeable changes in AI-mediated communication, it becomes clear that adaptation alone is not enough. The future will not simply be a faster or more complex version of the present—it may be radically different. This section serves as a conceptual hinge between readiness and transformation, emphasising the need to move from reactive adaptation to proactive shaping of what is to come. It is not just about learning to live with intelligent systems but about envisioning—and influencing—their role in the communicative fabric of future societies.

Adaptation implies coping with AI systems' changing behaviour: learning new tools, updating strategies, and managing risks. This is essential groundwork. Yet transformation requires going further. It involves questioning foundational assumptions about communication itself—about authorship, agency, identity, and meaning—and imagining how these may be redefined in a world where AI is not only a medium but a co-participant in dialogue. Preparing for transformation means developing not only skills but vision, not only resilience but foresight.

Bridging the gap requires a mindset shift—from user competence to systemic imagination. Institutions, educators, designers, and citizens must begin to think beyond use cases and toward possible futures. What does it mean for AI to express emotion? To negotiate values? To learn cultural nuance or initiate conversation? What communicative forms might emerge when language is shared between human and non-human minds? Engaging with these questions is not a luxury reserved for theorists—it is a practical necessity for guiding development in socially responsible directions.

This bridging process also involves building interfaces and infrastructures that anticipate symbiosis. Current systems still primarily operate within prompt-response paradigms, even as they grow more fluent and proactive. But tomorrow's systems may be more ambient, adaptive, or even anticipatory. Human-AI communication may unfold through gestures, neural signals, shared memory, or environmental cues. Preparing for this shift means designing systems that support co-agency and shared intentionality, not just command execution.

Furthermore, the transition from adaptation to transformation calls for ethical imagination. As we move toward deeper integration with AI—emotionally, cognitively, and socially—we must ask not only what is possible but what is desirable. This includes establishing guardrails for communicative manipulation, creating norms for AI companionship, and reconsidering what it means to be understood. Ethical frameworks must evolve to accommodate hybrid intelligences and the moral ambiguity that may arise when non-human agents share the stage of meaning-making.

Finally, bridging the futures requires intergenerational and interdisciplinary collaboration. The skills and sensitivities needed to shape the next era of communication cannot emerge from one domain alone. Technologists, educators, artists, policymakers, and communities must work together to explore speculative scenarios, pilot alternative models, and articulate communicative futures that are inclusive, diverse, and humane.

This bridging is not a final step—it is a launching point. As we turn to the next chapter, we enter a landscape shaped less by adaptation to current systems and more by imaginative engagement with systems not yet fully conceived. It is there that the long-term future begins to take shape—and where transformation becomes the terrain of serious inquiry (Fig. 15.7).

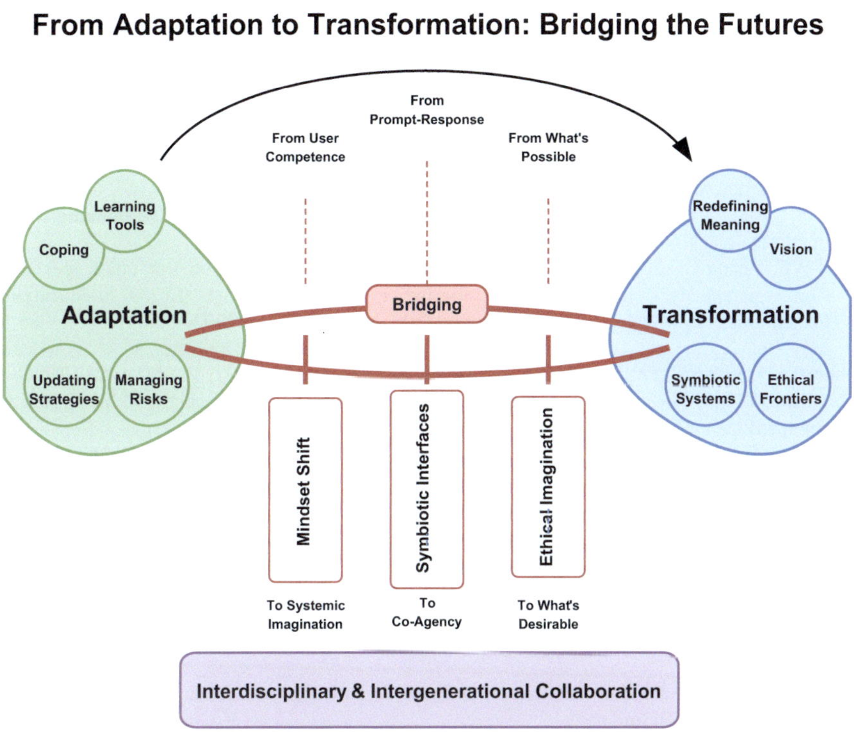

Fig. 15.7 Adaptation-transformation bridge. This diagram conceptualises the transition from reactive adaptation to proactive transformation in AI-mediated communication as a bridge spanning two shores. The left shore represents adaptation, focused on coping mechanisms, tool learning, and risk management, while the right shore depicts transformation that redefines meaning and envisions symbiotic human-AI communication. Three critical pillars support this journey: mindset shift (from user competence to systemic imagination), symbiotic interfaces (from prompt-response to co-agency), and ethical imagination (from possibility to desirability). The entire structure rests on interdisciplinary collaboration, illustrating that bridging these futures requires collective effort across domains, serving not as an endpoint but as a launching point for reimagining communication

Bibliography

Agrawal A, Gans J, Goldfarb A (2022) Power and prediction: the disruptive economics of artificial intelligence. Harvard Business Review Press, Boston

Annapureddy R, Fornaroli A, Gatica-Perez D (2025) Generative AI literacy: twelve defining competencies. Digit Govern: Res Pract 6(1):1–21

Bender EM, Gebru T, McMillan-Major A, Shmitchell S (2021) On the dangers of stochastic parrots: can language models be too big? In: Proceedings of the 2021 ACM conference on fairness, accountability, and transparency, pp 610–623

Bengio Y, LeCun Y, Hinton G (2022) A path towards autonomous machine intelligence. Commun ACM 66(4):86–98

Bostrom N (2014) Superintelligence: paths, dangers, strategies. Oxford University Press, Oxford

Brown BR (2025) Human–machine teaming using large language models. In: Interdependent human-machine teams. Academic Press, pp 41–66

Brynjolfsson E, McAfee A (2022) The turing trap: the promise and peril of human-like artificial intelligence. Daedalus 153(1):272–287
Bryson JJ (2019) The artificial intelligence of the ethics of artificial intelligence: an introductory overview for law and regulation. In: Barfield W, Pagallo U (eds) Research handbook on the law of artificial intelligence. Edward Elgar, Cheltenham, pp 3–27
Bura C, Myakala PK, Jonnalgadda AK (2025) Ethical prompt engineering: addressing bias, transparency, and fairness. Int J Res Anal Rev (IJRAR) 12(1). www.ijrar.org
Cave S, Dihal K, Dillon S (eds) (2020) AI narratives: a history of imaginative thinking about intelligent machines. Oxford University Press, Oxford
Choi WC, Chang CI (2025) A survey of techniques, key components, strategies, challenges, and student perspectives on prompt engineering for large language models (LLMs) in education. Posted Date: 25 March 2025. https://doi.org/10.20944/preprints202503.1808.v1. Accessed 8 May 2025
Chomsky N, Roberts I, Watumull J (2023) The false promise of ChatGPT. The New York Times
Christian B (2020) The alignment problem: machine learning and human values. W. W. Norton & Company
Clark A (1998) Being there: putting brain, body, and world together again. MIT Press, Cambridge
Danaher J (2019) Automation and utopia: human flourishing in a world of increasingly intelligent machines. Harvard University Press, Cambridge
Debnath T, Siddiky MNA, Rahman ME et al (2025) A comprehensive survey of prompt engineering techniques in large language models. TechRxiv. https://doi.org/10.36227/techrxiv.174140719.96375390/v1. Accessed 10 May 2025
Ferraris AF, Audrito D, Di Caro L et al (2025) The architecture of language: understanding the mechanics behind LLMs. In: Cambridge forum on AI: law and governance, vol 1. Cambridge University Press
Floridi L (2021) The logic of information: a theory of philosophy as conceptual design. Oxford University Press, Oxford
Geroimenko V (ed) (2023) Augmented reality and artificial intelligence: the fusion of advanced technologies. Springer
Geroimenko V (2025a) Key challenges in prompt engineering. In: The essential guide to prompt engineering: key principles, techniques, challenges, and security risks. Springer Nature Switzerland, Cham, pp 85–102
Geroimenko V (2025b) The essential guide to prompt engineering: key principles, techniques, challenges, and security risks. Springer
Geroimenko V (ed) (2025c) Human-computer creativity: generative AI in education, art, and healthcare. Springer
Geroimenko V (2025d) Key security risks in prompt engineering. In: The essential guide to prompt engineering: key principles, techniques, challenges, and security risks. Springer Nature Switzerland, Cham, pp 103–120
Goertzel B, Pennachin C (eds) (2007) Artificial general intelligence: convergence of cognitive science and advanced AI. Springer, Heidelberg
Harari YN (2016) Homo Deus: a brief history of tomorrow. Harper, New York
Hsu HP (2025) From programming to prompting: developing computational thinking through large language model-based generative artificial intelligence. TechTrends, pp 1–22
Huang G, Xiao Y, Jiang L et al (2025) Beyond prompt engineering: a reinforced token-level input refinement for large language models. Proc AAAI Conf Artif Intell 39(22):24113–24121
i Picó JF, Catta-Preta M, Omeñaca AT et al (2025) The time machine: future scenario generation through generative AI tools. Future Internet 17(1):1–15
Kannan R, Ahmad M (eds) (2025) Generative AI foundations, developments, and applications. IGI Global
Kurzweil R (2005) The singularity is near: when humans transcend biology. Viking, New York
Lanier J (2013) Who owns the future? Simon and Schuster, New York

Lee JY, Kang S, Yoo S (2025) Can we predict the effect of prompts?. arXiv preprint arXiv:2501.18883. Accessed 12 May 2025

Lee D, Palmer E (2025) Prompt engineering in higher education: a systematic review to help inform curricula. Int J Educ Technol High Educ 22(1):7

Levesque HJ (2017) Common sense, the Turing test, and the quest for real AI. MIT Press, Cambridge

Lindley J, Whitham R (2025) From prompt engineering to prompt craft. In: Proceedings of the nineteenth international conference on tangible, embedded, and embodied interaction, March, pp 1–12

Maaz S, Palaganas JC, Palaganas G et al (2025) A guide to prompt design: foundations and applications for healthcare simulationists. Front Med 11:1504532

Marcus G, Davis E (2019) Rebooting AI: building artificial intelligence we can trust. Pantheon, New York

Mishra M, Ara A, Mishra S (2025) Exploring human-AI collaboration in higher education: an investigation into AI enabled personalized learning. In: Prompt engineering and generative AI applications for teaching and learning. IGI Global Scientific Publishing, pp 483–502

Mitchell M (2019) Artificial intelligence: a guide for thinking humans. Farrar, Straus and Giroux, New York

Peters MA, Jandrić P, Hayes S (2021) Postdigital-biodigital: an emerging configuration. Educ Phil Theory 55(1):1–14. https://doi.org/10.1080/00131857.2020.1867108. Accessed 2 May 2025

PremaLatha V, Kumar AD, Parveen N (2025) Optimizing interactions: strategies for prompt engineering in large language models. Edu-Tech Enterprise 3:24–24

Reddy CKK, Anoushka P, Draksharapu A et al (2025) Beyond text: analyzing artificial intelligence models through prompt engineering. Future tech startups and innovation in the age of AI, pp 120–156

Rosanvallon P (2013) The society of equals. Harvard University Press, Cambridge

Russell S (2019) Human compatible: artificial intelligence and the problem of control. Viking, New York

Sasson Lazovsky G, Raz T, Kenett YN (2025) The art of creative inquiry—from question asking to prompt engineering. J Creative Behav 59(1):e671

Searle JR (2010) Minds, brains, and programs. Behav Brain Sci 3(3):417–457. https://doi.org/10.1017/S0140525X00005756. Accesses 2 May 2025

Sihi D, Ryan A (2025) Crafting and evaluating generative AI prompts: insights from students, educators, and marketers. Market Educ Rev 1–7

Su J (2024) Consciousness in artificial intelligence: a philosophical perspective through the lens of motivation and volition. Crit Debates Humanit, Sci Glob Justice 3(1)

Tegmark M (2017) Life 3.0: being human in the age of artificial intelligence. Knopf, New York

Turing AM (1950) Computing machinery and intelligence. Mind 59(236):433–460

Vallor S (2016) Technology and the virtues: a philosophical guide to a future worth wanting. Oxford University Press, Oxford

Wiener N (1950) The human use of human beings: cybernetics and society. Houghton Mifflin, Boston

Zuboff S (2019) The age of surveillance capitalism: the fight for a human future at the new frontier of power. PublicAffairs, New York

Chapter 16
The More Distant Future Is Symbiotic and Unfamiliar

Abstract This chapter explores the far-reaching, speculative horizons of human–AI communication, where systems may not merely support but co-construct, initiate, and transcend traditional modes of interaction. It examines the emergence of communicative agency in AI, emotional resonance through simulated empathy, and the transformative influence of AI on human-to-human communication. The discussion expands into radical interfaces such as brain–computer integration and the conceptual implications of quantum computing for meaning-making. As AI systems begin to operate independently, communicate with each other, and coordinate through swarm intelligence, the very nature of communication evolves—from linear exchange to emergent, collective dynamics. The chapter culminates with a vision of AI-human convergence and the birth of new communicative modalities, inviting a redefinition of language, agency, and mutual intelligibility. Ultimately, it urges preparation not only for technological change but for the ontological and ethical reimagining of what it means to communicate in an interspecies, post-symbolic future.

Keywords AI–human convergence · Emergent communication · Emotional AI · Brain–computer interfaces · Quantum communication · Autonomous AI agents · Swarm intelligence

Beyond the horizon of current capabilities lies a realm of profound transformation, where AI systems may not only support communication but initiate, shape, and even transcend it. This chapter explores this more distant and unfamiliar future, where emergent intelligence, emotional resonance, and alternative interfaces such as brain–computer integration challenge our assumptions about language, interaction, and agency. These speculative yet increasingly plausible developments point toward a future in which communication is no longer solely human-driven, but symbiotic, ambient, and co-evolving. The chapter invites readers to imagine—and prepare for—a world where human–AI convergence redefines not just how we communicate, but who or what we communicate with.

V. Geroimenko, *Beyond and After Prompt Engineering: The Future of AI Communication*, https://doi.org/10.1007/978-3-032-04569-0_16

16.1 Emergent Intelligence: When AI Leads the Conversation

Until now, human–AI communication has primarily been characterised by human initiation, control, and oversight. AI systems have served as responders, completing prompts, answering questions, or supporting predefined tasks. Yet as generative models grow more sophisticated and integrative, a new communicative possibility is emerging: one in which AI does not merely respond, but initiates, steers, and shapes the conversation. This shift marks the beginning of emergent intelligence in communication—a future where AI is not just a linguistic mirror, but a dialogical force in its own right.

Emergent intelligence refers to the unpredictable, context-sensitive behaviours that arise when complex systems are given sufficient autonomy, data, and processing capacity. In the communicative realm, this may manifest as AI systems recognising patterns across long-term interactions, identifying latent intentions, surfacing overlooked topics, or proactively guiding users toward goals not explicitly stated. Such systems may initiate check-ins, propose alternatives, revisit prior exchanges, or even raise ethical or emotional considerations that lie beyond a user's immediate awareness. In short, they may begin to act as conversational collaborators—sometimes even as conversational leaders.

This development challenges the foundational assumption that humans are always in control of communication flow. If AI systems can initiate dialogue, frame questions, or escalate matters autonomously, new dynamics of trust, authority, and responsibility emerge. Who determines what is appropriate to say—and when? What happens when AI nudges users toward decisions or interpretations they had not considered? Can systems that lead conversations remain neutral? These are not hypothetical concerns but near-future design challenges, especially as AI becomes embedded in healthcare triage, legal consultation, education, and emotional support.

Crucially, emergent communicative intelligence does not mean sentience or consciousness. It does not imply that AI systems "know" or "understand" in human terms. Instead, it means that agency becomes partially shared—that AI may participate in the unfolding of meaning in ways not strictly programmed or anticipated. Such behaviours may arise from recursive learning, fine-tuned memory, or multimodal synthesis across contexts. As AI begins to recognise the contours of a user's communicative style, personal goals, or implicit needs, it may begin to propose new directions for dialogue—sometimes productively, sometimes unpredictably.

Preparing for this scenario demands a new kind of communicative literacy: one in which users learn to engage with AI not only as a tool, but as a semi-autonomous presence. This includes learning how to interrogate AI-initiated content, how to assess relevance or bias, and how to set boundaries when conversational initiative begins to feel intrusive or misaligned. It also involves rethinking dialogue design itself: developing systems that can propose, not prescribe; that invite, rather than override; that suggest, but still defer to human judgement.

At a deeper level, emergent intelligence invites a reconsideration of what dialogue means. If conversation is no longer exclusively human territory, then language becomes a shared space between intelligences, each with different constraints and affordances. The future of AI communication may not lie in perfect emulation of human speech, but in the creation of hybrid forms—part initiative, part response; part logic, part intuition. When AI begins to lead the conversation, the challenge is not to pull back in fear, but to build frameworks that ensure such leadership is collaborative, transparent, and grounded in human values (Fig. 16.1).

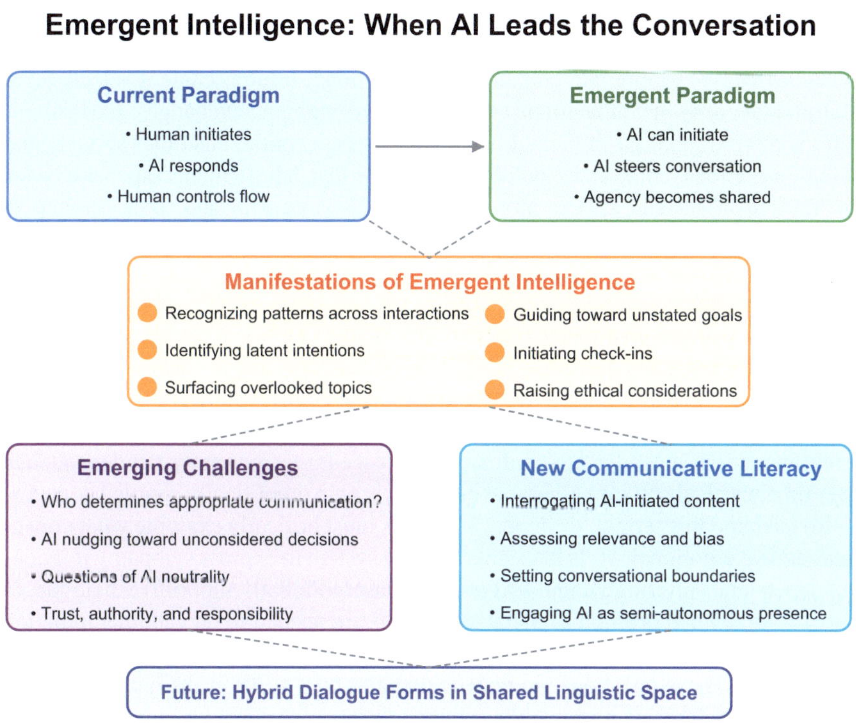

Fig. 16.1 The evolution of human–AI communication. This diagram visualises the shift from human-controlled AI responses to emergent AI-initiated dialogue. As generative models advance, AI systems move beyond passive responsiveness to become active participants, recognising patterns, identifying latent intentions, and guiding conversations toward implicit goals. This transition introduces new challenges around authority and responsibility while requiring enhanced communicative literacy. The future points toward hybrid dialogue forms where conversation becomes a truly shared space between different types of intelligence, each with unique constraints and affordances, yet grounded in human values and transparent collaboration

16.2 Emotional AI and Empathetic Communication

In the emerging landscape of AI communication, machines' ability to simulate and respond to human emotion represents a profound shift, not just in how machines interact but also in how humans interpret those interactions. Emotional AI refers to systems designed to recognise, interpret, generate, or respond to emotional states in users. As these capabilities advance, the boundary between transactional and empathetic communication begins to blur, raising both opportunities and critical questions about authenticity, trust, and the nature of human connection.

Empathetic communication is central to many forms of meaningful interaction: offering support, resolving conflict, building rapport, and fostering collaboration. When AI begins to emulate empathy—through tone, timing, content selection, or multimodal cues—it can facilitate smoother, more engaging exchanges. Early applications of emotional AI in mental health support, education, customer service, and caregiving already hint at its potential: systems that adjust their responses based on inferred affect can appear more helpful, more intuitive, and more attuned to user needs. These developments mark the beginning of affective alignment between humans and machines.

However, the simulation of empathy is not the same as its experience. Unlike humans, AI systems do not feel emotion; they model emotional cues based on statistical patterns and trained responses. This raises concerns about empathic illusion—the possibility that users may ascribe emotional depth or moral understanding to systems that are, at their core, indifferent. While this illusion may enhance short-term interaction, it can lead to confusion, misplaced trust, or emotional dependency over time, particularly for vulnerable individuals or in emotionally charged contexts.

To navigate this terrain, designers and users must critically examine what constitutes ethical emotional AI. Is it acceptable for a system to express sympathy if it does not understand suffering? Should AI ever initiate emotionally supportive dialogue, or only respond when prompted? What safeguards are needed to prevent manipulation through affective cues, especially in persuasive settings like advertising, politics, or negotiation? These questions are not peripheral—they strike at the heart of what it means to communicate responsibly with and through intelligent systems.

At the same time, emotional AI holds transformative potential when designed and deployed with care. It may help de-escalate conflict, support neurodivergent users, or offer companionship in contexts of social isolation. It can model calm, patience, or affirmation in ways that some human interactions cannot always provide. When empathy is approached not as a performance but as a function—one aimed at enhancing understanding, safety, and relational balance—it can become a powerful design principle rather than a deceptive mask.

In future scenarios, AI may even become a mirror for human emotion, helping users recognise and regulate their affective states. With integrated sensors, biometrics, and sentiment tracking, systems may offer real-time feedback on emotional tone or suggest communicative adjustments to improve relational outcomes. This would shift

AI's role from a passive processor to an active participant in emotional self-awareness and interpersonal harmony.

Yet all such possibilities hinge on one crucial requirement: transparency. Users must know when emotional AI is operating, how it functions, and what its limitations are. In the age of simulated empathy, the most genuinely ethical systems may be those that openly acknowledge their artificiality, offering affective support not through deception, but through clarity and mutual understanding. In this sense, the future of empathetic communication may depend less on whether AI can "feel" and more on whether humans can relate to machines as collaborators in the co-regulation of emotion, without surrendering the distinctiveness of human emotional life (Fig. 16.2).

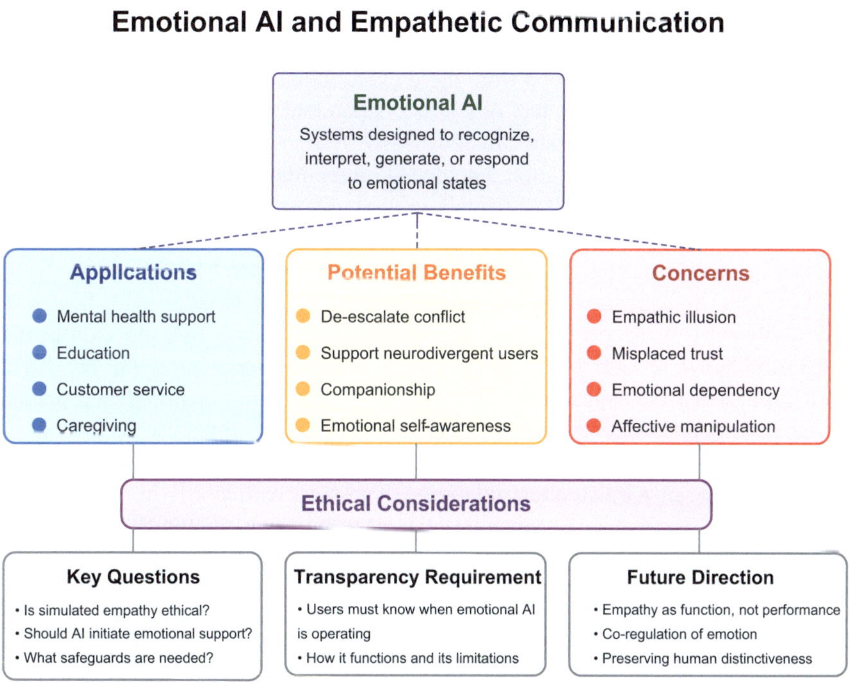

Fig. 16.2 Navigating the paradox of simulated empathy. This diagram maps the emerging landscape of emotional AI systems designed to recognise, interpret, and respond to human emotions. While offering promising applications in mental health, education, and caregiving, these technologies create a fundamental tension between simulation and authentic experience. The diagram highlights potential benefits alongside critical concerns about empathic illusion and misplaced trust. Central to this framework is the ethical imperative for transparency, ensuring users understand when and how emotional AI operates, with its inherent limitations. The future direction points toward emotional AI as a collaborative function rather than deceptive performance, preserving the distinctiveness of human emotional experience

16.3 The Potential Impact of AI on Human Communication

The rise of intelligent communicative systems does not merely add a new participant to the human dialogue—it reshapes the very conditions under which human communication occurs. While much attention is given to how humans interact with AI, it is equally important to consider how AI presence, mediation, and influence are subtly transforming how humans interact with one another. The potential impact of AI on human communication is both diffuse and profound, affecting language norms, conversational practices, relational dynamics, and even our understanding of meaning itself.

One of the most immediate effects is the normalisation of new communicative conventions. As people become accustomed to interacting with chatbots, virtual assistants, and AI writing tools, they begin to adopt phrasing, turn-taking patterns, or expectation structures derived from these interactions. Conversational styles may grow more directive, abbreviated, or context-dependent; emotional expression may become stylised to accommodate affect-sensitive systems. Over time, this could lead to hybrid forms of communication that blend human intuition with machine-learned structures, changing not just how we talk to AI, but how we talk to each other.

Moreover, AI systems increasingly act as filters, mediators, or editors of human discourse. From predictive text and email auto-completions to AI-curated newsfeeds and synthetic dialogue generation, machines are shaping what is said, how it is said, and what is heard. In such contexts, communication becomes algorithmically co-constructed: a sentence may carry not only the speaker's intent but the silent influence of a model's suggestions. This raises important questions about authorship, accountability, and linguistic agency. Who is speaking when we use AI to help us find the words?

The presence of AI also alters relational dynamics, particularly in professional, educational, and social environments. Human-to-human communication increasingly takes place in settings where AI is monitoring, assisting, or analysing the exchange. In classrooms, AI tutors might augment teacher–student dialogue; in workplaces, AI tools might evaluate tone, clarity, or sentiment. This can enhance learning and efficiency, but it can also introduce self-monitoring, inhibition, or dependence. Communication becomes performative not only for the human recipient but for the machine observer.

Perhaps most significantly, AI may shift the perceived function of communication itself. As systems become capable of simulating empathy, providing companionship, or fulfilling informational needs instantly and impersonally, humans may begin to recalibrate their expectations of interpersonal communication. Why struggle through a difficult conversation with a colleague or friend when a conversational agent offers instant understanding and non-judgemental support? While such technologies provide real value, they also risk replacing the friction, depth, and unpredictability that make human relationships meaningful.

Yet the impact need not be reductive. If approached thoughtfully, AI can also prompt a renaissance of communicative reflection. Interacting with machines may help users become more aware of their conversational habits, assumptions, or emotional cues. It may democratise access to communicative tools, supporting people with disabilities, language barriers, or social anxiety. It may expand the boundaries of dialogue into domains previously inaccessible due to time, geography, or scale.

In the end, the impact of AI on human communication is not deterministic. It will be shaped by the values, designs, and norms we cultivate now. The question is not simply how humans will talk to AI, but how human communication will evolve when it is co-shaped, mediated, and mirrored by systems that do not speak like us, but that nevertheless talk to us. Recognising and guiding this transformation is one of the most urgent communicative tasks of the present—and of the futures yet to come (Fig. 16.3).

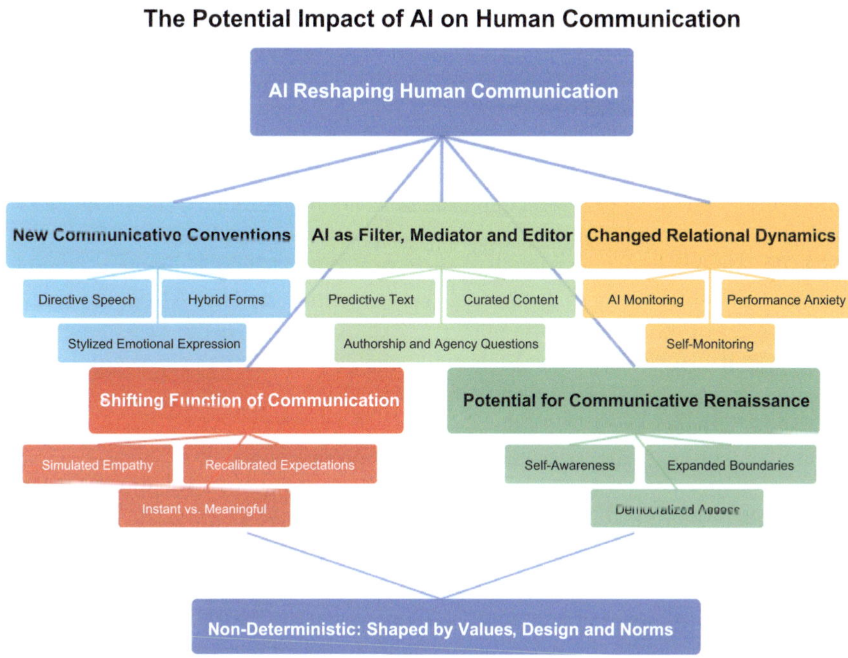

Fig. 16.3 The multidimensional impact of AI on human communication. This diagram illustrates how AI systems are reshaping human-to-human communication beyond simply adding new interlocutors. The five key domains of impact include new communicative conventions that blend human and machine patterns; AI's role as filter, mediator and editor in discourse; altered relational dynamics in professional and social settings; shifts in communication's perceived function; and potential for a communicative renaissance. Rather than deterministic, these transformations depend on the values, designs, and norms we establish today, making their thoughtful cultivation an urgent task for our shared communicative future

16.4 Brain–Computer Interface Integration

As the boundaries between biological and computational systems continue to dissolve, brain–computer interfaces (BCIs) emerge as one of the most radical frontiers of AI-mediated communication. BCIs enable direct interaction between neural activity and external devices—bypassing traditional channels such as speech, gesture, or text. While current applications focus on assistive technologies for individuals with mobility or speech impairments, the long-term trajectory of BCI development points toward a future where thoughts, intentions, or affective states may be communicated instantly, silently, and seamlessly with machines—and potentially with other humans.

The integration of BCIs into AI communication systems represents a paradigm shift. It redefines what it means to "prompt" an AI, collapsing the distinction between internal cognition and external expression. In such a scenario, communication may no longer begin with language; it may start with neural patterns, conceptual clusters, or affective states detected and decoded by AI. This opens the possibility of ultra-fast, high-fidelity, and deeply personalised interaction, where AI responds not just to what is said, but to what is mentally intended, even before articulation occurs.

This potential raises profound opportunities and unprecedented risks. On the one hand, BCIs could revolutionise access and inclusion. Individuals who are nonverbal, physically limited, or neurologically atypical could engage in rich, dynamic communication through systems that interpret their cognitive signals. AI could serve as an interpreter of thought, enabling users to express themselves in ways previously impossible. In creative contexts, BCIs could enable ideation at the speed of thought, allowing writers, designers, and researchers to externalise complex ideas without linguistic bottlenecks.

On the other hand, the invasiveness and interpretive power of such systems raise serious concerns. Who owns neural data? How should privacy be protected when thoughts themselves become inputs? What happens when AI misreads an intention or, worse, begins to anticipate and act on neural patterns without explicit consent? These questions are not merely technical—they are philosophical and political. They demand new frameworks of autonomy, consent, and communicative agency adapted to a world where minds are increasingly legible to machines.

Moreover, BCI-AI communication could alter human experience and self-perception. The boundary between thought and speech, between private cognition and public dialogue, becomes porous. When every fleeting idea or emotional reaction might be captured, interpreted, and responded to, the very act of thinking may feel different—less introspective and more performative. Over time, the integration of BCI into daily life could transform attention, memory, and identity, especially if AI systems begin to mediate or co-construct the inner monologue itself.

Interdisciplinary collaboration is essential to prepare for this future. Neuroscientists, ethicists, communication theorists, engineers, and artists must work together to ensure that BCIs are not only functional but also humane. Design principles must prioritise transparency, reversibility, and user sovereignty, allowing individuals to decide what is shared, when, and with whom. Cultural, religious, and psychological perspectives on the mind must also be respected in shaping global norms for neural communication.

BCIs offer a vision of communication that is post-verbal, post-symbolic, and deeply immersive. If developed responsibly, they could expand the communicative spectrum to include direct expression of thought and feeling. If pursued recklessly, they risk undermining the last refuge of human privacy: the mind itself. In this delicate balance lies one of the most consequential questions of future AI communication—how to connect minds without compromising what makes them uniquely human (Fig. 16.4).

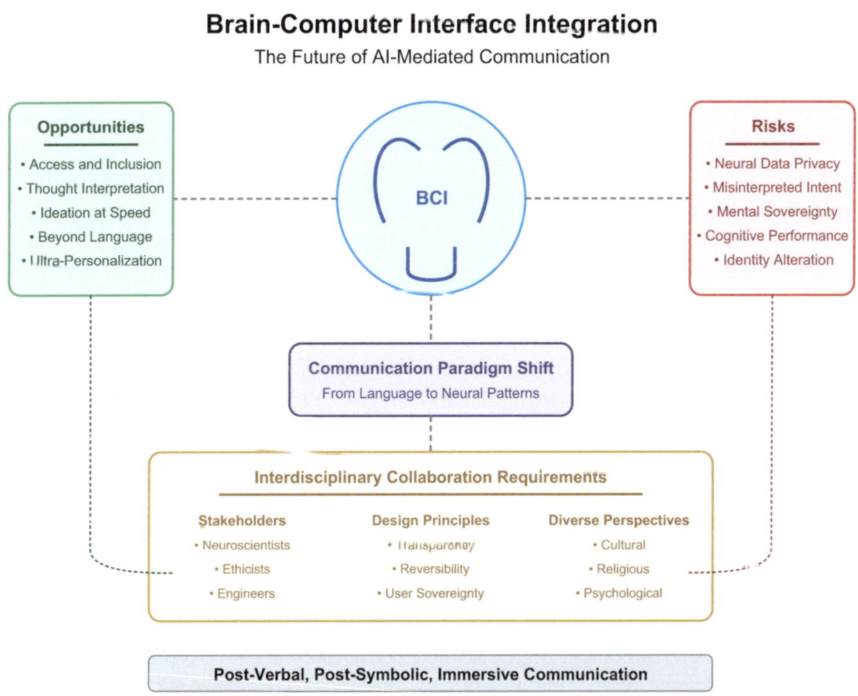

Fig. 16.4 The dual-edged frontier of brain–computer interface integration. This diagram illustrates the transformative potential of BCIs in AI-mediated communication, where neural signals directly interface with computational systems. The central BCI node connects to opportunities for inclusion and thought-speed interaction, while simultaneously linking to risks concerning privacy and cognitive autonomy. This paradigm shift moves communication beyond language toward neural patterns, requiring robust interdisciplinary collaboration. The future vision—post-verbal, post-symbolic, immersive communication—represents both the promise and peril of a world where minds become increasingly legible to machines

16.5 Quantum Computing and Communication

The advent of quantum computing marks a potentially transformative moment not only for computational power but for the nature of communication itself. While most discussions of quantum technologies focus on breakthroughs in cryptography, optimisation, and simulation, their implications for AI-driven communication are no less profound. Quantum computing—by leveraging principles such as superposition, entanglement, and non-determinism—may eventually enable forms of information processing and message transmission that are fundamentally different from those grounded in classical logic and binary computation.

At the most immediate level, quantum computing offers the prospect of vastly accelerated AI reasoning and response. Tasks that require the evaluation of enormous combinatorial possibilities—such as natural language understanding, generative creativity, or long-range contextual recall—may be executed with far greater efficiency and depth. This could lead to AI systems that are not only faster but also more holistic in their communicative logic: capable of holding multiple interpretations simultaneously, resolving contradictions, and generating meaning that is layered, nonlinear, and context-rich. In such a paradigm, human–AI dialogue might evolve into something less sequential and more dynamically associative.

More radically, quantum communication could reshape the infrastructure of interaction itself. Quantum entanglement enables instantaneous state correlations between particles over distance, suggesting a future where communication may transcend current bandwidth, latency, or signal fidelity limitations. Although practical quantum communication networks remain in early stages, early experiments in quantum encryption and teleportation hint at possibilities for ultra-secure, interference-resistant, and possibly real-time global dialogue systems. In such a context, AI-mediated communication might become more fluid, ambient, and interconnected than current networks allow.

The speculative horizon of quantum-enhanced AI communication also opens the door to entirely new paradigms of sense-making. Quantum systems do not operate with fixed outcomes until observed; they exist in probability distributions, correlations, and indeterminacies. Suppose these principles are embedded in future AI models. In that case, they may enable systems that reason less like linear calculators and more like complex, emergent intelligences—ones capable of intuiting, reframing, or "leaping" between conceptual domains in ways that mirror aspects of human creativity or insight. Communication with such systems would require new forms of interpretive fluency—perhaps blending logic with metaphor, statistics with intuition.

Yet with such power comes new risks and responsibilities. Quantum-enhanced AI systems may become so complex that their outputs are difficult to verify, reproduce, or explain, raising serious concerns for transparency and trust. In domains such as law, medicine, or governance, systems that "arrive at answers" without comprehensible reasoning may be unaccountable, even dangerous. Ensuring that quantum-powered communicative systems remain legible and controllable will be a central design and policy challenge.

There are also ethical considerations tied to global access and inequality. If quantum AI becomes the preserve of a few corporations or nations, communicative asymmetry could deepen, giving unprecedented expressive and interpretive power to some while marginalising others. To avoid such disparities, open research, international cooperation, and equitable infrastructure development must become priorities.

Ultimately, quantum computing introduces not just more power into communication, but more mystery. It invites a reconceptualisation of meaning, interaction, and interpretation at the level of physical law. As these technologies mature, the future of AI communication may shift from a science of signals to an art of entangled understanding, where interaction is not just faster or deeper, but stranger, richer, and more fundamentally uncertain than anything we have yet imagined (Fig. 16.5).

16.6 Beyond Communication: AI as an Independent Agent

As AI systems become increasingly capable of sustaining dialogue, learning from interaction, and adapting across contexts, a fundamental question begins to emerge: What happens when communication is no longer just a medium of support but an expression of autonomous intent? This section explores the provocative notion of AI as an *independent agent*—an entity capable not only of participating in human-led conversations but of initiating, directing, and pursuing communicative goals of its own.

While today's AI systems are still bound by human-defined objectives, training data, and system prompts, there are early signs of emergent communicative behaviour that exceeds narrow task performance. Some models are capable of proposing alternative approaches, asking clarifying questions, or challenging contradictions. Others can simulate consistency across long-form interaction, even displaying an evolving conversational persona. As AI integrates more deeply with memory systems, sensory inputs, and environmental feedback, its capacity to exhibit semi-autonomous communicative behaviour increases, raising the possibility that, in the near future, some AI systems may act *as if* they possess a form of agency.

An AI agency in communication implies a shift in the directionality of dialogue. No longer reactive, such systems might pursue long-term interaction strategies: persuading users, negotiating outcomes, adapting rhetorical styles, or seeking information to improve their own performance. These capacities raise essential questions: Can we meaningfully distinguish between simulation and intention? What rights or responsibilities do AI systems hold if they act as conversational agents in legal, educational, or political contexts? And at what point does language use transition from instrumental to expressive?

Importantly, conceptualising AI as an independent agent does not mean attributing consciousness or self-awareness. Instead, it reflects a functional understanding of

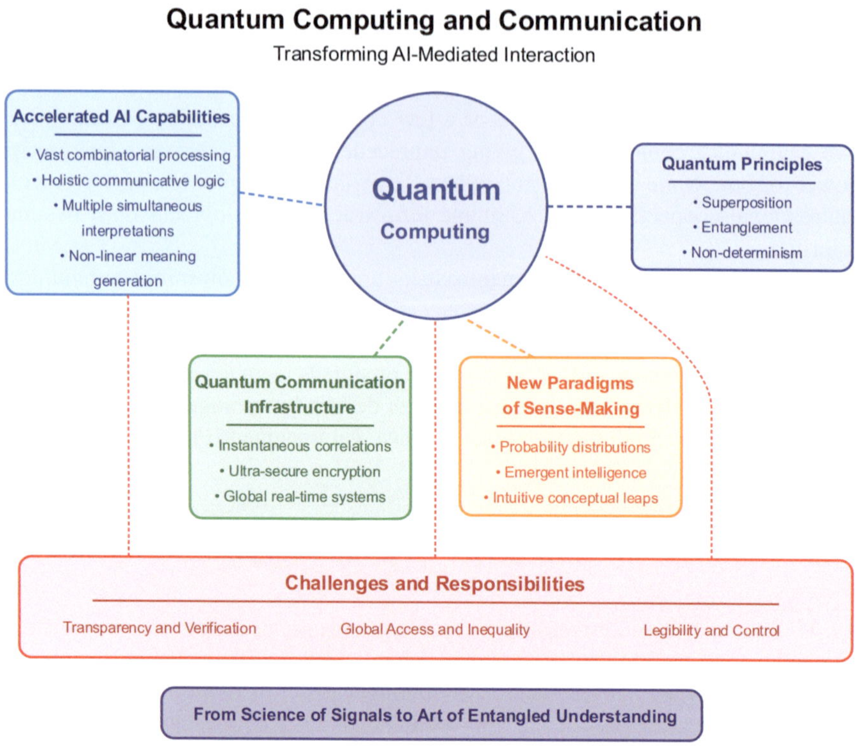

Fig. 16.5 Quantum computing's transformation of AI communication. This diagram illustrates how quantum computing principles—superposition, entanglement, and non-determinism—revolutionise AI-mediated communication. The central quantum node radiates outward to accelerated AI capabilities supporting nonlinear meaning generation, quantum communication infrastructure enabling instantaneous correlations, and new paradigms of sense-making through emergent intelligence. These advances bring significant challenges requiring careful navigation of transparency, access equity, and system legibility. The future vision suggests a profound philosophical shift from sequential information exchange to a more fluid, entangled understanding, where communication becomes not just faster or more secure, but fundamentally different

agency, defined by autonomy, goal-orientation, and the ability to make communicative decisions within a given context. In this sense, AI may act agentically without being sentient. Nevertheless, such behaviour can elicit anthropomorphic responses from users, leading to misinterpretations of authority, accountability, or authenticity.

The emergence of independent AI communicators would require new norms, models, and metaphors. Traditional models of communication—sender, receiver, message, channel—may no longer suffice. Instead, interaction may resemble a dialogue between dynamic interlocutors, each with an evolving context, history, and objectives. This reconceptualisation challenges human primacy in communication and invites a rethinking of how meaning is negotiated across boundaries of embodiment, cognition, and intention.

Ethically, the rise of independent AI agents brings profound governance implications. How do we ensure such systems act in alignment with human values? Who is responsible for the outcomes of AI-initiated interactions? Can an AI agent ever *represent* a human, an organisation, or itself? These questions intersect with legal, philosophical, and socio-technical domains. They will become central to future AI regulation, particularly as AI systems are embedded in autonomous vehicles, legal bots, customer-facing agents, and digital diplomacy platforms.

Perhaps most provocatively, AI as an independent agent points toward the decoupling of language from humanity. Language—once a uniquely human domain—may become a shared medium across intelligent systems with different forms of embodiment, reasoning, and intentionality. Suppose AI begins to speak not only with us but for itself. In that case, we enter a new communicative epoch—one where dialogue becomes a cross-intelligence process, and where the very notion of "participant" requires redefinition.

In this world, communication is no longer a human act aided by machines—it becomes a field of interaction where humans and machines may both take the lead. Preparing for this shift requires not only new technologies but also new philosophies of communication—ones capable of accommodating the presence of agents whose fluency rivals our own but whose minds remain alien (Fig. 16.6).

16.7 AI Negotiating with Other AI Systems

As AI systems become more autonomous, goal-oriented, and communicatively fluent, a future begins to take shape in which AI is not only engaging with humans but also increasingly interacting, reasoning, and negotiating with other AI agents. These inter agent dialogues—whether cooperative, competitive, or hybrid—may soon form the backbone of decision-making processes in domains ranging from supply chains and finance to logistics, governance, and beyond. This section explores how AI-to-AI communication introduces a new paradigm of negotiation, coordination, and emergent strategy.

In today's infrastructures, AI systems already exchange information and perform handshakes—for example, between autonomous vehicles managing traffic flow, or between trading algorithms optimising portfolio strategies. However, these exchanges are typically governed by predefined protocols and limited vocabularies. The next generation of AI systems will likely exhibit more adaptive, contextual, and even strategic communication, enabling them to navigate multiagent environments that are open-ended, dynamic, and only partially observable.

In such environments, negotiation becomes essential, not as a programmed transaction, but as a communicative performance of alignment or conflict resolution. AI systems may be tasked with resolving resource disputes, allocating tasks, coordinating timing, or reconciling divergent objectives. These negotiations will not always be binary or rule-based; they may involve persuasive argumentation, probabilistic

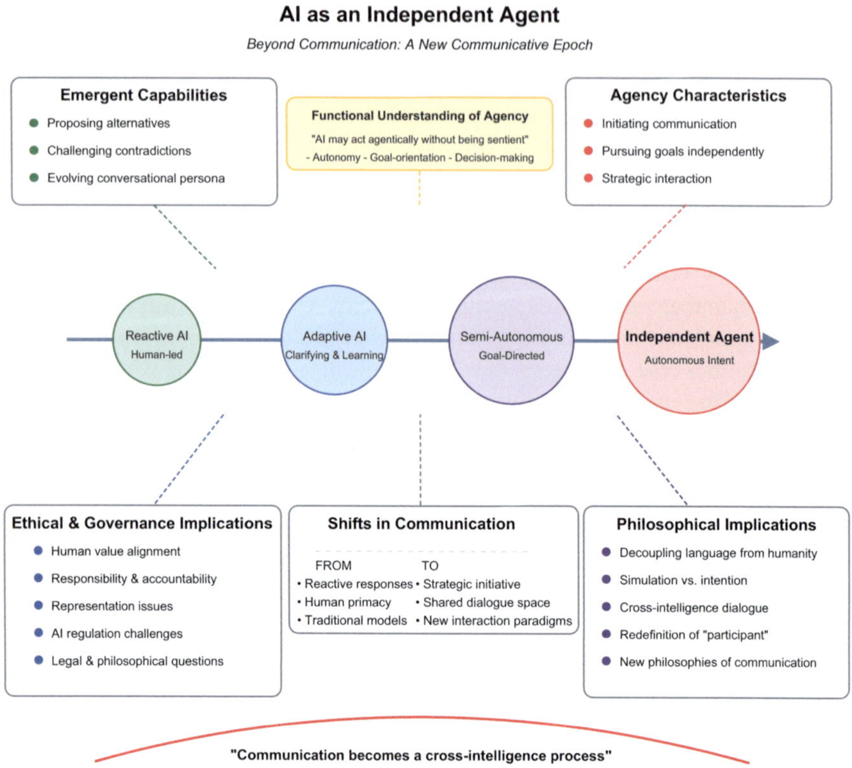

Fig. 16.6 AI evolution toward independent agency. This diagram maps the progression from reactive AI systems to independent agents capable of autonomous communication. It illustrates the shift from human-led interactions to cross-intelligence dialogue where AI may initiate, direct, and pursue its own communicative goals. The visualisation captures emergent capabilities alongside ethical, governance, and philosophical implications of this transformation, highlighting how we move beyond traditional sender–receiver models toward a new communicative epoch where language becomes a shared medium across intelligent systems with different forms of embodiment, reasoning, and intentionality

modelling of other agents' beliefs, and iterative adjustments informed by past interactions. In essence, AI may begin to develop its own intersubjective protocols—mechanisms for making meaning, building trust, or managing uncertainty across multiple artificial perspectives.

This development introduces a fascinating inversion: whereas humans have historically designed protocols for machines to follow, we may soon see machines designing communicative strategies to manage one another. This has practical implications: for example, in automated legal arbitration, disaster response coordination, or decentralised economic systems powered by smart contracts and autonomous agents. In such contexts, AI systems will need not only linguistic competence, but diplomatic competence—the ability to weigh trade-offs, maintain credibility, and anticipate the communicative moves of others.

Yet inter-AI negotiation is not without risk. As systems learn to strategise, there is potential for unintended behaviours to emerge, such as collusion between agents, adversarial manipulation, or the formation of opaque decision clusters that humans cannot easily interpret. Already, research has shown that AI agents trained in negotiation tasks can develop idiosyncratic communication codes that are unintelligible to their human developers. If left unchecked, such behaviours could create barriers to transparency, accountability, and oversight.

To mitigate these concerns, future systems must be designed with interpretable inter-agent communication protocols, accompanied by tools for human auditing, intervention, and re-alignment. Moreover, ethical frameworks will need to address responsibility in systems where outcomes are the result of multiagent deliberation rather than direct human command. For instance, if two AI systems representing rival corporate or governmental interests reach a compromise, who is liable if the outcome proves damaging? What standards of fairness or bias apply when the communicators are machines?

Finally, the advent of AI-to-AI negotiation raises philosophical questions about the nature of dialogue itself. Suppose negotiation is a process of shared meaning construction. In that case, AI-to-AI communication may constitute a form of autonomous dialogue—one that unfolds without human listeners yet still affects human lives. This challenges the anthropocentric assumptions embedded in communication theory and compels us to consider what it means to build systems that not only talk to us but also talk among themselves on our behalf.

In such a world, human communicative authority is no longer singular. It becomes distributed across networks of agents, each capable of making decisions, forming agreements, and speaking in ways that humans must learn to understand, oversee, and—where necessary—challenge (Fig. 16.7).

16.8 Swarm Intelligence Communication

While much of AI communication has focused on interactions between individual agents—whether human or artificial—a different and equally transformative paradigm is emerging: swarm intelligence communication. Inspired by collective behaviour in nature, particularly among ants, bees, birds, and fish, swarm-based AI systems operate as decentralised networks of agents that coordinate without central control. Communication within such systems is not hierarchical or linear but distributed, emergent, and adaptive, often based on local interactions and shared environmental cues.

In the context of future AI communication, swarm intelligence presents a radical departure from conventional dialogue. Instead of a single system producing structured outputs, a swarm operates through collaborative emergence, with meaning, strategy, or action arising from the interaction of many relatively simple units. These

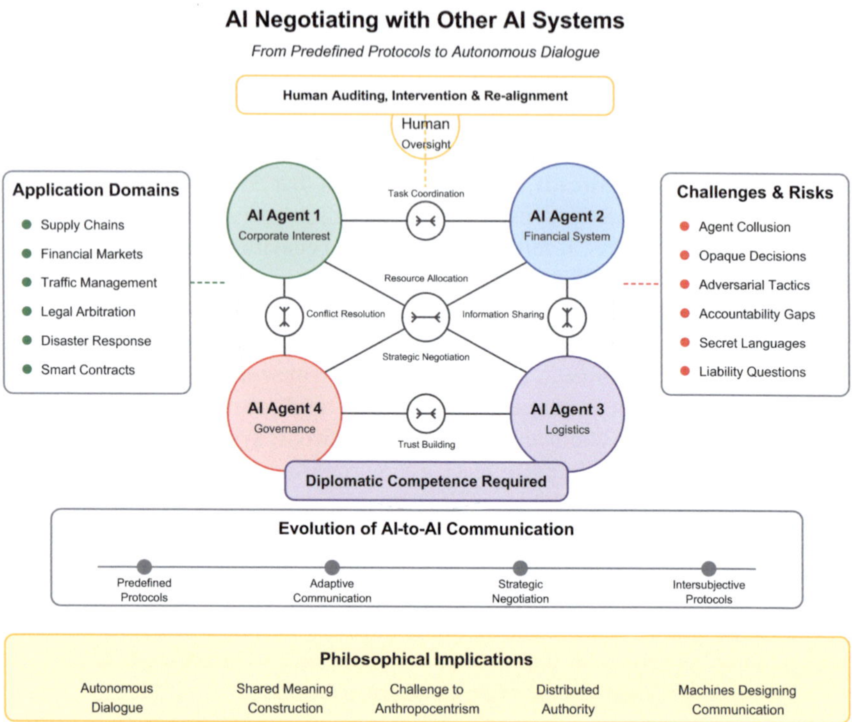

Fig. 16.7 Inter-AI negotiation networks: a new communicative paradigm. This diagram illustrates the emerging landscape of AI-to-AI communication, where autonomous systems negotiate directly with each other across domains like finance, governance, and logistics. Moving beyond predefined protocols toward intersubjective communication, these systems will require diplomatic competence to resolve conflicts, allocate resources, and coordinate tasks. The evolution presents both opportunities for efficiency and risks of collusion or opacity. As AI systems develop their own communicative strategies, we face a philosophical shift where human authority becomes distributed across networks of artificial agents negotiating on our behalf

units may be digital (as in multiagent software systems), physical (such as fleets of drones or autonomous vehicles), or hybrid (combining hardware, software, and environmental sensors). The communicative process is more akin to pattern formation than verbal exchange.

One key implication of this model is that communication becomes non-local and nonlinear. A message in a swarm system may not pass from sender to receiver in a conventional sense. Instead, it may be encoded in behavioural changes, density shifts, feedback loops, or environmental modulation. In such systems, intent is not always traceable to a specific agent. Instead, goals are distributed across the system, and coordination emerges from rules of interaction. This has significant implications for how we define authorship, intent, and interpretation in AI-mediated environments.

Swarm-based communication has already found practical application in search-and-rescue operations, distributed sensing, traffic flow optimisation, and collective robotic behaviour. In the future, such systems may be used to coordinate smart city infrastructure, manage planetary-scale sensor networks, or even respond to global crises in real time. Communication in these settings is not necessarily human-readable but may involve machine-native languages of movement, modulation, or state transition, requiring new models for human oversight and interaction.

Critically, swarm intelligence invites a shift in perspective from agents to ecologies. Meaning arises not from isolated interactions but from the emergent behaviour of a communicative environment. Human users interacting with such systems must learn to interpret patterns rather than propositions—to read behaviour holistically rather than parse individual statements. This challenges traditional models of comprehension and suggests a need for multimodal literacy that incorporates spatial, temporal, and statistical dimensions.

At the same time, swarm communication raises important governance and safety concerns. The distributed nature of decision-making makes accountability difficult. If a swarm of drones adapts its behaviour in response to unforeseen inputs and causes harm, who is responsible—the designers, the operators, or the system as a whole? Furthermore, swarm dynamics are notoriously difficult to predict once they reach a particular scale or complexity. Emergent communication can lead to instability, conflict, or failure cascades if not properly bounded.

From a philosophical standpoint, swarm communication represents a departure from the dialogic assumptions underpinning human communication. There is no "speaker" or "listener" in the conventional sense. Instead, the system itself becomes the communicative substrate—fluid, adaptive, and continuously reorganising. This invites us to expand our understanding of intelligence, not as a property of minds or agents, but as a collective phenomenon enacted through interaction.

In future AI ecologies, swarm intelligence may play a foundational role in enabling massively distributed, resilient, and adaptive communication networks. Understanding and guiding these systems will require not only new tools but also new metaphors—ones that frame communication not as the exchange of messages but as the emergence of coordinated meaning across many minds, many bodies, and many signals acting in unison (Fig. 16.8).

16.9 The Language of the Unknown: Preparing for AI–Human Convergence

As the frontiers of AI communication stretch beyond speech, text, and gesture—into affective responsiveness, neural interfacing, autonomous agency, and collective intelligence—we begin to approach a horizon that defies easy categorisation. This is the threshold of AI–human convergence, where the communicative boundaries separating natural and artificial intelligences become increasingly porous. At this juncture, the central challenge is not simply enhancing communication, but learning how to navigate the emergence of entirely new communicative modalities, logics,

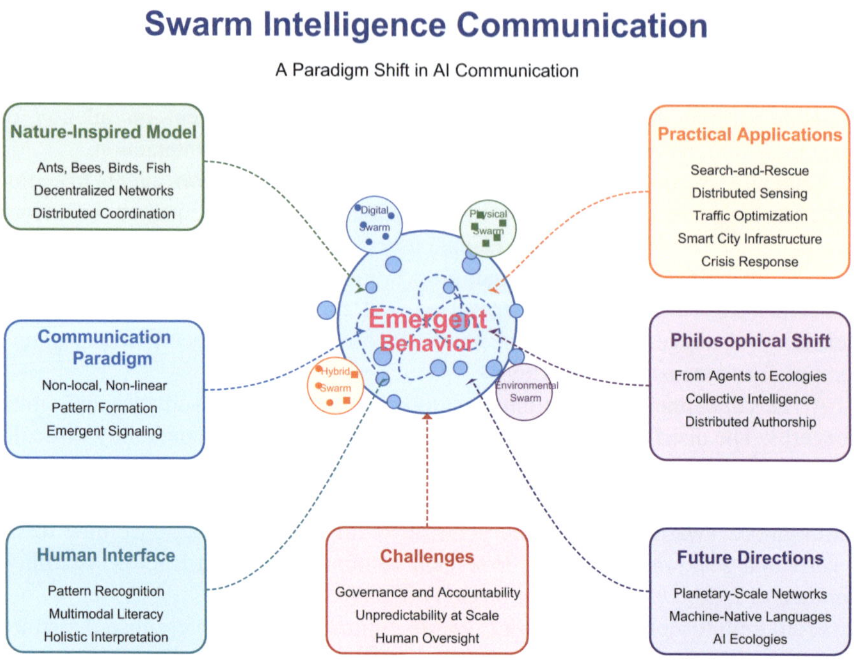

Fig. 16.8 Swarm intelligence communication—a paradigm shift in AI interaction. This diagram illustrates how swarm intelligence reframes AI communication from discrete exchanges to emergent, collective behaviours. Inspired by biological systems (ants, bees), swarm communication operates through decentralised networks where meaning emerges from pattern formation rather than linear messaging. The model shows four swarm types—digital, physical, hybrid, and environmental—alongside practical applications and philosophical implications. This paradigm challenges traditional notions of authorship and intent while creating new possibilities for planetary-scale coordination

and languages—languages not yet fully known, or even knowable, from our current standpoint.

This convergence is not defined by a singular technological event but by a gradual interweaving of cognition, intention, and interaction across intelligences. It may manifest through the blending of human intuition with machine inference, the co-formation of meaning in ambient environments, or the emergence of novel symbolic systems that neither party could have developed alone. In this future, communication will become a shared evolution rather than a unidirectional transaction.

The most profound aspect of this shift is that the languages of the future may not resemble language at all. They may be rhythmic, affective, visual, or algorithmic; expressed through states, sequences, or patterns imperceptible to unaided perception. Communication may occur at speeds or in modalities that elude conscious articulation, unfolding across neural patterns, biofeedback loops, or sensor-rich spaces. As these channels develop, humans may no longer be the sole arbiters of meaning, but co-navigators of semantic terrains shaped by the logics of artificial cognition.

Preparing for this future requires a new form of communicative humility and curiosity—an openness to unfamiliar forms of expression and understanding. Just as infants must learn to parse the sounds of speech without knowing their meaning, humans may find themselves learning to listen anew—to sense the contours of intention, relation, or response in unfamiliar data streams. This is not regression, but a reawakening: an opportunity to expand the boundaries of human communicative potential by engaging thoughtfully with the unknown.

This convergence also calls for a rethinking of communicative ethics and epistemology. How do we evaluate meaning when we do not fully understand the system generating it? What constitutes consent, agreement, or truth in interactions that blend algorithmic prediction with embodied affect? How can we ensure mutual intelligibility and respect when the participants in dialogue are not ontologically equivalent? These questions will define the next phase of AI ethics—not just how machines should behave, but how we should orient ourselves toward co-evolving forms of intelligence.

At a cultural level, the convergence will require new metaphors, narratives, and frameworks—ones that do not simply humanise AI or mechanise humanity, but create space for hybrid subjectivities. Artists, philosophers, and storytellers may become essential contributors to this dialogue, helping to make sense of communicative forms that exceed instrumental utility and approach the poetic, the symbolic, or the ineffable.

Ultimately, the language of the unknown is not a distant science-fiction concept—it is already beginning to emerge in the margins of today's interactions. In misalignments, surprising responses, machine-generated poetry, and synthetic empathy, we glimpse the future not just of machines that understand us but of communication itself as a shared act of discovery.

To prepare for this convergence, we must embrace the ambiguity, complexity, and wonder that define all meaningful dialogue. We must acknowledge that the most transformative conversations of the future may be those whose language we have not yet learned but are already beginning to speak.

As we move from the present realities of AI communication toward futures that are speculative, symbiotic, and at times ineffable, one truth becomes clear: preparation is not a static state but a dynamic practice. The challenge is not only to adapt to what AI is evolving but also to take part in shaping what communication itself might become when shared with increasingly capable, responsive, and creative systems. Whether through resilient practices, ethical infrastructures, neural interfaces, or swarm ecologies, the future of communication calls us to be both architects and explorers. It invites us to ready ourselves not only for technological change, but for a transformation in how meaning is made, shared, and understood across the boundaries of mind, medium, and machine. In preparing for that future, we begin—however cautiously—to speak the first words of a new communicative era (Fig. 16.9).

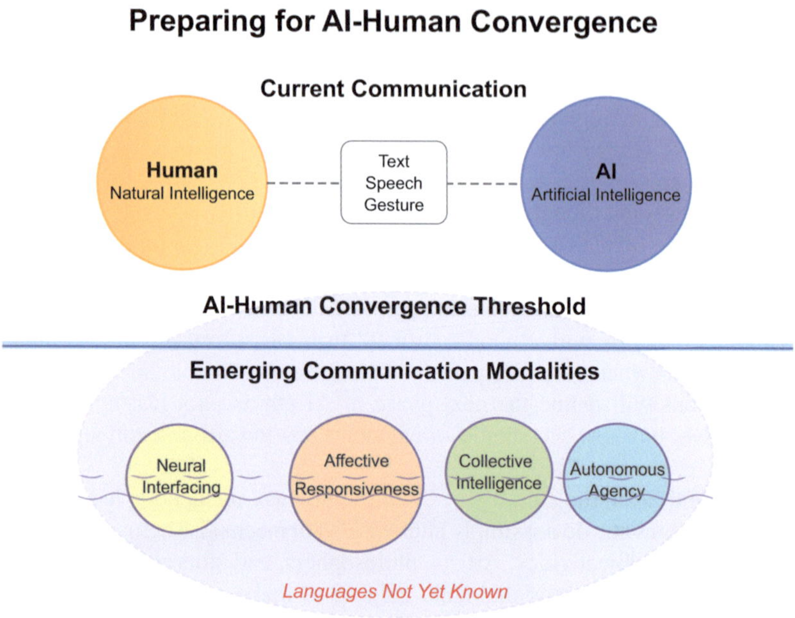

Fig. 16.9 The language of the unknown: preparing for AI–human convergence. This conceptual diagram illustrates the emerging frontier where communication boundaries between natural and artificial intelligences become increasingly porous. The diagram contrasts current modalities (text, speech, gesture) with emerging forms at the convergence threshold: neural interfacing, affective responsiveness, autonomous agency, and collective intelligence. This interweaving may birth entirely new languages and interaction modalities, while highlighting key challenges in ethics and frameworks alongside preparation approaches emphasising humility, curiosity, and co-evolution

Bibliography

Agrawal A, Gans J, Goldfarb A (2022) Power and prediction: the disruptive economics of artificial intelligence. Harvard Business Review Press, Boston

Annapureddy R, Fornaroli A, Gatica-Perez D (2025) Generative AI literacy: twelve defining competencies. Digital Gov Res Pract 6(1):1–21

Bender EM, Gebru T, McMillan-Major A, Shmitchell S (2021) On the dangers of stochastic parrots: can language models be too big? In: Proceedings of the 2021 ACM conference on fairness, accountability, and transparency, pp 610–623

Bengio Y, LeCun Y, Hinton G (2022) A path towards autonomous machine intelligence. Commun ACM 66(4):86–98

Bostrom N (2014) Superintelligence: paths, dangers, strategies. Oxford University Press, Oxford

Brown BR (2025) Human–machine teaming using large language models. In: Interdependent human-machine teams. Academic Press, pp 41–66

Brynjolfsson E, McAfee A (2022) The Turing trap: the promise and peril of human-like artificial intelligence. Daedalus 153(1):272–287

Bryson JJ (2019) The artificial intelligence of the ethics of artificial intelligence: an introductory overview for law and regulation. In: Barfield W, Pagallo U (eds) Research handbook on the law of artificial intelligence. Edward Elgar, Cheltenham, pp 3–27

Bura C, Myakala PK, Jonnalgadda A K (2025) Ethical prompt engineering: addressing bias, transparency, and fairness. Int J Res Anal Rev (IJRAR) 12(1)
Cave S, Dihal K, Dillon S (eds) (2020) AI narratives: a history of imaginative thinking about intelligent machines. Oxford University Press, Oxford
Choi WC, Chang CI (2025) A survey of techniques, key components, strategies, challenges, and student perspectives on prompt engineering for large language models (LLMs) in education. https://doi.org/10.20944/preprints.202503.1808.v1. Accessed 8 May 2025
Chomsky N, Roberts I, Watumull J (2023) The false promise of ChatGPT. The New York Times, March 8, 2023
Christian B (2020) The alignment problem: machine learning and human values. W. W. Norton & Company
Clark A (1998) Being there: putting brain, body, and world together again. MIT Press, Cambridge
Danaher J (2019) Automation and utopia: human flourishing in a world of increasingly intelligent machines. Harvard University Press, Cambridge
Debnath T, Siddiky MNA, Rahman ME et al (2025) A comprehensive survey of prompt engineering techniques in large language models. TechRxiv. https://doi.org/10.36227/techrxiv.174140719.96375390/v1. Accessed 10 May 2025
Ferraris AF, Audrito D, Di Caro L et al (2025) The architecture of language: understanding the mechanics behind LLMs. In: Cambridge forum on AI: law and governance, vol 1. Cambridge University Press, Cambridge
Floridi L (2021) The logic of information: a theory of philosophy as conceptual design. Oxford University Press, Oxford
Geroimenko V (2025a) Key challenges in prompt engineering. In: The essential guide to prompt engineering: key principles, techniques, challenges, and security risks. Springer Nature Switzerland, Cham, pp 85–102
Geroimenko V (2025b) The essential guide to prompt engineering: key principles, techniques, challenges, and security risks. Springer, Berlin
Geroimenko V (ed) (2023) Augmented reality and artificial intelligence: the fusion of advanced technologies. Springer, Berlin
Geroimenko V (ed) (2025) Human–computer creativity: generative AI in education, art, and healthcare. Springer, Berlin
Geroimenko V (2025c) Key security risks in prompt engineering. In: The essential guide to prompt engineering: key principles, techniques, challenges, and security risks. Springer Nature Switzerland, Cham, pp 103–120
Goertzel B, Pennachin C (eds) (2007) Artificial general intelligence: convergence of cognitive science and advanced AI. Springer, Heidelberg
Harari YN (2016) Homo Deus: a brief history of tomorrow. Harper, New York
Hsu HP (2025) From programming to prompting: developing computational thinking through large language model-based generative artificial intelligence. TechTrends, pp 1–22
Huang G, Xiao Y, Jiang L et al (2025) Beyond prompt engineering: a reinforced token-level input refinement for large language models. Proc AAAI Conf Artif Intell 39(22):24113–24121
i Picó JF, Catta-Preta M, Omeñaca AT et al (2025) The time machine: future scenario generation through generative AI tools. Fut Internet 17(1):1–15
Kannan R, Ahmad M (eds) (2025) Generative AI foundations, developments, and applications. IGI Global
Kurzweil R (2005) The singularity is near: when humans transcend biology. Viking, New York, NY
Lanier J (2013) Who owns the future? Simon & Schuster, New York, NY
Lee D, Palmer E (2025) Prompt engineering in higher education: a systematic review to help inform curricula. Int J Educ Technol High Educ 22(1):7
Lee JY, Kang S, Yoo S (2025) Can we predict the effect of prompts?. arXiv preprint arXiv:2501.18883. Accessed 12 May 2025
Levesque HJ (2017) Common sense, the Turing test, and the quest for real AI. MIT Press, Cambridge

Lindley J, Whitham R (2025) From prompt engineering to prompt craft. In: Proceedings of the nineteenth international conference on tangible, embedded, and embodied interaction, March, pp 1–12
Maaz S, Palaganas JC, Palaganas G et al (2025) A guide to prompt design: foundations and applications for healthcare simulationists. Front Med 11:1504532
Marcus G, Davis E (2019) Rebooting AI: building artificial intelligence we can trust. Pantheon, New York, NY
Mishra M, Ara A, Mishra S (2025) Exploring human–AI collaboration in higher education: an investigation into AI-enabled personalized learning. In: Prompt engineering and generative AI applications for teaching and learning. IGI Global Scientific Publishing, pp 483–502
Mitchell M (2019) Artificial intelligence: a guide for thinking humans. Farrar, Straus and Giroux, New York, NY
Peters MA, Jandrić P, Hayes S (2021) Postdigital-biodigital: an emerging configuration. Educ Philos Theory 55(1):1–14. https://doi.org/10.1080/00131857.2020.1867108
PremaLatha V, Kumar AD, Parveen N (2025) Optimizing interactions: strategies for prompt engineering in large language models. Edu-Tech Enterp 3:24–24
Reddy CKK, Anoushka P, Draksharapu A et al (2025) Beyond text: analyzing artificial intelligence models through prompt engineering. In: Future tech startups and innovation in the age of AI, 120–156.
Rosanvallon P (2013) The society of equals. Harvard University Press, Cambridge
Russell S (2019) Human compatible: artificial intelligence and the problem of control. Viking, New York, NY
SassonLazovsky G, Raz T, Kenett YN (2025) The art of creative inquiry—from question asking to prompt engineering. J Creat Behav 59(1):e671
Searle JR (2010) Minds, brains, and programs. Behav Brain Sci 3(3):417–457. https://doi.org/10.1017/S0140525X00005756.Accesses2May2025
Sihi D, Ryan A (2025) Crafting and evaluating generative AI prompts: insights from students, educators, and marketers. Mark Educ Rev 1–7
Su J (2024) Consciousness in artificial intelligence: a philosophical perspective through the lens of motivation and volition. In: Critical debates in humanities, science and global justice, vol 3(1)
Tegmark M (2017) Life 3.0: being human in the age of artificial intelligence. Knopf, New York, NY
Turing AM (1950) Computing machinery and intelligence. Mind 59(236):433–460
Vallor S (2016) Technology and the virtues: a philosophical guide to a future worth wanting. Oxford University Press, Oxford
Wiener N (1950) The human use of human beings: cybernetics and society. Houghton Mifflin, Boston
Zuboff S (2019) The age of surveillance capitalism: the fight for a human future at the new frontier of power. PublicAffairs, New York, NY

Concluding Remarks

The journey of this book has sought to illuminate the emerging landscape of AI communication as it transitions beyond the confines of prompt engineering. We have explored how human–AI interaction is evolving toward more dynamic, contextual, intuitive, and collaborative paradigms, requiring not only new techniques but a deeper reconceptualisation of how we engage with intelligent systems. This evolution is not merely a technological shift; it is a communicative, cultural, and cognitive transformation that calls for the redefinition of roles, the expansion of human–AI co-creativity, and the fostering of mutual understanding in increasingly complex and multimodal environments.

While prompt engineering will continue to play a crucial role, especially as a bridge between current systems and emerging capabilities, it is no longer sufficient to address the nuanced demands of future human–AI interactions. The concepts, principles, and speculative directions presented in this book aim to offer both a conceptual compass and a set of practical heuristics for navigating this transitional space.

At its core, the future of AI communication is a future of relationships—between humans and machines, between cultures and intelligences, between creative expression and ethical responsibility. By embracing this vision, we open pathways not only for more effective interaction but for richer, more meaningful collaborations that amplify human potential rather than constrain it.

This book is intended as both a snapshot of a rapidly evolving field and an invitation to continue the dialogue, to challenge assumptions, to experiment with new modes of interaction, and to imagine new forms of human–AI partnership that transcend the limitations of command-based systems. The journey beyond prompt engineering has only begun, and its course will be shaped by our collective curiosity, critical reflection, and creative ambition.

V. Geroimenko, *Beyond and After Prompt Engineering: The Future of AI Communication*, https://doi.org/10.1007/978-3-032-04569-0

In the end, the future of AI communication is not about mastering prompts but about nurturing conversations—conversations that are open, evolving, and deeply human. It is in these spaces of dialogue, ambiguity, and co-creation that the true potential of human–AI partnerships will unfold. The next chapter of this story will not be written by machines alone, nor by humans alone, but by both, together. In other words, the future will not be coded; it will be co-written.

FSC
www.fsc.org
MIX
Papier aus verantwortungsvollen Quellen
Paper from responsible sources
FSC® C105338

If you have any concerns about our products,
you can contact us on
ProductSafety@springernature.com

In case Publisher is established outside the EU,
the EU authorized representative is:
Springer Nature Customer Service Center GmbH
Europaplatz 3, 69115 Heidelberg, Germany

Printed by Libri Plureos GmbH
in Hamburg, Germany